Wills, Trusts, and Estates in Focus

Focus Casebook Series

WILLS, TRUSTS, AND ESTATES IN FOCUS

Naomi R. Cahn
Associate Dean and John Theodore Fey Research Professor of Law
George Washington University

Alyssa A. DiRusso
Whelan W. and Rosalie T. Palmer Professor of Law
Cumberland School of Law at Samford University

Susan N. Gary
Orlando J. and Marian H. Hollis Professor of Law
University of Oregon

Wolters Kluwer

Published by Wolters Kluwer in New York.

Wolters Kluwer Legal & Regulatory U.S. serves customers worldwide with CCH, Aspen Publishers, and Kluwer Law International products. (www.WKLegaledu.com)

To contact Customer Service, e-mail customer.service@wolterskluwer.com, call 1-800-234-1660, fax 1-800-901-9075, or mail correspondence to:

Wolters Kluwer
Attn: Order Department
PO Box 99
Frederick, MD 21705

Printed in the United States of America.

1 2 3 4 5 6 7 8 9 0

ISBN: 978-1-4548-8662-4

Library of Congress Cataloging-in-Publication Data

Names: Cahn, Naomi R., author. | Gary, Susan N., author. | DiRusso, Alyssa, 1974- author.
Title: Wills, trusts, and estates in focus / Naomi R. Cahn, Susan N. Gary, Alyssa DiRusso.
Description: New York: Wolters Kluwer, [2019] | Series: Focus casebook series | Includes index.
Identifiers: LCCN 2018058812 | ISBN 9781454886624 (casebound)
Subjects: LCSH: Trusts and trustees—United States. | Wills—United States. | Estate planning—United States. | LCGFT: Casebooks
Classification: LCC KF730.C29 2019 | DDC 346.7305—dc23
LC record available at https://lccn.loc.gov/2018058812

About Wolters Kluwer Legal & Regulatory U.S.

Wolters Kluwer Legal & Regulatory U.S. delivers expert content and solutions in the areas of law, corporate compliance, health compliance, reimbursement, and legal education. Its practical solutions help customers successfully navigate the demands of a changing environment to drive their daily activities, enhance decision quality and inspire confident outcomes.

Serving customers worldwide, its legal and regulatory portfolio includes products under the Aspen Publishers, CCH Incorporated, Kluwer Law International, ftwilliam.com and MediRegs names. They are regarded as exceptional and trusted resources for general legal and practice-specific knowledge, compliance and risk management, dynamic workflow solutions, and expert commentary.

Summary of Contents

Table of Contents

Chapter 13: Professional Ethics in Trusts and Estates

The Focus Casebook Series

Students reach their full potential with the fresh approach of the **Focus Casebook Series**. Instead of using the "hide the ball" approach, selected cases illustrate key developments in the law and show how courts develop and apply doctrine. The approachable manner of this series provides a comfortable experiential environment that is instrumental to student success.

Students perform best when applying concepts to real-world scenarios. With assessment features, such as Real Life Applications and Applying the Concepts, the **Focus Casebook Series** offers many opportunities for students to apply their knowledge.

Focus Casebook Features Include:

Case Previews and Post-Case Follow-Ups — To succeed, law students must know how to deconstruct and analyze cases. Case Previews highlight the legal concepts in a case before the student reads it. The Post-Case Follow-Ups summarize the important points.

Case Preview

Astrue v. Capato

This case concerns the meaning of "child" under a state's intestacy statute, because that definition turned out to be crucial for interpreting the federal Social Security Act. Although the U.S. Supreme Court rarely considers trusts and estates or family law issues, it was called on to determine a child's entitlement to receive Social Security benefits through a deceased parent. *Astrue* considers both the marital presumption and assisted reproductive technology. Eighteen months after her husband, Robert Capato, died of cancer, Karen Capato gave birth to twins conceived through in vitro fertilization using her husband's frozen sperm. Karen applied for Social Security survivors' benefits for the twins.

As you read the case, consider:

1. What was Robert Capato
2. What did Florida law pr
3. What did federal law pr
4. How does the Supreme (

Post-Case Follow-up

As a result of *Astrue v. Capato*, posthumously conceived children will only qualify for Social Security benefits if the state in which their parent died has recognized that children conceived and born after their parent's death are eligible to inherit from that parent. Because states have made different policy choices concerning reproductive technology and estate efficiency and fairness, posthumously conceived children in one state might qualify, while those across a state border might not. A difficult problem in drafting statutes governing posthumous children and inheritance is determining how long the estate will be left open for those children to come to fruition.

The Focus Casebook Series

Real Life Applications—

Every case in a chapter is followed by Real Life Applications, which present a series of questions based on a scenario similar to the facts in the case. Real Life Applications challenge students to apply what they have learned in order to prepare them for realworld practice. Use Real Life Applications to spark class discussions or provide them as individual short-answer assignments.

In re Estate of Javier Castro: Real Life Applications

1. Would the result have changed if Castro been unable to sign the will, but had asked one of his brothers to sign it on his behalf?

2. Assume the same facts as in the case, but instead of being written on the Samsung Tablet, it was written on a legal pad. How would the court have ruled?

3. If you had been representing Castro when he was in the hospital and physically incapable of signing a will, what steps would you have taken to ensure a valid signature on the will?

4. Cornelius, a new client, has consulted you about how to distribute his spouse's estate. He arrived in your office with an iPhone and the following story. His spouse recently died at home, alone. When he found the body, he found the iPhone next to it. Cornelius has brought you the phone and knows his spouse's password for her phone; he discovered that his spouse had typed a message on the phone entitled "My Will." The message stated that all probate property should be distributed to him and their children, and at the end of the message is his spouse's name in capital-typed letters. How would you advise Cornelius?

Applying the Concepts —

These end-of-chapter exercises encourage students to synthesize the chapter material and apply relevant legal doctrine and code to real-world scenarios. Students can use these exercises for self-assessment or the professor can use them to promote class interaction.

Applying the Concepts

1. Tina and Jake, a married couple, were driving together when they were in a serious car crash. Tina died immediately, and Jake remained in a coma after the crash. Tina's will provides "I leave all of my estate to Jake, if he survives me." Does Jake inherit from Tina in each of the following circumstances?

   a. Jake survived the coma but had a significant brain injury. A conservator was appointed for Jake and made all decisions for Jake until Jake died a year later.

   b. Jake died after two days

   c. Jake died after two mont

2. Cora's will gave the residue o
known as The U.C.L.A."
University of Southern Cali
California at Los Angeles (

Trusts and Estates in Practice

1. Alice's will leaves her estate to her wife, Gertrude, and if Gertrude does not survive, to a literary society. Gertrude's will leaves her estate to Alice, and if Alice does not survive, to Gertrude's brother, Michael. Alice and Gertrude are injured in a train accident. Alice dies one day after the accident, and Gertrude dies a week later. They have a joint bank account and each has a brokerage account in her own name. Write a letter to the personal representative of Alice's estate advising the personal representative as to who inherits Alice's property.

2. Terrence had two grandsons, Alex and Brandon, when he executed his will in 2012. Terrence's will included a provision given $10,000 to "each grandson of mine who survives me." In 2014, Alex transitioned from male to female. After Alex transitioned, Terrence continued to visit Alex at her college and attended her graduation in May 2015. Terrence told many family members that he "was very proud of Alex" when she graduated. When Terrence died in 2017, the probate court had to decide whether Alex should receive $10,000 from the estate. If you were the probate judge, how would you resolve this issue? Is there an ambiguity in the will? What if there were no evidence of how Terrence felt about Alex after her transition? How might the will have been drafted that would have avoided the problem?

Preface

Ensure student success with the Focus Casebook Series.

THE FOCUS APPROACH

In a law office, when a new associate attorney is being asked to assist a supervising attorney with a legal matter in which the associate has no prior experience, it is common for the supervising attorney to provide the associate with a recently closed case file involving the same legal issues so that the associate can see and learn from the closed file to assist more effectively with the new matter. This experiential approach is at the heart of the *Focus Casebook Series*.

Additional hands-on features, such as Real Life Applications and Applying the Concepts, provide more opportunities for critical analysis and application of concepts covered in the chapters. Professors can assign problem-solving questions as well as exercises on drafting documents and preparing appropriate filings.

CONTENT SNAPSHOT

This casebook focuses on clear communication of the fundamentals of wills, trusts, and estates. On completion of the course, students will have not only the comprehensive substantive knowledge base needed for advanced study in this field of law, but also a healthy degree of familiarity with various WTE-related resources. The student will emerge with the ability to perform well in a clinical or practice setting.

- Chapter 1 explores core trusts and estates issues of intent, testamentary freedom, and introduces trusts and estates practice.
- Chapter 2 examines intestacy laws that dictate the transmission of property when there is no will.
- Chapters 3 through 6 turn to wills, focusing on their execution, interpretation, and revocation, as well as will contests.
- Chapter 7 examines will substitutes (e.g., beneficiary designations and pay-on-death provisions) and the process of planning with will substitutes. It also considers the fast-changing law associated with planning for incapacity, such as health care, financial, and digital asset planning.
- Chapter 8 examines protection for the family, including the spousal right of election and the treatment of a spouse or children omitted from a will.

- Chapters 9 through 12 look at the law of trusts and the responsibilities of the fiduciaries charged with administering trusts, and include a brief description of charitable trusts. These chapters provide instruction on drafting, amending, or terminating a trust as well as building in flexibility.
- Chapter 13 explores professional responsibility issues in trusts and estates practice.
- Chapter 14 surveys the process of administering a decedent's estate with or without a valid will.
- Chapter 15 introduces estate tax law and its ramifications for sound estate planning.

RESOURCES

Casebook: The casebook is structured around text, cases, and application exercises. Highlighted cases are introduced with a *Case Preview,* which sets up the issue and identifies key questions. *Post-Case Follow-ups* expand on the holding in the case. *Real Life Applications* present opportunities to challenge students to apply concepts covered in the case to realistic hypothetical cases. *The Applying the Concepts* feature demands critical analysis and integration of concepts covered in the chapter.

Other resources to enrich your class include: Study Aid titles such as *Examples & Explanations: Wills, Trusts and Estates,* by Gerry W. Beyer. Ask your Wolters Kluwer sales representative or visit the Wolters Kluwer site at *wklegaledu.com* to learn more about building the product package that's right for you.

Acknowledgments

The three of us have benefitted enormously from working together, and the final product reflects an intensely collaborative process. A lagniappe from writing the book has been getting to know one another better!

In the process of working on this book, we benefitted immeasurably from the work of Professors Jerry Borison (Denver) and Paula Monopoli (Maryland). Susan and Naomi are so grateful to the two of them for their contributions to the final product and for their willingness to let us use material from our jointly-authored casebook. In addition, we would like to thank the following people: Mary Kate Hunter, Reference Librarian at George Washington University, answered countless inquiries with expertise and good humor, and Lillian White (George Washington) and Valerie Price (Cumberland) ably assisted administratively. We also thank our Deans—Marcilynn A. Burke at the University of Oregon, Blake Morant at GW, and Corky Strickland at Cumberland—for their support of this and other projects. Law students Priom Ahmed and Olivia Soloperto at George Washington University and Adelaide McGraw, Patrick Perry, and Kate Henderson at the Cumberland School of Law provided excellent research assistance. Several semesters of students at different schools have helped us develop these materials, providing useful critiques to guide us as we finalized the book. We are grateful to everyone who helped in the creation of this textbook, even if we neglected to list them here.

We also appreciate our work with the editorial staff at WK, particularly Richard Mixter, and we thank Jane Hosie-Bounar and Jessica Barmack (development editors), Kaesmene Banks (production editor), Adele Hutchinson (permissions editor), Anna Skiba-Crafts (copy editor), Michelle Williams (proofreader), Susan Junkin (indexer).

Thanks to those of you reading this book for your "trust" in us! Please let us know if you have any comments.

And to our families, thank you for your patience and support—of this book, and of everything else.

In addition, we gratefully acknowledge the following source for permission to reprint a portion of their work:

Joshua C. Tate, Personal Reality: Delusion in Law and Science, 49 CONN. L. REV. 891, 905-6 (2017). Reprinted by permission.

Wills, Trusts, and Estates in Focus

Introduction to the Law and Practice of Trusts and Estates

Welcome to trusts and estates! You might be taking this course for many reasons, ranging from interest in the field as a potential area of practice to needing to know more about a bar topic. Regardless of your reasons for enrolling in this course, you will find that trusts and estates is an interesting and challenging course for many reasons. Perhaps at the most basic level, trusts and estates is about people, money, and death. Everyone will die at some point, and, although many of us don't want to think about this, it is important to plan for that eventuality: deciding who will take care of minor children; dividing up assets; figuring out who will handle our digital presence; planning for incapacity; establishing a legacy; and if there are substantial resources, attempting to minimize tax liability. Underlying much of trusts and estates practice, you will see a range of human experience and emotions, including generosity and greed, and you also will see the complexity of relationships. But trusts and estates is also about professional responsibility, drafting, litigation, property ownership, contractual rights, health care planning, and so much more.

The primary goal of this chapter is to provide you with a historically grounded and contextual understanding of the role the law plays in trusts and estates. During the course, we will return to many of the topics introduced in this chapter. So for now, your focus should be on the policy issues and overall themes raised by trusts and estates and on the differing roles in legal practice played by trusts and estates lawyers. Note that we will sometimes use the term "wills, trusts, and estates" and sometimes the term "trusts and estates" to refer to this field.

Key Concepts

- The historical evolution of trusts and estates
- The primary sources of law in trusts and estates
- The special terminology of the trusts and estates field
- The basic concepts of freedom of testation and both default and override rules relating to public policy and family protection
- The practice of trusts and estates law

1

A. OVERVIEW

This course provides an overview of American inheritance law. It explores the theoretical and constitutional underpinnings of the American system for distributing property at death, and it also emphasizes the importance of lifetime planning for incapacity and property transfers. A variety of subjects are covered, ranging from (1) the rules that govern one's ability to direct the allocation of property at death by drafting a will (**testacy**); (2) the laws that govern the allocation of property when one dies without a will (**intestacy**); (3) the transfer of property both during lifetime and at death using trusts; (4) other tools, sometimes called nonprobate transfers or "**will substitutes**," used to transfer property at death; to (5) a series of other issues involved in lifetime estate planning, including gifts, planning for incapacity, and minimizing taxes.

We begin with a general introduction to the field of wills, trusts, and estates. Every adult with any type of property or with minor children should have some type of estate plan that adequately provides for management of property and health during incapacity and provides for minor children and distribution of assets upon death. An **estate plan** involves documentation of the tasks that manage and dispose of an individual's assets in the event of the individual's incapacity or death.

The major goal of many people who see a trusts and estates lawyer is to develop an estate plan, the general term that refers to a process that often starts with having a **will**, a legal document that expresses an individual's wishes concerning property distribution at death.

Many estate plans integrate **nonprobate transfers**, which are gratuitous grants of property that do not use a will, such as life insurance policies. A will is often integrated with a trust for continued management of the property. A **trust** is a legal relationship whereby property is held by one party for the benefit of another, and a trust can be established during a lifetime or through a will.

A complete estate plan will also include various "advance directives" that operate while a person is still alive, including: a financial **power of attorney**, which delegates financial decision making to another person or entity, and a health care **advance medical directive**, which sets out an individual's medical wishes in the case of **incapacity**, which is the inability to manage one's own property and business affairs. These documents help effectuate a client's intent.

***

Trusts and estates itself is an ancient area of law that is integrally related to property ownership and transmission. Once society establishes laws that govern private property, it can create rules specifying how—and whether—property can be transferred upon the death of the owner. In English law, it was the British Parliament's enactment of the Statute of Wills in 1540 that for the first time created a right to distribute property at death by a will. Joshua C. Tate, *Caregiving and the Case for Testamentary Freedom*, 42 U.C. Davis L. Rev. 129, 153-54 (2008). Many of the special terms you will see through the course are derived from, and left over from, this history. For example, you may see references to a "last will and testament," terminology that was in use in the 1500s. See Karen J. Sneddon, *In the Name of God, Amen: Language in Last Wills and Testaments*, 29 Quinnipiac L. Rev. 665, 694 (2011).

In the United States, each state has developed its own approach, largely built on the law of the country of origin of the initial settlers, generally England, France, or Spain. These early laws established numerous formalities for valid property transmission at death, such as the rules that there be three witnesses in order for a will to be valid. They were also characterized by a single-minded focus on wills as the only means by which an individual could indicate how property should be distributed post-death.

Over the past century there have been dramatic changes in trusts and estates law, including:

- The field has moved toward less formality in the requirements for a valid will.
- The field has become more accepting of nonprobate transfers, transfers that occur at death outside of the probate process, such as through life insurance or a **joint tenancy with right of survivorship**, a means for co-ownership of property that entitles a surviving co-owner to the share of a deceased co-owner.
- The types of property that can be transferred at death have expanded beyond real estate to include nearly all property an individual can own—not just stocks and bonds but also **digital assets**, electronic property like computer files, web domains, digital communications, and virtual currency.
- The laws of the states are becoming more similar as a result of the efforts of both the Uniform Law Commission (ULC), with its drafting of the **Uniform Probate Code** (UPC), a model act that sets out a state's approach to handling an individual's property at death; the **Uniform Trust Code** (UTC), a model law that sets out how a state can approach trusts, and other laws; as well as the American Law Institute (ALI), with its Restatements of Trusts and of Wills and Donative Transfers.
- The process of developing an estate plan, which gives directions for managing and disposing of an individual's assets in the event of incapacity or death, now typically involves the use of legal documents in addition to wills.
- Various legal documents that allow individuals to make advance arrangements for their incapacity have gained widespread legal and popular acceptance.
- The role of the lawyer has expanded beyond drafting wills, and professionalism in practice has assumed even more importance.
- "Self-help" planning is increasingly available through the Internet.
- The judicial process for probating wills or administering estates has been vastly simplified.

One core principle that has resisted change, however, is the significance of **freedom of donative intent**, sometimes known as **freedom of testation**. The dominant norm in American trusts and estates law has always been to allow property owners to do what they want with their property, during life and at death. This norm has been—and continues to be—subject to relatively few limitations. Property owners can make present or future gifts that are absolute or conditional, transfer their property in trust to benefit someone else (or even themselves), place restrictions on property they own, share their interests with other owners, and decide, upon death, who will own their property without the necessity of benefiting anyone in particular.

This respect for freedom of donative intent manifests itself most clearly in the general principle that a will dictates outcomes even if the choices made by the **testator**, the person who makes the will, seem inappropriate. However, as you will see, even this bedrock principle is subject to some limitations because of changing cultural norms concerning protection of dependent family members and various other public policy matters (discussed later in the chapter).

The respect for donative intent applies even when there is no explicit direction from the **decedent**, the person who has died, such as when there is no written document or an estate planner failed to adequately consider various contingencies when drafting documents. In these situations, state laws provide a set of default rules designed to approximate what the decedent would have wanted. The ultimate default rules are **intestacy** rules, establishing who gets the entire probate estate when an individual dies without a will.

Even where there is a will, however, default rules may be necessary. For example, assume that in her will, a testator left her house to her son. Before she died, she sold the house and bought a condominium. Does the son get nothing? Does he get the condominium? Or does he get the cash equal to the value of the house? In default of the testator's will addressing this question, a **rule of construction**, will apply to help resolve the situation. A rule of construction is typically either a judicial doctrine or statute that can help a court give meaning where the intent is unclear.

The themes of the book echo those throughout the field of trusts and estates. They include:

- The need to consider freedom of testation and respect for the testator's wishes balanced against rules dictated by legislatures and courts that restrict donative freedom in order to protect the living
- The potential tension between seeking to fulfill the individual's intent and the formalities that, though designed to protect it, may actually thwart that intent
- The use of other lifetime planning techniques
- The ethical issues that pervade estate planning

EXHIBIT 1.1   Trusts and Estates Formalities

An introduction to trusts and estates involves considering the four functions that formalities are commonly believed to serve:

- *The Evidentiary Function.* Formalities assure that there is permanent reliable evidence of the donor's intent that can be presented to a court, if needed.
- *The Channeling Function.* Formalities assure that the document enters the legal system in a manner that courts can process routinely and with few administrative hurdles.
- *The Ritual (Cautionary) Function.* Formalities assure that the donor's intent to dispose of property is serious, for example that an individual understands a particular document is a will and that the document is final and not a draft.

■ ***The Protective Function.*** Formalities assure that the donor is protected from her own lack of capacity, that the donor's intent is not the product of undue influence, fraud, delusion, or coercion, and that the document and signatures are not the products of forgery or perjury.

See Ashbel G. Gulliver & Catherine J. Tilson, *Classification of Gratuitous Transfers*, 51 Yale L.J. 1 (1941).

B. THE LEGAL SYSTEM GOVERNING TRUSTS AND ESTATES

Each year, approximately 2.5 million people die in the United States, and a majority of them do not have a will that explains how they want their property to be distributed. Who decides what happens to their property? How can people ensure their property is distributed as they wish? This course answers those questions.

As you will see, the laws governing trusts and estates are state laws, with federal laws having very little or no impact on the average estate. Because each state borrowed from the law of its particular colonial tradition to develop its own approach to trusts and estates law, many of the U.S. laws concerning trusts and estates are based on English common law, and are encrusted with history. Some states, primarily in the west, also have elements of Spanish law in addition to English common law; and Louisiana, which was once a colony of both Spain and France, has a unique set of trusts and estates laws. Trusts and estates practice involves a mix of common law and statutes. The primary federal law that impacts estates is the federal wealth transfer tax, which will be discussed at length in Chapter 15.

Although the course covers wills, estates, and trusts, different sets of law apply to wills and estates and to trusts. The laws applicable to wills and estates have generally been statutorily based, albeit with much case law, and with enormous variation among states. For example, one state might permit handwritten, unwitnessed wills signed only by the testator, while another state might only recognize wills signed by two witnesses. To bring some uniformity and clarity to the law and to eliminate many of the formal rules that were intent-defeating, the Uniform Law Commission (ULC) drafted the Uniform Probate Code (UPC) in 1969. After revisions to individual sections over the years, the ULC redrafted the entire UPC in 1990. The 1990 version has also been revised a few times, in particular in 2008, so it is impossible to describe any uniformity in terms of state adoptions. Some states have adopted the 1969 UPC, some have adopted the 1990 UPC as originally enacted, and others have incorporated some of the revisions. In addition, some states have not adopted either act as a whole but may have incorporated provisions from different versions.

Notwithstanding this lack of uniformity in adoptions of the UPC, the UPC has influenced statutes in states that are not "UPC states." Because of the impact of the UPC, this book uses selected provisions of the UPC to illustrate various aspects of U.S. probate law. In addition, to show you some of the variations among the states, the book uses statutes and cases from states that have not adopted the UPC.

In the trusts area, although the law developed primarily through cases, with relatively minimal statutory law, the Restatement has been particularly influential in the development of trusts law. In 2000, the ULC promulgated the Uniform Trust Code (UTC) to bring greater uniformity to the field and to provide a source of law for states with limited case law. The UTC codifies the common law in many respects, and to date it has been adopted in whole or in part by approximately half of the states. Like the UPC, however, its influence extends beyond the states that have enacted it. The UTC provides precise, comprehensive, and easily accessible guidance on trust law questions, and is a resource for trustees, lawyers, and courts. Rather than attempting to discuss the law of 50 states, this book primarily uses UTC provisions to explain trust law. We occasionally include the law of other states where we think it is pedagogically appropriate.

In addition to the UPC and the UTC, numerous other uniform laws, such as the Uniform Prudent Investor Act, the Uniform Power of Appointments Act, and others, are widely enacted and influential, and are discussed in depth in later chapters. The book, including the cases, frequently refers to the Restatements, which are often cited in the trusts and estates field.

C. TESTAMENTARY FREEDOM

The guiding principle in estate planning and estate administration is effectuating the transferor's intent, that is, the intent of the individual who is disposing of the property. As the UPC explains: "The underlying purposes and policies of this Code are . . . to discover and make effective the intent of a decedent in distribution of his property." UPC § 1-102(b)(2). Throughout the course, you will hear references to the "decedent's intent," the "settlor's intent," or the "testator's intent," and most of the default rules in the trusts and estates field are attempts to establish what the decedent would have wanted. As you will see, individuals enjoy broad freedom to craft their estate plans as they choose. Numerous policies support this freedom. See Mark Glover, *A Therapeutic Jurisprudential Framework of Estate Planning*, 35 Seattle U. L. Rev. 427, 444-45 (2012).

Perhaps the oldest policy is the notion that testators have a natural right to bequeath their property. Having created wealth by the sweat of their brows, testators are naturally free to do with it as they please—including passing it along to others.

One argument, tracing back to the thirteenth century, holds that freedom of testation creates an incentive to industry and saving. To the extent that lawmakers deny persons the opportunity to leave their possessions freely, the subjective value of property will drop, for one of its potential uses will have disappeared. As a result, thwarted testators will choose to accumulate less property, and the total stock of wealth existing at any given time will shrink.

Another argument for freedom of testation, also premised upon the goal of wealth enhancement, is that such freedom supports, as it were, "a market for the provision of social services. . . . The testator's power to bequeath encourages her beneficiaries to provide her with care and comfort—services that add to the total economic 'pie.'" Adam J. Hirsch & William K.S. Wang, *A Qualitative Theory of the Dead Hand*, 68 Ind. L.J. 1, 6-10 (1992).

On the other hand, while testamentary freedom is a bedrock principle, the law does not allow an individual unfettered discretion; it sets some limits on an individual's disposition of property. See Shelly Kreiczer Levy & Meital Pinto, *Property and Belongingness: Rethinking Gender-Biased Disinheritance*, 21 Tex. J. Women & L. 119, 125 (2011). For example, you are probably generally familiar with the **Rule Against Perpetuities**, which sets limits on the length of time that property can be encumbered. The law steps in at other points as well. The elective share rules preclude an individual from denying a surviving spouse a portion of the decedent spouse's estate. Similarly, the law will not allow a person to avoid creditors by leaving all of the debtor's property to others. The law also prevents "unreasonable restraints on alienation or marriage; provisions promoting separation or divorce; impermissible racial or other categorical restrictions; provisions encouraging illegal activity. . . ." Restatement (Third) of Property (Wills and Other Donative Transfers) § 10.1 (2003).

Moreover, unlimited freedom of testation raises various policy concerns.

First, it is difficult to anticipate future events. John H. Langbein, *Burn the Rembrandt? Trust Law's Limits on the Settlor's Power to Direct Investments*, 90 B.U. L. Rev. 375, 378 (2010). A living person has time to adjust her proposed estate plan and reconsider the consequences, while **dead hand control**, the disposition established by a will, is fixed. Id.

Second are concerns of "intergenerational equity between the interests of the present generation and future generations. . . . [T]he living may not have an incentive to incorporate fully the interests of future generations. Thus, their incentive to use and transfer property may diverge from what is socially optimal." Daniel B. Kelly, *Restricting Testamentary Freedom: Ex Ante Versus Ex Post Justifications*, 82 Fordham L. Rev. 1125, 1163 (2013).

Consider that dead hand control can tie up property for generations, preventing the property from being used for more productive purposes and restricting property recipients from maximizing the potential best uses of that property. Relatedly, Thomas Jefferson feared that the ability to inherit wealth would result in establishing an aristocracy. See Angus Deaton, *It's Not Just Unfair: Inequality Is a Threat to Our Governance*, N.Y. Times, Mar. 20, 2017, https://www.nytimes.com/2017/03/20/books/review/crisis-of-the-middle-class-constitution-ganesh-sitaraman-.html?mwrsm=Facebook&_r=0. Dead hand control can exacerbate income inequality.

Finally, other countries guarantee protection for family members by requiring that some portion of a decedent's estate pass to family. For example, in France, children are guaranteed a portion of their parents' estate. See Ray D. Madoff, *A Tale of Two Countries: Comparing the Law of Inheritance in Two Seemingly Opposite Systems*, 37 B.C. Int'l & Comp. L. Rev. 333, 334 (2014). By contrast, in the United States, outside of the state of Louisiana and Puerto Rico, the decedent is not required to leave any property to children, even minor children.

Outside of minimal limitations, courts are hesitant to restrict testamentary freedom, and some commentators have even suggested that testamentary freedom has expanded, such as through the abolition, in a number of jurisdictions, of the Rule Against Perpetuities. E.g., David Horton, *Testation and Speech*, 101 Geo. L.J. 61, 64 (2012).

Case Preview

Feinberg v. Feinberg

Max and Erla Feinberg had two children, Michael and Leila, and five grandchildren. When Max died in 1986, his will directed that all of his assets were to "pour over" into a trust that contained the restriction that is the focus of the case, a restriction on the marital choice of his grandchildren. That restriction only came into play on Erla's death in 2003. In *Feinberg*, the court struggles with where to draw the lines between following the testator's intent and fairness. The laws of both wills and trusts (like that of contracts) will not enforce provisions that are contrary to public policy.

As you read the case, think about:

1. What was the restriction that Max Feinberg sought to place on his grandchildren?
2. How does the court identify and describe the state's public policy?
3. What does the court state about the freedom of a testator to decide to whom to leave his property?
4. What issues does this case raise about why a state might wish to restrict dead hand control or to uphold it?

Who Are These People?

Max Feinberg was a wealthy Chicago dentist who died in 1986. His wife, Erla, died in 2003, and that's when all of the litigation started. Manya A. Brachear & Ron Grossman, *Jewish Disinheritance Upheld by Illinois High Court*, L.A. Times, (Sept. 26, 2009), http://articles.latimes.com/2009/sep/26/nation/na-jewish-disinherit26. Litigation on related issues between family members continued after 2009. E.g., In re Estate of Feinberg, 6 N.E.3d 310, *appeal denied*, 8 N.E.3d 1048 (Ill. 2014).

Feinberg v. Feinberg
919 N.E.2d 888 (Ill. 2009)

[The "beneficiary restriction clause" from Max Feinberg's estate plan] directed that 50% of the assets be held in trust for the benefit of the then-living descendants of [his children,] Michael and Leila during their lifetimes. . . . However, any such descendant who married outside the Jewish faith or whose non-Jewish spouse did not convert to Judaism within one year of marriage would be "deemed deceased for all purposes of this instrument as of the date of such marriage" and that descendant's share of the trust would revert to Michael or Leila. . . .

All five grandchildren married between 1990 and 2001. . . . Only Leila's son, Jon, met the conditions of the beneficiary restriction clause and was entitled to receive [a distribution from the trust].

This litigation followed, pitting Michael's daughter, Michele, against Michael, coexecutor[1] of the estates of both Max and Erla. The trial court invalidated the beneficiary restriction clause on public policy grounds. A divided appellate court affirmed, holding that "under Illinois law and under the Restatement (Third) of Trusts, the provision in the case before us is invalid because it seriously interferes with and limits the right of individuals to marry a person of their own choosing." 383 Ill. App. 3d at 997. In reaching this conclusion, the appellate court relied on decisions of this court dating back as far as 1898 and, as noted, on the Restatement (Third) of Trusts. . . .

We note that this case involves more than a grandfather's desire that his descendants continue to follow his religious tradition after he is gone. This case reveals a broader tension between the competing values of freedom of testation on one hand and resistance to "dead hand" control on the other. This tension is clearly demonstrated by the three opinions of the appellate court. The authoring justice rejected the argument that the distribution scheme is enforceable [], stating that its "clear intent was to influence the marriage decisions of Max's grandchildren based on a religions [sic] criterion." 383 Ill. App. 3d at 997. The concurring justice opined that while such restrictions might once have been considered reasonable, they are no longer reasonable. 383 Ill. App. 3d at 1000 (Quinn, P.J. specially concurring). The dissenting justice noted that [] the weight of authority is that a testator has a right to make the distribution of his bounty conditional on the beneficiary's adherence to a particular religious faith.

We, therefore, begin our analysis with the public policy surrounding testamentary freedom and then consider public policy pertaining to testamentary or trust provisions concerning marriage.

When we determine that our answer to a question of law must be based on public policy, it is not our role to make such policy. Rather, we must discern the public policy of the state of Illinois as expressed in the constitution, statutes, and long-standing case law. We will find a contract provision against public policy only "if it is injurious to the interests of the public, contravenes some established interest of society, violates some public statute, is against good morals, tends to interfere with the public welfare or safety, or is at war with the interests of society or is in conflict with the morals of the time." Thus,

> "In deciding whether an agreement violates public policy, courts determine whether the agreement is so capable of producing harm that its enforcement would be contrary to the public interest. The courts apply a strict test in determining when an agreement violates public policy. The power to invalidate part or all of an agreement on the basis of public policy is used sparingly because private parties should not be needlessly hampered in their freedom to contract between themselves. Whether an agreement is contrary to public policy depends on the particular facts and circumstances of the case." *Kleinwort Benson N. Am., Inc. v. Quantum Fin. Serv.*, 692 N.E.2d 269 (Ill. 1998).

Because, as will be discussed below, the public policy of this state values freedom of testation as well as freedom of contract, these same principles guide our analysis in the present case.

---

[1][The executor of an estate is the individual appointed by the court to manage and collect, the property of the decedent. The UPC refers to this individual as the "personal representative." UPC § 1-201(35). —Eds.]

PUBLIC POLICY REGARDING FREEDOM OF TESTATION

Neither the Constitution of the United States nor the Constitution of the State of Illinois speak to the question of testamentary freedom. However, our statutes clearly reveal a public policy in support of testamentary freedom. . . .

Under the Probate Act, Max and Erla had no obligation to make any provision at all for their grandchildren. Indeed, if Max had died intestate, Erla, Michael, and Leila would have shared his estate, and if Erla had died intestate, only Michael and Leila would have taken. Surely, the grandchildren have no greater claim on their grand-parents' testate estates than they would have had on intestate estates.

Similarly, under the Trusts and Trustees Act, "[a] person establishing a trust may specify in the instrument the rights, powers, duties, limitations and immunities applicable to the trustee, beneficiary and others and those provisions where not otherwise contrary to law shall control, notwithstanding this Act." Thus, the legislature intended that the settlor of a trust have the freedom to direct his bounty as he sees fit, even to the point of giving effect to a provision regarding the rights of beneficiaries that might depart from the standard provisions of the Act, unless "otherwise contrary to law. . . ."

The record, via the testimony of Michael and Leila, reveals that Max's intent in restricting the distribution of his estate was to benefit those descendants who opted to honor and further his commitment to Judaism by marrying within the faith. Max had expressed his concern about the potential extinction of the Jewish people, not only by holocaust, but by gradual dilution as a result of intermarriage with non-Jews. While he was willing to share his bounty with a grandchild whose spouse converted to Judaism, this was apparently as far as he was willing to go.

There is no question that a grandparent in Max's situation is entirely free during his lifetime to attempt to influence his grandchildren to marry within his family's religious tradition, even by offering financial incentives to do so. The question is, given our public policy of testamentary freedom, did Max's beneficiary restriction clause [] violate any other public policy of the state of Illinois, thus rendering it void? . . .

Michele argues that the beneficiary restriction clause discourages lawful marriage and interferes with the fundamental right to marry, which is protected by the constitution. She also invokes the constitution in support of her assertion that issues of race, religion, and marriage have special status because of their constitutional dimensions, particularly in light of the constitutional values of personal autonomy and privacy.

Because a testator or the settlor of a trust is not a state actor, there are no constitutional dimensions to his choice of beneficiaries. Equal protection does not require that all children be treated equally; due process does not require notice of conditions precedent to potential beneficiaries; and the free exercise clause does not require a grandparent to treat grandchildren who reject his religious beliefs and customs in the same manner as he treats those who conform to his traditions.

Thus, Michele's reliance on *Shelley v. Kraemer*, 334 U.S. 1 (1948), is entirely misplaced. In *Shelley*, the Supreme Court held that the use of the state's judicial process to obtain enforcement of a racially restrictive covenant was state action, violating the equal protection clause of the Fourteenth Amendment. *Shelley*, 334 U.S. at 19. This court, however, has been reluctant to base a finding of state action "on the mere fact that a state court is the forum for the dispute." *In re Adoption of K.L.P.*, 763 N.E.2d 741 (Ill. 2002). . . .

. . . Michele argues that the beneficiary restriction clause is capable of exerting an ongoing "disruptive influence" upon marriage and is, therefore, void. She is mistaken. The provision cannot "disrupt" an existing marriage because once the beneficiary determination was made at the time of Erla's death, it created no incentive to divorce.

Finally, it has been suggested that Michael and Leila have litigated this matter rather than concede to Michele's demands because they wish to deprive the grandchildren of their inheritance. The grandchildren, however, are not the heirs at law of Max and Erla and had no expectancy of an inheritance, so long as their parents were living, even if Max and Erla had died intestate. In addition, Michael and Leila are the coexecutors of their parents' estates and, as such, are duty-bound to defend their parents' estate plans. *Hurd v. Reed*, 102 N.E. 1048 (Ill. 1913) ("It is the duty of an executor to defend the will"), citing *Pingree v. Jones*, 80 Ill. 177, 181 (1875) (executor is "bound, on every principle of honor, justice and right" to defend the will, he "owes this, at least, to the memory of the dead who placed this confidence in him"). Although those plans might be offensive to individual family members or to outside observers, Max and Erla were free to distribute their bounty as they saw fit and to favor grandchildren of whose life choices they approved over other grandchildren who made choices of which they disapproved, so long as they did not convey a vested interest that was subject to divestment by a condition subsequent that tended to unreasonably restrict marriage or encourage divorce.

Incentive Trusts

Of course, parents (and grandparents) may have many motives in deciding how to leave their property and whether to include restrictions. Bill Gates, of Microsoft fame, explained: "'It's not a favor to kids to have them have huge sums of wealth,'" he said. "It distorts anything they might do, creating their own path." Amy Graff, *Bill Gates Explains Why He's Not Leaving His Fortune to His Children*, SFGate (Oct. 27, 2016, 10:44 AM), http://www.sfgate.com/mommyfiles/article/Bill-Gates-not-leaving-kids-fortune-Melinda-10414373.php. Lawyers may counsel their clients about including various "control from the grave" behavioral incentives and disincentives. Incentives often include making funds available for education, starting a business, or working in the nonprofit sector. Disincentives often include restricting funds if the beneficiaries abuse drugs, alcohol, or gambling, are not productive with their lives, or even do not maintain certain grade point averages. See *Greff v. Milam*, 51 So. 3d 29 (La. Ct. App. 5th Cir. 2010). These provisions are often not challenged, and, so long as they are not contrary to public policy, they will be upheld.

Post-Case Follow-Up

As already mentioned, the intermediate appellate court in *Feinberg* struck down this particular use of financial incentives in estate planning because of its impact on, and interference with, an individual's freedom to marry the person of their choice. Courts generally find that conditions requiring a potential beneficiary to divorce or become separated are invalid as a violation of public policy. These clauses, it is argued, allow the dead to exert too much control over the personal choices of the living. See Ruth Sarah Lee, *Over My Dead Body: A New Approach to Testamentary Restraints on Marriage*, 14 Marq. Elder's Advisor 55 (2012). On the other hand, as the Illinois Supreme Court noted, courts generally seek to preserve donative intent to the maximum extent possible.

Feinberg v. Feinberg: Real Life Applications

1. If Max Feinberg had consulted you about the advisability of the disinheritance clause in his will, what issues might you have raised with him relating to both legal and nonlegal matters?

2. You have been asked to advise Lily, the grieving widow of Alphonse. Alphonse and Lily were married and had two children, Nan and Omega. Alphonse recently died, and Alphonse's will provides: "I leave one-third of my estate to Nan, unless Nan should be so foolish as to marry before age 22. In that case, Nan shall receive nothing from my estate." Nan is currently 18 and unmarried, and Lily wants to know if Nan can receive all of the money now, or if distribution must wait until after Nan is 22 and is unmarried.

3. Based on the same facts as Problem 2, another provision in Alphonse's will provides: "I leave one-third of my estate to be paid to Omega to finance Omega's college and graduate school education." Lily wants your advice on whether this restriction on Omega's inheritance is legally enforceable.

D. INTRODUCTION TO TRUSTS AND ESTATES LEGAL PRACTICE

Trusts and estates is a versatile specialty. Practitioners have a variety of different practice options, including not just wealth transfer planning but also elder law, trust administration, nonprofit management, and government service. They may focus on the transactional or the litigation side. Most commonly, trusts and estates attorneys work in either small or large private law firms or in trust companies or banks.

But trusts and estates lawyers work in numerous other practice settings as well. Lawyers in legal aid offices, for example, provide assistance to lower-income older adults on a variety of planning and public benefits issues. You might consider a probate court clerkship or externship as an introduction to the types of matters that a trusts and estates attorney may face.

1. The Different Roles of Trusts and Estates Practitioners

Trusts and estates practitioners in private firms represent clients on a variety of issues related to estate planning and probate matters. Trust and estate attorneys in this type of practice help clients plan for lifetime management of their assets as well as the efficient and effective transfer of assets to family members, to other persons whom the clients wish to benefit, and to charities. Private practice might include preparing trust agreements, wills, financial powers of attorney, and health care medical directives. In some firms, trusts and estates lawyers litigate will contests or fiduciary conflicts, while in others, these matters are handled by the litigation department. Tax is a substantial part of the planning process for high-net-worth clients, and lawyers in firms servicing wealthy clients often obtain an LLM in taxation after completing their law degree.

Attorneys may help clients with comprehensive estate planning, they may represent executors of estates trying to manage the probate process, they may represent disgruntled heirs seeking to challenge the particular disposition of an estate, they may represent trustees of a trust, they may serve as tax advisers, or they may combine trusts and estates with family law or real estate expertise—and this is just the start of the list.

When an attorney begins working with an individual who is interested in estate planning, the lawyer will learn about the individual's familial relationships and charitable interests as well as engage in a comprehensive review of the client's financial situation. The relevant financial information ranges from bank accounts to investments to retirement accounts to real estate to trust beneficiary status to digital assets. Attorneys may help with general financial planning as well as tax issues; employee benefit planning; charitable gift planning; issues facing private foundations; and even with international law issues, such as for nonresidents with assets in the United States, and for U.S. citizens with substantial assets abroad.

In the trust administration area, attorneys may advise both corporate and individual trustees concerning compliance with the trust's terms and relevant law. They may also consult with beneficiaries concerning trust administration matters including concerns over distributions or trust accounts. Sometimes lawyers complete income tax returns for trusts and other estate planning entities, and sometimes accountants handle these matters. In some jurisdictions, lawyers serve as trustees or personal representatives, and maintain the obligations of a fiduciary with respect to all aspects of the administration of a trust or estate.

Many states have special courts, typically called probate courts (although they may have a different label in your state), that manage estate-related cases. Approximately 11 percent of all cases in general jurisdiction courts are probate estate matters. See Nat'l Center for State Courts, *Statewide Civil Caseload Composition in 26 States*, 2016 (n.d.). Florida is an interesting example. In that state, which has established a special probate court, more than 50,000 cases are filed per year.

Elder law has developed as its own legal specialty, and elder law practitioners must be familiar with trusts and estates concepts. Planning for incapacity overlaps both fields.

As you can see, there are numerous different aspects of trusts and estates practice, such as estate planning, wealth management, probate, trust administration, and litigation, and different work environments, including law firms, solo or boutique practice, planned giving offices of charities, financial institutions (where individuals may work as lawyers but also as trust officers, compliance officers, in risk management roles, etc.). And there is always a potential new client base; death never goes out of style.

2. The Demands and Rewards of Trusts and Estates Practice

Trusts and estates practice involves intellectually challenging and emotionally complex issues that are at the core of contemporary life. In addition, trusts and estates practice offers a glimpse into some of the most interesting and troublesome questions in our society—from the changing structures of family life, to end-of-life decision making, to advanced reproductive technologies. Trusts and estates involves various fundamental tensions in jurisprudence: e.g., between default rules (background rules) and individuals' actual preferences; between mandatory rules (society's absolute preferences) and individual autonomy; and between form and substance.

Practicing trusts and estates law requires competence in the field. Many of the cases and issues that arise in trusts and estates and through this casebook result from attorney involvement, or lack of involvement, in planning or drafting, and may raise issues of attorney competence. Consequently, professional responsibility issues appear throughout the course and are a critical part of trusts and estates practice.

Moreover, as you saw in *Feinberg*, trusts and estates law can also involve emotionally difficult issues. Individuals seeking legal help on how to plan for incapacity and to distribute money—or how to obtain an inheritance—often seek help from lawyers at fragile moments in their lives. Consider how much advice and counseling a lawyer should offer. Basic principles of professional responsibility require that you fully understand the client's wishes when you are drafting an estate plan. Likewise, if litigation ensues, the parties and the court must be able to interpret the property-transferring document, so the lawyer must draft the terms carefully.

Among other factors, raw emotion may contribute to many of the distinctive professional and ethical challenges that trusts and estates lawyers frequently face, matters explored in greater depth in Chapter 13, Professional Ethics in Trusts and Estates. The client's familial relationship may have been marked by divorce and remarriage and conflicts with children (or grandchildren) over life choices. The client's emotional vulnerability may affect the lawyer-client relationship. For example, as in *Feinberg*, a client may want to impose behavior controls on family members, while a lawyer may want the client to consider the impact of such restraints on family dynamics by looking into the future, long after the client has passed on. The client may misinterpret the lawyer's more dispassionate focus on tangible factors and resist the lawyer's explanations of why emotion-laden estate planning can lead not just to fractured family dynamics but to costly litigation.

Despite the emotional intensity frequently experienced by trusts and estates lawyers in their practice, a clinical study examining job satisfaction among lawyers in 12 primary areas of law found that tax, trusts, and estates lawyers had among the highest scores, while corporate and real estate practitioners had the lowest scores.

Lawrence R. Richard, *Psychological Type and Job Satisfaction Among Practicing Lawyers in the United States*, 29 Cap. U. L. Rev. 979, 1057 (2002). Trusts and estates is typically a people-focused practice with high amount of client contact and concrete tasks. It is also a practice that is welcoming to solo practitioners and does not require affiliation with a large firm to enter. See Alyssa A. DiRusso, *Turn-Key T&E: Building a Trusts and Estates Practice*, 29 Quinnipiac Prob. L.J. 96 (2016).

Moreover, practitioners typically have a great deal of autonomy, which is one of the elements that make lawyers satisfied with their careers. Indeed, a four-state study of lawyers found that experiences of autonomy as well as the choice of "work for internally motivated reasons (i.e., for enjoyment, interest, or meaning within subjects' belief systems) was also very highly predictive of well-being." Lawrence S. Krieger & Kennon M. Sheldon, *What Makes Lawyers Happy?: A Data-Driven Prescription to Redefine Professional Success*, 83 Geo. Wash. L. Rev. 554, 618 (2015). The authors' description of the ideal practice, which allows for autonomy, connectedness, and competence, describes how many trusts and estates lawyers feel about their professional roles. See Nancy Levit & Douglas O. Linder, The Happy Lawyer: Making a Good Life in the Law (2010) (including suggestions on how to find happiness in the law, ranging from working part-time to practicing mindfulness).

Chapter Summary

- Trusts and estates law encompasses planning for incapacity, planning for death, and planning for wealth transmission.
- The field of trusts and estates has developed a specific terminology that helps practitioners and courts understand the purposes and goals of estate planning action.
- Each state has enacted its own laws applicable to estates and to trusts, but the past half century has seen the development of an increasing number of uniform laws. The primary role for federal law is in taxation.
- The dominant theme of trusts and estates law is respect for donative intent, carrying out the wishes of the property owner. Even that fundamental principle has some limits based, for example, on public policy.
- The practice of trusts and estates is among the most rewarding of legal specialties. It encompasses a variety of potential roles, ranging from wealth adviser to bank fiduciary officer to elder law practitioner to probate judge.

Applying the Concepts

1. Your client, Erin, has $1,000,000. Erin is a widow who has four adult children, Alex, Betty, Cindy, and Derek. Erin wants to give money to Alex and Betty, but not to Cindy and Derek. Erin has retained you to draft her will and would like your professional opinion on the legality of effectuating her wishes. Erin wants

to divide the money between Alex and Betty because they have been providing caretaking while Cindy and Derek have not.

2. The same facts as in Problem 1, but Erin wants to give the money to Alex and Betty because they have been working in low-paying jobs, and Cindy and Derek are wealthy businesspeople. Can Erin do so under the law of wills?

3. The same facts as in Problem 1, but Erin is a devout Catholic and Alex and Betty are similarly devout, while Cindy and Derek are atheists. Can Erin exclude Cindy and Derek on this basis?

4. Jennifer and Ben have been married for 30 years, and they have three children. One of the children will remain dependent on Jennifer and Ben for care for the rest of her life. Jennifer wants to leave everything to Ben, and nothing to her children, including the one who cannot live independently. Is this permissible under the law of wills?

5. Dmitry is a doctor who has a spouse, four children, and ten grandchildren. Dmitry decides to give no money at all to family members, and to leave everything to a charity that provides international medical assistance, Health Care Without Borders. Is this permissible under the law of wills?

6. You are a staff member on your state legislature's trusts and estates committee. You have heard testimony on the importance of freedom of testation and on protecting the public fisc. You are currently considering three proposals:

   a. The state shall place no limits on dead hand control. Thus, for example, testators are permitted to direct that their survivors "burn the Rembrandts."
   b. The state shall place a 50 percent tax on the estates of all who die, in an effort to provide more money for state budgets.
   c. When an individual dies, all property shall be split among the closest surviving family members.

The ranking member of the legislative committee has asked for your analysis of the benefits and drawbacks of each of these proposals.

Trusts and Estates in Practice

1. You are considering becoming a trusts and estates attorney in your hometown. Which courses in law school do you think are most relevant to the practice (beyond Trusts and Estates and Estate Planning)?

2. One of your first tasks as a newly minted estates lawyer is to develop an initial client questionnaire for estate planning. What questions concerning personal information, family members, finances, and estate planning concerns will you

include? How would the questions be different for a client who is the executor of an estate? You might want to look at client intake questionnaires available online as a guide.

3. Has your jurisdiction adopted the UPC or the UTC? You can check on the Uniform Law Commission website as well as looking at your jurisdiction's statutes.

4. Spend some time in the local court that handles probate matters. What types of cases do you observe? Is there a special probate court or are such matters handled by a court of general jurisdiction?

5. Some law firms have changed the name of the practice group from "Trusts and Estates" to "Private Clients" or "Wealth Management." Why do you think that is? What is the common term for trusts and estates practitioners in the city of your law school?

Intestacy

Most Americans die without a valid will, or **intestate**. The primary goal of this chapter is to provide you with an understanding of what happens to property when someone dies intestate or when a will fails to dispose of all of the decedent's property. As we will see, the law supplies default rules that determine who will receive the decedent's property. These rules presume that the decedent wanted property to be inherited by close family members, but sometimes the people the decedent viewed as family are not considered family members under the statutes.

Focusing first on the share given to the surviving spouse, then on the share given to children, and then on the share given to more distant relatives, this chapter explores the background rules that serve as a "statutory will." The chapter also considers just what it means to be a spouse or a child—words that you might have thought, before taking this course, did not need a definition!

Key Concepts

- When intestacy rules apply
- Core assumptions of the intestacy system
- Methods of distribution among descendants and the different systems of representation
- Definition of family members

A. INTRODUCTION

About two-thirds of Americans today do not have a will. The intestacy rules are the state's default rules that determine what happens to the probate property of a decedent who died without a will. The intestacy statutes of the state where the decedent was domiciled at death will determine how probate property is distributed.

Intestacy concepts are useful even where there is a will. First, terminology from the intestacy statutes may be used in wills or other governing instruments, and the state's intestacy laws provide the meaning for those terms. Second, a will that is offered for probate can be invalidated in whole or in part. Third, a will may not dispose of the entire probate estate (as in the case of a will that leaves all the personal property to specified beneficiaries but does not specify what happens to the remainder of the estate). In each of these situations, the intestacy rules determine how the property not subject to the will is distributed.

As shown in Exhibit 2.1, the Uniform Probate Code (UPC) establishes which part of a decedent's probate estate passes by intestacy.

EXHIBIT 2.1   **UPC § 2-101. Intestate Estate**
(a) Any part of a decedent's estate not effectively disposed of by will passes by intestate succession to the decedent's heirs as prescribed in this Code, except as modified by the decedent's will.

The intestacy rules, codified by statute in each state, typically give the decedent's property to members of the decedent's family. Intestacy statutes generally (although not always!) establish the following priority: surviving spouse, children and their descendants, parents, descendants of parents, grandparents, and descendants of grandparents. In a few states, if there is no one else, then stepchildren and descendants of stepchildren or more remote relatives, such as descendants of great-grandparents, can inherit. As you will see, intestacy statutes follow rigid relationship rules based on legal status rather than the recipient's behavior toward the decedent, although a potential heir who murders or abuses the decedent may lose her inheritance as discussed in Chapter 5.

There are two theories concerning the goal of intestacy law: (1) the presumed intent theory; and (2) the duty theory. Under the presumed intent theory, the primary goal of intestacy statutes, as stated by the drafters of the UPC and by scholars, is to transfer property according to the probable intent of a decedent who dies without a will. The statutes try to reach the result that legislators believe most intestate decedents likely would want, with an understanding that anyone can execute a will and avoid the application of the statutes. This theory reflects a legislative presumption that most people would prefer that property pass to surviving family members, rather than to friends, cohabitants, favorite charities, or anyone else. Intestacy is thus a one-size-fits-all system.

The second theory focuses on the responsibility of the decedent to support the intestate's dependents, such as a spouse or children. Alyssa A. DiRusso, *Testacy and Intestacy: The Dynamics of Wills and Demographic Status*, 23 Quinnipiac Prob. L.J. 36, 56 (2009). Both theories lead to favoring close family members as the **heirs**, those who inherit through intestacy.

When there is no surviving spouse, children and their descendants are typically preferred over other relatives. When the decedent dies with both a surviving spouse and descendants, American intestacy statutes typically balance the interests of both in inheriting from the decedent. Early statutes provided a one-third share for the surviving spouse if the decedent left descendants, and a one-half share if there were no descendants. Susan N. Gary, *The Probate Definition of Family: A Proposal for Guided Discretion in Intestacy*,

Why Don't People Have a Will?

According to a 2015 Rocket Lawyer estate-planning survey by Harris Poll, 64 percent of Americans don't have a will. Of those without a will, about 27 percent said there isn't an urgent need for them to make one, and 15 percent said they don't need one at all.

Often, people don't have a will because they haven't gotten around to it yet, or because they believe wills are only for wealthy individuals. Jeff Reeves, *Plan Ahead: 64% of Americans Don't Have a Will*, USA Today (July 11, 2015, 1:30 PM, updated Apr. 26, 2016, 12:51 PM), https://www.usatoday.com/story/money/personalfinance/2015/07/11/estate-plan-will/71270548.

45 U. Mich. J.L. Reform 787 (2012). As you will see later in the chapter, modern statutes have evolved to increase the size of the surviving spouse's share, based in part on surveys and reviews of actual probated wills, although there is enormous variation between states.

With respect to determining who gets what portion of the probate estate via intestacy, the principal issues involve determining who qualifies as a family member entitled to take an intestate share, i.e., who are the decedent's heirs, and then calculating each heir's share. This chapter also explores the effect of lifetime transfers on the amount to which an intestate heir is entitled, examining whether the transfers were pure gifts, which do not affect the amount the heir will receive, or transfers that reduce the heir's share.

Heirs Putting on Heirs

Until an individual dies, there are no heirs; there are only apparent heirs. The determination of heirs, those who will inherit through intestacy, is not done until the individual's death, even though people may claim that they will inherit from a living individual. Moreover, under the UPC and in some states, the decedent can create a negative will that expressly disinherits potential heirs if the decedent dies with any intestate property. UPC § 2-101(b). At common law, these negative wills were not given effect.

B. SHARE FOR SURVIVING SPOUSE

Intestacy laws accord special status to spouses and descendants. Surviving spouses and descendants generally take to the exclusion of more remote heirs, including parents and siblings.

Before addressing the share of the surviving spouse, it is important to address who qualifies as the surviving spouse.

1. Who Is a Spouse?

An individual must first prove the appropriate status in order to inherit as a spouse. Just who qualifies? States recognize different ways of becoming a spouse, through either a ceremonial or a common law marriage; and they also recognize that even someone who was never validly married might have rights as a spouse if that person can prove putative spousehood or if state law accords members of a civil union or domestic partnership spousal rights. Certain methods of attaining the status of a spouse may be available in some states and not others, so choice-of-law issues are critical.

Qualifying as a surviving spouse is important: the surviving spouse is entitled to inherit from the decedent in intestacy as well as under the terms of a valid will

Why a Will?

One survey found that the three most important reasons respondents gave for having written a will were: (1) to ensure assets pass on to the right people (69 percent), (2) "to be sure my family is taken care of" (54 percent), and (3) "to prevent family disputes" (44 percent). In a new era of estate planning, protecting digital assets (Facebook account, online photos, passwords, and the like) is essential—yet 63 percent of respondents did not know what would happen to their digital assets when they died. *In a New Era of Estate Planning Rocket™ Lawyer Survey Shows That Only Half of Adults Have a Will*, Rocket Lawyer, http://www.marketwired.com/press-release/in-new-era-estate-planning-rocket-lawyer-survey-shows-that-only-half-adults-have-1637165.htm (last visited Mar. 28, 2012).

or trust that provides for a spouse. The surviving spouse will also be entitled to statutory benefits like the elective share and family allowances, which are discussed in Chapter 8.

Moreover, even if someone can prove a marriage, a subsequent divorce or annulment will make the spouse an ex-spouse. An ex-spouse does not qualify as an heir.

This section explores each of these classifications and their implications for inheritance rights below.

Legally Married Spouses

An individual who was legally married in a sanctioned ceremony to the decedent as of the date of death meets the definition of a surviving spouse. State law establishes both substantive restrictions (like age) and procedural restrictions (like the need for a valid license) in order for a marriage to be valid. If there is a technical irregularity, such as an invalid marriage license, then statutes in some states will invalidate the marriage; otherwise, due to the strong public policy in favor of upholding marriages, the noncompliance will not invalidate the marriage. Once a marriage is valid, it can only be ended by divorce, annulment, or death.

Common Law Spouses

In a small number of states, couples can create a common law marriage through their conduct and mental state even in the absence of a formal ceremony. In those states, couples can enter into a common law marriage by: (1) living together (in some states, for a certain amount of time); (2) holding themselves out as married; and (3) having the mutual intent to be married. Once formed, a common law marriage is valid *for all legal purposes* and can be dissolved only through formal divorce (there is no such concept as common law divorce). Accordingly, it is very important to distinguish common law marriage from "mere" cohabiting relationships. See Douglas E. Abrams et al., Contemporary Family Law 146-57 (5th ed., West Acad. Pub. 2019).

Many disputes over whether a valid common law marriage existed arise after the death of one partner, when mutual intent is often difficult to prove.

By 1900, about half the states permitted common law marriage, and today only a small number of states and the District of Columbia allow common law marriages. Joanna L. Grossman & Lawrence M. Friedman, Inside the Castle: Law and the Family in 20th Century America 80-81 (Princeton U. Press 2011).

Nonetheless, common law marriage has significance beyond the few states that recognize it. Once a valid common law marriage is established in a state that allows it, that marriage will be recognized elsewhere so long as the parties met the requirements of their home state. Indeed, the general conflict-of-laws rule is that a marriage validly contracted in one state will be recognized in all states, even in a state where it could not have been entered into in the first place, unless it is in contravention of that state's public policy.

Putative Spousehood

Unless precluded by applicable statute, a **putative spouse** is treated as a legal spouse for purposes of intestacy. A putative spouse is a person who cohabited with the decedent in the good-faith but mistaken belief that he or she was married to the decedent. For example, a couple might marry believing that a divorce was final—when in fact one member of the couple was still legally married to someone else. The second marriage is thus invalid under bigamy laws. Because neither the original nor the revised UPC explicitly denies rights to putative spouses, a putative-spouse doctrine is compatible with the UPC.

Conferring the status of "spouse" on a putative spouse is straightforward if the putative spouse is the only person claiming to be the decedent's surviving spouse. That person takes the share that a legal spouse would take. The problem becomes more complicated if there are multiple claimants—e.g., if the intestate decedent is survived by both a putative spouse and a legal spouse, or by two or more putative spouses. If there are multiple claimants, the court can exercise its power of equitable apportionment to divide the intestate estate among the claimants as appropriate in the circumstances. A potential starting point for apportionment would be to strike a ratio according to the length of time that each claimant cohabited with the decedent. Under this approach, for example, if one claimant cohabited with the decedent for 15 years and the other claimant cohabited with the decedent for five years, the starting point would be to award the first claimant three-fourths of the spouse's share and the latter one-fourth. A court might also consider other factors in arriving at the final division, such as the needs of each claimant and the number of the decedent's joint children with each claimant and their needs.

EXHIBIT 2.2   **Minnesota**

Minnesota's statute is modeled on the Uniform Marriage & Divorce Act, and it explicitly addresses the rights of a putative spouse versus a legal spouse as well as how long the putative spouse status lasts.

MINNESOTA STATUTES DOMESTIC RELATIONS § 518.055—PUTATIVE SPOUSE

Any person who has cohabited with another to whom the person is not legally married in the good faith belief that the person was married to the other is a putative spouse until knowledge of the fact that the person is not legally married terminates the status and prevents acquisition of further rights. A putative spouse acquires the rights conferred upon a legal spouse, whether or not the marriage is prohibited or declared a nullity. If there is a legal spouse or other putative spouses, rights acquired by a putative spouse do not supersede the rights of the legal spouse or those acquired by other putative spouses, but the court shall apportion property, maintenance, and support rights among the claimants as appropriate in the circumstances and in the interests of justice.

Minn. Stat. Ann. § 518.055

As the section notes, putative spouses acquire the rights of a legal spouse and may be able to share a decedent's estate with a legal spouse.

For example, Wendy and Harold were validly married. Harold then left town and married Sharon without divorcing Wendy. Sharon would be a putative spouse at Harold's death if she had a good-faith belief in the validity of the marriage and had not found out about his lack of a divorce from Wendy. Both Wendy and Sharon could claim a portion of Harold's estate at his death: Wendy as a legal spouse, and Sharon as a putative spouse. A court in a state that recognizes putative spousehood has the equitable jurisdiction to apportion Harold's estate in a manner that it considers appropriate and fair. Factors the court might consider are whether Sharon had a good-faith belief that the marriage was valid, the length of time Wendy and Sharon each cohabited with Harold, whether Wendy and Harold divided up their marital property when he left town, whether there are children of either relationship, and whether Harold's property was acquired during his relationship with Wendy or Sharon.

Case Preview

In re Ober

This case concerns whether the decedent was in a common law marriage at his death. In Montana, as in most states, a spouse is preferred over other family members as a court-appointed personal representative to administer an estate. See Mont. Code. Ann. § 72-3-502. In *Ober*, following the death of John Ober, his brother, Joseph, sought to be appointed as the personal representative. Selma Klein objected, and she sought appointment as the personal representative instead, claiming to be John's wife. The lower court found that the elements of a common law marriage had been satisfied, so it appointed Klein as the personal representative. The Montana Supreme Court considered whether Klein met the standard for establishing a common law marriage.

As you read the case, consider:

1. Which elements of common law marriage were at issue?
2. What evidence supported the existence of the common law marriage?
3. What evidence illustrated that Selma Klein was a cohabitant, not a spouse?
4. What, beyond the legal issues, might also have been at stake?

In re Ober
62 P.3d 1114 (Mont. 2003)

Cotter, J.

. . .

We restate the sole issue on appeal as follows:

Did the District Court err in finding that Selma Klein was the common-law wife of John Ober?

. . .

The State of Montana recognizes common-law marriages. See § 40-1-403, MCA. However, in order to establish a common-law marriage, the party asserting the existence of the common-law marriage must prove that: (1) the parties were competent to enter into a marriage; (2) the parties assumed a marital relationship by mutual consent and agreement; and (3) the parties confirmed their marriage by cohabitation and public repute.

In the instant case, Joseph and Leonard [another brother] (the Appellants) concede that both John and Selma were competent to enter into a marriage. The Appellants further concede that John and Selma lived together in Selma's home for several years prior to John's death. They allege, however, that Selma failed to establish that she and John assumed a marital relationship by mutual consent, and that their marriage was confirmed by public repute.

The Appellants contend that the evidence introduced at trial establishes that neither John nor Selma consented to assume a marital relationship. The Appellants support their contention with the following evidence introduced at trial: (1) Selma did not assume John's last name; (2) John and Selma maintained separate property and bank accounts; (3) John and Selma filed their taxes as "single" taxpayers; (4) John and Selma filed documents with the Farm Service agency as "single" persons; (5) John did not designate Selma as the beneficiary on his life insurance policy; (6) John did not report Selma as his spouse to his employer; (7) John granted his brother Benno Ober power of attorney in three separate documents; (8) John continued to pay rent on an apartment in Conrad, Montana, after he moved into Selma's home near Power, Montana; and (9) Selma continued to receive her widow's survivor benefit from the Social Security Administration under the name of her deceased husband, Frank Klein. The Appellants further maintain that no evidence exists to prove that Selma called John her husband, or that John called Selma his wife. The Appellants also question Selma's testimony that John proposed to her in 1987, and that the couple exchanged rings later that year. Finally, the Appellants assert that John was not wearing a ring in any of the photographs introduced into evidence at trial.

Selma counters that substantial evidence was introduced at trial to establish that she and John assumed a marital relationship by mutual consent. Specifically, Selma testified that John proposed to her in 1987. Selma stated that she accepted John's proposal, and that the couple discussed details of a marriage ceremony, such as location and potential members of the wedding party. Selma also testified that she and John exchanged rings shortly after his proposal. Selma stated that she wore her ring almost continuously during her common-law marriage to John, but that John wore his ring only sporadically. Selma further testified, as did Selma's grandson, that John's ring was cut off several years ago after John was involved in a minor accident which caused his hand to swell. Selma produced both her ring and John's "cut" ring at trial.

Selma testified that she was unaware her accountant had designated her a "single" person for tax purposes until it was brought to her attention by parties to the instant case. Additionally, Selma introduced address labels at trial which read "John or Selma Ober." Selma's granddaughter testified that John used address labels like those introduced every month when he paid his bills. Selma also introduced a photograph of herself at trial, which John had carried in his wallet. On the back of the photograph, in John's handwriting, were the words "my wife." Finally, Selma notes on appeal that no evidence was offered by the Appellants at trial to contradict the testimony regarding John's handwritten comment on the back of the photograph.

The facts of the instant case are similar to those in both *Hunsaker* and *Alcorn*. In *Hunsaker*, the surviving spouse testified that she had received a ring from her common-law husband. Hunsaker, 968 P.2d 281, 285-86 (1998). The surviving spouse further testified that the couple had displayed a grandfather clock in their home, which was engraved with their first initials intertwined over the letter "H." The "H" on the clock represented Hunsaker, her common-law husband's last name. Hunsaker, 968 P.2d at 282, 286. This Court determined that the ring and grandfather clock, combined with the surviving spouse's testimony that she "felt married," constituted sufficient evidence to establish that the couple mutually consented and agreed to a marital relationship. Hunsaker, 968 P.2d at 286.

In *Alcorn*, the surviving spouse testified that she had received a ring with a horseshoe design from her common-law husband. The surviving spouse also testified that the couple had incorporated the design into a walkway at their home, as the walkway contained their names etched in the concrete beneath intertwining horseshoes. In re Estate of Alcorn, 868 P.2d 629, 631 (1994). We concluded that the ring and concrete walkway, combined with the surviving spouse's testimony that the couple had agreed "that [they] were married," constituted sufficient evidence to indicate that the couple had mutually consented and agreed to a common-law marriage. Alcorn, 868 P.2d at 631.

This Court held in both *Hunsaker* and *Alcorn* that, based upon evidence in the record as well as testimony given by the surviving spouses, the burden of proving mutual consent to enter a marital relationship had been satisfied. In the instant case, the address labels and wallet photograph, when combined with Selma's testimony, could reasonably be construed to have the same effect. That is, although the Appellants introduced evidence to contradict Selma's assertion that she and John consented to a common-law marriage, the District Court weighed the testimony of the parties and found that John and Selma had indeed mutually consented to a marital relationship. The District Court, which was in the best position to observe Selma and her demeanor, accepted Selma's testimony regarding John's proposal, the wedding rings, and Selma's status as a "single" taxpayer. The District Court also concluded that John and Selma's use of separate bank accounts and surnames was not viewed as unusual by the community or indicative of their marital status. Moreover, we note that this Court "is unaware of any legal requirement that a wife assume the last name of her husband or that [husband and wife] list [each other] as beneficiaries on [their] insurance, retirement or health forms." Finally, public policy, as well as statutory law, favors the finding of a valid marriage. As such, we decline to disturb the District Court's assessment of the credibility of the witnesses, and conclude that the District Court did not err in finding that John and Selma assumed a marital relationship by mutual consent.

The Appellants' second assertion is that John and Selma failed to confirm their common-law marriage by public repute. The Appellants support their assertion with the testimony of several witnesses, who indicated that they believed John to be a bachelor. The Appellants further allege that the only witnesses to testify to John and Selma's common-law marriage were members or close friends of Selma's family.

A common-law marriage cannot exist if the parties have kept their marital relationship a secret. That is, to establish a valid common-law marriage, the couple must hold themselves out to the community as husband and wife. *Hunsaker*, 968 P.2d at 286. In the instant case, over thirty witnesses testified as to their opinions about the relationship between John and Selma. Members of Selma's family, as well as several members of their community, testified to their belief that John and Selma were legally married. One witness testified that she heard John call Selma his wife, and another witness stated that John and Selma had told her that they were married. As already noted, other witnesses testified to their belief that John was a bachelor. Finally, the Appellants both testified that they did not believe John and Selma to be in a marital relationship.

[T]he District Court was in the best position to assess the credibility of the witnesses. The District Court evaluated the testimony regarding John and Selma's reputation in their community, and concluded that John and Selma had in fact established a common-law marriage by public repute. After a careful review of the record, we find no error in the District Court's judgment. Therefore, we decline to disturb the District Court's conclusion that John and Selma confirmed their common-law marriage by public repute.

For the foregoing reasons, the judgment of the District Court is affirmed.

Post-Case Follow-Up

The Montana Court noted the strong public policy in favor of finding a valid marriage. Once a common law marriage has been established, then the parties are considered married for all intents and purposes, including for purposes of inheritance. *Ober* shows the complexity involved in establishing whether such a marriage exists after one of the alleged spouses has died, helping to explain why couples might want to obtain a state marriage license as a way to avoid the evidentiary difficulties in proving common law marriage.

In re Ober: Real Life Applications

1. Based on *Ober*, how would you advise a client couple who is common law married to ensure recognition that the surviving spouse has inheritance rights?

2. Abner is cohabiting with a nonmarital partner. Based on *Ober*, what advice do you give Abner to ensure that, by cohabiting, Abner is not entering into a common law marriage?

3. Jamie and Hayden both work at the same company in Montana. As a joke, they decide to profess their love to each other and pronounce themselves married. They tell other employees they were married, and jokingly refer to each other as "my loving spouse." Jamie meets Riley, and they decide to marry. Hayden claims that Jamie and Hayden are already married, so Jamie and Riley cannot marry. They marry anyway, and a month later, Jamie dies. Riley comes to you, seeking legal advice as to who is Hayden's spouse for purposes of being appointed to administer the estate. What is your advice? Why?

Civil Unions & Domestic Partnerships

A handful of states allow nonmarital partners to enter into legally sanctioned civil unions and domestic partnerships that confer inheritance rights in intestacy. Civil union statutes and some domestic partnership statutes explicitly state that couples are granted the same rights as if they were married. See, e.g., Wash. Rev. Code Ann. § 11.04.015; Wis. Stat. Ann. § 852.01. However, the UPC and the Restatement (Third) of Property do not currently provide for inheritance rights to those who are not "spouses," even if they have entered into a civil union. The Restatement drafters call this a "developing question," but they have not taken a position on it. For simplicity, this chapter will only use the term "spouse."

Cohabitants

Absent a contract, couples who live together without marital status (legal, putative, or common law and without entering into a civil union or registered domestic partnership) do not have intestacy rights in each other's estates. Taking affirmative action, such as getting married or entering into a more formal arrangement such as a legally sanctioned civil union, is a surrogate for intent to confer benefits like inheritance rights. In terms of policy, mere cohabitation without more has not yet been deemed, by most states, an adequate basis to confer these benefits. For a discussion of how the law fails to provide such legal protections to cohabitants, see Anna Stepien-Sporek & Margaret Ryznar, *The Consequences of Cohabitation*, 50 U.S.F. L. Rev. 75 (2016). The Uniform Law Commission is currently considering potential legal rights for nonmarital cohabitants.

2. Share of Surviving Spouse

Most intestacy statutes begin with a share for the surviving spouse, if one exists. After the spouse's share is determined, descendants or ancestors may be given a share, although in some situations, the spouse will take the entire estate. The amount provided for a surviving spouse differs from state to state. Before turning to the UPC, it is worth noting what surviving spouses receive in non-UPC states.

Non-UPC Share of Surviving Spouse

There is enormous variation among the states on the type of share that is left to the surviving spouse. In states that have not enacted the UPC, the surviving spouse is often entitled to one-third or one-half of the intestate estate if the decedent is survived by children (or descendants of deceased children), with the remaining portion passing to the decedent's descendants. Other variations exist. Some non-UPC statutes award half each to the surviving spouse and the descendants. See Exhibit 2.3 for Kentucky's law.

EXHIBIT 2.3   **Kentucky's Law**

Kentucky's law favors the decedent's children, parents, and siblings over the surviving spouse. For example, the real property of a person who dies intestate:

   "shall descend in common to his kindred, male and female, in the following order, except as otherwise provided in this chapter:

(1) To his children and their descendants; if there are none, then

(2) To his father and mother, if both are living, one (1) moiety each; but if the father is dead, the mother, if living, shall take the whole estate; if the mother is dead, the whole estate shall pass to the father; if there is no father or mother, then

(3) To his brothers and sisters and their descendants; if there are none, then

(4) To the husband or wife of the intestate."

Ky. Rev. Stat. Ann. § 391.010; see Ky. Rev. Stat. Ann. § 391.030 (addressing descent of personal property).

If the decedent is not survived by children (or descendants of deceased children), but is survived by one or both parents, the spouse's share in many non-UPC states is often one-half, with the other half going to the decedent's parent or parents. Approximately 20 states give the entire intestate estate to the surviving spouse if the decedent has no surviving descendants. Rebecca Friedman, *Intestate Intent: Presumed Will Theory, Duty Theory, and the Flaw of Relying on Average Decedent Intent*, 49 Real Prop. Tr. & Est. L.J. 565, 571-72 (2015). Some states favor a parent over a spouse in intestacy. In a few states, the spouse shares the intestate estate with the decedent's siblings if both parents have predeceased. See Restatement (Third) of Property (Wills and Other Donative Transfers) § 2.2 cmts. (1999).

A non-UPC approach. The Indiana statute shown in Exhibit 2.4 is an example of a non-UPC law that provides for the surviving spouse. As you read the statute, think about why—and when—a first (and only) spouse is treated differently from a subsequent spouse.

EXHIBIT 2.4   **Ind. Code Ann. § 29-1-2-1 (2017)**

(a) The estate of a person dying intestate shall descend and be distributed as provided in this section.

(b) Except as otherwise provided in subsection (c), the surviving spouse shall receive the following share:

    (1) One-half (½) of the net estate if the intestate is survived by at least one (1) child or by the issue of at least one (1) deceased child.

    (2) Three-fourths (¾) of the net estate, if there is no surviving issue, but the intestate is survived by one (1) or both of the intestate's parents.

    (3) All of the net estate, if there is no surviving issue or parent.

(c) If the surviving spouse is a second or other subsequent spouse who did not at any time have children by the decedent, and the decedent left surviving the decedent a child or children or the descendants of a child or children by a previous spouse, the surviving second or subsequent childless spouse shall take only an amount equal to twenty-five percent (25%) of the remainder of:

    (1) the fair market value as of the date of death of the real property of the deceased spouse; minus

    (2) the value of the liens and encumbrances on the real property of the deceased spouse.

The UPC Share of Surviving Spouse

Under the UPC, the surviving spouse is the preferred heir, but the surviving spouse's share is affected by which other family members also survive the decedent. Thus, the surviving spouse's share cannot be determined without reference to whether the following individuals also survive the decedent: (a) descendants who are joint descendants with the surviving spouse, (b) descendants who are not also descendants of the surviving spouse, (c) descendants of the surviving spouse who are not also descendants of the decedent, and (d) the decedent's parents.

Under the UPC, the surviving spouse receives the decedent's intestate estate *if* (1) the decedent left no surviving descendants and no parents; *or* (2) the decedent's surviving descendants are also descendants of the surviving spouse *and* the surviving spouse has no descendants who are not descendants of the decedent. The surviving spouse receives less *if* the decedent left no surviving descendants but does have at least one surviving parent. The surviving spouse receives even less *if* the decedent's surviving descendants are also descendants of the surviving spouse but the surviving spouse has one or more other descendants. And finally, the surviving spouse receives the least *if* the decedent has one or more surviving descendants who are not descendants of the surviving spouse. See Exhibit 2.5.

EXHIBIT 2.5 **UPC § 2-102. Share of Spouse**

The intestate share of a decedent's surviving spouse is:

(1) the entire intestate estate if:
    (i) no descendant or parent of the decedent survives the decedent; or
    (ii) all of the decedent's surviving descendants are also descendants of the surviving spouse and there is no other descendant of the surviving spouse who survives the decedent;

(2) the first $300,000 [+ COLA [cost of living adjustment]], plus three-fourths of any balance of the intestate estate, if no descendant of the decedent survives the decedent, but a parent of the decedent survives the decedent;

(3) the first $225,000 [+ COLA], plus one-half of any balance of the intestate estate, if all of the decedent's surviving descendants are also descendants of the surviving spouse and the surviving spouse has one or more surviving descendants who are not descendants of the decedent;

(4) the first $150,000 [+ COLA], plus one-half of any balance of the intestate estate, if one or more of the decedent's surviving descendants are not descendants of the surviving spouse.

For example, assume Reese died recently without a will. Reese's probate estate was worth $1,425,000. Reese is survived by her spouse, Josh, two children with Josh (Emma and Liam), and Josh's child, Noah (Reese's stepdaughter), from his first marriage that ended in divorce 15 years ago.

Part A: Josh is entitled to $225,000, plus 50 percent of $1,200,000 (the remaining value of the estate), for a total of $825,000. Emma and Liam split the other 50 percent of $1,200,000 ($600,000 for the two of them or $300,000 each).

Part B: Assume that Reese is also survived by one child from her first marriage to Mason. Josh is entitled to only $150,000, plus 50 percent of $1,275,000 (for a total of $787,500) and her three children split $637,500 equally. Josh would get the same amount even if he and Reese did not have joint children and even if Noah did not survive. This is because subsection (4) applies whenever the decedent is survived by descendants who are not related to the surviving spouse by blood or adoption.

The theory for these varying shares is that when the only surviving children are joint descendants of the decedent and the surviving spouse, then decedents view the surviving spouse "as occupying somewhat of a dual role, not only as their primary beneficiaries, but also as conduits through which to benefit their children." Lawrence W. Waggoner, *The Multiple-Marriage Society and Spousal Rights Under the Revised Uniform Probate Code*, 76 Iowa L. Rev. 223, 232-33 (1991).

By contrast, "the existence of children who are not joint children renders the conduit theory problematic. When a decedent is survived by children not descended from the surviving spouse, or by children of the surviving spouse not descended from the decedent, the decedent has a surviving spouse with divided

What's in a Name

Children constitute the generation immediately following the decedent. But what about **issue** and **descendants**? The two terms are synonyms, and refer to a multiple-generation class, beginning with the children, and also including all subsequent generations "down" the decedent's descending line. We will generally use the term "descendants" in this casebook, as that is what the UPC uses, although you will see that many state statutes and cases refer to "issue." Stepchildren are not "children" or "descendants" of the decedent for purposes of being eligible to take under UPC § 2-103(a)(1), so they are typically not entitled to a share in the intestate estate. On the other hand, if the decedent was not survived by one blood relative, however, the UPC allows stepchildren to inherit. See UPC § 2-103(b). Most non-UPC states do not allow stepchildren to take under any circumstances.

loyalties and, hence, a spouse who is a less reliable conduit." Id. Accordingly, the surviving spouse receives less when there are non-joint descendants.

C. SHARE TO CHILDREN, DESCENDANTS, AND PARENTS

Any portion of the property that does not go to the surviving spouse is distributed to remaining family members, with children and their children preferred to other relatives. If the decedent dies without a surviving spouse, then the surviving lineal descendants share the entire probate estate. If there is no surviving spouse and there are no surviving lineal descendants, then the estate is distributed to ancestors and other heirs, referred to as **"collateral heirs/relatives."**

The share available to descendants, ancestors, and collateral heirs varies from state to state. But, in all states, if there are *any* descendants of the decedent, then ancestors and collateral heirs will receive nothing. For example, even if the decedent is survived by parents, many siblings, nieces, nephews, aunts, uncles, and cousins, so long as the decedent is survived by only one grandchild, the grandchild will take the probate property.

Exhibit 2.6 shows how the UPC describes what is available to the lineal descendants.

EXHIBIT 2.6 **UPC § 2-103. Share of Heirs Other than Surviving Spouse**

> (a) Any part of the intestate estate not passing to a decedent's surviving spouse under Section 2-102, or the entire intestate estate if there is no surviving spouse, passes in the following order to the individuals who survive the decedent:
> (1) to the decedent's descendants by representation[.]

Only living descendants are entitled to a share. A deceased descendant's spouse does not take on behalf of a descendant; the only spouse who is entitled to take a share is the decedent's spouse. If a descendant is not living at the time of the decedent's death, lower-generation descendants take by a system generally referred to as "representation." In essence, these lower generations are entitled to share in the estate. We discuss the principal representation models below.

1. Just Who Is a Child?

Children inherit from their parents. At the core of most inheritance statutes is the definition of "child." A child is defined based on a legally established relationship with a parent, and does not include a stepchild, a foster child, or a descendant of a child. E.g., UPC § 1-201(5).

A major question then, is just how to establish the parent-child relationship. For that, state law (and the UPC) generally defer to state laws outside of the probate area.

The Marital Presumption

In about 60 percent of American families, where a child is born to married parents, determining the parent-child relationship is relatively easy. The **marital presumption** in effect in all states means that offspring of a married couple (regardless of the sex of the spouses) are presumed to be the children of their parents. The difficulty of rebutting that presumption depends on state law.

When parents have children with more than one partner, then the offspring are related by the **half-blood**. A half-blood relationship is between individuals who share only one parent. For example, while Jin and Barry are married, they have two children together: Corina and Tomas. After Jin and Barry divorce, Jin remarries and has two more children, Mateo and Nina. Corina and Tomas are related by full blood to one another and by half-blood to Mateo and Nina; correspondingly, Mateo and Nina are related by full blood to one another, and by half-blood to Corina and Tomas. At Jin's death, all four children qualify as Jin's descendants. If Corina subsequently died intestate survived by Tomas, Mateo, and Nina, would each take an equal share of the estate? The answer depends on state law. In some jurisdictions, such as Kentucky, a relative of the half-blood inherits only half the amount that a relative of the full blood inherits. See Ky. Rev. Stat. Ann. § 391.050. Under UPC § 2-107, however, they inherit equally.

Special Circumstances: Assisted Reproduction & Posthumous Children

The UPC defines assisted reproduction as a means of causing pregnancy other than by sexual intercourse. UPC § 2-115. When a husband's sperm and a wife's egg are used during their lifetimes, the resulting child is, pursuant to the marital presumption, marital. Assisted reproductive technology (ART) involving donor eggs, donor sperm, surrogacy, and posthumous conception have created challenges for inheritance law, regardless of whether the children are born to married or unmarried heterosexual or same-sex couples or to single parents. The UPC clarifies that a child born through assisted reproductive technology to married parents who use a third-party donor is a child of those parents, and not of the donor. But many states have not yet grappled with all of the possibilities created by new technology in defining the parent-child relationship pursuant to inheritance law.

For posthumous children, those born after the death of a parent, the traditional common law approach was that a child born within 300 days of a married parent's death was a child of that parent. What happens when a child is born after that time period?

EXHIBIT 2.7 **UPC § 2-120. Child Conceived by Assisted Reproduction Other than Child Born to Gestational Carrier**

(k) [When Posthumously Conceived Child Treated as in Gestation.] If, under this section, an individual is a parent of a child of assisted reproduction who is conceived after the individual's death, the child is treated as in gestation at the individual's death for purposes of § 2-104(a)(2) if the child is:

(1) in utero not later than 36 months after the individual's death; or
(2) born not later than 45 months after the individual's death.

Case Preview

Astrue v. Capato

This case concerns the meaning of "child" under a state's intestacy statute, because that definition turned out to be crucial for interpreting the federal Social Security Act. Although the U.S. Supreme Court rarely considers trusts and estates or family law issues, it was called on to determine a child's entitlement to receive Social Security benefits through a deceased parent. *Astrue* considers both the marital presumption and assisted reproductive technology. Eighteen months after her husband, Robert Capato, died of cancer, Karen Capato gave birth to twins conceived through in vitro fertilization using her husband's frozen sperm. Karen applied for Social Security survivors' benefits for the twins.

As you read the case, consider:

1. What was Robert Capato's intent? What sources indicate his intent?
2. What did Florida law provide with respect to posthumous children?
3. What did federal law provide with respect to defining the term "child?"
4. How does the Supreme Court reconcile state and federal law?

Astrue v. Capato
566 U.S. 541, 132 S. Ct. 2021 (2012)

Justice GINSBURG delivered the opinion of the Court.

. . .

I

Karen Capato married Robert Capato in May 1999. Shortly thereafter, Robert was diagnosed with esophageal cancer and was told that the chemotherapy he required might render him sterile. Because the couple wanted children, Robert, before undergoing chemotherapy, deposited his semen in a sperm bank, where it was frozen and stored. . . .

Robert's health deteriorated in late 2001, and he died in Florida, where he and Karen then resided, in March 2002. [His] will made no provision for children conceived after Robert's death, although the Capatos had told their lawyer they wanted future offspring to be placed on a par with existing children. Shortly after Robert's death, Karen began in vitro fertilization using her husband's frozen sperm. She conceived in January 2003 and gave birth to twins in September 2003, 18 months after Robert's death.

Karen Capato claimed survivors insurance benefits on behalf of the twins. The SSA [Social Security Administration] denied her application, and the U.S. District Court for the District of New Jersey affirmed the agency's decision. . . . [T]he District Court determined that the twins would qualify for benefits only if . . . they could inherit from the deceased wage earner under state intestacy law. Robert Capato died domiciled in Florida. . . . Under [Florida] law . . . a child born posthumously may inherit through intestate succession only if conceived during the decedent's lifetime.

The Court of Appeals for the Third Circuit reversed. Under § 416(e) [of the Social Security Act ("Act")], the appellate court concluded, "the undisputed biological children of a deceased wage earner and his widow" qualify for survivors benefits without regard to state intestacy law. . . .

II

. . .

"Child's insurance benefits" are among the Act's family-protective measures. An applicant qualifies for such benefits if she meets the Act's definition of "child," is unmarried, is below specified age limits (18 or 19) or is under a disability which began prior to age 22, and was dependent on the insured at the time of the insured's death.

. . . [W]e must decide whether the Capato twins rank as "child[ren]" under the Act's definitional provisions. [] Under the heading "Determination of family status," § 416(h)(2)(A) provides: "In determining whether an applicant is the child or parent of [an] insured individual for purposes of this subchapter, the Commissioner of Social Security shall apply [the intestacy law of the insured individual's domiciliary State]."

An applicant for child benefits who does not meet [the] intestacy-law criterion may nonetheless qualify for benefits under one of several other criteria the Act prescribes. First, an applicant who "is a son or daughter" of an insured individual, but is not determined to be a "child" under the intestacy-law provision, nevertheless ranks as a "child" if the insured and the other parent went through a marriage ceremony that would have been valid but for certain legal impediments. Further, an applicant is deemed a "child" if, before death, the insured acknowledged in writing that the applicant is his or her son or daughter, or if the insured had been decreed by a court to be the father or mother of the applicant, or had been ordered to pay child support. In addition, an applicant may gain "child" status upon proof that the insured individual was the applicant's parent and "was living with or contributing to the support of the applicant" when the insured individual died.

. . .

III

Karen Capato argues [that] "child" means "child of an [insured] individual," and the Capato twins . . . are undeniably the children of Robert Capato, the insured wage earner, and his widow, Karen Capato. . . .

A

Nothing in § 416(e)'s tautological definition ("'child' means . . . the child . . . of an individual") suggests that Congress understood the word "child" to refer only to the children of married parents. . . .

Nor does § 416(e) indicate that Congress intended "biological" parentage to be prerequisite to "child" status under that provision. As the SSA points out, "[i]n 1939, there was no such thing as a scientifically proven biological relationship between a child and a father, which is . . . part of the reason that the word 'biological' appears nowhere in the Act." Reply Brief 6. Notably, a biological parent is not necessarily a child's parent under law. Ordinarily, "a parent-child relationship does not exist between an adoptee and the adoptee's genetic parents." Uniform Probate Code § 2-119(a), Moreover, laws directly addressing use of today's assisted reproduction technology do not make biological parentage a universally determinative criterion. See, e.g., Cal. Fam. Code Ann. § 7613(b) (West Supp. 2012) ("The donor of semen . . . for use in artificial insemination or in vitro fertilization of a woman other than the donor's wife is treated in law as if he were not the natural father of a child thereby conceived, unless otherwise agreed to in a writing signed by the donor and the woman prior to the conception of the child."); Mass. Gen. Laws, ch. 46, § 4B ("Any child born to a married woman as a result of artificial insemination with the consent of her husband, shall be considered the legitimate child of the mother and such husband.").

We note, in addition, that marriage does not ever and always make the parentage of a child certain, nor does the absence of marriage necessarily mean that a child's parentage is uncertain. An unmarried couple can agree that a child is theirs, while the parentage of a child born during a marriage may be uncertain.

Finally, it is far from obvious that Karen Capato's proposed definition—"biological child of married parents," see Brief for Respondent 9—would cover the posthumously conceived Capato twins. Under Florida law, a marriage ends upon the death of a spouse. If that law applies, rather than a court-declared preemptive federal law, the Capato twins, conceived *after* the death of their father, would not qualify as "marital" children.

B

[T]he SSA finds a key textual cue in § 416(h)(2)(A)'s opening instruction: "In determining whether an applicant is the child . . . of [an] insured individual *for purposes of this subchapter*," the Commissioner shall apply state intestacy law.

. . .

Reference to state law to determine an applicant's status as a "child" is anything but anomalous.

. . .

The paths to receipt of benefits laid out in the Act and regulations, we must not forget, proceed from Congress' perception of the core purpose of the legislation. The aim was not to create a program "generally benefiting needy persons"; it was, more particularly, to "provide . . . dependent members of [a wage earner's] family with protection against the hardship occasioned by [the] loss of [the insured's] earnings." Califano v. Jobst, 434 U.S. 47, 52 (1977). . . . Reliance on state intestacy law to determine who is a "child" thus serves the Act's driving objective. True, the intestacy criterion yields benefits to some children outside the Act's central concern. Intestacy laws in a number of States, as just noted, do provide for inheritance by posthumously conceived children . . . and under federal law, a child conceived shortly before her father's death may be eligible for benefits even though she never actually received her father's support. It was nonetheless Congress' prerogative to legislate for the generality of cases. It did so here by employing eligibility to inherit under state intestacy law as a workable substitute for burdensome case-by-case determinations whether the child was, in fact, dependent on her father's earnings. . . .

V

Tragic circumstances—Robert Capato's death before he and his wife could raise a family—gave rise to this case. But the law Congress enacted calls for resolution of Karen Capato's application for child's insurance benefits by reference to state intestacy law. We cannot replace that reference by creating a uniform federal rule the statute's text scarcely supports.

For the reasons stated, the judgment of the Court of Appeals for the Third Circuit is reversed, and the case is remanded for further proceedings consistent with this opinion.

It is so ordered.

Post-Case Follow-Up

As a result of *Astrue v. Capato*, posthumously conceived children will only qualify for Social Security benefits if the state in which their parent died has recognized that children conceived and born after their parent's death are eligible to inherit from that parent. Because states have made different policy choices concerning reproductive technology and estate efficiency and fairness, posthumously conceived children in one state might qualify, while those across a state border might not. A difficult problem in drafting statutes governing posthumous children and inheritance is determining how long the estate will be left open for those children to come to fruition.

Astrue v. Capato: Real Life Applications

1. Just before his death, Robert Capato comes to you for estate planning advice to ensure that any posthumously conceived children will inherit. What advice do you give him about how to define "child"?

2. If the UPC had been in effect in Florida, how would that have affected the result in the case?

3. Quinn Jones has just died in a state where the UPC is in effect. Quinn's spouse, who is the executor of Quinn's estate, asks how long Quinn's estate must be kept open in order to ensure that all "children" are accounted for. What is your response?

Nonmarital Children

At common law, nonmarital children had no inheritance rights. That changed in early America, when they were given the right to inherit from their mothers. During the second half of the twentieth century, the Supreme Court decided a series of cases that recognized the rights of nonmarital children to inherit from their legally recognized fathers. Indeed, the UPC provides that marital and nonmarital children are treated equally with respect to inheritance. UPC § 2-117.

The real question remains proving parenthood, and a state's family law establishes the method for doing so. The matter of parenthood is more likely to arise with respect to fathers; the woman who gives birth is typically recognized as the mother, as is true in Exhibit 2.8. When parents are unmarried, paternity must be established in order for a man to be recognized as the legal father of a child. The two primary approaches to establishing paternity are adjudication and voluntary acknowledgment of some sort. The Uniform Parentage Act ("UPA"), last revised in 2017, sets out some of the more common ways of establishing parenthood, and many states have adopted variations of its approach. It provides methods for both mothers and fathers to establish parenthood.

EXHIBIT 2.8   UPA §§ 201 and 204

SECTION 201. ESTABLISHMENT OF PARENT-CHILD RELATIONSHIP.

A parent-child relationship is established between an individual and a child if:

(1) the individual gives birth to the child[, except as otherwise provided in [Article] 8];
(2) there is a presumption under Section 204 of the individual's parentage of the child, unless the presumption is overcome in a judicial proceeding or a valid denial of parentage is made under [another section of the Act;
(3) the individual is adjudicated a parent of the child [];
(4) the individual adopts the child;
(5) the individual acknowledges parentage of the child [unless the acknowledgement is rescinded or successfully challenged under other provisions of the Act];

(6) the individual's parentage of the child is established under [the provisions for assisted reproductive technology]; or

(7) the individual's parentage of the child is established under [the provisions for surrogacy].

SECTION 204. PRESUMPTION OF PARENTAGE.

(a) An individual is presumed to be a parent of a child if:

(1) except as otherwise provided under [other laws]:

(A) the individual and the woman who gave birth to the child are married to each other and the child is born during the marriage, whether the marriage is or could be declared invalid;

(B) the individual and the woman who gave birth to the child were married to each other and the child is born not later than 300 days after the marriage is terminated by death, [divorce, dissolution, annulment, or declaration of invalidity, or after a decree of separation or separate maintenance], whether the marriage is or could be declared invalid; or

(C) the individual and the woman who gave birth to the child married each other after the birth of the child, whether the marriage is or could be declared invalid, the individual at any time asserted parentage of the child, and:

(i) the assertion is in a record filed with the [state agency maintaining birth records]; or

(ii) the individual agreed to be and is named as a parent of the child on the birth certificate of the child; or

(2) the individual resided in the same household with the child for the first two years of the life of the child, including any period of temporary absence, and openly held out the child as the individual's child.

(b) A presumption of parentage under this section may be overcome, and competing claims to parentage may be resolved, only by an adjudication [] 6 or a valid denial of parentage [].

These two sections provide a framework for establishing parentage. As Section 204 notes, marriage is significant for establishing parentage; the other spouse is the parent of a child born during a marriage, conceived during marriage but born after its termination, and even a child conceived or born during an invalid marriage. For a child born before a valid or invalid marriage, other facts can confer the parentage presumption. Finally, an individual who "holds out" and lives with a child for the first two years of the child's life will be a presumptive parent. In addition to these methods, states may allow for voluntary acknowledgements of paternity in other documents, such as the one in Exhibit 2.9. Once this presumption arises, it is subject to attack only under limited circumstances.

EXHIBIT 2.9   **Sample: Virginia Acknowledgement of Paternity**

ACKNOWLEDGMENT OF PATERNITY
Virginia Department of Health/Division of Vital Records
(32.1-257, 32.1-261 or 32.1-269, Code of Virginia)

This statement is to acknowledge paternity of the child described herein. In order for the father's name to appear on the birth certificate of a child born out of wedlock, both biological (*natural*) parents must complete and sign this statement before a nota public.

PART 1 – CHILD

1. Full Name at Birth: _____
          (First)   *(Middle)*   *(Last)*   *(Suffix)*

2. Sex: _____   3. Date of Birth: _____

4. Place of Birth: _____   5. Birth Certificate Number *(If Known)*: _____

PART II – BIOLOGICAL MOTHER OF THE CHILD

6. Full Maiden Name: _____
          (First)   *(Middle)*   *(Maiden)*

7. Present Name: _____
          (First)   *(Middle)*   *(Last)*

8. Date of Birth: _____   9. Place of Birth *(State or Foreign Country)*: _____

10. Social Security Number: _____   11. Race or Color: _____

PART III – BIOLOGICAL FATHER OF THE CHILD *(NOTE: Items 17, 18, and 19 concern the father at the time of the child'*

12. Full Name: _____
          (First)   *(Middle)*   *(Last)*   *(Suffix)*

13. Date of Birth: _____   14. Place of Birth *(State or Foreign Country)*: _____

15. Social Security Number: _____   16. Race or Color: _____   17. Highest Level of Education Completed

18. Occupation: _____   19. Industry: _____

PART IV – BIOLOGICAL PARENTS' MARRIAGE *(IF APPLICABLE, You must complete this section and enclose a certified your marriage record)*

20. Place of Marriage: _____   21. Date of Marriage: _____
          (City/County and State, or Foreign Country)

PART V – PARENTS' ACKNOWLEDGMENT *(THIS ITEM MUST BE COMPLETED)*

22. We, being duly sworn, affirm that we are the biological parents of the child named above, we have read the rights and responsibilities statement provided on the reverse of our copy of this document, and we request that the father's information b shown on this child's birth certificate, and that the child's name be listed on the birth certificate as shown below.

Child's Name: _____
          (First)   *(Middle)*   *(Last)*   *(Suffix)*

23. a. Signature of Father: _____   24. a. Signature of Mother: _____

    b. Address of Father: _____   b. Address of Mother: _____

    _____   _____

25. Subscribed and sworn before me on: _____   26. Subscribed and sworn before me on: _____

27. Notary's signature: _____   28. Notary's signature: _____

29. Notary's address: _____   30. Notary's address: _____

    _____   _____

COMMONWEALTH OF VIRGINIA
DEPARTMENT OF SOCIAL SERVICES/DCSE
ALL VIRGINIA BIRTHING HOSPITALS
PATERNITY ACKNOWLEDGMENT RIGHTS AND RESPONSIBILITIES STATEMENT

Rights and Responsibilities of the Father
Please read and a trained hospital staff member will read to you the following statements before you sign the Acknowledgment of Paternity form.

1. I understand that my signature on the Acknowledgment of Paternity form establishes that I am the natural father of the named child for all legal purposes.
2. I sign the Acknowledgment of Paternity voluntarily and understand that I am under no obligation to do so. No pressure has been placed upon me to sign. I understand I take the following actions instead of signing this form:
   a. Seek the advice or representation of legal counsel
   b. Request that DNA testing be taken
   c. Have the matter of paternity determined by the court
3. I understand I will have the responsibility to provide support for my child.
4. I understand I will be responsible to pay such support until the child turns 18 years of age or beyond if required by law.
5. I understand after paternity is established, I have the right to request visitation with the custody of the child. Custody and visitation are decided in legal actions separate from the issues of paternity or child support.
6. I understand the Acknowledgment of Paternity may be used in any legal proceeding regarding this child.
7. I understand I have the right to talk to a staff person to clarify information on this statement and to ask any questions I have.
8. I understand I have the right to rescind this acknowledgment within sixty days from the date of signing unless and administrative or judicial proceeding involving this child has taken place earlier.

Rights and Responsibilities of the Mother
Please read and a trained hospital staff member will read to you the following statements before you sign the Acknowledgment of Paternity form.

1. I understand that my signature on the Acknowledgment of Paternity form means that I am I swear that I am the mother of the named child and that the person signing as the father is the biological father of the child.
2. I sign the Acknowledgment of Paternity voluntarily and understand that I am under no obligation to do so. No pressure has been placed upon me to sign. I understand I take the following actions instead of signing this form:
   a. Seek the advice or representation of legal counsel
   b. Request that DNA testing be taken
   c. Have the matter of paternity determined by the court
3. I understand after paternity is established, I have the right to request visitation with the custody of the child. Custody and visitation are decided in legal actions separate from the issues of paternity or child support.
4. I understand I have the right to talk to a staff person to clarify information on this statement and to ask any questions I have.
5. I understand I have the right to rescind this acknowledgment within sixty days from the date of signing unless and administrative or judicial proceeding involving this child has taken place earlier.

I have read and have been provided with an oral description of the rights and responsibilities statement above.	I have read and have been provided with an oral description of the rights and responsibilities statement above.

Signature of Father _____   Signature of Mother _____
Social Security Number _____   Social Security Number _____
Subscribed and Sworn before me on: _____   Subscribed and Sworn before me on: _____
In the _____ of _____ in the   In the _____ of _____ in the
Commonwealth of Virginia   Commonwealth of Virginia
Notary Signature: _____   Notary Signature: _____
My Commission Expires:_____   My Commission Expires:_____

Adopted Children

Historically, states often prevented adopted children from inheriting from or through their adoptive parents because of the lack of a blood relationship. See Naomi Cahn, *Perfect Substitutes or the Real Thing?*, 52 Duke L.J. 1077 (2003). Over time, states began to recognize that adopted children should be treated as "children" for purposes of inheriting both from and through their adoptive parents.

Consistent with this approach, they embraced the idea that the child would no longer be able to inherit from or through the genetic parents.

Adoption thus breaks the ties to the child's genetic family, and the adopting family becomes the child's legal family. If a child is placed for adoption, she is cut off from her genetic parents for purposes of inheritance law. She cannot inherit from them, nor they from her. Accordingly, a legally adopted child also falls within the definition of "child" in the intestacy statutes of all states. Adopted children may inherit both from and through their *adoptive* parents, and their parents may inherit from or through the adopted child. Assume Grandma Alice had one child, Betty, and Betty adopts Chloe. If Betty dies before her mother, Chloe can inherit from Alice through Betty if she establishes that she is Betty's child. UPC §§ 2-118 and 2-119, shown in Exhibit 2.10, continue this basic approach of treating the child as a member of the adopting family and not of the genetic family.

Although this is the general rule, some states and the UPC have established special rules for children adopted by the spouse of one of the genetic parents. While a stepparent can only adopt a child once the other parent's rights have been terminated, either voluntarily or involuntarily, these special rules preserve the ability of the child to inherit from the biological family. Under this exception, the child may inherit from the adopting stepparent and the stepparent's family as well as from both genetic parents and their families.

EXHIBIT 2.10   **UPC § 2-118. Adoptee and Adoptee's Adoptive Parent or Parents & UPC § 2-119. Adoptee and Adoptee's Genetic Parents**

UPC § 2-118. ADOPTEE AND ADOPTEE'S ADOPTIVE PARENT OR PARENTS

(a) **[Parent-Child Relationship Between Adoptee and Adoptive Parent or Parents.]** A parent-child relationship exists between an adoptee and the adoptee's adoptive parent or parents.

UPC § 2-119. ADOPTEE AND ADOPTEE'S GENETIC PARENTS

(a) **[Parent-Child Relationship Between Adoptee and Genetic Parents.]** Except as otherwise provided in subsection [b], a parent-child relationship does not exist between an adoptee and the adoptee's genetic parents.

(b) **[Stepchild Adopted by Stepparent.]** A parent-child relationship exists between an individual who is adopted by the spouse of either genetic parent and:
   (1) the genetic parent whose spouse adopted the individual; and
   (2) the other genetic parent, but only for the purpose of the right of the adoptee or a descendant of the adoptee to inherit from or through the other genetic parent.

For example, Alex and Franky were married ten years ago and had a child, Bella. Alex died in a car accident two years after Bella's birth. Franky later married Shirley, who adopted Bella. Bella is considered a child of Franky ("the genetic parent whose spouse adopted the individual" under UPC § 2-119(b)(1)) and Shirley (the adopting parent under UPC § 2-118). Bella is also considered a child of Alex for the purpose of inheriting from or through Alex. Thus, Bella could inherit from Franky and Shirley and, through them, from their families. Because Bella is also the child of Alex, Bella could have inherited from Alex when Alex died and, through Alex, can still inherit from Alex's relatives. UPC § 2-119(b)(2).

If Bella were to die first, then Franky and Shirley and their family members could inherit from Bella. However, Alex's family could *not* inherit from Bella. Under the stepparent adoption exception of UPC § 2-119(b)(2), the right to inherit belongs only to the child, not the other genetic parent or that parent's relatives. The exception only goes one way.

While inheritance law generally does not allow for such "double-dipping," the policy rationale for the UPC allowing an adoptee in the stepparent situation to inherit from both genetic parents and the new stepparent is to facilitate the stepparent's bonding with the adoptee. This serves society's interest in connecting the stepparent to the child by creating an emotional and legal bond between them. Adopting the child creates a legal support obligation on the part of the new adoptive/former stepparent as well. The stepparent may well be deterred from adopting the child if such an adoption were to prevent the child from inheriting from the child's biological grandparents.

Most stepparent adoptions occur after the death of one of the genetic parents. If the two genetic parents are divorced and one remarries, the new spouse of the remarrying genetic parent can only adopt the child once the parental rights of the other parent are terminated, typically because of abuse.

Case Preview

Fiduciary Trust Co. v. Wheeler

This case provides an illustration of the general rule concerning adopted children. A trust instrument, drafted in 1911, directed the trustee to distribute the principal under the "intestate laws of Maine then in force." As a 1957 case construing one part of the trust instrument made clear, at the date of the trust's execution, "an adopted child of someone, other than the person dying intestate, would not take under the then existing adoption statutes." Fiduciary Trust Co. v. Brown, 131 A.2d 191, 200 (Me. 1957). When the trust terminated in 2013, the court, in *Fiduciary Trust Co. v. Wheeler*, had to decide whether an adopted child could inherit from the trust pursuant to a different provision—and under a newer intestacy law.

As you read the case, consider:

1. What was the intent of the trust's creator? What facts are relevant to determine intent?

2. What are the terms of the trust concerning distribution of trust principal?
3. How does Maine's contemporary intestacy statute treat adopted children? Why is the contemporary statute relevant to a document that was initially drafted more than a century prior to the case?

Fiduciary Trust Co. v. Wheeler
132 A.3d 1178 (Me. 2016)

Opinion, MEAD, J.

Manchester H. Wheeler Jr. appeals from a summary judgment entered by the Superior Court (Kennebec County, Mullen, J.) in favor of Fiduciary Trust Company on Fiduciary's complaint to determine the proper method of distributing the principal of a trust of which Wheeler is a beneficiary....

I. BACKGROUND

The relevant facts in the summary judgment record are undisputed. Fiduciary is the acting trustee of the Elizabeth S. Haynes and Robert H. Gardner Trust, created in 1911 and amended in 1918. Pursuant to paragraph 1 of the trust, the trust's net income was to be paid to Elizabeth S. Haynes's two daughters, Hope Manchester Wheeler and Muriel Sturgis Haynes, or their issue....

Although paragraph 1 controls the distribution of trust income, paragraph 2—which is at issue here—governs the distribution of principal upon the trust's termination. Paragraph 2 provides, in pertinent part, "[t]wenty-one years after the death of the survivor of [Elizabeth S. Haynes's two daughters and a third person] the principal . . . shall be paid over to the persons . . . to whom and in which it would then have been distributed under the intestate laws of Maine then in force. . . ." Unlike paragraph 1, paragraph 2 does not rely on the word "issue"; instead, it defers to state intestacy laws to determine beneficiaries at the time of termination.

The trust terminated on December 26, 2013. On February 21, 2014, Fiduciary filed a complaint in the Kennebec County Probate Court asking that court to determine whether adopted children are entitled to a share of the principal pursuant to paragraph 2. [] On September 29, 2014, Fiduciary moved for a summary judgment on the ground that paragraph 2 invokes Maine intestacy laws applicable at the time of the termination, and 2013 Maine intestacy laws provided (and still provide) that adopted children inherit from or through their adoptive parents just as biological children inherit from or through their biological parents. See 18 A M.R.S. § 2-109(1) (2013) ("An adopted person is the child of an adopting parent. . . .").

Thus, pursuant to Fiduciary's proposed distribution scheme, Honora Haynes, the only living adopted child of Muriel S. Haynes and the only living person in her generation, would receive one-third of the trust principal. Wheeler, the biological great grandson of the settlor [the grandson of Hope Manchester Wheeler], objected to this distribution, contending that [the 1957 decision in *Brown*, the case that precluded adopted children from inheriting was controlling].

. . .

Because paragraph 2 involves intestacy laws that would be in effect at the time of termination, and because the time of termination was unknowable at the time of our decision in *Brown*, we did not construe—and could not have construed—paragraph 2. . . . Wheeler's argument that we should review paragraph 2 through the lens of our 1957 decision (i.e., that the settlor's intent was to exclude adopted children from the periodic net income payments from the trust) would require us to (1) examine intent regarding language that is unambiguous on its face; and (2) assume that the settlor did not wish for adopted children to share in the ultimate distribution of trust principal. Neither requirement is supported by law. By referring to and relying on future intestacy laws, rather than using the word "issue," paragraph 2 is unambiguous. The provision that "the principal . . . shall be paid over to the persons . . . to whom and in which it would then have been distributed under the intestate laws of Maine then in force" clearly provides that the intestacy laws in effect at the time of termination govern the distribution of trust principal. The 2013 Maine intestacy laws effective at the time of the trust's termination unequivocally provided that adopted children inherit from or through their adoptive parents just as biological children do. See 18-A M.R.S. § 2-109(1) ("An adopted person is the child of an adopting parent. . . ."). We have no basis to question the intention of the settlor of a trust where, as here, the terms are unambiguous.

The entry is:

Judgment affirmed.

Post-Case Follow-Up

This case shows how a state's intestacy laws can be relevant even when an individual does not die intestate. The trust at issue referred to "the intestate laws of Maine then in force." Rather than specify who would be entitled to a distribution of the money remaining in the trust at the time the trust terminated, the instrument provides flexibility. The court then simply needed to decide who would be entitled to inherit through intestacy, and Maine intestacy law, like that in effect in almost all other jurisdictions, treats an adopted child in the same manner as a genetic child. Note that an adult adoption would present different circumstances. While people generally think of adoption as involving minor children, a number of states allow the adoption of adults. One goal of adult adoption is to ensure inheritance by the "child" from and through the adoptive parent, even if the adoptive parent's will is challenged and ruled invalid. Historically, some same-sex couples used adult adoption to thwart a contest by disapproving family members of a bequest in the decedent's will to a partner. In other situations, it is (or has been) a standard technique to manipulate inheritance rules to bring an outsider into the line of inheritance. Consequently, while adult adoptees can inherit from their adoptive parents, they often may not inherit from nonparents who leave a class gift in a will or a trust to the "children" of the adoptee's parent or to their own "descendants."

Fiduciary Trust Co. v. Wheeler: Real Life Applications

The following facts apply to the questions set out below. Twelve years ago, Gabriel and Adele, who were married, gave birth to Hugo. Adele died shortly after Hugo's birth. When Hugo was two, Gabriel married Ines, and Ines then adopted Hugo.

1. If Gabriel died this year, may Hugo inherit from his estate?

2. If Ines died this year, may Hugo inherit from her estate?

3. If Adele's mother died this year, may Hugo inherit from her estate?

4. If Gabriel's father died this year, may Hugo inherit from his estate?

5. If Hugo died this year due to the negligence of a driver and there was a large damage award, who could inherit from his estate among the following individuals if the wrongful death statute in that state directs that such an award is paid to the decedent's estate: Gabriel, Ines, Gabriel's father, Ines's mother, and Adele's brother?

6. From whom may Hugo inherit if Gabriel and Ines are not married and Ines adopts Hugo?

Foster Children & Equitable Adoption

If there is no legal relationship between an adult and a child, the child cannot inherit. Thus, foster children cannot inherit through intestacy from their foster parents because even though foster parents may have certain rights with respect to their foster children, they are not the legal parents.

In some cases, a friend or relative takes in an orphaned child but fails to complete all the steps required for a legal adoption. The "parent" may hold the child out as a legal child, and the child may not know she is not legally adopted until the supposed parent dies. In extremely limited circumstances, courts use their broad remedial power to promote justice to find that there has been an "equitable adoption" as opposed to a "legal adoption." The child is thus able to inherit even without a formal adoption. While courts in over half the states have recognized this doctrine, other states have rejected the doctrine. Restatement (Third) of Property (Wills and Other Donative Trans.) § 2.5, cmt. k (1999). UPC § 2-122 ("Equitable Adoption") takes no position on the doctrine, thus allowing separate state law to control.

Even in states that recognize it, equitable adoption is difficult to establish. Some courts require the child claiming from the putative parent's estate to prove that an adoption proceeding had actually begun but had not been completed. They ground relief in an express or implied contract. Indeed, equitable adoption is also known as "adoption by estoppel" or "de facto adoption." Other courts are more flexible, allowing a child to bring a claim for equitable adoption if the guardian and the child treated each other as legal parent and child.

Equitable adoption is hard to establish and is successfully claimed in only *rare* cases. *The evidentiary threshold is steep.* For example, in *Wheeling Dollar Sav. &*

Trust Co. v. Singer, 250 S.E.2d 369, 373-74 (W. Va. 1978), the Supreme Court of West Virginia held that the doctrine of equitable adoption would be recognized by West Virginia but that it must be established by "clear, cogent, and convincing proof."

2. Just Who Is a Parent?

What happens if a child dies before a parent? The same rules for establishing the parent-child relationship discussed above in the context of the child also apply to the inheritance rights of parents. So, a person recognized as the parent would generally inherit from a deceased child in intestacy. But not always. Parents may have had their rights terminated; they may also be barred from inheriting if they have failed to support, or abandoned, their children. States vary widely in this area. For example, a New Jersey court held that the state intestacy statute does not condition the right of a parent to inherit from a child on the parent's support of the child. A child received a large settlement from a medical malpractice action, and the money was eventually placed in a trust that, upon the child's death, was to be distributed to her heirs under the law in effect at the time of her death. After the child died, the mother opposed the father's claim to one-half the trust property on the grounds that he had failed to support the child during her lifetime. In re Rogiers, 933 A.2d 971 (N.J. Super. Ct. App. Div. 2007). The appellate court affirmed the trial court's grant of a summary judgment to the father on his claim to the estate, noting that even a father who had abandoned his child could inherit.

By contrast, the UPC denies all parents—marital or nonmarital—the right to inherit from or through a child if their parental rights *could have been terminated.* See Exhibit 2.11. It makes clear that traditional grounds for termination of parental rights, such as abuse, are also grounds for disinheritance.

EXHIBIT 2.11   **UPC § 2-114. Parent Barred from Inheriting in Certain Circumstances**

(a) A parent is barred from inheriting from or through a child of the parent if:

(1) the parent's parental rights were terminated and the parent-child relationship was not judicially reestablished; or

(2) the child died before reaching [18] years of age and there is clear and convincing evidence that immediately before the child's death the parental rights of the parent could have been terminated under law of this state other than this [code] on the basis of non-support, abandonment, abuse, neglect, or other actions or inactions of the parent toward the child.

A growing number of states have a rule similar to UPC § 2-114 whereby a parent—married or otherwise—who has abandoned, failed to support, abused, or neglected a child may be barred from inheriting.

D. SHARE TO OTHER RELATIVES—AND ESCHEAT

The Table of Consanguinity in Exhibit 2.17 shows degrees of relationship, and it is helpful in understanding intestacy shares. You will notice the decedent is at the top of the column on the left, and the table includes the decedent's descendants, ancestors, and **collateral relatives**, the decedent's family members who are not descendants or ancestors.

If the decedent does not have a surviving spouse or descendants, then the estate passes to the first **parentela** (the first degree of relationship or first-line collaterals), which is the second column in the Table of Consanguinity. This line is headed by the decedent's parents. Below them are their descendants, i.e., the decedent's brothers and sisters, then nieces and nephews, and grand-nieces and nephews, and so on.

If there are no heirs in this relationship, then the estate passes through the second parentela, the column of people headed by the decedent's grandparents. In most jurisdictions, and under the UPC, the shares are divided into halves between the families of the maternal and paternal grandparents and then distributed to the appropriate heirs, employing the same representation system.

EXHIBIT 2.12 **Degree of Relationship**

Some states use a **degree-of-relationship** system, under which the intestate estate passes to the closest of kin, based on a system that counts degrees of kinship, rather than through the parentelic system. The counting system is as follows: count the steps (one step for each generation) up from the decedent to the nearest common ancestor, and then count the steps down from that common ancestor to the claimant. The total number of steps is the degree of relationship. The Table of Consanguinity in Exhibit 2.17 shows you the steps.

Ohio uses a pure degree of relationship system once there are no surviving grandparents and descendants of grandparents.

OHIO REV. CODE. ANN. § 2105.03—DETERMINATION OF NEXT OF KIN.

In the determination of intestate succession, next of kin <u>shall be determined by degrees of relationship</u> . . . .

OHIO REV. CODE. ANN. § 2105.06—STATUTE OF DESCENT AND DISTRIBUTION.

When a person dies intestate[, any property] shall descend and pass [] in the following course. . . .

    (l) [] if there are no surviving grandparents or their lineal descendants, then to the next of kin of the intestate, provided there shall be no representation among the next of kin. . . .

Finally, if there are no survivors in the first, second, or third parentela, states take a variety of approaches. Some, like New York, go up to the fourth parentela and pass property to great-grandparents and their descendants, the decedent's more distant cousins. See N.Y. Est. Powers & Trusts Law § 4-1.1. In some states, the personal representative must find more remote heirs, a time-consuming process. A more common alternative is for the intestate estate to **escheat** to the state if there are no relatives in the third parentela or closer. Escheat is when the probate estate is paid to the state. It is justified on the grounds that it is better for the estate to go to the state than to "laughing heirs," those who are so distant from the decedent that, when told they inherited, laugh all the way to the bank and shed no tears. Under the UPC, before the estate escheats, the decedent's stepchildren—the descendants of a deceased spouse—will take the estate. UPC § 2-103(b). In all states, once there are no heirs to take, the property does escheat to the state.

E. THE REPRESENTATION MODELS

The property that does not go to the surviving spouse is distributed through a system involving **representation,** which refers to what happens when a descendant has died and left surviving descendants to "step up" and represent them in the distributional scheme. This is why the earlier discussion of children and descendants is so important. The material that follows explains how each representation system works.

> ### "Per Stirpes" and "Per Capita"
>
> Both terms are from the Latin. **Per stirpes** means per bloodlines or per roots or stocks. (Note that it is stirpes, NOT stripes.) **Per capita** means per head or per person. Statutes use each term to distinguish different ways of inheriting through an ancestor.

Note that the representation systems come into play when at least one of the decedent's children died before the decedent and left surviving descendants. The representation system can also be useful when there are no descendants but more collateral relatives survive.

There are various representational variations throughout the states. However, there are three basic systems:

1. Strict (or "English") Per Stirpes
2. Modern Per Stirpes
3. The Current UPC Method—"Per Capita at Each Generation"

The concept of representation is more significant today than in the past because people are living longer and because it is not unusual for families to be comprised of many generations. If members of the family die "out of order," in other words, some children or grandchildren die before their parent, it becomes important to decide who is entitled to share in the decedent's probate estate.

In certain situations, all of the models give the same result. In others, two may give the same result while the other one will not. At times, especially if there are several generations of descendants involved, the three methods produce three different results. That said, there are a few rules that are common to all the systems:

- If there is at least one descendant, then relatives in the other parentela do not take anything.
- If *all* of the decedent's children survive the decedent, the representation rules are not necessary as the children do not need to be represented by others. The children will share the portion of the estate to which they are entitled equally.
- A representation system is only needed if, at the generation at which a distribution occurs, there is at least one descendant who has died, leaving descendants.
- A descendant who predeceases the decedent cannot be represented by spouse or stepchildren. Only an heir's children, grandchildren, or further descendants can stand in the heir's shoes as representatives. The representation rules require relationships by blood (consanguinity) or adoption, not marriage (affinity). Only the decedent's spouse qualifies as an heir.
- Only the highest surviving generation member of a family may receive a share; that person cuts off the rights of her descendants.

Once the intestate estate has been divided, all fractional shares should add up to one (a good way to check that you've done all of the math correctly).

The subsections following Exhibit 2.13 show how the different representation systems work, based on the following example.

EXHIBIT 2.13   Representation Systems

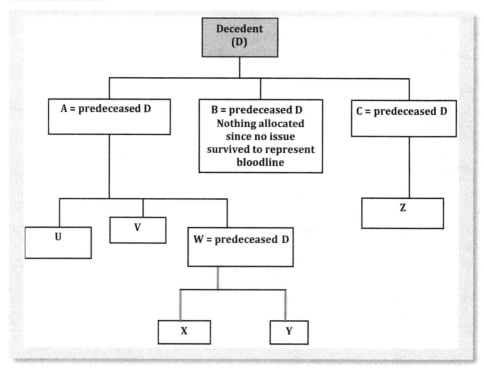

1. Strict Per Stirpes

The strict, or pure, per stirpes method establishes the number of shares based on the represented bloodlines at the first (or child) generation, *even if no child is alive at the decedent's death.* If a deceased child has descendants, those descendants divide the share of that deceased child. This method of representation, may also be called the **English**, **Classic**, or simply **per stirpes** method, and its goal is to distribute the decedent's property based on bloodlines, or "roots" or "stocks." The strict per stirpes approach, still in use in a number of the states, is traceable to pre-seventeenth-century English law.

Anyone receiving an inheritance through a parent or grandparent who predeceased the decedent divides the portion that the deceased parent or grandparent would have taken. Thus, each "grandchild or more remote descendant takes not only as a representative of his or her deceased parent, but has the right to share with his or her siblings or siblings' descendants the same portion of the decedent's estate as that descendant's parent would have taken if that parent had survived the decedent." Restatement (Third) of Property (Wills and Other Donative Trans.) § 2.3 (1999).

This approach is based on a belief that each of the decedent's children and those children's descendants should get an amount that is equal to the share of any other child of the decedent and that child's descendants. The goal is to divide up the estate into equal shares at the first generation, regardless of the number of people in subsequent generations.

Steps for Establishing the Strict Per Stirpes Share

1. Divide the decedent's estate so that each bloodline has an equal share, such that one share is set aside for each:

   a. living child of the decedent, if any, and
   b. deceased child with descendants then living who will represent them.
2. Distribute one share to each *living* member of the highest generation.
3. If any bloodlines with at least one survivor have not received a share, then distribute the probate property in the same manner as in Step 2. Repeat this generation by generation, putting each descendant who is represented at the top of the chart as if it was that person who was the decedent and whose property was being distributed.

Steps for Finding the Result for Exhibit 2.13 Under Strict Per Stirpes

1. Determine the number of shares by dividing the estate into as many equal parts as there are living children of the decedent, if any, and deceased children who are represented by their living descendants. Since B did not survive and did not leave any children, that potential share is lost. Thus, only two shares are created—one for the two children who each left descendants.

2. Z steps up to receive all of C's ½ share. Because A's bloodline receives ½, U and V receive ⅓ of that ½, or ⅙ each. The remaining ⅙ is distributed to W's two children.

3. Repeat Step 2 as to the ⅙ share to which W's bloodline is entitled. Doing this, X and Y each get ½ of that ⅙, or $\frac{1}{12}$ each of the intestate estate.

2. Modern Per Stirpes (1969 UPC/Modified Per Stirpes)

The modern per stirpes model of representation distributes the decedent's property per capita at the first generation where there are survivors and then by representation for descendants at lower generations.

In contrast to the strict per stirpes system where bloodlines are determined at the first generation of descendants whether there is anyone alive or not, the 1969 UPC per stirpes system drops down to the first generation where there are actual survivors; *in other words, shares are not created for a generation if everyone in that generation is dead.* Once the starting generation and primary shares are determined, the lower generations who represent their parents are locked into the share determined for their parent. On the other hand, moving down the family tree, if all members of a subsequent generation are deceased, then no shares are created for their generation, and their share drops down to the next generation where there are actual survivors.

Steps for Establishing the Modern Per Stirpes Share

1. Find the first generation where there are living descendants. At that generation, determine the number of shares by dividing the estate into as many equal shares as there are:
   a. living descendants of the decedent, if any, and
   b. deceased descendants with living descendants who will represent them.

Note that, unlike pure per stirpes, this system begins to divide the property into shares at the first generation where there are living descendants, not at the generation of the decedent's children.

2. Assign one share to each *living* member of this generation.
3. Repeat steps 1 and 2 for each generation.

Steps for Finding the Result for Exhibit 2.13 Under Modern Per Stirpes

1. Identify the generation closest to the decedent where there is at least one surviving member. Here, that is the second generation. Then we determine the number of shares by dividing the estate into as many equal parts as there are living descendants of the decedent at this level, if any (here, that is U, V, and Z), and deceased children who are represented by their living descendants (W). Thus, four shares.

2. Here, U, V, and Z each receive ¼.

3. Repeat the earlier steps for the remaining share. Since X and Y are both living, they each receive ½ of W's ¼ share, or ⅛.

Case Preview

In re Estate of Donald J. Evans

Evans illustrates the significance of the difference in the models when distributing the estate of an intestate decedent. It also highlights why terms like "per stirpes" and "by representation" should be fully defined in any documents using them.

Donald Evans died intestate. He was not married and did not have any children or other descendants. His three brothers were also dead, so his nearest relatives were the children of two of his brothers. One brother was survived by two daughters, while the other brother was survived only by a son. The court was required to determine how to distribute Evans's estate among the surviving family members based on the Nebraska intestacy statute. As you read *Evans*, consider:

1. Which model of representation does the Nebraska statute adopt?
2. Identify which system each party claimed in support of their claims.
3. Why didn't the court divide the estate into two shares, with one-half of the estate going to each of the brothers and their descendants?
4. Does the outcome of this case seem fair to you?

In re Estate of Donald J. Evans
827 N.W.2d 602 (Neb. Ct. App. 2013)

SIEVERS, Judge.

The decedent, Donald J. Evans, died intestate on October 2, 2011. . . . Donald was not married at the time of his death, and he had no surviving children or issue. Donald's parents were deceased at the time of his death. Donald had three brothers, Robert Evans, Stewart Evans, and Frederick Evans, but all three brothers predeceased Donald. Of the brothers, Robert did not have any children. Stewart had three children: Susan Evans Olson (Susan), Anna Evans, and Mary C. Evans. Anna predeceased Donald and did not have any children. Frederick had two children: Ted L. Evans and John Evans. John predeceased Donald and did not have any children. Thus, Donald was survived by nieces Susan and Mary (via Stewart) and nephew Ted (via Frederick).

PROCEDURAL BACKGROUND

[Ted] alleged that he had priority status as an heir entitled to at least 50 percent of the estate as a resident of Nebraska, whereas Susan and Mary were Colorado residents.

[] Mary filed an objection [], alleging that Ted was not entitled to 50 percent of the estate. . . .

Ted testified that Donald set up a will in 2010 with a bank, but that Donald tore up the will in September 2011, a month prior to his death. Ted testified that he, along with the bank officer who wrote the will, was present when Donald tore up his will. Ted testified that Donald also had the bank draw up a trust, but that he tore the trust document up at the same time he tore up his will.

. . .

Mary testified that a preliminary inventory of Donald's estate showed a value of $2.9 to $3 million. . . .

All of the parties, including Ted [and Mary] agree that § 30-2303 applies, which statute provides:

The part of the intestate estate not passing to the surviving spouse under section 30-2302, or the entire intestate estate if there is no surviving spouse, passes as follows:

(1) to the issue of the decedent; if they are all of the same degree of kinship to the decedent they take equally, but if of unequal degree, then those of more remote degree take by representation;

(2) if there is no surviving issue, to his parent or parents equally;

(3) if there is no surviving issue or parent, to the issue of the parents or either of them by representation; . . .

All parties agree that § 30-2303(3) applies and that the entire estate passes to the issue of the parents by representation. . . .

Ted claims that Susan, Mary, and he should take proportionate shares of the estate by representation, with Susan and Mary each inheriting one-quarter of the estate through their deceased father and Ted inheriting one-half of the estate through his deceased father. Ted reaches this result because § 30–2303(3) states that the issue of the parents take "by representation." . . . Mary counters that the estate is to be divided equally among the surviving heirs in the nearest degree of kinship, with Susan, Mary, and Ted each receiving an equal one-third share because they all have the same degree of kinship to Donald.

Neb. Rev. Stat. § 30-2306 (reissue 2008) provides the operative definition of the phrase "by representation," as used in § 30-2303(3), as follows:

If representation is called for by this code, the estate is divided into as many shares as there are surviving heirs in the nearest degree of kinship and deceased persons in the same degree who left issue who survive the decedent, each surviving heir in the nearest degree receiving one share and the share of each deceased person in the same degree being divided among his issue in the same manner.

Ted argues § 30-2306 means that the surviving issue of Stewart, namely Susan and Mary, would receive one share and that he, as the sole surviving issue of Frederick, would receive one share. Ted's end result would have Susan and Mary splitting Stewart's one-half share and Ted receiving Frederick's one-half share.

Ted misapplies § 30-2306. The portion applicable to our facts here provides: "If representation is called for by this code, the estate is divided into as many shares as there are *surviving heirs in the nearest degree of kinship*. . . ." § 30-2306 (emphasis supplied). Because none of Donald's brothers survived him, there are no surviving heirs in the nearest degree of kinship, namely Donald's siblings. Thus, the probate court must look to the next degree of kinship, or the next generation, which contains at least one surviving heir. The first generation which has living issue is composed of Donald's parents' grandchildren, who also are Donald's two nieces and his nephew. There must be at least one survivor in a degree of kinship. Here, because none of Donald's siblings survived him, the nearest degree of kinship to him containing a survivor was the generation containing two nieces and a nephew. And we note that Donald had no deceased nieces or nephews who have surviving issue. Susan, Mary, and Ted, who are all in an equal degree of kinship to one another, should, therefore, each receive a one-third share.

. . .

The parties are all applying a form of distribution traditionally referred to as "per stirpes distribution" in interpreting the words "by representation" found in § 30-2303(3) and defined in § 30-2306, but Ted is applying the older version of per stirpes distribution, referred to as "strict per stirpes," "classic per stirpes," or "English per stirpes." Mary is applying the modern version of per stirpes distribution, referred to as "modern per stirpes," "modified per stirpes," or "American per stirpes." . . . The difference between strict per stirpes and modern per stirpes is the generation at which shares of the estate are divided. Strict per stirpes begins at the generation closest to the decedent, regardless of whether there are any surviving individuals in that generation, whereas modern per stirpes begins at the first generation where there is living issue. Thus, the distinction between strict per stirpes and modern per stirpes will be most evident in instances where all of the heirs in the closest degree of kinship are deceased. In the present case, as earlier detailed, all of Donald's closest heirs, his parents and siblings, were deceased at the time of his death, and thus, the next generation with living members is Donald's parents' grandchildren: Susan, Mary, and Ted. [A]lthough the strict per stirpes system was the early standard for America, the majority of states now follow a different system of distribution.

[] 23 states have adopted some variation of modern per stirpes distribution, including Nebraska. Shumway explains that the distinction between modern per stirpes and strict per stirpes is that, in the latter system, the estate is divided into shares at the generation nearest the decedent regardless of whether there are living members, whereas in modern per stirpes, the estate is divided into equal shares at the nearest generation with surviving heirs. Nebraska is one of the 23 states that has adopted some variation of modern per stirpes distribution, because it has adopted the original 1969 Uniform Probate Code, a form of modern per stirpes. . . .

Susan, Mary, and Ted each take a one-third share of the estate, as they take by representation as defined in § 30-2306.

Post-Case Follow-Up

As the court held, the primary difference between pure per stirpes and the more modern systems is where the first division into shares occurs. Under the traditional system, this occurs at the generation closest to the decedent, even if there are no survivors in this generation; the more modern systems do not divide the estate into shares until they reach the first level with living descendants. The traditional system provides equity based on each distinct "bloodline," while the more modern systems are focused on equity at the generational level, so that all those who are of equal closeness to—or distance from—the decedent inherit equally. Note that even though the decedent had, at one point, drafted both a will and a trust, he revoked them both, so he died intestate.

In re Donald J. Evans: Real Life Applications

1. To what extent, if any, would the result have changed under the strict per stirpes system?

2. In *Evans*, Susan, Mary, and Ted were the children of the decedent's brothers. Would the result have changed and, if so, how, if:

   a. Susan were dead but was survived by her spouse?
   b. Susan were dead but survived by her three children?

3. In *Evans*, the third brother [Robert] had no surviving children. What would have been the result if he had left two surviving children:

   a. under the pure per stirpes system?
   b. under Nebraska law?

3. Per Capita at Each Generation—(1990 UPC)

The ULC adopted the "per capita at each generation" when it revised the UPC in 1990, as shown in Exhibit 2.14. This approach focuses on equality between members of a generation rather than on equality between bloodlines. It has been adopted by just over one-quarter of the states.

EXHIBIT 2.14 **UPC § 2-106. Representation**

(b) [Decedent's Descendants.] If, under Section 2-103(a)(1), a decedent's intestate estate or a part thereof passes "by representation" to the decedent's descendants, the estate or part thereof is divided into as many equal shares as there are (i) surviving descendants in the generation nearest to the decedent which contains one or more surviving descendants and (ii) deceased descendants in the same generation who left surviving descendants, if any. Each surviving descendant in the nearest generation is allocated one share. The remaining shares, if any, *are combined and then divided in the same manner* among the surviving descendants of the deceased descendants as if the surviving descendants who were allocated a share and their surviving descendants had predeceased the decedent. [Italics added.]

The UPC explicitly applies this system when "an applicable statute or a governing instrument calls for property to be distributed 'by representation' or 'per capita at each generation.'" UPC § 2-709. The system thus has significance beyond intestacy and is incorporated into the drafting process. A savvy drafter who wants a specific intestacy system to apply should use those words, such as "to be distributed per strict per stirpes" or include a definition of representation explaining the system that should be used.

Each living person in a particular generation who is entitled to a share gets exactly the same share as any other person within that generation who is entitled to a share.

Steps for Establishing the Per Capita at Each Generation Share

1. Begin at the first generation where there are living descendants. Divide the estate into equal shares based on the number of:
   a. living children of the decedent, if any, and
   b. deceased children in the same generation with descendants then living.

2. Assign one share per capita to each living member at this generation.

   Steps 1 and 2 are identical to the modern per stirpes method. It is the next step that is dramatically different.

3. Combine the remaining shares, if any, into a pot for sharing by lower generations.

4. Move down to the next generation and repeat steps 1 to 3 until the entire estate is distributed. That is, repeat the following:
   a. Divide the estate into equal shares based on the number of:
      i. living children of the decedent, if any, and
      ii. deceased children in the same generation with descendants then living.
   b. Assign one share per capita to each living member at this generation.
   c. Combine the remaining shares, if any, into a pot for sharing by lower generations.

Steps for Finding the Result for Exhibit 2.13

1. At the highest generation where there is at least one descendant who survives the decedent, determine the number of shares by dividing the estate into as many equal shares as there are living descendants of the decedent and deceased descendants who are represented by their living descendants. Since there was no one alive at the first generation (i.e., the child generation), we skip it and move directly to the second generation. At the second generation, there are three descendants of the decedent alive (U, V, and Z) and one descendant (W) who left descendants (X and Y). Therefore, four shares are created.
2. Distribute one share to each living descendant at that generation per capita. In this case, three of the four shares get distributed (to U, V, and Z).
3. The one share not distributed remains in the intestate pot to be shared by lower generations.
4. Repeat steps 1 to 3 as to the amount remaining in the pot. As a result, X and Y each receive 1/8.

Note that the result here is the same as with modern per stirpes, but, depending on the number of decedents and descendants, Steps 3 and 4 can lead to a different result.

F. REDUCING THE INTESTATE SHARE FOR ADVANCEMENTS

At common law, if a parent made a substantial gift to a child, then there was a presumption that the gift amount was an "**advancement**," a prepayment that diminishes the child's inheritance. The child had the burden of rebutting the presumption. Consequently, a transfer that took the form of an advancement was treated as a prepayment of some or all of the recipient's inheritance. It reduced the amount the heir would have otherwise received. The transfer may have been made in fee simple to the recipient or in the form of a nonprobate transfer, such as through a gratuitous transfer of a joint tenancy interest, or through being named the beneficiary of a life insurance policy.

Statutes in most states and the UPC reverse the common law presumption, so that all lifetime transfers to heirs are presumed to be gifts, not advancements. See Exhibit 2.15.

EXHIBIT 2.15 **UPC § 2-109. Advancements**

(a) If an individual dies intestate as to all or a portion of his [or her] estate, property the decedent gave during the decedent's lifetime to an individual who, at the decedent's death, is an heir is treated as an advancement against the heir 's intestate share *only if (i) the decedent declared in a contemporaneous writing or the heir acknowledged in writing that the gift is an advancement or (ii) the decedent's contemporaneous writing or the heir's written acknowledgment otherwise indicates that the gift is to be taken into account in computing the division and distribution of the decedent's intestate estate.* [Emphasis added.]

To rebut the presumption of a gift, the UPC specifies that the evidence must be in writing; oral (parol) evidence, no matter how persuasive, is not permitted. If the writing is from the *decedent*, it must have been drafted contemporaneously with the transfer and must specifically identify the transfer as an advancement or indicate in some clear manner that it was meant to reduce the amount to which the heir would have otherwise been entitled. The decedent's estate cannot subsequently try to transform an unqualified gift into an advancement. If the writing is from the *recipient*, it need not be contemporaneous but it must make a similar acknowledgment. For example, the recipient might write a letter stating, "Thank you, Dad, for the $15,000 to help me start my business. I understand the money will reduce my inheritance."

Evidence to prove that a transfer was intended as a loan is not as restricted. Unless the Statute of Frauds applies and requires a written instrument, other evidence of a loan may be introduced, such as proof of a repayment schedule.

A gift is an unqualified transfer so is not an advancement against inheritance through intestacy.

If the transfer is an advancement, then its value will be brought into a "hotchpot" calculation (see below for details) to determine if the recipient's share of the decedent's estate has been fully satisfied by the advance or if the recipient is entitled to more.

Even if the advancement exceeds the value of the recipient's calculated share of the estate, the recipient does not have an obligation to return the excess, unless the decedent's contemporaneous writing requires it. Note that an advancement only affects the share of the recipient. If the recipient predeceases the decedent, then the descendants of the advancee are still entitled to their share; the advancement is not taken into account in determining their share and the descendants of the advancee do *not* "step into the shoes" of the advancee. UPC § 2-109.

When a gift is deemed to be an advancement, then the estate must calculate whether the heir who received the advance has already received the amount to which she is entitled or whether she is entitled to more. This is accomplished through a method known as the "hotchpot."

EXHIBIT 2.16   Hotchpot Calculation

The UPC, which defers to the common law method of applying the hotchpot method, explains:
   Example: G died intestate, survived by his wife (W) and his three children (A, B, and C) by a prior marriage. G's probate estate is valued at $190,000. During his lifetime, G had advanced A $50,000 and B $10,000. G memorialized both gifts in a writing declaring his intent that they be advancements.

Solution. The first step in the hotchpot method is to add the value of the advancements to the value of G's probate estate. This combined figure is called the hotchpot estate.

In this case, G's hotchpot estate preliminarily comes to $250,000 ($190,000 + $50,000 + $10,000). W's intestate share of a $250,000 estate under § 2-102(4) is $200,000 ($150,000 plus 1/2 of $100,000). The remaining $50,000 is divided equally among A, B, and C, or $16,667 each. This calculation reveals that A has received an advancement greater than the share to which he is entitled; A can retain the $50,000 advancement, but is not entitled to any additional amount. A and A's $50,000 advancement are therefore disregarded and the process is begun over.

Once A and A's $50,000 advancement are disregarded, G's revised hotchpot estate is $200,000 ($190,000 + $10,000). W's intestate share is $175,000 ($150,000 plus 1/2 of $50,000). The remaining $25,000 is divided equally between B and C, or $12,500 each. From G's intestate estate, B receives $2,500 (B already having received $10,000 of his ultimate $12,500 share as an advancement); and C receives $12,500. The final division of G's probate estate is $175,000 to W, zero to A, $2,500 to B, and $12,500 to C.

UPC § 2-109, cmt.

Chapter Summary

- The intestacy rules apply to any of the decedent's probate property that does not pass by will. Thus, a decedent may die intestate or partially intestate.
- The decedent's heirs inherit through intestacy.
- Heirs may include the surviving spouse, descendants, ancestors, and collateral heirs. Those with the closest relationship to the decedent take first, and to the exclusion of more distant relatives.
- Under the UPC and in many states, the surviving spouse is preferred in distributing the decedent's intestate estate. State law determines who qualifies as a spouse; the parties may have undergone a ceremonial marriage, they may be common law married, or the individual may qualify as a putative spouse.
- Children and descendants inherit whatever portion does not go to the surviving spouse. Determining who is a child turns on state law establishing legal parentage. There is no distinction between children based on whether they are marital or nonmarital, and adopted children are treated equally with genetic children.
- Descendants take through a state-based "representation" system in which descendants "stand in" or represent their ancestors. The three most common representation systems are English or strict per stirpes, modern per stirpes, and per capita at each generation.
- A decedent's inter vivos gift to an heir might be treated as an advancement against the heir's share of the intestate estate, although the UPC presumes that such gifts are not advancements.

Applying the Concepts

1. Youssef and Alisha have lived together for 50 years. They have two children and four grandchildren who regularly come to visit them. Youssef recently died intestate with $1,000,000 in real estate in his name. In the following problems, analyze whether Alisha qualifies as a spouse for purposes of intestacy.

   a. What if Youssef and Alisha had a valid marriage ceremony 50 years ago?
   b. What if Youssef and Alisha lived in a state where common law marriage is recognized and they meet the criteria for a common law marriage?
   c. What if Youssef and Alisha were legally married but had been separated for ten years at the time of Youssef's death?
   d. What if Youssef and Alisha went through a marriage ceremony 50 years ago but, after Youssef's death, Alisha learned that he was still married to his first wife, Frieda? Would Frieda be entitled to anything from Youssef's estate? If so, how much?
   e. What if Youssef and Alisha separated last year?
   f. What if Youssef and Alisha were divorced last year?

2. Braden and Hermione were married in a valid marriage ceremony eight years ago. Braden died on June 23 of last year in a UPC state.

   a. At Braden's death, Hermione was pregnant with Mason, who was born on November 14 of last year. Does Mason qualify as a "child" of Braden for purposes of intestacy?
   b. What if two years after Braden's death, Hermione became pregnant, using his sperm, which was frozen before his death? Severus was born two years and nine months after Braden's death.

3. Fifteen years ago, Isaac and Jenn gave birth to Veronica. Unable to afford to raise Veronica, they gave her up for adoption when she was six weeks old. Newlyweds Nicolas and Olivia adopted Veronica.

   a. If Nicolas died this year, may Veronica inherit from his estate?   yes
   b. If Isaac died this year, may Veronica inherit from his estate?   no
   c. If Nicolas's mother died this year, may Veronica inherit from her estate if Nicolas survives?   no
   d. If Nicolas's mother died this year, may Veronica inherit from her estate if Nicolas has predeceased his mother?   yes
   e. If Jenn's father died this year, may Veronica inherit from his estate if Jenn is still alive?   no
   f. If Veronica died this year due to the negligence of a driver and there were a large damage award, who could inherit from Veronica's estate among the following individuals if the wrongful death statute in that state gives the award to Veronica's intestate heirs: Isaac, Jenn's mother, Olivia, Nicolas, Nicolas's mother?

4. Marco was married to Fanny, and they had one child, Camila. Marco and Fanny divorced, and Marco then married Ana. Ana and her first husband, Lucas, had one child together, Isaac. Marco and Ana had two children together, Xan and Yugo.

Marco died without a valid will and with a net probate estate of $2,000,000.

a. Determine the dollar value of Ana's share under UPC § 2-102. Be sure that you can identify which subsection is applicable.

Assume Marco is survived ONLY by the following:	Under the UPC, how much does Ana receive? Which section(s) appl(y/ies)?	Who might receive the balance and how much? Why?
1. Ana	100%	
2. Ana, Xan, and Yugo	100%	
3. Ana, Camila, and Fanny	$950,000	Camila
4. Ana and Isaac	100%	
5. Ana, Camila, Xan, and Yugo	$950k	Camila, Xan, Yugo
6. Ana, Camila, and Isaac	$950k	Camila
7. Ana, Xan, and Isaac	$1,075,000	Xan
8. Ana, Camila, Xan, Yugo, and Isaac	$950k	Camila, Xan, Yugo
9. Ana and Marco's mother	$1,550,000	M's mother
10. Ana, Marco's mother, Xan, and Yugo	100%	

b. Do your answers to Problems 3, 5, 6, and 8 change if Camila is dead, but survived by her child, Callie? Why or why not.

5. Alef and Polly, who were married, had two children, Bettina and Charlie. Bettina had two children, Elinore and Fernando, and one grandchild, Kriti, the child of Elinore. Charlie had four children, Georgio, Helena, Ina, and Josh. Georgio had one child, Lilah; Helena had two children, Mariana and Nanette; and Josh had one child, Oleander. If Alef dies intestate, survived by Fernando, Ina, Josh, Kriti, Lilah, Marian, Nanette, and Oleander, then who will inherit, and what proportion of Alef's estate will each person inherit?

6. The personal representative who is responsible for distributing Jacob's estate discovers a letter from Joseph, Jacob's son. Joseph's letter thanks Jacob for giving

him $100,000 to help start a coat business. Assume you are the personal representative and must decide who gets what.

a. The letter from Joseph acknowledges that it is meant to be an advance against whatever he might have received at Jacob's death. How does this note affect your decision?

b. The letter only says: "Thank you, Dad. I love you." How does this affect your decision?

c. What if there were no letter but Jacob told Joseph in front of their rabbi that the $100,000 was in lieu of his inheritance? How does this affect what you are willing to distribute to Joseph?

7. The personal representative of Rohan's estate has consulted you to determine how to distribute Rohan's estate. Rohan died intestate. Rohan is survived by his mother, his sister, his spouse, and two nieces (children of a deceased brother). How is Rohan's estate distributed?

Trusts and Estates in Practice

1. What are the requirements in your state for a valid ceremonial marriage? Does your state recognize common law marriage and putative spousehood? What about civil unions or domestic partnerships?

2. What are the different ways for determining parenthood in your state? Does your state publish a voluntary acknowledgement of paternity form?

3. Find your state's intestacy statute. What share of the estate is given to the surviving spouse? How does the existence of shared or non-shared descendants affect that share? What about the existence of parents?

4. What percentage of the intestate estate goes to surviving descendants? How does your state treat half-blood relationships? What happens to an adoptee's rights if a stepparent adopts?

5. Using the statute you used for Problem 3, describe the percentage or fraction of the intestate estate to which the decedent's children and grandchildren are entitled if the decedent is survived by (i) a spouse from a second marriage; (ii) an adult child of this second marriage; and (iii) two minor grandchildren of a child from the first marriage who died several years ago. Try to make the explanation one a layperson (your client) would understand, and avoid words such as "representation" and "per stirpes."

6. In practice, you will be required to explain technical legal concepts to your clients in a manner that they can understand. Translating legalese into layperson terms is a skill that is more difficult than you might think. Look at the intestacy

statute for the state where you grew up or where you intend to practice. Write a letter to your client, Kit Snow, of no more than one page, describing what the intestate rights are for Kit's spouse, Rosa Leslie, if Kit dies first and is also survived by an adult child from Kit's first marriage, two minor children from Rosa Leslie's marriage with Kit, Kit's mother, and Kit's brother.

7. Based on the same facts as in Problem 6, Kit would also like to know what would happen if Rosa's adult child Parker were to predecease her, because Parker has Stage III melanoma and has been given only two years to live.

8. You are a member of your state's probate law reform commission, and you are considering which of the three different representation systems to use for intestacy distributions. What are the equity arguments in favor of each? Which do you think is best suited to the reality of contemporary families in trusts and estates practice? Why?

EXHIBIT 2.17 Table of Consanguinity

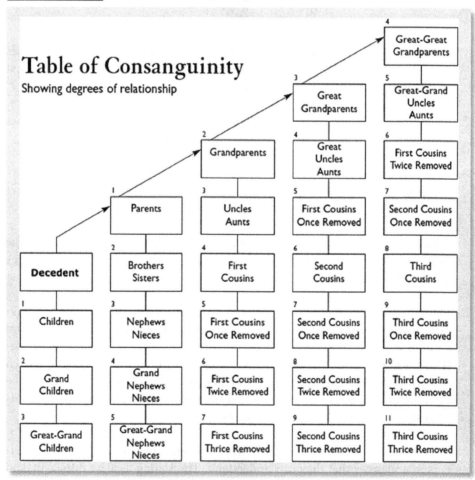

Creation of Wills

3

What is a **will**? A will is a document that disposes of the decedent's probate property at death. It allows a **testator** (the person who makes the will) to **devise**, or make a gift at death of, property. Wills can accomplish many things: transfer property at death; appoint an **executor**, who has the legal obligation to carry out the provisions of the will; nominate a **guardian** for minor children; exercise a testamentary **power of appointment** that selects the recipient of property the testator did not own; exclude or limit the right of an individual or class to receive property of the decedent passing by intestate succession; revoke an earlier will; or otherwise set out the decedent's wishes to take effect at death. A will does not become operative until the testator's death, and can be amended or revoked whenever the testator wishes, so long as the testator has capacity and complies with the requisite formalities each time. The term "will" also includes a **codicil**, a term that refers to a document that amends or supplements a prior will.

For a probate court to enforce those choices after the testator's death, the will must meet certain requirements as to how it is created. These requirements concern the document itself as well as the testator's testamentary capacity and intent, and they are built on both the 1677 English Statute of Frauds and the 1837 Statute of Wills. The formalities derived from both sources (Wills Act formalities) were very specific. Because compliance with the formalities was mandatory, wills could be declared invalid due to minor errors in the execution process, such as a signature that was not at the end of the will.

Today, a will must still comply with certain formalities, although there has been a movement to relax the rules a testator must follow for a will to be enforceable, with the goal of validating wills that represent the testators' wishes. The execution formalities that dictate the way in which a will must be written, signed, and witnessed continue to provide important protections.

Because a will takes effect after the person creating the will is deceased, the formalities protect against fraud and make the existence of recorded wishes of the decedent more likely.

This chapter explores these requirements in detail and the policy concerns that underpin

Key Concepts

- Requirements for the testator's mental abilities
- Formalities required for a valid will
- Doctrines that validate a will in the absence of compliance with the formalities
- What constitutes a will

them. The next section explores the formalities typically required for a valid will. It also describes doctrines that are designed to mitigate some of the harshness of the formal requirements. Finally, because this chapter is concerned with will drafting, we discuss the structure of a will, including the types of provisions that might be included in a will.

A. LEGAL REQUIREMENTS FOR THE TESTATOR

The testator must meet certain minimum requirements for a will to be valid.

1. Age and Mental Capacity

States typically require that the testator be age 18 and have **mental capacity** (be "of sound mind" or have "testamentary capacity") to make a will. For example, Uniform Probate Code (UPC) § 2-501 provides, "An individual 18 or more years of age who is of sound mind may make a will." While most states also allow people under the statutory age who are **emancipated minors** to make a will because they have been legally released from parental control, the number of such minors is minimal. The age of majority or contractual capacity and the age at which someone may execute a will are not necessarily the same. For example, persons who are at least 14 years old may execute wills in Georgia but are unable to enter contracts until reaching the age of 18. Another example is the state of Alabama, where persons who are 18 years old can execute wills, although legal minority lasts until the age of 19.

Being of "sound mind" to execute a will requires a level of mental capacity that is lower than the capacity required to enter into a contract or create an irrevocable trust, based on the assumption that individuals are competent to decide how to dispose of their property. For more detail on the level of capacity required to execute a variety of estate planning documents, see Robert Whitman, *Capacity for Lifetime and Estate Planning*, 117 Penn. St. L. Rev. 1061 (2013).

To meet the test for mental capacity, a testator "must be capable of knowing and understanding in a general way"; (1) the extent and character of her property; (2) the "natural objects" of her "bounty," who are generally recognized as the testator's close relatives; (3) how she is disposing of her property; and (4) how the other three elements interrelate. Restatement (Third) of Prop.: Wills and Other Donative Transfers § 8.1. Mental capacity

---

First and Last Pages of George Washington's 29-Page Will

Because wills are public documents, an internet search will easily lead you to wills of the rich and famous, including Heath Ledger, Jackie Kennedy, and George Washington. Although wills often are written in formal language, the testator's choices on how to distribute property, and on what property is listed in the will, gives you insight into what the testator (and the drafting attorney) thought was important.

The Papers of George Washington, http://gwpapers. virginia.edu/documents_gw/will/ will_manuscript_1.html.

must exist at the time of will execution, even if it does not exist before or afterwards. For example, Sam has Alzheimer's disease and is often disoriented. Nonetheless, if Sam executes a will during a lucid moment, then Sam will satisfy the test for mental capacity. See id., illus. 7. While this chapter is concerned with execution of the will, Chapter 4 discusses will challenges based on lack of capacity.

2. Testamentary Intent

The testator must not only have the mental capacity, but must also have **testamentary intent** for the creation of a valid will. Testamentary intent means that the decedent intended the document in question to be a will and to become operative at the person's death. A strong but rebuttable presumption of testamentary intent exists if the will contains language to that effect—i.e., as "This is my last will and testament." If such language is absent, a court may infer testamentary intent from other words in the document itself, such as "I give, bequeath, and devise." In some states, courts allow extrinsic evidence to establish testamentary intent in the absence of an express provision. To clarify, testamentary intent requires that the individual had the purpose of creating a legally binding document—not just that she created a good record as to whom she wanted to leave her property.

B. LEGAL REQUIREMENTS FOR EXECUTION OF A FORMAL WILL

Although there is enormous variation between states, each state typically requires the following three elements for a will to be valid. First, the will must be in writing. Second, the will must be signed by the testator. And third, the will must be properly witnessed. Some states also require **publication**, which means that the testator must declare to the witnesses that "this is my will."

As shown in Exhibit 3.1, the UPC sets out the typical requirements (although most states do not allow a notary as a substitute for two witnesses):

EXHIBIT 3.1   **UPC § 2-502. Formalities Required for a Valid Will**

> (a) **[Witnessed or Notarized Wills.]** Except as otherwise provided in subsection (b) and in §§ 2-503, 2-506, and 2-513, a will must be:
> (1) in writing;
> (2) signed by the testator or in the testator's name by some other individual in the testator's conscious presence and by the testator's direction; and
> (3) either:
>   (A) signed by at least two individuals, each of whom signed within a reasonable time after the individual witnessed either the signing of the will as described in paragraph (2) or the testator's acknowledgment of that signature or acknowledgment of the will; or

(B) acknowledged by the testator before a notary public or other individual authorized by law to take acknowledgments. . . .

(b) **[Extrinsic Evidence.]** Intent that a document constitutes the testator's will can be established by extrinsic evidence, including, for holographic[1] wills, portions of the document that are not in the testator's handwriting.

The Functions of Wills Act Formalities

Wills Act formalities are said to serve the four functions discussed in the first chapter. First, they serve the *Evidentiary Function* because formalities tend to enhance the reliability of wills as evidence of the decedent's intent by providing assurances of authenticity in place of the decedent's own court testimony. Second, the formalities serve the *Channeling Function* because they encourage standardization of wills, making it easier to identify the document as a will. Third, the *Ritual Function* is served because the formalities impress the testator with the legal significance of expressing testamentary intent. Fourth, the *Protective Function* is served because formalities can protect the testator from fraud or undue influence committed by individuals seeking to override the decedent's intent for their own benefit.

As we explore each of the formality requirements below—a writing, a signature, **attestation** (signing as a witness to authenticate the testator's execution of the will), and publication—ask yourself which of these functions the various requirements serve and how well they serve those functions.

1. The Writing Requirement

States require that a will be in writing, with a few minor exceptions. Courts are accustomed to paper writings, but the writing requirement is broadly construed to include, for example, words scratched on a car fender, so long as the markings are visible.

Some states will also recognize **nuncupative**, i.e., oral wills, under very limited circumstances. If oral wills are allowed, they generally must be executed while in fear of imminent death, often on the battlefield, in order to be valid; and states generally impose other requirements, such as limiting the amount of property that can be transferred through a nuncupative will and requiring the reduction of the spoken words to writing by the listener within a reasonable time.

States are beginning to respond to the development of electronic wills, as you will see in the *Castro* case below. The problem has been that existing Wills Acts are based on centuries-old law, and require that wills be "in writing;" they do not account for the possibility of electronic signatures or documents. Nevada adopted the first statute authorizing electronic wills in 2001, but only a few other states, including Arizona and Indiana, have enacted electronic wills statutes (as of the date of publication). The Uniform Law Commission (ULC) became involved in drafting a uniform law on electronic wills in 2017, http://www.uniformlaws.org/Committee.aspx-?title=Electronic%20Wills. Consider why it has taken states so long to move toward electronic wills.

2. The Signature Requirement

The testator must sign the will. In most cases, the testator will put a full signature on the signature line at the end of the will. The signature requirement shows that

---

[1][A **holographic will** is a will that is in the testator's writing and signed, but which need not be witnessed. —Eds.]

this is a particular testator's last will, and that the document is not a draft. But courts and legislatures do not require the testator's full signature, and most do not require a signature at the end of the will.

States have interpreted the signature requirement to include any symbol or mark that the testator considers to be her signature. The comments to UPC § 2-502 explicitly recognize this possibility, so that the testator may sign her full name, may make a cross or a mark, like an "X," or may use a term of relationship such as "Mom," "Grandpa," or "Auntie."

Moreover, many states, and the UPC, allow someone else to sign as a proxy for the testator. To be valid, the proxy must sign ". . . in the testator's conscious presence and by the testator's direction. . . ." UPC § 2-502(a)(2). While a proxy generally only signs if the testator is unable to do so herself, even with the guidance from another person, the testator's physical state is irrelevant as to the validity of the proxy's signature.

The testator's handwritten name at the end of the document unquestionably satisfies the signature requirement. However, only a few states still require that the signature be at the end of the document. Restatement (Third) of Prop.: Wills and Other Donative Transfers § 3.1, cmt. l (1999). Many states, and the UPC, do not specify a location for the testator's signature, and it might appear elsewhere on the will, such as in the margin or at the top.

If the testator signs somewhere other than the end of the document, it is more difficult to determine whether the name was intended to operate as a signature executing the will, as opposed to merely identifying the testator. In turn, this may be the basis for a challenge to the validity of the will.

Case Preview

In re Estate of Javier Castro

This case illustrates a court grappling with the complexities of modern technology. Javier Castro, the decedent, was hospitalized and knew that he would die soon. With no pen and paper available, his brother suggested writing a will on a Samsung Galaxy tablet. Castro dictated the terms to his brother, who recorded them on the tablet. Castro then signed the tablet, as did three witnesses. The court had to decide whether the tablet met the requisite statutory formalities so the document could be probated.

As you read *Estate of Javier Castro,* think about the following:

1. What did the statute require for a formal (attested) will?
2. What issues related to the statutory requirements did the court need to resolve?
3. How does the court's decision reflect the four functions for testamentary formalities?
4. What reasoning does the court use to determine that this document reflected the testator's intent?
5. Are there any other reasons to doubt the validity of the will?
6. Who would have inherited Castro's property had the will been invalidated?

In re Estate of Javier Castro
Case No. 2013ES00140 (Lorain Cnty. Ohio Ct. of Com. Pl. June 19, 2013)

. . .

This case concerns the creation and introduction on an electronic will. It appears to be a case of first impression in the State of Ohio.

The facts are as follows:

In late December 2012, Javier Castro presented at Mercy Regional Medical Center in Lorain, Ohio. He was told by medical personnel that he would need a blood transfusion. For religious reasons, he declined to consent to the blood transfusion. He understood that failure to receive the blood transfusion would ultimately result in his death.

On December 30, 2012, Javier had a discussion with two of his brothers, Miguel Castro and Albie Castro, about preparing a will. Because they did not have any paper or pencil, Albie suggested that the will be written on his Samsung Galaxy tablet. The Court is aware that a "tablet", is a one-piece mobile computer.[2] Tablets typically have a touchscreen, with finger or stylus pen gestures replacing the conventional computer mouse. . . .

Miguel and Albie both testified that Javier would say what he wanted in the will and Miguel would handwrite what Javier had said using the stylus. Miguel and Albie both testified that each section would be read back to Javier and that the whole document was *also* read back to Javier. Testimony was had that Javier, Miguel and Albie had discussions concerning each and every paragraph in the will. . . .

Miguel testified that later that same date [] Javier signed the Will on the tablet in his presence. Albie also testified that Javier signed the will in his presence. Oscar DeLeon, nephew of Javier, arrived shortly thereafter and became the third witness to the will. Oscar testified that he did not see Javier sign the will, rather Javier acknowledged in his presence that he had signed the will on the tablet.

After the will was executed, Albie retained possession of the tablet that contained the will. Albie testified that the tablet is password protected and has been in his continuous possession since December 30, 2012. Miguel and Albie testified that the will has not be altered in any way since it was signed by Javier on December 30, 2012. Both testified that the paper copy of the will presented to the Court on February 11, 2013 is an exact duplicate of the will in the tablet that was prepared and signed on December 30, 2012.

Javier, Miguel, Albie and Oscar were all over 18 years of age on December 30, 2012. Miguel, Albie and Oscar all testified that on December 30, 2012, Javier was of sound mind and memory and under no restraint. Specifically, testimony was had that Javier knew who his family members were, who his heirs were and what was the extent of his assets.

Dina Cristin Cintron, niece of Javier, testified that Javier told her that he had signed the will on the Samsung Galaxy notebook. Similar testimony was also received from Marelisa Leverknight and Steve Leverknight, that Javier told them he had signed the will on the tablet and that it contained his wishes.

---

[2]The Judge received a tablet as a Father's Day gift on 6/16/13.

Javier died on January 30, 2013.

. . . The will consists of three pages. The first two pages indicate that the will is the last will and testament of Javier Castro and has eleven numbered paragraphs. The eleven numbered paragraphs contain the naming of Miguel as Executor, dispositions of Javier's property along with instructions to the Executor. The copy of the will has a green background, with lines and black writing. It looks like a green legal pad.

The third page contains the signature of Javier Castro along with the signatures of Miguel, Albie and Oscar.

If the will were to be declared invalid, Javier's estate would pass by intestate succession under R.C. 2105.06. Javier had no lineal descendants. In this case, Benjamin Castro, Sr. and Maria Castro, Javier's father and mother, respectively, would inherit his estate. Benjamin Castro, Sr. and Maria Castro did . . . not contest the admittance of the will [and] if the will were to be declared invalid, [ ] would still distribute the assets according to Javier's wishes as stated in the will.

LAW AND DECISION

R.C. 2107.02 provides: "A person who is eighteen years of age or older, of sound mind and memory, and not under restraint may make a will." It uncontroverted from the testimony that Javier was over 18 years of age, was of sound mind and memory and not under any restraint to make this will. The medical condition that brought him to the hospital did not diminish his capacity to execute a will on December 30, 2012.

In R.C. 2107.03 provides the method for making a will. It states in part:

"Except oral wills, every will shall be in *writing,* but may be handwritten or typewritten. The will shall be *signed* at the end by the testator or by some other person in the testator's conscious presence and at the testator's express direction. The will shall be attested and subscribed in the conscious presence of the testator, by two or more competent witnesses, who saw the testator subscribe, or heard the testator acknowledge the testator's signature. . . ." (Emphasis added.)

The questions for the Court are as follows:

1) Is this a "writing" and was the will "signed" and,
2) Has sufficient evidence been presented that this is the last will and testament of Javier Castro.

R.C. 2107.03 requires only that the will be in "writing". It does not require that the writing be on any particular medium. Nowhere else in Chapter 21 is "writing" defined. Although not necessarily controlling, R.C. 2913.0l(F)[3] is instructive on the definition of a "writing." It provides: "Writing" means any computer software, document, letter, memorandum, note, paper, plate, data, film, or other thing having in or upon it any written, typewritten, or printed matter, and any token,

---

[3][This is from the definition section of the Ohio criminal code concerning "Theft and Fraud." —EDS.]

stamp, seal, credit card, badge, trademark, label, or other symbol of value, right, privilege, license, or identification." If the Court were to apply this definition of a writing to R.C. 2107.03, the document on the Samsung Galaxy tablet would qualify as a "writing". The writing in this contains of the stylus marks made on the tablet and saved by the application software. I believe that the document prepared on December 30, 2012 on Albie's Samsung Galaxy tablet constitutes a "writing" under R.C. 2107.03. . . .

The tablet application also captured the signature of Javier. The signature is a graphical image of Javier's handwritten signature that was stored by electronic means on the tablet. Similarly, I believe that this qualifies as Javier's signature under R.C. 2107.03. Thus, the writing was "signed" at the end by Javier.

Evidence was presented by six witnesses that Javier had stated that the document he signed on the tablet were his wishes and that it was his last will and testament. Testimony was elicited from all six witnesses that Javier never subsequently expressed any desire or intention to revoke, amend or cancel the will.

. . .

There is no statutory law or case law in Ohio concerning writing a will in electronic format. The State of Nevada allows for the creation of an electronic will.[2] If Javier's will had been created in Nevada, it would have complied with state law.

The Court finds that the document signed on December 30, 2012 on the Samsung Galaxy tablet is the last will and testament of Javier Castro and should be admitted to probate.

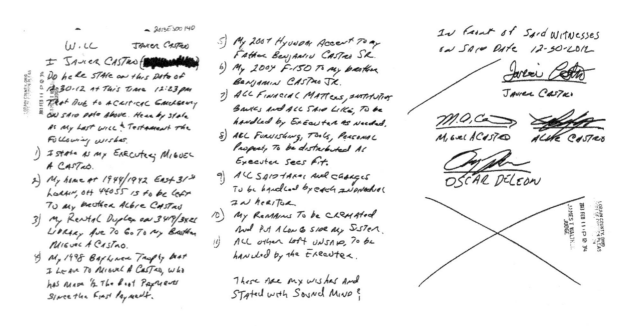

Post-Case Follow-Up

In *Castro*, the court held that the will was valid, concluding that the writing on the tablet met the statutory requirement that the will be "in writing," that Castro had in fact signed the will, and that the will was signed in the presence of two witnesses. The court was assured by the testimony that Castro intended the writing to be his will. Few other states have accepted electronic wills, although the Uniform Law Commission is drafting an electronic wills act. See Kyle B. Gee, *Beyond* Castro's *Tablet Will: Exploring Electronic Will Cases Around the World and Re-Visiting Ohio's Harmless Error Statute*, 26 Ohio Prob. L.J. 149 (2016).

In re Estate of Javier Castro: Real Life Applications

1. Would the result have changed if Castro been unable to sign the will, but had asked one of his brothers to sign it on his behalf?

2. Assume the same facts as in the case, but instead of being written on the Samsung Tablet, it was written on a legal pad. How would the court have ruled?

3. If you had been representing Castro when he was in the hospital and physically incapable of signing a will, what steps would you have taken to ensure a valid signature on the will?

4. Cornelius, a new client, has consulted you about how to distribute his spouse's estate. He arrived in your office with an iPhone and the following story. His spouse recently died at home, alone. When he found the body, he found the iPhone next to it. Cornelius has brought you the phone and knows his spouse's password for her phone; he discovered that his spouse had typed a message on the phone entitled "My Will." The message stated that all probate property should be distributed to him and their children, and at the end of the message is his spouse's name in capital-typed letters. How would you advise Cornelius?

3. The Witness Requirement

A formal will must also be "witnessed" in order to be valid. UPC § 2-502(a)(3)(A). The witnesses serve to "**attest**," or authenticate, the testator's execution (or acknowledgement) of the document as a will. Older statutes require three witnesses, but the UPC and almost every state now only require two. Pennsylvania does not require that wills be signed by witnesses, unless the testator did not sign with a full signature; but rather made a mark, or had someone else sign on her behalf. 20 Pa. Cons. Stat. § 2502. Nonetheless, even in Pennsylvania, wills drafted by lawyers must have the signatures of two witnesses, because two witnesses will be needed to prove the signature of the testator for the will to be admitted into probate. 20 Pa. Cons. Stat. § 3132.

The witnesses do not need to observe the testator actually sign the will. Even if the testator signs the will outside the presence of the witnesses, the witnesses can still attest if the testator later acknowledges to the witnesses that the signature is his (or that his name was signed by another) or that the document is his will. The acknowledgment does need to be expressly stated, but can be inferred through observation of the testator's conduct. UPC § 2-502(a)(3)(A) requires that the witnesses sign within a reasonable time after having witnessed either the testator's signing the will or the testator's acknowledging his signature on the will.

The witnessing requirement is often viewed as serving a protective function for the testator to ensure that making the will is her wish, and that the will is not signed under duress. In a dispute about testamentary capacity or the proper execution of the will, the witnesses can be required to testify in court as to their view of the testator's capacity and the circumstances surrounding the execution of the will.

The witnesses must be competent, and many states and the UPC permit an **interested witness** to serve, even though an interested witness is a beneficiary. See UPC § 2-505.

Interested Witnesses

Historically, if any of the witnesses were also beneficiaries of a will, then the entire will was void: an interested witness could not testify concerning the execution of the will. The beneficiary-witness was presumed to have an inherent conflict of interest and might provide false testimony to validate an ineffectively executed will.

Rather than invalidate the entire will and disinherit all beneficiaries, the law has developed to invalidate only the bequest to the interested witness rather than the entire will. Under these **purging statutes**, the witness could still attest to the will's validity, but would lose any bequest under the will. Under a newer form of purging statutes, the irrebuttable presumption against the interested witness was relaxed toward a rebuttable presumption that the gift to the interested witness was the product of undue influence. This allowed the interested witness to preserve her gift by rebutting the presumption. Even if she could not do so, some statutes provide that such a witness only forfeits that part of her devise that is greater than the amount she would have taken if the will were not valid, either under intestacy or under a prior will. See Restatement (Third) of Property: Wills and Other Donative Transfers § 3.1, cmt. o (1999).

In several states and under the UPC, there is no "interested witness" rule. UPC § 2-505(b). The general policy supporting this approach is that many bequests, which are not in fact the product of undue influence, may fail unjustly if an interested witness rule is applied. Many interested witness cases actually involve innocent family members who are witnesses because they are available. On the other hand, use of an interested witness may still be "suspicious." Restatement (Third) of Property: Wills and Other Donative Transfers § 3.1, cmt. o (1999). As a lawyer, best practices require that no beneficiary nor relative of a beneficiary should serve as a witness.

The Logistics and Timing of Signing

The requirement in UPC § 2-502(a)(3)(A) that two individuals "witness" the will means either they must observe the testator sign the will, or the testator must acknowledge to them that it is either her signature or her will.

In some states, the witnesses must sign in the presence of the testator and in the presence of each other. This has led to a number of cases interpreting the word "**presence**." At first, presence was defined as being in the "line of sight" of the testator when signing. This is still the standard in many states. This might be interpreted literally, or it could mean that, even if the testator did not see the witness, the testator could have done so without changing her position. Courts have also used the "**conscious-presence**" test, so that the will can be validated if the witnesses are within range of any of the testator's senses. That is, so long as the testator can sense the presence or actions of the witness (such as, they may be in earshot), then this satisfies the presence requirement. Restatement (Third) of Prop.: Wills and Other Donative Transfers § 3.1 cmt. p (1999).

As you saw in Exhibit 3.1, UPC § 2-502(a)(3) simply requires that there be "at least two individuals, each of whom signed within a reasonable time after he [or she] witnessed either the signing of the will . . . or the testator's acknowledgement of that signature or acknowledgement of the will." UPC § 2-502(a)(3) requires that the witnesses sign "within a reasonable time" after witnessing either the signing of the will or the testator's acknowledgement. The comments to the UPC note that witnesses might even be able to sign after the testator's death, so long as that otherwise satisfies the reasonable time requirement. Typically, a lawyer who oversees the execution of a client's will has the testator sign in front of the two witnesses who sign immediately after seeing the testator sign, so the questions of presence and timing are resolved quite easily. Under more unusual execution circumstances, one must consult state law to determine whether the presence and timing requirements are met; not all states are as generous as the UPC.

As an example, Bernard was in hospice care in his home when he signed a codicil. His caretaker, Alison, and his son, Mark, witnessed Bernard's signature from his bedside. Alison signed as a witness, but Mark did not at that time. Bernard died a week later, at which point Mark signed the codicil as a witness. This could satisfy the reasonable time requirement, serving the formalities function by protecting against fraud and mistake and ensuring authenticity. See In re Estate of Jung, 109 P.3d 97, 102 (Ariz. Ct. App. 2005).

Case Preview

Estate of Ray Merle Burton

Washington state law requires that a will be signed by two witnesses. In *Burton*, the court considered whether two different documents, each potentially disposing of the testator's estate, and each signed by a different individual, could be taken together to consider the decedent's will. The decedent had handwritten the two documents shortly before his death. Victor White, the beneficiary, had been the decedent's caretaker, and both documents left him all of the decedent' estate.

Richard Didrickson, the testator's cousin, argued that the alleged will had not met the witnessing requirement, and thus the decedent had died intestate. The first document could not be located. The second document, which contained the alleged testamentary statement, was on a blank portion of a preprinted health care directive form. The trial court held that Burton died intestate and the appellate court considered whether, without knowing the contents of the first document, the two documents could be considered counterparts that formed one will signed by two witnesses.

As you read the case, consider the following questions:

1. What are the different arguments that White makes? How do they fit together?
2. Why does the court conclude that there were not two witnesses?
3. What was the testator's intent?
4. Why does the court decide not to treat the two documents as constituting a will?
5. Which of the four different purposes of will formalities is implicated in the court's opinion?

Estate of Ray Merle Burton
358 P.3d 1222 (Wash. Ct. App. 2015)

MAXA, P.J.

Victor White appeals the trial court's order declaring that Ray Burton died intestate. RCW 11.12.020(1) states that wills must be signed by the testator and attested by two witnesses to be valid. White submitted evidence that Burton drafted and signed a document leaving his entire estate to White. The document was signed by one witness, but subsequently was lost. Burton later drafted a second, purportedly similar, document leaving his entire estate to White. That document was signed by a different witness. Richard Didricksen, Burton's legal heir, challenges the validity of the document under RCW 11.12.020(1). White argues that because two witnesses attested to Burton's testamentary intent to leave his estate to White, the documents together constituted a validly executed will. []

We hold that Burton's testamentary documents do not constitute a valid will because Burton did not strictly comply with the requirement in RCW 11.12.020(1) that two witnesses attest to a will. . . . Accordingly, we affirm the trial court's order declaring that Burton died intestate.

Burton was a successful businessman with substantial assets, including two gold mines and a number of collectible cars. He allegedly was estranged from his living relatives and considered himself without family. Beginning in 2011, White helped the elderly Burton with a variety of tasks around his home. At some point, Burton allegedly began to prepare White to take over his business dealings after he died. Burton was hospitalized for pneumonia in 2013, and after his release White became his caretaker. Burton also received home nurse visits, and later hospice care. Throughout this time, Burton apparently had no will.

Shortly before he died, Burton handwrote and signed a document in red ink that was witnessed and signed by Lisa Erickson, a nurse. Erickson stated in a declaration that the document was for the purpose of Burton leaving his property to White. However, Erickson provided no testimony regarding the actual language used in that document, and she does not know what happened to the document.

The day before he died, Burton handwrote another testamentary statement, again in red ink, on a blank portion of a preprinted healthcare directive form. He apparently needed some assistance from another nurse, Shirley Outson, to complete the writing. The final statement, which is difficult to read, appears to state:

> Thank Victor White remain my caretaker till I go to sleep/die. The transfer of Gold Mines Montecarlo and Black Hawk One, all my collector cars and real estate located at 36619 Mountain Hwy E, Eatonville, WA 98320. I wish all my worldly possessions to go to Victor White.

Clerk's Papers at 13. Burton signed the form below the statement, as did Outson. But no other witness signed the document.

Burton died on January 25, 2014. White petitioned the trial court to recognize Burton's statement on the healthcare directive form as his will and to name White as personal representative of Burton's estate. Didricksen, Burton's cousin and legal heir, moved for an order declaring that Burton died intestate. The trial court granted Didricksen's motion, finding that Burton had not executed a valid will and therefore had died intestate. [This appeal followed.]

ANALYSIS

A. Strict Compliance with Two Witness Requirement

White argues that the trial court erred by concluding that Burton died intestate because Burton complied with the requirements of RCW 11.12.020(1) and executed a valid will by creating two equivalent documents, each witnessed by a different person. We disagree.

. . .

RCW 11.12.020(1) requires that a will meet three basic formalities:

Every will shall be [1] in writing [2] signed by the testator or by some other person under the testator's direction in the testator's presence, and shall be [3] *attested by two or more competent witnesses,* by subscribing their names to the will, or by signing an affidavit that complies with RCW 11.20.020(2), while in the presence of the testator and at the testator's direction or request.

(Emphasis added). Attestation by two witnesses always is required, and Washington does not recognize "holographic" wills.

White argues that the healthcare directive document is a valid will that complies with the two witness requirement. But that document was signed by only one witness. Therefore, on its face the document does not comply with RCW 11.12.020(1).

However, White argues that two witnesses did attest to Burton's will. White claims that they attested to the will in counterparts, separately signing two counterpart documents describing the same testamentary gift. White notes that nothing in RCW 11.12.020(1) prohibits executing a will in counterparts and that no Washington cases address this situation.

Even if we assume that witnesses can attest to a will in counterparts, the facts here show that Burton's witnesses did not sign counterpart documents. . . . Having one witness sign one testamentary document and having another witness sign a different testamentary document does not constitute signing one document in counterparts.

White also argues that the two documents must be viewed as a single integrated document that was signed by two witnesses. However, even if we assume that these documents somehow formed a single will, there were no witnesses that signed that will. Erickson and Outson each signed a portion of the will, but neither witnessed the "integrated" document.

Without evidence that two witnesses signed the same document, or at least identical duplicates of that document, White cannot show that Burton complied with RCW 11.12.020(1). Because only one witness signed the healthcare directive document— the only testamentary writing signed by Burton in the record—we hold that Burton did not strictly comply with the two witness requirement in RCW 11.12.020(1).

Post-Case Follow-Up

The court construed the two-witness statutory provision as requiring that both witnesses sign the same document. Without evidence that two witnesses, one of whom had signed a document that was later lost, and the other of whom had signed a subsequent document, actually signed the same testamentary document (or at least identical duplicates of that document), the testator had not complied with the statutory requirement that two witnesses sign a will. This led the court to conclude that the decedent had not executed a valid will and had died intestate. The court defined the statutory purposes underlying formality requirements of the statute governing requisites of wills as to ensure that the testator has a definite and complete intention to dispose of his or her property and to prevent, as far as possible, fraud, perjury, mistake, and the chance of one instrument being substituted for another. *Burton* will return later in the chapter under another potential theory of validation.

Estate of Ray Merle Burton: Real Life Applications

1. What if both documents were produced, they were identical, and each was signed by a different witness?

2. What if only the health care power of attorney form had been produced, and it was signed by two witnesses?

3. Tia prepared a will. Her spouse, Seamus, and her only child, Dolores, acted as witnesses to Tia's will. In each situation below, have the execution formalities been met?

   a. Tia was unable to sign her will because she had had a stroke. She asked Seamus to sign her name, and he did, in her presence. Dolores was also there, watched Seamus sign their mother's name, and then both Seamus and Dolores signed the document as witnesses.

   b. Seamus and Dolores watched Tia sign her will, but did not themselves sign the document. Several weeks later, they signed the will as witnesses.

      i. Seamus and Dolores signed while Tia was still alive.

      ii. Seamus and Dolores signed after Tia's death.

   c. Tia signed her will. A week later, Seamus came to visit. Tia pulled out the will and asked him to sign it, which he did. A week after that, Tia called Dolores, who came over to Tia's house and signed the will. In both cases, Tia acknowledged to Seamus and Dolores that the signature on the will was hers.

   d. Tia bequeathed ¾ of her estate to Dolores and ¼ of her estate to her spouse, Seamus. Both Seamus and Dolores witnessed the will. How will the estate be distributed under: (1) the UPC; (2) the common law voiding approach; and (3) purging statutes?

The Self-Proved Will

To begin the probate process, the proponent must "prove" the will before it can be admitted into probate. Proving a will normally requires the testimony of the witnesses, either in court or by affidavit. Consequently, proponents had to track down the witnesses and have each witness execute an affidavit. Recognizing that finding witnesses to testify was becoming increasingly difficult in today's mobile society, states began to authorize "**self-proving affidavits**," executed at the time the testator executes the will. A self-proving affidavit is signed by the witnesses and a notary, and its purpose is to show that the will was properly signed by the testator and that the witnesses were present. Unless there is a self-proving affidavit, it may be necessary to find the witnesses after the testator's death so they can attest to the due execution of the will.

The self-proving affidavit may be executed as a separate document, signed and notarized immediately after the testator and witnesses sign the will. UPC § 2-504 below (Exhibit 3.2), combines the attestation (showing that the witnesses saw the testator sign the will) and the affidavit.

EXHIBIT 3.2   UPC § 2-504. Self-Proved Will

(a) A will may be simultaneously executed, attested, and made self-proved, by acknowledgment thereof by the testator and affidavits of the witnesses, each made before an officer authorized to administer oaths under the laws of the state in which execution occurs and evidenced by the officer's certificate, under official seal, in substantially the following form:

I, _____, the testator, sign my name to this instrument this ___ day of _____, and being first duly sworn, do hereby declare to the undersigned authority that I sign and execute this instrument as my will and that I sign it willingly (or willingly direct another to sign for me), that I execute it as my free and voluntary act for the purposes therein expressed, and that I am [eighteen] years of age or older, of sound mind, and under no constraint or undue influence.

_____

Testator

We, _____, _____, the witnesses, sign our names to this instrument, being first duly sworn, and do hereby declare to the undersigned authority that the testator signs and executes this instrument as [his] [her] will and that [he] [she] signs it willingly (or willingly directs another to sign for [him] [her]), and that each of us, in the presence and hearing of the testator, hereby signs this will as witness to the testator's signing, and that to the best of our knowledge the testator is eighteen years of age or older, of sound mind, and under no constraint or undue influence.

_____

Witness

_____

Witness

State of _____

County of _____

Subscribed, sworn to and acknowledged before me by _____, the testator, and subscribed and sworn to before me by _____, and _____, witness, this ___ day of _____. (Seal)

_____

(Signed)

_____

(Official capacity of officer)

For these purposes, the notary is considered a quasi-judicial figure. Once having attested under oath before the notary that they were witnesses "to the testator's signing, and that to the best of [their] knowledge the testator is eighteen years of age or older, of sound mind, and under no constraint or undue influence," the witnesses do not have to do so again in court, so the will "proves itself."

EXHIBIT 3.3   **UPC § 3-406. Formal Testacy Proceedings; Contested Cases**

In a contested case in which the proper execution of a will is at issue, the following rules apply:

(1) If the will is self-proved pursuant to Section 2-504, the will satisfies the requirements for execution without the testimony of any attesting witness, upon filing the will and the acknowledgment and affidavits annexed or attached to it, unless there is evidence of fraud or forgery affecting the acknowledgment or affidavit.

(2) If the will is notarized pursuant to Section 2-502(a)(3)(B), but not self-proved, there is a rebuttable presumption that the will satisfies the requirements for execution upon filing the will.

(3) If the will is witnessed pursuant to Section 2-502(a)(3)(A), but not notarized or self-proved, the testimony of at least one of the attesting witnesses is required to establish proper execution if the witness is within this state, competent, and able to testify. Proper execution may be established by other evidence, including an affidavit of an attesting witness. An attestation clause that is signed by the attesting witnesses raises a rebuttable presumption that the events recited in the clause occurred.

There are thus three options for witnesses:

1. Witnesses merely sign the witness lines on the will. A witness will need to establish proper execution.

2. Witnesses sign an attestation clause, which raises a rebuttable presumption of the truth of the recitals. A witness will still need to testify if that presumption is challenged.

3. Witnesses sign a self-proving affidavit. Under the UPC, this is a conclusive presumption that all the signature requirements imposed by its wills statute have been met and eliminates the need to have the witnesses testify upon the filing of the will to prove its authenticity (aside from the situations discussed above in UPC § 3-406 (1)).

Note that sometimes a witness "testifying" is done via deposition and signing an affidavit rather than an actual court appearance, but a witness may predecease the testator so that ends the window of time to get the information from them.

The Notarized Will

The signature of a notary is not required to validate a will. Nor, in most states, is notarization alone sufficient

---

Interview Checklist

When a client seeks to have a will drafted, the lawyer needs to ask some basic questions, even before getting to issues of how the client wants to dispose of the property. In addition to assessing whether the client has sufficient capacity to execute a will, it is important to find out information about the client's family. The client also needs to identify any and all real and personal property, including digital assets, however held, and to list any trusts of which the client might be a beneficiary. Trusts and estates lawyers have developed questionnaires that seek this information, and it is easy to find examples through the Internet.

to validate a will. By contrast, UPC § 2-502(a)(3)(B) allows acknowledgement by the testator before a notary public to substitute for having two witnesses. Thus, in jurisdictions that have adopted UPC § 2-502(a)(3)(B), only a notary's signature is necessary for due execution of the will.

A notarized will is not the same as a self-proved will. A notarized will allows the notary to substitute for the existence of any other witness and validate the will itself (but does not make it self-proving). This is a significant departure from the traditional attestation requirements. Indeed, most states have not adopted this approach. See Mark Glover, *Minimizing Probate-Error Risk*, 49 U. Mich. J.L. Reform 335, 404 n.199 (2016) (listing only two states that have adopted this approach).

4. Publication

Historically, the testator was required to "**publish**" the will by making it clear to the attesting witnesses that the document she was asking them to sign was her will, although there was no requirement that the witnesses be aware of the content of the will. Formal publication consists of the testator explicitly saying to the witnesses, "This is my will," but other steps will also be deemed to satisfy the publication requirement. For example, the testator could show the witnesses the first page of the will, or a lawyer could say to the witnesses, in front of the testator, that this was the testator's will. The testator's mere presence in the room to hear this statement by her lawyer would suffice as "publication." The testator need not say anything affirmative.

Most states no longer require publication. In those that do, strict compliance is necessary. In In re Estate of Griffith, 30 So. 3d 1190 (Miss. 2010), the witnesses who signed the will identified their signatures on the will. However, they testified that they were not informed of what they were signing and that the testator did not identify the document as a will when they signed it. The court ruled that witnesses must have some knowledge that the document they are witnessing is a will, once the will at issue failed.

Despite the fact that publication is no longer required in many states, estate planning attorneys routinely have the testator recite the particular "magic" words— "this is my last will"—to the witnesses during the signing ceremony as a matter of good form. This recitation is helpful if the witnesses are later called to testify in a will contest as to the testator's capacity and intent to make a will, and also reinforces the ritual function of the formalities.

C. LEGAL REQUIREMENTS FOR A HOLOGRAPHIC WILL

In addition to witnessed wills, about half of the states also recognize some form of handwritten will as valid without witnesses. If a will or a "material portion" of the will is written in the testator's handwriting and the testator has signed the document, then the will may be validated as a holographic will. Consider which of the functions of the formalities are served by recognizing a handwritten will.

States have taken one of three approaches to just what must be handwritten. First-generation statutes require that the testator handwrite the entire will, including all of its operative provisions. Second-generation statutes required that the signature and the *material provisions* (the dispositive provisions, such as "I leave my house to my spouse") be in the handwriting of the testator in order to be valid. Finally, third-generation statutes, of which UPC § 2-502(b), shown in Exhibit 3.4, is an example, only require that the signature and the *material portions* of the document be in the handwriting of the testator in order to be a valid holograph. The material portion consists of the words that identify the property and the devisee. Restatement (Third) of Prop.: Wills and Other Donative Transfers § 3.2, rptrs. note (1999). This means that the words of gifting, such as "I devise. . .", need not be in the testator's handwriting to validate a holographic will in states that have adopted the UPC's material portions language. Some states require that the date appear on the will in the testator's handwriting, but the UPC does not require a date.

As is true for a formally attested will, the testator must also have testamentary capacity and testamentary intent for the holographic will to be valid. These requirements help establish the dividing line between a will and other writings, such as to-do lists.

EXHIBIT 3.4   UPC § 2-502(b). Holographic Wills

> A will that does not comply with subsection (a) is valid as a holographic will, whether or not witnessed, if the signature and material portions of the document are in the testator's handwriting.

Case Preview

In re Estate of Melton

This case illustrates the types of documents that might be considered holographic wills. The testator executed a formal will leaving the bulk of his estate to his parents. He subsequently made a holographic codicil, leaving a small portion of his estate to a friend, Alberta (Susie) Kelleher. After his mother's death, the testator handwrote a letter to Kelleher, which appeared to give his entire estate to her, and he expressly disinherited his brother and daughter. Kelleher predeceased the testator, and, at the testator's death, he was survived by his daughter and two half-sisters. The Nevada Supreme Court considered whether the handwritten letter was a holographic will, and then, whether a will could include a disinheritance clause. The case illustrates the ease of writing a holographic will, and the relationship between formal instruments and holographic wills. *Melton* also shows that a will can include a disinheritance clause, at least in some states.

As you read the case, consider:

1. What is Nevada law with respect to the validity of holographic wills?
2. What are the arguments that the document at issue in this case is a will?
3. What are the arguments that the document as issue in this case is not a will?
4. Why does the court decide that a disinheritance clause can constitute a will?
5. Under which circumstances does Nevada permit escheat, even if the decedent leaves surviving relatives?

In re Estate of Melton
272 P.3d 668 (Nev. 2012)

PER CURIAM:

This is a dispute between the State and a testator's daughter and half sisters over his $3 million estate. At issue is the proper distribution of the estate of the testator, who, by way of a handwritten will, attempted to disinherit all of his heirs but was unsuccessful in otherwise affirmatively devising his estate. Under the common law, a disinheritance clause was unenforceable in these circumstances. In the proceedings below, after determining that the testator's handwritten will was a valid testamentary instrument that revoked his earlier will, the district court applied the prevailing common law rule, and thereby deemed the testator's disinheritance clause unenforceable. The court therefore distributed the testator's entire estate to his disinherited daughter, pursuant to the law of intestate succession, and rejected the claim that because he disinherited all of his heirs, his estate must escheat to the State to be used for educational purposes.

Crucially, however, the Nevada Legislature has enacted a statute providing, in pertinent part, that a will includes "a testamentary instrument that merely . . . excludes or limits the right of an individual or class to succeed to property of the decedent passing by intestate succession." NRS 132.370. We conclude that by its plain and unambiguous language, NRS 132.370 abolishes the common law rules that would otherwise render a testator's disinheritance clause unenforceable when the testator is unsuccessful at affirmatively devising his or her estate. Here, although the district court correctly determined that the testator executed a valid handwritten will that revoked his earlier will, the court erred in deeming the disinheritance clause contained therein unenforceable.

Finally, we consider whether an escheat[4] is triggered when, as here, a testator disinherits all of his or her heirs. We conclude that an escheat is triggered in such a circumstance because, when all heirs have been disinherited, the testator "leaves no surviving spouse or kindred" under NRS 134.120 pursuant to the plain and commonly understood meaning of that phrase. Accordingly, the district court erred in determining that the testator's estate does not escheat.

---

[4][The term "escheat" is discussed in the intestacy chapter; and means that the decedent's property is transferred to the state. —EDS.]

Because the disinheritance clause contained in the testator's will is enforceable, we reverse the judgment of the district court. As the testator disinherited all of his heirs, his estate must escheat.

FACTS AND PROCEDURAL HISTORY

The 1975 Will

In 1975, William Melton executed a formal will. The will was comprised of two forms, which Melton and three witnesses signed. Melton devised most of his estate to his parents and devised small portions to his brother and two of his cousins, Terry Melton and Jerry Melton. He also indicated that his daughter was to receive nothing. In 1979, Melton executed a handwritten codicil on the back of one of the 1975 will forms that provided his friend, Alberta (Susie) Kelleher, should receive a small portion of his estate (both will forms and the codicil are hereinafter referred to as "the 1975 will").

The 1995 Letter

In 1995, Melton sent a handwritten letter to Kelleher. It reads:

> 5-15-95
> 5:00 AM
>
> Dear Susie
> I am on the way home from Mom's funeral. Mom died from an auto accident so I thought I had better leave something in writing so that you Alberta Kelleher will receive my entire estate. I *do not* want my brother Larry J. Melton or Vicki Palm or any of my other relatives to have *one penny* of my estate. I plan on making a revocable trust at a later date. I think it is the 15 of [M]ay, no calendar, I think it['s] 5:00 AM could be 7:AM in the City of Clinton Oklahoma
> Lots of Love
> Bill
> /s/ William E. Melton
> AKA Bill Melton
> [Social Security number]

Discovery of the 1975 will and the 1995 Letter

Kelleher died in 2002, thus predeceasing Melton, who died in 2008. Shortly after Melton's death, respondent John Cahill, Clark County Public Administrator, initiated a special administration of Melton's estate. During this administration, it was discovered that Melton had a daughter, respondent Vicki Palm. The 1995 letter was also discovered. Initially, Palm and respondent Elizabeth Stessel were appointed co-administrators of Melton's estate. But the district court suspended their powers after determining that a disinterested party should administer the estate because a dispute over the proper distribution of the estate had arisen between Melton's half sisters, appellants Linda Melton Orte and Sherry L. Melton Briner, appellant State of Nevada, respondents Bryan Melton and Robert Melton, and Palm. The district court therefore appointed Cahill to be the special administrator of Melton's estate. Thereafter, Cahill obtained access to Melton's safe deposit box and discovered the 1975 will. The appraised net value of Melton's estate is approximately $3 million.

The Parties and Their Respective Positions

Melton's daughter

Palm, Melton's only known child, initially argued that the 1995 letter is not a valid will, and that Melton's estate therefore should pass to her under the statutes governing intestate succession. Following the discovery of the 1975 will, however, she argued that the 1995 letter is a valid will and that it revoked the 1975 will. Palm argued that although the 1995 letter is a valid will, it is ineffective because the only named devisee, Kelleher, predeceased Melton. Thus, she maintained that Melton's estate should pass through intestacy, under which she has priority pursuant to NRS 134.100.

Melton's half sisters

In the proceedings below, Melton's half sisters contended that the 1995 letter is not a valid will, and therefore, the 1975 will is still effective. In addition, they argued that if the 1995 letter is a valid will, it does not effectively revoke the 1975 will. . . . Although Melton's half sisters were not named as devisees in the 1975 will, they asserted that under Nevada's antilapse statute, NRS 133.200, they could take their parent's share of Melton's estate.

The State

The State asserted that the 1995 letter is a valid will that revoked the 1975 will. It argued that the Legislature's revisions to the Nevada Probate Code in 1999 provide for the enforcement of disinheritance clauses, even when an estate passes by intestate succession. Thus, the State contended that because Melton expressly disinherited all of his relatives in the 1995 letter, his estate must escheat.

The District Court Order

After extensive briefing by the parties, the district court [] distributed Melton's estate to Palm pursuant to the intestate succession scheme. Melton's half sisters and the State each appealed.

   . . .

Standard of Review

Whether a handwritten document is a valid will is a question of law reviewed de novo. . . .

The 1995 Letter Is a Valid Will

Melton's half sisters assert that the 1995 letter is simply a letter and nothing more. They emphasize that the 1995 letter was discovered amongst miscellaneous papers in Melton's home, in contrast to the 1975 will, which was found carefully placed in a safe. Thus, Melton's half sisters argue that if Melton intended for the 1995 letter to be his will, he would have treated it as carefully as the 1975 will. Therefore, they contend that because the 1995 letter is not a valid will, the 1975 will still controls the distribution of Melton's estate.

Nevada law gives holographic wills the same effect as formally executed wills. NRS 133.090(3). "A holographic will is a will in which the signature, date and material provisions are written by the hand of the testator, whether or not it is witnessed or notarized." NRS 133.090(1).

The 1995 letter was written, signed, and dated by Melton. It contains the material provisions of a will because it provided that Kelleher should receive Melton's estate and that his relatives should receive nothing. Although Melton did not store the 1995 letter in the same manner that he stored the 1975 will, its validity as a holographic will does not depend upon him doing so. Melton's testamentary intent is evinced by his references to his mother's funeral, her untimely death, and his statement that he "had better leave something in writing." Accordingly, we conclude that the 1995 letter is a valid holographic will.

The Disinheritance Clause Contained in the 1995 Letter Is Enforceable

. . .

The Proper Distribution of Melton's Estate Under the 1995 Letter Is an Escheat

We now turn to the proper distribution of Melton's estate under the terms of the 1995 letter. The State argues that because Melton disinherited all of his heirs in the 1995 letter, an escheat is triggered.

. . .

The law disfavors escheats . . . the Legislature [] determined that testamentary freedom has primacy over the policy disfavoring escheats. Thus, when, as here, a testator disinherits all of his or her heirs, the law's disfavor of escheats does not prevent an estate from passing to the State. Accordingly, we conclude that Melton's estate must escheat to the State.

CONCLUSION

Because the disinheritance clause contained in Melton's will is enforceable, we reverse the judgment of the district court. As Melton disinherited all of his heirs, his estate escheats.

Post-Case Follow-Up

Nevada has a second-generation holographic will statute. Here, the entire document was in the testator's handwriting, so it would have been valid regardless of the type of holographic statute in place. The court looked at various statements within the document to determine whether there was testamentary intent or whether this was just a letter, and found that Melton had written the letter with the requisite seriousness. The decision shows that holographic wills must satisfy both the "holographic" and "will" requirements; a letter can be both a letter and a will, or simply a letter.

In re Estate of Melton: Real Life Applications

1. Melton apparently wrote the letter to Kelleher on a drive back from his mother's funeral. Would the letter have qualified as a holographic will if it came into existence in the following way: Melton was driving, and he dictated his wishes to Nellie, a passenger in the car. Nellie wrote down Melton's wishes on a legal pad, and then, at the next rest stop, Melton signed and dated the statement.

2. Using the facts of the case, imagine that Melton was not returning from his mother's funeral but had just visited her. The document introduced for probate is as follows:

   Dear Susie
       I am on the way home from visiting Mom. I don't like her or any other family member. I *do not* want my brother Larry J. Melton or Vicki Palm or any of my other relatives to have *one penny* of my estate. I plan on making a revocable trust at a later date. I think it is the 15 of [M]ay, no calendar, I think it[']s 5:00 AM could be 7:AM in the City of Clinton Oklahoma
       Lots of Love
       Bill
       /s/ William E. Melton

   Should a judge consider this a valid will? Why or why not?

3. Olaf printed a draft will form from a Web site on the Internet, and filled in all the blanks with a pen in his own handwriting, as set out in Exhibit 3.5. How would different holographic will statutes deal with this document?

EXHIBIT 3.5 **Last Will and Testament**

I, *Olaf Biskup*, whose address is *716 Forsyth Dr., St. Louis, Missouri, 63101*, being of sound and disposing mind and memory, do make, publish, and declare the following to be my Last Will and Testament, hereby revoking all Wills made by me at any time heretofore.

1. I hereby appoint *Dmitry Romanov*, as executor of this, my Last Will and Testament. If *Dmitry Romanov* does not survive me, I hereby appoint *Marie Antoine* as executor of my estate. I direct that no executor serving hereunder shall be required to post bond.

2. I direct my Executor to pay all my funeral expenses, administration expenses of my estate, including inheritance and succession taxes, state or federal, which may be occasioned by the passage of or succession to any interest in my estate under the terms of this instrument, and all my just debts, excepting mortgage notes secured by mortgages upon real estate.

3. All the rest, residue, and remainder of my estate, both real and personal, of whatsoever kind or character, and wherever situated, I give, devise, and bequeath to spouse, *Tatiana*, to be *Tatiana's* absolutely and forever, so long as we are married at my death.

4. If my spouse does not survive me, all the rest, residue, and remainder of my estate, both real and personal, of whatsoever kind or character, and wherever situated, I give, devise, and bequeath to *Anastasia, Eugene, and Nicholas*, my *children* to be theirs absolutely and forever.

IN WITNESS WHEREOF, I have hereunto set my hand and seal at this *25th* day of *June*, 2017.

Olaf Biskup
Signature
716 Forsyth Dr., St. Louis, Missouri, 63101
Address

D. WHAT CONSTITUTES THE WILL?

When a lawyer drafts a will, it is generally clear what actually constitutes the will. The pages will be numbered sequentially, the lawyer may ask the testator to initial each page, and one clause in the will follows another. But wills are not always that tidy. The document sought to be probated might consist of a formal will, codicils, or other pieces of paper to which the will refers.

This section first addresses the doctrine of **integration**, which provides that the will consists of the papers that were present when the will was executed, and that the testator intended to be part of the will. We then consider different methods through which independent events and additional documents that were not present at the time of execution might actually constitute parts of the will.

1. Integration

The goal of integration is to ensure that the document treated as a testator's will consists of the pages that the testator intended to be part of the will at the time of execution. Pursuant to the doctrine of integration, pages that were present when the will was executed and that the testator intended to be part of the will are indeed treated as part of the will. Anything that was subsequently added and that was not executed with the required formalities is not part of the will, subject to the exceptions discussed below.

There are many actions a lawyer can take at the time the will is drafted and executed to lessen the likelihood that someone might contest the validity of the will on integration grounds. For example, the attorney can draft the will with the pages and lines numbered, use one font type and size, and carry sentences from one page to the next so it is clear they were drafted at the same time. At the end of the execution ceremony, the document can be stapled, with the testator and witnesses initialing and dating each page. At the end of the chapter, we have listed the steps in a sample will execution ceremony.

But not all wills are executed in this way. The testator may have written the will on a variety of scattered papers, so it may be difficult for the proponent to establish which papers were present at the time of the execution. If the papers are produced in the probate court and are unnumbered, and if it appears that pages or provisions were later added or deleted, a court is likely to conclude that the writing, or at least portions of it, do not constitute the testator's valid will.

For example, Terry prints a five-page will from the Internet, writes in specific bequests, and then clips together the pages. On April 20, 2017, while two neighbors are visiting, Terry shows them the will and asks them to sign as witnesses. Terry then unclips the pages, puts the last page on top, signs it, and has the neighbors sign as witnesses. After the neighbors leave, Terry piles the papers back together. At Terry's death, Terry's spouse finds a ten-page stack of loose pages labeled "will" in Terry's safe. The court will have to determine which pages were present when the will was signed, and then determine whether the other pages were executed with testamentary formalities.

2. Acts of Independent Significance

A will may rely on material that goes beyond the actual document. A provision may refer to an external circumstance that is significant regardless of its impact on the will. Terry's will might state: "I leave a bequest of $15,000 to the winner of the Nobel Prize for Peace in the year of my death, a bequest of $15,000 to the hospital in which I die, and the residue of my property to the person to whom I am married at my death." Under the **doctrine of acts [or events] of independent significance**, these terms are valid, even though the identity of the Nobel Peace Prize winner, the hospital in which the testator will die, and the testator's spouse cannot be determined as of the time of the will's execution. The doctrine allows the testator's property distribution in the will to be affected by: (1) any fact, act, or event existing or occurring outside the four corners of the will so long as (2) it is an otherwise objective event that occurs without regard to the testator 's plan of disposition. For example, these events might include purchasing a new car or house, the enactment of legislation, or the birth or adoption of a child. It also includes the actions of third parties, ranging from the identity of their children to the drafting of their wills. The testator's will may state: "I leave the residue of my property to the residuary beneficiaries identified in my deceased mother's will."

The doctrine is "universally accepted." Restatement (Third) of Prop.: Wills and Other Donative Transfers § 3.7 (1999). Consider what would happen in its absence: class gifts, residuary devises, and a number of other bequests might fail because of the traditional rule that all the provisions governing which property is to be distributed to whom must be clearly stated in the four corners of the will itself. Of course, some events are too closely linked to the testator's actions to qualify as events of independent significance and may invite a will contest. Such an event would include, for example, "the property in the drawer next to my bed." In such a situation, the testator might manipulate the types of property in order to affect property disposition.

The UPC approach is set forth in Exhibit 3.6.

EXHIBIT 3.6   **UPC § 2-512. Events of Independent Significance**

> A will may dispose of property by reference to acts and events that have significance apart from their effect upon the dispositions made by the will, whether they occur before or after the execution of the will or before or after the testator's death. The execution or revocation of another individual's will is such an event.

3. Including Additional Non-Attested Documents

Even a non-attested document might be incorporated into the will. Terry's April 20, 2017 will might refer to another document, stating: "I leave my jewelry to the persons identified on a typed list dated January 15, 2017 in my blue jewelry box." When Terry's spouse goes to the jewelry box, there may indeed be such a list. This list may serve to supplement the will, and, if so, the persons on the list will receive the jewelry through the **doctrine of incorporation by reference**. This doctrine permits a will to include a separate writing that has not been executed with the testamentary formalities.

There are three requirements for a writing to be incorporated by reference: (1) the document must be in existence at the time the will is executed; (2) the document must be sufficiently described so it can be readily identified; and (3) the language of the will must show the intent to incorporate the separate document. Restatement (Third) of Prop.: Wills and Other Donative Transfers § 3.6 (1999); see UPC § 2-510. If these elements are satisfied, then the document is deemed to be part of the will, as if the document were literally typed into the will or attached to it as an exhibit. Note that the document need not be in the room when the testator is signing the will. While most states accept the doctrine of incorporation by reference, not all do. The doctrine is limited to documents that are in existence as of the time of the will's execution, so the testator cannot make subsequent changes without observing the will execution formalities.

The UPC and some states recognize an exception to this doctrine, allowing for the inclusion of a subsequent, or subsequently modified, memo under certain limited conditions. Under this exception, an unattested memo is permitted to supplement the will, even if created or amended after the will's execution if: (1) the testator explicitly refers to the separate document in the will; and (2) the separate document disposes only of items of tangible property, other than money, that are described "with reasonable certainty." UPC § 2-513. The separate document does not need to list separately each item of personal property, so could refer to "all my tangible personal property in my apartment." Provisions in the will control if there is a direct conflict between the will and provisions in this separate memorandum. On the other hand, if the testator wants the memorandum to take priority over any contrary provisions in the will, then, as the comments to the UPC note, the testator can explicitly state in the will that the "written statement or list takes precedence over any contrary devise in the will."

In a state without a statute like UPC § 2-513, a memorandum executed after the date of the will cannot be given effect. The doctrine of incorporation by reference could apply to a memorandum executed before the will, but not to revisions made after the date of the will. The memorandum cannot be considered an act of independent significance because it has no significance other than the testator's wishes for the transfer of his property. In a state that has adopted UPC § 2-513, however, the memorandum will be read together with the will and implemented by the court. It illustrates the trend toward fewer formalities in the process of validly passing property at death.

4. Republication by Codicil

When a will is amended through a separate, attested document, that second document is termed a **codicil**. For the codicil to be effective as a change to the will, it must comply with the same testamentary formalities as the original will.

The codicil also serves as a **republication** of the earlier will. **Republication by codicil** is the process of treating the earlier will as though it had been executed as of the date of the codicil. Restatement (Third) of Prop.: Wills and Other Donative Transfers § 3.4 (1999).

Recall the example discussed under incorporation by reference. Terry's April 20, 2017 will stated that: "I leave my jewelry to the persons identified on a typed list dated January 15, 2017 in my blue jewelry box." The list was incorporated by reference because it existed on the date Terry executed his will. But what if Terry's spouse finds the list and discovers that Terry has typed at the bottom of the list: "I also give my grandfather's gold pocket watch to my nephew, Jason." Terry signed the addition and dated it May 1, 2017. The addition was not in existence when Terry executed his will, so the gift to Jason cannot be given effect under incorporation by reference. Now assume that Terry executes a codicil on July 1, 2017, changing the personal representative. The date of the will moves forward to July 1, 2017, and the change to the list is now incorporated by reference. Jason gets the watch, as his uncle intended. The Restatement notes that republication by codicil should be applied *only* if it effectuates the testator's intent. Id.

E. RELAXING THE FORMALITIES

Courts in many jurisdictions are strict about compliance with the requirements of the Wills Act, and, in those jurisdictions, an instrument may be denied probate based on a minimal defect in execution.

Consider the issues involved when an inadvertent defect occurs in executing documents. This can happen easily when lawyers are rushed or clients are nervous about taking such a serious and final act as signing their last will. For example, spouses might execute wills at the same time and may sign each other's wills by mistake. If a court requires strict compliance with the formalities, the wills fail the execution requirements.

The doctrines of substantial compliance and harmless error attempt to validate wills that have not satisfied all the formalities. The doctrine of substantial compliance asks whether a will has substantially complied with the formalities. If so, the court can treat the will as if it had been executed in compliance, and then consider any other issues that might affect validity. In contrast, the doctrine of harmless error excuses compliance with the formalities if the testator's intent is clear.

1. Substantial Compliance

Substantial compliance is a curative doctrine that fixes problems when the Will Act formalities have not been strictly followed. Some courts have moved toward acceptance of the substantial compliance doctrine since it was proposed in the latter quarter of the twentieth century. Professor John Langbein is the American scholar most closely associated with encouraging the adoption of the intent-furthering doctrine of substantial compliance. His 1975 article, *Substantial Compliance with the Wills Act*, 88 Harv. L. Rev. 489 (1975), proposed a test for substantial compliance that would treat a defectively executed document as compliant with Wills Act formalities, notwithstanding a formal defect. He suggested that there be a rebuttable presumption of invalidity where a will has been defectively executed, with rebuttal dependent on strong evidence of intent and satisfaction of the purposes of the Wills Act. Substantial compliance allows for a determination that documents could be construed as to satisfy the requisite formalities, so it does not undercut the purpose of the Wills Act.

Case Preview

Estate of Ray Merle Burton (continued)

In *Burton*, White, the proponent was unsuccessful in getting the documents, including the health care directive form, probated as a properly attested will. White then turned to a claim that the documents were in substantial compliance with the statute, so that the will should be deemed valid. In support of this claim, White pointed to cases where wills had been probated notwithstanding irregularities concerning the signatures of witnesses.

As you read the case, consider:

1. Under what circumstances might Washington courts use the doctrine of substantial compliance?
2. Why does the court decide not to apply substantial compliance to the facts here?
3. What policies would be undermined by applying substantial compliance to this case?

Estate of Ray Merle Burton
358 P.3d 1222 (Wash. Ct. App. 2015)

(continued)

B. SUBSTANTIAL COMPLIANCE

White argues that even if Burton did not strictly comply with the two witness requirement in RCW 11.12.020(1), we should conclude that he executed a valid will because he substantially complied with that requirement. We disagree.

1. Legal Principles

Under the substantial compliance doctrine a party complies with statutory requirements by "satisfaction of the substance essential to the purpose of the statute." Courts may invoke the doctrine where a party has "substantially complied with the requirements crucial to the underlying design intended by the legislature." Murphy v. Campbell Inv. Co., 486 P.2d 1080 (1971). However, some statutes are not susceptible to substantial compliance. See, e.g., Medina v. Pub. Utility Dist. No. 1 of Benton County, 53 P.3d 993 (2002) (failure to comply with a statutory time limitation cannot be considered substantial compliance with the statute).

2. Substantial Compliance and RCW 11.12.020(1)

Washington courts have not applied the substantial compliance doctrine to the requirements of RCW 11.12.020(1). The only Washington case that even mentions substantial compliance with regard to RCW 11.12.020(1) is *In Re Estate of Ricketts*, 773 P.2d 93 (1989). In that case, the two witnesses to a will codicil did not subscribe their names to the codicil, but instead signed an affidavit that was stapled to it. It was undisputed that this procedure did not strictly conform with the requirements of the version of RCW 11.12.020(1) then in effect. But the proponent of the will cited to a number of cases approving probate of wills despite irregularities in the placement of witnesses' signatures.

. . .

Ricketts could be interpreted as accepting the notion that a testator can comply with RCW 11.12.020(1) through substantial compliance. . . .

3. Substantial Compliance with Will Validity Provisions

Even assuming that substantial compliance is sufficient to satisfy the two witness requirement of RCW 11.12.020(1), Didricksen argues that there was no substantial compliance here. We agree.

The deficiency with Burton's testamentary documents was more than merely technical or procedural. The fundamental problem is that only Erickson saw and witnessed the first document and only Outson saw and witnessed the second, *different* document. If Erickson and Outson had seen an identical document but both signatures for some reason were not on that document, White's substantial compliance argument might be more compelling. But the fact that Erickson and Outson signed different documents precludes any finding of substantial compliance of the requirement in RCW 11.12.020(1) that two witnesses attest to the will.

Applying substantial compliance here also would work against the purposes of RCW 11.12.020. The statutory purposes underlying the formality requirements of the statute are "to ensure that the testator has a definite and complete intention to dispose of his or her property and to prevent, as far as possible, fraud, perjury, mistake and the chance of one instrument being substituted for another." Here, the risk of mistake—if not fraud—would be high if we allowed probate of a testamentary document signed by only one witness when the second "witness" never saw that document.

We hold that under the facts of this case, Burton's healthcare directive document did not substantially comply with RCW 11.12.020(1).

Post-Case Follow-Up

As the court explained, under the "substantial compliance doctrine" a party complies with statutory requirements by satisfaction of the substance essential to the purpose of the statute. Courts may invoke the substantial compliance doctrine where a party has substantially complied with the requirements crucial to the underlying design intended by the legislature. Although the court was willing to apply the substantial compliance doctrine, it decided that the purposes of the formalities required by the will statute would be undermined if the document(s) were allowed to be probated. The fact that two witnesses to wills signed two different testamentary documents precluded any finding of substantial compliance with the statutory two-witness requirement for a valid will.

Estate of Ray Merle Burton: Real Life Applications

1. Under the facts of the case, if one witness signed the original will, and a second signed a copy of that original, would the court have found substantial compliance?

2. Assume that the court had both documents, the first signed by Erickson and the second on the health care directive form. Would the court have found substantial compliance?

3. Wally signed his will, leaving all of his property to his daughter, Ella. The witnesses to the will did not sign at the end of the will, but instead signed the self-proving affidavit, a separate document that was attached at the end of the will. Ella has offered the will for probate, but Wally's two daughters from his second marriage, Drucilla and Anastasia, have challenged the will as not showing the requisite formalities. How will a court rule?

2. Harmless Error

The doctrine of substantial compliance allows a court to excuse an otherwise defective execution based on clear and convincing evidence that the defective execution nonetheless fulfills the goals of the formalities. Pursuant to substantial compliance, a court ultimately deems the will to have complied with the formalities, notwithstanding the defect.

As an alternative designed to effectuate the decedent's intent, the UPC provides a "harmless error" rule (Exhibit 3.7) that excuses compliance with the formalities if the will proponent can establish testamentary intent by clear and convincing evidence.

EXHIBIT 3.7 **UPC § 2-503. Harmless Error**

Although a document or writing added upon a document was not executed in compliance with Section 2-502, the document or writing is treated as if it had been executed in compliance with that section if the proponent of the document or writing establishes by clear and convincing evidence that the decedent intended the document or writing to constitute (1) the decedent's will, (2) a partial or complete revocation of the will, (3) an addition to or an alteration of the will, or (4) a partial or complete revival of his [or her] formerly revoked will or of a formerly revoked portion of the will.

This provision gives courts statutory authority to excuse a formality if a "defect in execution was harmless in relation to the purpose of the statutory formalities." Restatement (Third) of Prop.: Wills and Other Donative Transfers § 3.3, cmt. b (1999). Harmless error does not excuse all defects in will execution. First, the proponent of the defective will must establish by clear and convincing evidence that the decedent intended the document to be his will. Second, as the UPC explains, "The larger the departure from Section 2-502 formality, the harder it will be to satisfy the court that the instrument reflects the testator's intent." UPC § 2-503 cmt.

The goal of the harmless error doctrine is to balance respect for the testator's intent with determining just what the testator's intent actually was and ensuring that the document reflects the testator's actual intent. Some states have adopted the harmless error rule. See Haw. Rev. Stat. Ann. § 560:2-503 (2017); David Horton, *Tomorrow's Inheritance: The Frontiers of Estate Planning Formalism*, 58 B.C. L. Rev. 539, 560 (2017) (listing ten states). Many states, however, do not apply the harmless error doctrine.

Case Preview

In re Macool

The following case illustrates how a court might apply the harmless error rule to an instrument that appears not to be in compliance with traditional will formalities. In *Macool*, the court was faced with a document that the testator neither saw nor approved. The document was nonetheless proffered for probate on the basis that the testator's handwritten notes and the drafting attorney's testimony established the testator's intent that the draft drawn up by the attorney be her "last and binding will." The testator's "untimely" demise prevented her from reviewing the draft, but the court considered whether her intent was established by "clear and convincing evidence" so the will could be probated under New Jersey's harmless error doctrine.

As you read the case, consider:

1. What problems does the court identify with considering the document as a will?
2. What testimony do the document proponents offer to show that this was Ms. Macool's will?
3. How does the doctrine of harmless error apply to the alleged will?
4. Would substantial compliance have been a more useful doctrine?
5. Should the court have applied the harmless error doctrine?

In re Macool
3 A.3d 1258 (N.J. Sup. Ct. App. Div. 2010)

FUENTES, J.A.D.

. . . The facts underlying this case are so uniquely challenging that they have the feel of an academic exercise, designed by a law professor to test the limits of a student's understanding of probate law. But this case is not, of course, a mere didactic exercise.

We are confronted here with the real life story of Louise R. Macool, a woman who sadly died before she had the opportunity to definitively indicate whether the document drafted by her attorney accurately reflected her wishes as to the disposition of her estate. In this context, our task is to determine whether the Chancery Division correctly construed and applied the provisions of *N.J.S.A.* 3B:3-3.[1]

After examining the record developed before the trial court, we affirm the court's judgment declining to admit into probate a will that was not reviewed by decedent before her demise. We reject, however, the part of the court's ruling that construes *N.J.S.A.* 3B:3-3 as requiring that the writing offered as a will under the statute bear in some form the signature of the testator as a prerequisite to its admission to probate. . . .

As correctly found by the trial court, the salient facts of this case are undisputed. Louise and Elmer Macool were married for forty years; this was, for both, their second marriage. Although they did not have biological children together, Louise raised Elmer's seven children from his prior marriage as if they were her own. These children are defendants Muriel Carolfi[3] and Michael Macool, as well as James Macool, William Macool, Helen Wilson, Isabel Macool, and Mary Ann McCart. In addition to her seven step-children, Louise also had a very close relationship with her niece, plaintiff Mary Rescigno, whose mother died in childbirth.

Attorney Kenneth Calloway drafted wills for both Elmer and Louise Macool. On September 13, 1995, Louise executed a will naming her husband Elmer as the sole beneficiary of her entire estate, and also naming her seven step-children, step-granddaughter Theresa Stefanowicz, and step-great-grandson Alexander Stefanowicz as contingent beneficiaries.[5] Elmer Macool was named as executor of her estate, and her stepsons James and Michael Macool were named as contingent co-executors.

On May 23, 2007, Louise executed a codicil to her will naming her stepchildren Muriel Carolfi and Michael Macool as contingent co-executors. Calloway drafted and witnessed both the September 13, 1995 will and the May 23, 2007 codicil.

Elmer Macool died on April 26, 2008. Less than a month later, on May 21, 2008, Louise went to Calloway's law office with the intent of changing her will. Toward that end, she gave Calloway a handwritten note that read as follows:

> *get the same as the family* <u>*Macool gets*</u>
>   *Niece*
>   *Mary Rescigno [indicating address] If any thing happen[s] to Mary Rescigno [,] her share goes to he[r] daughter Angela Rescigno. If anything happen[s] to her it goes to her 2 children. 1. Nikos Stylon 2. Jade Stylon*

Niece + Godchild LeNora Distasio [indicating address] if anything happe[ns] to [her] it goes back in the pot
    I [would] like to have the house to be left in the family Macool.
    I [would] like to have.

1. *Mike Macool [indicating address]*
2. *Merle Caroffi [indicating address]*
3. *Bill Macool [indicating address]*

Jake

According to Calloway, after discussing the matter with Louise and using her handwritten notes as a guide, he "dictated the entire will while she was there." Either later that afternoon or the next morning, Calloway's secretary typed a draft version of Louise's will, with the word "Rough" handwritten on the top left corner of the document. When asked to explain what the word "rough" meant in this context, Calloway indicated:

> I mean [] it was the rough will. It had not been reviewed by me to make changes if I deemed any changes had to be made from what I believed I dictated. And I had reviewed it but I never got a chance to even tell my secretary to do it up and let's move.

The draft will names as residuary beneficiaries[6] Louise's nieces Mary Rescigno and Lenora Distasio, as well as all of her step-children, Theresa Stefanowicz, and Alexander Stefanowicz. Although the draft will substantially reflects Louise's handwritten notes, it does not provide a statement naming Angela Rescigno's two children as contingent beneficiaries of Rescigno's share of the estate. In addition, the draft makes only an oblique reference to the provision in the handwritten document to keep the house "in the family Macool," stating that "Michael Macool, Merle Caroffi, and William Macool be responsible to maintain . . . and to *try* to keep the home in the family *as long as possible.*" (Emphasis added.)

Louise left Calloway's office with the intention of having lunch nearby. Calloway expected her to make an appointment to review the draft will sometime after he had reviewed it. Sadly, Louise died approximately one hour after her meeting with Calloway. She thus never had the opportunity to see the draft will.

II

This matter came before the trial court as an action filed by plaintiff Mary Rescigno seeking to invalidate decedent's 1995 will and 2007 codicil, admit into probate the 2008 draft will that decedent neither read nor signed before her death, and for an award of counsel fees pursuant to Rule 4:42-9(a)(3).

    . . .

---

[5][A contingent beneficiary is one who is eligible to take a distribution only if the first-named beneficiaries have predeceased. —Eds.]

Plaintiff's principal argument in support of her position is grounded on *N.J.S.A.* 3B:3–3, which provides as follows:

Although a document or writing added upon a document was not executed in compliance with *N.J.S.A.* 3B:3-2, the document or writing is treated as if it had been executed in compliance with *N.J.S.A.* 3B:3-2 if the proponent of the document or writing establishes by clear and convincing evidence that the decedent intended the document or writing to constitute: (1) the decedent's will; (2) a partial or complete revocation of the will; (3) an addition to or an alteration of the will; or (4) a partial or complete revival of his formerly revoked will or of a formerly revoked portion of the will.

. . .

The trial court found that plaintiff failed to establish, by clear and convincing evidence, that the draft will prepared by Calloway met the requirements for admissibility to probate under *N.J.S.A.* 3B:3-3. In so doing, the court focused on the statutory language requiring "the proponent of the document or writing [to establish] by clear and convincing evidence that the decedent intended *the document or writing* to constitute [her will]." *Ibid.* (emphasis added).

Before we address the court's ruling with respect to the draft will, we must first distinguish decedent's handwritten notes from what was once commonly referred to as a "holographic will." *See In re Will of Smith*, 108 *N.J.* 257, 262, 528 *A.*2d 918 (1987). Under *N.J.S.A.* 3B:3-2a, a will must meet three specific requirements: it must be "(1) in writing; (2) signed by the testator or in the testator's name by some other individual in the testator's conscious presence and at the testator's direction; and (3) signed by at least two individuals, each of whom signed within a reasonable time after each witnessed either the signing of the will as described in paragraph (2) or the testator's acknowledgment of that signature or acknowledgment of the will."

Under the current provisions in *N.J.S.A.* 3B:3-2b, "[a] will that does not comply with [the requirements of *N.J.S.A.* 3B:3-2a] is valid as a writing intended as a will, whether or not witnessed, if the signature and material portions of the document are in the testator's handwriting." Stated differently, a so-called holographic will must have all material testamentary provisions in the handwriting of the testator and must also be signed by the testator. Here, although decedent's handwritten notes arguably meet the first requirement, they fail to meet the second one because decedent did not sign her notes.

We next address plaintiff's argument that under *N.J.S.A.* 3B:3-3, the draft will should be admitted because there is clear and convincing evidence that decedent intended this document to constitute her will, or alternatively, a partial revocation of her prior will. In addressing this argument, we distinguish between evidence showing decedent's general disposition to alter her testamentary plans and evidence establishing, by clear and convincing evidence, that decedent intended the draft will prepared by Calloway to constitute her binding and final will.

---

[6][A residuary beneficiary is the recipient of any money and assets remaining in the estate once estate expenses, taxes, and all other bequests have been satisfied. —EDS.]

In this respect, we agree with the trial court that the record clearly and convincingly shows that decedent intended to alter her testamentary plan to include Rescigno and Distasio when she met with Calloway in 2008. Decedent's handwritten notes, Calloway's testimony, and the draft will itself all support this finding. The court found, however, that plaintiff failed to establish, by clear and convincing evidence, that decedent intended the document denoted by Calloway as a "rough" draft to be her last and binding will. We agree.

Decedent's untimely demise prevented her from reading the draft will prepared by her attorney. She never had the opportunity to confer with counsel after reviewing the document to clear up any ambiguity, modify any provision, or express her final assent to this "rough" draft. Indeed, Calloway testified that although decedent's handwritten notes named Angela Rescigno's two children as contingent beneficiaries, he intentionally did not include them in the draft will because it was his practice to exclude "a third generation unless she told me that the first two were very old."

The trial court treated this omission as a minor discrepancy. We view it as evidence that this document was a work in progress, subject to reasonable revisions and fine tuning. Calloway's customary procedure or "practice" notwithstanding, decedent's notes clearly indicate that she wanted these two children specifically named as contingent beneficiaries. We have no way of knowing whether decedent would have approved of Calloway's approach or insisted that her wishes be strictly followed.

. . .

We hold that for a writing to be admitted into probate as a will under *N.J.S.A.* 3B:3–3, the proponent of the writing intended to constitute such a will must prove, by clear and convincing evidence, that: (1) the decedent actually reviewed the document in question; and (2) thereafter gave his or her final assent to it. Absent either one of these two elements, a trier of fact can only speculate as to whether the proposed writing accurately reflects the decedent's final testamentary wishes.

Although this holding effectively disposes of plaintiff's case, in the interest of completeness we will address the trial court's ruling requiring that a writing offered under *N.J.S.A.* 3B:3-3 be signed by the testator. Here again we are confronted with a dearth of case law authority. . . .

. . . [W]e are satisfied that a writing offered under *N.J.S.A.* 3B:3-3 need not be signed by the testator in order to be admitted to probate. . . .

A variation of the facts presented here offers a compelling case for construing *N.J.S.A.* 3B:3-3 as not requiring the testator's signature. Had decedent been able to read the draft will prepared by Calloway and thereafter express her assent to its content in the presence of witnesses or by any other reasonably reliable means, the trial court's misgivings concerning the absence of her signature would have been seen as needlessly formalistic and against the remedial purpose that animates *N.J.S.A.* 3B:3-3.

V

By way of summary, we affirm the trial court's ruling denying plaintiff's application to probate a draft will that was never read by decedent Louise Macool. To be admitted into probate under *N.J.S.A.* 3B:3-3, the proponent of a writing intended to constitute the testator's will must prove, by clear and convincing evidence, that: (1) the decedent actually reviewed the document in question; and (2) thereafter expressed his or her final assent to it.

Post-Case Follow-Up

The court carefully considered whether a document that was in draft and that the testator had not signed could be admitted to probate. The court first asked whether there was clear and convincing evidence that the document was the testator's will, but found inadequate evidence. On the other hand, the court held that had there been such evidence, the absence of a signature would not have prevented probate. This holding illustrates the focus of the harmless error rule not on the lack of formalities, but on the testator's intent. Although only a small number of American states have adopted the harmless error rule, it is enshrined in the UPC, so more states may adopt it in the future. Several foreign jurisdictions, including several provinces in Australia, have adopted similar rules. See Stephanie Lester, *Admitting Defective Wills to Probate, Twenty Years Later: New Evidence for the Adoption of the Harmless Error Rule*, 42 Real Prop. Prob. & Tr. J. 577 (2007).

In re Macool: Real Life Applications

1. What if the lawyer had given Louise Macool the draft, and she took it with her, signed it, and left it on the table in the restaurant?

2. Using the same facts as in Problem 1, what result if the chef in the restaurant where she was eating lunch was talking to her, and she took the draft, told the chef it was her will, showed him where she had signed it, asked him to sign it as a witness—which he did—and she then died?

3. What result if Macool had signed the handwritten note when she gave it to Callaway? Would it have mattered if the draft will differed from the signed handwritten note?

4. Consider the following actual case. The decedent created a document through an online legal drafting service. The proponent alleged that in preparing the will, the decedent (who worked in a laboratory at Yale's School of Medicine) logged into her computer, created an account with the legal drafting service, and completed a lengthy process to determine with specificity her exact wishes, including providing all her pertinent information and her social Security number. Should the court validate the document under the harmless error rule?

F. CHOICE OF LAW

A testator might execute a will in one state and then move to another. Is the will still valid even if the second state has s different execution requirements? Yes, most states recognize the validity of wills executed in other jurisdictions as long as the will was executed in conformity with the laws of the state or the country where it was initially executed. Restatement (Third) of Prop.: Wills and Other Donative Transfers § 3.1 (1999). Exhibit 3.8 shows the UPC's statement of this general rule:

EXHIBIT 3.8   UPC § 2-506. Choice of Law as to Execution

> A written will is valid if executed in compliance with Section 2-502 or 2-503 or if its execution complies with the law at the time of execution of the place where the will is executed, or of the law of the place where at the time of execution or at the time of death the testator is domiciled, has a place of abode, or is a national.

The comments to this section note that it applies regardless of whether the will is executed in another state or another country.

A testator might also choose to include a provision specifying which state's law will control various substantive provisions. While the law of the state where the testator was domiciled at death controls the disposition of personal property, the law of the state where real property is located controls disposition of real property. Most states will allow these choice-of-law provisions in the will to control. Thus, in order to define the group of potential heirs as broadly as possible to prevent escheat, a will might provide: "My heirs shall be determined according to Massachusetts law."

G. COMMON PROVISIONS IN WILLS

Lawyer-drafted wills typically have standard provisions. The first clause in the will is commonly called the **exordium** or the preamble. This section identifies the testator and also acknowledges that the testator intends the document to be the testator's will. The exordium also typically states that by making this will, the testator is revoking all prior wills; sometimes the testator explicitly lists the prior wills that are revoked.

Foreign Wills

The Uniform International Wills Act (UIWA) has been enacted either on its own or as Part 10 of Article 2 of the UPC in approximately 15 states. It implements the 1972 UNIDROIT "Convention Providing a Uniform Law on the Form of an International Will." The Convention's purpose is to establish safe harbor guidelines for a universal form of will that will be accepted internationally, even if the will does not comply with a particular country's local requirements. As noted, jurisdictions in the United States will typically recognize, probate, and enforce foreign wills, so long as they were executed in accordance with the law of the jurisdiction where they were executed (there are some exceptions); the UIWA is designed to give certainty to wills executed in compliance with the legislation.

Such a clause might provide:

I, BeLinda D. Testator, of 2000 Main Street, Anytown, State, make this as my LAST WILL, and hereby revoke all prior wills and codicils.

Next, the testator identifies family members. The easiest way to identify the children is to list all the children by name, and then to include language that acknowledges any additional children who are born to or adopted by the testator after the date of signing the will. Identifying the children in this manner avoids any mistakes that unintentionally leave a child out of the will.

My spouse's name is Franklin D. Spouse. All references in this will to my "spouse" are to said named spouse. I have two children, Ella and Fitzgerald. All references in my will to my "child" or "children" are to these named children and all also include any children born to or adopted by me after the date of this will.

The will also includes a list of **devises,** or dispositive provisions, the actual gifts made by the will. While the term "devise" was historically used only for dispositions of real property, "legacy" was used for gifts of money, and "bequest" referred to dispositions of anything else. Today, these words are generally used interchangeably.

Devises can take the form of an outright gift or can be made to an already existing trust or trust created by the will, and the beneficiaries can be individuals, classes of individuals ("my grandchildren"), or entities. Devises can be of money, personal property, real property, virtual currency, etc.; nearly everything in which a testator has an ownership interest at death can be transferred. Devises take one of four forms: *specific, demonstrative, general,* and *residuary.* A **specific devise** refers to a particular item, such as "my car" or "the jewelry I inherited from my grandmother," or "the beach house" or "the stocks in my account at ABC Brokerage." Here's an example:

I hereby give my books to Local Library.

A **demonstrative devise** is a gift from a specific source. For example, a testator could direct that her caretaker receive "$50,000 from my bank account at DEF Bank." If there is only $40,000 remaining in the account, then that will go to the caretaker, and remaining amount will be taken from other assets.

A **general devise** is a gift of property payable from any asset in the testator's estate. For example, a testator might direct: *I hereby give $10,000 to each of my children.*

The executor can take the $10,000 from any estate asset to satisfy the devise.

The final type of gift is a **residuary devise.** Residuary devises distribute the **residue:** all assets remaining after the other devises and estate debts have been satisfied. Although this clause does give the "leftovers," it is often the bulk of the value of the estate, in part because it may include financial assets that are not specifically granted to anyone. A typical provision might read:

I leave the residue of my estate to my spouse.

A will also includes various administrative provisions. One is a provision that nominates a person to serve as the personal representative who will be responsible for administering the estate, and also typically names a contingent personal representative, in case the first one cannot serve or declines to serve. Note that the will "nominates" the executor, because the court appoints the executor. The following is sample language for the nomination of an executor and a substitute executor:

I nominate my spouse as the executor of my estate and of this will. If my spouse should fail to qualify or otherwise cease to act as executor, then I nominate my child, Ella, as executor.

The will typically contains a paragraph that addresses the payment of all estate debts, such as final medical expenses, funeral expenses, attorney's fees, and any expenses incurred in the administration of the estate, such as the personal representative's phone calls to beneficiaries, postage, probate costs, mileage for going to secure the decedent's assets, or any other expense incurred in the administration of the estate.

Sample language for the payment of debts is as follows:

I direct my executor to pay my funeral expenses, my medical expenses, the costs of administration of my estate, and all of my enforceable debts, other than those secured by property specifically devised under this will, or secured by property passing outside of this will, as my executor, with sole discretion, determines shall be paid.

And, as mentioned in the previous section, the testator might include a provision specifying which state's laws control substantive provisions.

Finally, the testator and witnesses must sign the will.

The testator typically signs a clause like the following, which declares the instrument to be a will and states the date of will execution.

IN WITNESS WHEREOF, I sign my name this _____ day of _____, 201_____ in _____[City], [State].

The witnesses might sign something like the following:

SIGNED, after the Testator declared this to be his Last Will, in the presence of each of us, we, at his request, in his presence, and in the presence of each other, have signed our names as attesting witnesses.

_____residing

at_____

Witness _____residing

at_____

Witness

A self-proving affidavit, discussed above, might also appear after the witnesses' attestation.

Remember that, as a lawyer drafts a will, there are a number of interesting and important ethical concerns that frame that work. These include whether a lawyer: (1) can represent members of the same family, or a testator and beneficiary, in drafting wills; (2) can name herself a fiduciary in the will; (3) can name herself as a beneficiary in a client's will; and (4) has a duty to contact a client about changes in the law that affect her estate plan if the attorney keeps the will she drafted. These ethical issues are addressed in Chapter 15, Professional Responsibility, and this section focuses on the provisions themselves.

Signing the Will

After an attorney has interviewed the client and has drafted the will, often after additional consultation and perhaps a few exchanges of drafts (assuming this is an attorney-drafted will), the next step is for the client to execute the will (and any other instruments included in the estate plan, such as trusts). Many attorneys have developed formulaic and ritualistic will-signing ceremonies to make sure that everything goes smoothly and no step is forgotten. Following a formal script can also help protect the will from subsequent challenges based on fraud, undue influence, or lack of mental capacity. Of course, the clients are often nervous. Signing a will is a serious and important step that involves acknowledging one's own mortality. Clients often joke and get easily distracted when visiting the lawyer's office for the actual signing ceremony.

We have listed below some of the steps that might be involved in actual execution of the will. Some of the steps are legally required, while others are included to protect against subsequent challenge. Following these steps should also ensure that other jurisdictions will respect the will.

WILL EXECUTION CEREMONY

1. Make sure all pages of the actual and current will are present, and proofread the will once more to ensure it is free from grammatical mistakes and reflects the testator's intentions.

2. The ceremony should take place in an office that has space for the witnesses and the testator. Once everyone has arrived and the ceremony starts, it should not be disturbed. The lawyer should introduce everyone, and make sure the witnesses and testator can see and hear one another.

3. The lawyer should explain how the ceremony will proceed and the significance and general purpose of the ceremony.

4. The attorney should review the will with the client; this is often done in private, before the witnesses arrive. The attorney can also establish the testator's testamentary intent and mental capacity by making sure the testator understands the transaction, comprehends generally the nature and extent of property to be disposed of, remembers who are the natural objects of his or her bounty and understands the nature and effect of the desired disposition.

5. With a pen (often a blue one!), the testator should initial each page of the will, either in the margin or at the bottom. This has two functions: it shows that the testator read each page, and it shows the pages that were present at the ceremony, thereby preventing tampering with the will. This step is not legally required, and some lawyers omit this step, especially if the will is long. If the will is 50 pages, the testator might miss a page, leading to questions later, and the testator might get irritated at having to initial every page of a long document.

6. The testator signs, with a full signature, and dates the will on the last page. The witnesses should watch the testator sign.

7. Ask the witnesses to read the attestation clause and then sign the will, again with a blue pen.

8. If there is a self-proving affidavit, then that too is completed with the requisite formality. The witnesses sign the affidavit, and the notary signs the affidavit and affixes the notarial seal.

9. Following the ceremony, the lawyer should make copies for the client. The lawyer should instruct the client on the appropriate safeguarding of the original will, such as keeping the will in a safe deposit box. The lawyer should keep a copy of the will and the copy can indicate that the testator has the original, assuming that the lawyer does not keep the original.

Many of these steps are adapted from Gerry W. Beyer, *The Will Execution Ceremony* (2011), http://www.professorbeyer.com/Archive/new_site/Articles/Will_Ceremony.html (last visited June 28, 2017).

Chapter Summary

- The law of wills requires certain formalities at the time of execution in order for a will to be valid.
- States generally impose three requirements for the validity of a formal will. The instrument must be: (1) in writing, (2) signed by the testator, and (3) signed by the requisite number of witnesses.
- About half the states permit "holographic" wills, which do not need to be witnessed, but must be in the testator's handwriting.
- The will constitutes the documents present at execution, along with documents subsequently executed with the requisite formalities. Through additional doctrines, the will may refer to events of independent significance and, in limited situations, include additional unattested documents.
- Because of the harshness of the requirements of complying with Wills Act formalities, states have begun to adopt curative doctrines. The doctrine of "substantial compliance" allows a court to examine a document to determine whether it expresses testamentary intent and whether the formalities observed are sufficient to serve the underlying functions of testamentary formalities (i.e., cautionary, evidentiary, protective, and channeling).
- The "harmless error" rule excuses noncompliance with the Wills Act requirements of signature and/or attestation where there is clear and convincing evidence of the decedent's intent to treat the document as her will. Under the harmless error rule, a court can dispense with the testamentary formalities entirely (not true of substantial compliance).

Applying the Concepts

For Problems 1-3, consider whether the following instruments strictly comply with the requirements of UPC § 2–502(a):

1. Tommie recently died. The only evidence of how Tommie wanted property to be disposed of is the following, which was found, written in black marker, on Tommie's blue jeans: "I want all of my property to go to my partner, Jaya." Tommie's handwritten signature follows the statement. Jaya has offered the blue jeans for probate, but Tommie's only child, Walinga, claims that Tommie died intestate. What advice do you give Jaya?

2. Using the facts of Problem 1, what if both Jaya and Walinga had been present when Tommie uttered the same words and she told them to write down what she had said? What if Tommie drew the words in the air with her finger?

3. Carson was bleeding profusely, and no help was in sight. Carson had a smart-phone.

    a. Carson recorded a video in which Carson recited: This is my last will and testament, and I want all of my property to be given to the Glen Echo Citizens Association.

    b. Carson used the smartphone to send an email to Lily Lawyer, describing the disposition of Carson's estate, with Carson's full name at the end.

4. Ralph signed a will drafted by his lawyer; two administrative assistants from the lawyer's office, Claudia and Elizabeth, witnessed Ralph's will. Ralph's will included an affidavit similar to the one included in UPC § 2-504. The affidavit was executed and notarized. Ralph's cousin contests the will and alleges that Ralph was not of a sound mind at the time of the signing of the will and that the witnesses were not in Ralph's conscious presence when he signed the will. You are the attorney for the proponents of the will. What objection(s) would you make to Claudia and Elizabeth being called as witnesses to testify about the execution formalities? As to what other areas of inquiry might Claudia and Elizabeth have to testify regardless of the self-proved affidavit?

5. Tia's will devised "my grandmother's diamond engagement ring to my child, Ria." After Tia's death, Tia's personal representative looked through Tia's papers and found both the will and an undated, typed piece of paper signed by Tia that says: "Grandmother's engagement ring to stepchild, Mia."

    a. Who will receive the ring, Ria or Mia? Why?

    b. Assume that Tia's will also contained a clause providing: "I might leave a written statement or list disposing of items of tangible personal property. If I do, then my written statement or list is to be given effect to the extent authorized by law and is to take precedence over any contrary devise or devises of the same item or items of property in this will." Who will receive the ring? Why?

7. Ian's will, which was executed on March 30, 2017, devised his bank account at Local Bank to "the person identified in a letter found in my safe at Local Bank." At Ian's death, when the safe deposit box was opened, it contained an unsigned letter stating that the bank account at Local Bank was to go to his friend, Pat.

   a. Will Pat receive the bank account identified in the letter if the letter is dated March 15, 2017?
   b. Does your answer change if the letter is dated April 1, 2017?
   c. What if the letter is dated April 1, 2017, and it is signed?

Trusts and Estates in Practice

1. What are the requirements for a valid will in your jurisdiction? How many witnesses? Can a notarized will be valid without any other witnesses? Does your jurisdiction accept the doctrine of substantial compliance or harmless error? Does your jurisdiction accept holographic wills?

2. You have drafted wills for Han and for Lia, and they are coming to your office later today to sign the wills. Make a list of the actions you need to take in advance of the meeting to prepare for the ceremony with Han and Lia. Who will you choose as witnesses? Why? What qualities would influence you as the drafting attorney in selecting the best witnesses? Would you be more or less inclined to choose a relative instead of a stranger, a young person instead of an old person, or a home health care aide instead of a neighbor?

3. Han and Lia have just arrived in your office, and they are ready to sign their wills. Role play the will execution ceremony itself, explaining to Han, Lia, and anyone else present what the procedure will involve.

4. Plan out what you will say to, or do with, Han and Lia and any other participants at the conclusion of the ceremony (in this regard, a checklist might be helpful for the clients).

5. Han and Lia want to know if you will keep the will for them. What advice will you give Han and Lia about where the will should be kept?

6. Consider the risks involved in allowing electronic documents to be deemed valid wills. If you were to draft a Model Electronic Wills Act, how would you protect against those risks? What type of record would qualify as an "electronic will"?

7. Does your jurisdiction recognize the memorandum at death doctrine? What are the limitations, if any?

4

Amendment and Revocation of Wills

A testator does not need to commit to a will forever. A will may be **amended** (altered), **revoked** (voluntarily retracted by the testator), or changed in a number of different ways. First, a testator may revoke an entire will by physical act, if the testator does so with the intent to revoke. In some jurisdictions, partial revocation by physical act is possible, leaving the rest of the will standing.

Second, as long as a testator remains competent, the testator can choose to revoke or amend a will by executing a document with the same formalities as required for a will. That is, a testator may change a will by written amendment (called a **codicil**) or may instead execute a new will that effectively revokes the old will. Even if the later document does not explicitly revoke part or all of the prior will, the new will or codicil is effective to revoke any provisions in the prior will that are inconsistent with the new document.

Third, provisions in a will may also be automatically revoked by operation of law upon certain changed circumstances of the testator, such as marriage, divorce, or birth or adoption of children. These sorts of changes to the will happen without direct involvement with the document itself, although the document can override the default rules.

Once fully revoked, wills are normally no longer effective. However, even a revoked will may be entitled to probate if the will is **revived** (reinstated) or if the doctrine of **dependent relative revocation** applies because the revocation was conditional on a mistaken understanding of the testator.

Key Concepts

- How to revoke a will in writing by codicil or later will
- How to revoke a will by physical act
- When a testator may revoke only certain provisions but not the entire will
- When dependent relative revocation or revival may reverse the revocation of a will
- When changed circumstances automatically revoke will provisions

A. INTRODUCTION

A testator may choose to revoke a will at any time during life and capacity. For purposes of revoking a will, **capacity** is not a comprehensive test of competence, but rather the ability to meet a fairly liberal legal standard. Capacity commonly requires both **legal capacity**—generally having obtained a sufficient age under the state statute—and **mental capacity**. Section 8.1(b) of the Restatement (Third) of Property defines mental capacity sufficient to revoke a will to require that the testator "be capable of knowing and understanding in a general way the nature and extent of his or her property, the natural objects of his or her bounty, and the disposition that he or she is making of that property, and must also be capable of relating these elements to one another and forming an orderly desire regarding the disposition of the property." Restatement (Third) of Property: Wills and Other Donative Transfers § 8.1(b) (1999).

The threshold of capacity is the same for revoking a will as it is for executing it in the first place. The standard applies regardless of whether the will is revoked by writing or by physical act, in full or in part. If a testator lacks mental capacity and attempts to revoke his will, a will contest can prevent the revocation from being recognized and a petition can be filed for the probate of the original will. Contesting wills based on lack of capacity or other grounds is discussed in Chapter 6 on Will Contests. For a discussion of how an estate plan may be altered during a person's incapacity, see Chapter 7 on Nonprobate Transfers and Planning for Incapacity.

B. REVOKING A WILL BY WRITING

As a practicing lawyer, you will find that the most common way in which a client's will is revoked is by writing. A testator may use a writing to revoke a will by **express revocation**, in which the testator specifically states that a will is revoked, or **revocation by inconsistency**, in which a later document has terms that override an earlier document. Often, a writing revokes both by express revocation and by inconsistency. Section 2-507(a) of the Uniform Probate Code (UPC) provides the standard rule that a testator may revoke a will (or part of it) "by executing a subsequent will that revokes the previous will or part expressly or by inconsistency." Restatement (Third) of Property: Wills and Other Donative Transfers § 4(a). Nearly all will forms, or wills generated by professional legal document assembly software, include an express revocation clause stating that the will is the "last will" of the client, and that it "revokes all prior wills and codicils" made by the client.

1. Express Revocation in Writing

A testator can execute a new will or codicil that expressly states an intent to revoke the will. The language in most will forms, quoted above, does exactly this. Such an express revocation of all prior wills also revokes all prior codicils, since the term "will" includes codicils. To the extent state law allows alternative paths to the valid execution of a will, such as recognizing holographic wills in addition to attested wills, any method may be used to revoke regardless of the method used to execute the will being revoked. A validly executed holographic will may therefore be revoked in full or in part by an attested writing, and a validly executed attested will may be revoked in full or in part by a valid holographic writing. To the extent compliance with formalities for will execution may be excused by the harmless error rule in some states, compliance with formalities in revocation is likewise excusable under UPC § 2-503.

2. Revocation by Inconsistency

Rather than expressly revoking a prior will, a testator may effectively revoke part or all of it by validly executing a later will that overrides the earlier provisions. Because the most recent validly executed document takes precedence over earlier documents, provisions that are inconsistent in the earlier document are revoked when a new provision overrides it.

For example, if Tina's will leaves "all of my estate to Mom," and Tina then validly executes a new will leaving "my stamp collection to Ivan," the original will is *partially* revoked by inconsistency, because the will is revoked with respect to the bequest of the stamp collection, even though no language from the new will references the original will. Although the bequest of "all of my estate" to Mom included the stamp collection, the later bequest to Ivan overrides the earlier will; thus, Ivan will receive the stamp collection, and Mom will receive everything else.

If Tina writes a third will that leaves "all of my estate to LaVonne," the first will, leaving everything to Mom, and the second will, leaving the stamp collection to Ivan, would both be completely revoked by inconsistency. It is therefore not strictly necessary to include a provision expressly revoking prior wills in new wills, so long as the later will makes a complete disposition of the testator's property. It is still best practice to include express revocation language, however, as it is a clear statement of the testator's intent.

3. Using Codicils to Revoke or Amend Will Provisions

A codicil is an amendment to a will. Because revocations by writing may be made expressly or by inconsistency, a codicil revokes the part of the previous will that it overrides. Professionally drafted codicils generally revoke both expressly and by inconsistency, such as by stating "I hereby revoke article 3 in its entirety and replace it with the following new article 3: I appoint my mother, SHILOH COHN, to serve as Personal Representative of my estate." When codicils are used to amend a will, the will itself is entitled to probate as modified by the later codicils.

C. REVOKING A WILL BY PHYSICAL ACT

As stated above, practicing lawyers almost always draft documents for clients to execute to perform the work of revoking a will. As an alternative to revoking by writing, a testator may revoke her own will by a physical act performed upon the will with the intent to revoke, such as ripping the will into pieces. A testator may also direct another to perform the act in his presence. For revocation by physical act, the same standards for capacity, and the same grounds for a will contest, apply as in the case of will execution or revocation by subsequent writing.

As discussed below, states vary in the types of acts that can be used to revoke wills, but the list of revocatory acts is generally designed to connect with the testator's intent to revoke the will. The UPC is generous in its description of revocation methods and focuses primarily on the intent of the testator. The Michigan Pattern Jury Instructions in Exhibit 4.1 provide an example of the types of revocatory acts deemed sufficient; and § 2-504(a)(2) of the UPC provides that a testator may revoke a will or part of it:

> by performing a revocatory act on the will, if the testator performed the act with the intent, and for the purpose of revoking the will or part of it or if another individual performed the act in the testator's conscious presence and by the testator's direction. For purposes of this paragraph, a "revocatory act on the will" includes burning, tearing, canceling, obliterating, or destroying the will or any part of it. A burning, tearing, or canceling is deemed a "revocatory act on the will," whether or not the burn, tear, or cancellation actually touched any of the words on the will.

EXHIBIT 4.1   Michigan Pattern Jury Instructions

(79 Mich. B.J. 1704, December 2000)

WILL CONTESTS: REVOCATION OF WILL BY PHYSICAL MEANS, SJI2d 170.31

A [will/part of a will] may be revoked by being [burned/torn/cancelled/obliterated/destroyed] by [a decedent/another person in decedent's conscious presence and by [his/her] direction] with the intent and for the purpose of revoking [the will/any part of the will].

★ (Cancelling can include a striking out, as drawing one or more lines through, crossing out or otherwise marking out.)
★ (Obliteration can include a blotting out and erasing, or a smudging.)
★ (There is no requirement as to what amount or in what manner the [cancellation/obliteration] is accomplished as long as it is done with the decedent's intention of revoking [the will/any part of the will].)
★ (A [burn/tear/or cancellation] can be a revocation even if it does not touch any of the words on the will.)

The contestant has the burden of proving that [the will/a part of the will] was revoked by being [burned/torn/cancelled/obliterated/destroyed] by [the decedent/another person in the decedent's conscious presence and by [his/her] direction] with the intent and for the purpose of revoking [the will/any part of the will].

1. Formalities Required for Revoking a Will by Physical Act

Generally, revoking by physical act requires: (1) an appropriate physical act (2) performed on the will (or in some states, to the words of the will), (3) made with intent to revoke, (4) by the testator or in the testator's conscious presence and as directed by the testator. Note the overlap with the formalities we have encountered earlier with respect to will execution: intent remains central, action by proxy is permitted, and the testator is expected to perform certain actions as directed by the statute.

2. Which Physical Acts Cause Revocation

There is broad consensus that tearing, destroying, obliterating, or burning are sufficient actions to revoke a will by physical act. Some states add "cancelling," which is generally interpreted to mean drawing lines through words but may also include an express statement on the face of the will that it is cancelled, null and void, or revoked. States vary as to whether such a revocation must be written on top of the words of the will or whether it is sufficient to write on the back or in the margin. Some states, like those modeled after the UPC, permit revocation by any act clearly intended by the testator to revoke the document. A qualifying act of revocation must be performed on the will itself—not a draft or a copy. If there are duplicate original wills, all duplicates must be revoked—which is why having a client execute duplicate originals is not a good practice technique.

Case Preview	***In re Will of Powers***
	Formalities in revocation can be as technical as those in execution. Even when it is relatively clear what the testator wanted and expected to happen, failing to jump through the correct hoops can result in an ineffective revocation. In the case that follows, a woman includes a note on her will indicating her intent to revoke it and replace it with the plan presented in an attached document; but she never formally executed the replacement. As you read the case, consider:

1. What method of revocation did the testator attempt to use?
2. Why was the attempted revocation ineffective?
3. Why was the replacement language not given effect?
4. What happens to the original will?

In re Will of Powers
17 N.Y.S.3d 385 (Oneida Cty. Surr. Ct. 2015)

LOUIS P. GIGLIOTTI, J.

The decedent, Patricia E. Powers, executed a Last Will and Testament on November 4, 2003. This Will was drafted by Donald R. Gerace, Esq., who also supervised its execution and served as one of the two attesting witnesses. Article IX of the Will nominates Attorney Gerace as executor. The testator died on April 24, 2014. On September 22, 2014 Attorney Gerace petitioned to have the Will admitted to probate and to have Letters Testamentary[1] issued to him.

Decedent's sole distributee, i.e. her mother Patricia Dunn Powers, filed objections to the admission of the Will to probate by and through her attorney-in-fact James F. Powers, Jr. The objections assert that actions taken by the testator nearly four years after signing the Will, as hereinafter described, worked to revoke it.

Prior to her death decedent was receiving periodic payments from a structured settlement, which apparently continue following her death. Article VI of the Will divides these settlement proceeds equally between the decedent's nieces, Shannon Patricia Johnson and Shelby Kaitlyn Johnson.

The Will is typewritten but at the top of the first page there is handwritten, in red, the following:

> This Last Will & Testament is no longer valid. After *Much* (2 years) of consideration, I have written a new one—enclosed & handwritten which should be honored until I get this handwritten one to my Lawyer to be "officially changed". e.g . . . typed up like this one. Patricia E. Powers 8/22/2007

There is no dispute among the interested parties that the handwriting and signature were placed at the top of the Will by the testator.

The handwritten note refers to a "new" Will "enclosed and handwritten". In an affidavit sworn to on December 23, 2014, James F. Powers, Jr. alleges that . . . he discovered the Will in decedent's residence he noticed the handwriting and signature of the testator, in red, on the top of the first page and also found attached thereto 12 smaller sheets of paper containing the testator's handwriting and signed on the last page by her.

It is significant that none of the testator's handwriting, placed only at the top of the first page of the Will, touched or obliterated any part of the words on that page. Also, even though in this handwritten note the testator stated that she intended to get the attached "new" Will to her lawyer to be "officially changed", she never did so despite the passage of nearly seven years.

In his affidavit sworn to on January 14, 2015, the attorney-proponent, Donald R. Gerace, states that he represented the decedent between 1995 until the date of her death. He also states that he had contact with her at least 2-3 times per year, including a conference at his office approximately four months before her passing

---

[1][Letters Testamentary are forms issued by a court that give the personal representative authority to act with respect to the assets of the estate. —EDS.]

to discuss her health and legal affairs. At no time did she indicate to him that she wanted to make out a new Will or that she had revoked the November 4, 2003 Will.

Objectant's counsel asserts that, by her actions described above, the testator cancelled the Will thereby causing it to be revoked pursuant to EPTL § 3-4.1(a)(2)(A)(i). That section reads as follows:

(2) A will may be revoked by:
    (A) An act of burning, tearing, cutting, *cancellation*, obliteration, or other mutilation or destruction performed by: (italics and bold added)
        (i) The testator.

As there was no burning, tearing, cutting, obliteration or other mutilation or destruction of the Will, the issue is whether the testator's actions, as described above, cancelled it. Objectant's counsel cites several cases in support of his contention that is does. . . .

Objectant's counsel asserts that this case is most similar to the facts in *In re Parson's Will*, 119 Misc. 26 (1922), wherein the Court found a cancellation. In that case the testator wrote these words across the face of the Will:

> "This Will is hereby revoked Geo. W. Parsons."

The Court held that when words of revocation and signature are written directly across the face of the Will it obliterates or cancels other words, thereby expressing the intent of the testator to annul them. However, in this case the testator's placement of her handwriting on the Will makes it quite evident that she was avoiding contact with the words of the Will as none of her writing obliterated or cancelled a single letter.

In support of his motion to strike the objections, the attorney-proponent of the Will cites *Matter of Akers,* 74 A.D. 461, aff'd. 173 N.Y. 620. In *Matter of Akers* the Will was written on ruled legal cap paper in the handwriting of the testator. On the first page of the Will, in the blank marginal space running lengthwise, was written in the handwriting of the testator the words:

> "This Will and Codicil is revoked, Jany 14/96".

Under this line was the signature of the testator. Just as in this case, in *Matter of Akers* none of the words or the testator's signature were written across, nor did they come in contact with, any of the typewritten words of the Will. The Court in *Matter of Akers* ruled as follows:

> "There can be no such thing as a cancellation of an instrument, either as a physical fact or as a legal significance, unless the instrument thereof is in some way defaced or obliterated."

As mentioned above, Objectant's counsel only asserts that the testator's conduct caused a cancellation of the Will. However, the Court notes that even if it were argued that the testator's handwritten note at the top of the Will revoked it by writing [See EPTL § 3-4.1(a)(1)(B)], that contention would fail as it was not executed with the formalities required by statute.

Based on the foregoing, the Court finds that the actions of the testator, purportedly taken on August 22, 2007, do not constitute a valid cancellation, nor a written revocation, of the Will offered for probate in this proceeding.

...

This constitutes the Decision and Order of this Court.

Post-Case Follow-Up

Note that just as in the case of will execution, testators must adhere to proper formalities for will revocation. The testator wanted to execute a new will, but did not return to her attorney in time and the new plan remained merely a draft. Instead, a will that the testator apparently no longer wanted is entitled to probate because it was not validly revoked. Following the formalities required to revoke a will is every bit as important as following the formalities to execute the will in the first place. Remember that formalities should perform specific functions to ensure that a will accurately represents a testator's true preferences.

In re Will of Powers: Real Life Applications

1. Why was the note in handwriting not given effect as a holographic revocation? If state law does recognize holographs, should this language be sufficient to revoke the document?

2. You represent a client who has just executed a will. How do you advise him as to the proper methods to revoke the document? Is legal supervision of revocation necessary, or can the rules be explained plainly enough (and can one expect clients to follow them)?

3. You are a state legislator in a state that currently has a statute requiring revocation by physical act to affect the words in the will. Should your state allow revocation by physical act where the action does not affect the words of the will? Should your state adopt the harmless error rule, which would apply to attempted revocations much in the same manner as attempted will executions?

---

3. Presumption of Proper Revocation of Lost Will

If a will can be traced to the possession of a testator and the will cannot be found after the testator's death, a presumption will arise that the testator effectively revoked the will by physical act. This presumption of revocation is rebuttable. For example, if a proponent of the will could show that the will was destroyed in a house fire rather than by the testator's direct action on the will, the contents of the will could be proven (often by drafts supplied by the attorney, but sometimes by oral evidence), and the will can be entitled to probate. If the presumption of revocation is not rebutted, however, a missing will is presumed to have been revoked properly. This may seem ironic: testators who clearly want to revoke a will but fail to comply with the formalities die with wills that are entitled to probate, while testators who casually dispose of their wills or permanently misplace them are deemed to have revoked their wills properly.

Case Preview

Johnson v. Fitzgerald

Although a will that was in the possession of the testator is presumed revoked if it is missing at the death of the testator, this is merely a presumption; a will proponent can overturn the presumption (and show the will was in fact revoked) by providing sufficient evidence. In reading the case, consider the following questions:

1. What standard of evidence is applied to overcome the presumption of revocation?
2. How can the will be proved and admitted to probate if it is missing?
3. Does admitting the will to probate further the intent of the testator?
4. Does overturning the presumption of revocation ensure that the will at issue will be probated as written, or is this just the first step in the process?

Johnson v. Fitzgerald
751 S.E.2d 313 (Ga. 2013)

Lonnie L. Michael ("the Testator") died on September 29, 2010. He had executed a will on November 22, 2002. However, the original of that will could not be found. Nevertheless, Michael King Fitzgerald, who was named executor in the November 22, 2002 will, offered a copy of the will for probate in solemn form,[2] requesting that it be admitted to probate upon proper proof. Danny Johnson, Michael D. Gwirtz, and Patricia A. Gwirtz ("Caveators"),[3] the Testator's heirs at law, filed a caveat, asserting, inter alia, that the November 22, 2002 will had been revoked

---

[2][As discussed further in Chapter 14 on Estate Administration and the Probate Process, many states offer both formal and informal methods of probate. Solemn form probate is a formal probate procedure, which is necessary if any parties object to the probate of the will. —Eds.]

[3][A "caveator" is a party who brings a will contest, which is sometimes called filing a "caveat." Other jurisdictions use the term "contestant" instead of "caveator" and "contest" instead of "caveat." —Eds.]

by the Testator's subsequent destruction of it. After hearing evidence and argument, the probate court admitted the will to probate. Caveators appealed to the superior court, and the case was tried before a jury, which found in favor of the propounded will, which the trial court then admitted to probate in solemn form. After the denial of their motion for new trial, Caveators appealed to this Court. For the reasons that follow, we affirm.

Caveators [contend] there was no evidence authorizing the jury to find that the propounded will was the true last will and testament of the Testator. Under the governing law, if the original of a will cannot be found for probate, there is a presumption that the testator intended to revoke that will. OCGA § 53-4-46(a). But, "[t]hat presumption can be overcome if a copy is established by a preponderance of the evidence to be a true copy, and if it is shown by a preponderance of the evidence that [he] did not intend to revoke it. OCGA § 53-4-46(b)." Warner v. Reynolds, 546 S.E.2d 520 (Ga. 2001). . . .

Put simply, under the propounded will, $50,000 was bequeathed to the Bogart Baptist Church to be used for its cemetery fund, and $50,000 was bequeathed to Fitzgerald; the will named a trust which benefitted the Lonnie L. Mitchell Foundation as the residuary beneficiary. And, there was ample evidence that, after November 22, 2002, the Testator intended this residuary bequest, and thus the propounded will, to continue in force. On June 5, 2003, the Testator executed a document guiding the trust referenced in the will, and he amended the trust on January 12, 2006; these actions would have had no purpose if the Testator did not intend to fund the trust through the residual clause of the propounded will. Further, in discussions with his attorney about the 2006 trust amendment, the Testator understood that his assets had risen to a point that the church originally named as the primary beneficiary of the trust might not have need for the full amount, and he wished to give the trustees more flexibility to fund charitable contributions from the money that would come to the trust from the will.

Additionally, in 2004, the Testator told the pastor of the Bogart Baptist Church that he was leaving money for the cemetery fund in his will; the Testator also expressed disdain for what he considered his relatives' greed, stated that he did not wish them to have his money, and did not express a contrary sentiment thereafter. Wills that the Testator executed before the execution of the propounded will were introduced, and were consistent with the propounded will in the amount left for the cemetery fund, and the exclusion of Caveators. Although Caveators moved to exclude these prior wills from evidence, contending that they were irrelevant, the trial court properly ruled that they were relevant to the issues to be tried; such wills can show a consistent testamentary scheme, supporting an inference of that testamentary intent carrying into the period during which revocation is presumed.

Accordingly, the jury was authorized to find by a preponderance of the evidence that Fitzgerald had rebutted the presumption of revocation. . . .

Judgment affirmed.

All the Justices concur.

Post-Case Follow-Up

Note the interplay between the statute and case law here. It is the statute on will revocation that sets the standard of "preponderance of the evidence." The court is bound by the standard articulated in the statute, rather than relying on prior case law based on an earlier statute. Note also that although conversations about what a testator wanted to have happen to his assets would not be sufficient to constitute a will or to convey an interest to beneficiaries, these conversations are taken into account in determining whether the testator intended his will to be revoked.

Johnson: Real Life Applications

1. You represent a client who wants to keep her estate plan secret from her children because her eldest is her favorite child. Years ago, she wrote a will dividing her estate equally among her three children, but she wants to revoke it and have the property pass according to the terms of a prior will, in which she left everything to her firstborn. She thinks the children will be less angry if the later will is just mysteriously missing as opposed to there being evidence that she actively revoked it. What do you advise your client? Does she need to watch what she says around others?

2. You are responsible for drafting your firm's document retention policies. How does the presumption—that a will in the possession of a testator missing at death is presumed to be revoked—weigh into your decision of whether the executed documents should be retained by the client or by the attorney?

D. PARTIAL REVOCATION OF A WILL

Sometimes clients want to make modest changes to a will while leaving the majority of an estate plan in place. In all states, part of a will may be revoked by writing. In some states but not others, part of a will may alternatively be revoked by physical act.

1. Partial Revocation or Amendment by Writing

All states permit the revocation or amendment of part of a will by the valid execution of a codicil. When a codicil is validly executed, portions of the original will that are not inconsistent with the provisions of the codicil continue to remain effective. It is therefore possible to make modest changes to a client's documents, such as altering selection of a personal representative, while leaving the majority of the estate plan in place. Particularly where a change is minor and the level of capacity of the testator is questionable, the execution of a noncontroversial codicil may draw less rancor (and litigation) than the execution of a new will. Aside from these situations, because a codicil must be executed with the same formality as the underlying will, and the original will may still be electronically stored, it may be simpler to execute a new will to ensure clarity.

Codicils may sometimes complicate an estate plan, making it unclear whether a bequest was intended to be increased, decreased, or eliminated. For example, if the original will left "$10,000 to Macey" and a codicil leaves "my Dell stock, worth $9,000, to Macey," is the stock in the codicil in addition to the cash, or in place of it? Under the common law, gifts in a codicil were presumed to be cumulative and added to those made in an earlier will. Under modern law and the UPC, there is no such presumption, and it is a matter of whether the testator intended the gifts to be cumulative that matters: a rule that may require litigation to determine intent. When changing dispositions of property, it is generally better practice to execute a new will if the client's health allows it.

2. Whether Partial Revocation by Physical Act Is Effective

Only some states recognize partial revocation by physical act. The states that do not permit such partial revocations theorize that because removing a bequest results in a substantive change to the provisions of the will and the bequests to other beneficiaries, all changes to the document short of revoking it entirely must be done both in writing and in compliance with testamentary formalities.

The UPC authorizes partial revocation as a way of furthering the testator's intent, using the phrase "a will or any part thereof" when discussing revocation by physical act or in writing. Practicing lawyers are creatures of writing by nature and thus rarely make changes by physical act. This rule therefore has more impact on individuals who want to alter their wills without the assistance of an attorney and may be unsure or incorrect as to the legal consequence of striking through or otherwise damaging only part of the language of a will. Where a state does recognize partial revocation by physical act, the same acts that are used for total revocation may also be used for partial revocation. For example, if a state statute allowed revocation by "cutting," a testator could use scissors to trim unwanted parts from the will and leave the rest remaining.

E. AUTOMATIC WILL REVOCATION DUE TO CHANGED CIRCUMSTANCES

Most will revocations occur because of the intentional efforts of the testator. There are a few changes in life circumstances, however, when the law automatically revokes part or all of a will based on the presumed intent of the testator. The theory animating these rules is that the will has become "stale"—that there has been a substantial enough change that a typical decedent would have intended to adapt the will to reflect the change, but he missed the final deadline. In these instances, the law attempts to further the presumed intent of the testator by altering the disposition under the will to adapt to these changed circumstances. Some older statutes have vague references to "changed circumstances" justifying revocation of bequests, but most modern statutes specify which circumstances should result in changes. Under § 4.1(b) of the Restatement (Third) of Property, a marriage dissolution constitutes changed circumstances that justify revocation of bequests favoring the former spouse. A testator's marriage or the birth or adoption of children are changed circumstances that do not result in revocation, but may result in changes in the way property is distributed.

1. Divorce and Marriage

In most U.S. states, a final divorce settlement or annulment of a marriage revokes all provisions in the will in favor of the former spouse. These statutes typically include revocation of transfers of property, rights to determine who receives property, and nominations to serve in fiduciary roles such as executor of the will or trustee of a testamentary trust. Some states and the UPC revoke provisions in favor of former in-laws as well. The will itself is not entirely revoked (unless the spouse is the sole beneficiary), but rather the provisions benefitting the former spouse are not given effect, and the property passes as if the spouse had predeceased the testator. Many states also apply this rule revoking gifts to the ex-spouse to nonprobate transfers such as revocable trusts and beneficiary designations. The UPC provides that "express terms" to the contrary in a will or other document, a court order, or a contract relating to the divorce will supersede UPC § 2-804 (see Exhibit 4.2), but those circumstances are rare.

EXHIBIT 4.2 **UPC § 2-804. Revocation of Probate and Nonprobate Transfers by Divorce; No Revocation by Other Changes of Circumstances**

(b) [Revocation Upon Divorce.] Except as provided by the express terms of a governing instrument, a court order, or a contract relating to the division of the marital estate made between the divorced individuals before or after the marriage, divorce, or annulment, the divorce or annulment of a marriage:

(1) revokes any revocable

    (A) disposition or appointment of property made by a divorced individual to his [or her] former spouse in a governing instrument and any disposition or appointment created by law or in a governing instrument to a relative of the divorced individual's former spouse,

    (B) provision in a governing instrument conferring a general or nongeneral power of appointment on the divorced individual's former spouse or on a relative of the divorced individual's former spouse, and

> **(C)** nomination in a governing instrument, nominating a divorced individual's former spouse or a relative of the divorced individual's former spouse to serve in any fiduciary or representative capacity, including a personal representative, executor, trustee, conservator, agent, or guardian; and
>
> **(2)** severs the interests of the former spouses in property held by them at the time of the divorce or annulment as joint tenants with the right of survivorship [or as community property with the right of survivorship], transforming the interests of the former spouses into equal tenancies in common.

The general rule is that divorce will revoke provisions in favor of the former spouse, but there is some variation throughout the states. Where states do have statutes revoking transfers upon divorce, some apply only to probate transfers and some apply to nonprobate transfers as well. States also vary as to whether a revocation on divorce statute has any effect on bequests or fiduciary appointments of relatives of the former spouse (ex-in-laws). In *When an Ex Can Take It All: The Effect—and Non-Effect—of Revocation on a Will Post-Divorce*, 74 Md. L. Rev. 969, 975 (2015), Molly Brimmer explains the several main categories of variation: (1) explicit revocation on divorce statute; (2) implied revocation, despite the absence of an explicit revocation on divorce statute; and (3) no revocation on divorce statute and no implementation of implied revocation on divorce. Notably, some nonprobate transfers, such as beneficiary designations for a retirement plan governed by ERISA, are not subject to state revocation-on-divorce statutes because federal law preempts state law. See Egelhoff v. Egelhoff, 532 U.S. 141 (2001). It is better for clients to reassess all estate planning—both probate and nonprobate transfers—than to allow the default rules to apply following a divorce.

Although divorce often causes a will to be revoked automatically, marriage does not. At common law, a woman's will was revoked upon her marriage and a man's will was revoked upon the birth of a child within a marriage. Under modern law, neither marriage nor birth of children revokes a will, and the rules that do apply are consistent regardless of the sex of the testator.

Even though marriage does not revoke a testator's will, a spouse is often entitled to certain rights to the decedent's property. These rights, including the elective share and rights of an omitted spouse, are discussed in more detail in Chapter 8. Property may therefore pass to a surviving spouse rather than another beneficiary named in the will, so to this extent, the provision in favor of the beneficiary is "revoked" to allow the property to pass to the spouse. (Technically, the provision in favor of the other beneficiary "abates" to fund the spouse's share; abatement is discussed in more detail in Chapter 5.)

2. Birth or Adoption of Descendants

When a testator has children (by birth or adoption) after she has executed her will, the will is not revoked. Children born or adopted after the will was executed may, however, have rights to the testator's property that override provisions that favor other beneficiaries. This is similar to the rights of an omitted spouse, as mentioned above, and the rights of these omitted descendants are discussed in Chapter 8. The enlarging of a class of children or descendants may also affect the number of ways a bequest is split; such as when a testator leaves her jewelry "to my grandchildren," and additional grandchildren are born or adopted over the years. None of these events, however, is a legal "revocation" of the original will.

3. *Cy Pres* and Charitable Bequests

Transfers to a charitable organization may be modified by the doctrine of *cy pres*, discussed more fully in Chapter 9. *Cy pres* applies to modify a condition in a transfer made to a charity where it cannot realistically be carried out as written due to a change in circumstances after execution of the document. For example, if a testator sets aside funds in his will to cure a specific disease, it may no longer be possible to carry out as written if the disease is cured. When a court applies *cy pres*, it attempts to further the donor's intent by modifying the original transfer to be *cy pres comme possible* (as near as possible) to the donor's original intent while adapting to the changed circumstances. The modification may not actually be as near as *possible* to the original bequest, yet the hope is that it remains consistent with the charitable intent of the donor without triggering the concerns of impracticability, wastefulness, or similar problems that the bequest caused as originally worded. The application of *cy pres* is not a revocation of a provision in a will, but it can alter who receives the property or how the terms of the bequest are carried out.

F. DEPENDENT RELATIVE REVOCATION AND REVIVAL OF WILLS

Most of the time, revocation of a will is permanent. In some instances, however, the revocation of the will may be undone under the doctrines of dependent relative revocation or revival. These doctrines seek to further testator intent by negating acts of revocation and leaving previously revoked documents in place. They can apply to wills or to codicils, regardless of the method used to revoke the document.

1. Dependent Relative Revocation

The doctrine of **dependent relative revocation** (DRR) can negate the effect of a testator's revocation of her will if that revocation was conditioned on certain mistakes. Most states recognize the doctrine of dependent relative revocation, and the UPC commentary to § 5-207 acknowledges that states have developed their own doctrines on DRR. The extent to which a state needs to resort to dependent relative revocation depends in part on whether the state recognizes other doctrines, such as partial revocation, because those doctrines may effectuate the testator's intent more efficiently.

In re Estate of Virginia E. Murphy

The doctrine of dependent relative revocations helps rescue testators from their own mistakes, but its remedy is limited to negating the act of revoking the will. The doctrine will nullify a prior revocation if: (1) the revocation was conditional on the testator's mistaken understanding; and (2) the testator is closer to her ideal plan with the revoked will reinstated than she would be if the revocation were effective. The case that follows shows both of these criteria in action. Notice that the testator executed a later will that expressly revoked prior wills, but under the assumption that the portions of her later will would not be thrown out due to a will contest. The court applies a dependent relative revocation analysis to determine whether the testator would not have expressly revoked the entire prior will had she known the later will would not be entitled to probate in its entirety. In reading the case, consider the following questions:

1. How does the court articulate the doctrine of dependent relative revocation?
2. What facts triggered the application of dependent relative revocation?
3. Why could the court not just consider all of the evidence and piece together the estate plan it seems the decedent wanted, instead of merely unrevoking her will?
4. Does the doctrine of dependent relative revocation come closer to granting the decedent her testamentary intent than if the doctrine did not apply?

In re Estate of Virginia E. Murphy (Rocke v. American Research Bureau)
184 So.3d 1221 (Fla. Dist. Ct. App. 2015)

Lucas, Judge.

At the age of 107, Virginia E. Murphy passed away, leaving behind an estate worth nearly twelve million dollars, a series of wills, a phalanx of potential heirs, and extensive litigation. Following a trial, appeal, and remand from this court, the probate court entered an order in which it concluded that the vast majority of Mrs. Murphy's estate should pass through intestacy. For the reasons explained below, we are compelled to reverse the probate court's order following remand because it failed to apply the presumption of dependent relative revocation to Mrs. Murphy's last will.

I

A

Born in 1899, Virginia Murphy died on September 6, 2006, after more than a decade of declining health and acuity. Her parents and husband predeceased her, and she had no children or siblings. In the years before her passing, Mrs. Murphy executed a number of wills prepared by her longtime attorney, Jack S. Carey, including her last will and testament dated February 2, 1994 ("1994 will"). When Mrs. Murphy died, Mr. Carey filed a Petition for Administration submitting the 1994 will to probate. The 1994 will named Mr. Carey as personal representative of Mrs. Murphy's estate; and it purported to leave the bulk of that estate to Mr. Carey, Gloria DuBois (Mr. Carey's legal assistant), and George Tornwall (Mrs. Murphy's accountant, who died the year before Mrs. Murphy passed away).

Upon learning of the probate proceedings, Mrs. Murphy's second cousin, Jacqueline "Jackie" Rocke, a devisee under one of Mrs. Murphy's prior wills, filed an objection to the residuary devises in the 1994 will. In her objection, Ms. Rocke alleged undue influence[4] on the part of Mr. Carey and Ms. DuBois over Mrs. Murphy.

. . .

We briefly summarize the testamentary schemes set forth in the last six of Mrs. Murphy's wills that were admitted into evidence below, as they are all pertinent to this appeal:

May 10, 1989, Will ("1989 Will").

This will, the earliest of the wills admitted into evidence, included a specific bequest to Ms. Rocke in the amount of $150,000 and specific bequests to Mr. Tornwall, Mr. Carey, and Ms. DuBois in the amount of $50,000 each and devised the entire residuary of the estate to Northwestern University's medical school.

June 11, 1991, Will ("1991 Will")

This will contained specific bequests to the Northwestern University medical school in the amount of $500,000, Ms. Rocke in the amount of $400,000, and Mr. Tornwall, Mr. Carey, and Ms. DuBois in the amount of $100,000 each, with the residuary of the estate divided in equal fourths between Ms. Rocke, Mr. Tornwall, Mr. Carey, and Ms. DuBois.

February 4, 1992, Will ("February 1992 Will")

This will, nearly identical to the 1991 will, also contained specific bequests to Northwestern University's medical school in the amount of $500,000, Ms. Rocke in the amount of $400,000, and Mr. Tornwall, Mr. Carey, and Ms. DuBois in the amount of $100,000 each, while the residuary of the estate was divided in equal

---

[4]Chapter 6 explains will contests, including those based on undue influence. For purpose of understanding how dependent relative revocation works in the *Murphy* case, the critical point is that bequests forced by undue influence are not given effect. —EDS.

fourths between Ms. Rocke, Mr. Tornwall, Mr. Carey, and Ms. DuBois. Ms. Rocke argued below and on appeal that this will's residuary devises (excluding Mr. Carey, Mr. Tornwall, and Ms. DuBois's devises) should have been the controlling testamentary scheme for probate of the residuary estate.

August 25, 1992, Will ("August 1992 Will")

This will included specific bequests to the medical school of Northwestern University in the amount of $500,000, Ms. Rocke in the amount of $400,000, and Mr. Tornwall, Mr. Carey, and Ms. DuBois in the amount of $100,000 each, but the residuary of the estate was now divided into equal thirds between Mr. Tornwall, Mr. Carey, and Ms. DuBois.

January 29, 1993, Will ("1993 Will")

The 1993 will contained specific bequests to Northwestern University's medical school in the amount of $500,000, Ms. Rocke in the amount of $400,000, Ms. DuBois in the amount of $150,000, and Mr. Tornwall and Mr. Carey in the amount of $100,000 each. The residuary of the estate was devised in equal thirds between Mr. Tornwall, Mr. Carey, and Ms. DuBois.

1994 Will

This will, like the 1993 will, included specific bequests to Northwestern University's medical school in the amount of $500,000, Ms. Rocke in the amount of $400,000, Ms. DuBois in the amount of $150,000, and Mr. Tornwall and Mr. Carey in the amount of $100,000 each. The residuary of the estate was again devised in equal thirds between Mr. Tornwall, Mr. Carey, and Ms. DuBois.

In addition to these testamentary documents, the probate court also considered the testimony of Mr. Carey, Ms. DuBois, Ms. Rocke, and other witnesses who had been involved with Mrs. Murphy's estate planning. By nearly all accounts, Mrs. Murphy maintained few personal relationships in the final decades of her life; she never knew anyone in her extended family other than Ms. Rocke, with whom she had enjoyed a close, social relationship since the early 1960s. Over time, Mr. Carey and Ms. DuBois built their own relationship with Mrs. Murphy (Ms. DuBois would eventually manage Mrs. Murphy's day-to-day finances for several years) founded upon Mr. Carey's service as her counsel. While Mrs. Murphy's health and mental awareness diminished, Mr. Carey and Ms. DuBois' share of the estate grew under the wills Mr. Carey drafted.

After the conclusion of the trial, on August 1, 2008, the probate court entered its Order on Objection to Petition for Administration and Order Admitting Will to Probate ("Order on Objection"). The Order on Objection included thorough and detailed findings that Mr. Carey and Ms. DuBois had, in fact, exerted undue influence through their confidential, fiduciary, and personal relationships with Ms. Murphy in order to become residuary devisees of her estate. The probate court further concluded that the residuary devises in the 1994 will were void but that "[t]he remainder of the provisions of the will are valid and shall control the disposition of the assets specifically devised." The court then admitted the 1994 will to probate, excluding its residuary devises, and ordered that "the rest, residue and remainder [of the estate] shall pass by the laws of intestate succession" as a lapsed gift.

Implicit in the probate court's determination was that the 1994 will's revocation clause, revoking all of Mrs. Murphy's prior wills, remained valid, so that the vast majority of Mrs. Murphy's estate would now pass to her intestate heirs who were, as yet, still unknown. Suffice it to say, none of the litigants were particularly satisfied with that result.

. . .

We begin by examining the legal construct at the heart of this appeal, the doctrine of dependent relative revocation. Founded in the common law of early eighteenth century England, the doctrine was first adopted by the Florida Supreme Court, which explained:

> This doctrine has been stated and reiterated by many courts since it was first expounded in 1717, but stated simply it means that where [a] testator makes a new will revoking a former valid one, and it later appears that the new one is invalid, the old will may be re-established on the ground that the revocation was dependent upon the validity of the new one, [the] testator preferring the old will to intestacy.

Stewart v. Johnson, 194 So. 869, 870 (1940). Grounded in the axiom of probate law that intestacy should be avoided whenever possible, the doctrine of dependent relative revocation, our court has observed, is "a rule of presumed intention" that creates a rebuttable presumption that the testator would have preferred to have a prior will effectuated over statutory intestacy. The presumption's application hinges on whether "the provisions of the present invalid will are sufficiently similar to the former will." . . . In cases of undue influence,[5] if a prior will is sufficiently similar to an invalidated will then the presumption arises but may be rebutted by evidence that "the revocation clause was not invalidated by undue influence and that it was not intended by the decedent to be conditional on the validity of the testamentary provisions" of the will.

. . .

We find no reason to erect a barrier between admissible evidence and the task of sifting similarities between wills that have been affected by undue influence. Rather, we join the courts of our sister states to hold that, in cases involving undue influence, a probate court is not confined to the testamentary documents when determining whether the doctrine of dependent relative revocation should apply. . . . Upon a finding of undue influence, a probate court may consider any relevant, admissible evidence to decide if the testator intended a will's revocation clause to be conditional upon the will's efficacy.

Comparing Mrs. Murphy's wills in the appropriately broad light, and in the light of all the evidence, we find there were sufficient similarities between Mrs. Murphy's 1994 will and her prior wills to support the application of the doctrine of dependent

---

[5][Undue influence is a common ground for a will contest and is discussed thoroughly in Chapter 6. Broadly speaking, undue influence occurs when a third party exerts such extreme influence over the testator's freedom to choose the disposition of her property that she changes it to reflect the third party's preferences rather than her own. Provisions in a will that are procured by undue influence are not entitled to probate. —Eds.]

relative revocation to the 1994 will. We discern several contours of similarity that were unrefuted in the record.

First, Mrs. Murphy's execution of six wills over a period of five years evidences a sustained concern about the disposition of her property upon her death. Mrs. Murphy prized her right to dictate how her property should be divided, and she exercised that right, repeatedly, in the final years of her life. No one seriously disputes that she preferred testacy over intestacy. And that is, of course, the very foundation for the doctrine of dependent relative revocation's application.

Moreover, the testamentary documents themselves evince an overall pattern of similarity. Each of Mrs. Murphy's wills employed a similar testamentary scheme in which Mrs. Murphy made numerous specific bequests to charities and caregivers while limiting the division of the residuary of her estate to a few devisees. Although their respective proportions varied from will to will, the identities of the devisees and beneficiaries within the six wills, overall, remained fairly constant. Indeed, in its Order on Remand, the probate court observed, "Over the course of six wills, the changes in specific bequests were insubstantial." The variance the probate court fixed upon, the alteration of residuary devisees, is likewise modest once the effect of Mr. Carey and Ms. DuBois' undue influence is properly taken into account. When Mr. Carey and Ms. DuBois are removed from consideration, there is only one change between the six wills' residuary clauses that did not involve Mr. Carey or Ms. DuBois' illicit gain over the residuary estate: the change between the 1989 will and the 1991 will, which exchanged Northwestern University's medical school and Ms. Rocke's respective positions as a specific beneficiary and a residuary devisee. For her part, Ms. Rocke appeared repeatedly throughout Mrs. Murphy's wills, either as a residuary devisee, a designee of a specific bequest, or both.

Finally, the extrinsic evidence proffered before the probate court further demonstrated the appropriateness of applying the presumption in this case. With the exception of four individuals, including Ms. Rocke, none of the forty-eight intestate heirs ultimately identified in the Final Order Determining Beneficiaries and Respective Shares were mentioned within any of Mrs. Murphy's six wills. In contrast to the close relationship she had with Ms. Rocke, it appears Mrs. Murphy never knew her intestate heirs, and they never knew her. The intestate heirs' ancestral ties to Mrs. Murphy apparently remained forgotten until this litigation (and an heir search firm) brought them to light. Intestacy, in this case, would usurp the repeated testamentary dispositions of Mrs. Murphy's property throughout her wills, dispositions that were invariably tied to individuals she cared about or charities and institutions which she supported. Cf. In re Jones' Estate, 352 So. 2d 1182 (Fla. Dist. Ct. App. 1977) (applying doctrine because testator's wills demonstrated a strong aversion to intestacy by their expressed intention to disinherit the decedent's daughter). We hold, as a matter of law, that Mrs. Murphy's six wills were sufficiently similar to give rise to the doctrine of dependent relative revocation's presumption.

. . .

Stripping the undue influence that spanned the residuary devises of Mrs. Murphy's last six wills leaves two alternative residuary devises that remained untainted: the medical school of Northwestern University or Ms. Rocke. Northwestern University would receive the entire residuary of Mrs. Murphy's estate under the express provision of the 1989 will. Ms. Rocke would stand to receive all of the residuary estate by operation of law under the February 1992 will as the only remaining residuary devisee in that will. See § 732.5165 (establishing that any part of a will procured by undue influence is void, "but the remainder of the will not so procured shall be valid if it is not invalid for other reasons"). The question then becomes which devise from which will should determine the disposition of the residuary estate.

From our review of the evidence proffered below, the February 1992 will's residuary clause, which includes the last untainted residuary disposition Mrs. Murphy made, controls the disposition of her residuary estate. Although it is true Mr. Carey and Ms. DuBois procured part of the February 1992 will's residuary clause through their illicit efforts, the probate court made no finding—as, indeed, no one has ever argued—that Ms. Rocke was, in any way, associated with that exertion of undue influence over Mrs. Murphy. The February 1992 will would remain perfectly intelligible and true to Mrs. Murphy's repeated indications of preferring testacy over intestacy had the probate court excised Mr. Carey and Ms. DuBois' devises and left Ms. Rocke's to stand. . . . The court must honor the last uninfluenced residuary devise Mrs. Murphy made: to her cousin, Jackie Rocke.

In conclusion, we hold that in cases of undue influence over a testator, the presumption from the doctrine of dependent relative revocation requires only a showing of broad similarity between a decedent's testamentary instruments. We further hold that a probate court may consider any admissible extrinsic evidence when measuring similarity for purposes of the doctrine's application. Consistent with sections 90.302(2) and 733.107(2), we hold that when the doctrine's presumption arises the burden of proof then shifts to the opponent of the presumption to show that the testator held an independent, unaffected intention to revoke the otherwise affected will.

Having clarified the doctrine's application, we find that the presumption under the doctrine was established here and was not rebutted. The probate court erred and should have admitted the February 1992 will to probate with Ms. Rocke receiving the residuary of the estate as the last remaining devisee. Accordingly, we reverse the order of the probate court and remand with directions to enter an order consistent with this opinion.

Reversed and remanded; conflict certified.

Post-Case Follow-Up

You will notice that the court did not require that substantial similarity between the documents be proven in order for the doctrine of dependent relative revocation to apply. Dependent relative revocation should apply to negate the intent behind a revoking act where the testator's plan for distribution of her estate is more closely matched with the revoked document functioning than with it out of the picture. Note also the limits of dependent relative revocation: all it can do is unrevoke a will; it cannot correct the testator's mistake by giving her the estate plan that evidence suggests she wanted. Not all mistakes trigger DRR; the mistake normally relates to an attempted substitute estate plan that fails. Some states also use DRR for a mistake of fact recited in the will.

In re Estate of Virginia E. Murphy: Real Life Applications

1. If you were the judge in this case, how important would the similarity of the documents be to you? Is the more critical factor: (1) how the series of wills compare to each other; or (2) how the will that would be probated compares to how the decedent's property would pass in intestacy?

2. What if the testator had made significant lifetime transfers to the charities named in the case? Would that affect your decision as to which dispositive plan the testator would have preferred? Does it make it more or less likely that a decedent would want to benefit a party under her will if she has already benefitted them during life?

3. Assume that there was no will contest at issue, but Mrs. Murphy validly revoked her 1993 will by physical act, shortly thereafter writing what she believed would be a valid holographic will in 1994. Assume the holographic will is not admissible in Mrs. Murphy's state because only attested wills are allowed. Should the doctrine of dependent relative revocation apply to allow the 1993 will to be admitted to probate? Can it be used to probate the 1994 will?

2. Revival of Revoked Wills

The doctrine of **revival** applies when a will that has previously been revoked is reinstated to legal enforceability. A testator may always deliberately revive a will by re-executing a previously revoked will according to testamentary formalities (attested or holographic, if permitted by the state). In some states, this is the only method of reviving a will; there is no automatic revival. See *In re Estate of Alburn*, 118 N.W.2d. 919 (Wis. 1963). In other states, a will is automatically revived under certain circumstances that demonstrate the testator's intent that it be reinstated.

Under the UPC and similar statutes, the revival of a revoked will occurs under circumstances indicating the testator's intent, with different presumptions arising depending on whether it is a will or a codicil that is revoked and which method of revocation was used. Specifically, when a testator revokes an entire will by physical act, revival occurs only if the circumstances of the revocation or the testator's statements show the testator intended the revocation of the later will to reinstate the earlier one. When a testator revokes a codicil by physical act, revival of the provision of the earlier will that was overridden by the codicil is automatically revoked unless there is evidence that the testator did not intend such an outcome. Finally, if a later will revokes an earlier will which by its terms revoked an even earlier will, the later will must show an intent to revive the even earlier will for revival to occur. The provisions from the Uniform Probate Code are shown in Exhibit 4.3.

Using the UPC as an example, let's work through several fact patterns. First say Lisa executed Will 1 giving her daughter Lauren $10,000 and her daughter Leah the rest. Later, Lisa executed Will 2 expressly revoking Will 1 and leaving everything to her church, and then changed her mind and revoked Will 2 by burning. The default rule is that Will 1 is not automatically revived—Lisa would need behavior or statements, like telling her bridge club that she had decided not to leave everything to the church after all, to show that it was her intent to revive Will 1 in order for it to be effective. If instead Will 2 was only a codicil, stating that Lisa should not receive the $10,000 but that Lisa's church should receive the money, Lisa burning Will 2 would be effective to reinstate the transfer of $10,000 to Lauren in Will 1, without specific evidence as to her intent (although evidence could prove it was not her intent to reinstate the gift to Lauren). Finally, assume that instead of burning Will 2, Lisa executed Will 3, which expressly revoked Will 2. Under these facts, Will 3 would need to include language showing that Lisa wanted Will 1 to be effective; otherwise, the $10,000 gift to Lauren remains revoked.

EXHIBIT 4.3 **UPC § 2-509 Revival of Revoked Will**

(a) If a subsequent will that wholly revoked a previous will is thereafter revoked by a revocatory act, the previous will remains revoked unless it is revived. The previous will is revived if it is evident from the circumstances of the revocation of the subsequent will or from the testator's contemporary or subsequent declarations that the testator intended the previous will to take effect as executed.

(b) If a subsequent will that partly revoked a previous will is thereafter revoked by a revocatory act, a revoked part of the previous will is revived unless it is evident from the circumstances of the revocation of the subsequent will or from the testator's contemporary or subsequent declarations that the testator did not intend the revoked part to take effect as executed.

(c) If a subsequent will that revoked a previous will in whole or in part is thereafter revoked by another, later, will, the previous will remains revoked in whole or in part, unless it or its revoked part is revived. The previous will or its revoked part is revived to the extent it appears from the terms of the later will that the testator intended the previous will to take effect.

G. CONTRACTUAL WILLS

A testator is generally free to make whatever disposition she wishes of her property. She may voluntarily, however, limit that testamentary freedom by contract. These limitations most frequently occur in the context of divorce agreements. It may also arise when one person agrees to care for another during the patient's final years of life, based on the patient's agreement to leave a share of his estate to the caregiver.

1. Contracts to Make a Will

To the extent an individual is able to make a contract regarding the transfer of property, he may enter into a contract to execute a will that includes terms conveying that property. As the reader will fondly remember from the first year of law school, the subject of contracts has an entire body of law relating to the enforceability of agreements. In the context of contracts to make a will, all basic rules of contract law continue to apply. In addition, a contract to make a bequest in favor of a beneficiary must also comply with probate law.

Generally, the additional level of regulation that probate law provides is to require sufficient evidence of the contract, either on the face of the will itself, or in another signed writing. Although contracts in general may be oral, a contract to make or revoke a will must be written, because of the execution formalities inherent in wills. Writing is also clearly the most reliable method of recording the terms of an agreement. A contract to make a will (or to refrain from making or revoking a will) generally requires that the will itself states the key components of the contract, that the will expressly refers to a contract and extrinsic evidence can expressly prove its terms, or a writing providing evidence of the contract that the decedent has signed. The UPC includes the statute shown in Exhibit 4.4 with respect to contracts regarding wills.

EXHIBIT 4.4 | **UPC § 2-514. Contracts Concerning Succession**

> A contract to make a will or devise, or not to revoke a will or devise, or to die intestate, if executed after the effective date of this [article], may be established only by (i) provisions of a will stating material provisions of the contract, (ii) an express reference in a will to a contract and extrinsic evidence proving the terms of the contract, or (iii) a writing signed by the decedent evidencing the contract. The execution of a joint will or mutual wills does not create a presumption of a contract not to revoke the will or wills.

Case Preview

Matter of Attea

Contracts to leave a will benefiting a certain party are enforceable if they meet the criteria for enforcement under both contract law and probate law. The remedy to the injured party, however, is damages against the estate—in stark contrast from the most common remedy in a will contest: denial of probate. In the following case, a nun allegedly took a vow of poverty that entailed passing any assets she might own to her congregation upon her death. Her will instead left some of her estate to charity and some to family members. The congregation sued on several grounds, including breach of contract to make a will. If the nun did make an enforceable contract to leave her entire estate to the congregation, the congregation would have the right to sue the estate on the breach of contract claim and pursue the recovery of the assets. When reading this case, consider the following questions:

1. When is the proper time to bring a claim for breach of contract to make a will?
2. Can a claim for breach of contract to make a will be combined with various other claims raised in a will contest, such as fraud or undue influence?
3. Does a contract to make a will have any effect on whether a will that does not comply with that agreement should be denied probate?
4. Is a claim that a contract to make a will has been breached really a will contest at all, or is it a separate contract claim?

Matter of Attea
49 Misc. 3d 218 (N.Y. Sur. 2015)

Barbara Howe, J.

Decedent, a long-time professed nun of the Congregation of the Sisters of St. Joseph [hereafter, the Congregation] died at age 82 on March 26, 2014, leaving a probate estate worth nearly two million dollars. She was survived by three brothers, Joseph Attea, William Attea, and Martin Attea. Her Will, dated August 31, 1994, has been offered for probate in this court by Joseph H. Spahn [hereafter, Joseph], husband of decedent's predeceased sister Mary Spahn [hereafter, Mary]. Preliminary letters testamentary were issued to Joseph on April 29, 2014.

Decedent entered the Congregation in 1950 and lived as a member of the Congregation until the time of her death. She executed a Declaration of Final Profession on August 29, 1959, which included taking vows of poverty, chastity and obedience according to the Congregation's Constitution. Pursuant to those vows, she executed a Will on June 18, 1979 [hereafter, the "1979 Will"], leaving all her property upon her death to the Congregation and naming the president thereof as her executrix.

On November 15, 1982, decedent was involved in an accident as a passenger in a vehicle allegedly owned and operated by the Congregation, and she suffered severe physical injuries. On August 14, 1984, upon a petition by decedent's sister Mary, Erie County Court appointed Mary as guardian of decedent's property, and authorized her to pursue a claim for damages arising out of the 1982 accident.

Mary's action on behalf of decedent was settled in the amount of $1,700,000. Mary then returned to County Court with respect to the disposition of the net settlement proceeds—roughly $1,100,000—and County Court made the following directions in its December 1, 1988 Order:

> "ORDERED, that any proceeds received by Mary A. Spahn, as Conservator of Sister George Marie Attea, Conservatee, as the result of the settlement of the personal injury claim of the said Sister George Marie Attea, be deposited in any bank, trust company or savings and loan association where such deposits will be insured by the United States Federal Government or its agencies and that the proceeds of said settlement are also authorized to be deposited in a high interest yield account such as

an insured 'savings certificate' or an insured 'money market' account or said monies may be invested in one or more insured or guaranteed United States treasury or municipal bills, notes or bonds."

In the years following the automobile accident, decedent needed ongoing nursing care. She continued to reside with the Congregation and was cared for by other nuns to the extent possible, with additional professional treatment as necessary. Mary died on April 26, 2000. Decedent's 1994 Will leaves certain personal property to Joseph, and divides the residuary estate into many shares. Five (5) shares are given to Joseph Attea, two (2) shares go to William Attea, two (2) shares go to Martin Attea, and two (2) shares go to Joseph. Six (6) shares are given to the Congregation, and the remaining shares are left to various Roman Catholic charitable institutions.

Verified objections to probate were filed on August 14, 2014, by the Congregation, which allege, [among other grounds for denial of probate]:

"Acceptance of the Will to probate would violate the vow of poverty taken by Sister George Marie upon her admittance to the Sisters of St. Joseph and breach their contract, and therefore it would be inequitable to do so."

. . . the Congregation's legal submission generally frames the issue:

"Though arising in the domain of sacred vows and canon law, this case is in law a straightforward matter of equity and contract principles, and the remedy is clear. Sister George Marie Attea ('Sister George Marie') took a vow of poverty when she joined the Congregation of the Sisters of St. Joseph of Buffalo ('Sisters of St. Joseph' or the 'Congregation') in 1959. Pursuant to that vow, she pledged to leave all her worldly goods to the Congregation upon her death. Sister George Marie executed a will to that effect. That a later will was executed—after Sister George Marie suffered severe brain damage in a terrible car accident and been declared impaired and unable to care for her property—should not overcome her vows and obligations".

. . .

The estate correctly notes that the existence of a contract purporting to govern the testamentary dispositions of decedent has no effect on whether her 1994 Will is valid. In Matter of Coffed, 46 N.Y.2d 514, 519 [1979], our Court of Appeals, citing long-established authority, reiterated that:

"[c]onceptually, the contract to make a testamentary provision is separate and distinct from the will itself. While the contract might be enforceable in equity, from a technical standpoint it has no effect upon the will's status as a legal instrument. Thus, this court has previously held that a document purporting to be a will may not be denied probate merely because the testator 'bound himself to a different disposition of [his] property by contract' (Matter of Higgins, 264 N.Y. 226, 229; see, also, Matter of Davis, 182 N.Y. 468)" (emphasis added).

These principles were noted more recently by the Appellate Division, Second Department, in Matter of Murray, 84 A.D.3d 106, 116 [2011]:

"[A] will may not be denied probate on the ground that the testator previously bound himself to a different disposition of [his] property by contract' [citations omitted].

Put differently, the enforceability of the terms of a will does not affect the will's status as a legal instrument' (Matter of Coffed, 46 N.Y.2d 514, 519 [1979]), nor does it determine if the will should be admitted to probate (id.)"

Here, the Congregation's [] objection to probate of decedent's 1994 Will has nothing to do with whether the Will itself is valid. The fact that decedent may have bound herself to a different disposition of her property by way of a prior agreement—an issue which I need not and do not decide, and on which I express no opinion at this juncture—is not a basis for this Court to deny probate of the 1994 Will if it is otherwise valid. If the 1994 Will is ultimately admitted to probate, the Congregation may well seek relief as to the alleged assets of the estate premised upon its "prior contract" theory, but that is clearly a matter for another day. And, in a similar vein, there is no present basis for adjudicating the "prior contract" issue or the "constructive trust" issue, as those matters are irrelevant to any issue actually now before me, namely, the validity of the 1994 Will. As such, those other matters may not be entertained in this probate proceeding.

Accordingly, I hereby deny the Congregation's motion for summary judgment in all respects, and I dismiss the Congregation's fourth objection to probate as a matter of law.

Post-Case Follow-Up

Note that the best the Congregation can hope for in this case is to litigate the enforceability of the contract after the will has been admitted to probate. Because the Congregation is also bringing will contest claims (including lack of capacity and undue influence), it may be a good long time before it is decided whether the will is admitted to probate or not. This would also be the case if someone else were bringing a will contest or if probate of a will was delayed due to tax, creditor, or insolvency issues.

Matter of Attea: Real Life Applications

1. You represent Cody, who was married to Kaitlan and with whom he had eight children. The divorce settlement required that Kaitlan provide for Cody and their eight children in her will. Kaitlan instead remarried and had eight more children, and left a validly executed will leaving all of her property to her children from her second marriage. Advise Cody as to: (1) whether Cody can commence a will contest to prevent probate of Kaitlan's will; and (2) whether and when Cody can bring a cause of action for breach of contract to execute the will as required by the divorce agreement.

2. Again, you represent Cody in the fact pattern mentioned above, but you are now at the point in time where the divorce agreement is being finalized. Should Cody insist Kaitlan execute a will that benefits him and their children? Are there alternative methods for their support that might be superior?

---

2. Contracts to Not Revoke a Will

Although in most cases agreements concern dispositions to be made under a will, a contract may also be made not to revoke a will or never to execute a will. Such a commitment alters the ability of a potential testator to dispose of his assets as he sees fit; and agreements not to revoke or alter are subject to the same rules regarding evidence of the agreement and enforceability as contracts to make a particular disposition.

In some states, when spouses execute a **joint will,** in which one document executed by both spouses governs the disposition of assets of the couple, courts will find an implied agreement not to revoke the will without consent of the other spouse. Obtaining agreement from a deceased spouse is obviously impossible, which means that such an agreement not to revoke a will leaves a surviving spouse with little agility to adjust her estate plan to changed circumstances such as family status or tax law. It is therefore better practice to avoid the use of joint wills and have each spouse execute his or her own document, with a specific contract regarding gratuitous transfers if that is what the couple wants.

3. Nonprobate Alternatives to Will Contracts

The remedy for a party suffering damages from a breach of a contract to make a will is to commence litigation against the estate of the breaching party after the will has been admitted to probate. Not only does such a remedy require patience—or a waste of time, depending on your perspective—it may not gather the claimant significant assets, because debts of higher priority (and costs of the lawsuit) may have reduced the size of the probate estate. Moreover, because the remedy only lies against the probate estate, nonprobate transfers are immune to such claims.

Because of these risks, the well-informed attorney will generally recommend alternatives to entering into a contract to make a will. For example, a divorce agreement might require the ex-spouse to maintain a life insurance policy in a certain amount with the children or former spouse as beneficiary. Instead, a trust may be funded to make the payments that would otherwise be required under the terms of the will. These alternatives escape both the risk of an insolvent estate and the delay that occurs when a party's remedy is merely a lawsuit against the estate.

Chapter Summary

- A revocation in writing may be effective either by express revocation of part or all of a previous will or by inconsistency with it. To the extent that there are multiple testamentary documents, the terms of the latest validly executed document control and override the provisions in any earlier document.

- A revocation by physical act will be effective to revoke a will or codicil in its entirety so long as the testator has intent to revoke the document and performs the appropriate physical act, such as burning, tearing, or cancelling. In some states, partial revocation by physical act is permitted and testators may delete limited provisions of their wills and leave the rest standing. In others, physical revocation must revoke either the entire document or none of it.

- Under automatic operation of law, all or part of a testator's will may be altered if the testator divorces, marries, or has children. Divorce often results in partial revocation of a will. While marriage and birth or adoption of children does not automatically revoke any part of a will, it may create rights in these individuals to the decedent's property and thereby alter the estate plan.

- Most revocations are permanent and a revoked will is not entitled to probate. The effect of revocation, however, may be reversed if the doctrine of dependent relative revocation applies because the testator would not have revoked the will if he were not under a misunderstanding of the consequences of its revocation.

- Revoked wills are also entitled to probate if the doctrine of revival applies. A will is revived when the testator expressly reinstates the document by executing it again or if state law triggers automatic revival either when the testator revokes a revoking document or when he does so intending the previously revoked document to be revived.

- An individual may make a contract to make a will, to refrain from making a will, or not to revoke a will, but planning for property transfers through nonprobate alternatives is often more efficient. The remedy for breach of a contract to make, or not make, a will is a lawsuit against the decedent's estate.

Applying the Concepts

1. Determine whether revocation has occurred under the following facts and explain why or why not (assume the decedent intended to revoke the document).

   a. A week after Collin's death, the personal representative finds that a single page out of Collin's ten-page will is torn in half.

   b. An executor finds a sheet of paper attached to Alessandra's will where Alessandra has handwritten, "I revoke my entire will." The sheet is notarized and signed by two witnesses.

    c. Zhu-Zhu tells her sister Amy to destroy her will. Amy shreds the will, and at Zhu-Zhu's death, the pieces are found in Zhu-Zhu's recycling bin.

    d. Jae tore off the entire left margin of each page of his six-page codicil.

2. A large portion of estate work concerns which asset goes to which person. This can become more complicated when there have been numerous changes made to the will. Beneficiaries of a will are also often very invested in the asset distribution. In each of the following scenarios, who gets what?

    a. Mallie executed Will 1 in 2012. In Will 1 she left her entire estate to her mother. She then executed Will 2 in 2015, expressly revoking Will 1. Will 2 left her entire estate to her brother. In 2016, Mallie tore up Will 2 with the intent to revoke it.

    b. In Charles Michael's will it states, "I leave to my wife $200,000." Charles Michael drew a line through "wife" and wrote in "Meghan," which is the name of his sister.

    c. In Will 1, Ricky put "I leave my sports car to James." Ricky later executed Will 2, which partially revoked his earlier Will 1. Will 2 replaced "James" with "Frederick." Ricky burned the portion of Will 2 that devised the sports car.

3. Harun executed a will leaving half of his estate to his son and half to his daughter. He later learned that his daughter had perished in a car accident. He then executed a new will that stated, "because my daughter died I leave my entire estate to my son." Harun dies before discovering that his daughter survived the crash.

    a. How will Harun's estate be distributed?

    b. Assume Harun did not execute an entirely new will, and instead just crossed out the section that left his daughter half of his estate and hand wrote in the margin "I leave my entire estate to my son." Does this make a difference? How will the estate be distributed now?

4. Ana's business partner, Jackson, has just died and she is becoming increasingly apprehensive about the content of his will. Jackson had told Ana that he left her his interest in their business, but Ana never actually checked to make sure this was true. Nevertheless, Ana is determined to gain control of her partner's interest in the business. Consider UPC § 2-514.

    a. Ana and Jackson had a contract agreeing she would receive his interest in their business after his death. Will this be enough to solidify her claim to the business?

    b. Jackson had recently remarried and never updated his will to reflect the new marriage. Does this change your previous answer?

    c. The previously mentioned contract only has Ana's signature. Does this matter?

5. Assume you are a practicing estates attorney presented with each of the following scenarios. Respond to the questions and include an explanation of your response.

a. Marteki lawfully executed a will. She then made a second will that partially revoked her first will. She then revoked the entire second will. She wants to know if her first will is still valid. Consider UPC § 2-509.

b. Vivienne wants to revoke her will. She is 90 years old and while she is usually lucid, she does have occasional bouts of dementia. How would you suggest she revoke her will? What risks arise if Vivienne revokes her will?

c. Jacob recently died, leaving behind a will. Unfortunately, less than 24 hours after Jacob's death, his house burned down. The police found a few pages of the will, which shows signs of having been ripped prior to catching fire. Jacob's estate wants to determine if the will can be probated. Has revocation occurred?

d. Mia and Lee Nakayama were careful to retain separate wills. Before his death, Lee tore apart his will with the clear intent to revoke. It was only after Lee's death that Mia realized it was her will that had been torn apart. Lee's will was still locked in the safe at home. Has Lee's will been revoked? Has Mia's will been revoked?

Trusts and Estates in Practice

1. One of your clients, Jamillah, approaches you with the following factual situation. Two years ago, she divorced her husband, Christian, after 30 years of marriage. Within a year of the divorce, Christian married Indira; nine months after that marriage, Christian died. Jamillah knows that his will was never altered and still has provisions leaving her a good portion of his estate. Jamillah also informs you that she had a conversation with Christian a week before his death where he explicitly stated that he was not going to change his will because he wanted her to receive the property he initially bequeathed to her. Jamillah knows that Christian had left her their vacation home in Malibu, several cars, and at least $300,000, and also designated her as beneficiary of his life insurance policy. She also expects that the will is likely to designate her as personal representative, because she clearly has in-depth knowledge about his assets. Jamillah wants to know what the likelihood is that she will receive any of these assets. Role-play with the student next to you and take turns providing oral advice on whether it is appropriate for Jamillah to serve as personal representative and how likely it is she will receive assets from Christian's estate.

2. Based on the previous problem, assume that it is Christian's second wife, Indira, not his ex-wife Jamillah, who approaches you with the following fact scenario. Indira does not think that her deceased husband, Christian, ever updated his will following their marriage and the birth of their first child. Additionally, Indira believes Christian was never legally married to Jamillah, making his recent nuptials his first legal marriage. She informs you that his "ex-wife" Jamillah has been going on about a divorce settlement that never actually occurred. Indira wants to know if the will does not mention Indira, and if it leaves the majority of the

assets to Jamillah, then what are the chances that Indira will receive any assets? Does the fact that she is his first legal marriage partner make a difference?

3. Keiko is a longtime client of your firm and recently came in for a consultation. In Keiko's will, executed five years ago, she left her brother a third of her estate. Unfortunately, she and her brother are now no longer speaking, and she now does not want to leave her brother any of her estate. Keiko states that she already revoked the portion of her will that included her brother, and also admits that at a future date, her feelings toward her brother may change. She explains that if her sentiments change, Keiko has instructed her husband to amend her will if he thinks that she would want her brother to inherit any assets. He will justify this by claiming the removal was a mistake conditioned on her dislike of her brother. Keiko is not concerned because she also might just erase the line she drew through the provision and it will be fine. Your firm's partner has instructed you to write Keiko a three-paragraph letter explaining whether any of these revival methods work.

4. During a firm meeting, one of the partners brings up an issue involving a client, which is a nonprofit charitable university ("University"). An alumni, Judge Patel, has left a will that specifically directs that a $200,000 bequest is to go toward the start up of a law program at the University. The University recently decided not to proceed with the initiation of a law program, but instead to develop a physical therapy program. Further, the University is concerned because a sheet of paper was found in Judge Patel's house that stated: "I no longer designate the University as a beneficiary of my will." Draft a memo explaining whether or not the University will be entitled to receive any assets.

5. Changes that occur within a family dynamic play a large role in the administration of an estate. Divorce, death, estrangement, and marriage are just some of the events that can completely alter a client's estate planning needs. A common scenario often involves happily married couples with a solid family situation who want a joint will. As an estate attorney, it is important to look to the future, to help clients understand that life is often uncertain and this should play an important factor in planning one's estate. Write a paragraph dictating how you would clarify this to a client. Remember that clients often do not want to think of the possibility of an unpleasant future, so handle your explanation tactfully.

6. Laws on revocation, revival, and amendment differ from state to state. When researching and drafting memos for firms, it is important to keep in mind the areas in which states are not uniform. Write a legal research memo detailing any of the differences between your state laws and the UPC in the areas of revocation, revival, and amendment.

Wills—Construction and Interpretation

When a testator dies with a valid will, the testator's estate will be distributed according to the directions the testator provided in the document. Several types of problems can cause the need to interpret the document. Sometimes language is ambiguous or a mistake was made in drafting. Changes in the people or property named in a will may make the testator's intent uncertain. To assist a court in **construing** (interpreting) language in a will, the law has developed **rules of construction** that seek to direct an interpretation most likely to reach a testator's desired outcome. These rules of construction apply only if the testator has not provided adequate instruction. The personal representative may ask a court for guidance, or potential beneficiaries may bring competing arguments about how the will should be construed. The court will look first at the language in the will. If the testator's intent is clear, the court will follow the language in the will. If the testator's intent is not clear, however, the court may use a rule of construction to help interpret a provision in the will. The court's determination will usually affect who takes the testator's property.

In this chapter, we look at how a court interprets provisions in a will, and we examine how changes to people or property between the time of execution and the time that the testator dies affect the disposition of the property. We also examine statutes that seek to give effect to a testator's likely intent when a will has not anticipated changes that occurred after the testator executed the will.

Key Concepts

- Requirements for the use of extrinsic evidence to interpret ambiguous language in a will
- Rules of construction that assist courts in interpreting wills
- Rules that apply when a beneficiary predeceases a testator
- Rules that apply when property identified in a will is not owned by the testator at death

A. AMBIGUITY AND MISTAKE

In connection with interpreting a will, two competing policies are at play. As you already know, *giving effect to the testator's intent* is an important goal of wills law. Many legal rules support this goal. The countervailing concern, however, is the *integrity of evidence* when the most important person involved—the testator—can no longer speak. Through the rules that govern wills, the court seeks to effectuate the testator's intent by protecting the will as the best evidence of what the testator intended, although in some circumstances the court may consider other evidence.

In this section, we consider how the court approaches ambiguities and mistakes in wills, beginning with the plain meaning rule, then discussing the traditional distinction between ambiguity and mistake, and concluding with law reform efforts to permit reformation of wills affected by a mistake.

1. The Plain Meaning Rule

When a court interprets language in a will, the court begins with the plain meaning of the words. The court seeks to determine the testator's intent by using the common (plain) meaning of the words used by the testator and by looking only at the information contained within the four corners of the will itself. Even if other information exists that could aid in interpreting the will, traditionally, a court does not consider evidence that is extrinsic to the will, because only the will itself was executed with will formalities. The majority of states still follow this traditional rule.

Although terms in a will are given their ordinary meaning, a court typically uses intestacy statutes to define terms that have special meanings in the context of gratuitous transfers. For example, a reference to a "spouse," "child," or "descendant" usually has the meaning assigned to those terms by state intestacy law (assuming the document did not include its own definition). For example, if a will says "I leave the residue of my estate to my children," a court will probably interpret "children" to mean the testator's legal children and not the testator's stepchildren, even if the testator raised the stepchildren together with the testator's legal children. A careful lawyer will draft a definition in the will, explaining whether the testator intends to include the stepchildren.

> **Estate of White, 9 Cal. App. 194 (1970)**
>
> In *Estate of White*, the will made a gift of "unpublished manuscripts" to Ms. Kimball, who had assisted the testator with his written work. A completed manuscript had been accepted for publication before the testator's death, but had not yet been published. If the book contract was considered an "unpublished manuscript," Ms. Kimball would be entitled to the royalties under the contract. If the book contract did not come within the meaning of the gift to Ms. Kimball, the royalties would go to the testator's brother under another provision of the will. The court determined that the plain meaning of an "unpublished manuscript" applied. The manuscript was not yet published, and Ms. Kimball received the rights to the royalties.

2. Interpreting Ambiguous Language

A provision in a will is **ambiguous** if it is susceptible to multiple reasonable interpretations. Although a court will start with the words used in the will, if the court finds the meaning of the words ambiguous, the court can use **extrinsic evidence** to construe the meaning. For example, a will might make a gift to someone with instructions that could be considered **mandatory** or **discretionary**. If the instructions are mandatory, the testator may have meant to create a trust, but if the instructions are discretionary, the testator may have intended an outright gift. The court will need to consider extrinsic evidence to determine whether the testator intended to create a trust. See, e.g., *Estate of Kearns*, 36 Cal. 2d 531, 225 P.2d 218 (1950).

Patent Ambiguity

Sometimes, an ambiguity is obvious on the face of the will. For example, a will might say, "I give one-third of my estate to Tom and one-third of my estate to Janelle." Did the testator mean to divide the estate between Tom and Janelle, or should the remaining one-third go by intestacy? The ambiguity appears on the face of the document. Historically, courts referred to this type of ambiguity as a **patent ambiguity**.

Latent Ambiguity

In other cases, extrinsic evidence must be used to uncover the ambiguity. The will might have said, "I give one-half of my estate to Tom Honjo and one-half of my estate to Janelle Gordon." The provision does not appear ambiguous on its face, but the personal representative discovers that the testator had a good friend named Tom Honjo and a nephew named Tom Honjo. The personal representative will ask the court to construe the provision, because otherwise the personal representative could be liable for distributing half the estate to the wrong person. The court will have to consider extrinsic evidence to determine who the testator intended to receive a share of the residue. This type of ambiguity was historically called a **latent ambiguity** because extrinsic evidence was needed to expose the ambiguity.

Courts that distinguished between patent and latent ambiguities admitted extrinsic evidence in connection with latent ambiguities, because the extrinsic evidence was already necessary to show that the ambiguity existed. Those courts did *not* admit extrinsic evidence to resolve a *patent* ambiguity, but simply treated the problem as a mistake that could not be fixed by construing the provision.

Modern Approach to Ambiguity

Most courts today allow extrinsic evidence to construe any language that is considered, by the court, ambiguous. Thus, a strategy for a lawyer seeking the use of extrinsic evidence will be to argue that a provision is ambiguous. The lawyer may be using extrinsic evidence to reveal the ambiguity, but once the court determines that the provision is ambiguous, the court can then consider extrinsic evidence in reaching its decision.

3. Reforming a Will to Fix a Mistake

Reforming a will means that a court uses extrinsic evidence to fix a **mistake** in a will. In effect, the court is *adding* language or *changing* the language that the testator used. Using extrinsic evidence as a basis for fixing a mistake involves a particular risk, because the best witness to the actual intended meaning of the words—the testator—cannot contradict whatever extrinsic evidence is offered. By the time the will is given effect, the testator is dead. In the case of ambiguous language, the court gives effect to the language in the document and may use evidence outside the will to determine what the testator meant when the testator used that language. For a mistake, the language could be given effect as written, but extrinsic evidence shows that the testator intended something else. Thus, to fix a mistake, the court is adding to what appears on the face of the will. In this section, we will discuss the conditions under which extrinsic evidence can be used to reform a will to fix a mistake.

Mistake

A will can contain a mistake for a variety of reasons. A client might give the lawyer drafting the will incorrect information, a testator drafting a will without the help of a lawyer might not understand the meaning of a legal term, or a lawyer might not draft the will accurately.

Consider the following examples of mistakes in wills:

Lawyer Fails to Ask Questions to Get Sufficient Information

Pedro told his lawyer to give the residue of his estate to his cousins, telling the lawyer that the cousins were his only relatives. The lawyer drafted the will, giving the residue to Pedro's intestate heirs, thinking that doing so would result in a division among the cousins. After Pedro's death, Pedro's elderly aunt demands a share of Pedro's estate. Pedro had not mentioned her to the lawyer because he had lost contact with her, and considered his cousins to be his closest family members. He would have mentioned her to the lawyer if asked, but Pedro's focus was on his cousins, the people he wanted to benefit from his estate.

Under the plain meaning of the will, which is not ambiguous, Pedro's elderly aunt will receive a share of the estate, even though that was not Pedro's intent.

Testator Uses a Legal Term Incorrectly

Bernice handwrote her will, stating, "I direct that my good friend, Ramona, be the executor of my estate." Assuming that the document complies with execution formalities, it is Bernice's will because it appoints an executor, but it does not say who should get Bernice's property.

Extrinsic evidence might show that Bernice thought that the word "executor" meant the person who would handle the property, pay the creditors, and then keep whatever property remained. Bernice had no close relatives, and extrinsic evidence might also show that she wanted Ramona to *have* her property. If the court refuses to reform the will to give effect to Bernice's intent, the property will go to distant relatives under the intestacy statute. The plain meaning of the will is to appoint Bernice in the role of managing the estate, but because the will does not say who should get the property, the property will be distributed through intestacy.

Lawyer Was Sloppy in Preparing the Will

When Erica met with her lawyer, she explained that she wanted to change the charity that would receive the residue of her estate and make a few other changes to gifts of money to family members. Rather than preparing a codicil, the lawyer thought it best to draft a new will. The new will made the changes requested, but inadvertently left out a bequest to Erica's niece. The prior will, and the lawyer's notes, show that Erica intended to make the gift to her niece. Without reformation, however, the niece will not receive the gift.

In each of these examples, the testator's intent will be thwarted if the court applies the plain meaning rule and refuses to fix the mistake in the will.

As the examples above illustrate, the line between ambiguity and mistake is not always clear. In the example of a will disposing of only two-thirds of the testator's estate, the language might be ambiguous, or it might be a mistake that happened because the person drafting the will forgot to name the person who was supposed to take the remaining one-third. In either case, evidence outside the will might be available to guide the court in determining the actual intent of the testator. However, in most jurisdictions, only if the court deems the language *ambiguous*, rather than a mistake, can the court consider extrinsic evidence.

Note that if a mistake caused by the drafting lawyer cannot be fixed, the beneficiaries who were supposed to inherit may have a malpractice claim against the lawyer. In the example above involving the gift to Erica, the niece who failed to receive the gift to which she was entitled might be able to sue the lawyer, depending on the jurisdiction. Pedro's cousins may also be able to sue Pedro's lawyer. If a court is willing to fix the mistake, the lawyer avoids liability and the estate is distributed as the testator intended. (For a discussion of malpractice issues, see Chapter 13.)

The majority rule has been and continues to be that extrinsic evidence will not be permitted to reform a mistake in a will. However, the Restatement (Third) of Property: Wills and Other Donative Transfers § 12.1 (2003), Uniform Probate Code (UPC) § 2-805, and courts in a few states have begun to permit reformation of wills to fix mistakes. As discussed in Chapter 11, trust law has always permitted reformation to fix a mistake. Courts and legislatures are beginning to decide that it makes sense to allow courts to fix mistakes in wills, too, at least if clear and convincing evidence (the standard used in UPC § 2-805) establishes both the mistake and the testator's intent.

Estate of Duke

In *Estate of Duke*, the court is asked to reconsider the rule preventing the use of extrinsic evidence to reform a mistake in a will that was unambiguous. The probate court followed the traditional common law rule and refused to consider evidence of the testator's intent. The Supreme Court of California concluded that the "categorical bar on reformation of wills" was no longer justified. The Court adopts the rule that a will can be reformed using extrinsic evidence, if clear and convincing evidence establishes that the will contains a mistake based on the testator's intent at the time the will was made and also establishes what the testator intended.

As you read the case, consider:

1. What do you think Mr. Duke intended when he wrote his will?
2. Why do you think the Supreme Court was willing to adopt a new rule for California?
3. Do you think the Court would have approached the issue the same way if a lawyer had drafted the will?
4. What safeguards does the Supreme Court impose on any reformation actions?

Estate of Duke
61 Cal. 4th 871 (2015)

Cantil-Sakauye, C.J.

I. FACTS

In 1984, when Irving Duke was 72 years of age, he prepared a holographic will in which he left all of his property to "my beloved wife, Mrs. Beatrice Schecter Duke," who was then 58 years of age. He left to his brother, Harry Duke, "the sum of One dollar." He provided that "[s]hould my wife . . . and I die at the same moment, my estate is to be equally divided—[¶] One-half is to be donated to the City of Hope in the name and loving memory of my sister, Mrs. Rose Duke Radin. [¶] One-half is to be donated to the Jewish National Fund to plant trees in Israel in the names and loving memory of my mother and father—[¶] Bessie and Isaac Duke."

Irving further provided in his will that "I have intentionally omitted all other persons, whether heirs or otherwise, who are not specifically mentioned herein, and I hereby specifically disinherit all persons whomsoever claiming to be, or who may lawfully be determined to be my heirs at law, except as otherwise mentioned in this will. If any heir, devisee or legatee, or any other person or persons, shall either directly or indirectly, seek to invalidate this will, or any part thereof, then I hereby give and bequeath to such person or persons the sum of one dollar ($1.00) and no more, in lieu of any other share or interest in my estate."

. . .

Irving died in November 2007, leaving no spouse or children. In February 2008, a deputy public administrator for the County of Los Angeles obtained the will from Irving's safe deposit box. In March 2008, two charities, the City of Hope (COH) and the Jewish National Fund (JNF), petitioned for probate and for letters of administration. In October 2008, Robert and Seymour Radin (the Radins) filed a petition for determination of entitlement to estate distribution. The Radins are the sons of Irving's sister, Rose Duke Radin, who predeceased Irving. Their petition alleged that they are entitled to the distribution of Irving's estate as Irving's sole intestate heirs.

The Radins moved for summary judgment. They did not challenge the validity of the will. Instead, they asserted that the estate must pass to Irving's closest surviving intestate heirs, the Radins, because Irving did not predecease Beatrice, nor did Irving and Beatrice "die at the same moment," and there is no provision in the will for disposition of the estate in the event Irving survived Beatrice. In opposition to the motion, COH and JNF offered extrinsic evidence to prove that Irving intended the will to provide that in the event Beatrice was not alive to inherit Irving's estate when Irving died, the estate would be distributed to COH and JNF. The probate court concluded that the will was not ambiguous, and on that ground, it declined to consider extrinsic evidence of Irving's intent, and granted summary judgment for the Radins.

The Court of Appeal affirmed based on our opinion in Estate of Barnes, [63 Cal. 2d 580 (1965)] . . . .

We granted review to consider whether the rule applied in [Barnes] should be reconsidered. For the reasons set forth below, we hold that the categorical bar on reformation of unambiguous wills is not justified and that reformation is permissible if clear and convincing evidence establishes an error in the expression of the testator's intent and establishes the testator's actual specific intent at the time the will was drafted.

II. DISCUSSION

California law allows the admission of extrinsic evidence to establish that a will is ambiguous and to clarify ambiguities in a will. As COH and JNF acknowledge, however, California law does not currently authorize the admission of extrinsic evidence to correct a mistake in a will when the will is unambiguous. To evaluate whether there are circumstances in which this court should authorize the admission of extrinsic evidence to correct a mistake in an unambiguous will, we first consider whether the Legislature [has] acted in a manner that restricts the authority of courts to develop the common law in this area. [The Court concludes that it has not.] Second, we consider whether the common law rule categorically barring the reformation of wills is warranted, in light of the evolution of the law of probate and modern theories of interpretation of writings, and we conclude that the categorical bar on reformation is not justified. [The Court examines the use of extrinsic evidence in other probate matters and states that any concerns about the reliability of evidence for a will reformation proceeding can be addressed by requiring clear and convincing evidence.] Third, we consider principles of *stare decisis*, and conclude that a change in the law is warranted to allow the reformation of an unambiguous will when clear and convincing evidence establishes that the will contains a mistake in the expression of the testator's intent at the time the will was executed and also establishes the testator's actual and specific intent at the time the will was executed. Finally, we conclude that the remedy of reformation is potentially available with respect to the theory of mistake articulated by COH and JNF in this case. Therefore, we will direct the case to be remanded for the probate court's consideration of whether clear and convincing evidence establishes that the testator intended, at the time he drafted his will, to provide in his will that his estate was to pass to COH and JNF in the event his wife was not alive at the time the testator died.

. . .

D. The Charities Have Articulated a Valid Theory that Will Support Reformation if Established by Clear and Convincing Evidence

COH and JNF contend that Irving actually intended at the time he wrote his will to provide that his estate would pass to COH and JNF in the event Beatrice was not alive to inherit his estate when he died, but that his intent was inartfully expressed in his will and thus there is a mistake in the will that should be reformed to reflect his intent when the will was drafted. Their contention, if proved by clear and convincing evidence, would support reformation of the will to reflect Irving's actual intent.

. . .

III. CONCLUSION

We hold that an unambiguous will may be reformed to conform to the testator's intent if clear and convincing evidence establishes that the will contains a mistake in the testator's expression of intent at the time the will was drafted, and also establishes the testator's actual specific intent at the time the will was drafted. We reverse the judgment of the Court of Appeal and remand the matter to the Court of Appeal with directions to remand the case to the trial court for its consideration of extrinsic evidence as authorized by our opinion.

Post-Case Follow-Up

In *Estate of Duke*, the Supreme Court abandoned precedent and adopted a new rule applicable to unambiguous wills in California. Under the case, a will that contains a mistake can be reformed to give effect to the intent of the testator. The party proposing reformation must be able to establish, by clear and convincing evidence, two things: (1) that the will contains a mistake when the language is compared with the testator's intent at the time the will was drafted, and (2) what the testator's actual specific intent was when the will was drafted. In California, a court can use extrinsic evidence to interpret ambiguous language in a will and can also use extrinsic evidence to reform a will to carry out the testator's intent, if the requirements set forth in *Estate of Duke* are met.

Estate of Duke: Real Life Applications

1. If you were the draftsperson for Irving Duke's will, what language would you have drafted to ensure that the charities received their property if Beatrice predeceased Irving?

2. Tonya's will gives the residue of her estate to three charities. She decides to add some specific bequests to family members and to add a fourth charity as a residuary beneficiary, so she asks her lawyer to draft a new will for her. When the lawyer drafts the will, the new specific bequests are added but the new charity is left out. When Tonya dies, the fourth charity, which knew about the bequest from a conversation between Tonya and the president of the charity, comes to you to ask what it can do. Advise the charity. What kinds of evidence would support an argument that the will should be reformed?

B. WHAT DOES "SURVIVE" MEAN?

A beneficiary under a will must **survive** the testator to take a bequest. The same **requirement of survival** applies to an heir of a decedent who dies intestate. The meaning of "survive" for purposes of wills and intestacy depends on state law, which we examine in this section. In addition, a will can define what "survive" means *for the purposes of that document*. For example, a will might say, "I give my jewelry to my sister, Elizabeth, if she is living on the 30th day after the day of my death." If Elizabeth dies a week after the testator, she has not met the requirement of survival provided in the will.

For will substitutes and trusts, survival is not required unless the document says so. Many of these other instruments do require a beneficiary to survive in order to take, but not all do. If the instrument does not require that a beneficiary survive, assets passing under the instrument to a predeceasing beneficiary are distributed to the beneficiary's estate. As with wills, a will substitute or trust instrument can include a definition of survival. If the document requires survival but does not include a definition of survive, the meaning of survive in the document will depend on state law, as explained here in connection with wills and intestacy.

1. Survival When Will Is Silent on Meaning of "Survive"

If a document does not require a longer (or shorter) period, survive means to survive under state law. States that have adopted a statute like UPC § 2-702 provide that a beneficiary will "survive" someone only if the beneficiary lives at least 120 hours (five days) after the person's death. The Uniform Law Commission developed **the 120-hour rule** to address problems that occur when the testator and beneficiary die in close succession.

EXHIBIT 5.1   **UPC § 2-702. Requirement of Survival by 120 Hours**

(a) [Requirement of Survival by 120 Hours Under Probate Code.] For the purposes of this Code, except as provided in subsection (d), an individual who is not established by clear and convincing evidence to have survived an event, including the death of another individual, by 120 hours is deemed to have predeceased the event.

(b) [Requirement of Survival by 120 Hours Under Governing Instrument.] Except as provided in subsection (d), for purposes of a provision of a governing instrument that relates to an individual surviving an event, including the death of another individual, an individual who is not established by clear and convincing evidence to have survived the event by 120 hours is deemed to have predeceased the event.

(c) [Co-owners with Right of Survivorship; Requirement of Survival by 120 Hours.] Except as provided in subsection (d) if it (i) is not established by clear and convincing evidence that one of two co-owners with right of survivorship survived the other co-owner by 120 hours, one-half of that property passes as if one had survived by 120 hours and one-half as if the other had survived by 120 hours and (ii) there are more than two co-owners and it is not established by clear and convincing evidence that at least one of them survived the others by 120 hours, the property passes in the proportion that one bears to the whole number of co-owners.

(d) [Exceptions.] Survival by 120 hours is not required if:

   (1) the governing instrument contains language dealing explicitly with simultaneous deaths or deaths in a common disaster and that language is operable under the facts of the case; [or]

   (2) the governing instrument expressly indicates that an individual is not required to survive an event, including the death of another individual, by any specified period or expressly requires the individual to survive the event by a specified period; but survival of the event or the specified period must be established by clear and convincing evidence[.]

The deaths of testator and beneficiary may be simultaneous, with no evidence that one person died before the other, or one person may survive by a few minutes. To avoid the need to determine the time of death in most cases where that determination would be difficult, and also to avoid transferring property through a survivor's estate if two people die within a few days of each other, UPC § 2-702 adopts 120 hours as a default rule for survival.

If an inheritance depends on which person died first, family members may present medical evidence about a person's last moments to try to establish that the person survived, even for a few minutes. The five-day survival period does not avoid all contentious determinations of when death occurred, but it makes them less likely when a property owner and beneficiary die in a common accident. Issues such as the timing of the removal of life support remain; a beneficiary might be kept on life support for 120 hours so that the beneficiary would be deemed to have survived the testator.

2. Time of Death

Usually a death certificate indicating the time of death will provide clear evidence of the date and time of death. However, when someone is kept alive through medical intervention or has disappeared, rules of construction help determine when death occurred.

The UPC provides **rules of construction** for a determination of death. States that have adopted the **Uniform Determination of Death Act** may refer to their statutes, and states that have not adopted the Act can use the language provided in UPC § 1-107(1).

> ### *Janus v. Tarasewicz*, 482 N.E.2d 418 (Ill. App. 1985)
>
> In a case that spurred the development of the 120-hour rule, two families fought over which newlywed spouse died first after they each took Tylenol tainted with cyanide. The spouses collapsed at nearly the same time, and the case involved reports from the paramedics who arrived at the house and medical personnel at the hospital. The litigation determined who would receive the proceeds of an insurance policy on the husband's life, which named his wife as the beneficiary. If the wife survived, her estate received the proceeds which then went to her family. If the husband survived, the proceeds went through his estate to his family. After years of what must have been painful litigation, the wife's family won.

The UPC uses five years as the period after which a person can be presumed to be dead. State law with respect to that period varies, but all states have some process for declaring a person dead after a long disappearance.

EXHIBIT 5.2 **UPC § 1-107. Evidence of Death or Status**

1. Death occurs when an individual [is determined to be dead under the Uniform Determination of Death Act] [has sustained either (i) irreversible cessation of circulatory and respiratory functions or (ii) irreversible cessation of all functions of the entire brain, including the brain stem. A determination of death must be made in accordance with accepted medical standards].
2. A certified or authenticated copy of a death certificate purporting to be issued by an official or agency of the place where the death purportedly occurred is prima facie evidence of the fact, place, date, and time of death and the identity of the decedent. . . .
3. An individual whose death is not established under the preceding paragraphs who is absent for a continuous period of 5 years, during which [the individual] has not been heard from, and whose absence is not satisfactorily explained after diligent search or inquiry, is presumed to be dead. [The] death is presumed to have occurred at the end of the period unless there is sufficient evidence for determining that death occurred earlier.

C. BENEFICIARIES WHO FAIL TO SURVIVE

Changes can happen between the time the testator executes a will and the time the testator dies. Some changes involve the people included in the will, and some changes involve property distributed through the will. A careful lawyer will draft to anticipate as many changes as possible, although no will can anticipate every change that might occur. This section examines the rules that apply when a beneficiary named in a will predeceases the testator. Section D then covers the issues involving changes in property.

1. Lapse

As just discussed, a person named as a beneficiary in a will must survive the testator in order to take under the will. If the beneficiary does not survive, as defined in the document or by law, the gift **lapses**. A lapsed gift will be distributed as the will provides, and if the will does not indicate what happens when a particular gift lapses, the common law or statutes provide default rules.

Under the common law, if a specific, demonstrative, or general devise lapses, the gift is distributed with the residue. Traditionally, if a residuary beneficiary predeceased the testator, the share was distributed through intestacy. For example, if Ellyn's will gives the residue of her estate to Angela, Brooke, and Carina, and Carina predeceases Ellyn, one-third of the residue would go to Ellyn's intestate heirs. If Angela and Brooke are Ellyn's intestate heirs, that result seems sensible. If, however, Ellyn wants to give her estate to three close friends because she is estranged from her relatives, giving those relatives one-third of the estate cuts against Ellyn's wishes.

When a testator provides for residuary takers, the testator has indicated who should take all the remaining property in the estate, so giving a lapsed residuary share to the other residuary takers would seem to carry out the likely intent of most testators. For that reason, some courts have applied the "residue of the residue" rule so that a lapsed residuary devise will be distributed to the remaining residuary beneficiaries. UPC § 2-604 takes that approach. Of course, if all residuary beneficiaries predecease the testator, the residue must be distributed through intestacy.

EXHIBIT 5.3 **UPC § 2-604. Failure of Testamentary Provision**

(a) Except as provided in Section 2-603, a devise, other than a residuary devise, that fails for any reason becomes a part of the residue.

(b) Except as provided in Section 2-603, if the residue is devised to two or more persons, the share of a residuary devisee that fails for any reason passes to the other residuary devisee, or to other residuary devisees in proportion to the interest of each in the remaining part of the residue.

2. Anti-Lapse Statutes

A will can—and should—provide instructions in case a beneficiary predeceases the testator. The direction may be simply that the gift lapses: "I give my mother's engagement ring to Anne, but if Anne fails to survive me, this gift shall lapse and be distributed with the residue." Alternatively, the will could provide for a gift to someone else: "if Anne fails to survive me, I give my mother's engagement ring to Beatrice, if she survives me, and if Beatrice fails to survive me, to Christine, and if Christine fails to survive me . . . ."

Often, wills do not indicate what should happen when a gift lapses. For example, Jamie might want her estate to go to her two children, Sander and Alex. She does not imagine that one of the children could die before she does. A lawyer should raise the issue, but if the lawyer forgets to do so or if Jamie is drafting her own will, the will may fail to address the possibility that a child might predecease the testator. Then if Sander predeceases Jamie, the residue-of-the-residue rule would give Sander's share of the residue to Alex. If Sander left children, Jamie would probably want those children—Jamie's grandchildren—to inherit Sander's share. To address this presumed intent of most testators, legislatures and the Uniform Law Commission have developed statutes called "anti-lapse statutes."

An anti-lapse statute applies only if the will does not provide for an alternative taker for the gift or indicate the testator's intent that the anti-lapse statute not apply. As UPC § 2-601 says, rules of construction like the anti-lapse statute apply "[i]n the absence of a finding of contrary intention."

State anti-lapse statutes vary, but the statutes usually limit application to a beneficiary who is related to the testator in the manner required by the statute. The statutes create a substitute gift to the descendants of the beneficiary. The UPC provides an example of an anti-lapse statute.

EXHIBIT 5.4 **UPC § 2-603. Antilapse; Deceased Devisee; Class Gifts**

(b) [Substitute Gift.] If a devisee fails to survive the testator and is a grandparent, a descendant of a grandparent, or a stepchild of either the testator or the donor of a power of appointment exercised by the testator's will, the following apply:

> **(1)** . . . if the devise is not in the form of a class gift and the deceased devisee leaves surviving descendants, a substitute gift is created in the devisee's surviving descendants. They take by representation the property to which the devisee would have been entitled had the devisee survived the testator.
>
> **(2)** . . . if the devise is in the form of a class gift, other than a devise to "issue," "descendants," "heirs of the body," "heirs," "next to kin," "relatives," or "family," or a class described by language of similar import, a substitute gift is created in the surviving descendants of any deceased devisee. The property to which the devisees would have been entitled had all of them survived the testator passes to the surviving devisees and the surviving descendants of the deceased devisees. Each surviving devisee takes the share to which he [or she] would have been entitled had the deceased devisees survived the testator. Each deceased devisee's surviving descendants who are substituted for the deceased devisee take by representation the share to which the deceased devisee would have been entitled had the deceased devisee survived the testator. For the purposes of this paragraph, "deceased devisee" means a class member who failed to survive the testator and left one or more surviving descendants.
>
> **(3)** For the purposes of Section 2-601, words of survivorship, such as in a devise to an individual "if he survives me," or in a devise "to my surviving children," are not, in the absence of additional evidence, a sufficient indication of an intent contrary to the application of this section.

No Contrary Intent

A well-drafted will provides for what happens if a beneficiary predeceases the testator. If Shelley's will says, "I give $1,000 to my niece, Renee, and if Renee does not survive me, I give $1,000 to Toni," and then Renee predeceases Shelley, Toni gets $1,000. The will failed to say what happens if Toni also predeceases Shelley so, if both Renee and Toni fail to survive Shelley, the anti-lapse statute may apply.

Rather than make a substitute gift in her will, Shelley may want the money to be distributed with the residue if Renee does not survive her. The will might say, "I give $1,000 to my niece, Renee, and if Renee does not survive me this gift shall lapse." Shelley's will indicates her intent that the anti-lapse statute should not apply. In both of these examples, her contrary intent is clear.

But what if Shelley's will had said, "I give $1,000 to my niece, Renee, if she survives me," and Renee did not survive? Does the requirement of survival mean that Shelley does not want the anti-lapse statute to apply? The answer depends on state law. UPC § 2-603(b)(3) says that a requirement of survival, without more, is not sufficient to serve as an indication of contrary intent.

The comment to this UPC section, regarding the question of whether a survival requirement indicates contrary intent, has been litigated frequently. A concern of courts has been that the language may simply be boilerplate and not a considered decision of the testator.

The purpose of UPC § 2-603(b)(3) is to remind lawyers to draft more specific information about the testator's intent. The UPC position on words of survival may still be a minority rule, especially for older documents that predate the promulgation of this UPC provision, but a drafting lawyer should be careful to address lapse directly.

Related to the Testator

Most, but not all, anti-lapse statutes apply only to beneficiaries related to the testator as required in the statute. A typical statute applies to anyone who would be an intestate heir of the testator under the state's intestacy statutes. The UPC adds the testator's stepchildren to testator's grandparents and descendants of the grandparents.

Although the requirement that the beneficiary be related to the testator covers many beneficiaries, anti-lapse statutes do not apply to all gifts under a will. For example, if Shelley's will said, "I give $1,000 to my friend, Renee," the anti-lapse statute will not apply.

Anti-lapse statutes also do not typically apply to the spouse of the testator. If Shelly's will gives the residue of her estate to her spouse, Renee, the UPC's anti-lapse statute would not apply.

If Shelley and Renee were raising two children who were biologically Renee's children, but who were not legally Shelley's children, a gift to the children if Renee predeceased Shelley should be drafted into the will. The anti-lapse statute will not apply to Shelley's will.

Descendants

The UPC's anti-lapse statute creates a substitute gift for the descendants of the deceased beneficiary. If the beneficiary has no descendants, the anti-lapse statute will not apply and the gift to the beneficiary will be distributed with the residue or if the beneficiary was the sole residuary taker, by intestacy. The anti-lapse statute will not give the beneficiary's devise to the beneficiary's heirs (other than descendants) or to devisees under the beneficiary's will.

For example, if Shelly's will says, "I give $1,000 to my niece, Renee," and Renee predeceases Shelley, $1,000 will be distributed to Renee's descendants who survive Shelley. If Renee had one child, Renee's child will receive $1,000. If Renee had several children, one of whom predeceased the testator, and several grandchildren, the gift will be given to her surviving descendants, divided under the rules of intestacy.

3. Class Gifts

A class gift is one made to a group of people who all share some common relationship with the testator. Often, though not always, the gift to a class is a gift of a piece of property the class should share.

The common law treatment of class gifts assumes that the testator would want the surviving members of the class to have the gift, rather than having a class member's share lapse and become part of the residue. Thus, if a devise to a group of people is determined to be a class gift, a lapse of a devise to a member of a class is divided among the surviving members of the class.

For example, Lenora executes a will that leaves a $15,000 devise to "my nieces, Ariana, Bailey, and Caroline." Ariana died in 2014, leaving no descendants. When Leila died in 2018, Bailey and Caroline survived her. Bailey and Caroline will each receive $7,500.

The UPC's anti-lapse statute applies to class gifts and overrides the class gift rules. Some class gifts, like gifts to "descendants" or "issue," are already in the form of multi-generational gifts.

For example, if Jamie's will gives the residue of her estate to her descendants, and one of her two children predeceases her, that child's descendants will take the share that their parent would have taken. The anti-lapse statute is not needed for those types of class gifts.

Other class gifts do not include a substitute gift to the next generation, so the standard anti-lapse analysis will apply: Is the predeceased member of the class related to the testator? If so, did the predeceased class member leave descendants? Is the will silent on what should happen if a class member does not survive the testator?

If a lapse of a class gift complies with the anti-lapse requirements, the statute will create a substitute gift. In the example of Lenora's gift to her nieces, the anti-lapse statute would apply. If Ariana had descendants who survived Lenora, her share would go to her descendants, if any. If the gift had been to a class consisting of Lenora's college roommates, Ariana, Bailey, and Caroline, then the lapsed gift to Ariana would not be covered by the anti-lapse statute because Ariana was not related to Lenora.

Case Preview	***Estate of Tolman v. Jennings***

This case concerns whether language in the will of Nellie G. Tolman indicated Nellie's intent that the anti-lapse statute not apply. At issue was interpretation of language disinheriting any heirs of Nellie not named in the will. If the anti-lapse statute applied, Betty Jo's son would take the residue intended for Betty Jo. If the anti-lapse statute did not apply, the residue would pass by intestacy to all of Nellie's grandchildren.

As you read the case, consider:

1. Why was paragraph 7 included in the will?
2. How are the parties related to Nellie and to each other?
3. The court determines that paragraph 7 did not express Nellie's intent that the anti-lapse statute not apply. Does that interpretation seem correct? What do you think Nellie wanted?

Estate of Tolman v. Jennings
104 Cal. Rptr. 3d 924 (Ct. App. 2010)

The opinion of the court was delivered by Judge LICHTMAN.

Deborah C. Tomlinson, granddaughter of decedent Nellie G. Tolman, appeals from the order denying her petition to determine persons entitled to distribution from Tolman's estate. Applying Probate Code section 21110, an anti-lapse provision, the trial court concluded that Tolman's grandson Michael Jennings (respondent) was among those entitled to inherit the residue of the estate, as issue of his mother Betty Jo Miller, the predeceased residual beneficiary. The court rejected appellant's contention that the will reflected Tolman's controlling intent that Jennings and other issue of Miller not take from the estate. We affirm the order.

FACTS

The record reflects that Tolman was married to Lloyd E. Tolman, who predeceased her, and with whom she had two children, Lloyd C. Tolman and Betty Joe Miller. Appellant and Laurie Onan are the surviving children of Lloyd C. Tolman, and thus granddaughters of the decedent. Respondent is the surviving son of Miller, and grandson of the deceased. Additionally, Tolman was survived by three great-grandchildren, who are children of respondent's deceased sisters and grandchildren of Miller (hereafter Miller's grandchildren).

Tolman's 1981 will bequeathed all of her property to her husband. It provided, however, that if he predeceased her, her granddaughters, appellant and Onan, each would receive $10,000, and the remainder of the estate would go to Tolman's daughter, Miller. The bequests to appellant and Onan each provided that if the designee predeceased Tolman, "this gift shall lapse." No such proviso, or any alternative disposition, appeared in the residual bequest to Miller.

Paragraph seven of the will stated: "Except as otherwise specifically provided for herein, I have intentionally omitted to provide herein for any of my heirs who are living at the time of my demise, and to any person who shall successfully claim to be an heir of mine, other than those specifically named herein, I hereby bequeath the sum of ONE DOLLAR ($1.00)."

As stated, Miller died before Tolman, requiring resolution of the proper disposition of Miller's residual bequest. The named executor being deceased, appellant and respondent each filed petitions for probate of the will and for letters of administration with the will annexed. Appellant's petition estimated the value of the estate's property at slightly under $1 million.

Shortly after filing the petition for probate, appellant filed under section 11700 a petition to determine persons entitled to distribution. The petition alleged that neither Jennings nor Miller's grandchildren were entitled to inherit under the will, which did not provide for them. However, they were asserting entitlement under section 21110, subdivision (a). That subdivision provides that if a transferee by will fails to survive the transferor, "the issue of the deceased transferee take in the transferee's place." Subdivision (b) of section 21110 qualifies subdivision (a) by providing: "The issue of a deceased transferee do not take in the transferee's place if the instrument expresses a contrary intention or a substitute disposition. . . ." Appellant alleged that the will's paragraph seven expressed Tolman's intention that an heir whom she had not named in the will should not inherit.

In its statement of decision, the trial court ruled in favor of respondent, and Miller's grandchildren. The court first observed that Tolman's gift of the residue to Miller, unlike her gifts to appellant and Onan, did not provide for lapse should Miller not survive Tolman. This omission did not "express an intention that the issue of Betty Jo Miller not succeed to her share."

It had been stipulated, the court noted, that Miller's descendants were "heirs." Appellant accordingly asserted that paragraph seven of the will barred them from taking pursuant to it, while the descendants argued that their right to take was not as heirs, but was solely based on their "being the lineal descendants of a deceased devisee, Betty Jo Miller." The court stated the issue as being whether paragraph seven was sufficient, under section 21110, subdivision (b), to preclude Miller's descendants from taking as lineal descendants.

The trial court concluded that paragraph seven did not have that effect. . . . The court ruled that paragraph seven "did not contain specific language that would be sufficient to bar a lineal descendant's right to inherit as the issue of a named deceased beneficiary," and therefore respondent and Miller's grandchildren should take under section 21110. The order denying appellant's petition followed.

DISCUSSION

. . .

In paragraph seven of her will, Tolman expressed her intent not to provide for any of her unmentioned heirs, and limited to $1.00 the recovery of any person outside the will who successfully claimed to be her heir. The trial court ruled that this provision did not manifest an intention to preclude Miller's issue from succeeding to the residue of the estate under section 21110, subdivision (a). The court's ruling is strongly supported by the facts and reasoning of the two decisions on which it principally relied.

In *Larrabee v. Tracy*, 134 P.2d 265 (Cal. 1943), the . . . executor contended that the plaintiff had been disinherited, under a clause in the will that disinherited all persons " 'claiming to be or who may be lawfully determined to be my heirs at law, except as otherwise mentioned in this will.' The Supreme Court held that plaintiff had been entitled to her mother's bequest under former section 92."

. . .

Equally if not more instructive is *Pfadenhauer*, 324 P.2d 693 (Cal. Ct. App. 1958). The will there contained a paragraph in which the testatrix declared her purposeful intent not to provide for any person not mentioned in the will, " 'whether claiming to be an heir of mine or not,' " and bequeathed only $1.00 to anyone who contested or objected to the will's provisions. The provision concluded, "I specifically have in mind all of my relatives not herein specifically mentioned, and it is my will and wish that none of my said relatives other than those specifically herein mentioned receive anything from my estate." The will left shares of the residue to two of the testatrix's daughters, and also to the two children of one of those daughters (grandchildren).

They sought a determination that they were entitled to the entire residue, because the other predeceased daughter's numerous descendants were excluded under the paragraph just quoted.

[The court held that the anti-lapse statute applied.]

Both cases support the contention that exclusion of unmentioned heirs or relatives from the will's dispositions, or an intent to disinherit those who contest those dispositions, does not sufficiently express or manifest an intent to arrest the operation of the anti-lapse law following a legatee's death. These decisions provide a guide for measuring the intent of testators whose wills have been drafted with presumptive knowledge of the cases and their interpretations. From both perspectives, the trial court here reached a sound decision.

DISPOSITION

The order under review is affirmed. Respondent shall recover costs.

Post-Case Follow-Up

The court concluded that the anti-lapse statute should apply, despite the inclusion of general disinheritance language in the will. The case points to the importance of stating clearly for each gift what should happen if a beneficiary predeceases the testator. A clear explanation in the will would have avoided the costs and hard feelings of litigation.

Estate of Tolman: Real Life Applications

1. How would you draft the gift to Betty Jo Miller to indicate that the anti-lapse statute should not apply? How would you draft the gift to indicate that it should apply?

2. Arnold comes to you for estate planning. He wants to make gifts to his two brothers, $40,000 to his brother Baker and $60,000 to his brother Cedric. The residue of the estate should be used to create a trust that will provide income to Arnold's surviving spouse for life, with the remainder going to Arnold's descendants when the surviving spouse dies. If either Baker or Cedric predeceases Arnold, that sibling's share should go to the other sibling. If both siblings predecease Arnold, the devises should be distributed with the residue. How would you draft the will provisions to accomplish Arnold's wishes?

D. CHANGES IN PROPERTY

Changes that occur after a testator executes a will may affect the property the testator owned at the time the will was made. The testator may no longer own property identified in the will or the property may have changed. The rules in this section explain whether a beneficiary will receive a gift when the property has changed or the testator no longer owns the property and also explain which beneficiaries lose their bequests when the property in the estate has decreased in value.

1. Abatement

Before the personal representative makes distributions to beneficiaries, the testator's debts, the expenses of administering the estate, and any taxes owed by the testator or the estate must be paid. Sometimes after payment of all the debts and expenses not all of the devises made in the will can be made. The doctrine of **abatement** provides the rules for determining which devises are reduced or eliminated to pay debts or bequests of higher priority.

Although a testator can specify the order of abatement by including a provision on abatement in the will, provisions on abatement are not common. Instead, the common law and statutes like UPC § 3-902 provide the court with an order of abatement.

Bequests abate by category—residuary, general, and specific. The residuary devises abate first, because the residue is the property left over after the payment of debts and expenses and specific and general devises. General devises abate next, and specific devises abate last. Bequests in the same category abate on a pro rata basis, based on the size of each bequest relative to the total amount of bequests in that category. Sometimes, courts will alter the order of abatement if the ordinary abatement priority clearly conflicts with the testator's intent. UPC § 3-902(b).

Another way to think about abatement is to think about the order in which gifts are made: specific, then general, then the residue.

For example, Alan's will provides: "my mother's pearl necklace to Samantha, my car to Trevor, $10,000 to Ursula, $20,000 to State University, and the residue to Valentina." When he executed his will, Alan's estate was worth about $500,000, and he intended to leave most of it to his daughter, Valentina. Unfortunately, significant medical expenses in the last years of his life depleted his estate. After the payment of debts and expenses, Alan's estate consists of the pearl necklace, the car, and $40,000. Samantha will get the necklace, Trevor the car, Ursula $10,000, State University $20,000 and Valentina will get only $10,000.

If at Alan's death his remaining estate held only the necklace and $12,000, Samantha will get the necklace and the remaining $12,000 will be divided between the two general devisees on a pro rata basis. The total devised in the will was $30,000, so Ursula's share of $10,000 represents one-third of the total and State University's share represents two-thirds. Ursula will get $4,000 (one-third of $12,000) and State University will get $8,000. Valentina will get nothing. The residuary devise abates first, even though Valentina was Alan's highest priority.

UPC § 2-903(b) allows a court to alter the order of abatement if "the testamentary plan or the express or implied purpose of the devise would be defeated by the order of abatement" in the statute. In a state that has adopted this provision, a court might hold that the order of abatement should be altered because applying it frustrates the intent of the testator, and would provide at least some distribution to Valentina.

2. Ademption

A will may include specific devises of property that the testator owns at the time the will is executed. However, years later, when the testator dies, the testator may no longer own that particular property. The testator may have sold the property or exchanged it for something similar, or the property might have been destroyed or stolen. When property is no longer in the estate at the testator's death, it is said to have **adeemed**, or to have been subject to **ademption**. Because the testator's interest in the property has been extinguished, ademption is sometimes referred to as **ademption by extinction**.

The beneficiary named to receive adeemed property can no longer receive it because the property is no longer there. The testator's will can provide for changes in any property specifically devised, but if the will does not indicate whether the beneficiary should receive a substitute gift, then the doctrine of ademption, combined with **non-ademption statutes**, provide rules of construction. The doctrine of ademption applies only to specific devises.

Identity Theory

To determine whether ademption applies, courts often use an **identity theory**. If the will makes a gift of specific property and the testator does not own the property at death, the gift is adeemed and the beneficiary receives nothing.

Change in Form, Not Substance

Some courts have been willing to examine whether the property has changed in form but not substance. Using this analysis, the property is still there, it is just somewhat different in form. The policy behind the change-in-form rule is that the testator would not have intended that the gift be adeemed.

For example, Eugene's will states, "I give my 2008 Volvo to Phoebe." When Eugene dies, he no longer owns the 2008 Volvo, because he had traded it in and

> ### Acts of Independent Significance
>
> In Chapter 3 we discussed the use of a term in a will that has significance beyond the will, significance that is independent from the use of the term in the will. A testator can use a word with independent significance to avoid some problems with ademption. For example, rather than saying in the will, "I give Bobbie Sue my 2012 Subaru Outback," the will could say, "I give Bobbie Sue the car I own at my death." Then, if the testator trades the Subaru in for another car, Bobbie Sue will get the new car. Of course, if the reason for the gift to Bobbie Sue was that she liked and wanted the specific car, then the will provision could indicate that the devise would adeem if the testator did not own the car at death.

bought a 2016 Volvo. Under the identity theory, Phoebe would get nothing, but if the court is willing to consider the new car a change in form and not substance, Phoebe would get the 2016 Volvo. Sometimes application of the change-in-form approach is fairly easy, but it can be more difficult. If when Eugene dies his only car is a Maserati, one could argue that it is still a car and therefore just a change in form, or one could argue that the difference in value makes the change one of substance. If Eugene sells the Volvo and buys a pickup truck, will Phoebe be entitled to the truck under the change-in-form theory?

Intent Theory in Non-Ademption Statutes

The UPC has adopted an **intent theory** in its non-ademption provision. The goal is to give effect to the testator's intent under several common scenarios. The non-ademption statute does not attempt to determine a testator's actual intent, but instead creates a substitute gift based on the presumed intent of testators in the situations covered by the statute.

UPC § 2-606 provides guidance to courts faced with various scenarios:

- Subsections (a)(1)-(4) cover situations where the specifically devised property was disposed of and a balance is still owed to the testator when the testator dies. These subsections give the beneficiary the right to collect the balance due in lieu of the property. The beneficiary is not entitled to any amounts already collected by the testator.
- Subsection (a)(5) applies where the testator has replaced the specifically devised property with property that represents a change in form.
  - The comment to this provision notes that "subsection (a)(5) does not import a tracing principle into the question of ademption, but rather should be seen as a sensible 'mere change in form' principle."
- Finally, subsection (a)(6) applies when the testator manifested a plan of distribution at the time of execution of the will and ademption would frustrate that plan.
  - Subsection (a)(6) will create a substitute general devise in an amount equal to the value of the property when it was disposed of, but only if evidence shows that the testator would not have intended for the beneficiary to receive nothing. This provision should be applied narrowly.

EXHIBIT 5.5   **UPC § 2-606. Nonademption of Specific Devises; Unpaid Proceeds of Sale, Condemnation, or Insurance; Sale by Conservator or Agent**

(a) A specific devisee has a right to specifically devised property in the testator's estate at the testator's death and to:

(1) any balance of the purchase price, together with any security agreement, owed by a purchaser at the testator's death by reason of sale of the property;

(2) any amount of a condemnation award for the taking of the property unpaid at death;

(3) any proceeds unpaid at death on fire or casualty insurance on or other recovery for injury to the property;

(4) any property owned by the testator at death and acquired as a result of foreclosure, or obtained in lieu of foreclosure, of the security interest for a specifically devised obligation;

(5) any real property or tangible personal property owned by the testator at death which the testator acquired as a replacement for specifically devised real property or tangible personal property; and

(6) if not covered by paragraphs (1) through (5), a pecuniary devise equal to the value as of its date of disposition of other specifically devised property disposed of during the testator's lifetime but only to the extent it is established that ademption would be inconsistent with the testator's manifested plan of distribution or that at the time the will was made, the date of disposition or otherwise, the testator did not intend ademption of the devise.

(b) If specifically devised property is sold or mortgaged by a conservator or by an agent acting within the authority of a durable power of attorney for an incapacitated principal or a condemnation award, insurance proceeds, or recovery for injury to the property is paid to a conservator or to an agent acting within the authority of a durable power of attorney for an incapacitated principal the specific devisee has the right to a general pecuniary devise equal to the net sale price, the amount of the unpaid loan, the condemnation award, the insurance proceeds, or the recovery.

Sometimes, property is sold by a conservator for a testator or by an agent acting under a power of attorney for an incapacitated testator. The person selling the property may inadvertently (or perhaps on purpose) change the testator's plan for distribution of property. If the testator no longer has capacity, the testator may not know about or consent to the sale and may not be able to execute a codicil to adjust the will. Subsection § 2-606(b) provides for a substitute gift to the beneficiary whose devise is adeemed when the testator is incapacitated.

For example, Cornelia's will gives her house to her adult daughter, her stock account to her adult son, and the residue of her estate to her descendants (currently her two children). The specific devises of the house and the stock have approximately the same value. After Cornelia develops dementia, her son is appointed as her conservator (a person who will handle her financial matters—we will discuss conservators in Chapter 7). He moves her to a memory care facility and sells her house. Without a statute like § 2-606(b), the son would receive the stock account and half the residue and the daughter would receive only half the residue. Under § 2-606(b) the daughter will receive an amount equal to the net sales price of the house as a substitute gift for the devise of the house.

Satisfaction

Sometimes an item of specifically identified property may no longer be in the estate because the testator gave the property to the beneficiary named in the will. This situation might be referred to as **ademption by satisfaction**. The property is adeemed, but the beneficiary has the property, so no substitute gift is necessary. However, if the will makes a general devise to a beneficiary, a court probating the will may be faced with another interpretative question—whether a lifetime transfer from the testator to a beneficiary was meant to be in lieu of a bequest in the will or whether it was meant to be in addition to the bequest. This situation presents the issue of **satisfaction**.

Historically, some courts allowed parol evidence (oral testimony) of the testator's intent that the lifetime transfer be in satisfaction of the bequest under the will. The more modern rule is to require a writing of some sort, either by the testator or by the beneficiary to evidence the testator's intent. UPC § 2-609 takes this approach, requiring a statement in the will directing the deduction of a lifetime gift, a contemporaneous writing by the testator, or a written acknowledgment by the beneficiary that the gift is in satisfaction of the devise.

Because written records regarding the treatment of a lifetime gift to someone also named in a will are uncommon, the requirement of a writing means that most gratuitous transfers during life will be treated as gifts (or possibly loans) and will not reduce the amount a beneficiary receives under a will. The requirement of a writing is similar to the modern approach for the doctrine of **advancement** in intestacy. We discussed advancement in Chapter 2.

For example, Gina's will makes a gift of $30,000 to Betty. During Gina's lifetime, she gives Betty $10,000. When Gina dies, she still has assets in her estate sufficient to distribute $30,000 to Betty. The issue is whether Betty should get the full $30,000 under the will. If the doctrine of satisfaction applies, the testamentary gift has been partially satisfied by the $10,000 lifetime gift. Betty would receive $20,000 from the estate rather than $30,000. Under modern statutes, Betty will receive the full $30,000 from the estate (in addition to the $10,000 she has already received) unless a writing indicates the testator's intent that the gift under the will be reduced by the amount of the lifetime gift.

Accessions and Non-Ademption

If a will contains a bequest of shares of stock in a specific company, the doctrine of **accessions** traces the changes in the shares owned by the testator at death. This doctrine provides specific guidance as to whether stock has adeemed or has merely changed in form and as to the treatment of stock splits and dividends. UPC § 2-605 provides guidance with respect to various changes that may occur. The shares originally devised may not be in the estate because another company purchased the shares and the estate instead owns shares in the acquiring company. If so, UPC § 2-605(a)(2) provides for a substitute gift of the shares of stock that replaced the specifically identified shares. Alternatively, the company might have issued additional stock shares to shareholders as a result of stock splits or stock dividends. Subsections (a)(1) and (a)(3) give the beneficiary the increased number of shares. Cash dividends paid before death do not become part of a devise of stock.

EXHIBIT 5.6   **UPC § 2-605. Increase in Securities; Accessions**

> (a) If a testator executes a will that devises securities and the testator then owned securities that meet the description in the will, the devise includes additional securities owned by the testator at death to the extent the additional securities were acquired by the testator after the will was executed as a result of the testator's ownership of the described securities and are securities of any of the following types:
>   (1) securities of the same organization acquired by reason of action initiated by the organization or any successor, related, or acquiring organization, excluding any acquired by exercise of purchase options;
>   (2) securities of another organization acquired as a result of a merger, consolidation, reorganization, or other distribution by the organization or any successor, related, or acquiring organization; or
>   (3) securities of the same organization acquired as a result of a plan of reinvestment.

Case Preview

In re Estate of Magnus

When one company acquires another, someone who owned shares in the company that was acquired will no longer own shares in that company. If a will made a gift of those shares, the shares would seem to be adeemed. Accessions statutes provide that the beneficiary will get the shares in the acquiring company that are equivalent to shares the testator owned in the acquired company and devised to the beneficiary. In *Estate of Magnus*, the court applies a statute like UPC § 2-605 to a slightly different situation. The acquiring company had purchased the acquired company, paying the shareholders cash for their shares. Dorothy Magnus had received cash for some of her shares, but she had neglected to exchange all of her shares for cash. The court must determine whether a gift of shares is adeemed when the stock certificates exist, but the company does not.

As you read the case, consider:

1. How does the court distinguish between stock tendered by Dorothy before her death and stock tendered by her personal representative after her death?
2. If Heileman no longer existed at the time of Dorothy's death, what do the shares found after her death represent?
3. What property will be distributed to the trustee of the testamentary trust Dorothy created for her friends and the college?

In re Estate of Magnus
444 N.W.2d 295 (Minn. Ct. App. 1989)

FORSBERG, J.

Donald and Gerald Sweeney appeal from an order of the probate court finding a specific devise to a trust adeemed under [Minnesota statute similar to 2-605]. We affirm in part, reverse in part and remand.

FACTS

Dorothy B. Magnus died testate on August 17, 1988, at the age of 85. By order dated October 5, 1988, Magnus' last will and testament and the first codicil thereto (hereinafter, the "will"), were formally admitted to probate.

Article III of the will made the following provisions for Donald and Gerald Sweeney (appellants):

> I bequeath all of the shares of the capital stock of Heileman Brewing Company owned by me at the time of my death to my Trustees hereinafter named to hold, administer and distribute the same as follows, to-wit:
>
> 1. During the lifetime of my friends, Donald Sweeney and Gerald Sweeney, now residing in Delray Beach, Florida, my Trustees shall pay all of the income of the said trust to said Donald Sweeney and Gerald Sweeney in equal shares and to the survivor thereof.
>
> 2. Upon the death of the survivor of said Donald Sweeney and Gerald Sweeney the said Heileman Brewing Company stock shall be distributed to Saint Mary's College, Winona, Minnesota, to be added to the scholarship endowment fund created by Paragraph B, Article V of this my Last Will and Testament.

In late 1987, Amber Acquisition Corp. and the Heileman Board of Directors completed a sale whereby Amber controlled 92.8% of Heileman shares by October 1987. In February 1988, the Heileman shareholders approved a reverse stock split in which Heileman made payments to all remaining shareholders of $40.75, in cash, for each share held. The new ownership made funds available in escrow accounts at various banks to enable former shareholders to present their certificates and receive the cash payments.

Prior to her death, Magnus tendered 17,549 shares and received for them $715,121.75 in cash. Following Magnus' death, the personal representative located certificates for 6,749 shares of Heileman in a safe deposit box. The personal representative surrendered the certificates and received proceeds of $275,021.75. . . .

ANALYSIS

The probate court ordered:

> 1. The bequest under article 3 of the decedent's will is fully adeemed and fails in its entirety under [Minnesota statute similar to UPC §2-605] because the decedent had no ownership interest in Heileman Brewing Co. at the time of her death.

2. All proceeds received by the estate for the Heileman stock certificates found in the decedent's safe deposit box are a part of the residue of the estate.

Therefore the only question under consideration by this court is whether the probate court properly applied [Minnesota statute similar to UPC §2-605]. . . .

[The court concluded the stock of Heileman was a security within the meaning of the statute.]

The next issue is whether these are securities "of the same entity." One could argue the "indebtedness" to testator is owed by the escrow agent rather than Heileman. However, the statute apparently foresees this situation by including a provision avoiding ademption when the amounts are owed "by reason of action initiated by the entity." We believe the stock redemption was the type of action contemplated by the framers of the UPC.

Additionally, the securities were acquired by testator as a result of ownership interest in Heileman. The framers of this law note this is an essential element in bringing the transaction within the purview of this statute. . . .

We therefore conclude, as a matter of law, the probate court erred in holding the devise of the found stock certificates adeemed under [Minnesota statute similar to UPC §2-605] and remand with instructions to order the funds acquired thereof distributed to the trustee under the terms of article 3 of the testator's will.

Post-Case Follow-Up

In *Magnus*, the court was able to use the accessions statute to salvage some of the gift to the trust for the testator's friends and the college. Thus, the accessions statute provides a way to carry out the likely intent of the testator, at least partially, rather than force the harsh result of complete ademption. The shares that had been converted to cash before the testator's death were adeemed, so the sale of Heileman resulted in a reduction of almost three-quarters of the value of the intended gift to the trust. Why did Dorothy not change her will after the sale of Heileman?

In re Estate of Magnus: Real Life Applications

1. If you were drafting the will for Ms. Magnus, what could you have done so that her friends and the college would have received the gift she intended?

2. Ben's will included a gift of ABC Corp. stock to his friend, Stan. About five years before Ben's died, ABC Corp. was purchased by XYZ Enterprises. Ben received 100 shares of XYZ stock in exchange for his shares of ABC stock. When Ben dies, he owns 50 shares of the XYZ stock. He had sold the other 50 shares and reinvested the proceeds in the stock of a craft brewery in his home town. Advise Stan. Is he entitled to the XYZ stock, the craft brewery stock, or nothing?

3. Exoneration

At common law, if a devise of property did not provide instructions about paying off a mortgage on the property prior to distributing the property to a beneficiary, the silence would be construed to mean that the personal representative must pay off the mortgage prior to distribution. This is the doctrine of **exoneration**, which refers to whether a devise of property will pass subject to a debt or whether that debt obligation will be "forgiven" by paying it from the residue of the estate.

UPC § 2-607 and many state statutes reverse the common law rule and provide that if the will is silent, the devised property is distributed with the mortgage attached. For people with modest estates, the house may be the primary asset, and a direction to pay off the mortgage may shift the value of devises under the will.

For example, if Terrill owned a house worth $200,000, with a mortgage of $150,000 at the time of his death, and a bank account holding $50,000 in cash, he might have devised the house to his daughter, Roberta, and the bank account to his daughter, Sienna, with the intention of making equal gifts to the children. If the will is construed to pay off the mortgage before distributing the house, the entire bank account will be used to pay the mortgage, although it will not be sufficient to pay the entire mortgage, and Sienna will receive nothing.

This nonexoneration rule regarding mortgages applies even if there is a general provision that instructs the personal representative to pay all debts, such as the following: "I direct my personal representative to pay my funeral and burial expenses, claims against my estate, and expenses of estate administration." For exoneration to occur under UPC § 2-607, the testator must give the personal representative a specific instruction to pay the particular debt. For example, a will might say, "I direct my personal representative to pay the mortgage on my personal residence before transferring title to the beneficiary named above."

Courts in some states continue to follow the common law rule. For example, in Estate of Fussell v. Fortney, 730 S.E.2d 405 (W. Va. 2012), the court found that a clause that simply required the personal representative to "pay just debts" was sufficient to require exoneration of the mortgage. Careful drafting can address the issue.

E. APPORTIONMENT

Historically, if a testator failed to specify from which source taxes were to be paid, the default rule was that they would be paid from the residuary estate. However, many states have reversed that rule by statute and provide in **apportionment** statutes that in the absence of a clear direction to pay taxes out of the residue, each bequest shares the tax burden pro rata. This rule evolved as will substitutes became more popular; taking the taxes out of the residue may eliminate a residuary beneficiary altogether if large will substitute gifts trigger tax to the decedent's estate.

As always, the default rules yield to direct statements of intent in the will. Most form books give the attorney drafting the will the option of directing that: (i) estate taxes be deducted from the residue; or (ii) each gift, either limited to those stated in the will or all gifts including nonprobate transfers, must contribute its pro rata share. The form will often simply provide that estate taxes will be paid from the residue. In many estates, that will be in keeping with the testator's overall estate plan, but in some cases, paying taxes from the residue can cause serious unintended consequences, as the example below explains. The attorney should always consider the preferences of the testator and the overall estate plan before deciding how to address apportionment in the will.

For example, Donald's will contained a provision directing that all taxes be paid from the residue of his estate. The will primarily benefited his spouse and children, and the plan was designed to avoid estate taxes on Donald's death and minimize taxes on his spouse's death. Donald owned a large and valuable piece of land, which he left to a friend with whom he had a long-term secret relationship. The transfer to the friend was made using a transfer-on-death (TOD) deed, and the lawyer who had drafted the will did not know about the land, the friend, or the TOD deed. Because of the value of the estate and structure of the estate plan, taxes were due on the value of the land. The taxes were paid by the residue, which meant that Donald's spouse and children bore the burden of the taxes incurred because land was transferred to Donald's friend.

F. DISCLAIMERS

When a beneficiary prefers not to receive a bequest, the beneficiary can **disclaim** the gift and refuse to accept it. When property is disclaimed, the property is distributed as if the person disclaiming, the **disclaimant**, predeceased the testator. The will may direct what happens to the property, or an anti-lapse statute may cause the property to be distributed to the disclaimant's descendants. The disclaimant cannot direct where the property should go, and the disclaimant can have no control over the ultimate disposition of the property. A person can disclaim property received through wills, will substitutes, and intestacy.

Often disclaimers are used for tax planning. A senior family member may disclaim a gift, causing the gift to go instead to a younger family member. If the disclaimer meets the federal tax requirements for a qualified disclaimer, the beneficiary disclaiming the property will be treated as never having owned the property for tax purposes. Disclaimers may also be used for personal reasons. A beneficiary may not need the gift and may want the alternate beneficiary to receive it.

In some circumstances, disclaimers may be effective to defeat creditors' rights. Some courts do not regard a disclaimer as a fraudulent conveyance because the disclaimant is treated as if the disclaimant never received the interest. If the federal government is the creditor, however, a disclaimer will not be permitted to avoid a tax lien. Drye v. United States, 528 U.S. 49 (1999). The effect of a disclaimer on eligibility for government benefits such as Medicaid is mixed. Compare Tannler

v. Wis. Dep't of Health & Soc. Serv., 564 N.W.2d 735 (Wis. 1997) (disclaimed assets counted toward the eligibility requirements for Medicaid benefits), with *Estate of Kirk*, 591 N.W.2d 630 (Iowa 1999) (disclaimer was allowed to prevent government from collecting Medicaid claims).

Some states have statutory requirements for valid disclaimers, for example requiring that the disclaimant not have accepted any interest in the property and notify the person holding the property in writing. For a disclaimer to be valid for federal tax purposes, the disclaimer must meet the requirements of Internal Revenue Code § 2518, including the requirement that the disclaimer be completed within nine months of the creation of the interest in the beneficiary. In the case of a will, the nine-month period begins to run on the date of the testator's death.

G. FORFEITING PROPERTY DUE TO BAD BEHAVIOR OF BENEFICIARY

Behavior plays a limited role in American inheritance law. The legal rules are based on documents and legal relationships and not on the way family members treated a decedent. Good behavior is not rewarded. For example, under intestacy a dutiful child will not receive a larger share of a parent's estate than an estranged child. Bad behavior may result in the loss of an inheritance, but the behavior must be very bad. This section looks at statutory rules that reduce or eliminate the share a person would otherwise have received, based on the person's behavior.

1. Killing of Testator by Beneficiary or Heir

If a beneficiary named in a will killed the testator, or an intestate heir killed a person who died with an intestate estate, statutes in most states provide that the beneficiary or heir should not receive property from the decedent. These statutes are sometimes referred to as **slayer statutes**. From a policy standpoint, an individual should not benefit from wrongdoing, and in terms of the decedent's intent, the assumption is that most people would not want their murderers to inherit.

Slayer statutes do not apply to all situations in which a beneficiary or heir caused the decedent's death. The beneficiary might have stabbed her husband with the intent to kill him, or she might have killed him in self-defense as he tried to strangle her. The beneficiary may have accidentally caused a house fire that resulted in the death of her mother by falling asleep with a lit cigarette, or she might have started the fire hoping that her bedridden mother would die. The testator might have died under suspicious circumstances, but the evidence may not have been sufficient to convict anyone of murder.

Slayer statutes typically apply only to killings that could be prosecuted as felonies and that involve the element of intent. Even if the killer is not convicted of killing the decedent, or if the conviction is not final, an interested person (someone who will take if the killer does not) can petition the probate court to conduct a separate proceeding to determine whether under the civil standard—a preponderance of the evidence standard—the killer would be found accountable for the killing. Such a finding by the probate court is sufficient to trigger the forfeiture provisions under the statute.

If a beneficiary or heir comes within the statute, the statute then revokes any bequest to the decedent's killer. Under many statutes, including the UPC, the revoked provisions are given effect as if the killer disclaimed them. Although the UPC prevents the killer from taking, the fact that it treats the killer as having disclaimed the interest means that the killer's descendants may take the property, either under the document or under an anti-lapse statute. Some states also bar the killer's descendants from inheriting. See, e.g., Cal. Prob. Code § 250.

UPC § 2-803 applies to will substitutes, including revocable trusts, life insurance, any property transferred with a beneficiary designation, and jointly held property. As with devises under a will, the killer will be treated as disclaiming any transfer the killer would have received under a will substitute. If property is owned in joint tenancy or tenancy by entirety, the statute severs the tenancy and treats the property as if it had been owned by the killer and the decedent as tenants in common. The effect is that the killer does not receive the decedent's half of the property but does not lose the killer's half. States vary in whether their statutes apply to will substitutes.

EXHIBIT 5.7   UPC § 2-803. Effect of Homicide on Intestate Succession, Wills, Trusts, Joint Assets, Life Insurance, and Beneficiary Designations

(b) **[Forfeiture of Statutory Benefits.]** An individual who feloniously and intentionally kills the decedent forfeits all benefits under this [article] with respect to the decedent's estate, including an intestate share, an elective share, an omitted spouse's or child's share, a homestead allowance, exempt property, and a family allowance. If the decedent died intestate, the decedent's intestate estate passes as if the killer disclaimed his [or her] intestate share.

(c) **[Revocation of Benefits Under Governing Instruments.]** The felonious and intentional killing of the decedent:

   (1) revokes any revocable (i) disposition or appointment of property made by the decedent to the killer in a governing instrument, (ii) provision in a governing instrument conferring a general or nongeneral power of appointment on the killer, and (iii) nomination of the killer in a governing instrument, nominating or appointing the killer to serve in any fiduciary or representative capacity, including a personal representative, executor, trustee, or agent; and

   (2) severs the interests of the decedent and killer in property held by them at the time of the killing as joint tenants with the right of survivorship [or as community property with the right of survivorship], transforming the interests of the decedent and killer into equal tenancies in common.

(e) **[Effect of Revocation.]** Provisions of a governing instrument are given effect as if the killer disclaimed all provisions revoked by this section or, in the case of a revoked nomination in a fiduciary or representative capacity, as if the killer predeceased the decedent.

(f) **[Wrongful Acquisition of Property.]** A wrongful acquisition of property or interest by a killer not covered by this section must be treated in accordance with the principle that a killer cannot profit from his [or her] wrong.

(g) **[Felonious and Intentional Killing; How Determined.]** After all right to appeal has been exhausted, a judgment of conviction establishing criminal accountability for the felonious and intentional killing of the decedent conclusively establishes the convicted individual as the decedent's killer for purposes of this section. In the absence of a conviction, the court, upon the petition of an interested person, must determine whether, under the preponderance of evidence standard, the individual would be found criminally accountable for the felonious and intentional killing of the decedent. If the court determines that, under that standard, the individual would be found criminally accountable for the felonious and intentional killing of the decedent, the determination conclusively establishes that individual as the decedent's killer for purposes of this section.

2. Abuse of Testator by Beneficiary

A few states have adopted statutes that revoke a gift to a beneficiary based on abuse of the testator by the beneficiary. Elder abuse is increasingly a problem, and statutes may revoke devises if the beneficiary is liable for physical abuse or financial abuse of an elder person or other dependent adult. Elder abuse is more difficult to establish than death, so these statutes may use a clear and convincing evidence requirement, rather than the preponderance requirement used in statutes that apply to death caused by a beneficiary. A few states also have statutes that revoke the inheritance of a parent who abused or abandoned a child.

Chapter Summary

- A court can use extrinsic evidence to construe ambiguous language in a will.
- The traditional and majority rule is that a court cannot reform a will to fix a mistake, but the UPC and cases in a few states now permit a court to use extrinsic evidence to reform a mistake in a will.
- A beneficiary must survive a testator in order to take under a will.
- A will can provide a definition of "survive," but if the will is silent, a beneficiary must survive by 120 hours. If a beneficiary fails to survive a testator, the gift lapses and is distributed with the residue, unless the will or an anti-lapse statute provides for a different result.
- Anti-lapse statutes apply to create a substitute gift for the beneficiary's descendants, but only if the beneficiary is related to the testator as defined in the statute,

the beneficiary left descendants who survive the testator, and the testator's will does not indicate the testator's intent that the anti-lapse not apply.

- A class gift is a gift to a group of people the testator considers as a group. If a member of the group predeceases the testator, the surviving members of the group divide the gift, unless an anti-lapse statute applies.

- If assets in an estate are insufficient to pay all devises in a will after creditors and expenses have been paid, the devises abate (go unpaid) in the following order: residuary devises, general devises, and specific devises. Multiple devises in a category abate pro rata.

- If an item of property is specifically devised in a will and the testator does not own the item when the testator dies, the gift is adeemed and the beneficiary will not take a substitute gift unless a non-ademption exception applies.

- If a testator devises shares of stock in a company that is acquired by another company, the beneficiary will receive any shares the testator owns in the acquiring company as a result of the acquisition.

- Under the doctrine of accessions, a gift of shares of stock will include shares acquired through stock splits or stock dividends.

- If a testator owns property subject to a mortgage, the doctrine of exoneration directs the personal representative to pay the mortgage before distributing the property. However, if a nonexoneration statute applies, the mortgage will not be paid.

- If a beneficiary disclaims a devise under a will, the property passes as if the beneficiary predeceased the testator.

- Slayer statutes prevent a beneficiary or intestate heir who caused the death of the decedent feloniously and with intent from inheriting. The slayer will be treated as disclaiming the inheritance.

Applying the Concepts

1. Tina and Jake, a married couple, were driving together when they were in a serious car crash. Tina died immediately, and Jake remained in a coma after the crash. Tina's will provides "I leave all of my estate to Jake, if he survives me." Does Jake inherit from Tina in each of the following circumstances?

   a. Jake survived the coma but had a significant brain injury. A conservator was appointed for Jake and made all decisions for Jake until Jake died a year later.
   b. Jake died after two days in the coma.
   c. Jake died after two months in the coma.

2. Cora's will gave the residue of her estate to "The University of Southern California known as The U.C.L.A." Two schools located in southern California, the University of Southern California (usually known as USC) and the University of California at Los Angeles (UCLA) are fighting over the bequest. You represent

the personal representative. How do you advise the personal representative? How do you decide which school receives the residue?

3. Timothy died with a will leaving $20,000 to Kimberly, $30,000 to Lena, and the residue to Maura. If Kimberly predeceases Timothy, who takes Timothy's estate under the following circumstances, assuming that UPC § 2-603 has been adopted?

   a. Kimberly is a friend of Timothy and is survived by two children, Owen and Paul.
   b. Kimberly is Timothy's spouse and is survived by Owen and Paul, children from Kimberly's prior marriage to Adam.
   c. Kimberly is Timothy's niece and is survived by her children, Owen and Paul.
   d. Kimberly is Timothy's niece and is survived by her spouse, Jasmine.

4. Ted's will gives his house (worth $200,000) to Alfred, 100 shares of ABC Corp. stock (worth $200,000) to Ben, $50,000 to Carla, and the residue (worth about $300,000) to David.

   a. At Ted's death he owned no ABC Corp. stock because he had sold it. He invested the proceeds in corporate bonds. What, if anything, does Ben get?
   b. At Leonard's death he owned no ABC Corp. stock because ABC had merged with XYZ Corp. Leonard owned 100 shares in XYZ Corp. that he obtained as the result of the merger. He owned 100 additional shares in XYZ that he purchased after the merger. What, if anything, does Ben get?
   c. About a year before he died, a conservator was appointed for Leonard. The conservator sold Leonard's house for $300,000 when Leonard had to move to assisted living. When Leonard died, he owned the ABC Corp. stock (assume no merger) and $500,000 in other investment assets. How is Leonard's estate distributed?
   d. Assume that when Leonard died he still owned his house (worth $300,000), he owned the ABC Corp. stock (worth $250,000), and he had $100,000 in a bank account. How is Leonard's estate distributed?
   e. Now assume that when Leonard died he owned his house (worth $300,000) and he had $100,000 in a bank account. He had debts of $200,000. How is Leonard's estate distributed?

5. Tessa left $90,000 total to "my nieces." Tessa had three nieces when she executed the will, Anita, Benita, and Caterina. Anita predeceased Tessa, leaving two children. Who takes the $90,000? What if the gift had been to "my college roommates," and Anita, Benita, and Caterina were the college roommates?

6. Kip killed his parents and was convicted of their murders. Each of them had a will leaving everything to the other and then, if the other did not survive, to their two children, Kip and his sister. When Kip killed his parents, he was unmarried and had no children. What happens to his parents' estates? What if Kip had three children when his parents died?

Trusts and Estates in Practice

1. Alice's will leaves her estate to her wife, Gertrude, and if Gertrude does not survive, to a literary society. Gertrude's will leaves her estate to Alice, and if Alice does not survive, to Gertrude's brother, Michael. Alice and Gertrude are injured in a train accident. Alice dies one day after the accident, and Gertrude dies a week later. They have a joint bank account and each has a brokerage account in her own name. Write a letter to the personal representative of Alice's estate advising the personal representative as to who inherits Alice's property.

2. Terrence had two grandsons, Alex and Brandon, when he executed his will in 2012. Terrence's will included a provision given $10,000 to "each grandson of mine who survives me." In 2014, Alex transitioned from male to female. After Alex transitioned, Terrence continued to visit Alex at her college and attended her graduation in May 2015. Terrence told many family members that he "was very proud of Alex" when she graduated. When Terrence died in 2017, the probate court had to decide whether Alex should receive $10,000 from the estate. If you were the probate judge, how would you resolve this issue? Is there an ambiguity in the will? What if there were no evidence of how Terrence felt about Alex after her transition? How might the will have been drafted that would have avoided the problem?

3. Jamal has a stock portfolio worth $5 million that constitutes the bulk of his estate. When Jamal dies, his will provides that the residue of his estate goes to his son, Micah, and if Micah does not survive Jamal, to Micah's descendants by representation. Micah has built a tech business that he recently sold for a substantial amount of money. He is married and has three children—a daughter born of the marriage and two stepchildren who are his wife's sons from a prior marriage. Micah has not adopted the stepsons, but considers them part of his family. Advise Micah as to whether he should disclaim the residue of his father's estate and what will happen if he disclaims. What additional information would you want? What steps should Micah take if he wants to disclaim the property and make sure his stepsons take?

4. Does your state permit reformation of wills to fix a mistake? The answer may be found in a statute or in case law.

5. Who does the anti-lapse statute in the state where your law school is located cover? Compare it to the UPC anti-lapse statute.

6. Does the state where your law school is located have a non-ademption statute, and if so, what types of ademption does it cover?

6

Will Contests

Not every will makes it through probate. Documents that appear to be valid wills can be challenged. Sometimes a potential testator lacks sufficient capacity to execute a legal document as important as a will. Other times a testator does not execute the will according to the formalities required by statute. In some circumstances, a third party comes between the testator and the estate plan. If a will is the result of **undue influence**, where the plan of the decedent is overcome by significant outside pressure, or if the will is the result of **fraud**, where a person deliberately misleads the testator as to the nature or contents of the will or relevant external facts, the will is not entitled to probate. Likewise, if the will is executed by the testator under **duress**, where he or a loved one is subject to force or threat of force or other wrongful acts, the will is not entitled to probate. Beneficiaries or heirs who would have received the property if it passed as (they believe) the testator wanted may find themselves in the position of **contesting the will**—bringing litigation to show that a will is not entitled to probate. Often multiple grounds to contest the will may be brought in one will contest; see Appendix 6.1 for a Petition Contesting Will.

A. LEGAL AND MENTAL CAPACITY

In order to execute a valid will, an individual must have both legal capacity and mental capacity. Legal capacity is generally simple to assess and depends largely on age. Mental capacity is more nuanced.

Key Concepts

- Will contests based on the grounds that the testator lacked the baseline legal capacity or mental capacity to make a will
- Will contests based on the grounds that the testator executed a will as a result of undue influence
- Will contests based on the grounds that the testator executed a will as a result of fraud or duress
- Will contests based on the grounds that the testator failed to execute a will properly
- Standing to contest a will
- No-contest clauses and strategies to minimize probate litigation

1. Legal Capacity Age Requirement

All states require that an individual have obtained a certain age to have legal capacity to execute a will. States also often permit certain substitutes for age such as **emancipation** (being granted adult status as a minor) to have legal capacity to make a will. Section 2-501 of the Uniform Probate Code (UPC) provides that "[a]n individual 18 or more years of age who is of sound mind may make a will." Georgia allows testators as young as 14 to make a will, so long as the testator is not "laboring under some legal disability arising either from a want of capacity or a want of perfect liberty of action." Ga. Code Ann., § 53-4-10. The majority of states recognize the right to make a will around the same age as majority, which is typically 18. Some states have also allowed individuals to make a will younger than the statutory age if the testator is married or in military service. Marriage or military service normally triggers emancipation, so a married minor or minor serving in the military may have the right to execute a will even if the statute is silent.

A strange quirk of the laws allowing younger individuals to execute wills is that a person may have the right to execute a will before he or she is able to hold title to property. For example, in Alabama, an individual age 18 or older may execute a will, but 19 is the age of majority. A will executed by a person who is a minor with respect to property ownership may still be effective to nominate guardians or executors as well as to convey property the testator owns at death, assuming he or she attains the age of majority before death.

The Montana Supreme Court Describes the UPC Mental Capacity Test

A Montana court, following the Uniform Probate Code approach to mental capacity, described the test as follows:

[A] testator is competent if he is possessed of the mental capacity to understand the nature of the act, to understand and recollect the nature and situation of his property and his relations to persons having claims on his bounty whose interests are affected by his will. . . . The "testator must have sufficient strength and clearness of mind and memory to know, in general, without prompting, the nature and extent of the property of which he is about to dispose, and the nature of the act which he is about to perform, and the names and identity of the persons who are to be the objects of his bounty, and his relation towards them." (Citations omitted.) Therefore, testamentary capacity requires that the testator be aware of three elements: (1) the nature of the act to be performed, (2) the nature and extent of the property to be disposed of, and (3) the objects of his or her bounty. In re Estate of Prescott, 8 P.3d 88, 93 (Mont. 2000).

---

2. Mental Capacity

In addition to possessing legal capacity, an individual must possess mental capacity in order to execute a valid will. The capacity required is a bare minimum baseline in which the testator understands (1) the consequence of the will she is executing, (2) the natural objects of her bounty (who her relatives and her beneficiaries are; which individuals fall within this category vary by state), and (3) what property she has to convey. Most states also require that the testator understand how these three criteria relate to each other.

It is possible for a testator to pass this baseline test even if there are impediments to full and complete capacity, such as advanced age, psychiatric disorders, or drug or alcohol abuse. When a will contestant alleges that the testator lacked mental capacity, the focus of the court should be on the ability of the testator to meet the specific criteria for mental capacity and not whether the testator is at a peak level of functioning. For example, a testator with declining cognitive abilities should be able to execute a will during a **lucid interval**, a time at which the tests for capacity are met even if only for a short while.

Case Preview

In re Estate of Ryan

How much capacity is enough? In the case that follows, a cancer patient used online resources to prepare a will that favored a son with a disability over other family members. The patient was in poor physical and mental health and did not have the assistance of an attorney. The patient's daughter challenged the will as ineffective due to lack of capacity. As you read the case, consider:

1. What is the test for mental capacity as articulated by the court?
2. In what ways were the decedent's abilities or behaviors questionable?
3. Did the decedent still meet the test for mental capacity despite these abilities and behaviors?
4. Which party had the burden of proving capacity or lack of capacity in *Estate of Ryan*? State law varies as to which party is assigned the burden of production of evidence and the burden of persuasion; how is which party has the burden relevant in determining the outcome of a case?

In re Estate of Ryan
2008 Mont. Dist. LEXIS 348 (2008)

FINDINGS OF FACT, CONCLUSIONS OF LAW, ORDER, AND DECREE

This matter came on for hearing on July 16, 2008. From the evidence presented, the Court enters the following:

Findings of Fact

Robert Lee Ryan, Sr., died testate on November 15, 2007.

On November 29, 2007, Patrick S. Ryan, son of the decedent, filed an application for informal probate of will and for informal appointment of a personal representative. . . . Cheryl Ryan petitioned this Court to establish supervised administration[1] of the Estate of Robert Lee Ryan, Sr., and made numerous other allegations.

---

[1]Supervised administration requires more oversight by the court than informal administration and is more appropriate where there is conflict in an estate.

The Court determined that there were no grounds to establish supervised administration of the Estate and subsequently denied the substantive motion of Petitioner Cheryl Ryan. However, the Court determined that some of Cheryl Ryan's allegations could be construed as a challenge to the testamentary capacity of Robert Lee Ryan, Sr., and set a hearing on this issue.

Cheryl Ryan, as the contestant of the validity of the will of Robert Lee Ryan, Sr., had the burden of establishing the lack of testamentary capacity. No substantive evidence of lack of testamentary capacity by Robert Lee Ryan, Sr., was presented by Cheryl Ryan.

Ron Glueckert and Stacey Velarde, the individuals who witnessed the execution of Robert Lee Ryan, Sr.'s will, testified that at the time the will was executed, Robert Lee Ryan, Sr., was fully aware of the nature and extent of the property to be disposed of and was aware of the objects of his bounty.

Gary Bartle and Rom Frances testified that at the time the will was executed, Robert Lee Ryan, Sr., was fully aware of the nature and extent of the property to be disposed of and was aware of the objects of his bounty.

The will itself is significant evidence of the decedent's testamentary capacity. Robert Lee Ryan, Sr., prepared it himself over a period of time, using internet resources, without the assistance of an attorney. The will itself contains the elements to establish capacity. He recites that the document is his last will and testament; he lists his children and grandchildren; and he goes into considerable detail about his assets. The will also contains detailed trust provisions for the share of one child, Robert Lee Ryan, Jr., who has a disability. These trust provisions were created evidencing Ryan Sr.'s knowledge of the special needs of his son. Further, the trust provisions were structured so as to minimally impact any other benefits that his son might be receiving from governmental or other agencies.

At the time the will was prepared, Robert Lee Ryan, Sr., lived alone, drove himself around town, managed a rental property, paid his bills, went to the store, and managed to feed himself.

The proposed findings of fact filed by Cheryl Ryan on or about July 18, 2008, contain various references to medical records that were received into evidence from the VA Hospital at Fort Harrison. While the medical records may not technically be admissible as evidence, the Court has considered them. These records show that Robert Lee Ryan, Sr., suffered from a variety of maladies, including possible depression, along with lung, colon, and prostate cancer. Further, he was on a variety of medications and was a rude and difficult patient for the nurses and doctors at the VA Hospital. However, Cheryl Ryan did not present any expert testimony whatsoever that would indicate that any of these maladies or medications prevented Robert Lee Ryan, Sr., from knowing what he was doing when he signed his will. Indeed, the only evidence presented as to Robert Lee Ryan, Sr.'s capabilities at the time that he signed his will showed that he had the requisite testamentary capacity in February 2005 to execute his will.

From the foregoing Findings of Fact, the Court enters the following:

Conclusions of Law

. . .Once a will has been admitted to probate, the law creates a presumption that the decedent was competent and of sound mind. *In re Estate of Bodin,* 144 Mont. 555, 398 P.2d 616 (1965). "At this point it becomes incumbent upon the contestants to overcome the presumption by a preponderance of the evidence . . . the evidence must be clear and satisfactory to overcome the presumption of due execution of the will (including the mental capacity of the testatrix)." *Id.,* at 559, 398 P.2d at 619 (citation omitted).

The contestants of a will have the burden of establishing the lack of testamentary capacity. Cheryl Ryan has presented no substantive evidence showing lack of testamentary capacity by Robert Lee Ryan, Sr. Therefore, she has not met the requisite burden of proof. The validity of the will is confirmed.

Testamentary capacity requires that the testator be aware of three elements: (1) the nature of the act to be performed, (2) the nature and extent of the property to be disposed of, and (3) the objects of his or her bounty. The evidence presented by the Estate established that Robert Lee Ryan, Sr., was aware that he meant to execute a will; was aware of the nature and extent of his property; and was aware of his children and the greater need of one child for support.

A testator may have significant health problems, periods of confusion, or eccentric habits, and still retain the legal capacity to execute a valid will. . . .

Order and Decree

The Court hereby ORDERS that the request for supervised administration or a finding that the decedent did not have testamentary capacity IS DISMISSED as having no basis whatsoever.

The Court hereby DECLARES that the will executed by Robert Lee Ryan, Sr., was validly executed and probate of the will is CONFIRMED.[2]

Post-Case Follow-Up

The testator in *Ryan* was quite ill with cancer, appeared to have depression (a mental illness), was on a variety of medications, and was rude and difficult. No evidence was introduced to show that this in any way interfered with his ability to understand the implications of his will, who his family and beneficiaries were, what property he owned, and how those factors related to each other. Consequently, the will contest failed. Note that the legal test for capacity to execute a will is a lower baseline than capacity in other contexts, such as entering contracts. The legal test for capacity is a matter of balancing the autonomy of the individual with

---

[2][The holding of the District Court of Montana was affirmed by the Montana Supreme Court, which noted that "[o]n appeal, Cheryl Ryan raises a number of arguments which are, unfortunately, difficult to follow and generally without appropriate supporting authority." The court notes that she was a pro se litigant, which she may have been at the District Court level as well. In the Matter of the Estate of Robert Lee Ryan, Sr., 2009 MT 155N (2009). —Eds.]

the expectations of others. With a contract, both parties expect the agreement to be enforced and to have their rights respected. With a will, only the testator has rights; the beneficiaries have no right to receive a bequest, except to the extent the testator wants it. For that reason, mental capacity for purposes of will execution is appropriately a pretty low standard.

In re Estate of Ryan: Real Life Applications

1. Sylvia has come to your office for estate planning services. She admits to having been institutionalized for schizophrenia many years ago, but is now living independently. Is it possible for Sylvia to have capacity to execute a will? How should you determine whether she has sufficient capacity?

2. Umberto lives in an assisted care facility due to his progressing dementia. He has good days and bad days. The law in his state allows for holographic wills. (See Chapter 3.) What do you advise him? Why would an attested will be preferable to a holographic will where both are permitted?

3. Insane Delusion

Even if a testator meets the general test for mental capacity, a will or part of it may be denied probate if the testator suffered from an **insane delusion** at the time the will was executed. An insane delusion is a false belief that the testator is fixated upon even in the face of overwhelming contrary evidence and that affects the testator's will. For example, a father might believe his child to be possessed by the devil, and for that reason exclude the child from his estate plan. See Greenwood v. Greenwood (1790) 163 Eng. Rep. 930 (K.B.).

An insane delusion is more than a mistake or misunderstanding—it requires blind adherence to a completely irrational conclusion. If the belief is mistaken, yet has some basis in reason, it is not an insane delusion. For example, if the father in the case above merely believed that his daughter was associated with atheists, based on the behaviors he observed in her friends, and for that reason cut her out—there would be no basis for overturning the will based on an insane delusion, even if the conclusion the father drew as to her atheist associations was incorrect.

In order for an insane delusion to invalidate a bequest, the bequest must be a result of the insane delusion. Some states will presume that an insane delusion caused a bequest, but others will require proof of causation. If the false belief is entirely irrelevant to the estate plan, there is no ground to void a bequest based on insane delusion. For example, if Antonio believes that the local police are controlled by the mob, but wouldn't have benefited the police anyway and leaves his entire estate to his wife Evangeline, there are no grounds to void the bequest to Evangeline.

Note that the effect of a finding of insane delusion will be to invalidate only the portion of the will affected by the delusion. The rest of the will stands. While an overall lack of capacity invalidates the entire will, a court can use a finding of insane delusion to strike a problematic provision without disrupting the entire plan.

Courts have struggled with the application of the insane delusion doctrine, particularly with respect to how strongly against evidence a belief must be in order to be considered "insane." Professor Tate describes this conflict as follows:

> The *Restatement (Third) of Donative Transfers* addresses mental capacity in Section 8.1. The first paragraph of Section 8.1 states generally that "[a] person must have mental capacity in order to make or revoke a donative transfer." If the donative transfer takes the form of a will or will substitute, the testator must be capable of understanding "[t]he nature and extent of his or her property, the natural objects of his or her bounty, and the disposition that he or she is making of that property," and "must also be capable of relating these elements to one another and forming an orderly desire regarding the disposition of the property." If the testator cannot satisfy this general test of mental capacity, the will is void. The doctrine of insane delusion is not addressed in the text of Section 8.1 of the *Restatement (Third) of Donative Transfers*. A comment to the section, however, defines an insane delusion as "a belief that is so against the evidence and reason that it must be the product of derangement." The comment clarifies that "mere eccentricity does not constitute an insane delusion," and "[a] belief resulting from a process of reasoning from existing facts is not an insane delusion, even though the reasoning is imperfect or the conclusion illogical." Nevertheless, even though a person who "suffers from an insane delusion is not necessarily deprived of capacity to make a donative transfer," a donative transfer will be invalid "to the extent that it was the product of an insane delusion."
>
> The *Restatement* definition of insane delusion raises two difficult issues, one relating to the definition of an insane delusion and the other relating to the consequences of such a delusion. First, how are courts to determine whether a belief is "so against the evidence and reason that it must be the product of derangement?" Is the test satisfied if there is even a slight possibility that the delusion might be based in fact? Second, how is a court to determine whether a will was "the product of an insane delusion" when the testator is dead and cannot explain the reasons for his or her testamentary choices? Courts have wrestled with these issues for years, with inconsistent and sometimes dubious results. [B]oth components of the insane delusion test are difficult to apply, partly because factfinders sometimes disregard factual evidence supporting a testator's choices when the result fails to comport with their own notions of fairness.

Joshua C. Tate, *Personal Reality: Delusion in Law and Science*, 49 Conn. L. Rev. 891, 905-06 (2017).

The test of insane delusion, therefore, requires a careful analysis of the facts to determine whether the estate plan was a result of some deranged and targeted belief of the testator, or was the testator's legitimate (even if unfair) choice unencumbered by such a delusion. The New York Appellate Court engages with such an analysis in the following case.

In re Estate of Zielinski

In the case that follows, a cancer patient executed a will leaving her estate to her sister and brother-in-law, excluding her son. Among other things, the patient believed that her son was receiving directions from "a device" and was responsible for putting balloons in her body. Her son alleged that the testator lacked mental capacity and suffered from an insane delusion. As you read the case, consider:

1. What is the test for insane delusion as articulated by the court?
2. What specific facts support the conclusion that the testator had an insane delusion?
3. Did the insane delusion influence the way the testator distributed her estate?
4. What is the relationship between the tests for insane delusion and mental capacity?

In re Estate of Zielinksi
2008 A.D.2d 275 (N.Y. App. Div. 1995)

PETERS, Justice

Cecilia Zielinski (hereinafter decedent) was admitted to the hospital on May 30, 1992 and diagnosed with colon cancer shortly thereafter. While in the hospital, she was seen on a daily basis by her sister, Barbara Moczulski (hereinafter proponent) and her sister's husband. On or about June 23, 1992 while still in the hospital, decedent executed a will, in the presence of proponent, which provided for the distribution of her residuary estate in equal shares to proponent and proponent's husband. Neither decedent's only son, Eugene J. Zielinski, her two grandchildren, her five great-grandchildren nor any of decedent's other lineal decedents were named as beneficiaries. Her assets consisted of a house and approximately 200 savings bonds worth approximately $360,000. Such bonds were purchased by decedent over a 20-year period and were either in the sole name of an intended beneficiary, in the joint name of decedent and a beneficiary, or in decedent's name with "payable on death" designations to a beneficiary. Every beneficiary was either decedent's grandchild or great-grandchild. No bonds were issued in the name of proponent, proponent's husband or any of decedent's other siblings.

On the day that the will was executed, decedent also signed a power of attorney in favor of proponent. Pursuant to the power of attorney, proponent attempted to redeem each and every one of decedent's savings bonds but was successful in redeeming only those bonds held in decedent's name or jointly by decedent and either one of her grandchildren or great-grandchildren. Decedent died on September 25, 1992. On November 6, 1992, after holding a check for the proceeds of the bonds, proponent placed the funds, totaling $354,944.08, in a bank account in decedent's name. As the sole beneficiaries under decedent's will, proponent and her husband became the beneficiaries of these proceeds.

When proponent brought a petition for probate of the will in Surrogate's Court, [decedent's son] Zielinski filed objections which claimed, *inter alia,* that decedent lacked testamentary capacity. He thereafter joined decedent's grandchildren and great-grandchildren (hereinafter collectively referred to as the challengers) in a separate action against proponent in Supreme Court to recover the proceeds of the bonds. A consolidated nonjury trial was held in Surrogate's Court which resulted in a denial of the petition for probate and a direction to proponent to pay the named beneficiaries in accordance with the amounts they would have received had the bonds not been redeemed. Proponent appeals.

In a nonjury trial, while our power to review the evidence is as broad as that of the trial court, we will not disturb the trial court's decision if it is found to be supported by the weight of the credible evidence. Based upon the evidence adduced at trial, we agree with Surrogate's Court that proponent made a prima facie showing of the requisite testamentary capacity. The burden thereby shifted to the challengers to show that decedent's mind was affected by an insane delusion regarding her son. Noting the difficulty of such burden, we nonetheless find that Surrogate's Court properly concluded that decedent was suffering from an insane delusion which directly affected her decision not to leave anything to her son. With proponent thereafter failing to demonstrate that the delusions had a reasonable basis, we find that the credible evidence supports Surrogate's Court's determination.

The expert testimony of Abdul Hameed, the consulting psychiatrist at the hospital where decedent had been admitted, indicated that decedent was diagnosed on the date of her admission as suffering from a delusional disorder regarding her son. Such psychiatrist testified that decedent told him that Zielinski had injected her in her buttocks and that her husband (since deceased) and her doctors had been involved in the plan. Hameed further testified that when he next examined decedent on June 9 and 10, 1992, she continued to verbalize these delusions. He opined that patients with this disorder could be competent in some respects and delusional with respect to others.

Testimony of a second psychiatrist, Zoser Mohammed, who examined decedent on June 15, 1992, confirmed Hameed's diagnosis. Decedent told Mohammed that her husband broke her legs and that Zielinski was getting instructions from a "device" that turned the world inside out. Mohammed confirmed that a person could exhibit appropriate behavior apart from the specific delusion. Testimony from decedent's attending nurses confirmed the delusional statements regarding decedent's son. Two additional psychiatrists, one proffered by proponent and the other by the challengers, confirmed such diagnosis after their review of the medical records. Both testified that such delusions may have directly affected decedent's decision to exclude Zielinski from the will.

Lay testimony included that of Patricia Russo, an employee of Zielinski, who knew decedent since 1979. She testified that decedent continuously made delusional statements from 1979 to 1992 regarding the placement of balloons in her stomach by Zielinski, that her husband ran over her legs and put someone else's legs on her, that Zielinski injected chemicals into her, and that there was a conspiracy by and between her husband, her son and her doctors. Donna Loro, another employee of Zielinski, testified that from as far back as 1965, decedent told her of a conspiracy between decedent's husband, her dentist and her son in trying to put needles into her to make her ill, and Loro reiterated decedent's tales of "balloons" and "devices."

Zielinski's former spouse, Jean Smith, testified similarly and advised that such statements dated from 1973 when she first met decedent. She added that decedent advised her that her husband and doctors pushed her eyes back into her head and that decedent regularly spit into a jar to save as evidence of what Zielinski and [decedent's] husband had done to her. Zielinski and one of his employees testified to finding approximately 25 to 30 one-gallon jars in decedent's closet, apparently filled with the saliva she had saved. Zielinski's current spouse, Lynn Zielinski, testified that when she met decedent in 1979, decedent told her about her legs being substituted and the balloons. She further confirmed prior testimony about the "devices" and the spitting into a jar. While she testified that decedent mostly blamed her husband, after decedent's husband became ill such witness testified that decedent's focus shifted to Zielinski. All such witnesses, including Zielinski, testified that there was no basis for such statements and that there existed a good relationship between Zielinski and decedent.

Recognizing that there was testimony indicating that decedent was capable of leading a normal life, we note that a person suffering from an insane delusion can still be competent to manage their own affairs and, if the person's behavior is not centered on the subject of the delusion, can appear to be normal (*see, Matter of Honigman*, 8 NY2d 244, 250, supra). Moreover, where, as here, the credibility of both the lay and expert witnesses was a substantial factor in the determination of Surrogate's Court, this Court will be deferential to the trial court's determinations, so long as such conclusions were not against the weight of the credible evidence. We find that they were not.

Even if it could be said that decedent had general testamentary capacity, she could, at the same time, have an insane delusion which controlled the testamentary act, thus rendering it invalid (*see, Matter of Brush*, 1 AD2d 625). "'In order to invalidate a will it is not necessary that the intellect . . . be in total eclipse . . . . There is a partial insanity and a total insanity. Such partial insanity may exist as respects particular persons . . . while as to others the person may not be destitute of the use of reason'" (supra, at 628). We find that the testimony fully supports the conclusion that decedent was suffering from an insane delusion regarding her son and that this delusion directly affected her decision not to leave anything to him under her will. We further find that Surrogate's Court properly determined that proponent failed to show that the delusions had a rational basis. Although suggesting possible reasons for the exclusion of Zielinski from the will, we find that there was no evidence presented of any reasonable basis for the delusion. Rather, there was sufficient credible evidence that Zielinski had a good relationship with decedent and that her delusions were chronic. Based upon the expert testimony, decedent was not capable of lucid intervals where it could have been determined that decedent had the requisite testamentary capacity at the time of the execution of the will. . . .

Finding the remaining contentions raised to be without merit, we affirm the decree and judgment of Surrogate's Court in their entirety.

Post-Case Follow-Up

In this case, the testator suffered from chronic bizarre misbeliefs that colored the way she saw her son. Notice that the intent of the insane delusion doctrine is not to save the son from disinheritance, but to save the mother from doing something that she would regret if she were able to understand what she was doing. How does the doctrine of insane delusion further that intent?

In re Estate of Zielinski: Real Life Applications

1. Imagine that Mrs. Zielinski's bizarre beliefs were directed not at her husband and son, but at her neighbor. The will still bequeaths everything to her sister and brother-in-law. Is the will entitled to probate?

2. You are designing a screening form for clients of your solo law practice to determine whether they have sufficient mental capacity to execute a will. Is determining whether the potential client can identify her relatives and her assets and understands the consequences of her estate plan sufficient? What else do you need to know? How can you discover it?

B. UNDUE INFLUENCE

A will is not entitled to probate if it does not reflect the true testamentary intent of the decedent—if instead the decedent executed an unwanted estate plan owing to the manipulations of a third party. A will, or any part of it, that is procured by undue influence is therefore invalid. State statutes often provide that a will (or part of it) resulting from undue influence is not entitled to probate, but the details of what actions qualify as undue influence is commonly developed by case law.

1. The Test of Undue Influence

A will or bequest is the product of undue influence if the testator is manipulated into making a testamentary gift the testator did not want to make. It happens when a person takes unfair advantage of the testator, particularly if that testator is especially vulnerable or dependent. The Restatement provides that "A donative transfer is procured by undue influence if the wrongdoer exerted such influence over the donor that it overcame the donor's free will and caused the donor to make a donative transfer that the donor would not otherwise have made." Restatement (Third) of Property: Wills and Other Donative Transfers, § 8.3(b). Influence must be substantial and forceful to be undue—mere requests or suggestions as to the path of an estate plan do not invalidate bequests.

Because the nature of undue influence is often private—just between the testator and the person taking advantage—direct evidence of undue influence can be hard to find. Circumstantial evidence can be sufficient to show that the testator was manipulated into executing an unwanted will. A contestant lacking direct evidence would normally prove undue influence through circumstantial evidence by showing "(1) the donor was susceptible to undue influence, (2) the alleged wrongdoer had an opportunity to exert undue influence, (3) the alleged wrongdoer had a disposition to exert undue influence, and (4) there was a result appearing to be the effect of the undue influence." See Restatement (Third) of Property: Wills and Other Donative Transfers, § 8.3(b), cmt. e.

Case Preview

Mueller v. Wells

In the case that follows, an elderly woman was persuaded by her mail carrier and caretaker, Michelle Wells, to execute a will in favor of Ms. Wells that cut out her relatives. The relatives alleged undue influence. As you read the case, consider:

1. What is the test for undue influence as articulated by the court?
2. Who has the burden of proving undue influence?
3. How does the burden shift in undue influence cases where a will contestant has made an initial showing and prima facie case of undue influence?
4. Which facts does the court consider important in determining whether undue influence occurred?

Mueller v. Wells
367 P.3d 580 (Washington 2016)
Supreme Court of Washington, en banc

Yu, Justice

This case involves a will contest and whether the will proponents presented sufficient evidence to rebut a presumption of undue influence. The trial court invalidated the will at issue, finding that it was the product of undue influence. The trial court's factual findings were not challenged on appeal, but the Court of Appeals reversed and remanded for a new trial, holding that the trial court failed to make findings of direct evidence to support its conclusion of undue influence, relying solely on the presumption of undue influence to invalidate the will. . . . We reverse the Court of Appeals and reinstate the trial court's judgment invalidating the will as a product of undue influence.

FACTUAL AND PROCEDURAL HISTORY

Eva Johanna Rova Barnes was born on July 17, 1916, in Bellingham, Washington. She died at her home in Poulsbo, Washington, on June 27, 2011, just a few weeks before her 95th birthday. Barnes' will was admitted to probate on July 1, 2011. Respondent Michelle Wells was appointed personal representative. . . but was later removed by the court and replaced by her husband, Dennis Wells. Barnes' estate includes an acreage of land located on Rova Road that was homesteaded by her parents. The property contains her residence and a rental property in which the petitioners (the Rovas)[3] shared a one-half interest. Barnes' probated will completely disinherited the Rovas in favor of Wells and her husband. Wells became acquainted with Barnes as Barnes' rural mail carrier, and the two became friends after Barnes' husband and daughter passed away. After Barnes suffered a fall in her home, Wells became her caretaker.

The Rovas challenged the validity of Barnes' will for lack of testamentary capacity and undue influence by Wells. After a five-day bench trial, the trial court issued 83 findings of fact and 23 conclusions of law, finding that while Barnes had testamentary capacity when she executed the will in contest, the will was invalid as a result of Wells' undue influence. The trial court found that Barnes' increasing dependence on Wells coincided with Barnes' estrangement from her family and that Wells made numerous false statements that "fanned the flame" of Barnes' unfounded anger and mistrust of the Rovas. Wells became the only person close to Barnes on a consistent basis, eventually replacing Barnes' niece as her attorney-in-fact and assuming the role of caretaker after Barnes fell in her home. Isolated from her family and friends, physically and mentally impaired, and totally dependent on Wells, it is indisputable that Barnes was highly vulnerable to undue influence.

Throughout her relationship with Barnes, Wells and her husband were struggling financially. After Wells became more involved in her life, Barnes began writing checks to Wells and Wells' family members for various services and expenses. Just days before Barnes passed away, Wells paid her own mortgage with a check issued from Barnes' personal bank account. Barnes was in or close to being in a coma when Wells wrote this check. The check posted on the same day that Barnes passed away.

> ### Undue Influenced Explained in *Cresto v. Cresto*
>
> The Kansas Supreme Court defined undue influence as follows in the case of Cresto v. Cresto, 358 P.3d 831 (Kansas 2015):
>
> > This court has defined undue influence as "'such coercion, compulsion or constraint that the testator's free agency is destroyed, and by overcoming his power of resistance, the testator is obliged to adopt the will of another rather than exercise his own.'" In other words, the testator becomes "the tutored instrument of a dominating mind, which dictates to him what he shall do, compels him to adopt its will instead of exercising his own, and by overcoming his power of resistance impels him to do what he would not have done had he been free from its control."

---

[3] The Rova family are descendants of Eva Rova Barnes' parents, so presumably her nieces/nephews or their children.

On appeal, Wells did not challenge the trial court's findings of fact but assigned error to the conclusions that the Rovas had established a presumption of undue influence that Wells failed to rebut, and that Barnes' will was invalid because it was a product of Wells' undue influence.

ANALYSIS

The right to testamentary disposition of one's property is a fundamental right protected by law. *Dean v. Jordan,* 79 P.2d 331 (1938). A will that is executed according to all legal formalities is presumed valid. Nevertheless, a will executed by a person with testamentary capacity may be invalidated if "undue influence" existed at the time of the testamentary act. "Undue influence" that is sufficient to void a will must be "something more than mere influence but, rather, influence 'which, at the time of the testamentary act, controlled the volition of the testator, interfered with his free will, and prevented an exercise of his judgment and choice.'"

. . . The trial court properly invalidated the will in contest for undue influence under the *Dean* framework.

A. Establishing the Presumption of Undue Influence

When challenging the validity of a will, the will contestant bears the burden of proving the will's illegality by "clear, cogent, and convincing" evidence. *Dean,* 79 P.2d 331. Circumstantial evidence may be used to establish suspicious facts that raise a presumption of undue influence. If the presumption is raised, the will proponent must produce evidence to rebut the presumption. *Dean,* 79 P.2d 331. The absence of rebuttal evidence may be sufficient to set aside a will, but the contestant retains the ultimate burden of proof. *Id.*

The court in *Dean* identified certain suspicious facts and circumstances that could raise a presumption of undue influence:

> The most important of such facts are (1) that the beneficiary occupied a fiduciary or confidential relation to the testator; (2) that the beneficiary actively participated in the preparation or procurement of the will; and (3) that the beneficiary received an unusually or unnaturally large part of the estate. Added to these may be other considerations, such as the age or condition of health and mental vigor of the testator, the nature or degree of relationship between the testator and the beneficiary, the opportunity for exerting an undue influence, and the naturalness or unnaturalness of the will.

Whether the existence of the so-called *Dean* factors raises a presumption of undue influence is a highly fact-specific determination that requires careful scrutiny of the totality of the circumstances.

The trial court properly held that the facts raised a presumption of undue influence based on the presence of all the *Dean* factors and other considerations. We reaffirm the *Dean* factors and find that the undisputed facts in this case substantially support the trial court's conclusion of undue influence.

1. Opportunity—existence of a fiduciary or confidential relationship

The first *Dean* factor establishes that a confidential or fiduciary relationship may give rise to a presumption of undue influence. The crux of these relationships is a level of trust that leads the testator to believe that the beneficiary is acting in his or her best interests, creating an opportunity for the beneficiary to exert undue influence.

The trial court's findings of fact were sufficient to meet this *Dean* factor. A fiduciary relationship inheres in the role of attorney-in-fact, and it is undisputed that Wells was Barnes' attorney-in-fact at the time the will in contest was signed. Wells exercised her power of attorney by signing checks on behalf of Barnes. These facts are sufficient to find that a fiduciary relationship existed.

2. Causation—active participation in procurement of the will

The second *Dean* factor requires that the beneficiary's actions bring about or affect the testamentary instrument. In this case, although Wells was not present in the room when Barnes signed the will, she was Barnes' sole means of transportation and drove Barnes to the series of meetings that led to the execution of the new will.

While the mere act of driving Barnes to the meeting with her attorney is not sufficient in and of itself to satisfy this *Dean* factor, the new will was executed on the heels of what appeared to be Wells' systematic manipulation of Barnes. Wells alienated Barnes from her family by making numerous false statements that "fanned the flame" of Barnes' unfounded anger towards the Rovas. Wells suggested that the Rovas had deliberately destroyed Barnes' address book—an irreplaceable item of great sentimental value to Barnes—when John Rova helped Wells unclutter Barnes' home, which had been declared unsafe due to Barnes' hoarding tendencies. She also accused John of trying to "throw Ms. Barnes under the bus" and stated that the Rovas wanted to put Barnes in a nursing home—untrue statements that "acted to further poison" Barnes' relationship with the Rovas. Wells also falsely told the rental property tenants that the Rovas were "greedy villains" who intended to evict them in order to sell the land, develop the property, and become millionaires. Wells further isolated Barnes by changing her long distance calling plan, making it difficult for family and friends to reach her by phone.

When viewed in the context of these actions, driving Barnes to the meeting in which she executed a new will can be reasonably seen as the last act in Wells' campaign to influence Barnes. These findings support the conclusion that the will would not have come into being but for Wells' activities and influence on Barnes.

3. Result—unusually or unnaturally large bequest

Under the third *Dean* factor, the effect of undue influence must manifest in the testamentary instrument in an "unnatural" or "unusual" way. *See In re Estate of Peters*, 264 P.2d 1109 (1953) ("If fraud or undue influence had actually been exercised, we would expect to find some indication of this in the way in which the property was devised and bequeathed."). "Unusualness" or "unnaturalness" can be measured by comparison to the decedent's previous testamentary instruments or bequests to other beneficiaries.

The trial court found that Barnes' new will was a "radical departure" from her prior wills. Both of Barnes' prior wills included the Rovas: first as alternate beneficiaries, then as primary beneficiaries following the death of Barnes' husband and daughter. The will in contest completely disinherited the Rovas in favor of Wells and her husband as the sole beneficiaries. Wells and her husband were never named as beneficiaries in Barnes' prior wills, yet they received the entirety of Barnes' estate in the new will, leaving nothing to the prior beneficiaries. These facts are sufficient to support the conclusion that the Wells received an unusually and unnaturally large bequest.

4. Other considerations

In addition to the three main factors, *Dean* enumerates other considerations that could weigh in favor of finding undue influence. *Dean*, 79 P.2d 331. These considerations speak to the testator's vulnerability to undue influence due to mental or physical infirmity and the nature of the relationship with the beneficiary.

. . . Barnes was elderly—nearly 95 when the will was executed—and "extremely vulnerable to undue influence due to physical limitations, [and] some degree of cognitive impairment." *Id.* Barnes was dependent on Wells as her caregiver, and Wells' constant presence created ample opportunity to exert undue influence over Barnes.

The trial court cited the unnaturalness of the will as a "critical factor" in its decision. A will is unnatural "when it is contrary to what the testator, from his known views, feelings, and intentions would have been expected to make." *In re Estate of Miller*, P.2d 526 (1941). The bequest to the Wells was "unnatural" in that they were not natural objects of Barnes' bounty: Wells was 51 years younger than Barnes, she and her husband were unrelated to Barnes, and Wells became consistently involved with Barnes only in the last few years of Barnes' life. In contrast, the Rovas are Barnes' closest living relatives and direct lineal descendants of the property's homesteaders. They grew up near Barnes and spent a significant amount of time on the property. Up until the last few years of her life, the Rovas shared a close family relationship with Barnes, celebrating her 90th birthday together and including her in important family events, like the wedding of Karen Bow's daughter. Under these circumstances, the trial court stated that it "cannot conceive of Ms. Barnes disinheriting the [Rovas] and making this absolutely radical and unnatural change to her prior wills unless she was subjected to undue influence that the evidence suggests she was vulnerable to."

The trial court's conclusion that all the *Dean* factors and other considerations were present is sufficiently supported by its findings of fact.

B. Effect of the Presumption of Undue Influence

If the facts raise a presumption of undue influence, the burden of production shifts to the will proponent, who must then rebut the presumption with evidence sufficient to "balance the scales and restore the equilibrium of evidence touching the validity of the will." However, the will contestant retains the ultimate burden of proving undue influence by "clear, cogent, and convincing" evidence.

1. Wells failed to rebut the presumption of undue influence

. . . [The appellate court] reversed based on its own reweighing of the evidence in favor of an alternative theory for upholding the will—that "[t]he trial court's unchallenged findings of fact contain more than sufficient evidence that Barnes changed her will for a valid reason, unaffected by undue influence: that she had grown apart from, was suspicious of, and disliked the Rovas."

This was error—the appellate court's role is to review findings supporting the conclusions the trial court *did* reach, not to look for evidence supporting an alternate conclusion the court *could have* reached. Wells does not challenge any of the trial court's findings or offer any evidence disputing the presence of the *Dean* factors, but selectively restates the trial court's findings to support her alternative theory for Barnes' will. While Wells' story may be persuasive in isolation, we must defer to the weight given to all the evidence by the trial court and its credibility assessment that the facts Wells points to do not balance the scales against the overwhelming evidence of undue influence.

2. The Rovas met their burden of proving undue influence by clear, cogent, and convincing evidence

Whether or not the presumption of undue influence is established or rebutted, the will contestant bears the ultimate burden of proving the will's illegality by "clear, cogent, and convincing" evidence. *Dean*, 194 Wash. at 671, 79 P.2d 331. We have long recognized that circumstantial evidence alone can be sufficient to support a finding of undue influence. However, a will contestant cannot rely solely on the weight of the presumption to invalidate a will, *Dean*, and "mere suspicion of undue influence is not enough," *In re Estate of Mitchell*, 249 P.2d 385 (1952). Rather, the contestant must establish undue influence by producing direct or circumstantial "positive evidence." *Dean*, 79 P.2d 331.

Here, the trial court properly found that the evidence met the clear, cogent, and convincing standard in order to find undue influence. The trial court did not delineate which evidence went to any particular proposition, but we have never held that evidence of the presumption could not also be considered as direct or circumstantial evidence of actual undue influence. As the taking of testimony unfolds at trial, the trial court must consider the evidence as a whole, regardless of which party offers it. The trial court's extensive findings of fact established an unrebutted presumption of undue influence based on the *Dean* factors, supported by further positive evidence of Wells' systematic influence over Barnes and active efforts to isolate and alienate Barnes from the Rovas. Taken together, the findings are easily sufficient to establish undue influence.

The Rovas met their burden and, under the appropriate standard of review, the trial court's conclusions are sustainable. We reverse the Court of Appeals and reinstate the trial court's judgment.

CONCLUSION

The Court of Appeals exceeded the proper function of appellate review in these types of cases. We reaffirm the *Dean* factors and reiterate that the substantial evidence standard of review applies on appeal. Applying this precedent to the case before us, we reverse the Court of Appeals and reinstate the trial court's conclusion that Eva Johanna Rova Barnes' will is invalid due to undue influence exercised by Michelle Wells.

Case Preview

In Mueller v. Wells, the will contestants were able to provide sufficient evidence of undue influence. They were also able to provide sufficient evidence to raise the presumption of undue influence, which shifted the burden to the proponent to provide evidence that the will was valid. In Mueller v. Wells, the contestant still bore the ultimate burden of proving undue influence, but in many states, the burden of persuasion rests with the will proponent after the burden to produce evidence has been triggered. If the party who holds the burden of persuasion does not meet that standard, the other party wins.

Mueller v. Wells: Real Life Applications

1. Assume that instead of litigating, Michelle Wells and the Royas want to enter into alternative dispute resolution (ADR). Should the fact that burden shifting is triggered in litigation be relevant in the ADR context? Should it inform whether you advise a client to settle or to go to trial?

2. You represent a daughter who believes that her father's estate plan was manipulated by his ex-wife. What facts do you need to gather to determine whether there are grounds for an undue influence claim?

2. Evidentiary Burden-Shifting in Undue Influence Litigation

In undue influence cases, there are often only two people who really know what happened: the decedent, who is not around to give testimony, and the alleged undue influencer, who is likely to have a biased view of the facts. For that reason, many states recognize burden-shifting to allow undue influence claims to prevail under circumstances where the undue influence cannot be disproved, and not only in circumstances where the will contestant has sufficient evidence to prove undue influence directly.

To take this route to prevailing on an undue influence claim, the contestant must first present enough evidence to trigger the presumption of undue influence. The elements of the claim vary somewhat by state, but often the law requires some combination of a "confidential relationship," "suspicious circumstances," and an "unnatural bequest." The variety in articulation of the rule happens because succession is a state law issue, with language developed in case law serving as precedent.

A "confidential relationship" exists where one party relies on another in a fiduciary capacity, such as when a person has appointed another as agent under a power of attorney. It also exists where the testator is subservient to the alleged influencer, such as an employer-employee relationship. There are "suspicious circumstances" if the alleged undue influencer procured the attorney to write the will, ostracized the testator from her family members, or engaged in other similar activities. An "unnatural disposition" occurs if an unrelated individual gets a sizeable bequest or if there are substantial inequalities in the gifts given to individuals of the same degree of relationship (for example, one nephew receiving the entire estate and other nieces and nephews excluded). See Restatement (Third) of Property: Wills and Other Donative Transfers, § 8.3 and comments following. A new will that is substantially inconsistent with the distribution pattern of prior wills may also be an "unnatural disposition."

If the will contestant is successful at establishing the presumption of undue influence, the procedural burden for the case shifts. It then becomes the onus of the alleged undue influencer to come forward with evidence disproving undue influence by a preponderance of the evidence—to show that the plan truly reflected the wishes of the decedent. This evidence may be hard to produce, so as a practical matter, many undue influence cases are won by this burden-shifting technique.

The purpose of denying a will probate when it is a result of undue influence is to respect and protect the right of decedents to make individual choices with respect to their own property. Sometimes people take advantage of vulnerable testators and this doctrine helps counterbalance that threat. Applying the doctrine, however, is not always easy or objective. Determining whether a testator's will accurately reflects "true" wishes requires a judgment call about what an individual is likely to want, and societal biases and preconceptions color what a judge or jury is likely to see. Undue influence cases may be brought by family members who disapprove of choices made by the decedent and therefore don't perceive a will as reflecting the decedent's truest intentions. For example, if the decedent and his romantic partner had a long-term relationship but never married, the decedent's parents might challenge a will leaving everything to the partner based on undue influence. The romantic partners may have given each other power of attorney, used the same lawyer, and left their estates to each other even though they are not related. If the court shares the parents' disapproval of the relationship, the court may find that their relationship and interactions triggered the presumption of undue influence. Imagine the difficulty the surviving partner will have in trying to prove a negative—that he did not unduly influence the decedent.

C. FRAUD, DURESS, MISTAKE, AND TORTIOUS INTERFERENCE WITH AN EXPECTANCY

As discussed with respect to undue influence, a will should not to be entitled to probate if it does not reflect the wishes of the testator, since the primary purpose of a will is to further the intent of the testator. Two doctrines similar to undue influence, in that they interfere with testamentary intent, are fraud and duress. Fraud most commonly occurs when someone deliberately misleads the testator as to a fact, the testator reasonably believes it, and the testator then changes her estate plan based on the fraudulent information. Duress occurs when the testator is coerced into executing (or refrained from revoking) a will by a wrongful act, often a threat of force or violence to the testator or another. Mistake, not based on undue influence, fraud, or some other cause of action, is not in itself grounds for a will contest. **Tortious interference with an expectancy** is a new tort claim that may be available under certain circumstances to intended beneficiaries or heirs who cannot be made whole by a will contest.

1. Fraud

A will is induced by fraud when a wrongdoer (1) knowingly or recklessly, (2) makes a false representation to the donor, (3) about a critical fact, (4) intending to lead the testator to make a transfer he would not otherwise have made, which (5) causes the transfer. See Restatement (Third) of Property: Wills and Other Donative Transfers § 8.3(d) cmt. j.

The false representation may be either: 1) **fraud in the execution**, which involves a misrepresentation about the nature or contents of the document the testator is signing; or 2) **fraud in the inducement**, which is when the misrepresentation concerns an external fact relevant to the pattern of distribution among beneficiaries.

Fraud in the execution happens when someone lies about what language is in the document, or leads the testator to believe he is signing something other than a will. For example, if an attorney drafted a will and indicated to the client that the will left the property to the client's son as requested, and in fact the will left the estate to the attorney, that would be fraud in the execution. Telling the client he was signing a deed when in fact she was signing a will would also be fraud in the execution.

Fraud in the inducement is more common, and it occurs when someone lies about a relevant fact—generally something to do with an intended beneficiary or property. For example, if a brother convinces Mom that his sister has a drug addiction and would waste an inheritance on heroin, when in fact the sister is clean and sober, and Mom leaves her estate to the brother based on the false representation, that would be fraud in the inducement. Either type of fraud interferes with testamentary intent, so courts invalidate bequests caused by fraud.

2. Duress

A will is induced by duress when a wrongdoer (1) performs or threatens to perform, (2) a wrongful act, (3) that coerces the transferor to make a transfer, (4) that the transferor would not otherwise have made. See Restatement (Third) of Property: Wills and Other Donative Transfers § 8.3(c). Duress normally includes force or a threat of force. An example of duress would be to threaten to kill or kidnap the testator's daughter if he did not execute a will favoring the person making the threat. Obviously, bequests procured by duress do not reflect the true testamentary intent of the decedent and therefore should not be considered valid in probate. If you have a gun to your head, the will is going to include whatever the assailant requires, regardless of whether it reflects your true testamentary wishes.

In order for a threat or action to constitute duress, it must be "wrongful"—something that the person did not have the right to do. For example, say Raul is taking care of his aging mother, Gertrude. Raul may threaten to leave and never to speak to his mother again unless she leaves him her entire estate instead of splitting it equally among all siblings in the family. This is not duress because, although nasty, it is within Raul's legal rights to abandon his mother. The threats may constitute undue influence, however, depending on other facts such as Gertrude's dependency on Raul and how susceptible she is to his manipulation.

3. Mistake

Fraud, duress, or undue influence may lead a testator to be mistaken as to facts that affect the estate plan. In the absence of these separate causes of action, however, mistake alone is not a reason to bring a will contest. See *Estate of Smith*, 61 Cal. App. 4th 259 (1998). If a testator is mistaken as to the consequences of the language in the document, or as to an external fact that would have affected how the will distributed his estate, there is no relief in the form of a will contest for such a problem. In some states, bringing a case to construe the will may offer some relief, but most states require ambiguous language to allow a court to construe a will, do not allow extrinsic evidence to contradict the terms of the document, and will not reform the document, even if the unambiguous terms were included by mistake. See Chapter 5. Malpractice claims may also be possible for certain kinds of mistakes that should have been corrected by the lawyer, like failure to proofread or improper oversight of the execution ceremony, but this again is not a will contest.

4. Tortious Interference with an Expectancy

Tortious interference with an expectancy (or inheritance) is altogether different from a traditional will contest. In fact, the tort claim is normally available only

> ### Comparing Undue Influence and Duress
>
> It can be difficult to distinguish duress from undue influence, in part because the same facts may very well raise both claims. The Surrogate's Court of New York explained the distinction in *In Re Estate of Rosasco*, 19 Misc. 3d 1109 (2008), as follows:
>
> > There are two principal categories of undue influence in the law of wills, the forms of which are circumscribed only by the ingenuity and resourcefulness of man. One class is the gross, obvious and palpable type of undue influence which does not destroy the intent or will of the testator but prevents it from being exercised by force and threats of harm to the testator or those close to him. The other class is the insidious, subtle and impalpable kind which subverts the intent or will of the testator, internalizes within the mind of the testator the desire to do that which is not his intent but the intent and end of another. . . . The former category is also known as "duress."

if a will contest is not. To prevail in a claim for tortious interference, the plaintiff must prove: (1) the existence of an expectancy; (2) intentional interference with the expectancy through tortious conduct; (3) causation; (4) damages; and (5) (in most states) that the probate remedies were exhausted through no fault of the wronged party. See Restatement (Second) of Torts § 774B. A typical tortious interference claim would mimic a fraud, duress, or undue influence cause of action, but also have an additional wrongdoing that prevented the will contest—such as fraud in concealing the fact of the testator's death or other relevant facts. For example, in the case of Schilling v. Hererra, 952 So. 2d 1231 (Fla. App. 2007), a caretaker persuaded an ill and elderly testator to favor her in estate planning documents—and then concealed from the testator's brother the fact that the testator had died. Here, the brother had a valid tortious interference claim, because the fraud relating to his sister's death caused him to miss the statute of limitations for filing an undue influence will contest.

Although the facts surrounding tortious interference claims are less common than those in will contests, these claims are often in a client's best interest to pursue when available—because punitive damages are possible in a tort claim. The remedy for a will contest is simply to have the property pass as if the improper provision in the will or the will itself did not exist. With a tortious interference claim, the intended beneficiary may receive not only the property she expected under the will or intestate distribution, but additional money to punish the wrongdoer as well. About half of states recognize this tort, and the trend appears to be in the direction of more states recognizing it.

D. IMPROPER OBSERVATION OF WILL EXECUTION FORMALITIES

Because a will must typically be executed in compliance with statutory formalities, wills that do not observe these formalities normally are not entitled to probate. Interested parties may therefore bring a will contest on the grounds that the will was not executed with sufficient formalities as required by state statute. If that is true, and no curative doctrine comes to the rescue, the entire will is denied probate. Allegations that a will execution did not comply with statutory formalities may be combined with a claim based on lack of testamentary intent, like undue influence or fraud, and/or a claim based on lack of mental capacity.

As you will recall, a will is entitled to probate only if it complies with statutory requirements for execution. All states have provisions allowing attested wills, and they vary somewhat as to the requirements surrounding their execution. A large number of states also permit holographic wills and admit a will to probate to the extent it complies with state requirements for a valid holograph. Finally, some states will apply curative doctrines, such as substantial compliance or the harmless error rule, to admit documents that do not quite meet the strict standard the statutes require for being probated. The steps for executing a valid attested or holographic will, as well as a discussion of the curative doctrines, can be found in Chapter 3 on Will Creation.

E. STANDING TO CONTEST AND NO-CONTEST CLAUSES

Not every family member or friend may bring a cause of action to contest a will. Only parties with standing to sue have such a right. Even parties who do have standing to sue may be discouraged from doing so by the use of a **no-contest clause**, which eliminates bequests made to beneficiaries who sue. Estate planning clients can also take additional steps to attempt to minimize the risk of a successful will contest.

1. Standing to Bring a Will Contest

In order to have standing to bring a will contest, a person must be a potential beneficiary or heir. The individual may be a beneficiary under the current will who would receive more if a will contest successfully eliminated a certain bequest, or alternatively a beneficiary under the prior will that would be valid if the contested will were denied probate. Regardless of whether there is a prior will that would be entitled to probate, an heir may bring a will contest.

Keep in mind that the determination of who an heir might be is made at the time of the testator's death (give or take a little time to provide for near-simultaneous deaths). A court therefore knows the statutory priority of surviving relatives. A parent of a decedent is not an heir if a descendant of the decedent survived, and a nephew of the decedent is not an heir if a spouse survived. There is no longer a theoretical exploration of who one's heirs might be, as we considered in Chapter 2 on Intestacy; the class of takers is now closed. This means that relatives who are not heirs and who are not otherwise beneficiaries do not have standing to sue. For example, a sibling of an unmarried childless adult might have been an heir if the sibling outlived both parents, but if either parent is alive, the sibling is not an heir and does not have standing (unless the sibling is a beneficiary under the will).

2. No-Contest Clauses

As a means of discouraging individuals who have standing to contest the will to refrain from doing so, some wills include no-contest clauses. A no-contest clause (sometimes called an *in terrorem* or a *forfeiture* clause) is a provision in a will that states that any beneficiary who brings a will contest or similar challenge will forfeit any bequest in his favor under the will. A no-contest clause can help ward off frivolous suits and also provide some deterrent against borderline claims. In order to be effective, however, a will with a no-contest clause must give the beneficiary a bequest to lose. One dollar, for example, would not provide any real disincentive; the bequest needs to be substantial enough to have a deterrent effect on would-be contestants. This strategy can be a tough sell to a client, because it requires her to transfer something of value to someone the client does not want to benefit, but that the client suspects will fight the disposition she has made in her will. No-contest clauses not only have the negative side effect of skewing the estate plan to include benefits to would-be challengers, they are often unenforceable, an issue discussed in the following case.

Case Preview

Parker v. Benoist

What happens to beneficiaries who bring a will contest in the face of a no-contest clause? In the case that follows, a daughter brought an unsuccessful will contest alleging that her brother had unduly influenced their father. The will included a no-contest clause, but the daughter brought the contest because she genuinely believed her father's medical condition and drug use made him susceptible to undue influence. As you read the case, consider:

1. What did the will provide should happen if a beneficiary contested the will?
2. What did in fact happen to the bequest to the beneficiary who contested the will?
3. Why does the court choose this standard of enforcement for no-contest clauses?

Parker v. Benoist
160 So. 3d 198 (Mississippi 2015)

Kitchens, Justice, for the Court:

Bronwyn Parker and William Benoist are siblings who litigated the will of their father, Billy Dean "B.D." Benoist, in the Chancery Court of Yalobusha County. In 2010, B.D. executed a will which significantly altered the distributions provided by a previous will that B.D. had executed in 1998. Bronwyn alleged that William had unduly influenced their father, who was suffering from dementia and drug addiction, into making the new will, which included a forfeiture clause that revoked benefits to any named beneficiary who contested the will. Bronwyn lost the will contest and her benefits under the new will were revoked by the trial court. In this appeal, we must determine whether Mississippi law should recognize a good-faith and probable-cause exception to a forfeiture *in terrorem* clause in a will. We hold that it should, and that Bronwyn has sufficiently shown that her suit was brought in good faith and was founded upon probable cause. Accordingly, we reverse the decision of the chancery court that excluded Bronwyn from the will, and we render judgment in her favor to allow her to inherit in accordance with her father's 2010 will. . . .

FACTS AND PROCEDURAL HISTORY

. . . In 2008, B.D.'s mind and memory began to deteriorate. William testified that it was due to his drinking and characterized his father's condition as "slight dementia." William testified that his father's mind suffered when he drank heavily, but would snap right back during periods of lucidity. During that time, B.D. also was taking Lortab for back pain. According to William, B.D. would take "a couple [of Lortabs] in the morning, a couple at night, and that pain medicine messed [his] mind up." . . . In 2009, William's wife filed for divorce. The divorce was very difficult for William financially, and B.D. supplied him substantial assistance.

In 2009, B.D. began seeing Dr. Cooper McIntosh, an internist in Oxford, Mississippi. He complained of falling and dizziness. The doctor listed the numerous drugs that B.D. was taking, and stated in a report that B.D. had "significant dementia." B.D. went to Dr. McIntosh several times that year, at times appearing confused. At one point, William called on B.D.'s behalf requesting Lortab, but when B.D. was examined, he did not appear to be in pain. At trial, Dr. McIntosh testified that he "never saw [B.D.] where I would say he was incompetent over, what, almost two years, a year and a half." In June of 2009, B.D. was diagnosed with mild dementia at a V.A. hospital in Jackson. Eventually, Bronwyn became so concerned about her father's increased drinking, depression, and dementia that she wanted to get power of attorney over him. Bronwyn also became concerned about significant withdrawals that were made from B.D.'s trust account and his private Merrill Lynch account, which were sent directly to William. Near the end of his life, B.D. also conveyed a large portion of his real estate to William.

In 2010, B.D. executed a new will ("the 2010 will"). When B.D. died less than a year later, William submitted the 2010 will for probate. Bronwyn, until that point unaware of the new will, entered the 1998 will for probate. She also filed a complaint requesting that the court. . . void any benefits William had received due to his undue influence upon B.D., and grant any legal and equitable relief to Bronwyn to which she was entitled. . . .

She argued that the terms of the 2010 will, combined with the substantial *inter vivos* gifts from B.D. to William, robbed her of much of what she should have inherited under the 1998 will. She also alleged that William was behind the drafting and execution of B.D.'s 2010 will. She contended that William had hidden a document which granted both William and Bronwyn B.D.'s power of attorney, and instead turned B.D. against Bronwyn's husband Walt by convincing him that Walt wanted to use some of B.D.'s property for a commercial development. William argued that Walt and Bronwyn were collaborating against B.D., and that they were going to use Bronwyn's inheritance under the 1998 will in a way which was contrary to B.D.'s wishes. He stated that his father's gifts to him all were aboveboard and simply were the gifts a loving father would give to a son who was having a tough time. . . .

After a trial in the Chancery Court of Yalobusha County, the jury found that the 2010 will was valid and enforceable. The jury unanimously found that there existed a confidential relationship between William and B.D., but it did not find that William had exerted undue influence over B.D. Further, the 2010 will included a forfeiture provision which stated that any beneficiary of the will who instigated a will contest, "regardless of whether or not such proceedings [we]re instituted in good faith and with probable cause," would have his or her benefits under the will revoked. The chancellor found the provision enforceable and held that Bronwyn was no longer a beneficiary of the will. . . .

ANALYSIS

I. Whether the law of Mississippi should recognize a good faith and probable cause exception to forfeiture provisions in wills.

The forfeiture clause in the 2010 will stated:

> If any beneficiary hereunder (including, but not limited to, any beneficiary of a trust created herein) shall contest the probate or validity of this Will or any provision thereof, or shall institute or join in (except as a party defendant) any proceeding to contest the validity of this Will or to prevent any provision thereof from being carried out in accordance with its terms (*regardless of whether or not such proceedings are instituted in good faith and with probable cause*), then all benefits provided for such beneficiary are revoked and such benefits shall pass to the residuary beneficiaries of this Will. . . .

(emphasis added).

A hearing was held on the applicability of the forfeiture clause. By order, the chancellor held that the forfeiture clause was enforceable, "as testators enjoy the right to do as they wish, subject to existing laws." Because Mississippi law did not prohibit such a clause, "the clause contained in B.D. Benoist's Will is valid and enforceable." Under the terms of the clause, Bronwyn was denied any benefits under the will and ordered to pay all attorney fees and court costs associated with the will contest. The chancellor never determined whether Bronwyn's suit was brought in good faith. Because she lost, the forfeiture provision automatically cut her out of the will. We hold that such a provision is unconstitutional under Mississippi's Constitution, void as against public policy, and fundamentally inequitable, and we join the large number of jurisdictions which permit a good-faith and probable-cause exception to forfeiture clauses in wills.

While this may be a case of first impression in Mississippi, this issue has been confronted by courts for hundreds of years, and most of them have held that forfeiture clauses in wills are unenforceable when a will contest is brought in good faith and based upon probable cause. The logic for a good-faith exception is simple: courts exist to determine the truth. A forfeiture clause that operates regardless of a party's good faith in bringing suit to ascertain the validity of a will frustrates the fundamental purpose of a court, which is to determine whether a will is valid or not. . . .

The Restatement (Third) of Property supports the position that a probable-cause exception should be made to forfeiture provisions in will contests. *Restatement (Third) of Property: Wills and Donative Transfers* § 8.5 (2003). "A provision in a donative document purporting to rescind a donative transfer to, or a fiduciary appointment of, any person who institutes a proceeding challenging the validity of all or part of the donative document is enforceable unless probable cause existed for instituting the proceeding." *Id.* The Restatement does acknowledge that forfeiture clauses may serve a valuable purpose in deterring "unwarranted challenges to the donor's intent by a disappointed person seeking to gain unjustified enrichment," or preventing "costly litigation that would deplete the estate or besmirch the reputation of the donor," or discouraging "a contest directed toward coercing a settlement—the so-called strike suit." *Id.*, cmt. b. However, enforcing such a provision without a probable-cause exception would defeat "the jurisdiction of the court to determine the validity of a donative transfer." *Id.* Essentially, the Restatement reasons that unlimited enforceability of forfeiture clauses frustrates the fundamental purpose of the courts to ascertain the truth.

Additionally, permitting a good-faith and probable-cause exception to challenges to wills containing forfeiture provisions is firmly in line with the maxims of equity. . . . For a court of equity to protect and enforce property rights, it must be able to hear disputes regarding those rights. Without a good-faith exception to forfeiture clauses, the testator's will would frustrate the very object of equity. This cannot be allowed.

The weight of authority, logic, and fairness is firmly on the side of a probable-cause and good-faith exception. . . . The determination of good faith and probable cause should be inferred from the totality of the circumstances.

II. Whether Bronwyn Parker's challenge to the 2010 will was made in good faith and founded upon probable cause.

We find that there is sufficient evidence before us to determine whether Bronwyn's challenge to the 2010 will was undertaken in good faith and founded upon probable cause. . . .

Bronwyn's claim was based upon the fact that she understood her parents' intentions in the mutual reciprocal wills from 1998 to be that she and her brother "share and share alike." It cannot be disputed that those were the wishes of her mother, Mary, who died shortly after her will was executed. Mary's will explicitly stated that her children were to inherit equally the remainder of her trust upon the death of B.D. Mary's and B.D.'s 1998 wills provided that the estate of the latter-deceased parent would be given to William and Bronwyn, "in equal shares, per stirpes." At least until 2010, Bronwyn was under the impression that the estate would be divided according to the 1998 will. Further, she testified about B.D.'s failing mental and physical health toward the end of his life, and even William testified about B.D.'s alcoholism and use of strong prescription pain killers. Bronwyn knew that Dr. McIntosh had prescribed two drugs used to treat "cognition problems." Dr. McIntosh's records state that, when he prescribed those drugs for B.D., B.D. was suffering from "significant dementia."

Further, large withdrawals were made from B.D.'s trust account and his private Merrill Lynch account, which were sent directly to William. B.D. also conveyed a large portion of his real estate to William around the time the 2010 will was executed. Bronwyn understandably was worried about these *inter vivos* gifts. The gifts severely depleted B.D.'s estate, rendering much smaller the amount of property that Bronwyn and William would have shared and shared alike under the 1998 will. Overall, Bronwyn argues that her father's failing mental state, his erratic behavior, and his dependence on alcohol and pain killers made him vulnerable to the suggestions of William, an unemployed man experiencing a difficult divorce who convinced B.D. to give him large sums of money beyond what he would have received under the provisions of his father's 1998 will.

We find that Bronwyn's will contest was brought in good faith and was founded on probable cause. . . . Based on the totality of the circumstances, Bronwyn had a reasonable expectation that her will contest would be successful and has provided significant evidence that she instituted the contest in good faith. . . . The claim was not frivolous or made to cause vexatious litigation. The evidence presented by Bronwyn "would lead a reasonable person, properly informed and advised, to conclude that there was a substantial likelihood that the challenge would be successful." *Restatement (Third) of Property: Wills and Other Donative Transfers* at § 8.5 cmt. c. No evidence was adduced that showed bad faith on Bronwyn's part. Based upon the totality of the circumstances, Bronwyn satisfied her burden of proof to demonstrate that her will contest was brought in good faith and was founded upon probable cause. Accordingly, we reverse the judgment of the chancery court and render judgment in favor of Bronwyn on the forfeiture clause issue. The 2010 will is valid except for the forfeiture clause, and Bronwyn cannot be cut out of the will for bringing her good-faith suit to determine its validity. . . .

CONCLUSION

We hold that forfeiture provisions in wills in Mississippi are enforceable unless the will contest has been founded upon probable cause and made in good faith. This is in accord with the majority of U.S. jurisdictions, the Restatement of Property, and the Uniform Probate Code, and most faithfully conforms to our state constitutional guarantees of access to courts and the maxims of equity. Under the totality of the circumstances, Bronwyn Benoist Parker's will contest was based upon probable cause and was brought in good faith. Accordingly, the forfeiture provision in B.D.'s will is unenforceable against her. We reverse the decision of the Chancery Court of Yalobusha County in this regard, and render judgment in Parker's favor to the effect that she is entitled to her inheritance as provided in her father's 2010 will. . . .

Post-Case Follow-Up

The rule followed by the court in Parker v. Benoist is very common. Although no-contest clauses have a loud bark, so long as the contestant's suit is not frivolous, they generally have no bite. Enforcing a no-contest clause under any circumstances would make it easy to commit undue influence, fraud, or duress simply by inserting the clause into the document. Therefore no-contest clauses may provide some deterrent effect, but should not be taken literally to mean that there will be no contest.

Parker v. Benoist: Real Life Applications

1. You represent the brother of a wealthy unmarried doctor who has left the majority of her estate to the American Cancer Society, in addition to gifts of $50,000 each to her son, her daughter, and her brother. The will contains a no-contest clause such as the one quoted in Parker v. Benoist. There is no evidence of wrongdoing by the charity, but when she executed her will the doctor was in her late nineties and had some health problems. How would you guide your client in deciding whether to bring a will contest based on lack of capacity?

2. You are drafting model language for your firm's wills. Should the firm routinely include a no-contest clause? Under what circumstances should the firm include or exclude the clause?

3. You are representing a client who wants to include a no-contest clause in his will. What do you tell him about the reasoning for including it and how likely it is to be effective?

3. Planning to Avoid a Will Contest

In addition to considering the inclusion of a no-contest clause, there are several practical steps a lawyer may advise for a client who expects a will contest may arise. First, nonprobate transfers, discussed in more detail in Chapter 7, provide several benefits over transfers in a will. Wills are a matter of public record, whereas nonprobate transfers are private, and therefore less likely to come to the attention of or to raise the ire of a neglected would-be beneficiary. Transfers over time, such as transfers in trust or a series of gifts, are harder to contest than a will because they show the client's ongoing commitment to a consistent plan to benefit a particular individual or organization. Lawyers should also advise clients to refrain from using inflammatory language to cut out unwanted relatives.

It is also often helpful to have the client have a family meeting with relatives who may be expecting to receive property. Sometimes it is the secrecy of the will itself that causes the problems as much as the actual disposition of property that the will provides. The omitted beneficiary is less likely to be offended (and bring suit) if the client explains that she is giving property to a child out of medical need, or to a charity out of a sense of commitment to the cause, rather than intending to illustrate lack of love for the omitted beneficiary.

There are additional steps a lawyer can take to minimize the risk of a will contest when there are warning signs that one may arise. If the client's capacity is questionable, the lawyer should advise medical examinations and maintain doctor records relating to level of mental functioning. Ensuring that the client comes to meetings with the lawyer alone, rather than with someone who might exert (or be accused of exerting) undue influence can also help protect against such claims. It is also good practice to maintain a thorough record of client communications, paricularly a series of documents prepared by the client explaining the intended estate plan. Finally, more drastic measures, such as using adoption to remove the standing of those likely to contest, may be worth considering for large transfers where contest is almost certain.

Chapter Summary

- A testator must have both legal capacity and mental capacity to execute a valid will. Legal capacity is granted by statute to individuals who have attained a certain age or substitute for maturity such as marriage, military service, or emancipation.
- Mental capacity exists if a testator understands the nature of her possessions, her loved ones, her estate plan, and how those three elements relate to each other. Even if a testator has mental capacity, provisions in a will may be denied effect if they are a result of an insane delusion—an irrational belief that cannot be overcome despite evidence to the contrary and that affected those provisions.
- A testator's will must result from testamentary intent and should be denied probate if it is the product of undue influence, fraud, or duress. Undue influence exists when the decisions of the testator are overcome by the pressure of the influencer and the will fails to state the testator's own plans. Fraud exists when the testator is deliberately misled by a third party as to the contents or legal effect of the will or facts relevant to the plan of distribution the testator chose. Duress exists when the testator executes the will under force or threat of force. Wills executed under any of these circumstances do not set forth the true testamentary intent of the decedent and are not entitled to probate.
- If any grounds for contest exist, an interested party may "contest the will" and bring litigation alleging that the will is not entitled to probate. An interested party must have standing to bring the will contest, which arises if the party is a beneficiary under a prior will or would have taken as an heir under the state intestacy statutes if no valid will had been left.
- If a drafting lawyer anticipates a will contest, some strategies may minimize the likelihood that an interested party will bring a lawsuit. Properly structured no-contest clauses provide some disincentive to beneficiaries named in the will. These clauses provide that a beneficiary who contests a will and loses forfeits her bequest, but the clauses are generally not enforced against a beneficiary who has probable cause to bring a claim.

Applying the Concepts

1. Ethel is a grandmother in her eighties who lives in an assisted living facility. She uses a wheelchair and has good days and bad days with respect to her dementia. Ethel's daughter normally handles her financial affairs, but there is no formal guardianship. Does Ethel have the necessary capacity to execute a will?

2. Matilda was a scientist who gradually developed a belief that Earth was being overtaken by life-forms from a distant planet. Matilda was otherwise decisive and managed her affairs well. Two years before she died, Matilda executed her only will, leaving her entire estate to the Society for Research of Extraterrestrial Intelligence, a charity to which she donated during life and where she served on the board for several years and until her death. Matilda's will is currently in probate, with one of her children, Leo, challenging its validity on the ground that his mother suffered from an insane delusion. Applying the concepts you have learned, how is the judge of probate most likely to rule?

3. Jayden has always relied on the advice of his twin, Hayden. When Jayden raised the idea of writing a will in favor of his fiancée, Brittany, Hayden talked him out of it. Jayden died with no will and Hayden received the entire estate through intestacy. Does Brittany have grounds for a claim of undue influence?

4. Building on the facts in Problem 3, assume that Jayden left his twin, Hayden, his entire estate under an existing will but raised the idea of a new will favoring his fiancée. Assume also that Jayden was unusually vulnerable to influence by Hayden and relied on him in all matters, that the twins lived together and were often alone with each other, and that this combined with Hayden receiving the entire estate is sufficient to trigger burden-shifting in his state. What are examples of evidence Hayden would need to produce to disprove undue influence if Brittany brings a will contest?

5. Mary was a member of a tightly knit religious group known for its followers' intense devotion. Mary executed a will leaving almost her entire estate to Father Jones, the charismatic leader of the group. Years later, she regretted the decision and made an appointment with her lawyer to revoke her will, allowing the property to pass to her two adult children. Using his connections with a surgeon who was a member of the group, Father Jones had Mary admitted for heart palpitations; she was sent into surgery and died. If Mary's children were to challenge Mary's final will leaving her estate to Father Jones, would they have a case on grounds of duress? See Latham v. Father Divine, 85 N.E.2d 168 (N.Y. 1949).

Trusts and Estates in Practice

1. Giuseppe has come to your office to have a new will drafted. You had asked Giuseppe to bring a thorough list of his assets so that you would be able to form a detailed picture of his estate. He has arrived at your office with a list of his assets, including land holdings, bank account information, and personal property. However, the personal property contained in the list is not specific and merely lists items such as "cars," "books," and "antiques." Does the lack of detail regarding the property Giuseppe owns preclude you from drafting the will? Research the law of your state regarding the required elements for testator capacity and determine whether you would face problems in connection with drafting Giuseppe's will.

2. Five years ago, you drafted a will for Sunny, then age 20, which left her entire estate to her boyfriend, Rogan. Sunny became a country music star and earned significant income, but died a young and tragic death in a pickup truck accident. Sunny's mother and sole heir, Addy, wants to have the will declared void because Sunny irrationally and inaccurately believed that Addy's neighbor was secretly heading a terrorist organization. Sunny's will does not mention Addy or her neighbor. In one short paragraph, explain whether Addy has grounds to contest the will. If time allows, research the law in the state where you attend law school to determine the test for insane delusion.

3. Jean comes to your office explaining that her mother, Nancy, has left her entire estate to the two nurses who were her primary caregivers in the last months of her life. The nurses told Nancy that Jean was wasting Nancy's money and wanted to put her in a nursing home. On what grounds may Jean contest the will? Write a letter to Jean in which you explain the elements of each relevant claim. What additional information would be useful? See Puckett v. Krida, 1994 Tenn. App. LEXIS 502 (1994).

4. You represent Olivia, who comes from an argumentative family and wishes to leave her entire estate to her best friend and exclude her family members.

   a. In a letter to Olivia, explain what a no-contest clause is and what its benefits and downsides may be.
   b. Research the law in the state where you are attending law school to determine under what circumstances no-contest clauses are enforced.

5. A senior partner has come to you to ask about a plan of action to represent the firm's client, Zachary. Zachary states that Sal, the boyfriend of his mother Isabella, prevented Zachary from receiving his inheritance from Isabella by lying to her about Zachary's whereabouts and concealing Zachary's attempts to contact his mother. Assume that the will leaving all of Isabella's estate to Sal has already been admitted to probate, but Zachary only recently learned of the details pertaining to Sal's actions. Compose a memorandum addressing the following questions:

   a. Can Zachary bring a claim for tortious interference with an expectancy under the law of the state where you are in school?
   b. If such a course of action is plausibly available, does the fact that the probate proceedings have been concluded bar the course of action?
   c. What are the potential damages and remedies in this case?

EXHIBIT 6.1   Petition Contesting Will

NO. 05-770-P3

IN THE MATTER OF THE	§ § §	IN THE PROBATE COURT
GUARDIANSHIP OF	§ § §	NUMBER THREE OF
MARY ELLEN LOGAN BENDTSEN, AN ALLEGED INCAPACITATED PERSON	§ §	DALLAS COUNTY, TEXAS

FILED (stamp)

<u>ORIGINAL PETITION CONTESTING WILL</u>

TO THE HONORABLE JUDGE OF SAID COURT:

Now comes **FRANCES ANN GIRON**, ("Contestant") and files this Original Petition Contesting Will contesting the probate of the purported February 22, 2005 Will (the "Purported Will"), and respectfully shows the Court as follows:

I.
<u>DISCOVERY LEVEL 3</u>

1.   Discovery is intended to be conducted under Level 3 of TEX. R. CIV. P., Rule 190.1. Contestant requests the Court to order a Level 3 discovery plan and dictate the discovery rules and deadlines in this case.

II.
<u>THE DECEDENT</u>

2.   **MARY ELLEN LOGAN BENDTSEN**, ("Decedent"), died testate, on March 2, 2005, in Dallas, Dallas County, Texas, at the age of eighty eight (88) years. The Decedent was domiciled and had a fixed place of residence in Dallas County, Texas.

III.
<u>THE CONTESTANT</u>

3.   **FRANCES ANN GIRON** ("Contestant"), presently resides at 6361 Westblanc, Plano, Texas 75093. Contestant is the Respondent's daughter.

ORIGINAL PETITION CONTESTING WILL, Page 1   S:\05-931\Contest_Petition.wpd

IV.
JURISDICTION AND VENUE

4.   This Court has jurisdiction under TEX. PROB. CODE §5 and venue under TEX. PROB. CODE §6 because Decedent was domiciled and had a fixed place of residence and his principal Estate was in Dallas County on the date of his death.

V.
SERVICE

5.   Service upon **DIXIE L. M. TIDWELL** ("Applicant"), a party of record, will be accomplished by serving her attorney of record, Edwin C. Olsen IV, with a copy of this Contest, pursuant to TEX. PROB. CODE §34.

VI.
FACTS

6.   The Decedent was married one time to Christian Bendtsen and he pre-deceased her on August 8, 1986. Contestant was the only child of that marriage.

7.   Execution of the Purported Will was obtained at a time when the Decedent was weak and infirm and was under the control of others.

8.   The Decedent died on March 2, 2005.

9.   The Purported Will of the Decedent dated February 22, 2005 was signed and executed at a time when she lacked testamentary capacity and was unduly influenced.

10.   The Purported Will is invalid.

11.   The Purported Will has not been admitted to probate and should not be admitted to probate.

VII.
WILL CONTEST

12.   Contestant alleges that the Purported Will should be set aside because it was not executed according to the formalities required by Texas law.

13.   Contestant alleges that the Purported Will should be set aside because it was executed without testamentary intent.

14.   Contestant alleges that the Purported Will should be set aside because Decedent lacked the necessary testamentary capacity to make a Will at the time it was executed.

15.   Contestant alleges that the Purported Will should be set aside because Decedent was unduly influenced to sign the Purported Will by the compulsion and arguments of others.

16.   Such efforts to obtain the Purported Will were of such strength as to overcome Decedent's desires and her free agency to make the Purported Will, in part, due to her inability to resist them through weakness and fear and/or because of her desire for peace.

17.   For all of the above reasons, Contestants request that the Purported Will be found invalid, set aside and not admitted to probate.

VIII.
ATTORNEY'S FEES

18.   Contestant hired Judith P. Kenney & Associates, P. C. to represent her in this matter, to contest the Purported Will and to thereby defend the Will dated October 23, 2002. Contestant and her attorneys have acted in good faith with just cause and are entitled to attorney's fees under TEX. PROB. CODE §243. Contestant request

that their reasonable attorney's fees and expenses incurred in this proceeding be paid by the Estate.

IX.
PRE-JUDGMENT AND POST-JUDGMENT INTEREST

19. Contestant seeks recovery of pre-judgment and post-judgment interest at the highest rate allowed by law on all damage awards, attorney's fees, and/or reimbursements.

WHEREFORE, PREMISES CONSIDERED, Contestant prays that the Court consider this pleading, that notice and citation be issued as required by law to all persons interested in this Estate and upon hearing, grant all of her requested relief including, but not limited to:

a.) Ordering this case to be a Level 3 case;

b.) Dictating the discovery rules and deadlines for this case;

c.) Finding that the purported February 22, 2005 Will of the Decedent is invalid;

d.) Setting the Purported Will aside;

e.) Admit to probate the Will dated October 23, 2002;

f.) Awarding actual damages;

g.) Awarding costs, attorney's fees and expenses;

h.) Awarding interest at the highest rate allowed by law; and

i.) Granting general relief.

Respectfully submitted,

JUDITH P. KENNEY & ASSOCIATES, P.C.

By: *Nat M. Kenney, III*
Judith P. Kenney
State Bar Number 11311600

Nat M. Kenney, III
State Bar Number 11311650

One Bent Tree Tower
16475 Dallas Parkway
Suite 740
Addison, Texas 75001
(972) 713-6133
(972) 713-6233 FAX
(800) 862-3663

ATTORNEYS FOR CONTESTANT

CERTIFICATE OF SERVICE

I hereby certify that on the ___3rd___ day of March, 2005, a true and correct copy

of the above and foregoing was forwarded to the counsel of record listed below:

Edwin C. Olsen, IV
11318 Cotillion Drive
Dallas, Texas 75228
Attorney for Dixie L. M. Tidwell, Applicant

Nat M. Kenney, III
Nat M. Kenney, III

Nonprobate Transfers and Planning for Incapacity

Historically, property was transmitted at death through the probate process. However, beginning in the second half of the twentieth century, **will substitutes** or **nonprobate transfers** grew in popularity as an alternative to probate. The terms each refer to legal mechanisms for transmitting property at death outside of the probate process. Through such legally recognized nonprobate transfers, a person can exert ownership rights over property during his or her lifetime, but designate someone else to receive that property at death without involving the probate court. You are probably already familiar with this type of transfer from your Property class through the concept of joint tenancies with rights of survivorship, and you will become familiar with additional types that are used in estate planning.

This chapter addresses and defines various types of property transfers that occur at death outside of probate. The chapter first discusses some of the most common types of nonprobate transfers and looks at some of the most common problems with them, including changing a beneficiary designation. We will also explore why nonprobate transfers have become such a significant part of the legal landscape, examining their benefits and drawbacks, and showing the need to develop a comprehensive estate plan that incorporates both nonprobate transfers and wills.

Finally, we look at how an individual can plan for financial and medical care upon incapacity, exploring the most common instruments that individuals draft to handle this contingency. Both planning for incapacity and nonprobate transfers are relatively new tools (within the past century) in estate planning, which is why they are discussed in this chapter. Moreover, both will substitutes, particularly revocable trusts, are useful for incapacity planning.

Key Concepts

- The types of nonprobate transfers
- Reasons for using nonprobate transfers
- Differences between probate and nonprobate transfers
- Planning for property management upon disability
- Planning for medical care upon disability

A. INTRODUCTION TO WILL SUBSTITUTES/NONPROBATE TRANSFERS

More people have will substitutes than wills.[1] While wills have historically required near-perfect compliance with formalities such as the testator's signature, witnessing, publication, and other requirements, will substitutes have fewer such requirements. Indeed, nonprobate transfers are not controlled by probate law. Instead, they are controlled by contract law (since many are commercial agreements between a company and the customer, such as life insurance policies and financial accounts), by property law (such as joint tenancies with right of survivorship), or by trust law (as you will see later this semester). The differing sets of laws also affect other matters, such as the level of competency one must possess in order to execute the documents and, more importantly, the process for distributing the property that is subject to their provisions.

While will substitutes may function to pass property at death just as a will does, the historical "explanation for why a will substitute is not a will is that a will substitute transfers ownership during life—it effects a *present* transfer of a *nonpossessory future* interest or contract right," which is recognized as an ownership interest, but actual possession does not occur until the donor has died. Restatement (Third) of Property: Wills and Other Donative Transfers § 7.1 (2003). Although these are the historical underpinnings of the rule, beneficiaries of most nonprobate transfers do not in reality have any significant rights to the property during the lifetime of the owner, and the beneficiary designation generally may be changed freely. They are thus comparable to wills when it comes to the timing of the transfer of property.

The lesser number of formalities surrounding will substitutes—business contracts, joint ownership, and, in some respects, trusts—has profoundly affected the law of testamentary transfers, and vice versa. While the laws of wills and will substitutes are more alike today than in the past, they are still not the same. This has led the drafters of the Uniform Probate Code (UPC) and state property inheritance laws to attempt to make the two even more uniform. *See* Grayson M.P. McCouch, *Probate Law Reform and Nonprobate Transfers*, 62 U. Miami L. Rev. 757 (2008).

Will Substitutes and Attorney Review

Even though people typically create will substitutes without consulting an attorney, it is important for an estate planning attorney to review will substitutes because they must be considered when developing a comprehensive estate plan for a client. Attorneys need to address such issues as whom the client has designated as a beneficiary and whether the client has changed beneficiaries to reflect changes in the client's family. (For example, divorce should prompt such changes.) In addition, if too much property is transferred outside probate directly to named beneficiaries, the probate estate may not be sufficient to pay the taxes and debts of the decedent, possibly leaving the burden to transferees of nonprobate property.

---

[1] Jeffrey M. Jones, *Majority in U.S. Do Not Have a Will*, Gallup (May 18, 2016), http://www.gallup.com/poll/191651/majority-not.aspx; Bureau of Labor Statistics, *Employee Benefits in the United States—March 2016*, https://www.bls.gov/news.release/pdf/ebs2.pdf.

B. THE MOST COMMON FORMS OF WILL SUBSTITUTES

There are numerous types of will substitutes. See UPC § 6-101. The most common forms include: (1) life insurance, (2) retirement accounts, (3) joint bank accounts and joint brokerage accounts holding stocks and securities, (4) accounts or deeds with a payable-on-death or transfer-on-death designation, and (5) inter vivos trusts. Each will be discussed below.

1. Life Insurance

Life insurance is just what it sounds like: insurance on the life of a person. It generally takes the form of a contract that guarantees payment if the insured person dies. That payment can be made to any beneficiary named in the life insurance contract. Typically, a spouse, child, or, in the business context, a business entity will be named. The individual pays a **premium** to obtain life insurance coverage. A premium is simply the amount of money the owner pays for the insurance policy, and it can be paid as a lump sum or in installments over time. For example, Kojo takes out a $100,000 life insurance policy and names Dahlia as the beneficiary of the policy. Kojo pays an annual premium for the policy. When Kojo dies, Dahlia receives $100,000 from the insurance company by following procedures, such as producing a certified copy of the death certificate (these procedures are discussed in Chapter 14, Estate Administration and the Probate Process).

The two most common types of life insurance are term and permanent. A term life insurance policy protects the insured for a specified amount of time. A term life insurance policy has no investment component, and for that reason, term insurance is cheaper when a person is younger and more expensive as a person ages. Such a policy offers protection for a particular amount of time and expires thereafter. "This period could be as short as one year or provide coverage for a specific number of years such as 5, 10, 20 years or to a specified age such as 80 or in some cases up to the oldest age in the life insurance mortality tables. . . . If you die during the term period, the company will pay the face amount of the policy to your beneficiary. If you live beyond the term period you had selected, no benefit is payable." New York State Dept. Fin. Services, Life Insurance Resource Center, http://www.dfs.ny.gov/consumer/cli_basic.htm.

Permanent life insurance is—well, permanent, so long as the premiums are paid. Permanent insurance is designed to provide coverage for the insured person's entire lifetime, and it pays out to the beneficiary when the insured individual dies. Many different insurance products, beyond the scope of our discussion here, provide various types of permanent insurance. Some more common insurance options are whole life or universal life policies. Insurance policies other than term insurance typically have an investment component, and the premiums are set higher than for term insurance, so that the premiums both pay for the insurance and increase the size of the investment account associated with the policy. Income earned on the investment account can be used to pay the premiums over time, although additional premiums may be due, depending on the type of product chosen and the amount of the early premiums. Other kinds of insurance policies, such as accidental death and dismemberment insurance and business travel accident insurance, may also have a death benefit payable to a beneficiary upon the insured's death.

Without delving into the details of insurance law, anyone who has an insurable interest in a person may take out a policy on that person's life. Normally, the insured buys the policy on her own life. However, a family member or a trust whose beneficiaries are family members may also buy a policy on someone's life. The owner of the policy decides who the beneficiaries are. In addition, the owner may borrow against the value of the policy if the policy has an investment component to it. These rights are sometimes referred to as "the incidents of ownership," especially in the tax context.

For example, Freda owned a life insurance policy that specified, at her death, that the insurance company should pay the proceeds of the policy to Freda's only child, Sydney, if Sydney survives Freda, and if not, to Freda's probate estate. If Sydney survives Freda's death, the proceeds will pass to Sydney directly and will not be added to Freda's probate estate. If Sydney does not survive Freda, the insurance company will pay the proceeds to Freda's estate, and the money will be included in the probate estate.

At any point, the person who acquires the life insurance policy can change the beneficiary. Because life insurance is governed by contract law, however, a beneficiary designation change can only be done if the owner complies with the means for changing the beneficiary required by the life insurance policy.

Case Preview

Hillman v. Maretta

The next case illustrates the importance of complying with company procedures to change a beneficiary. Warren Hillman and Judy Maretta were married. In 1996, Warren named Judy as the beneficiary of his federal life insurance policy. They divorced in 1998 and, four years later, he married Jacqueline. Warren died unexpectedly in 2008. Because Warren had never changed the named beneficiary under his life insurance policy, it continued to identify Judy as the beneficiary at the time of his death despite his divorce and subsequent remarriage.

After Warren's death, Judy filed a claim for benefits and collected the proceeds. Jacqueline then sued Judy, alleging she was entitled to the proceeds under Virginia law. Virginia law revokes a life insurance beneficiary designation upon divorce, but if policies are covered by federal law, then federal law requires respect for the beneficiary designated on the policy itself.

As you read the case, consider the following:

1. On what basis did each party claim the insurance proceeds?
2. Did Warren Hillman take the requisite steps to change the beneficiary?
3. What did Virginia state law provide with respect to the beneficiary designation? What does the Court suggest is the policy rationale for the Virginia law?
4. What did the Court decide was the relationship between Virginia state law and federal insurance law?

Hillman v. Maretta
133 S. Ct. 1943 (2013)

Justice SOTOMAYOR delivered the opinion of the Court.

The Federal Employees' Group Life Insurance Act of 1954 (FEGLIA), 5 U.S.C. § 8701 *et seq.*, establishes a life insurance program for federal employees. FEGLIA provides that an employee may designate a beneficiary to receive the proceeds of his life insurance at the time of his death. § 8705(a). Separately, a Virginia statute addresses the situation in which an employee's marital status has changed, but he did not update his beneficiary designation before his death. Section 20-111.1(D) of the Virginia Code renders a former spouse liable for insurance proceeds to whoever would have received them under applicable law, usually a widow or widower, but for the beneficiary designation. Va. Code Ann. § 20-111.1(D). This case presents the question whether [Virginia law] is pre-empted by FEGLIA and its implementing regulations. We hold that it is.

I

A

In 1954, Congress enacted FEGLIA to "provide low-cost group life insurance to Federal employees." H.R. Rep. No. 2579, 83d Cong., 2d Sess., 1 (1954). The program is administered by the federal Office of Personnel Management (OPM). 5 U.S.C. § 8716. . . . The program is of substantial size. In 2010, the total amount of FEGLI insurance coverage in force was $824 billion.

FEGLIA provides that, upon an employee's death, life insurance benefits are paid in accordance with a specified "order of precedence." 5 U.S.C. § 8705(a). The proceeds accrue "[f]irst, to the beneficiary or beneficiaries designated by the employee in a signed and witnessed writing received before death." Ibid. "[I]f there is no designated beneficiary," the benefits are paid "to the widow or widower of the employee." Ibid. Absent a widow or widower, the benefits accrue to "the child or children of the employee and descendants of [the] deceased children"; "the parents of the employee" or their survivors; the "executor or administrator of the estate of the employee"; and last, to "other next of kin." *Ibid.*

To be effective, the beneficiary designation and any accompanying revisions to it must be in writing and duly filed with the Government. See ibid. ("[A] designation, change, or cancellation of beneficiary in a will or other document not so executed and filed has no force or effect"). An OPM regulation provides that an employee may "change [a] beneficiary at any time without the knowledge or consent of the previous beneficiary," and makes clear that "[t]his right cannot be waived or restricted." 5 CFR § 870.802(f). Employees are informed of these requirements through materials that OPM disseminates in connection with the program.

. . .

In 1998, Congress amended FEGLIA to create a limited exception to an employee's right of designation. The statute now provides that "[a]ny amount which would otherwise be paid to a person determined under the order of precedence . . . shall be paid (in whole or in part) by [OPM] to another person if and to the extent expressly provided for in the terms of any court decree of divorce, annulment, or legal separation" or related settlement, but only in the event the "decree, order, or agreement" is received by OPM or the employing agency before the employee's death. 5 U.S.C. § 8705(e)(1)-(2).

FEGLIA also includes an express pre-emption provision. That provision states in relevant part that "[t]he provisions of any contract under [FEGLIA] which relate to the nature or extent of coverage or benefits (including payments with respect to benefits) shall supersede and preempt any law of any State . . . . which relates to group life insurance to the extent that the law or regulation is inconsistent with the contractual provisions." § 8709(d)(1).

This case turns on the interaction between these provisions of FEGLIA and [the] Virginia statute. (Section A) of the Virginia Code provides that a divorce or annulment "revoke[s]" a "beneficiary designation contained in a then existing written contract owned by one party that provides for the payment of any death benefit to the other party." A "death benefit" includes "payments under a life insurance contract." § 20.111.1(B).

In the event that Section A is pre-empted by federal law, [] Section D creates a cause of action rendering a former spouse liable for the principal amount of the insurance proceeds to the person who would have received them had Section A continued in effect.

B

. . .

Hillman filed a claim for the proceeds of Warren's life insurance, but the FEGLI administrator informed her that the proceeds would accrue to Maretta, because she had been named as the beneficiary. Maretta filed a claim for the benefits with OPM and collected the FEGLI proceeds in the amount of $124,558.03.

Hillman then filed a lawsuit in Virginia [], arguing that Maretta was liable to her under Section D for the proceeds of her deceased husband's FEGLI policy. The parties agreed that Section A, which directly reallocates the benefits, is pre-empted by FEGLIA. Maretta contended that Section D is also pre-empted by federal law and that she should keep the insurance proceeds.

The Virginia Supreme Court [] entered judgment for Maretta. The court found that FEGLIA clearly instructed that the insurance proceeds should be paid to a named beneficiary. The court reasoned that "Congress did not intend merely for the named beneficiary in a FEGLI policy to receive the proceeds, only then to have them subject to recovery by a third party under state law." It therefore concluded that Section D is pre-empted by FEGLIA [].

We granted certiorari []. We now affirm.

II

. . .

The regulation of domestic relations is traditionally the domain of state law [], and "family and family-property law must do 'major damage' to 'clear and substantial' federal interests before the Supremacy Clause will demand that state law will be overridden." But family law is not entirely insulated from conflict pre-emption principles, and so we have recognized that state laws "governing the economic aspects of domestic relations . . . must give way to clearly conflicting federal enactments."

A

[] Maretta insists that Congress [enacted FEGLIA] to ensure that a duly named beneficiary will receive the insurance proceeds and be able to make use of them. If Maretta is correct, then Section D would directly conflict with that objective, because its cause of action would take the insurance proceeds away from the named beneficiary and reallocate them to someone else. We must therefore determine which understanding of FEGLIA's purpose is correct.

We do not write on a clean slate. In two previous cases, we considered federal insurance statutes requiring that insurance proceeds be paid to a named beneficiary and held they pre-empted state laws that mandated a different distribution of benefits. The statutes we addressed in these cases are similar to FEGLIA . . . . FEGLIA creates a scheme that gives highest priority to an insured's designated beneficiary. 5 U.S.C. § 8705(a). . . .

Section D interferes with Congress' scheme, because it directs that the proceeds actually "belong" to someone other than the named beneficiary by creating a cause of action for their recovery by a third party. It makes no difference whether state law requires the transfer of the proceeds, as Section A does, or creates a cause of action, like Section D, that enables another person to receive the proceeds upon filing an action in state court. In either case, state law displaces the beneficiary selected by the insured in accordance with FEGLIA and places someone else in her stead. As in [an earlier case], applicable state law "substitutes the widow" for the "beneficiary Congress directed shall receive the insurance money," and thereby "frustrates the deliberate purpose of Congress" to ensure that a federal employee's named beneficiary receives the proceeds. *Ibid.*

One can imagine plausible reasons to favor a different policy. Many employees perhaps neglect to update their beneficiary designations after a change in marital status. As a result, a legislature could have thought that a default rule providing that insurance proceeds accrue to a widow or widower, and not a named beneficiary, would be more likely to align with most people's intentions. Or, similarly, a legislature might have reasonably believed that an employee's will is more reliable evidence of his intent than a beneficiary designation form executed years earlier.

But that is not the judgment Congress made. Rather than draw an inference about an employee's probable intent from a range of sources, Congress established a clear and predictable procedure for an employee to indicate who the intended beneficiary of his life insurance shall be. []FEGLIA evinces Congress' decision to accord federal employees an unfettered "freedom of choice" in selecting the beneficiary of the insurance proceeds and to ensure the proceeds would actually "belong" to that beneficiary. . . .

There is further confirmation that Congress intended the insurance proceeds be paid in accordance with FEGLIA's procedures. Section 8705(e)(1) of FEGLIA provides that "[a]ny amount which would otherwise be paid . . . under the order of precedence" shall be paid to another person "if and to the extent expressly provided for in the terms of any court decree of divorce, annulment, or legal separation." This exception, however, only applies if the "decree, order, or agreement . . . is received, before the date of the covered employee's death, by the employing agency." § 8705(e)(2). This provision allows the proceeds to be paid to someone other than the named beneficiary, but if and only if the requisite documentation is filed with the Government, so that any departure from the beneficiary designation is managed within, not outside, the federal system.

. . . In short, where a beneficiary has been duly named, the insurance proceeds she is owed under FEGLIA cannot be allocated to another person by operation of state law. Section D does exactly that. We therefore agree with the Virginia Supreme Court that it is pre-empted.

* * *

Section D is in direct conflict with FEGLIA because it interferes with Congress' objective that insurance proceeds belong to the named beneficiary. Accordingly, we hold that Section D is pre-empted by federal law. The judgment of the Virginia Supreme Court is affirmed.

It is so ordered.

[A concurring opinion by Justice Thomas has been omitted.]

Justice ALITO, concurring in the judgment.

I concur in the judgment.

[] FEGLIA seems to me to have two primary purposes or objectives.

The first is administrative convenience. It is easier for an insurance administrator to pay insurance proceeds to the person whom the insured has designated on a specified form without having to consider claims made by others based on some other ground. . . .

The second purpose or objective is the effectuation of the insured's *expressed* intent above all other considerations . . . .

FEGLIA prioritizes the insured's *expressed* intent.

Post-Case Follow-Up

The case provides a number of important lessons. First, it shows the need to revisit estate planning whenever there is a change in family structure. Second, it reinforces the rule that individuals must comply with the underlying contract in order to effectuate a valid change in beneficiary. Third, it is in accord with various Supreme Court decisions indicating that state statutes that automatically rescind rights upon divorce do not apply to life insurance or retirement plans controlled by federal law, such as the Employee Retirement Income Security Act of 1974 (ERISA). *E.g., Egelhoff v. Egelhoff,* 532 U.S. 141 (2001); *Kennedy v. Plan Adm'r for DuPont Sav. and Inv. Plan,* 555 U.S. 285 (2009). For employees with nonprobate assets controlled by federal law, it is thus particularly important to reassess beneficiary designation procedures upon divorce.

Hillman v. Maretta: Real Life Applications

1. What steps could Warren Hillman have taken to ensure that his wife would receive the life insurance?

2. Based on the facts of the case, consider what would have happened if Judy Maretta had predeceased Warren. Who would have received the life insurance proceeds?

3. *Hillman* concerns a life insurance policy for federal employees. Suppose that Warren had also purchased a life insurance policy from a large private insurance company, naming Judy as the beneficiary. As was true for the FEGLIA policy, imagine that Warren did not change the beneficiary designation after the divorce. Who would have received those proceeds under Virginia law?

2. Pensions/Retirement Plans

Most workers have access to some type of **pension**, which is often the greatest asset that an individual has to pass at death. A pension is a retirement plan in which a specific amount is paid every month to a retiree. Retirement benefits can take the form of either a (1) defined benefit plan, or (2) defined contribution plan.

An employer that offers a **defined benefit plan** provides employees with a guaranteed level of fixed monthly payments, based on a fixed formula that accounts for factors such as salary, years of service, and age. Benefits are generally payable to the employee or to the employee and spouse jointly for life, and there is little or no flexibility in naming beneficiaries. Because the benefit is a series of payments during life, there is no balance in the account at death and no need to designate a beneficiary for a transfer effective upon death. Under a defined benefit plan, the employer bears the risk that investment results will be poor, because a set amount is payable under the plan even if assets underperform. For this reason, defined contribution accounts are increasingly more popular.

By contrast, a **defined contribution plan** does not offer a guaranteed payment. Instead, the payments from a defined contribution plan are based on the amount of money contributed and the rate of return on the money invested. Defined contribution plans therefore place the risk of poor investment performance on the employee, because the employer is not promising a fixed payment, but merely the right to whatever balance accrues in the account. These plans may be funded by employee contributions, employer contributions, or a combination of the two. Most plans are administered by employers, but individuals may also establish independent retirement accounts. **Individual Retirement Accounts** (IRAs) are retirement savings accounts that can offer various tax breaks. The most common types of IRAs are accounts that you open on your own rather than ones provided by a business. Note that IRAs are not employee benefit plans, but instead serve as a vehicle for holding funds that are set aside for retirement.

Just as with insurance contracts, the individual designates the beneficiary of a defined contribution retirement plan account on a form (or online selection) provided by the investment company or retirement plan administrator. A retirement plan must **vest** before benefits are paid. Vesting refers to the amount of time a participant must work before earning a nonforfeitable right to a retirement benefit. Once the plan is vested, the accrued benefit is retained even if the worker leaves the employer before reaching retirement age.

After the owner of a defined contribution retirement account dies, the person listed as the beneficiary has the legal right to take control of the account. The rate at which the beneficiary may withdraw assets from the account is set by federal tax law. As with life insurance, the person who contributes to a retirement account can control the distribution of the money remaining in the account at death by designating the beneficiary.

Individual Retirement Accounts (IRAs) are not employee benefits plans. IRAs are retirement savings accounts in which individuals can set aside a capped sum each year for retirement. IRAs are attractive because individuals need not go through their employers to open an IRA (making IRAs appealing to the self-employed) and because taxation of account funds can be deferred until the funds are withdrawn. If the funds in an IRA are withdrawn too early, the account holder is penalized.

Much of the law associated with retirement plans in the workplace is preempted by federal law, pursuant to ERISA. See 29 U.S.C. § 1002. If the covered employee is married, ERISA restricts the employee's selection of beneficiary—basically limiting the choice to the person's spouse unless the spouse signs a fully informed waiver of that right. 26 U.S.C. §§ 401(a)(11)(A) and (13)(C)(iii). (These issues are discussed further in the context of *Hillman*, earlier in the chapter.) This requirement does not apply to IRAs, because they are not covered by ERISA. In either situation, so long as the beneficiary is not the individual's estate, the annuity or retirement proceeds will escape probate.

Beneficiary Designation via Superwill

Because nonprobate assets are subject to trust, contract, or property laws, those laws control beneficiary designations. Thus, for example, a beneficiary designation can only be changed by compliance with the underlying contract. However, one state—Washington—allows for a superwill. People can change beneficiary designations for nonprobate assets by will, see Wash. Rev. Code Ann. § 11.11.020 (West), although there are some exclusions, such as joint tenancies with right of survivorship. See id. § 11.11.010(7)(a); see also Stewart E. Sterk & Melanie B. Leslie, *Accidental Inheritance: Retirement Accounts and the Hidden Law of Succession*, 89 N.Y.U. L. Rev. 165, 237 (2014). The state does include trusts. *Manary v. Anderson*, 292 P.3d 96 (Wash. 2013).

3. Nonprobate Bank and Brokerage Accounts

Individuals can establish various types of bank and brokerage accounts that will pass outside of probate.

Checking and savings accounts, certificates of deposit between a depositor and a financial institution, and brokerage accounts can be set up in several different ways. As discussed below, an individual needs to ensure that the account ownership reflects the owner's intent. Some accounts will avoid probate, while others will not. The ownership structure is designated on a form supplied by the institution, and is typically filled out online. There are few formal requirements involved in the execution of the form. Although UPC § 6-204 provides a sample form for use by banks, most banks create their own instead. Moreover, state laws concerning presumptions about what kind of account has been established vary.

Single-Party Accounts

A single-party account is an account titled in the name of one person. When that person dies, the balance in the account is probate property. UPC § 6-212(c).

Multiple-Party Accounts

A multiple-party account is defined in UPC § 6-201(5) as "an account payable on request to one or more of two or more parties, whether or not a right of survivorship is mentioned." An individual can choose between four different types of multiple-party accounts, which give each party different rights during life and at death: a tenancy in common, a joint tenancy with right of survivorship, one with a payable-on-death designation, and one that provides lifetime rights for the party added to the account but does not provide after-death rights (sometimes called a "**convenience account**").

A tenancy in common for a bank account is rare. If one exists, the share of the account owned by the decedent is probate property.

A **joint tenancy** account provides each person named on the account with the right to make withdrawals while both (or all) are alive and, and, based on the assumption that it is a **joint tenancy with right of survivorship**, then provides that at the death of one joint tenant, the other joint tenant(s) becomes the owner(s) of the entire account. You may already be familiar with joint tenancies from your Property course. A bank account with a joint tenancy operates in a similar manner to a joint tenancy in real property. Joint accounts may be savings or checking accounts that include cash, or brokerage accounts that include investments. Spouses, parents and children, and domestic partners often establish joint tenancy accounts for savings and to pay household expenses. If an account is established as a joint account, for example, "Stuart and Nina, as joint tenants" or "Stuart and Nina, jointly," most (if not all) states presume it to be a joint tenancy with right of survivorship, not a tenancy in common. Joint tenancy accounts can have more than two account owners.

Joint tenancy has different consequences during life and at death. While the joint tenants are alive, the account is presumed to be owned by each party in proportion to that person's net contribution; joint ownership does not mean, for example, that if there are two joint tenants, they are each entitled to half of the account—unless each has contributed half. Instead, unless there is clear and convincing evidence otherwise, the assumption is that no gift is intended. See UPC § 6-211(b). If one party withdraws more than that party is entitled to, the UPC Comments state that the rights between parties in this situation are governed by general law other than the UPC. Generally, if one party feels defrauded, that person will have a claim of conversion, and in many situations, the withdrawal will be considered a gift.

By contrast, when one joint tenant dies, the survivor is presumed to be entitled to the account, regardless of the amount contributed. See UPC § 6-212(a).

For example, Mirna and Sean signed a signature card indicating their intent that a new account at Community Bank be a joint account with right of survivorship. Mirna contributed 90 percent of the funds. If Sean withdraws 50 percent of the funds, then Sean is liable to Mirna for conversion (although she may decide not to sue him or may simply ask that he return the funds). If Mirna dies first, the account will not be included in Mirna's probate estate, and Mirna cannot, by will, designate a new joint owner; Sean will become the sole owner of the account. Then, when Sean dies, with the account titled in Sean's name alone, the account will be included in Sean's probate estate. Sean can designate, by will, who should receive the money in the account, or it may be disposed of through the will's residuary clause.

If the person who opens the account wants to provide for survivorship rights but not permit access to the account during the owner's lifetime, the owner can use a payable-on-death (POD) designation. A POD designation provides that any amount remaining upon the death of the account owner will be transferred to the POD designee. See UPC §§ 6-201(8); 212(b)(2). POD designations are generally only employed with single-party accounts; most multiple-party accounts are held in joint tenancy. A sample form from the UPC is shown in Exhibit 7.1.

In all respects, the account holder is the owner and the only person who has access to the funds in the account while she is alive. The beneficiary stated on the POD designation form has no rights to the account and cannot withdraw funds during the life of the owner. See UPC § 6-211(c). The POD designation simply means that the account does not go through probate. The account holder can revoke or change the POD designation at any time, and the beneficiary has no vested rights in the POD designation.

For example, Prerna had a savings account at Community Bank. She signed a POD designation form that said "payable on death to Quinn." During Prerna's life, only she can use funds in the account. When Prerna dies, the account will be excluded from her probate estate and Quinn will become entitled to any funds remaining in the account. At any point during her lifetime, Prerna can change the POD designation to someone else; she has no fiduciary obligations to Quinn, and Quinn does not have a vested interest in the account. Prerna could also remove the POD designation altogether.

A predecessor to POD accounts, and a term for them in some states today, is a **Totten trust**. The Court of Appeals of New York, the highest court in the state, permitted a person to deposit money in a savings account for the benefit of a third party. See In re Totten, 71 N.E. 748 (N.Y. 1904). At a time when nonprobate transfers were much less common, the court treated the savings account as an inter vivos trust instead of a testamentary trust.

Where securities are involved, the designation takes the form of a transfer-on-death (TOD) designation, which functions in the same way with respect to securities. It thus provides a nonprobate means for holding securities.

EXHIBIT 7.1 **Uniform Single- or Multiple-Party Account Form (from UPC Sec. 6-204)**

UNIFORM SINGLE- OR MULTIPLE-PARTY ACCOUNT FORM

PARTIES [Name One or More Parties]:

_____

OWNERSHIP [Select One And Initial]:
_____SINGLE-PARTY ACCOUNT
_____MULTIPLE-PARTY ACCOUNT
   Parties own account in proportion to net contributions unless there is clear and convincing evidence of a different intent.

RIGHTS AT DEATH [Select One And Initial]:
_____SINGLE-PARTY ACCOUNT
   At death of party, ownership passes as part of party's estate.
_____SINGLE-PARTY ACCOUNT WITH POD (PAY ON DEATH) DESIGNATION

[Name One Or More Beneficiaries]:

_____

   At death of party, ownership passes to POD beneficiaries and is not part of party's estate.
_____MULTIPLE-PARTY ACCOUNT WITH RIGHT OF SURVIVORSHIP
   At death of party, ownership passes to surviving parties.
_____MULTIPLE-PARTY ACCOUNT WITH RIGHT OF SURVIVORSHIP AND POD (PAY ON DEATH) DESIGNATION

[Name One Or More Beneficiaries]:

_____

   At death of last surviving party, ownership passes to POD beneficiaries and is not part of last surviving party's estate.
_____MULTIPLE-PARTY ACCOUNT WITHOUT RIGHT OF SURVIVORSHIP
   At death of party, deceased party's ownership passes as part of deceased party's estate.
AGENCY (POWER OF ATTORNEY) DESIGNATION [Optional]
   Agents may make account transactions for parties but have no ownership or rights at death unless named as POD beneficiaries.

[To Add Agency Designation To Account, Name One Or More Agents]:

_____

[Select One And Initial]:
_____AGENCY DESIGNATION SURVIVES DISABILITY OR INCAPACITY OF PARTIES
_____AGENCY DESIGNATION TERMINATES ON DISABILITY OR INCAPACITY OF PARTIES

The final type of account is a **convenience account**, which does not have survivorship rights (and is thus a probate asset). A "depositor" (primary account holder) can create such an account for the limited purpose of giving a "convenience depositor" access to the funds in the account to make deposits and to withdraw funds only for the depositor. The convenience depositor has neither an ownership interest in the account nor rights to the balance in the account upon the death of the depositor, which distinguishes it from a "true" joint account or a POD account. See, e.g., *Convenience Accounts*, Fla. Stat. Ann. § 655.80. A jurisdiction might have its own distinct statutory provisions to distinguish between these accounts and accounts that have survivorship benefits.

Convenience accounts are useful if the depositor is disabled and needs someone else to have access to the account to withdraw money on the depositor's behalf, such as for paying bills. An elderly parent might add a child or a caretaker to an account for this reason. The intent of the account owner is to allow the other person to have access to the account while the original owner is alive, but not to transfer the account balance to the other person at the owner's death.

Unfortunately, the standard form used by banks usually creates a "joint account" and does not offer the account owner the choice of a "convenience" account, nor does it even necessarily explain whether a joint account has survivorship rights. This can result in confusion when the owner dies because of the lack of clarity of the decedent's intent. The other person named on the account and the owner's probate beneficiaries or heirs might each claim ownership based on a lack of clarity of what the account owner intended when she established the account. In some states, evidence of the account owner's intent when she created the account can be used to show that the person named on the account should not receive the funds, while in other states, the form is determinative and no other evidence is permitted.

Case Preview

Matter of Corcoran

The following case shows the difficulties sometimes encountered in distinguishing between a joint tenancy with right of survivorship account and a convenience account, since access to each type of account by the parties during life is similar. The case addresses the applicability of presumptions concerning joint bank accounts to a brokerage account. The decedent's daughter, the executor of her mother's estate, held several different accounts in joint tenancy with her mother, and she became sole owner after her mother's death. One of her brothers then sued her, claiming that the accounts were not intended to have the survivorship feature, and the daughter may have unduly influenced her mother.

As you read the case, consider:

1. What claims does the daughter have to the various accounts at issue in the case? What evidence supports those claims?
2. What is the difference in ownership structure between the brokerage account and the bank account?
3. How does New York banking law address the brokerage account?
4. What presumptions from that law apply to the case? How can those presumptions be rebutted?

Matter of Corcoran
63 A.D.3d 93 (N.Y. 3d Dept. 2009)

Decedent, who died on December 9, 2005, was survived by her four children. In her will, decedent appointed respondent, her daughter, as executor, bequeathed her house and its contents to respondent, disinherited her two eldest sons and divided the remainder of her estate equally between respondent and petitioner, her third son.

After respondent filed an application to settle the estate, petitioner commenced this proceeding [and] a jury trial was commenced for the purpose of resolving four limited issues: (1) whether decedent opened certain joint accounts with the intent to create a joint tenancy with respondent or for convenience only; (2) whether decedent placed assets in these accounts with the intention that they would pass outside of her probate estate directly to respondent; (3) whether a confidential relationship existed between respondent and decedent such that the burden of proof shifted to respondent; and (4) whether respondent exercised undue influence over decedent or committed fraud or coercion against her. Upon the close of petitioner's proof, [the lower court] dismissed the petition. This appeal by petitioner ensued.

Petitioner argues that the presumption set forth in Banking Law § 675 does not apply to [two] of decedent's joint accounts—namely, a Charles Schwab brokerage account [] and a Trustco Bank account. Banking Law § 675(a) provides, in pertinent part, that "[w]hen a deposit of cash . . . has been made . . . in or with any banking organization[2] . . . in the name of [the] depositor . . . and another person and in form to be paid or delivered to either, or the survivor of them, such deposit . . . and any additions thereto made, by either of such persons . . . shall become the property of such persons as joint tenants." When an account has been formed in accordance with the statute, and the "survivorship" language appears on the account's signature card, a presumption arises that the parties intended to create a joint tenancy with rights of survivorship (see Banking Law § 675[b]).

First addressing the Charles Schwab brokerage account, we cannot agree with petitioner's assertion that, despite its clear survivorship language, the statutory presumption does not apply because it is an investment account rather than a traditional bank account. Both this Court as well as other Departments apply the Banking Law § 675(b) presumption to joint brokerage and investment accounts. Indeed, this Court recently rejected an argument similar to that advanced by petitioner here, finding that the application of the presumption is not altered by "[t]he fact that the deposit is not made into a traditional banking account, but instead into a joint brokerage or investment account" (Fehring v. Fehring, 874 N.Y.S.2d 266).

With the presumption applicable to the Charles Schwab account, the burden shifted to petitioner to either establish fraud, undue influence or lack of capacity (see Banking Law § 675[b]); or tender direct or circumstantial proof to support an inference "that the joint account was established as a convenience and not with the

---

[2]"Banking organization" means and includes "all banks, trust companies, private bankers, savings banks, safe deposit companies, savings and loan associations, credit unions and *investment companies*" (Banking Law § 2[11] [emphasis added]).

intention of conferring a present beneficial interest on the other party to the account." Mindful that a [] motion for judgment as a matter of law may be granted only when, viewing the evidence in a light most favorable to the nonmoving party and according him or her the benefit of every favorable inference which can be drawn, "there is no rational process by which the fact trier could base a finding in favor of the nonmoving party" . . . we find that it was error for Surrogate's Court to grant the motion in favor of respondent on this account.

"A major factor in determining whether a bank account is opened as a matter of convenience or as a joint account is the conduct and statements of a surviving cotenant" Matter of Camarda, 406 N.Y.S.2d 193 (App. Div. 1978). Here, the evidence demonstrated that decedent had exclusive possession of the checks for this account and that respondent did not receive account statements, never withdrew any funds from the account to pay her own expenses, considered this account to be her mother's and did not know where the funds in the account would go upon decedent's death. Furthermore, decedent's will, executed nearly three months after she opened this account, leaves all of her estate, save her house, to petitioner and respondent equally. Since the Charles Schwab account constitutes more than one-half of her estate, decedent's testamentary disposition is arguably inconsistent with an intent to give respondent alone rights of survivorship in the majority of her estate. While the above-mentioned circumstantial proof is certainly not conclusive as to decedent's intent at the time the account was created, we simply cannot say that there is no rational process by which the jury could have found that the account was opened as a matter of convenience.

Turning to the joint Trustco Bank account, we agree with petitioner that the presumption of joint tenancy under Banking Law § 675 does not apply, as the signature card for this account bears no specific language of survivorship. In the absence of the statutory presumption, the burden remained on respondent to establish that decedent intended to create a joint tenancy with survivorship rights. As the record is devoid of any proof as to this account or decedent's intent when it was opened, respondent failed to meet her burden in this regard and it was therefore error for [the lower] Court to grant a directed verdict in her favor as to this account.

Petitioner's remaining contentions have either been rendered academic by our decision or have been reviewed and found to be unavailing.

Post-Case Follow-Up

New York banking law applies a presumption of joint tenancy when a bank or an investment account is opened in the name of multiple parties and survivorship language is used. New York allows that language to be rebutted, although some states find that use of survivorship language is conclusive. Gregory Eddington, *Survivorship Rights in Joint Bank Accounts: A Misbegotten Presumption of Intent*, 15 Marq. Elder's Advisor 175, 204 (2014). The strength of the presumption counsels care in opening up such accounts. Other jurisdictions have different approaches. For example, UPC § 6-212 simply provides that "on death of a party sums on deposit in a multiple-party account belong to the surviving party or parties."

Matter of Corcoran: Real Life Applications

1. Based on the facts of the case, if the Trustco account had been set up with survivorship language, would that have changed the outcome? Why or why not?

2. After suffering a stroke, Lillian had a difficult time handling her affairs. Lillian put the name of her grandchild, Glynnis, on her checking account at State Bank, so that Glynnis could pay Lillian's bills. The account was funded with Lillian's Social Security checks. Two years later, Lillian executed a will stating, "I leave my house to my grandchild, Glynnis. The rest of my estate is to be divided between my three children, Nigel, Minna, and Kim." State Bank only had joint tenancy accounts available. Eighteen months later, Lillian died. At the time of her death, Lillian had $71,000 in her State Bank checking account. Who gets the $71,000 under New York law?

3. Using the facts of the previous problem, what is the result if Lillian opens a new account in her own name, and then designates it as POD to Glynnis?

4. Concurrently Owned Real Property

When real property is held in certain forms, then it too becomes nonprobate property. The options are joint tenancy, tenancy by the entirety, or, in some states, transfer-on-death deeds (each term is discussed further below). Joint tenancy is probably the most commonly used device that avoids probate because it is easy to understand and inexpensive to create, although the principles of property law are somewhat different from those of banking law. Under a joint tenancy arrangement, each owner has the immediate right to possess the entire property. When one of the owners dies, title passes by operation of property law exclusively to the surviving joint tenant or tenants. Because the decedent has no ownership interest in the property, the property passes outside of probate. This is also true for **tenancies by the entirety**, which are joint tenancy arrangements that can only be entered into by married people.

By contrast, a tenancy in common does not have a survivorship element: the interest of a deceased co-tenant is probate property that will be transferred via will or intestacy. A transfer-on-death deed, available in some states, is similar to a POD designation for a bank account: the property owner lists the TOD beneficiary on the deed and records the deed. The beneficiary will then receive the property upon the owner's death without the need for probate court proceedings.

Once a joint tenancy has been created, a joint tenant cannot devise the joint tenancy interest. Instead, if a joint tenant wants to sever the joint tenancy so that someone other than the other joint tenant will receive the property at death, the person must convert it to a tenancy in common.

For example, Norman and Oona buy a house as joint tenants. Norman decides to leave his interest to his daughter, Dahlia. To sever the joint tenancy, Norman arranges to transfer his interest in the property to Edwin, and Edwin and Oona become tenants in common. Edwin, by prior arrangement, then transfers the property back to Norman. Norman and Oona have become tenants in common, and Norman can leave the property to Dahlia by will. Regardless of whether Norman writes the will, the property will pass via probate succession.

Joint tenancies are characterized by the coexistence of what are referred to as the four unities: the unity of interest, the unity of title, the unity of time, and the unity of possession. Most states have modified the common law with respect to the four unities by relaxing the requirements and providing that an estate with all the characteristics of a common law joint tenancy can be created through a conveyance from the grantor directly to herself and others as grantees, without the intervention of a third party.

For example, many years ago, Patty bought a beach house in Alabama and titled it in her name alone. She wants to give her son, Duncan, a half interest in the beach house immediately. Patty anticipates that she will die before Duncan, meaning that the half interest she has retained will pass to Duncan upon her death. Today, this can be easily accomplished by quitclaiming the beach house to Duncan and herself as joint tenants with rights of survivorship. In the past, this could only be accomplished with the assistance of a straw person (or intermediary) who acquired transitory title. (Of course, if Duncan dies first, then his interest will pass to Patty.)

A variation of joint tenancy is tenancy by the entirety. About half the states recognize tenancy by the entirety, often limited to real property. Tenancies by the entirety are reserved for married people (or those treated as married under state law) with the property considered as owned by the marriage. One tenant cannot unilaterally convey that person's interest in the property to a third party, nor can courts order the property divided on the motion of only one tenant. The rules for a tenancy by the entirety are more restrictive than those for a joint tenancy. Property owned as a tenancy by the entirety cannot be levied upon by a creditor during the marriage unless the creditor has a judgment against both spouses. In many states, if a creditor has a judgment against only one spouse, the creditor can get a lien against the property but cannot foreclose on it; the creditor is entitled to take half the proceeds only if and when the property is sold. In other states, a creditor of one spouse is precluded from even putting a lien on the property and may never collect against the entirety property. Divorce terminates a tenancy by the entirety, converting ownership into a tenancy in common.

For example, Hubert and Willie hold title to their house as tenants by the entirety. If Hubert wishes to sell or give away his half interest in the house, he needs Willie's agreement and signature on the deed. Likewise, if a creditor gets a judgment against Hubert individually, the house may not be levied upon and foreclosed to satisfy the judgment. If Willie and Hubert divorce, then the creditor can foreclose upon Hubert's half of what has become a tenancy in common.

Most spouses and people registered as domestic partners or parties in a civil union own bank accounts, brokerage accounts, and their homes and other real estate either as joint tenants with rights of survivorship or as tenants by the entirety. This ensures that the survivor receives the property. When real property is involved, the joint tenancy must be in writing to comply with the statute of frauds.

5. Inter Vivos Trusts

As Chapters 9 through 11 discuss, trusts may be testamentary or inter vivos. Unless an inter vivos trust terminates upon the settlor's death and distributes all of the property to the settlor's estate, then such a trust is a nonprobate transfer. A revocable trust is actually the paradigmatic will substitute because the revocable trust is not asset-specific like the other nonprobate devices and allows the settlor virtually complete control over the assets. A testamentary trust can only be established via will, so it is *not* a nonprobate transfer.

C. WHY USE NONPROBATE TRANSFERS?

Nonprobate transfers are used for a variety of reasons. While many people think nonprobate transfers became a part of the legal landscape so decedents could avoid the time and expense of probate proceedings, most, with the exception of revocable living trusts, developed more organically, and they can satisfy various purposes. Estate planners can use will substitutes to engage in sophisticated tax planning (as well as to ensure orderly transmission of property). Will substitutes allow an individual to continue to control assets during life, and then have those assets transferred at death outside of the probate process. Employers use will substitutes to clarify who will receive an employee's benefits upon death. Will substitutes are useful in establishing continuity of property rights between family members. And will substitutes, such as life insurance, provide financial benefits to the surviving beneficiaries.

Moreover, changing a will substitute does not require the same level of formality as changing a will. And, unlike wills, they are not filed in court, but remain confidential.

Many people believe that nonprobate transfers can be used to avoid estate taxes. Chapter 15 will provide more details, but most nonprobate transfers are still subject to the estate tax. If the client retains the power to determine who receives the property at death—which is the case in all revocable trusts and other changeable beneficiary designations—the property will be subject to estate tax, whether the transfers are probate or nonprobate.

Moreover, will substitutes themselves cannot shield all of the decedent's assets from probate. As estate planners recognize, it is difficult to avoid probate completely. If the decedent owns any property at death that was not titled in the name of a trust or dealt with by another will substitute, probate may be required. This is especially likely for personal items, such as jewelry, art, and electronic equipment. It is also possible that some property that the decedent intended to pass by a will substitute may be forced into the probate estate because of certain events, such as the death of intended beneficiaries.

Finally, almost all clients will have both a will and multiple types of property. Overselling the benefits of "will substitutes" may create the false impression that as a lawyer, clients would have no need for a will.

D. PLANNING FOR INCAPACITY

Estate planning today goes beyond preparing a will or a trust; it also includes planning for incapacity. The demographics make it easy to understand the need to plan for incapacity to ensure that an individual's health and financial care can be managed when the individual is no longer able to do so. The number of people over the age of 65 in the United States is continuously increasing. In 2015, for example, the number of people aged 65 and over was approximately 47.8 million.[3] Moreover, Alzheimer's disease and related dementias have become increasingly prevalent, with 5.4 million people having this disease in 2016.[4]

It is not just the elderly, however, who need to plan for their incapacity; all adults should do so as well. There are more than 2 million traumatic brain injuries in the United States per year, and such injuries may cause some forms of mental disability.

In the absence of advance planning, default rules specify who can act as a **surrogate**, that is, a substitute who can act to make decisions for the incapacitated person. Another person, or the government, might petition the court for the appointment of a **guardian** or **conservator**, a fiduciary with court-ordered responsibility for managing the affairs of another. The court will then hold a hearing to evaluate whether the individual is able to manage the individual's own personal (including health) and business affairs. If the court determines that the person is unable to do so, then a court-appointed fiduciary will assume that role.

The two major elements of planning for incapacity involve managing health care and financial decision making. As with all of wills, trusts, and estates law, statutory default rules determine what will happen if the individual did not engage in advance planning and did not prepare written instructions. Default rules are just that: while they are designed to reflect presumed intent, they do not necessarily yield the result the individual would have wanted, and they may not be efficient in an emergency, particularly if they involve a court process. This section focuses on both aspects of planning for incapacity.

---

[3]A Profile of Older Americans: 2016, U.S. Dept. of Health and Human Services, https://www.giaging.org/documents/A_Profile_of_Older_Americans__2016.pdf.
[4]2016 Alzheimer's Disease Facts and Figures, Alzheimer's Ass'n, https://www.alz.org/documents_custom/2016-facts-and-figures.pdf.

One useful legal document is a **power of attorney** (POA), which authorizes one person to act on behalf of another. A POA can be used for financial purposes, such as for banking, business purposes, the purchase or sale of real estate, or medical dealings, and may also be used to delegate decision making in other contexts. The person who signs the POA and authorizes another person to act on his or her behalf is the **principal**. The person authorized to act on behalf of the principal is called the **agent** or **attorney-in-fact**. Notwithstanding the name, neither an agent nor an "attorney-in-fact" needs to be a lawyer.

1. Financial Planning

Advance planning allows an individual to control who should make financial decisions in the event of her incapacity, ensuring that the process is private and not subject to court supervision. The individual can choose representatives who she believes will effectuate her plan and her wishes. As discussed in Chapter 8, while a revocable living trust is a good way to plan for the management of financial issues during disability, the trust may not include all of a person's property—and many people do not have a trust at all. Consequently, an individual who wants to ensure that someone else will step in when she becomes disabled is likely to use a power of attorney.

Different Aspects of Planning for Incapacity: Health Care

When a client plans for incapacity, this may also involve planning for the care of minor children and counseling about issues of how to finance health care. Since children under the age of majority (18 in most states) are presumed to be legally incapacitated, parents should plan for the care of their children in the event the parents die or become incapacitated.

Planning for the financing of care can involve discussions of qualifying for **Medicaid** and/or **Medicare**. Medicaid is a jointly funded federal-state program that provides health coverage to people with low incomes and few resources. Medicare is the federal health care insurance program that provides coverage for people age 65 or older, people under age 65 with certain disabilities, and people of all ages with end-stage renal disease. While most of the more than 55 million people who receive Medicare are 65 or older, almost one-sixth of recipients are under 65 and have a qualifying disability.

Powers of Attorney

Powers of attorney are routinely created instruments. They are frequently used for single transactions, such as by one spouse so the other spouse can act on her behalf in the sale of their home if she anticipates being out of town during the closing, or on a more comprehensive basis, allowing the agent to act for the principal in numerous matters when the principal is incapacitated. This chapter focuses on the latter use.

The capacity standard for appointing an agent is typically the same as that required to enter into a contract, a high standard, which requires that the individual have a reasonable understanding of the act in which she is engaging. See Lawrence A. Frolik & Mary F. Radford, *"Sufficient" Capacity: The Contrasting Capacity Requirements for Different Documents*, 2 NAELA J. 303, 313, 315-16 (2006). And this means that the power of attorney has to be created when the principal has capacity.

Differences Between an Agent and a Trustee

While both an agent and a trustee have fiduciary obligations, there are important differences in their roles, including the following:

- A trustee has legal title to property, while an agent does not.
- A trustee only controls the property in the trust; an agent can act on behalf of all of the principal's property.

Establishing a trust can be a complex effort, while the power of attorney form is simple. Third parties (e.g., banks) may be more familiar with, and more likely to honor, a trustee's actions than an agent's efforts.

There are also more options when establishing a trust. For example, a revocable trust might designate an alternate trustee to act when the initial trustees have either become incompetent or deceased. Moreover, because of how property is titled, the creation of the trust provides financial institutions with advance notice about the accounts or properties held in trust; agents do not provide such notice. See, e.g., Paul Sullivan, *Power of Attorney Is Not Always a Solution*, N.Y. Times, Aug. 22, 2014, https://www.nytimes.com/2014/08/23/your-money/power-of-attorney-can-have-its-own-complications.html.

Under common law, powers of attorney expired once the principal became incapacitated. Today, the UPC assumes that all powers of attorney are **durable** (i.e., they last during a principal's incapacity) and are effective immediately, although the principal can provide otherwise. See UPC §§ 5B-104, 110. Some attorneys engaged in estate planning use a **springing power of attorney** that only becomes effective upon the occurrence of a future event—most frequently, the principal's incapacity. Springing powers, however, can create difficulties because they require proof that the specified event has occurred.

Every state authorizes durable powers of attorney (DPOA). When used properly, powers of attorney can enhance the principal's autonomy and ensure continuity in an individual's financial matters. Unfortunately, there is often little independent oversight of them, and the agent's scope of power can be unclear. So long as the agent is authorized to take certain actions by the power of attorney, and the exercise of this authority complies with the agent's fiduciary responsibilities, then the agent can act. This section explores issues involved in the implementation of powers of attorney, including the parameters for the agent's authority and the potential for abuse when an agent acts inconsistently with the delegated duties.

Agent's Responsibilities

The utility of a power of attorney depends on the trustworthiness of the agent. Thus, the principal, and the lawyer advising the principal, should think about what qualities to consider when choosing an agent. The agent has a fiduciary obligation to the principal, but the parameters of this obligation are not entirely clear. Accordingly, common law concepts of fiduciary obligations such as loyalty and due care, similar to those discussed in Chapter 11, are highly relevant. This section provides a brief review of those principles focused on powers of attorney. Note that these responsibilities are also relevant in the health care context discussed later in the chapter.

Many state statutes do not specifically set forth the agent's duties, and there is wide variation even among those states that do. A single state may impose different standards for different decisions made pursuant to a DPOA, and there is enormous discretion for differing interpretations of the decision-making standards employed.[5]

---

[5] *See* Nina A. Kohn, *Elder Empowerment as a Strategy for Curbing the Hidden Abuses of Durable Powers of Attorney*, 59 Rutgers L. Rev. 1 (2006).

Banks or other financial institutions that respect the power of attorney are generally protected if they can show that they relied on the agent in good faith, treating the agent in the same way as they would treat the principal. Some banks may request additional proof beyond the power of attorney form itself. States may even have laws that impose liability on an entity that does not honor the agent's request. *See* Lawrence Frolik, *Keep Powers of Attorney in Check*, 45 Trial 42, 44 (2009).

Unfortunately, elder law attorneys and probate judges routinely deal with cases where an agent has defrauded the principal. Breaches can occur when the power of attorney is created, as when the principal is coerced into signing a form; breaches may also occur when the agent engages in: (i) actions that exceed the delegated authority—such as making gifts in the absence of explicit permission to do so; and (ii) self-dealing—such as when an agent uses the principal's money for his own benefit rather than for the principal.[6]

Springing or Not?

Consider the benefits and drawbacks of using a springing or an immediately effective power of attorney. Both are "durable" in that they survive the principal's incapacity. But some have argued that the immediately effective power of attorney undercuts the principal's autonomy, and people may be reluctant to sign a document in which they relinquish control immediately. See John C. Craft, *Preventing Exploitation and Preserving Autonomy: Making Springing Powers of Attorney the Standard*, 44 U. Balt. L. Rev. 407, 465 (2015). When would you recommend a springing power of attorney? An immediately effective power of attorney? Consider why banks are reluctant to permit withdrawals if a power is a springing power unless there is clear evidence of incapacity.

Case Preview

Matter of Ferrara

The following case is about the gift-giving authority of an agent under a power of attorney. George Ferrara had executed a power of attorney designating his brother and nephew as his agents. The nephew used the power of attorney to make some financial gifts to himself. After Ferrara died, the primary beneficiary under his will, the Salvation Army, sued the nephew, claiming that the gifts were unauthorized.

As you read the case, consider:

1. What does New York law provide with respect to the scope of a power of attorney?
2. What authority were the agents given under the power of attorney? What is the standard that the court uses to evaluate the agents' exercise of that authority?
3. What actions constituted breach of the power of attorney?
4. What evidence supports the breach?

---

[6]Lori A. Stiegel & Ellen VanCleave Klem, ABA Comm. on Law and Aging, *Power of Attorney Abuse: What States Can Do About It* (2008), http://assets.aarp.org/rgcenter/consume/2008_17_poa.pdf.

Matter of Ferrara
852 N.E.2d 138 (N.Y. 2006)

READ, J.

Article 5, title 15 of the General Obligations Law prescribes what a statutory short form power of attorney must contain, specifies the powers that the form may authorize and defines their scope. On this appeal, we hold that an agent acting [pursuant to] a statutory short form power of attorney that contains additional language augmenting the gift-giving authority must make gifts pursuant to these enhanced powers in the principal's best interest.

I.

On June 10, 1999, decedent George J. Ferrara, a retired stockbroker who was residing in Florida at the time, executed a will "mak[ing] no provision . . . for any family member . . . or for any individual person" because it was his "intention to leave [his] entire residuary estate to charity." Accordingly, in the same instrument he bequeathed his estate to a sole beneficiary, the Salvation Army, "to be held, in perpetuity, in a separate endowment fund to be named the 'GEORGE J. FERRARA MEMORIAL FUND' with the annual net income therefrom to be used by the Salvation Army to further its charitable purposes in the greater Daytona Beach, Florida area." On August 16, 1999, decedent executed a codicil naming the Florida attorney who had drafted his will and codicil as his executor, and otherwise "ratif[ied], confirm[ed] and republish[ed] [his] said Will of June 10, 1999." Decedent was single, and had no children. His closest relatives were his brother, John, and a sister, and their respective children.

According to John Ferrara's son, Dominick Ferrara, after decedent was hospitalized in Florida in December 1999, he and his father "were called to assist."

On January 25, 2000, ten days later, decedent signed, and initialed where required, multiple originals of a "Durable General Power of Attorney: New York Statutory Short Form," thereby appointing John and Dominick Ferrara as his attorneys-in-fact, and allowing either of them to act separately "IN [HIS] NAME, PLACE AND STEAD in any way which [he] [him]self could do, if [he] were personally present, with respect to the following matters [listed in lettered subdivisions (A) through (O)] as each of them is defined in Title 15 of Article 5 of the New York General Obligations Law to the extent that [he was] permitted by law to act through an agent."

Subdivisions (A) through (O) of the pre-printed form listed various kinds of transactions; in particular, subdivision (M) specified "making gifts to my spouse, children and more remote descendants, and parents, not to exceed in the aggregate $10,000 to each of such persons in any year." Decedent authorized his attorneys-in-fact to carry out all of the matters listed in subdivisions (A) through (O). Critically, decedent also initialed a typewritten addition to the form, which stated that "[t]his Power of Attorney shall enable the Attorneys-in-Fact to make gifts without limitation in amount to John Ferrara and/or Dominick Ferrara."

Dominick Ferrara insists that this provision authorizing him to make unlimited gifts to himself was added "[i]n furtherance of [decedent's] wishes," because decedent repeatedly told him in December 1999 and January 2000 that he "wanted [Dominick Ferrara] to have all of [decedent's] assets to do with as [he] pleased." When asked if he and decedent had discussed making gifts to other family members—including his father, John, the other attorney-in-fact—Dominick Ferrara replied that they had not, again because "[m]y Uncle George gave me his money to do as I wished." Dominick Ferrara acknowledges that decedent made no memorandum or note to this effect, and only once expressed these donative intentions in the presence of anyone else— Dominick's wife, Elizabeth. Dominick Ferrara sought out an attorney in New York City "to discuss [his] Uncle's wishes," and this attorney provided him with the power of attorney that decedent ultimately executed.

The power of attorney was notarized by an attorney with whom Dominick and Elizabeth Ferrara were acquainted. This attorney testified that she attended the signing at the Ferraras' behest, and was acting as a notary only, not as an attorney for either the Ferraras or decedent. Specifically, she rendered no legal advice to decedent, who read the form in her presence before signing it. The attorney and Dominick Ferrara generally agree that it was Dominick who explained the form's provisions to decedent; she does not recall the word "gift" having been mentioned.

Decedent's condition deteriorated. He was admitted to the hospital on January 29, 2000, and never left. Decedent died on February 12, 2000, less than a month after moving to New York, and approximately three weeks after executing the power of attorney. During those three weeks, Dominick Ferrara transferred about $820,000 of decedent's assets to himself, including [] IBM stock and about $300,000 in cash from the certificates of deposit, multiple bank accounts and the sale of [decedent's] Florida property. After decedent's death, he filed a 1999 federal income tax return for decedent, and collected a refund in the amount of roughly $9,500. Dominick Ferrara testified that he does not recall what happened to any of the $300,000 in cash, but that he still owns the IBM stock.

The Salvation Army found out about decedent's will . . . [and] commenced a proceeding [in NY Surrogate Court]. . . .

II.

Section 5-1501 of the General Obligations Law sets out the forms creating a durable and nondurable statutory short form power of attorney. By these forms, the principal appoints an attorney-in-fact to act "IN [HIS] NAME, PLACE AND STEAD" with respect to any or all of 15 categories of matters listed in lettered subdivisions (A) through (O) "as each of them is defined in Title 15 of Article 5 of the New York General Obligations Law"; specifically, the 15 categories in subdivisions (A) through (O) are interpreted in corresponding sections 5-1502A through 5-1502O of the General Obligations Law (id.).[7]

---

[7] . . . The 15 categories are real estate transactions; chattel and goods transactions; bond, share and commodity transactions; banking transactions; business operating transactions; insurance transactions; estate transactions; claims and litigation; personal relationships and affairs; benefits from military service; records, reports and statements; retirement benefit transactions; gifts to specified beneficiaries not to exceed $10,000 to each per year; tax matters; and all other matters. . . . [citations omitted].

As relevant to this case, in 1996 the Legislature amended section 5-1501(1) to add lettered subdivision (M), authorizing the attorney-in-fact to "mak[e] gifts to [the principal's] spouse, children and more remote descendants, and parents, not to exceed in the aggregate $10,000 to each of such persons in any year." Section 5-1502M construes this gift-giving authority []

> "to mean that the principal authorizes the agent . . . [t]o make gifts . . . either outright or to a trust for the sole benefit of one or more of [the specified] persons . . . only for purposes which the agent reasonably deems to be in the best interest of the principal, specifically including minimization of income, estate, inheritance, generation-skipping transfer or gift taxes."

. . . Thus, section 5-1502M unambiguously imposes a duty on the attorney-in-fact to exercise gift-giving authority in the best interest of the principal. . . .

[T]he best interest requirement is consistent with the fiduciary duties that courts have historically imposed on attorneys-in-fact. "[A] power of attorney . . . is clearly given with the intent that the attorney-in-fact will utilize that power for the benefit of the principal" (Mantella v. Mantella, [3d Dept. 2000]). Because "[t]he relationship of an attorney-in-fact to his principal is that of agent and principal . . . . the attorney-in-fact must act in the utmost good faith and undivided loyalty toward the principal, and must act in accordance with the highest principles of morality, fidelity, loyalty and fair dealing."

In short, [regardless of the form of the gift-giving power], the best interest requirement remains. Thus, Dominiçk Ferrara was only authorized to make gifts to himself insofar as these gifts were in decedent's best interest, interpreted by section 5-1502M as gifts to carry out the principal's financial, estate or tax plans. Here, Dominick Ferarra clearly did not make gifts to himself for such purposes. Rather, he consistently testified that he made the self-gifts "[i]n furtherance of [decedent's] wishes" to give him "all of his assets to do with as [Dominick] pleased." The term "best interest" does not include such unqualified generosity to the holder of a power of attorney, especially where the gift virtually impoverishes a donor whose estate plan, shown by a recent will, contradicts any desire to benefit the recipient of the gift. Accordingly, the order of the Appellate Division should be reversed, without costs, and the matter remitted to Surrogate's Court for further proceedings in accordance with this opinion.

Post-Case Follow-Up

In *Ferrara*, the court affirmed the broad power given to an agent to act on behalf of the principal. Yet it also noted that this power is limited by the agent's fiduciary duty to act for the benefit of the principal. Agents have potentially broad powers. For example, they may be able to claim an elective share of an estate or to change beneficiaries of life insurance policies. E.g., In re Weidner, 938 A.2d 354, 360 (Pa. 2007). State law may also permit the agent to change a retirement plan beneficiary designation. See Mark R. Caldwell, Elliott E. Burdette & Edward L. Rice, *Winning the Battle and the War: A Remedies-Centered Approach to Litigation Involving Durable Powers of Attorney*, 64 Baylor L. Rev. 435, 464 (2012). Note that

New York, like most states, sets out basic formalities concerning valid powers of attorney. States vary in their statutory requirements for a power of attorney, and may require that it be witnessed or notarized. Even when state law does not require a power of attorney to be notarized, it is best practice to do so, as may be necessary for certain real estate filings. Following *Ferrara*, New York amended its statute to require that if the principal grants the agent the authority to make total annual gifts of more than $500 to one person or charity, that power must be included in a separate Statutory Major Gifts Rider that must be signed in the presence of two witnesses or in a comparable form. N.Y. Gen. Oblig. §§ 5-1501 to 1514. New York also now requires that principals and agents both sign the power of attorney.

Matter of Ferrara: Real Life Applications

1. Consider the scope of Dominick's authority. Could he have changed George's will?

2. Do you think the court would have found Dominick's actions problematic if he had given himself a $10,000 gift? What about a $50,000 gift?

3. If New York law had required two witnesses for a power of attorney, would that have prevented the abuse in *Ferrara*?

Agent Liability

An agent may face a range of potential civil claims, including fraud and conversion. Criminal laws, such as theft, may also be relevant, and some states have adopted specialized laws that criminalize abuse or exploitation of the authority granted by a power of attorney. For example, in Utah, an individual who "unjustly or improperly uses a vulnerable adult's power of attorney or guardianship for the profit or advantage of someone other than the vulnerable adult" is guilty of the criminal offense of "exploitation." Utah Code Ann. § 76-5-111(4)(a)(iv). More generic criminal laws may also apply. When an agent, who had unlimited authority to make a gift, misused that authority as a "license to steal" rather than expend the funds for the principal's benefit, a court found him guilty of both "theft by unlawful taking" and "theft by failure to make required disposition of funds received." He was sentenced to "an aggregate term of 30 to 60 months in prison." Commonwealth v. Patton, 2014 WL 10575182, at *4 (Pa. Super. Ct. Sept. 19, 2014).

The right to a remedy, including criminal prosecution, may not really help a principal who has been defrauded. By the time the principal (or someone acting in the principal's interest) actually discovers the agent's breach, the principal may not be able to afford litigation. Moreover, the agent may have dissipated the assets, and the lack of clarity in many power of attorney statutes may undercut the lawsuit. Might springing powers ameliorate these problems? See Craft, *supra*, at 425.

Uniform Power of Attorney Act

In an effort to curb abuses like those on display in *Ferrara*, the Uniform Law Commission drafted the Uniform Power of Attorney Act (UPAA) in 2006. The Act establishes relatively straightforward procedures so that individuals can arrange for a surrogate to handle their property if they are incapacitated. It also focuses on protecting the principal by promoting her autonomy and preventing fraud. The Act sets out both mandatory and discretionary duties.[8]

Unempowering Powers

Even a valid power of attorney is not necessarily accepted by all financial institutions. Financial institutions may want customers to use the institution's own form, rather than a state or lawyer-drafted form. Even if state law requires the institutions to accept a durable power of attorney and protects them from liability, some agents may still experience problems using the power of attorney. See Paula Span, *Finding Out Your Power of Attorney Is Powerless*, N.Y. Times, May 6, 2016, https://www.nytimes.com/2016/05/10/health/finding-out-your-power-of-attorney-is-powerless.html.

Dealing with Digital Assets

Among the types of property that a surrogate decision maker may manage are **digital assets**. More than half of all individuals over the age of 65 use the Internet or email, as do even higher proportions of the rest of the population. As our lives become increasingly dependent on the Internet, people accumulate different categories of digital property. Digital assets include any digital file that is stored on your computer, on your phone, on a separate disc, or on the Internet (in the cloud), and any online account that requires you to enter a username and password to access. The average American believes that her digital assets have substantial value. [9]

Most people, however, probably have not considered how to manage their digital life if they become incapacitated or how to dispose of digital assets upon death, regardless of whether they have drafted a will. Indeed, even if they do engage in planning, they cannot be confident that their wishes will be carried out. Consequently, new methods are being developed to use wills or trusts to dispose of digital assets, even though the policies of Internet providers can limit the exercise of individual autonomy. See Natalie M. Banta, *Inherit the Cloud: The Role of Private Contracts in Distributing or Deleting Digital Assets at Death*, 83 Fordham L. Rev. 799, 802 (2014). Notwithstanding the uncertainty, estate planning attorneys have developed language to include in wills, trusts, and powers of attorney indicating how their clients want their fiduciary to manage their digital assets. Fiduciaries need to distinguish between digital property that can be transferred and property subject to contractual rights specifying that the particular asset disappears upon death. For example, users may only have a license to use music; that license terminates upon the user's death. For example, a sample (and simple) clause might

---

[8]See Linda S. Whitton, *Understanding Duties and Conflicts of Interest—A Guide for the Honorable Agent*, 117 Penn St. L. Rev. 1037, 1040 (2013). In 2010, the UPAA became Article 5B of the UPC.

[9]Robert Siciliano, *How Do Your Digital Assets Compare?*, McAfee Blog Central, May 14, 2013, http://blogs.mcafee.com/consumer/digital-assets.

state: "My fiduciary shall have the power to access, handle, manage, distribute, and dispose of my digital assets."

The Uniform Law Commission has developed a model law in this area that would allow personal representatives of estates, conservators of protected persons, agents acting pursuant to a power of attorney, and trustees of trusts to access digital property. The Revised Uniform Fiduciary Access to Digital Assets Act permits fiduciaries to manage digital property like computer files, Web domains, and virtual currency. It also strives to balance the accountholder's privacy interests with the needs of fiduciaries by restricting access to electronic communications such as the contents of emails and social media accounts unless the original user has indicated consent to disclosure in a will, trust, power of attorney, or other record, such as an online tool that sets out the account owner's wishes for the asset.[10]

As of late 2018, the legislation had been enacted in more than 40 states.

Four Categories of Digital Assets

For planning purposes, individuals typically need to consider four categories of digital assets, although there can be some overlap among the different types, and this list may change as new products become available.

- Personal assets include information generally found on a computer or smartphone or uploaded to a Web site, such as photos, important personal documents, playlists, and banking and medical records.
- Social media assets include Web sites where you connect with others, such as Facebook, Twitter, gaming sites, and blogs. These accounts can include personal information, photos, and videos.
- Financial assets include online bill payment, bank, and investment accounts, as well as other business-related accounts, such as sites through which you make purchases or sales.
- Business accounts include business-related records (e.g., online databases for storing documents) and other information, such as notes about clients (for lawyers) or patients (for physicians).

See, e.g., Gerry W. Beyer & Naomi Cahn, *Digital Planning: The Future of Elder Law*, 9 NAELA J. 135 (2013).

Agents Versus Conservators

An individual can plan for incapacity through the use of trusts and a power of attorney, but those documents may not address all of the issues associated with incapacity. When an individual has not engaged in thorough planning (or in any planning at all), then someone else may need to manage the incapacitated person's

---

[10]See Uniform Law Comm., *Fiduciary Access to Digital Assets Act, Revised (2015)*, http://www.uniformlaws.org/Act.aspx?title=Fiduciary%20Access%20to%20Digital%20Assets%20Act,%20Revised%20 (2018).

personal and financial matters. In these situations, states allow for the appointment of conservators (or guardians), court-appointed fiduciaries given responsibility for managing matters on behalf of an incapacitated person (the **ward** or person under conservatorship).

A court appoints a conservator only after a relative or friend of the potential ward or a governmental entity petitions the court to do so. Once the petition has been filed, the court will conduct a hearing to determine whether the individual can manage his or her own financial matters. States vary in the procedural protections available to the potential ward; some states permit the proceedings to continue without the attendance of the person. If the court determines that the person is unable to manage the person's own affairs, then a court-appointed fiduciary will assume that role as a substitute decision maker. States typically try to allow the ward to maintain as much autonomy as possible. The Uniform Law Commission has drafted a Uniform Guardianship and Protective Proceedings Act that sets out model procedures for states, and the act was adopted by almost 20 states before its revision in 2017.[11]

Several differences exist between conservators appointed by a court and agents acting pursuant to a power of attorney: (1) it takes a court action to begin and end a conservatorship, but the principal can initiate or revoke a power of attorney at any point during capacity; (2) conservators are appointed only upon incapacity of the principal, but powers of attorney can only be established while the principal has capacity; (3) conservators are subject to court supervision, but agents are generally not; and (4) conservatorships are relatively rare, while estate planners routinely include powers of attorney when developing plans for clients.

2. Health Care Decisions During Incapacity

A competent person has the right to make her own decisions about medical treatment, including rights associated with life-prolonging treatment. In the event of incapacity, however, an individual may be utterly unable to express her wishes, even with appropriate assistive devices. This section discusses the primary means of delegating decisional authority.

Advance Medical Directives

Statutory default provisions typically are only necessary when an individual has not already indicated her preferences in a valid instrument. Planning for health care incapacity involves two major types of advance medical directives: living wills and health care powers of attorney (these terms are defined below). Many states will combine these into one document

---

[11]See *Guardianship, Conservatorship, and Other Protective Arrangements Act*, Uniform Law Comm., http://www.uniformlaws.org/Committee.aspx?title=Guardianship,%20Conservatorship,%20and%20Other%20Protective%20Arrangements%20Act; uniformlaws.org.

A **living will** is a written document in which an individual specifies preferences regarding life-sustaining medical care in case of incapacity, and it is limited to end-of-life (EOL) decisions or irreversible illnesses that result in a vegetative state. It is directed to medical professionals and concerns specific treatment decisions. State statutes generally allow an individual to indicate a preference either for or against further medical treatment when the person becomes terminally ill, when the person becomes permanently unconscious, or when death is imminent. Through a living will, a person may, for example, state a preference to receive, not to receive, or to receive for a stated period, life-sustaining artificial nutrition and hydration if there is no reasonable expectation of recovery. While the execution requirements for a living will vary, states typically require that the document be in writing and be signed, and many also require witnesses and a notary. A living will only becomes effective once the patient is unable to communicate her own decisions. States generally provide immunity to medical professionals who follow their patient's instructions in a living will, although states may not impose liability if a medical professional fails to comply with a living will. See Lawrence A. Frolik & Melissa C. Brown, Advising the Elderly or Disabled Client ¶ 23.07 (2d ed. 2018) (discussing procedural issues and legal effects of living wills).

Living wills typically provide guidance on the desirability of life-sustaining measures, such as ventilators and tube feeding. But living wills also have limitations. "They typically contain broad pronouncements about the patient's wishes that are insufficiently flexible to deal with the ambiguities of real clinical decisions. In addition, living wills are based on people's predictions about how they will react to hypothetical situations that may occur far in the future. Research has shown that people often respond to real-world medical situations very differently than they might have anticipated." Carl H. Coleman, *Research with Decisionally Incapacitated Human Subjects: An Argument for a Systemic Approach to Risk-Benefit Assessment*, 83 Ind. L.J. 743, 774 (2008). Moreover, a living will does not become effective until certain requirements are met, such as the need to have two physicians certify that the individual is terminally ill or in a persistent vegetative state and unable to make her own medical decisions. (And there isn't necessarily a universally agreed upon definition of these terms.) Finally, state statutes control the legally binding nature of living wills.

A client's decision as to whether to execute a living will is a personal one and may be difficult. When a client expresses her wishes in writing, however, it lifts a substantial burden from the relatives or proxy decision makers who must guess as to what the client would have wanted. Although many well-meaning relatives may assume their loved one wants to fight for life at all costs, some would instead choose to die in peace. Over 88 percent of doctors elect to decline aggressive medical interventions in the event of terminal illness. See Bryan Walsh, *Why Your Doctor Probably Has a "Do Not Resuscitate" Order*, Time (May 29, 2014), http://time.com/131443/why-your-doctor-probably-has-a-do-not-resuscitate-order.

In contrast to a living will, a **health care power of attorney** appoints a surrogate decision maker and generally allows the principal to include treatment instructions. A health care power of attorney (sometimes also called a "health care proxy") is a written document that gives legal authority to another adult to make health care decisions on behalf of the principal. These forms are springing and only take effect

Medicare Coverage

Beginning in 2016, Medicare covers advance care planning with health care providers, allowing physicians and other health care professionals to be compensated for such discussion with their patients. See *Medicare Program; Revisions to Payment Policies Under the Physician Fee Schedule and Other Revisions to Part B for CY 2016*, Dep't of Health and Human Serv., 80 Fed. Reg. 70,886, 70,955 (Nov. 16, 2015), https://www.gpo.gov/fdsys/pkg/FR-2015-11-16/pdf/2015-28005.pdf.

The Four Ws

Pragmatically, in discussing end-of-life wishes, such conversations need to go beyond the contents of the legally binding documents. These more fundamental questions "boil down to the four Ws:

- Who should speak for you when you can't?
- What should they be saying?
- When do you want these issues raised?
- Where do you want to spend your final time—at home or in a hospital?

Essentially, you need to let folks know how you want to live your life at its end." Amos Goodall, *How to Plan for End-of-Life Wishes*, Centre Daily Times (Mar. 17, 2017 2:32 PM), http://www.centredaily.com/living/article139165628.html.

when the individual loses physical or mental capacity. Thus, they can be revised while the individual still has capacity. A health care power of attorney may be simple and merely appoint an agent and explain what rights the agent has. A client must carefully consider whom to name as an agent, as that person will be making critical health care decisions for the principal.

Alternatively, it may be a "hybrid" form that incorporates both the appointment of an agent with directions that would otherwise be found in a living will. A hybrid advanced directive can be more comprehensive than a living will and can address not only the principal's preferences regarding continuation or termination of artificial life support but also instructions about any medical treatments that the principal may wish to undergo or to avoid, such as surgery or chemotherapy. For state-specific forms, see Download Your State's Advance Directives, Nat'l Hospice & Palliative Caring Org. (2017), http://www.caringinfo.org/i4a/pages/index.cfm?pageid=3289.

All hospitals that participate in Medicare or Medicaid must respect patients' advance directives and their choice of visitors, regardless of the existence of a legal relationship between the patient and the visitor. The regulations protect, among others, same-sex partners. See 42 C.F.R. §§ 482.13(h)(2), 485.635(f)(2).

Advance medical directives may be cumbersome to use during an emergency. See Beverly Petersen Jennison, *Reflections on the Graying of America: Implications of Physician Orders for Life-Sustaining Treatment*, 12 Rutgers J.L. & Pub. Pol'y 295, 307-08 (2015). Beginning in Oregon in the early 1990s, Physician Orders for Life-Sustaining Treatment (POLST) developed as an additional means for implementing a patient's wishes. POLSTs are (as their name suggests) direct orders signed by a health care professional. Unlike advance medical directives, which are appropriate for all adults, POLSTs are best suited for people with a serious illness or frailty, with a short (one-year) life expectancy, and they complement advance directives. They provide medical directions for current treatment and guide the response of Emergency Medical Personnel. POLST programs are developing across the country and are not yet available in all states. For more information and a sample POLST form, see *Nat'l POLST Paradigm*, http://www.polst.org.

Chapter Summary

- Will substitutes, like wills, allow property to be transferred at death. Unlike property subject to a will, the property subject to a will substitute passes outside of probate.
- Will substitutes typically are not subject to the same statutory formalities as a will.
- Will substitutes are not governed by probate law but are instead governed by contract, property, or trust law.
- The most common forms of will substitutes are life insurance contracts, retirement accounts, jointly owned bank or brokerage accounts, revocable inter vivos trusts, multiple-party accounts with banks and other financial intermediaries, payable or transfer-on-death arrangements, and joint ownership with right of survivorship accounts or property.
- Planning for incapacity typically includes drafting documents for both financial and medical care and, increasingly, for handling digital assets.
- Through a power of attorney, the principal can authorize an agent to act on behalf of the principal on various financial transactions. States vary as to the formalities through which such a transfer can occur, such as whether it must be witnessed or notarized, and how explicitly certain powers, such as gift-giving, must be authorized.
- For medical care, a person may designate an agent in a durable power of attorney for health care. The person may also sign a living will, expressing the person's decisions as to whether be kept alive through the use of medical technology when the person is in a terminal condition and unable to communicate the person's wishes to decline further treatment.

Applying the Concepts

1. Devin died with a will. The estate consists of the following assets: checking account, savings account, car, house, retirement account with the decedent's niece as beneficiary, and life insurance policy with decedent's late husband named as beneficiary. Which assets are probate assets and which are nonprobate assets? Explain your reasoning.

2. Scarlett and Rhett established a joint checking account with right of survivorship. Scarlett made all the contributions to the account. Scarlett's will left the checking account to her daughter, Tara. When Scarlett dies, who is entitled to the joint checking account? What if they lived in Washington?

3. Afia and Lulu owned a beach house as tenants in common. Afia married, and she and her spouse decided to move to the other side of the country. Afia sold

her share of the house to Nicky. Nicky died suddenly just after the sale. Nicky's will leaves the beach house to Polo. How is the beach house currently owned?

4. Using the same facts as in Problem 3, does your answer change if Afia and Lulu originally owned the house in a joint tenancy with right of survivorship?

5. Marion has two children, Delilah and Sanford. Marion gets along well with Delilah, but is estranged from Sanford, and Marion's will leaves the entire estate to Delilah. When Marion begins to need more care, Sanford moves Marion to the state where he lives. Marion signs a power of attorney, naming Sanford as the agent. Sanford then transfers the money in Marion's bank account to an account in Sanford's name. He tells Delilah he will use the account for Marian's care. Assume the Uniform Power of Attorney Act applies.

   a. Advise Delilah. Is there anything she can legally do? Is there anything she should do?
   b. If you represented the bank where Marion's bank account is located, would you advise the bank to allow Sanford to withdraw the money?
   c. Now assume that Marion had created a revocable trust before she became ill. After Sanford became Marion's agent under the power of attorney, he revoked the trust. Advise Delilah on whether she can challenge the revocation.
   d. If you represented the bank that is serving as trustee of Marion's trust, what would you recommend when Sanford revokes the trust?

Trusts and Estates in Practice

1. What presumptions does your state law provide with respect to joint bank accounts?

2. You are developing a new estate-planning questionnaire for your firm. Draft three questions about nonprobate assets. Draft three questions that focus on digital assets.

3. Discussions about planning for incapacity may be quite sensitive. Think about how you might begin such a discussion. Will your questions differ depending on the age of the client? Why or why not?

4. What kinds of advance medical planning are permitted in your state? Does your state recognize POLSTs? What statutory forms exist?

5. Locate your state's statutes concerning financial powers of attorney. What do the statutes provide with respect to a determination of the principal's incapacity? Do the statutes include authorized forms one may use? If so, consider how you would fill them out on your own behalf or what advice you might give a family

member. What powers should be given to the agent? How often should the form be revised? You can compare the form in UPC § 5B-301.

6. You are a member of your state's legislature, and the chair of the probate committee. Consider whether your jurisdiction should enact legislation to protect against agents' fraud pursuant to a power of attorney. For example, should entities to which a power of attorney is presented have an obligation to perform further investigations, or should an agent be required to give periodic accountings to the principal or a third person? *See* Frolik, *supra*; the Uniform Power of Attorney Act, *supra*.

7. Consider how you yourself would fill out the advance medical directives for your state. Think about how you would advise a family member to do so. What advice would you give about whom to choose as an agent?

Family Protection

The law typically respects freedom of testation, and a testator is generally free to leave property to anyone. However, the state does place some restrictions on testation based on public policy, as discussed in Chapter 1. Among the few restrictions are protections for surviving family members: the surviving spouse is generally protected against both intentional and unintentional **disinheritance** (being prevented from inheriting), while children are only sometimes protected against unintentional disinheritance.

Recall the discussion in Chapter 2 regarding intestacy. If the decedent dies without a will, or if a will fails to dispose of all of the probate property, then the state's default rules supply the principles for disposing of the decedent's property in a way designed to effectuate what the decedent presumably intended. By contrast, this chapter examines how the law applies when the decedent affirmatively chooses not to leave property to family members—or apparently fails to do so. This chapter illustrates the tension between freedom to leave property as one chooses and protection of the "natural objects of one's bounty," who are presumed to be close family members.

This chapter begins by describing the two systems of property ownership during marriage: the **community property system**, which assumes property gained by a spouse during marriage is owned equally by both spouses, and the **common law system**, which treats the title to property as determinative of the power to dispose of such property. The chapter then turns to: (i) the opportunity for a surviving spouse to take an "**elective share**," or a specified amount to which the surviving spouse is entitled if the decedent did not leave the spouse a sufficient share of the marital estate via will or if such a share would be preferable to the result in intestacy; (ii) the means for waiving an elective share; and (iii) the protection against accidental

Key Concepts

- Analyzing the various forms of protection against the disinheritance of the surviving spouse
- Contrasting the two primary systems of marital property ownership
- Understanding the methods for overriding statutory protections
- Calculating the share of a surviving spouse omitted from a premarital will
- Determining the share of a child omitted from a parent's will

disinheritance when the testator executed a will before marriage or omitted a child. In most states, the child must be born after the execution of the will in order to inherit as an omitted child.

A. OVERVIEW OF THE TWO MARITAL PROPERTY SYSTEMS

Although the differences have become less pronounced over time, two distinct marital property systems still exist in this country. In this section, we compare the community property and the common law (or separate property) approaches to marital property. Regardless of the system in the state in which the couple lives, the surviving spouse may still be entitled to federal benefits, such as Social Security and the deceased spouse's retirement benefits (as governed by ERISA). Moreover, state law may protect the surviving spouse's right to remain in the marital home through the homestead exemption, and may also provide a state-mandated personal property set-aside (discussed in Chapter 14, Estate Administration and the Probate Process). As a general rule, the state in which the couple lived at the time they acquired the property will ultimately determine its character as either community property or common law separate property, although states may make some adjustments to account for migrating couples.

EXHIBIT 8.1 Sample Homestead Allowance Provisions

UPC § 2-402. HOMESTEAD ALLOWANCE. A decedent's surviving spouse is entitled to a homestead allowance of [$22,500]. If there is no surviving spouse, each minor child and each dependent child of the decedent is entitled to a homestead allowance amounting to [$22,500] divided by the number of minor and dependent children of the decedent. The homestead allowance is exempt from and has priority over all claims against the estate. Homestead allowance is in addition to any share passing to the surviving spouse or minor or dependent child by the will of the decedent, unless otherwise provided, by intestate succession, or by way of elective share.

IDAHO CODE ANN. § 15-2-402

The homestead allowance is exempt from and has priority over all claims against the estate except as hereinafter set forth. The homestead allowance is in addition to any share passing to the surviving spouse or minor or disabled child by the will of the decedent unless otherwise provided in the will, or by intestate succession, or by way of elective share. The amount of the homestead allowance shall be fifty thousand dollars ($50,000). The homestead allowance is not a right to claim ownership of, or succession to, any homestead owned by the decedent at the time of the decedent's death but is only the right to claim the sum set forth above. The right to a homestead allowance is determined as follows:

(a) If there is a surviving spouse of the decedent, the surviving spouse shall be entitled to a homestead allowance.

(b) If there is no surviving spouse, and there are one (1) or more children under the age of twenty-one (21) years whom the decedent was obligated to support or children who were in fact being supported by the decedent and who are disabled, []then each such minor or disabled child is entitled to a portion of the homestead allowance in the amount of the homestead allowance divided by the number of such minor or disabled children entitled to receive the homestead allowance.

1. Community Property

Eight states follow a community property (or comparable civil law) model when it comes to property acquired by earnings of either spouse during the marriage: Arizona, California, Idaho, Louisiana, Nevada, New Mexico, Texas, and Washington. Based on patterns of colonization and territorial acquisition, these states were influenced by Spanish civil law and, in the case of Louisiana, by both Spanish and French law. Although it does not share a similar history, the state of Wisconsin is now considered a ninth community property state based on the enactment of a marital property statute that effectively tracks the modern approach of community property states to the ownership of assets. Wis. Stat. ch. 766 ("Property Rights of Married Persons; Marital Property"). Alaska and Tennessee permit married couples to opt into a community property system. In community property states, most property acquired during marriage is characterized as owned by the community of both spouses as a whole, regardless of which spouse earned it. This is because marriage is viewed as an economic partnership. Property acquired before the marriage, or property received by gift, devise, or bequest during the marriage, remains the separate property of the spouse holding that property. States vary as to the details on how income from separate property should be categorized and what sorts of management powers spouses have over community property.

Historically, under the community property system, even though the community property was considered to belong equally to both parties, marital partners were not regarded as equals. A husband was still given complete authority over the community property, including his wife's earnings. But that approach has changed, and the spouses now have co-equal rights to community property while they are living.

At death, each spouse is able to dispose of one-half of the community property. The surviving spouse owns the other one-half of the community property because the community was severed—not because she received it from her spouse—resulting in each spouse owning and having the power to convey half of the property. Sometimes, the testator provides that the surviving spouse can choose between receiving the community property share or transferring the one-half share of the community property to a trust under the will containing both spouses' shares of the community property. Under this process, which has traditionally been called a **widow's election**, the surviving spouse would receive all income for life in exchange for relinquishing an ownership interest in one-half of the community property. See Pamela L. Rollins et. al., *Remainders of the Day: The Demise of Gradow*, 12 Prob. & Prop. 31 (May/June 1998).

In a community property state, there is no separate statute to protect the surviving spouse from disinheritance because the nature of marital property already serves the function of allocating a reasonable share to the survivor. If there is no community property (or very little community property) compared to the separate property, however, then there is no protection for the surviving spouse.

EXHIBIT 8.2 **California Statute**

> **CAL. PROB. CODE § 100(A)**
> Upon the death of a person who is married or in a registered domestic partnership, one-half of the community property belongs to the surviving spouse and the other one-half belongs to the decedent.

2. Common Law Property

Historically, the common law vision of the marital relationship assumed the loss of a wife's legal identity. The common law approach to marital property rights flowed directly from this understanding of the marital relationship. In this approach, there was no notion of a marital enterprise representing the cumulative efforts of both spouses—there was simply the husband who owned all of the property except for his wife's realty, which she controlled.

Married women gradually acquired property rights through the passage of the **Married Women's Property Acts**, beginning in the mid-nineteenth century. But the concept of a marital community did not take hold in the common law states. Instead, traditional common law property concepts, which extolled the virtues of individual rights, were extended to married women. The property was either the husband's or wife's, depending on who supplied the purchase funds, and in whose name the property was titled, which in reality meant that it mostly belonged to the husband because husbands were typically the breadwinners. In contrast to community property states, common law property states established that the nonfinancial contributions of a homemaker spouse did not give rise to ownership rights, and the spouse who held title to the property could dispose of it, subject to **dower** and **curtesy**. Upon her spouse's death, the widow received "dower," a life estate in one-third of her husband's real property. Because the widow received only a life estate, she could not control the ultimate

> **Moving Out of a Common Law State**
>
> What happens when a spouse moves from a common law state that recognizes the elective share to a community property state that does not? Some community property states will recognize elective-share-type rights in so-called quasi–community property, which is property that was acquired in a common law state that would have been community property if it had been acquired in a community property state.

disposition of the property. A surviving husband was protected through "curtesy," through which he received a life estate in all of his deceased wife's property (not just her real property), but only if at least one child had been born during the marriage. See Susan N. Gary, *The Oregon Elective Share Statute: Is Reform an Impossible Dream?*, 44 Willamette L. Rev. 337 (2007). The rights to dower or curtesy have been superseded by the elective share, described below.

B. THE ELECTIVE SHARE

Today, in all the common law states (save Georgia, which provides a different form of protection), a surviving spouse is protected through what is typically known as the elective share, or a forced or statutory share that is taken out of the decedent spouse's estate. See Terry L. Turnipseed, *Why Shouldn't I Be Allowed to Leave My Property to Whomever I Choose at My Death? (Or How I Learned to Stop Worrying and Start Loving the French)*, 44 Brandeis L.J. 737, 739 (2006).

1. The Development of the Elective Share

First generation elective share statutes (some of which still exist) gave a surviving spouse the right to take one-third of the deceased spouse's probate property, based on the old dower rule. Unlike dower and curtesy (the male equivalent of dower), however, these elective share statutes were gender-neutral and gave the surviving spouse a full ownership interest as opposed to a life estate. Restatement (Third) of Property: Wills and Other Donative Transfers § 9.1 (Am. Law Inst. 2003).

Some states have moved past the first generation elective share statutes and, currently, state laws differ significantly on the operation of the elective share. For example, the elective share percentage might be affected by whether there are surviving and joint descendants. However, in some states, the surviving spouse may receive up to one-half of the decedent's estate in the absence of descendants.

States also vary as to the type of property subject to the elective share. Property ownership has shifted so that an increasing amount of a decedent's property passes outside of probate through, for example, life insurance or payable-on-death bank accounts, and revocable trusts. Such types of ownership, discussed in Chapter 7 on nonprobate transfers, have become standard in estate planning, useful both in case of the settlor's incapacity as well as to avoid probate. Because of the increase in property being transferred through nonprobate means, elective share statutes based on the decedent's probate estate began to be seen as too limited in what was eligible for the surviving spouse to take. This change in property ownership decreased the amount available as part of the elective share. Moreover, estate planners realized that nonprobate assets, such as trusts, could be used to shield the property from the elective share. Concerns arose, therefore, about decedent spouses perpetrating "fraud on the elective share."

In some states, the elective share still applies only to probate property, meaning that the surviving spouse has minimal protection against intentional disinheritance if the decedent has made extensive use of nonprobate transfers. Sometimes, courts step in to solve the problem, using theories such as **illusory transfer** or fraud on the surviving spouse's share to apply the elective share to property held in **revocable trusts**. A judicial solution, however, means that each case requires a fact-specific analysis. In some states, little effort is made to expand the reach of the elective share. In an increasing number of states, however, legislatures apply the elective share to an expanded (or "augmented") "estate" that includes property that passes outside of probate as well as property conveyed by will (or as a result of intestacy).

Case Preview

In re Estate of Thompson

Thompson shows how a court adapted its understanding of the estate subject to the elective share based on newer forms of property ownership. A year before his death, H. Ripley Thompson executed a revocable trust, which on his death gave his wife a cash gift of $100,000. By contrast, previous wills and trusts had been much more generous to his wife, but the final trust was executed after the spouses separated. After her husband's death, his wife filed with the court to take her elective share and sought to include the property in the trust in the husband's estate solely for purposes of calculating the elective share. The relevant Arkansas statute defines the elective share amount by reference to "dower" or "curtesy," and such rights vary; for example, if there are surviving children, the spouse is entitled to a one-third life estate, while if there are no children, the spouse is entitled to one-half of the property in fee simple. Ark. Code §§ 28-11-301, 307 (West).

As you read *Estate of Thompson*, consider the following:

1. What would the wife have received without taking an elective share?
2. What did Arkansas law provide with respect to the composition of the estate from which the elective share would be taken?
3. Why did the executor argue that the revocable trust was not included in the elective share?
4. What significance did the court accord to the decedent's actions during his lifetime toward his spouse?
5. What was the legal basis for the lower and appellate courts' decisions to include the revocable trust?
6. What happens to the trust as a result of the court's opinion?
7. What is the major source of disagreement between the majority and the dissent?

In re Estate of Thompson
434 S.W.3d 877 (Ark. 2014)

Donald L. Corbin, Associate Justice.

Appellant, Vance Thompson as executor as trustee of the H. Ripley Thompson Revocable Trust ("the Trust"), appeals the order of the Woodruff County Circuit Court finding that Appellee Anne L. Thompson's election to take against the will of her husband, the Decedent, H. Ripley Thompson ("Ripley" or "the Decedent"), was valid and that, because the Decedent's intent in creating the Trust was to deprive Appellee of her elective share in her husband's estate ("the Estate"), the assets held by the Trust must be included in his Estate for purposes of determining her elective share. . . . [W]e affirm.

. . . Appellee alleged that she had married the Decedent on July 15, 2001, that they had remained husband and wife until his death on February 20, 2010, and that, because the Decedent had no children, she was his sole heir. She also alleged that she previously had a successful career as a registered nurse, but that she had left her career at her husband's request because he had promised to take care of her. Appellee attached to her amended complaint her deceased husband's will, dated May 29, 2009 ("the 2009 Will"), that had been admitted to probate and to which she had filed a petition to set aside and an election to take against. She also attached to her amended complaint the [] H. Ripley Thompson Revocable Trust, also dated May 29, 2009 []. Appellee attached as an exhibit to her amended complaint the petition she had filed in probate court to have the 2009 Will and the 2009 Trust (collectively "the 2009 Will and Trust") set aside on grounds of incapacity and undue influence, or alternatively, to elect to take against the 2009 Will. For her cause of action in her amended complaint, Appellee sought the imposition of a constructive trust on the 2009 Trust assets for her elective share; alternatively, she sought a declaration that the 2009 Will and Trust were invalid as a result of undue influence and lack of testamentary capacity. []

. . .

According to the facts alleged in the amended complaint, upon the Decedent's death, the property of the Trust was all personalty[1] and valued in excess of $5.8 million, while the inventory of the Estate showed all personalty valued at $230,471. Appellee alleged that, pursuant to Arkansas Code Annotated section 28-39-401(b)(1), her elective share of the Estate should be calculated as one-half of the total of the estate assets plus the Trust assets, or $3,015,209.

The circuit court held a three-day hearing on the complaint, [and held that] the Trust assets would be included as part of the Estate for the limited purpose of calculating Appellee's elective share.

. . . The circuit court's findings [included that early in 2008], Appellee was diagnosed with breast cancer. . . . By 2008, the Decedent's health was precarious, and he had a medical history of heart disease, type-2 diabetes, and dementia, as well as other health-related complications. The Decedent executed the 2009 Will and Trust while he was in [a] nursing home, where he remained until his death in 2010.

---

[1][**Personalty** is all property that is not real property, money, or investments. —Eds.]

. . .

[] First, Appellant contends that the elective share of a surviving spouse is limited to property owned by the deceased spouse at the time of his or her death, and the circuit court therefore erred in interpreting Arkansas Code Annotated section 28-39-401(a) (Repl. 2012) to include the assets of the Trust in the Decedent's Estate. Second, Appellant contends that the evidence does not support the finding that Appellee was defrauded of her statutory rights to the Decedent's property. Third, Appellant contends that Appellee failed to prove fraud on her marital rights. . . .

. . . Appellant's first argument for reversal of the circuit court's order is that the circuit court erred in ruling that the property owned by the Trust at the time of the Decedent's death should be subject to Appellee's elective share because the Decedent did not own the Trust property at the time of his death. . . . He maintains the general proposition that, upon a settlor's[2] death, title to property held in an inter vivos revocable trust becomes irrevocable, such that, regardless of the nature of the rights retained over the assets by the settlor during his lifetime, the property ceases to be owned by the settlor upon his death and is removed from his or her estate.

. . . .

[] The circuit court ultimately concluded that the assets of the Trust would be included in the Decedent's Estate for the limited purpose of calculating Appellee's elective share due to the fact that the Decedent's intent in amending the Trust in 2009 was to deprive Appellee of her marital rights to his property. For the reasons explained below, we cannot say that this finding was clearly erroneous.

Arkansas law gives a surviving spouse the right to elect to take a share of the estate of his or her deceased spouse against the will of the deceased. Ark. Code Ann. § 28-39-401. This elective share is the equivalent of the spouse's dower or curtesy rights, as well as any homestead rights and statutory allowances. The statute provides in pertinent part as follows:

> 28-39-401. Rights of surviving spouse—Limitations.
>   (a) When a married person dies testate as to all or any part of his or her estate, the surviving spouse shall have the right to take against the will if the surviving spouse has been married to the decedent continuously for a period in excess of one (1) year.
>   (b) In the event of such an election, the rights of the surviving spouse in the estate of the deceased spouse shall be limited to the following:
>   (1) The surviving spouse, if a woman, shall receive dower in the deceased husband's real estate and personal property as if he had died intestate. The dower shall be additional to her homestead rights and statutory allowances; and
>   (2) The surviving spouse, if a man, shall receive a curtesy interest in the real and personal property of the deceased spouse to the same extent as if she had died intestate. The curtesy interest shall be additional to his homestead rights and statutory allowances. . . .

. . . Arkansas law is well settled that the surviving spouse's elective interest can vest only in property that the deceased spouse owned at the time of death. And . . . the parties did not dispute that the Trust had become irrevocable upon the Decedent's death. Thus, generally speaking, in the absence of fraud, the assets of the Trust would have remained assets of the Trust after the Decedent's death. That is not the case here. . . .

---

[2][A **settlor** is a person who creates a trust. —Eds.]

. . . Appellant challenges the circuit court's finding that the Decedent intended to defraud Appellee of her statutory rights to his property [and that] no "evil" intent existed. [] The important consideration is the settlor's intent.

. . .

In the present case, the circuit court . . . concluded quite clearly and unequivocally that, in this case, the Decedent's "intent, as the Grantor of the 2009 H. Ripley Revocable Trust was to defraud [Appellee] and deny her statutory rights, pursuant to Arkansas Code Annotated § 28-39-401(a) to the property held by the 2009 Trust."

The circuit court went on to state the bases for that opinion. The circuit court first noted that the 2002 Trust and the 2004 Trust provided Appellee with income for life from the Trust's net income, gave her the right to invade the principal for extraordinary expenses, and gave her annual withdrawal rights of $5,000 or 5% of the net fair-market value of the principal on the date of withdrawal. In contrast, the circuit court observed, the 2009 Trust provided nothing to Appellee except the $100,000 bequest, but only if she did not contest the 2009 Will and Trust. . . .

The circuit court observed in its order that while Appellee and the Decedent lived together, he showered her with gifts of great value, including cash, and that while they were living together he ensured that she would be provided for after his death through his 2002 and 2004 Wills and Trusts. The circuit court further observed that it was not until they were separated, and after she had filed for separate maintenance, that he redrafted his 2009 Will and Trust "in order to leave her basically nothing." The circuit court thus found that in the early years of the marriage, the Decedent provided for Appellee quite well and had no intent to deprive her of her marital rights to his property, but that in the latter years of the marriage, the Decedent stopped providing for Appellee to the extent that she "felt impelled to file for separate maintenance." The circuit court found that the Decedent's intent to deprive Appellee of her marital rights manifested sometime in 2008 when his health had begun to deteriorate and the parties were no longer living together.

The circuit court noted other indicators of the Decedent's intent to deprive Appellee of her marital rights to his property, such as the change in Appellee's status as trustee. In the 2002 Trust and the 2004 Trust, Appellee was to be a co-trustee; but, with the 2009 amendment, the Decedent and Vance Thompson were named as co-trustees; Appellee was not. Because Appellee was removed from all participation in the 2009 Trust, the circuit court concluded that "[c]learly, [the Decedent's] intent was to deprive her of her statutory rights to his property." The circuit court pointed out still further indicators of the Decedent's intent, such as the fact that the 2009 Will and Trust had been executed while he was in a nursing home and that less than a year had passed between the execution of the 2009 Will and Trust and the Decedent's death. . . .

The circuit court's ultimate conclusion was that "[the Decedent's] intent was to deprive [Appellee] from receiving from his testamentary estate," and therefore that her "election to take against the 2009 Will and Trust . . . [was] valid" and that "the assets transferred to the Trust by [the Decedent] must be included in the calculations to determine [Appellee]'s elective share."

. . . Thus, while it is true that, as Appellant argues, a testator can devise his property however he chooses and can exclude or disinherit his spouse, the testator's choices do not prevent the surviving spouse from gaining his or her elective share.

. . . Appellant contends that, in order to prove that the Decedent's actions in amending the Trust in 2009 constituted a fraud on her marital rights, Appellee was required to meet the elements of a fraud claim with evidentiary proof, and that she failed to do so. This argument is without merit for several reasons.

First, Appellant cites no authority for the proposition that "fraud on marital rights" as that phrase is used in the estate-planning context is to be analyzed under the traditional test for common-law fraud. [W]e note that other courts have expressly rejected the idea that "fraud on marital rights" in this context is akin to common-law fraud. Thus, . . . we conclude that Appellee was not required to prove the elements of common-law fraud.

. . . Accordingly, we hold that once a circuit court determines that a settlor had the intent of depriving his or her spouse of marital-property rights when creating or amending an inter vivos revocable trust, the effect of that intent is to have the trust assets included in the settlor's estate for the limited purpose of calculating the surviving spouse's elective share. The intent to defeat the marital rights or the elective share will not invalidate any other lawful purpose of the trust.

. . . Accordingly, we affirm the order appealed.

Baker and Hart, JJ., dissent.

Josephine Linker Hart, Justice, dissenting.

The majority holds that the assets of a revocable trust should be included in a decedent's estate for the purpose of calculating the elective spousal share. Because this holding is contrary to established Arkansas probate law and will thwart the use of many traditional estate-planning tools, I respectfully dissent.

. . . Contrary to our case law and the plain language of the [elective share] statutes, the majority grafts onto our state jurisprudence a new source from which a [elective share] interest can be taken: personalty in which the spouse did not have an accrued [elective share] interest. . . . Further, in permitting Thompson, on her claim of fraud, to take an elective share in the trust, the majority states that the "Decedent's intent to deprive Appellee of her marital rights in his property is evident on the face of the Will and Trust documents." Under the majority's conception of the law, *any* transfer of personalty to a person other than the spouse would compel the conclusion that the spouse was defrauded by the transfer and deprived of her marital rights.

The ramifications of this new law are broad and upend the use of familiar tools of estate planning. In creating this new law, the majority permits a surviving spouse to make a fraud claim and to take an elective share not only in trusts, but also in any property or accounts held in pay on death, transfer on death, or co-ownership registration with the right of survivorship, as well as in the proceeds of insurance over which the decedent held an exercisable general power of appointment, all of which are used as estate-planning tools. The confusion to follow this opinion is indeed disturbing.

. . .

Because the majority rejects black-letter Arkansas probate law and undercuts well-established methods of estate planning, I respectfully dissent.

Baker, J., joins in this dissent.

Post-Case Follow-Up

Although there was little doubt that the literal words of the statute did not include the revocable trust, the court focused instead on the purpose of the statute. It noted the twin public policies concerning the importance of protecting the testator's intent and of protecting the surviving spouse. The dissent notes that the majority effects a fundamental change in the property subject to the elective share, expanding it beyond the probate estate and beyond the language of the elective share statute. While the majority reaches this result through statutory interpretation and a discussion of fraud, the "augmented" estate is a fundamental component of some states' elective share statutes and of the Uniform Probate Code's (UPC's) approach to the elective share. Not all states include nonprobate property in the property subject to the elective share.

In re Estate of Thompson: Real Life Applications

1. Based on the facts of the case, assume it is 2002 and that H. Ripley Thompson has approached you to represent him in estate planning.

   a. He wants to ensure that there is no need for his wife to elect against his will, and he wants to provide for her. What advice do you give him?

   b. He wants to protect assets for his existing family, rather than permitting up to half of his estate be given to his new wife. What steps should he take?

2. You are a member of the Arkansas state legislature, reviewing the outcome of the case.

   a. What steps can you take to ensure that the augmented estate concept does not take hold in Arkansas?

   b. You like the idea of including assets beyond the probate estate in the property to which the elective share is applied. Which assets should be included? Why?

3. In *Thompson*, the parties were married for approximately a decade. As a member of the legislature, you are not sure that ten years is the appropriate time for the vesting of full entitlement to the elective share. Will you draft legislation that provides a sliding scale based on the number of years of marriage? If so, how many years would yield full entitlement? Or should marriage itself serve as the dividing line?

2. The Contemporary UPC

The UPC recognizes the increasing amount of property that is transferred through nonprobate means with its reliance on using an **augmented estate** as the basis for elective share calculations; the augmented estate under the UPC is the combined value of both spouses' assets. And, the UPC also takes into account the length of the marriage, although regardless of the length of the marriage the surviving spouse receives a minimum amount (called the **supplemental amount** in the UPC). The overall goal is to effectuate an economic-partnership theory of marriage by equalizing marital assets at death and to provide a base level of support so the surviving spouse will not be left destitute. In taking this partnership approach to marriage, the UPC elective share is far closer to community property principles than the traditional elective share.

The elective share is calculated in two steps. The first step is determining the composition of the augmented estate by sweeping in equivalent property of both the decedent and the surviving spouse. The augmented estate is calculated by adding: (1) the value of the decedent's net probate estate; (2) the value of the decedent's nonprobate transfers to persons other than the surviving spouse as well as to the surviving spouse; and (3) comparable assets from the surviving spouse that would have been part of the augmented estate had the surviving spouse died first (the surviving spouse's net assets at the decedent's death, plus the surviving spouse's nonprobate transfers to others). See Uniform Probate Code Part II, Elective Share of Surviving Spouse, General Cmt. (Unif. Law Comm'n 2009).

The second step is determining what percentage of the augmented estate will constitute the elective share. The percentage depends on the length of the marriage, with a surviving spouse who has been married less than one year receiving only minimal amount, and spouses who have been married 15 years or more receiving a full elective share, or 50 percent of the augmented estate. UPC § 2-203.

The net effect of creating the augmented estate and using a sliding scale based on years of marriage is that, in a long-term marriage where the decedent spouse owned a majority of the assets, the surviving spouse receives a significant share of assets acquired during the marriage. The surviving spouse in a short-term, later-in-life marriage, where few assets are presumed to be acquired during the marital partnership, receives relatively little.

If the surviving spouse chooses the elective share, then that amount is satisfied first through the decedent's probate and nonprobate transfers to the surviving spouse and the marital portion of the surviving spouse's assets. If these amounts do not satisfy the elective share amount, then the decedent's probate and nonprobate transfers to others are proportionately used to make up the balance.

C. WAIVING THE ELECTIVE SHARE

The elective share provides protection against unilateral disinheritance, but it can be validly waived, through a **premarital (or prenuptial) agreement**, which is an agreement entered into prior to marriage, or other agreement during the marriage. Such waivers are particularly common where one of the potential spouses has family members from a previous relationship. The elective share waiver ensures that the decedent's property benefits the earlier family. Attorneys frequently include such provisions in premarital agreements.

The waiver can be partial or full, can occur before or during marriage, and must be by done by a written agreement that was signed by both parties. The UPC incorporates the approach of the **Uniform Premarital Agreement Act (UPAA)**, which is in effect in approximately half of the states, albeit with variations. The general goal is to validate the parties' choices concerning the financial term of their marriage. The statute builds in various, albeit minimal, procedural requirements, such as protection against an agreement entered into involuntarily or under duress and the need for adequate financial disclosure. UPC § 2-213; see, e.g., In Re Estate of Pattanayak, 2016 WL 4527592, at *1 (N.J. Super. Ct. App. Div. Aug. 30, 2016). The UPAA provides that a voluntary agreement will not be enforced only if the agreement is not only unconscionable *but also* that the parties did not provide informed consent based on adequate knowledge of the other's financial status. In its comments to Section 9, the UPAA notes that the burden of proof is on the person seeking to invalidate the agreement. UPAA § 6, cmt., *available at* www.nccusl.org.[3]

Case Preview

In re Estate of Shinn

This case shows a court applying a variation of the Uniform Premarital Agreement Act. Although the UPAA does contemplate that an agreement including an elective share waiver can be unenforceable, the burden on the party attacking the agreement is high. Stacey, the surviving spouse of Edward Shinn, sued her husband's estate, seeking to declare their premarital agreement unenforceable and to recognize her right to receive an elective share of her husband's estate. Edward had three children from a previous marriage, which ended in an acrimonious divorce—perhaps prompting him to seek the premarital agreement at issue in the case.

As you read *Shinn*, consider the following:

1. What were the circumstances under which Stacey learned of the agreement?
2. What were the terms of the agreement?
3. What did New Jersey law provide with respect to the enforceability of the agreement?
4. What public policy did the court rely on to justify its decision?

---

[3]The UPAA has been updated, but only a few states have adopted the new version. Uniform Premarital and Marital Agreements Act. (Unif. Law Comm'n 2012), http://www.uniformlaws.org/shared/docs/premarital%20and%20marital%20agreements/2012_pmaa_final.pdf.

In re Estate of Shinn
925 A.2d 88 (N.J. Super. Ct. App. Div. 2007)

FISHER, J.A.D.

. . .

I

Stacey and Edward met in August 1991 and, by September 1992, began living together in Edward's rented townhouse. In August 1994, Edward purchased a home in Rockaway, where they thereafter resided together.

Stacey and Edward became engaged in December 1994, and agreed to a small wedding in Hawaii in August 1995. Approximately one month before the wedding, Stacey planned to visit her mother and sister in Florida. The night before this trip, Edward presented Stacey with a draft of an agreement prepared by his attorney.

The agreement included, among other things, a waiver of Stacey's right to an elective share of Edward's estate. . . . In addition, the agreement contained limits on Stacey's right to alimony upon a dissolution of the marriage. Edward also agreed that in the event of his death, Stacey would be entitled to receive a death benefit of $100,000.

Stacey left for Florida the day after receiving a copy of the agreement. She conversed with a New Jersey attorney about the agreement while in Florida. Stacey's attorney, Alan Rich, Esq., then contacted Edward's attorney, Edward Rosen, Esq., and, on July 17, 1995, Rosen forwarded to Rich a copy of the agreement.

Following his review of the agreement, Rich requested that Rosen provide the financial information that was referenced, but not included, within the agreement; Rosen immediately sent to Rich a copy of a document entitled "Financial Statement of Edward H. Shinn, IV, as of July 18, 1995," and advised Rich to append this document, as Rider A, to the agreement.

The financial statement revealed Edward's ownership of: a certificate of deposit (in the amount of $20,000); 100% of the stock in Edward Shinn United Crane, Inc. (valued at $635,000); 50% of the stock in Shinn Brothers Associates Inc. (valued at $80,000); 50% of the stock in Shinn Brothers Properties Inc. (valued at $6,750); a loan receivable due from Shinn Brothers Properties Inc. (in the amount of $52,000); 1.83% ownership of commercial rental properties referred to as Kenilworth Properties (the value of which was described on the document as "not available"); 6.66% ownership of commercial rental properties referred to as Lakewood Properties (the value of which was described as "not available"); 6% of the stock in United Crane & Shovel Service Co. Inc. (the value of which was described as "not available"); and the Rockaway residence (the equity of which was valued at $60,000 based upon an original purchase price of $290,000 and an outstanding mortgage of $230,000).

The financial statement did not disclose: Edward's earnings (of approximately $300,000 per year); his financial obligations relating to his purchase of the entity later known as Edward Shinn United Crane, Inc.; an annuity[4] of $95,022.32; and a

---

[4][An annuity is an insurance product that an individual purchases in order to receive fixed amounts at a later date. —EDS.]

pension payable to Edward at age 55 of $892.76 per month and at age 60 of $1,539.65 per month. And, as already mentioned, the financial statement failed to attribute a value to Kenilworth Properties, Lakewood Properties, or United Crane & Shovel Service Co., Inc. As a result of these omissions, the figures provided by the financial statement indicated that Edward had a net worth of only $853,750. Contrary to this representation, it was revealed at trial that in applying for life insurance in 1992 and again in 1995, Edward represented his net worth to be in excess of $6,000,000.

On July 25, 1995, Rich expressed to Rosen that there were problems with the agreement, including the lack of a complete statement of Edward's financial condition. Rosen responded that Stacey and Rich had already received all the information they were going to get.

On July 26, 1995, Rich met with Stacey. He attempted to negotiate changes in the agreement and obtain additional financial information, but Rosen reiterated Edward's intractable position and advised that Stacey would have to sign the agreement as is or the marriage was off. When this response and Rich's advice that she not sign the agreement was relayed, Stacey left Rich's office in tears. She called Edward a few minutes later, and pleaded for him to give Rich additional information as well as his consent to the changes in the agreement that Rich sought. Edward summarily refused, saying that Stacey "had to sign it the way it was or [they] weren't getting married." This further upset her, but Stacey returned to Rich's office and signed the agreement.

Stacey and Edward married in Hawaii on August 16, 1995. On May 17, 1996, Stacey gave birth to Samantha.

Following Samantha's birth, Edward and Stacey went to Rosen's office to sign wills. Edward's will directed, among other things, that upon his death Stacey would receive the Rockaway home, and that his estate would pay off the mortgage on that property. The remainder of Edward's estate was to be split equally between all four of his children and held in trust until they reached the age of thirty.

After a short illness, Edward died on May 19, 1998 at the age of 46.

A few months later, Stacey commenced this action [] seeking, among other things, a judgment that would both declare the premarital agreement unenforceable and recognize Stacey's right to receive her elective share of Edward's estate.

II

N.J.S.A. 3B:8-1 permits a surviving spouse to elect a right to take one-third of the augmented estate of a deceased spouse. That specific right, however, may be waived, in whole or in part, by written agreement. Specifically, N.J.S.A. 3B:8-10 expresses the Legislature's intent that an elective share may be waived "by a written contract, agreement or waiver, signed by the party waiving *after fair disclosure*" (emphasis added).

Subsequently, in 1988, the Uniform Premarital Agreement Act, was enacted in this State, N.J.S.A. 37:2-31 to -41. This act defines more thoroughly than N.J.S.A. 3B:8-10 when a premarital agreement may be enforced, and it also governs all types of premarital agreements, not just those that contain a waiver of an elective share:

The burden of proof to set aside a premarital or pre-civil union agreement shall be upon the party alleging the agreement to be unenforceable. A premarital or pre-civil union agreement shall not be enforceable if the party seeking to set aside the agreement proves, by clear and convincing evidence, that:

a. The party executed the agreement involuntarily; or
b. The agreement was unconscionable at the time enforcement was sought; or
c. That party, before execution of the agreement:

(1) Was not provided full and fair disclosure of the earnings, property and financial obligations of the other party;

(2) Did not voluntarily and expressly waive, in writing, any right to disclosure of the property or financial obligations of the other party beyond the disclosure provided;

(3) Did not have, or reasonably could not have had, an adequate knowledge of the property or financial obligations of the other party; or

(4) Did not consult with independent legal counsel and did not voluntarily and expressly waive, in writing, the opportunity to consult with independent legal counsel.

d. The issue of unconscionability of a premarital or pre-civil union agreement shall be determined by the court as a matter of law.

[N.J.S.A. 37:2-38.]

. . .

The trial judge concluded that he had been presented with clear and convincing evidence that Edward made neither "fair disclosure" nor "full and fair disclosure." In his thorough oral decision, the judge found, among other things, that the book value of $635,000 listed in the agreement for Edward Shinn United Crane, Inc. grossly understated that entity's true value, observing that although the experts who testified disagreed about its value, the lower of the valuations "was more than three times the book value of the asset." In addition, the judge found that there was an inadequate disclosure of Edward's interest in Shinn Brothers Properties, although the value of this business was "much more modest," as well as an inadequate disclosure of Edward's interests in other listed properties and entities since the agreement said only that the value of those interests was "not available." And, the judge found that the agreement failed to contain a statement of Edward's yearly income of approximately $300,000, or an indication of the union benefits he was then receiving, or all the cash on deposit in banks he then possessed.

The judge explained the significance of Edward's failure to provide the disclosure required by the statutes in the following way:

> See, the point of the disclosure is that somebody's being asked—actually, both parties are asked to give up something under the agreement, but practically in this agreement, the only party really giving up anything is [Stacey]. The reason for that was that [Edward] did not give up anything. He did nominally, but he gave up his right to an elective share; he gave up his right to alimony, . . . and [he gave up his right to] shar[e] by way of equitable distribution in the assets of his wife, but she didn't have any assets.
>
> Her disclosure indicates that she actually had a negative net worth at the time she entered into the agreement. She had, you know, credit card and other consumer

indebtedness of $9,000 or so. She had less than $200 cash in the bank. She has a 1990 automobile. And she was making perhaps $15,000 a year as a bartender. Actually, I'm not sure whether she was still working when she signed the agreement; but in any event, if she was, that's the kind of money she was making.

Ed Shinn, on the other hand, had this very valuable business; he was making $300,000 a year, and he had a lot of other tangible . . . assets that Stacy didn't have.

So when she surrendered [] elective share rights, she was actually surrendering something that was conceivably worth a good bit of money. When Ed Shinn surrendered those things, it did not mean anything economically because, even in the absence of the agreement, even if he hadn't shed those things, they would not have been worth anything or would not have been worth much. So she was giving up a lot.

Now the point . . . of the full disclosure [required by statute] is, that if someone's going to consent to give up their rights, they have to understand what they're giving up.

. . .

The trial judge also found that the agreement did not contain an adequate written waiver of the right to full financial disclosure. . . .

In fact, the judge indicated that some of the statements in the agreement's waiver provisions were "just contrary to fact" and were "[f]latly, totally wrong." Specifically, the judge pointed to the statement in the opening recitals that erroneously proclaimed that "the full nature and complete extent" of each party's property and sources of income were "heretofore disclosed to the other. . . ."

The judge emphasized that Edward's disclosures "were not accurate" because Edward "deliberately" refused to answer Rich's questions.

The judge also concluded that the circumstances set forth in N.J.S.A. 37:2-38(c)(3) were applicable because Stacey had no true understanding of Edward's property or financial obligations. He explained that, even though there was some evidence that Stacey lived comfortably with Edward before they married, knew that he had met all of her financial needs during that time, and had had some contact with his business, Stacey actually "had no real detailed sense of how much [Edward] was worth," and she "had no idea of what his income was." . . .

. . . The trial judge's findings were thorough and well-supported by the evidence adduced during a nine-day trial. . . .

. . .

Here, Edward had no right to rely upon the future enforceability of the agreement. He stonewalled the requests of Stacey and her attorney for additional financial information in the face of the Legislature's declaration that he make "fair disclosure," N.J.S.A. 3B:8-10, or "full and fair disclosure," N.J.S.A. 37:2-38. Having deliberately refused to make such a disclosure and having failed to obtain a waiver of disclosure as permitted by these statutes, Edward had no right to assume that the agreement would be enforced in the future, and those who now seek to benefit from his inequitable conduct cannot invoke the doctrine of equitable estoppel to defeat Stacey's legislatively-created right to be free from this unenforceable agreement.

. . .

[R]emanded for further proceedings in conformity with this opinion. We do not retain jurisdiction.

Post-Case Follow-Up

The court in *Shinn* carefully reviewed the facts underlying the premarital agreement to determine the validity of the waiver. As it stated, the standard it applied (which varies slightly from the Uniform Act) was that a prenuptial agreement is unenforceable if it was not executed voluntarily, it was unconscionable, or the disclosure standard had not been met. Note that in the vast majority of cases, premarital agreements are upheld because there is such disclosure, and waivers in premarital agreements are standard clauses. Consider that Edward did provide for Stacey in his will, but under the opinion, her elective share would have far exceeded the value of the home.

In re Estate of Shinn: Real Life Applications

1. Suppose you had been Edward Shinn's attorney for the premarital agreement. What would you have done differently? How would you have counseled him on the importance of disclosure?

2. You are a probate court judge in New Jersey. Georgia Moe Hansen (Georgia) married Lyle K. Hansen (Lyle) on October 14, 1995. Both spouses had been married previously and each had children from the prior marriage. They signed a prenuptial agreement that included a provision waiving each other's elective share rights. When Georgia died, Lyle challenged their prenuptial agreement. At trial, Lyle presented evidence establishing that: (1) it was decedent, and not he, who first raised the issue of a prenuptial agreement and requested that one be executed prior to the wedding; (2) the agreement was prepared by decedent's attorneys, at her request and in accordance with her direction. At the same time, Georgia's estate showed that: (1) Lyle readily acceded to decedent's request that they enter into a prenuptial agreement and willingly signed the instrument because he did not want any of decedent's money or property, he only wanted to be her husband; (2) Lyle was advised to obtain the services of independent counsel; (3) Lyle was given an adequate opportunity to read the instrument before he signed it; and (4) prior to executing the prenuptial agreement, Lyle was provided with detailed disclosure of decedent's $2.5 million net worth. Is the agreement likely to be upheld?

3. Using the same facts as in the previous problem, what if Lyle introduces the following additional facts? (a) the prenuptial agreement was executed only a few hours prior to the parties' wedding, (b) Lyle did not seek or obtain independent legal counsel and the agreement was not read by him nor to him before he signed it, (c) Lyle was not specifically advised that the agreement provided for a waiver of his right to elect against decedent's will, and (d) he was not furnished with a copy of the agreement. If you were the judge, what would be your decision about the validity of the prenuptial agreement?

D. PROTECTING AGAINST UNINTENTIONAL DISINHERITANCE

The law protects the surviving spouse and children from disinheritance when a testator has not updated a will to reflect some changes in circumstances. Most states have statutes: (1) protecting a spouse against disinheritance as a result of a premarital will; and (2) protecting a child of a testator not provided for in the testator's will executed before the birth or adoption of the child. These unintentionally omitted (or **pretermitted**) family members are typically entitled to a specified share of the testator's estate.

1. Pretermitted/Omitted Spouse

At common law, a woman's marriage revoked her premarital will; for men, a premarital will was revoked upon the birth of a marital child. Today, instead, most states provide protection for both through elective share or omitted spouse statutes, and there is no automatic revocation of a will upon marriage or birth of a child. While the elective share protects against intentional disinheritance, the omitted spouse statutes assume that the disinheritance was unintentional. The omitted spouse statutes thus provide a substantial share for the surviving spouse based on an assumption about the amount that the testator would probably have wanted the spouse to have, had the testator updated the premarital will to include the spouse.

Generally, the only portion of the estate available for distribution to omitted spouses is the property available for probate. The omitted spouse statutes typically only apply to property that may be passed by will—not will substitutes such as life insurance, individual retirement accounts, joint tenancies or other payable-on-death contractual arrangements. Alan Newman, *Revocable Trusts and the Law of Wills: An Imperfect Fit*, 43 Real Prop. Tr. & Est. L.J. 523 (2008). This means, at least in a separate property jurisdiction that has something other than a probate-only approach to the elective share, an omitted spouse must calculate the amount available pursuant to the elective share before deciding whether to claim as an omitted spouse or whether to claim an elective share.

Under the UPC, where there is a will executed prior to the testator's marriage to his or her surviving spouse, the surviving spouse is entitled to take an intestate portion of the testator's estate. UPC § 2-301. The surviving spouse's portion is limited to a share in property that is not devised to the testator's children born prior to the current marriage, and who are a child or adolescent of the surviving spouse.

Moreover, the UPC provides three exceptions to the surviving spouse's entitlement, precluding the surviving spouse from taking if:

(1) it appears from the will or other evidence that the will was made in contemplation of the testator's marriage to the surviving spouse;

(2) the will expresses the intention that it is to be effective notwithstanding any subsequent marriage; or

(3) the testator provided for the spouse by transfer outside the will and the intent that the transfer be in lieu of a testamentary provision is shown by the testator's statements or is reasonably inferred from the amount of the transfer or other evidence.

UPC § 2-301.

For example, under the UPC, assume that Grant's premarital will leaves everything to his parents. Grant subsequently marries Xandra. When Grant dies, Grant is survived by his parents, Xandra, and their three children, Alef, Beta, and Chandini. Xandra will receive her intestate share, which is the entire estate. (Of course, this would not be the conclusion in some states which have different intestacy schemes that require the spouse to share with the descendants, regardless of whether the descendants are also descendants of the surviving spouse.)

Assume instead that Grant's premarital will devised all of the estate "to my three children, Alef, Beta, and Chandini, in equal shares," and that Alef, Beta, and Chandini are children from Grant's first marriage, which ended in divorce. Several years later, Grant married Xandra. Grant never updated the will. Grant is survived by Alef, Beta, and Chandini and by Grant's spouse, Xandra. Xandra's right under UPC § 2-301 is to take an intestate share in that portion of Grant's estate not left to Grant's children born prior to the marriage. In this case, Xandra is not entitled to anything.

2. Omitted Children

A testator can intentionally disinherit a child, and the testator's decision will be enforced—although, as discussed in Chapter 6, the will may be challenged. The one exception is in Louisiana, where if there are children who are under the age of 24 or are incapable of caring for themselves, mentally or physically, they are "forced heirs." La. Civ. Code art. 1493 (2009). Although intentionally omitting children from a will may seem unfair or unusual, many testators leave their entire estate to a spouse, perhaps with the expectation the spouse will care for the children. Parents have an obligation to support their children during life, but absent a child support agreement or other contract to the contrary, there is no obligation for a parent to support a child after the parent's death, even during a child's minority.

Protecting the Omitted Child

Even though children have no right to inherit from their parents, most states have omitted (or pretermitted) child statutes that protect children who have been disinherited unintentionally. These statutes protect children born after the execution of a parent's will, and some laws even protect children alive at the time of the will's execution under some circumstances. See Restatement (Third) of Property: Wills and Other Donative Transfers § 9.6 (Am. Law Inst. 2003).

Because it is not always clear whether the testator intentionally left out a child, states have adopted different approaches to determine the children's rights. Statutes vary on numerous issues, including the following:

■ Which children have standing to contest their exclusion? Some statutes also include grandchildren and other descendants as omitted heirs.
■ Do the protections only include children who were born or adopted after the execution of the will, or all children omitted from the will, regardless of whether they were living when the will was executed?

- To what share is an omitted child entitled?
- Is the share limited to taking against probate property or does it include nonprobate property as well?
- What types of evidence, if any, are admissible to show the testator's intent?

Case Preview

Gray v. Gray

The issue in this case was whether a child born during the testator's second marriage could inherit as an omitted child. During his second marriage, John drafted a will that left all of his property to his wife, Mary, and nothing to his two children from a previous marriage. After the will was drafted, John and Mary had a child, Jack. John and Mary then divorced, and the divorce settlement required the testator to establish a trust for Jack. John never changed his will.

The court had to decide whether Jack, who was born after the testator executed his will, had any rights under Alabama's omitted child statute.

As you read *Gray*, consider the following:

1. How could Jack claim as an omitted child if the testator had two children living when he executed the will?
2. What would Jack have received under the probate court ruling? What will he receive now?
3. What argument was most convincing to the appellate court?
4. Which interpretation of the statute, the majority's or the dissent's, seems closer to the intent of the statute?
5. Does the statute adequately respond to the changing family in America?

Gray v. Gray
947 So. 2d 1045 (Ala. 2006)

SEE, Justice.

. . .

In 1981, John executed his will. At that time, John was married to Mary Rose Gray and had two children from a prior marriage, Robert B. Gray and Monica L. Muncher. John's will devised all of his estate to his wife Mary and did not include his two children. In 1984, John and Mary gave birth to John Merrill "Jack" Gray III. In 1989, John and Mary divorced. John and Mary's divorce judgment and property settlement included a provision creating a trust for Jack, which states that "[o]ne-half of all assets, inheritance or disbursements of any kind received by the Husband from his mother's estate shall be placed in trust for his son, Jack." Pursuant to [Alabama law], even though John's will devised all of his estate to Mary, Mary would not inherit under John's will upon his death because John and Mary divorced. In 2004, John died without having changed his will.

William Terry Gray, the executor of John's estate, petitioned the Jefferson County Probate Court to probate John's will. Jack petitioned the probate court for an order finding that he is entitled to a share of John's estate under Ala. Code 1975, § 43-8-91, which provides in full:

"(a) If a testator fails to provide in his will for any of his children born or adopted after the execution of his will, the omitted child receives a share in the estate equal in value to that which he would have received if the testator had died intestate unless:

"(1) It appears from the will that the omission was intentional;

"(2) When the will was executed the testator had one or more children and devised substantially all his estate to the other parent of the omitted child; or

"(3) The testator provided for the child by transfer outside the will and the intent that the transfer be in lieu of a testamentary provision be reasonably proven."

The executor moved the probate court to dismiss Jack's petition. The executor argued that Ala. Code 1975, § 43-8-91(a)(2), applies because John had two children when he executed his will and devised substantially all of his estate to Jack's mother, Mary. Therefore, the executor argued, Jack was not entitled to his intestate share of John's estate. The executor also argued that Ala. Code 1975, § 43-8-91(a)(3), applies because, he argued, John provided for Jack in a nontestamentary transfer in lieu of a testamentary transfer when he established a trust in Jack's favor upon his divorce from Jack's mother. Robert and Monica, John's children from his previous marriage, also moved the probate court to dismiss Jack's petition under Ala. Code 1975, § 43-8-91(a)(3).

The probate court granted Jack's petition, holding that Jack is entitled to a distribution from John's estate equal in value to the share he would have received had John died intestate. The executor appeals the order of the probate court.

. . .

ANALYSIS

The executor argues that the probate court erred in holding that Jack is entitled to a share of John's estate. He argues that Ala. Code 1975, § 43-8-91, excludes Jack from taking a share because of the exception set forth in subparagraph (a)(2): "When the will was executed the testator had one or more children and devised substantially all his estate to the other parent of the omitted child." Specifically, he notes that when John executed his will, John had two children from a prior marriage and John devised all of his estate to Mary, the mother of Jack, the omitted child.

. . .

In determining whether Jack may benefit from § 43-8-91, we give the words of the applicable statute their plain, ordinary, and commonly understood meaning, and we interpret the language to mean what it says.

. . .

Section 43-8-91 states that, if a child is born subsequent to the execution of a will and the will fails to provide for the child, the omitted child is entitled to a share of the testator's estate, except in certain circumstances. One of those exceptions is that an omitted child is not entitled to a share of the estate if "[w]hen the will was executed the testator had one or more children and devised substantially all his estate to the other parent of the omitted child."

In 1981, when John executed his will, he had two children by a prior marriage, and his will devised all of his estate to Jack's mother Mary. Therefore, § 43-8-91(a)(2) applies, and Jack may not receive a share of John's estate.

Jack argues that the exception[] should not apply to him because, he says [it] "does not appear to contemplate a situation wherein the testator has children, divorces their mother, remarries, executes a will that makes no provision for any children whatsoever, than [sic] has a child with that second wife."[5] However, § 43-8-91(a)(2) states only two conditions for excluding an omitted child from an intestate share of the testator's estate: (1) the testator had one or more children at the time he executed his will, and (2) the testator's will devised substantially all of the testator's estate to the other parent of the omitted child. Because the statute is one of substance and is in derogation of the common law, we must construe it strictly and not extend its reach beyond its terms. Jack's argument, therefore, fails. The fact that John's other children were from a prior marriage is immaterial. . . .

CONCLUSION

We reverse the probate court's order and remand the case to the probate court for further proceedings consistent with this opinion.

REVERSED AND REMANDED.

LYONS, Justice (dissenting).

. . .

The main opinion relies upon the confluence of (a) the existence of more than one child at the time the testator executed his will and (b) a devise of his entire estate to his then wife, who would later bear the pretermitted child. Of course, the children then in being were the result of the union of the husband and his first wife.

The legislature created an exception to the rule permitting an omitted child to inherit when, at the time of the execution of the will, the testator, as a parent of one or more children, devises substantially all his estate to "the other parent of the omitted child." § 43-8-91(a)(2). The only rational basis for such an exception is an intent to deny relief to a child then in being who is omitted from the will and whose *other* parent, under the terms of the will, is entitled to a devise and to whom, ostensibly, the omitted child can look for an inheritance. . . .

. . .

. . . . I would therefore read the exception set forth in § 43-8-91(a)(2) as inapplicable to this proceeding because, at the time of the execution of the will, there was no "*other* parent of an omitted child" or, in other words, the testator had no parenting relationship with the devisee and therefore no basis to assume from the terms of his will an attitude of favoring her to the exclusion of *their* children.

---

[5][Note, original footnote callout number has been moved up. —EDS.] The legislature might well have assumed that in a case like this one it could anticipate that the child would be protected in the divorce proceeding, either directly or by a distribution of a share of the marital assets to the custodial parent. In this case, as we have previously noted, Jack was provided for in the divorce proceeding by the creation of a trust.

Post-Case Follow-Up

In *Gray*, the court was faced with a statute that seemed to apply to the situation—the will did leave everything to the omitted child's other parent—and the court held that Jack did not have rights as a pretermitted child. Of course, that child had not been born when the will was written, a point particularly important to the dissent, which notes that there is no basis to assume that the testator would have favored his wife over his child. The statutory presumption that the other parent will take care of the omitted child is not relevant when the omitted child does not yet exist. Consider whether the court might have more appropriately decided the case under § 43-8-91(a)(3) because, as the executor argued, the trust for Jack showed he was provided for outside of the will. Finally, note that, as you've learned already, divorce revokes any revocable disposition in a governing instrument so, when the will was drafted, Mary stood to inherit. But by the time the will become operative at the testator's death, Mary stood to inherit nothing.

More on Gray v. Gray

Jack Gray graduated cum laude from the Cumberland School of Law, where he presented this case as a student in Professor DiRusso's wills class. In a paper he wrote during law school, Jack provided some additional facts about his family and the case. His father was born to a prominent local family, and after graduating from law school, opened up a small general practice. Jack notes that there is no evidence that his father actually ever did any work that involved wills or trusts. John and Mary were married for 14 years, and it was John's alcoholism that contributed to the divorce. Indeed, the Alabama bar suspended John's license to practice law because of his addiction. Jack only met his half siblings once, at his father's funeral.

John's brother, Terry, was the executor of the estate, and Jack sought an informal resolution of his claims before filing to protect his rights in probate court. Terry was not willing to compromise, so the lawsuit, which was ultimately resolved by the Alabama Supreme Court, resulted. Jack now practices law in a mid-size firm in Birmingham, Alabama.

Gray v. Gray: Real Life Applications

1. You are an attorney in Alabama. John Gray's children from his first marriage have consulted you about representing them as omitted children. What will you advise them concerning the validity of their claim under the Alabama omitted child statute?

2. Assume the same facts as in Question 1, except that John drafted his will in 1979, while he was still married to his first wife and before he had any children. That will left everything to his first wife. Will you represent the two children now?

3. Assume the same facts as in *Gray*, except that John's will left everything to his brother. Jack has consulted you about representing him. Consider whether he has a valid claim under the Alabama omitted child statute. Will you represent him in seeking a share of his father's estate?

4. Had John Gray consulted you for advice about rewriting his will after his divorce, what issues would you have explored with him?

Omitted Child Statutes

Some omitted child statutes apply to both omitted children of the testator and omitted descendants of a deceased child of the testator (e.g., grandchildren of the testator). See, e.g., Alexander v. Estate of Alexander, 93 S.W.3d 688, 691 (Ark. 2002) (Arkansas's omitted child statute explicitly refers to the "issue of a deceased child of the testator," and the court refused to permit extrinsic evidence of the testator's intent); In re Estate of Treloar, 859 A.2d 1162 (N.H. 2004) (New Hampshire's omitted child statute, which refers to "issue of a child," gave grandchildren inheritance rights).

The UPC Approach

UPC § 2-302 presumes that the failure to mention children born or adopted after execution of the will is unintentional and allows those children to inherit a share of the estate as if the decedent had died intestate. On the other hand, under the UPC and in some states, an omitted child is not entitled to a share of the decedent's estate if all or "substantially all" of the estate is left to the other parent of that child. Moreover, the UPC, and most states, specifically refer only to a "child" who is omitted.

In Exhibit 8.3 the UPC explains its approach:

EXHIBIT 8.3   **UPC Omitted Child Approach**

UPC § 2-302 cmt.

No Child Living When Will Executed. If the testator had no child living when he or she executed the will, subsection [UPC § 2-302] (a)(1) provides that an omitted after-born or after-adopted child receives the share he or she would have received had the testator died intestate, unless the will devised, under trust or not, all or substantially all of the estate to the other parent of the omitted child. If the will did devise all or substantially all of the estate to the other parent of the omitted child, and if that other parent survives the testator and is entitled to take under the will, the omitted after-born or after-adopted child receives no share of the estate.

One or More Children Living When Will Executed. If the testator had one or more children living when the will was executed, subsection (a)(2) [] provides that an omitted after-born or after-adopted child only receives a share of the testator's estate if the testator's will devised property or an equitable or legal interest in property to one or more of the children living at the time the will was executed; if not, the omitted after-born or after-adopted child receives nothing. . . .

Subsection (a)(2) is illustrated by the following example.

Example. When G executed her will, she had two living children, A and B. Her will devised $7500 to each child. After G executed her will, she had another child, C.

C is entitled to $5,000. $2,500 (1/3 of $7,500) of C's entitlement comes from A's $7,500 devise (reducing it to $5,000); and $2,500 (1/3 of $7,500) comes from B's $7,500 devise (reducing it to $5,000).

> Variation. If G's will had devised $10,000 to A and $5,000 to B, C would be entitled to $5,000. $3,333 (1/3 of $10,000) of C's entitlement comes from A's $10,000 devise (reducing it to $6,667); and $1,667 (1/3 of $5,000) comes from B's $5,000 devise (reducing it to $3,333).
>
> Subsection (b) Exceptions. To preclude operation of subsection (a)(1) or (a)(2), the testator's will need not make any provision, even nominal in amount, for a testator's present or future children; under subsection (b)(1), a simple recital in the will that the testator intends to make no provision for then living children or any the testator thereafter may have would be sufficient.

The New Hampshire Approach

Note that most states, like the UPC, cover only an after-born child. A few states, like New Hampshire, take a different approach, although that number is dwindling.

> Every child born after the decease of the testator, and every child or issue of a child of the deceased not named or referred to in his will, and who is not a devisee or legatee, shall be entitled to the same portion of the estate, real and personal, as he would be if the deceased were intestate.

N.H. Rev. Stat. § 551:10.

Chapter Summary

- There are two systems of marital property ownership: community property and common law. In the community property system, any property acquired during the marriage, other than by gift or bequest or devise, is jointly owned. Under the common law system, title controls.
- The elective share of the surviving spouse is a statutory provision found in most common law state probate codes. In community property states, each spouse receives an ownership interest in half of the property that the couple acquires during the marriage (other than by gift, bequest, or devise), so no elective share protection is necessary.
- The elective share protects the decedent's surviving spouse against intentional disinheritance by allowing the surviving spouse to claim some part of the decedent's estate, regardless of the existence of a will. The percentage that the spouse can claim, as well as the property subject to the elective share, varies by state.
- The elective share can be waived through a valid premarital or marital agreement that complies with the state's procedural and substantive requirements.
- When a will was executed before marriage, then the surviving spouse is generally entitled to a specified share of the testator's estate unless there is evidence that: (a) the will was made in contemplation of the marriage; (b) the will expresses the intention that it be effective notwithstanding any subsequent marriage; or (c) the testator provided for the spouse by transfer outside the will and there is a showing of intent that the transfer be in lieu of a testamentary transfer.

■ Under certain circumstances, a child of the testator—or, in some states, a descendant of the testator—who was not provided for in the testator's will may be entitled to a specified share of the testator's estate as an omitted or pretermitted child. Most statutes, including the UPC, only provide protection for a child who was born or adopted after the will was executed.

Applying the Concepts

1. Arturo and Monsy were married to each other for more than 20 years and did not have a prenuptial agreement. Arturo died, survived by Monsy and their only child, Connie. Arturo's will left nothing to Monsy, and Arturo made no nonprobate transfers to Monsy. Arturo had $500,000 left in his estate. Arturo made one nonprobate transfer to Connie (via a revocable inter vivos trust) worth $100,000. What result under the UPC? What result under an Arkansas-style statute?

2. When in his late 20s, Arnie executed a will devising his entire estate to his brothers and sisters. Later, Arnie married Boni. Three years later, Arnie died in an airplane crash. Arnie was survived by Boni and by his brothers and sisters. What is Boni entitled to?

3. Han and Wu enjoyed a long and happy marriage, which produced two children, Anya and Bud. Wu died. Wu's will devised her entire estate to Han if he survived her, and if not, to Anya and Bud in equal shares. Han's will, executed at the same time, devised his entire estate to Wu if she survived him, and if not, to Anya and Bud in equal shares. Five years after Wu's death, Han married Yolanda. He never changed his will after the marriage. A few months later, Han suffered a heart attack and died. Han was survived by his second wife, Yolanda, and by Anya and Bud. Han's net estate was valued at $150,000. How will Han's estate be distributed?

4. Denaya's father, Guido, recently died, and his will left none of his assets to her or to her younger sister. Her older brother and her mother each received one-half of her father's estate pursuant to the will that he drafted 25 years ago. Denaya would like to claim some part of Guido's estate. What rights does Denaya have under the UPC? What additional facts do you need to know?

5. Your client, Pru, desires to leave nothing to Pru's oldest child, Rami, and everything to Rami's siblings, Sami and Tami. What language should Pru use in a will to make this intent clear?

6. When Jorge wrote his will in 1999, he and Inez were good friends. In his will, he specifically named her in this bequest, "I leave Inez $20,000." Later, in 2012, Jorge and Inez married. Jorge never updated his will, and died in 2019 with a probate estate worth $450,000. Can Inez be considered an omitted spouse even though she is specifically named in the will?

Trusts and Estates in Practice

1. Do you live in a community property or common law state? What statutory authority indicates your state's system?

   a. Which system better protects the economic interest of a surviving spouse?
   b. In which system would a wealthy testator prefer to live?
   c. What assumptions about marriage are built into each system?

2. For your state, locate any applicable elective share statutes and determine the following:

   a. Can the surviving spouse choose an elective share if the decedent died intestate as well as with a will?
   b. Against what property can the elective share be claimed? Is it only the probate estate or is it an augmented estate? What is included in the augmented estate? Note that the statute may have been interpreted by case law, although unless instructed otherwise, please focus only on the statute.

3. Imagine you are in a non-UPC state. You are a member of your state bar's trusts and estates committee considering adoption of the UPC approach to the elective share. Will you recommend adoption? Why or why not?

4. Find your state's statutes concerning an omitted spouse.

   a. Under what circumstances can the surviving spouse claim?
   b. What is the surviving spouse's share?

5. Find your state's statutes concerning omitted children.

   a. Does it apply to all children omitted from a will? If not, then which children can claim?
   b. What is the share that an omitted child can claim?
   c. What are the exceptions under which an omitted child cannot claim?
   d. Does it apply only to children or to other descendants as well?

6. Ray and Lyle are about to marry. Each has previously been married and has children from the previous marriage. What advice do you give them about waiving an elective share through an agreement? Why? Would your advice change if this was a first marriage for both? Can you represent both of them?

7. Ray and Lyle have decided on a mutual prenuptial waiver. What does your state require in order for the waiver to be valid? Please draft a provision that waives the elective share. It may be helpful to find a form and then adapt it. After drafting the waiver, draft a cover letter to the client explaining what requirements must be satisfied in order for the waiver to be valid and that explains the meaning of the waiver.

Creation of Trusts

Trusts are incredibly flexible—and useful—estate planning tools. In this chapter, we learn what a trust is, how to create a trust, and some of the potential uses for trusts. After we cover the requirements for a trust, we will look at the special uses of revocable trusts, a powerful **will substitute**. Charitable trusts have their own unique set of rules, which we discuss at the end of this chapter.

Lawyers use trusts for a variety of purposes: to protect assets from being squandered by an irresponsible family member, to manage assets for a child who is still a minor, or for a beneficiary who is unsophisticated with financial and investment matters; to hold assets in a way that will provide tax benefits or minimize creditor exposure; or to set aside assets for a loved one with special needs in a manner that will not cause them to lose government benefits. The possible uses for trusts are as varied as the needs of the settlor—a person who creates a trust.

A settlor creates the trust and funds it, therefore a settlor can dictate the terms of a trust. In this chapter, we consider the limits the law places on the settlor's control. In Chapter 11, we consider whether the law should give beneficiaries some ability to change the terms of the trust.

Key Concepts

- The elements necessary to have a valid trust
- Restrictions imposed on the creation of a trust
- Considerations in choosing a trustee
- The role of revocable trusts in planning for disability and as will substitutes
- The rules that distinguish charitable trusts from private trusts

A. TRUST TERMINOLOGY

Trust law, like all areas of the law, has a specific vocabulary that must be understood and used correctly in discussing trusts. The first step in appreciating the role of trusts is defining the relevant terms, so we start there. The **settlor** (sometimes also called donor or grantor) is the person who creates a trust by transferring property to the **trustee**. The trustee holds legal title to the property and manages the property for the **beneficiary** or beneficiaries. The beneficiaries hold beneficial title (also called "equitable title") to the trust property—the trust is held for their benefit. A trust may have several beneficiaries with present interests and may also have beneficiaries with future interests. The beneficiaries have the right to enforce the trust—make sure the trustee is fulfilling the trustee's duties—and can take the trustee to court if the trustee **breaches** the trustee's **fiduciary duties**.

Although lawyers try to use the vocabulary precisely, people creating trusts without the assistance of lawyers may not. A court can find that a trust exists even if the parties never used the word "trust," and the use of the word "trust" does not necessarily mean that a court will find that a trust was created.

EXHIBIT 9.1   **A Schematic Way to Think About a Trust**

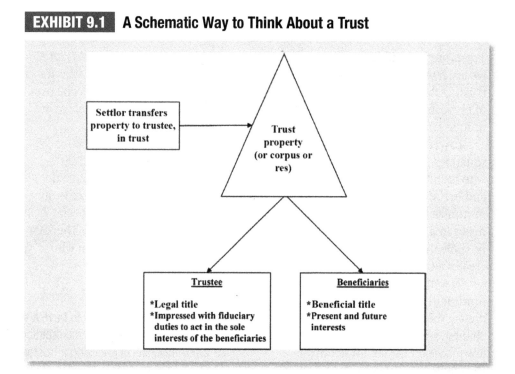

1. Beneficiaries

The trustee owes fiduciary duties to all beneficiaries, including beneficiaries whose interests are remote and contingent. To limit the classes of beneficiaries who must receive notice or must consent in certain situations, the Uniform Trust Code (UTC) creates the concept of **qualified beneficiary**. This subset of beneficiaries consists of beneficiaries who, on the date the determination of who the beneficiaries are is made, are beneficiaries to whom the trustee may or must make distributions (**distributees** or **permissible distributees**), would be distributees or permissible distributees if the interests of the first group ended, or would be distributees or permissible distributees if the trust terminated.

2. Mandatory and Default Rules

Trust law establishes both mandatory and default rules. Mandatory rules apply to all trusts and cannot be changed by the settlor. There are relatively few mandatory rules, but they serve to safeguard the interests of the beneficiaries who might otherwise have no way to protect their rights—and might not even know about the trust. Much of trust law is default law; the settlor can establish the terms of the trust in a written document.

3. Types of Trusts

Inter Vivos or Testamentary

If a settlor creates a trust during the settlor's lifetime, the trust is called an **inter vivos trust**. A settlor can also create a trust at death, and then the trust is called a **testamentary trust**. A testamentary trust is created by will, with a provision directing the personal representative of the probate estate to transfer property to a trustee, normally named in the will. The terms of the trust, explaining how the trust assets will be administered and distributed, are written into the will. A testamentary trust will be created through the probate process. That is, the will itself does not create the trust; the will must be admitted to probate.

Private or Charitable

A **private express trust** is a trust created intentionally by the owner of property for private beneficiaries and not for a charitable purpose. A **charitable trust** is an express trust created for a charitable purpose or with a charity as a named beneficiary.

Revocable or Irrevocable

A **revocable trust** is one the settlor can modify or revoke, while an **irrevocable trust** is one the settlor cannot change. Testamentary trusts are always irrevocable because a testamentary trust is not created until the settlor dies, and the settlor cannot revoke the trust after death. Of course, while the settlor is alive, the settlor can revoke the will and prevent the trust from being created at death. Some inter vivos trusts, usually ones created for tax planning reasons, are irrevocable. The most common type of revocable trust is a certain type of trust created as a will substitute and to plan for the settlor's incapacity. This trust may be called a "revocable living trust," and when a lawyer refers to a "revocable trust," the lawyer almost always means this type of trust. We will look at these revocable living trusts at the end of this chapter.

The Uniform Trust Code

Trust law developed as common law, over centuries. The Uniform Trust Code (UTC), approved by the Uniform Law Commission in 2000, mostly codifies the common law, although it makes a few changes to the common law. The UTC has been adopted by 33 jurisdictions as of 2018 and is increasingly influential. We will use some sections of the UTC in our discussions, but you should be aware that not all states have adopted it, and adopting states often make changes to uniform acts. As with all statutes, cases continue to explain and interpret the trust statutes, so we will also examine cases to help understand trust law rules.

4. Presumption of Revocability Under the UTC

The UTC provides that all trusts created after its enactment are revocable unless the terms of the trust "expressly provide that the trust is irrevocable." UTC § 602(a). The UTC reverses the common law rule that a trust is presumed to be irrevocable unless the settlor reserves, in the terms of the trust, the right to revoke the trust. The UTC drafters changed the presumption based on an assumption that people working without lawyers are more likely to be attempting to create revocable trusts (with the flexibility and retention of control that goes along with them) than irrevocable ones. The changed presumption protects those most likely to make a mistake. A trust drafted by a lawyer should state clearly whether the trust is revocable or irrevocable. Many states still retain the common law rule that a trust is presumed to be irrevocable unless the trust instrument explicitly states otherwise.

5. Merger

If a trustee and the trust's only beneficiary are the same person, the interests in the trust merge and the trust ceases to exist. The doctrine of **merger** will terminate the trust early, even if purposes remain, because the legal interests and the beneficial interests are held by the same person. Although a revocable living trust, created by the settlor for the settlor's benefit, would appear to be subject to merger, a revocable living trust should always provide for what happens to the property when the settlor dies. The remainder beneficiaries are beneficiaries even though the settlor can revoke their interests. Thus, merger normally does not apply to a revocable living trust.

6. Resulting Trust

If a trust created for private beneficiaries (not a charitable trust) fails to make a complete disposition of property or can no longer be administered because it lacks a valid purpose, the term **resulting trust** is used. The remaining property returns to the settlor or is distributed through the settlor's estate. For example, if a settlor creates a trust that directs the trustee to pay for a child's college education but does not say what happens if property remains after the child graduates from college, the trust becomes a resulting trust. The trustee cannot distribute the remaining property to the child, because the terms of the trust did not direct the trustee to do so. Instead the trustee must distribute the property to the settlor, or if the settlor is dead, to the settlor's estate. The UTC does not discuss resulting trusts.

7. Constructive Trust

A **constructive trust** is a legal fiction typically used to prevent unjust enrichment. A constructive trust is an equitable remedy that a court can use to transfer title as required by law to the legal owner but direct that the legal owner holds the property subject to a constructive trust, with the duty to transfer the property to the rightful owner. Thus, the structure of a trust—legal title held by one person and beneficial title held by another—can be used by the court to fix a problem. Because a constructive trust is a remedy and not really a trust, the UTC does not apply.

B. ELEMENTS OF A TRUST

An examination of the **elements of a trust** assists students—and the court—in making a determination of whether a trust exists as a legal relationship between the settlor and the trustee. For most written trusts, it is clear that many, and usually all, of the following elements exist. If there is an oral trust, the question of whether these elements exist may require further inquiry by the court.

This section looks at what happens when a property owner transfers property to someone else. The property owner may be creating a trust, making a gift, or making a promise to make a gift in the future. A determination of whether a trust exists will determine who ultimately receives the property. Notice that the list of elements of a trust does not include the requirement of a writing or execution formalities. A lawyer will always use a written instrument to create a trust, and a number of the problems discussed in this section occur when a property owner attempts to transfer property without the assistance of a lawyer.

EXHIBIT 9.2   **Elements of a Trust**

- The trust must be established for a valid, legal purpose.
- The settlor must be competent when creating the trust.
- The trust must have a trustee.
- The settlor must have intended to create a trust.
- The trust must be funded, i.e., must have some property (called corpus or res).
- The settlor must identify an ascertainable beneficiary. (As this section explains, the UTC modifies this requirement.)

1. Valid, Legal Purpose

A trust must have a valid purpose—a reason the trustee holds and manages the property. For example, a trust might be created to provide for the care of children if their parents die while they are minors, for the education of a niece, for safe management of assets in case the settlor becomes incapacitated, or for the support of a spouse for life with the remaining assets given to descendants from a prior marriage. If the purpose is accomplished and a valid purpose no longer exists for the trust, the trust terminates. At that point, the trustee will distribute the trust assets as directed by the terms of the trust, or if the terms do not state where the assets should go, the trust will become a resulting trust and revert to the settlor or the settlor's estate.

If the purpose of the trust or any term of the trust is illegal or contrary to public policy, the trust or the offending term will be held invalid and unenforceable. UTC § 404. For example, if a settlor creates a trust to hide beneficial ownership of the settlor's assets from known creditors or from the government (before applying for government benefits such as Medicaid), the trust purpose is illegal and the trust will be unenforceable, at least as to those creditors or the government. Similarly, a trust term that directs the trustee to purchase illegal drugs for distribution would be invalid. If the trust has other purposes, the trust can continue for those other purposes, but if the only purpose is illegal, the trust will terminate.

A trust provision that is against "public policy" is also unenforceable, but public policy for the purpose of holding a trust provision invalid can be difficult to determine. Recall the *Feinberg* case in Chapter 1. At issue in that case was a trust provision that took away benefits under the trust from any grandchild who married outside the Jewish faith or whose spouse did not convert to Judaism within a year of the marriage. A grandchild argued that the restriction was a restraint on marriage and therefore against public policy, but the court let the restriction stand. The interpretation of public policy will vary from state to state and will change according to social norms, but courts rarely use public policy to invalidate a trust provision.

Provisions that interfere with family relationships, for example, by encouraging divorce, encouraging neglect of parental duties, or discouraging contact between siblings, likewise may be found to be against public policy. In *Estate of Romero*, 847 P.2d 319 (N.M. 1993), the court invalidated a provision that permitted the decedent's minor sons to live in his house only if their mother—the decedent's ex-wife—did not live there with them!

2. Competent Settlor

The settlor of a trust must be mentally competent to establish the trust. In some situations, the competency required to create a trust and to execute a will are the same; in others, it is different. We discussed the standard of capacity required to execute a will in Chapter 3. In general terms, the testator must understand who the natural objects of the testator's bounty are, the nature and extent of the testator's property, the plans the testator has for the disposition of the property, and how those interrelate. Because a testamentary trust is created in a will, the standard of capacity required to create a testamentary trust is the same as the standard to execute a will.

Irrevocable Inter Vivos Trusts

For an irrevocable inter vivos trust, the level of capacity required is the standard to make a gratuitous transfer: the settlor must not only have the understanding required for wills but also understand the effect that creating a trust has on the settlor's future financial security and ability to support any dependents. The law imposes this requirement because a decision to part with property during life affects the settlor's ability to care for the settlor and any dependents. Thus, the standard to create an inter vivos trust is higher than the standard to execute a will or create a testamentary trust. See Restatement (Third) of Trusts § 11, cmt. c (2003).

Revocable Trusts

For revocable trusts, the question of what standard to use is complicated by the fact that a revocable trust serves both lifetime and testamentary functions. The UTC applies the wills standard to revocable trusts. UTC § 601. Capacity challenges are less frequent with trusts than with wills. For a revocable trust, a capacity challenge would relate not just to the moment of execution, but to the ongoing interactions the settlor has with the trust.

3. Trustee

A trustee holds title to the property interests held in trust. For example, if David gave Terrence some money to hold in trust for Tina, the title of a bank account opened to hold the trust assets might read like this: "Terrence Taylor, as trustee of the Tina Taylor Trust, dated March 17, 2017." The trustee's duties include managing and investing the property and making distributions to the beneficiaries, as directed by the terms of the trust. The law imposes strict fiduciary duties on the trustee, who must always act in the sole interests of the beneficiaries and avoid self-dealing with trust assets. A trustee who fails to comply with all the fiduciary duties may face removal or financial penalties.

The existence of a trustee is an important issue in determining whether a trust exists; courts focus on what the settlor intended when the settlor transferred property to someone else: Did the settlor intend to impose a mandatory duty on a trustee to act on behalf of a beneficiary? Did the settlor intend something else?

A trust must have a trustee, but a trust will not fail for lack of a trustee because a court will appoint a trustee if necessary. Although a trust cannot continue indefinitely without a trustee, the lack of a trustee will not cause the termination of the trust. Usually, the trust instrument names a trustee and successor trustees in case the named trustee cannot or will not serve, dies, resigns, or is removed. The trust instrument may appoint more than one trustee to serve as co-trustees at the same time, and then the survivor can continue if the other trustee resigns. If the trust instrument is silent as to successor trustees, or if no successor named by the settlor is able to serve, UTC § 704(c)(2) provides that the beneficiaries, acting unanimously, can appoint a trustee. If the beneficiaries cannot agree, the court can appoint a trustee.

We will consider three issues in connection with the trustee: how the settlor chooses a trustee, how a trustee accepts the duties of a trustee, and how a trustee resigns.

Choosing a Trustee

Given the important role a trustee plays in administering the trust on behalf of the beneficiaries, a settlor must choose a trustee carefully. A settlor can serve as the trustee, ask a family member or a close personal friend to be the trustee, or decide that a professional trustee such as a bank will be best. The settlor should discuss the trust with the intended trustee in advance to make sure the person or institution is willing to serve. If the intended trustee is a family member, information about the duties of a trustee will be helpful. Some lawyers provide informational brochures outlining the duties of a trustee, which can be shared with prospective trustees.

In deciding who should serve as trustee, the settlor should consider possible conflicts of interest and family dynamics. A trustee has to act impartially with respect to all beneficiaries, which becomes more challenging if the trustee is also a beneficiary of the trust or is related to a beneficiary. For example, if a settlor creates a testamentary trust providing a life estate for the settlor's second spouse and the remainder in the trust to the children of a first marriage, naming either the spouse or a child as trustee may cause difficulties. If a trust is created to provide for the college education of the settlor's grandchildren, naming one of the settlor's three children, all of whom have children who are beneficiaries of the trust, creates a conflict for the trustee.

A family member may be a good choice as trustee, because a family member may be in a better position than a professional trustee to know the needs of the beneficiaries. The settlor should consider the person's experience in managing money, general sense of responsibility, and ability to work with the beneficiaries. Family members and close personal friends may decline fees or serve for less than the fees charged by a professional trustee, and for a trust with limited assets, cost will be a factor.

In contrast to a family member, a professional trustee has experience with accounting and investment management and will not face conflicts of interest in making distribution decisions. However, a professional trustee will charge fees for the services the trustee provides, and most banks and trust companies have minimum asset requirements for management. For smaller trusts, individuals who serve as professional fiduciaries may be an option. Due to concerns about the quality of the services provided by some of these professional fiduciaries, California enacted a statute regulating them. Professional Fiduciaries Act, Cal. Bus. & Prof. Code § 6501. The statute makes licensing mandatory and requires initial and continuing training, record keeping, and reporting. Other states may have less regulation, so care in choosing a trustee is essential.

A settlor may decide that the best choice will be co-trustees. Two family members can serve together, bringing different skills and serving as a check on each other, although family conflict may be a risk. Alternatively, a settlor may chose a family member and a professional trustee to act together. The family member can provide guidance on the needs of the beneficiaries, and the professional trust can provide investment guidance and accounting.

Acceptance

A person or institution named as a trustee need not accept the designation as trustee, but a person who accepts property from a settlor and takes control of the property will most likely be deemed to have accepted the position of trustee. No formal acceptance of the position is required. In drafting trust instruments, lawyers typically provide for the signatures of the settlor (to signify intent) and the trustee (to signify acceptance), but the settlor's intent and the trustee's acceptance can be established in other ways if either fails to sign the document. The terms of the trust may provide a method of acceptance by the trustee, but that method may not be exclusive and even if it is, substantial compliance is usually sufficient. See UTC § 701(a)(1). Performing the duties of a trustee will constitute acceptance, UTC § 701(a)(2), but a person designated as trustee can act to protect the property without that action being considered an acceptance if the person sends a refusal of the trusteeship to the settlor or, if the settlor is dead or incapacitated, to a beneficiary. UTC § 701(c)(1).

Resignation

A trustee can resign from the position, but the trustee remains liable for any acts or omissions that occurred while the person was acting as trustee. Usually, the trust instrument provides the process for resignation, but if the trust instrument is silent on trustee resignation, then the trustee must look to common law or statutes. Under the common law, a trustee had to get court approval to resign. UTC § 705 now permits the trustee to resign after following procedures in the statute, including giving notice to the qualified beneficiaries. Some states may still apply the common law rule requiring court approval, so a well-drafted trust should include a process for trustee resignation. Many documents also give one or more people the right to remove a trustee. Aside from resignation or removal, a trustee will also cease to serve upon death or incapacity.

After a trustee ceases to serve, the successor trustee named in the trust instrument will become the trustee without court appointment. The trust instrument may, instead of naming a successor, direct the beneficiaries to appoint a successor, which they can do by following the procedure specified in the trust instrument. If the trust instrument neither names a successor nor provides a way to name a successor, the court will appoint a successor.

4. Intent to Create a Trust

The creation of a trust involves the transfer of property to a person, with the settlor's *intent* that the person hold the property in trust. In most estate planning situations, with a lawyer advising a client, the client will execute a trust document. That trust document, labeled as a **Declaration of Trust** (if the settlor will serve as the initial trustee) or a **Trust Agreement** (if the trustee is someone else), is usually sufficient to show that the settlor intended to create the trust. Without a trust document, however, it may not be clear whether the property owner intended the property to be held in trust or intended something else—an outright gift, a power of appointment, or a promise to make a gift in the future.

A determination of what the property owner intended will establish whether a trust exists, which in turn will affect the ultimate ownership of the property. If the property owner intended to hold the property until death and make a testamentary gift at that time, the property still belongs to the property owner. If the property owner intended to make an outright gift to someone, perhaps with an explanation or request, the property will belong to the other person. If the property owner actually intended to create a trust, then the person holding the property will hold it as a trustee and not for the person's own benefit. In this section we look at different ways to interpret a property owner's intent, and the problems that arise when the intent is not clear.

Inter Vivos Gift in Trust or Ownership Retained

A property owner may declare, orally or in writing, that the property owner holds the property as a trustee. A declaration of trust may be sufficient to create a trust, but when title to the property is not transferred into the name of the owner as trustee, a trust may not be created. Confusion can result if the property owner's intent is not clear. If title to property is not transferred into the name of the trustee or a deed associated with an attempted declaration is not recorded, a court may refuse to find the creation of a trust. If so, the property will be in the owner's estate when the owner dies and will be distributed under the owner's will or by intestacy.

Intent to Create a Trust or Gift with Explanatory or Precatory Language

When a document purporting to create a trust exists, the language is important in determining whether the person writing the document actually intended to create a trust. A property owner need not use the word "trust" or "trustee" in establishing a trust, but the intent to create a trust must be clear. If the property owner makes a gift to someone and expresses the "hope" or "desire" that the recipient use the property in a particular way, perhaps for the benefit of someone else, the property owner may be merely explaining the reason for the gift or recommending how the gift should be used. Unless the owner intended to create a trust, **precatory** language may create a moral obligation, but it does not create a legal obligation with respect to the use of the property. Unfortunately, language does not always clearly convey the intent of the property owner.

Case Preview

In re Estate of Bolinger

When Harry Bolinger died, his will gave all his property to his father, even though Harry had three minor children when he executed his will. He may have intended to create a trust for his children, with his father as trustee. Alternatively, he may have intended to give the property to his father outright, with precatory language encouraging his father to use the property for the benefit of the children. Unfortunately, Harry's intent is not clear, and because Harry is dead, the court must determine his intent by examining the language in the will. Harry's father thinks he owns the property outright, while Harry's children argue that the property belongs to them.

As you read the case, consider:

1. What evidence did the court consider in trying to determine Harry's intent?
2. What makes language "precatory"?
3. How does the *Stapleton* case support Marian's argument?
4. How does the dissent distinguish *Stapleton*?

In re Estate of Bolinger
943 P.2d 981 (Mont. 1997)

NELSON, J.

Harry Albert Bolinger, III, (Decedent), died March 23, 1995. . . . The November 15, 1984 will so offered for probate devised all Decedent's estate to Hal [Bolinger, decedent's father], or, in the event that Hal predeceased Decedent, to Hal's wife (Decedent's step-mother), Marian. Specifically, the Fifth paragraph of the will, the language of which is at issue here, provides:

> I intentionally give all of my property and estate to my said father, H.A. Bolinger, in the event that he shall survive me, and in the event he shall not survive me, I intentionally give all of my property and estate to my step-mother, Marian Bolinger, in the event she shall survive me, and in that event, I intentionally give nothing to my three children, namely: Harry Albert Bolinger, IV, Wyetta Bolinger and Travis Bolinger, or to any children of any child who shall not survive me. I make

this provision for the reason that I feel confident that any property which either my father or my step-mother, Marian Bolinger, receive from my estate will be used in the best interests of my said children as my said beneficiaries may determine in their exclusive discretion.

The will nominated Hal as personal representative with Marian as the alternate. Hal subsequently renounced his right to serve as personal representative and suggested the appointment of Marian, who petitioned to be appointed on November 6, 1995. Decedent's children objected, contending, among other things, that the will was void as a matter of law because of undue influence or constructive fraud on the part of Hal, and, in the alternative, that the will created a trust on behalf of the children. [The court found no undue influence or constructive fraud.] . . .

On the basis of the discovery responses and depositions provided as part of the summary judgment proceedings, the District Court found that both Hal and Marian believed that the language in the *Fifth* paragraph of Decedent's will created a trust (although in a second deposition Marian contended that she was mistaken in her initial impression in this regard). The court also found that Marian believed that at the time Decedent's will was drafted and executed, the children were minors and that Decedent used the language in the will to prevent his ex-wife from obtaining control over his estate. The court also agreed with Professor Folsom [an expert witness] that, when read in its entirety, the *Fifth* paragraph of the will expressed Decedent's intention that all of his property must be used in the best interests of his children. The court found that the subject or res of the trust was all of Decedent's property and that the testator's purpose in creating the trust was to ensure that his assets would be used in his children's best interests. The court then concluded that Decedent having thus manifested his intention, and, on the basis of the criteria and authorities argued by the children, an express trust for the children's benefit was created under the *Fifth* paragraph of Decedent's will.

On appeal from the District Court's decision, Marian argues that proof of an express trust requires clear and convincing evidence that the trustor intended to create a trust and that devises, bequests and gifts that do not contain any restrictions on use or disposition of the property involved do not create an express trust. She contends that the use of "precatory" words by a testator, that is words which express only a wish or recommendation as to the disposition of property, are not sufficient to establish an intention to create a trust. She cites, among other cases, our decision in *Stapleton v. DeVries*, 535 P.2d 1267 (Mont. 1975), in support of her position in this regard. . . .

In support of the District Court's decision, the children argue that where the testator manifests his intention to create a trust, no particular form of words or conduct is necessary, and that, providing that the trustor indicates with reasonable certainty the subject, purpose and beneficiary of the trust, an express trust is created. The children contend that, under the facts here and under these criteria, the language used by Decedent in the *Fifth* paragraph of his will created an express trust in their favor. They maintain that a trust must be construed in a manner so as to implement the trustor's intent and that, here, Decedent clearly expressed his intention that his property be used for the benefit of his children. . . .

. . . [I]n the case at bar, we will address the first issue [creation of a trust] in the context of those legal principles which, we believe, have remained historically constant . . . . In this regard, we also note that under the present Trust Code, §72-33-103, MCA, provides that "[e]xcept to the extent that the common law rules governing trusts are modified by statute, the common law as to trusts is the law of this state."

Taking this approach, it is clear that a trust is created only if the testator demonstrates that he or she intends that a trust be created. . . .

[U]nder the Trust Code the law is that "[a] trust is created only if the trust or properly [sic] manifests an intention to create a trust." Section 72-33-202, MCA.

Moreover, in our case law, we continue to cite to the general rule that in the construction of trusts it is the trustor's intent that controls and that to determine that intent we look to the language of the trust agreement. In that regard, our rules of construction with respect to testamentary instruments are well settled:

> The words of the instrument are to receive an interpretation which will give some effect to every expression, rather than an interpretation which will render any of the expressions inoperative. The will is to be construed according to the intentions of the testator, so far as is possible to ascertain them. Words used in the instrument are to be taken in their ordinary and grammatical sense unless a clear intention to use them in another sense can be ascertained. In cases of uncertainty arising upon the face of the will, the testator's intention is to be ascertained from the words of the instrument, taking into view the circumstances under which it was made, exclusive of his oral declarations. . . .
>
> "The object, therefore, of a judicial interpretation of a will is to ascertain the intention of the testator, according to the meaning of the words he has used, deduced from a consideration of the whole instrument and a comparison of its various parts in the light of the situation and circumstances which surrounded the testator when the instrument was framed."

Furthermore, "[n]o particular form of words or conduct is necessary for the manifestation of intention to create a trust," Restatement (Second) of Trusts §24 (1959), and "words of trusteeship are not necessarily conclusive," George T. Bogert, Trusts §11 at 24 (6th ed. 1987). Nonetheless, we have held that "express trusts depend for their creation upon a clear and direct expression of intent by the trustor," and that the burden of proof to establish the existence of a trust is upon the party who claims it and must be founded on evidence which is unmistakable, clear, satisfactory and convincing. . . .

From [the language in the will] it is clear that Decedent intended to accomplish several things under this paragraph of his will. First, he "intentionally" devised outright all of his property and estate to his father, and in default of that bequest, then to his step-mother, Marian. Second, it is also clear that Decedent "intentionally" devised nothing to his three children. Third, Decedent desired to make some explanation as to why he disposed of his estate in the foregoing manner. To this end, he added to the otherwise unequivocal language of the first sentence of the *Fifth* paragraph, a second sentence with the explanation that he made this provision because he felt "confident" that any property which either his father or his step-mother, Marian, received from his estate would ["will"] be used in the best interests of his said children as Hal or Marian may determine in their exclusive discretion. It is the language in this second sentence which is at issue and which the District Court determined created an express trust in favor of the children.

The use of this latter sort of qualifying language in a will or instrument is referred to as "precatory" language. As stated in Bogert, *supra* §19 at 41:

> Usually, if a transferor of property intends the transferee to be a trustee, he directs him to act in that capacity, but sometimes he merely expresses a wish or recommendation that the property given be used in whole or in part for the benefit of another. Words of this latter type are called "precatory" and are generally construed not to create a trust but instead to create at most an ethical obligation.

In weighing the effect of precatory expressions the courts consider the entire document and the circumstances of the donor, his family, and other interested parties.

The author of this treatise notes that the primary question in construing precatory language is whether the testator meant merely to advise or influence the discretion of the devisee, or himself control or direct the disposition intended. Bogert, *supra* §19 at 42. Here, in Marian's favor, the author notes that "the settlor must have explicitly or impliedly expressed an intent to impose obligations on the trustee and not merely to give the donee of the property *an option to use if for the benefit of another.*" Bogert, *supra* §19 at 42 (emphasis added). Put another way, considering the language of the entire instrument and the situation of the alleged settlor, his family, and the supposed beneficiaries at the time the will was executed, "was it natural and probable that the donor intended the donee to be bound by an enforceable obligation *or was he to be free to use his judgment and discretion?*" Bogert, *supra* §19 at 42 (emphasis added). Moreover, "[w]here a donor first makes an absolute gift of property, without restriction or limitation, and later inserts precatory language in a separate sentence or paragraph, the courts are apt to find that there was no intent to have a trust." Bogert, *supra* §19 at 43.

We have addressed the use of such language in a prior decision relied on by Marian. In *Stapleton*, 535 P.2d at 1268, the decedent's will provided as follows:

> I give, devise and bequeath to my beloved wife, Amanda DeVries, all the balance, residue and remainder of my property of whatever nature, kind or character which I may own at the time of my death to have and to hold as her sole and separate property. I do this with the knowledge that she will be fair and equitable to all of my children, the issue of myself and my former wife as well as the issue of herself and myself.

When Amanda died leaving all her property to her children and nothing to the decedent's children by his first marriage, the latter sued claiming that a constructive trust was created by decedent's will in their favor. Reversing the trial court's summary judgment in the plaintiffs' favor, we ruled that the language was clear on its face—Amanda was given decedent's property outright and the remaining precatory language did not create a trust for the benefit of the children by decedent's first marriage. . . .

Similarly, in the case at bar, the language used by Decedent clearly and unambiguously makes an outright gift to his father, and in default of that gift, to his stepmother and specifically excludes his children. Then, in a separate sentence, Decedent explains the reason for this distribution, expressing his "confidence" that the devisees will use his estate for the children's "best interests" in the devisees' "exclusive discretion." This language does not impose any sort of clear directive or obligation (other than, perhaps, a moral or ethical one) on either Hal or Marian. The purported trustee is given no direction as to how the supposed settlor intends his estate to be used to further the "best interests" of the children and neither does Decedent provide any guidance as to what those best interests might include. Decedent imposes no restrictions on the purported trustee, but, rather, leaves in that person the "exclusive discretion" as to how the estate will be used for the children's best interests, expressing his "confidence" that will be accomplished. Decedent's statement of reasons for devising his estate to Hal and Marian, neither limits nor restricts the gift to them any more than did the language at issue in *Stapleton* and in *Miller* limit or restrict the bequests made in those cases. The bottom line is that, under the precatory language used by Decedent, his devisees had complete discretion as to how to use the property given them outright. . . .

We hold that the District Court erred in its legal conclusion that the *Fifth* paragraph of Decedent's will created an express trust for the benefit of Decedent's three children. Accordingly, we reverse and remand for further proceedings consistent with this opinion.

Reversed and remanded.

LEAPHART, J., dissenting.

I dissent . . . .

The language used in the Bolinger will is distinguishable from and more conclusive than that used in *Stapleton*. In *Stapleton*, the decedent's will devised the property to the beneficiary "to hold as her sole and separate property." Such a "sole and separate property" provision is absent in the Bolinger will. Secondly, in *Stapleton*, the testator made the devise knowing that the beneficiary would be fair and equitable to all his children (i.e. children from both marriages). The beneficiary was thus under no obligation to segregate the devised property or to treat it any differently than her sole property. In contrast, Bolinger provided that "any property" received from his estate was specifically tagged for use "in the best interests of [his] children." In other words, his father or step-mother were not to commingle the property with their own property, nor were they to treat it as their sole and separate property with some vague understanding that they would then be fair and equitable to all concerned. Rather, Bolinger was confident that this *specific property* "will be used in the best interests of my children." [Emphasis in original.] The language in the Bolinger will is more than precatory, it is peremptory.

As the court recognizes, no particular form of words is necessary for the manifestation of an intent to create a trust, Restatement (Second) of Trusts §24, express trusts depend upon a clear and direct expression of intent by the trustor. Bolinger clearly intended that the property passing maintain its separate identity and that his father or step-mother, as trustees, use the property solely for the benefit of his children, who were, at the time of the will, minors.

I would affirm the decision of the District Court.

Post-Case Follow-Up

Bolinger demonstrates the difficulty of determining intent after a testator's death. The court finds that the children did not meet the standard of clear and convincing evidence of intent to create a trust, but the dissent finds that Harry "clearly intended" that the property be held in trust for the benefit of his children. Both sides in this dispute had good arguments, because the language in the will could be interpreted both ways. A lawyer drafting Harry's will could have made the intent clearer. Litigation could have been avoided with good drafting.

In re Estate of Bolinger: Real Life Applications

1. If Harry Bolinger had asked you to draft his will, what words would you have used in drafting to create a trust for minor children? What words would you have used to draft a gift to his father, with precatory suggestions as to its use?

2. Shirley brings you a will written by her sister, Angelica, who has just died. The will says, "I give my entire estate to my sister, Shirley, so that she can take care of our mother as long as our mother lives." Angelica is survived by Shirley, their mother, and their brother, Ben. What is the effect of the will? Does Shirley take the property outright or in trust? What information would be helpful as you advise Shirley? What evidence would a court consider?

3. When Beth and Joshua divorced, they entered into a settlement agreement providing that Joshua would transfer $100,000 to Beth for the college education of their two children. Their older daughter, Nicole, is now ready for college and when she asks her father for help with tuition, he explains that her mother is holding money for her. Beth says she used the money for living expenses, including summer camps and music lessons for the children. Advise Nicole.

Transfer into Trust or Promise to Make a Gift in the Future

A gift requires intent and delivery of property. For example, if a mother, Maude, hands her son, Scott, a $100 bill and says "Happy Birthday," this is a completed gift. But what if Maude calls Scott to tell him she has put $100 in a birthday card and will give it to him when he visits, but then dies before she is able to give it to him? Maude's intent to make a gift is clear in both cases, but delivery was not completed in the second case and Scott will not receive the gift. Scott might argue that Maude had intended to hold the property in trust for him: a declaration of trust does not require delivery of the property to the trustee (the settlor is the trustee) or to the beneficiary. Although this strategy may work in some circumstances, courts are reluctant to find a declaration of trust any time an inter vivos gift fails due to lack of delivery. Delivery can be constructive or symbolic, and sometimes a court will refuse to find a trust but use constructive delivery to get the property to the intended recipient. Another strategy for Scott, then, is to argue that by putting the money in an envelope with his name on it, Maude had made symbolic delivery.

5. Property (aka Corpus or Res)

A trust must have property to be a valid trust. The trust property can be as minimal as a $20 bill stapled to the trust document, especially if the plan is to fund the trust from the settlor's estate after death. The trustee must hold the property, so trustee would need to receive the $20 (or some other amount) and hold it for trust purposes. Usually, however, the trust property is the property the settlor transfers to the trustee for management in the trust. Even if a settlor signs a trust instrument, until the settlor transfers property to the trustee, the trust does not exist. The trust document, by itself, does not create the trust. The lack of property is rarely an issue for a testamentary trust, unless no property remains at death to transfer into the trust, but with an inter vivos trust, a settlor sometimes forgets to transfer property into the trust, and then the trust does not exist. Under the Uniform Testamentary Additions to Trusts Act, adopted in many states, an unfunded trust may be given effect if certain requirements are met. We discuss the statutory requirements in connection with revocable trusts, in Section C.

Property held in trust that can be titled (such as real estate, bank and securities accounts, vehicles, patents, and copyrights) should be retitled in the name of the trustee because the trustee, not the trust, has legal ownership of the property. The best practice for transferring property to a trust is to change the title to indicate that the property is now held by the trustee. A typical way to title property, to show ownership by the trustee in the trustee's fiduciary capacity, would be as follows: "Lorna Park, as trustee of the Jennifer Hong Trust, dated March 25, 2017." The date of the trust is often used as an identifier for the trust. Jennifer Hong may have more than one trust, and although the trusts may have different names, using the date will clarify which trust holds the property.

> ### Professor Yahuda's Library—Trust, Gift, or Neither?
>
> After Professor Yahuda's death, his widow announced that she had given her husband's library to Hebrew University in Israel. She began the work of cataloguing and crating the books for shipment and said, when asked, that she could not sell the books because she had given them to the university. When she died, the books remained in the warehouse in the United States, in her name, and her will did not include the university as a beneficiary. Hebrew University argued that she had held the books in trust and that her actions were consistent with those of a trustee. The court concluded that although she may have had the requisite donative intent to make a gift, she had not completed the gift before her death, so the library was still part of her estate. Although she had donative intent, the facts did not show that she intended to create a trust. The court said, "A gift which is imperfect for lack of a delivery will not be turned into a declaration of trust for no better reason than that it is imperfect for lack of a delivery." Id. at 644. Hebrew University tried again, and in a second case, Hebrew University Ass'n v. Nye (II), 223 A.2d 397 (Conn. 1966), the court found that the delivery of a memorandum listing most of the books constituted constructive delivery of the gift. Hebrew University got the library.

What about items that do not have a separate document establishing ownership, such as furniture, jewelry, coin collections, and silver? Tangibles can be "scheduled" to show that they have been transferred into the trust. The trust instrument will have a schedule attached identifying the assets Ms. Hong is transferring to the trust. The schedule should be sufficient to establish that her tangibles are now the property of the trustee.

What if Ms. Hong lists on Schedule A, attached to the trust instrument, "Bank Account #4589, in the Bank of San Francisco" and does not change the ownership documents at the bank? Will listing the bank account (and other assets that have formal title documents) on the schedule, without changing the registration at the bank, cause the account to be subject to the terms of the trust? If the settlor creates a trust with someone else as trustee, title must be transferred to the name of the trustee. If, however, the settlor declares that she now holds the property as trustee and does not change title, is Schedule A sufficient to establish that the property is now held in the trust? The answer depends on state law. Some states require registration for real property or for any assets with registered title, like bank accounts. See, e.g, N.Y. Est. Powers & Trust Law § 7-1.18(b).

UTC § 401(2) permits the inclusion of property in a trust by declaration, but the comment to that section explains that reregistration of the property is best. In a state that has adopted the UTC, scheduling the property may be sufficient, but a lawyer would advise clients to reregister any asset that has formal title. Cases in a few states have held that listing the property on an attached schedule was sufficient to cause the property to be held in the trust, when the settlor declared herself trustee of the assets. See Rose v. Waldrip, 730 S.E.2d 529 (Ga. Ct. App. 2012); Ladd v. Ladd, 323 S.W.3d 772 (Ky. Ct. App. 2010); Samuel v. King, 64 P.3d 1206 (Or. Ct. App. 2003); Taliaferro v. Taliaferro, 921 P.2d 803 (Kan. 1996); Estate of Heggstad, 20 Cal. Rptr. 2d 433 (Ct. App. 1993). Even with these cases, reregistration continues to be the safest and best practice to avoid litigation and ensure that the property will be treated as held in trust by the trustee.

6. Beneficiary

The beneficiary plays an essential role in a trust because the beneficiary has standing to enforce the trust. Without someone with the legal authority to force the trustee to comply with the terms of the trust, a trust fails. Under the common law only a charitable trust could exist without an identifiable beneficiary. A charitable trust must have a charitable purpose, and the state Attorney General has the authority to enforce the purpose of the trust. Charitable trusts are discussed at the end of this chapter.

The UTC now permits the creation of an animal trust or a "trust for a purpose," with rules that limit the scope of these trusts. Because these trusts do not have identifiable beneficiaries, someone other than the beneficiary, named in the trust instrument or, if the trust instrument is silent, by the court, will have the authority to enforce the trust.

Identifiable Person or Class

Under the common law, a beneficiary has to be either an identifiable person or a class of identifiable persons so that the court knows who has the authority to enforce the trust. A class like "children" or "descendants" works because the members of those classes can be identified, even if the membership will change over time and even if some members are not yet born. Other people can represent minor and unborn beneficiaries and can enforce the trust on their behalf.

Case Preview

Clark v. Campbell

Sometimes a testator will want to give items of personal property to friends without identifying each item of personal property and each friend who should receive that item. In Clark v. Campbell, a testator faced with this common problem thought he could solve it by giving the people managing his estate the authority to distribute the personal property among his friends. At issue in this case is whether the testator intended to create a trust and if so, whether he did create a trust. The case is from 1926, and the court uses the rather archaic term "cestui que trust" to mean "beneficiary."

As you read the case, consider:

1. What does the court say about the need for identifiable beneficiaries?
2. What language in the will shows the intent to create a trust?
3. What might the testator have intended instead of a trust?

Clark v. Campbell
133 A. 166 (N.H. 1926)

Snow, J.

The ninth clause of the will of deceased reads:

> My estate will comprise so many and such a variety of articles of personal property such as books, photographic albums, pictures, statuary, bronzes, bric-a-brac, hunting and fishing equipment, antiques, rugs, scrap books, canes and Masonic jewels, that probably I shall not distribute all, and perhaps no great part thereof during my life by gift among my friends. Each of my trustees is competent by reason of familiarity with the property, my wishes and friendships, to wisely distribute some portion at least of said property. I therefore give and bequeath to my trustees all my property embraced within the classification aforesaid in trust to make disposal by the way of a memento from myself, of such articles to such of my friends as they, my trustees, shall select. All of said property, not so disposed of by them, my trustees are directed

to sell and the proceeds of such sale or sales to become and be disposed of as a part of the residue of my estate.

By the common law there cannot be a valid bequest to an indefinite person. There must be a beneficiary or a class of beneficiaries indicated in the will capable of coming into court and claiming the benefit of the bequest. This principle applies to private but not to public trusts and charities. . . . The basis assigned for this distinction is the difference in the enforceability of the two classes of trusts. In the former, there being no definite cestui que trust to assert his right, there is no one who can compel performance, with the consequent unjust enrichment of the trustee; while, in the case of the latter, performance is considered to be sufficiently secured by the authority of the Attorney General to invoke the power of the courts. . . .

Where a gift is impressed with a trust, ineffectively declared, and incapable of taking effect because of the indefiniteness of the cestui que trust, the donee will hold the property in trust for the next taker under the will, or for the next of kin by way of a resulting trust. The trustees therefore hold title to the property enumerated in the paragraph under consideration to be disposed of as a part of the residue, and the trustees are so advised. . . .

Case discharged.

Post-Case Follow-Up

In Clark v. Campbell, the testator was faced with a common problem: the desire to distribute items of personal property to a large number of people. The court viewed the language in the will as an attempt to create a trust, so the gift failed. A class like "friends" does not work as a class of identifiable beneficiaries, because a court cannot determine for certain who the settlor's friends are and therefore who has rights in the trust. The result of this decision is that the personal property was distributed with the residue of the estate or perhaps, depending on whether the will included a residuary clause, to the testator's intestate heirs. In either case the testator's wish that his friends be given "a memento from myself" was not accomplished.

Clark v. Campbell: Real Life Applications

1. The court could have construed the language in the will as an outright gift to the three trustees (named earlier in the document) in their individual capacities, with the precatory request that they distribute the personal property to the testator's friends. Why didn't the court resolve the case this way? Do you think the three people named would have wanted an outright gift of the tangibles?

2. How would you redraft the ninth clause of the will to make the gift an outright gift to three people to distribute among the testator's friends?

3. If Clark had come to you for estate planning assistance, what options would you have outlined for him to ensure that his friends would receive some property? Explain the advantages and disadvantages of each option.

Honorary Trust

Under the common law, trusts without ascertainable beneficiaries fail. A court will sometimes find an honorary trust when the owner of property attempts to transfer the property to a devisee in trust for a noncharitable purpose and without an identifiable beneficiary. A court must establish an honorary trust, so a settlor of an improper trust cannot be sure that an honorary trust will be created. Courts sometimes impose honorary trusts for purposes such as the care of graves and the care of animals. Honorary trusts cannot last beyond a state's perpetuities period.

If a court creates an honorary trust, the person who received the property as the intended trustee, usually under a will, holds the property for the benefit of the persons who would take the property owner's estate as beneficiaries or heirs. The person holding the property is given the power to make distributions to carry out the settlor's wishes, but that power is not mandatory as it would be for a trustee. Thus, the person the owner intended to make the trustee is actually trustee for the benefit of the persons who will take the owner's estate, but is permitted to carry out the owner's wishes if the person chooses to do so. No one can enforce the intended trust, and carrying out the owner's intent is entirely up to the person holding the property. If the person chooses not to carry out the owner's wishes, the person must hold the property for the takers of the owner's estate.

Trust for a Purpose

UTC § 409 responds to the desire of some property owners to create trusts for a noncharitable purpose, without an identifiable beneficiary. The most common type of purpose trust is a trust for the care of a cemetery or a cemetery plot. Another example is a trust providing for the distribution of items of personal property among the friends of a decedent. UTC § 409 provides that a trust created for a noncharitable purpose and without an identifiable beneficiary will be enforced by a person designated by the settlor or, if the trust document does not designate someone, then a person appointed by the court. A trust under this section cannot last longer than the state's Rule Against Perpetuities, because the trust has no identifiable life in being. Of course, a state that has abolished its Rule Against Perpetuities would need no restriction on duration.

A trust for a purpose might have a purpose that would benefit the community but not qualify as a charitable purpose (we examine the meaning of "charitable purpose" at the end of this chapter). For example, Genevra wants to encourage her neighbors to plant more flowers in their front yards. She creates a trust for this purpose, contributing enough money to fund small grants to several people in the neighborhood each year. The trustee selects the grant recipients. The purpose is probably not a charitable one because the benefit goes to her neighborhood, and there is no identifiable beneficiary, but the trust might qualify as a trust for a purpose.

Trust for an Animal

A trust for a pet fails under the common law, because an animal does not have legal rights and therefore does not "count" as a beneficiary capable of enforcing the trust. Also, an animal does not "count" as a life in being for purposes of the Rule Against Perpetuities, so the trust would violate the Rule. Despite the invalidity of pet trusts under the common law, people have attempted to create trusts for pets and for animals such as horses. When faced with a trust for an animal, a court might find an honorary trust, but often the court would hold the attempted trust invalid.

One option for a pet owner is to give the pet and a bequest of money to a friend, with the hope that the friend will care for the animal. However, the friend will be under no obligation to use the money for the pet's care. Many pet owners want assurance that their pets will receive proper care, and the law has responded with statutes permitting pet or animal trusts. Most states have adopted either Uniform Probate Code (UPC) § 2-907(b), providing for pet trusts, or UTC § 408, providing for animal trusts (trusts that can include animals that might not be considered pets, such as farm animals). The statutory provisions are substantially similar.

EXHIBIT 9.3   **UPC § 408. Trust for Care of an Animal**

(a) A trust may be created to provide for the care of an animal alive during the settlor's lifetime. The trust terminates upon the death of the animal or, if the trust was created to provide for the care of more than one animal alive during the settlor's lifetime, upon the death of the last surviving animal.

(b) A trust authorized by this section may be enforced by a person appointed in the terms of the trust or, if no person is so appointed, by a person appointed by the court. A person having an interest in the welfare of the animal may request the court to appoint a person to enforce the trust or to remove a person appointed.

(c) Property of a trust authorized by this section may be applied only to its intended use, except to the extent the court determines that the value of the trust property exceeds the amount required for the intended use. Except as otherwise provided in the terms of the trust, property not required for the intended use must be distributed to the settlor, if then living, otherwise to the settlor's successors in interest.

Like a "trust for a purpose," a trust for an animal will be enforced by someone named in the trust instrument or appointed by the court. The trust will terminate when the animal dies, and the remaining property will be distributed as provided in the trust instrument, or if the trust instrument does not say what should happen to the property, it will be returned to the settlor. If the settlor is not living when the trust terminates, the remaining property will pass through the settlor's estate. Drafting an animal trust requires attention to these requirements. The settlor must consider not only who should be the trustee but also who should be named to enforce the trust and what should happen to any property remaining when the animal dies. Practitioners recommend including instructions for the care of the animal, to guide the trustee in making distributions.

For example, a pet trust created for Sandra's dog, Fluffy, could name Sandra's sister as the trustee and Sandra's friend as the person to enforce the trust. Fluffy might live with Sandra's sister, the friend, or with another person. Sandra would fund the trust with enough money to take care of Fluffy, and she might include instructions related to expenses the trustee should cover, such as annual visits to the vet, shots and medications, a particular type of dog food, and the cost of boarding in a kennel when the caregiver is away on vacation. Depending on the resources available, Sandra might also provide that the trustee should spend money for more extraordinary expenses to maintain Fluffy's health, including surgeries and medications. Instructions about less routine expenses are helpful for the trustee, so that the person enforcing the trust and the trustee will both understand Sandra's wishes. The trust instrument should also provide for what happens when Fluffy dies. The property could be distributed to Fluffy's caregiver, in appreciation for the care, or to a local Humane Society. If the remaining property will go to the caregiver, Sandra may not want to name the caregiver as trustee, to avoid a conflict of interest in decisions about spending on Fluffy.

C. FORMALITIES

The elements of a trust do not include a requirement of a writing, a signature by the settlor, or signatures by witnesses (the formalities required for a will). Nonetheless, a lawyer typically drafts a trust instrument with places for the settlor to sign (to help indicate intent to create a trust) and for the trustee to sign (to indicate acceptance of the trusteeship). Notarization is often included. If the settlor will hold the trust property as trustee, only one person will sign, so a notarization will provide extra evidence if the settlor's signature and intent to create the trust are challenged.

If an oral trust can be proved, it will be valid, except that special problems arise if the property in the attempted trust is real property. This section examines the problems associated with oral trusts and then considers secret and semi-secret trusts, which involve a combination of a written document and oral instructions.

1. Oral Trusts of Personal Property

Both the common law and UTC § 407 permit an oral trust. The UTC requires clear and convincing evidence to establish an oral trust, but proof of any oral trust is difficult. Lawyers do not recommend using an oral trust, but oral trusts do occur in situations in which property owners act without the advice of a lawyer.

2. Oral Trusts of Real Property

In most states the Statute of Frauds will prevent the enforcement of an oral trust created for land. For example, imagine that Arthur (the transferor) executes a deed giving his friend, Logan (the transferee and intended trustee), his house. Arthur tells Logan, "I'm giving you the house because my sister, Hannah, is in a bad marriage. She plans to divorce her spouse soon, and after the divorce is finished, I want you to transfer the house to Hannah." The transfer to the intended trustee is not void, and Logan has legal title to the land, but the attempted oral trust will not be enforced as a trust. Thus, Hannah has little protection if Logan decides to ignore Arthur's wishes. Several rules have developed to keep the transferee in this kind of situation from taking the property for personal purposes. The problem is that the transferee can choose to carry out the trust voluntarily, but if the transferee fails to do so, the intended trustee cannot be sued for breach of trust.

Partial Performance

If the transferee begins to perform the duties of a trustee, the trust can be enforced under the doctrine of partial performance. This doctrine may also apply if the beneficiary has acted in reliance on the trust and the intended trustee has permitted the reliance.

Constructive or Resulting Trust

If the transferee used fraud, undue influence, or duress to cause the property owner to transfer the property to the transferee, or, if at the time of the transfer, the transferee was in a "confidential relation" to the property owner, a court may impose a **constructive trust**. If the court does so, the transferee will hold the trust property under a constructive trust for the intended beneficiaries. If neither of these conditions applies, a court may find that the transferee holds the property as a resulting trust (i.e., the trust fails and the property returns to the settlor) or as a constructive trust for the benefit of the property owner, unless the property owner is dead or incapacitated, in which case the transferee will hold the property for the intended beneficiaries, rather than for the heirs or beneficiaries of the property owner.

If the property owner declared herself trustee of the property and there is no transferee, the property owner holds the property outright, free of trust. But if the property owner declared herself trustee and then became incapacitated or died, the court may impose a constructive trust for the intended beneficiaries to avoid unjust enrichment. Of course, someone will have to have sufficient evidence to prove the existence of the trust and the identities of the beneficiaries.

For fraudulent behavior, undue influence, or duress to result in the imposition of a constructive trust, the transferee must have intended not to act as trustee at the time of the transfer. The rule does not apply if the transferee intended to act as trustee but then, after accepting the property, changed her mind. In that situation, the transferee has assumed fiduciary responsibilities. Proving fraud or the lack of fraud or undue influence or duress may be difficult.

Case Preview

Gregory v. Bowlsby

After Catherine Bowlsby died, her children received some of her property. Her husband, Benjamin Bowlsby, asked his children to transfer to him the real property they had inherited from their mother. He promised to farm the land for their benefit and then give them back the land on his death. After he remarried, he gave an undivided interest in the property to his new wife. On her death, the children sued to get their property back. At issue are whether the agreement between the children and their father created an oral trust, and if not, whether the court should use a constructive trust to return the property to the children.

As you read the case, consider:

1. Why did the oral exchange between the children and their father not create a trust?
2. Were the children in a confidential relationship with their father?
3. Did their father use fraud, undue influence, or duress to cause them to transfer the property?
4. How does the court discuss the imposition of a constructive trust on the property?

Gregory v. Bowlsby
88 N.W. 822 (Iowa 1902)

DEEMER, J.

It appears from the amended and substituted petition, which, under the record, must be treated as presenting the facts, that plaintiffs are the children and heirs at law of defendant Benjamin Bowlsby and of Catherine S. Bowlsby, now deceased, and that the defendant M.J. Bowlsby is the second wife of her codefendant; that Catherine S. Bowlsby died intestate, seised of the real estate in dispute; that at the request of defendant Benjamin Bowlsby certain of the plaintiffs met the father at the home of Frank Davison, a son-in-law, and that the father then and there requested them to deed him their interest in the real estate left by his deceased wife, in order that he might use and farm the land to better advantage, and that he then and there verbally agreed that he would hold the land, would not sell or dispose of the same, and that the net proceeds and accumulations thereof should and would at his death descend to the children of Catherine Bowlsby, as provided by law; that, believing in said promises, and that such an arrangement was valid, they executed a deed of bargain and sale to their father of their interest in the real estate theretofore owned by their mother, which deed recited a consideration of $1, the receipt whereof was acknowledged by the grantors; that by reason of the relations existing between them and their father these plaintiffs accepted his statements and promises without taking legal advice, and relied on him to advise them as to their rights and protect them in the premises; that neither defendant nor his attorney, who was present with him, advised them that the arrangement could not be enforced. It further appears from the allegations of this petition that the conveyance was procured by mistake on the part of these plaintiffs, induced by the representations made to them by said defendant; that said defendant paid nothing for the conveyance, and that the sole consideration therefor was his agreement as aforesaid. It is further alleged that said defendant did not intend to carry out the arrangement or agreement on his part, but made the representations and agreement aforesaid for the sole purpose of cheating and defrauding plaintiffs out of their interest in the land of their deceased mother; that after his marriage to his codefendant he conveyed to her an undivided one-third interest in the property received from plaintiffs, but that this conveyance was without consideration, and was made with intent to cheat and defraud these plaintiffs; that his codefendant, when she took the conveyance, knew of the terms and conditions under which her husband received his deed from these plaintiffs. The prayer is that these deeds be canceled, that plaintiffs be adjudged to be the owners of an interest in the property, that their title be quieted, and that an accounting be had of the rents and profits of the real estate. The demurrer was the general equitable one, and as further grounds therefor it is claimed that the alleged oral agreement is within the statute of frauds.

[The court states that a trust with respect to land cannot be established without a writing based on the Statute of Frauds.]

. . . we have one question left, and that is, was there such a fraud perpetrated by defendant Benjamin Bowlsby as entitles plaintiffs to the relief asked? . . . If there is any cause of action stated, it is for the declaration and establishment of a constructive trust, growing out of the alleged fraud of the defendants. While some facts are recited for the purpose of showing fiduciary relations between the parties, we apprehend they are insufficient for that purpose. A father bears no such confidential or fiduciary relations to his adult children as to bring transactions between them relating to the lands of either under suspicion. He may deal with them as with strangers, and no presumption of fraud or undue influence obtains. It is charged, however, that, with intent to cheat and defraud, defendant made the representations charged, fully intending at the time he made them not to carry them out, but to obtain the title to the land, and thus defraud the grantors. Does this make such a case of fraud as that a court will declare a constructive trust in the land in favor of the grantors? This instrument was in the exact form agreed upon by the parties, and there was no promise to execute defeasances or other instruments to witness the trust. The sole claim is that defendant made the promises and agreements with intent to cheat and defraud the plaintiffs. Mere denial that there was a parol agreement as claimed will not constitute a fraud. If it did, the statute would be useless. Nor will a refusal to perform the contract be sufficient to create a constructive trust. But the statute was not enacted as a means for perpetrating a fraud; and if fraud in the original transaction is clearly shown, the grantor will be held to be a trustee ex maleficio. If, then, there was a fraudulent intent in procuring the deed without intention to hold the land as agreed, and pursuant to that intent the grantor disposed of the property, or otherwise repudiated his agreement, equity will take from the wrongdoer the fruit of his deceit by declaring a constructive trust. Mere breach of or denial of the oral agreement does not, as we have said, constitute a fraud. . . .

We think the petition on its face recites facts showing a constructive trust, and that the demurrer should have been overruled. Reversed.

Post-Case Follow-Up

A court may be willing to impose a constructive trust *either* if the person got the property through fraud *or* if the person was in a "confidential relation" with the person who transferred the property. A determination of who is in a "confidential relation" with the property owner may be difficult for a lawyer advising a client. In Gregory v. Bowlsby, the court did not consider the parent-child relationship to create a confidential relation, but on other facts involving overreaching by a parent—or a child, if the parent is of diminished capacity—it might. Although the court did not find a confidential relationship, the court found that the facts as recited in the petition could result in a constructive trust. The facts indicated that Mr. Bowlsby had intended at the outset to defraud his children.

If the children had transferred property other than land to their father, they might have been able to establish the creation of an oral trust. For example, children might be persuaded to transfer shares of stock in a family business to their father to manage. Depending on the circumstances, such a transfer could have been made with the intent to create a trust. The persons making the transfer would have to provide clear and convincing evidence to establish that intent, but on facts similar to the ones in **Gregory v. Bowlsby**, that could work.

Gregory v. Bowlsby: Real Life Applications

1. Would a court today be more or less likely to find a confidential relationship based on the facts in this case?

2. If the property involved in the case had not been real property, could the children have argued for the existence of an oral trust based on these facts?

3. Pamela tells you that her son, Ryan, convinced her to transfer her house to him. Now Ryan is planning to evict Pamela and sell the house. What questions would you ask Pamela? What information would help you in assisting her?

3. Secret and Semi-Secret Trusts to Be Given Effect at Death

Sometimes a testator will attempt to create a testamentary trust without putting the terms of the trust in the will. This may happen because the testator is trying to hide the real gift being made or perhaps just because it seems easier. Strict rules apply to what information can be considered in connection with a will, and oral conversations cannot be given effect.

For example, Juno might tell Aaron that she wants to make a gift to Cori but does not want the gift to be public. She asks Aaron if she can make the gift to him under her will, with the understanding that he will transfer the money to Cori. Aaron agrees and Juno's will says "I give $10,000 to Aaron." The gift is a secret trust because the existence of the trust cannot be determined on the face of the will. Aaron is not supposed to keep the property, so if Juno's intent to make the gift in trust can be proved, a court will enforce the trust. Aaron must give the $10,000 to Cori. If the court did not enforce the trust, Aaron would receive the property and would be unjustly enriched if he refused to give it to Cori. Juno attempted to create an express trust, and a court is unlikely to impose a constructive trust on the property. If Aaron always intended to keep the property and fraudulently told Juno he would give it to Cori, perhaps a court would be willing to impose a constructive trust.

If the will instead indicates that Aaron is supposed to hold the property as trustee but does not provide the terms of the trust, the trust is a semi-secret trust. The will might say, "I give my personal property to Aaron, to distribute according to the conversations we have had." The traditional rule is that a court will not enforce a semi-secret trust. See Oliffe v. Wells, 130 Mass. 221 (1881). The trust fails because the terms cannot be proved. The intended trustee, Aaron, will hold the property as a resulting trust and must distribute the property through the estate of the testator, to the residuary beneficiaries, or if none, to the testator's intestate heirs. The Restatement (Third) of Trusts § 18 (2003) states that a court should impose a constructive trust on behalf of the intended beneficiaries of a semi-secret trust, but the majority rule is still that a court will not enforce a semi-secret trust.

D. REVOCABLE TRUSTS

Most of the trust rules discussed in this chapter apply equally to revocable trusts and irrevocable trusts, but the particular purposes and functions of revocable trusts deserve additional consideration. In this section we examine the structure of a typical revocable trust and consider advantages and disadvantages of revocable trusts, as compared with wills. For a general overview of revocable trusts, see Bradley E.S. Fogel, *Trust Me? Estate Planning with Revocable Trusts*, 58 St. Louis U. L.J. 805 (2014).

1. Structure of a Typical Revocable Trust

A settlor creates a revocable trust during life, and the settlor retains control over the property, often serving as the trustee. Even if someone else serves as trustee, the settlor can request distributions from the trust, amend the trust, or revoke the trust at any time. The trust typically provides that a successor trustee can step in if the settlor becomes unable to manage financial matters. Thus, a revocable trust is an excellent tool in planning for the possibility of incapacity. The successor trustee will be able to use the settlor's property for the settlor's benefit without the expense or public nature of a court hearing. To make the incapacity planning effective, most or all of the settlor's assets will be held in the trust.

At death, the settlor's power to revoke the trust ends, and the trust becomes irrevocable. Usually, the settlor will have also executed a pour-over will, which will distribute the residue of the probate estate to the trustee of the revocable trust. A pour-over will "pours" any probate assets into the revocable trust. A pour-over will can pick up an asset that the settlor may have forgotten to transfer into the trust or an asset like a personal injury claim that arises at the time of the settlor's death and becomes part of the settlor's probate estate. Any assets that pass under a pour-over will must go through probate. These assets will distributed, ultimately, as part of the revocable trust, but the benefit of avoiding probate, which applies to all assets held in the revocable trust at death, is lost.

The settlor may also name the revocable trust as the beneficiary of other non-probate assets, such as life insurance. Those assets will be distributed to the revocable trust outside of probate, and the trust will then serve as the dispositive document when the settlor dies. All of the settlor's assets will pass under the terms of the trust to the desired beneficiaries. By naming the trust, rather than the estate, as the beneficiary, the settlor can keep information about these other assets private.

2. Funding a Revocable Trust

When a settlor creates a revocable trust, the settlor should fund the trust with something, even if most of the assets will be transferred later. The trust will not be created until an asset is held in trust. If the settlor wants to avoid probate, the settlor should transfer all of the settlor's assets to the trustee before death. Any assets left in the decedent's name at death will go through probate, unless another will substitute applies. The probate assets may be distributed to the trust under a pour-over will, but these assets will be administered in probate and the benefits of probate avoidance will have been lost.

If a settlor is not ready to transfer title to property into the name of the trustee, the settlor may create a revocable trust as a "standby trust," to be funded primarily at death. The settlor funds the trust with a small amount of money or other assets, so that the trust is created, but then provides for the rest of the funding to occur at death. The settlor might name the trustee as the beneficiary of a life insurance policy or the settlor might rely on a pour-over will to distribute probate property to the trustee.

Sometimes a settlor will execute a trust instrument that creates a revocable trust but forget to fund the trust. When a lawyer finishes preparing a revocable trust for a client, the lawyer will typically offer to transfer title to assets but will also explain that the settlor can save legal fees by transferring title himself. The settlor may prefer to transfer the property himself, but then procrastinate or forget, resulting in an unfunded trust. If a revocable trust remains unfunded at the settlor's death (no assets at all), then the trust does not exist. Prior to adoption of the Uniform Testamentary Additions to Trusts Act (UTATA), the fact that the trust did not exist raised questions about whether the provisions for distribution of the decedent's property could be given effect. UTATA fixed that problem and allows the revocable trust to be treated as an inter vivos trust, as if it had been funded before the settlor's death.

Without UTATA, if the trust does not exist at the settlor's death, the doctrine of incorporation by reference might be used to incorporate the written trust instrument into the will. See Chapter 3 for the rules on incorporation by reference. However, only the document in existence at the time the will is executed can be incorporated by reference. Therefore, if the will was executed before the trust document was prepared or if the trust document was amended after the will was executed, the document or changes written after the execution of the will cannot be given effect.

Faced with settlor (and sometimes lawyer) mistakes that resulted in unfunded revocable trusts and ineffective dispositive documents, the Uniform Law Commission developed UTATA, now included in the UPC. A revocable trust will be considered an inter vivos trust as long as the will identifies the trust and the trust is funded either during the settlor's life or at the settlor's death. Under UTATA, even if the trust did not exist at the settlor's death (because it had no property), it will be treated for purposes of distributions after death as if it existed.

EXHIBIT 9.4   **UPC § 2-511. Testamentary Additions to Trusts**

(a) A will may validly devise property to the trustee of a trust established or to be established (i) during the testator's lifetime by the testator, by the testator and some other person, or by some other person, including a funded or unfunded life insurance trust, although the settlor has reserved any or all rights of ownership of the insurance contracts, or (ii) at the testator's death by the testator's devise to the trustee, if the trust is identified in the testator's will and its terms are set forth in a written instrument, other than a will, executed before, concurrently with, or after the execution of the testator's will or in another individual's will if that other individual has predeceased the testator, regardless of the existence, size, or character of the corpus of the trust. The devise is not invalid because the trust is amendable or revocable, or because the trust was amended after the execution of the will or the testator's death.

(b) Unless the testator's will provides otherwise, property devised to a trust described in subsection (a) is not held under a testamentary trust of the testator, but it becomes a part of the trust to which it is devised, and must be administered and disposed of in accordance with the provisions of the governing instrument setting forth the terms of the trust, including any amendments thereto made before or after the testator's death.

(c) Unless the testator's will provides otherwise, a revocation or termination of the trust before the testator's death causes the devise to lapse.

3. Advantages of a Revocable Trust

Although people often think of using a revocable trust to avoid probate, the use of a revocable trust as a tool for incapacity planning may be the more important reason to recommend that a client use a revocable trust. If a person has done no advance planning and begins to lose mental capacity, a family member or other person may need to file a conservatorship over the property, so that someone else—a court-appointed conservator—can manage the property for the incapacitated person. In some cases, a person may be forgetful but not legally incapacitated, and a legal conservatorship may not be appropriate. The family may have difficulty stepping in to assist the person with financial matters, and the person may then be vulnerable to financial abuse. An advantage of a revocable trust is that a trustee can manage the person's property and no conservatorship will be needed. The person can choose the successor trustee and can provide guidance in the terms of the trust as to how the determination of incapacity is to be made and how the property should be managed and used.

Property held in a revocable trust will not go through the probate process after the settlor dies. By avoiding probate, the settlor saves costs associated with probate, although the cost of preparing a revocable trust instrument is typically more than that of a will. In some states, like California, the court closely supervises administration of a probate estate. That close supervision is costly and time-consuming, so a revocable trust may be used as a less expensive alternation and to provide for quicker distribution of assets.

A revocable trust can provide a comprehensive estate plan, just as a will would, and can direct the distribution of property or the creation of further trusts. The trust instrument will not be filed with the probate court and will not be a public document, so the use of a revocable trust can benefit people for whom privacy is important. The revocable trust is also useful when a settlor owns real property in another state. Real property held in the decedent's name will require a separate probate proceeding in the state in which the property is located, but if a revocable trust holds the property, the trust will control the distribution of the property. Thus, in addition to planning for incapacity, a revocable trust can provide a number of advantages, depending on a person's circumstances.

4. Disadvantages and Misconceptions

The probate process may provide greater creditor protection than administration using a revocable trust. The claims period for creditors in probate can be short (e.g., four months), while creditors seeking property in a trust may have a longer statute of limitations. Also, despite common misconceptions to the contrary, revocable trusts do not provide income or transfer tax benefits.

Whether costs are an advantage or disadvantage depends on the circumstances of the property owner. Preparation of a revocable trust will typically be more expensive than a will, and that cost will be paid by the client herself, rather than by the estate.

A client may not want to incur the additional upfront cost, even if some probate avoidance savings result. Costs may also be incurred to have title to property transferred into the trustee's name, and if the settlor does not act as trustee, the trustee may take fees. After the death of a settlor with a revocable trust, there will be some costs to administer the trust, just as there are with a will, to transfer the property as directed in the document.

5. Rules that Differ from Rules Applicable to Other Trusts

Although most trust law applies to revocable trusts, a few rules are different. This paragraph highlights the key differences. Under UTC § 601 and the laws of some states the, capacity to execute a revocable trust is the same as the capacity to execute a will, while the capacity to execute an inter vivos trust is higher. The duties a trustee owes to beneficiaries are constrained as long as the settlor of a revocable trust is alive. Under UTC § 603(a) the trustee owes duties only to the settlor, and not to other beneficiaries, as long as the settlor is alive. Some states have modified this section of the UTC to provide that if the settlor lacks capacity, the trustee owes duties to other beneficiaries as well as to the settlor. These future beneficiaries can keep an eye on the trustee when the settlor becomes unable to do so.

Because a revocable trust is used as a will substitute, some states apply rules that developed in wills law to revocable trusts. These rules, which do not apply to irrevocable trusts, include revocation of provisions for the benefit of a spouse after divorce and revocation of provisions for a person who killed the settlor.

E. CHARITABLE TRUSTS

Charitable organizations play a significant role in the United States, and the nonprofit sector continues to grow in size and importance. Some charities are organized as charitable trusts, but a charity can also be organized as a nonprofit corporation or as an unincorporated association. Many of the issues we will examine apply to all types of charities, however organized. Some of the rules that apply to all charities derive from trust law, due in part to the idea that someone (a director or trustee) is managing property for the benefit of others and therefore should be subject to fiduciary principles, while some rules are derived from other sources of law. The American Law Institute is engaged in a project to provide guidance on the law of nonprofit organizations, and many observers expect that project to unify, to an even greater extent, the rules that apply to charitable trusts and nonprofit corporations. See Restatement of the Law, Charitable Nonprofit Organizations (current project of the American Law Institute), https://www.ali.org/publications/show/charitable-nonprofit-organizations.

A charitable trust is a trust with a charitable purpose. For example, the provision of scholarships to law students, restoration of wetlands, and distribution of food to people in need are all charitable purposes. In general, the trust law that applies to private express trusts applies to charitable trusts as well. In several ways, however, charitable trusts are subject to different rules. A charitable trust need not have an ascertainable beneficiary, and instead must have a charitable purpose. If a charitable trust does not have an ascertainable beneficiary, then who can enforce the trust? Traditionally that role falls to the state attorney general, but sometimes others can challenge the trustee of a charitable trust. Another difference is that the Rule Against Perpetuities does not apply to charitable trusts. Because a charitable trust can, in theory, last forever, the law developed special modification rules called "*cy pres*" and "deviation."

Although charitable trusts must be organized for a charitable purpose and need not have an ascertainable beneficiary, some charitable trusts do name specific beneficiaries that are consistent with a charitable purpose. For example, a trust to pay all of the income to State University in perpetuity would be a valid charitable trust because of its educational purpose, regardless of the fact that it also has a named beneficiary.

1. Charitable Purpose

The Uniform Trust Code defines charitable purpose as "the relief of poverty, the advancement of education or religion, the promotion of health, governmental or municipal purposes, or other purposes the achievement of which is beneficial to the community." UTC § 405(a). This statement tracks the common law definition and aligns the UTC with the common law.

In general, a charitable purpose must benefit the public and not specific individuals, although a charitable trust can make distributions to a few people, as long as they are chosen from a sufficiently large and indefinite class. For example, a charitable trust might provide one scholarship each year, as long as the pool of potential recipients is large and not defined in some way that related to the settlor. A settlor could create a charitable trust to provide a college scholarship to one graduate of South City High School who was interested in studying music. A settlor could not, however, create a charitable trust to grant scholarships to the settlor's nieces and nephews. The settlor could create a private trust for scholarships to family members, but that trust would be a private express trust and not a charitable trust.

Although "beneficial to the community" sounds like it could cover a lot of activities, courts have construed the phrase narrowly. The phrase has permitted the development of new ways to benefit the public—environmental protection is now a charitable purpose—but it does not convert merely benevolent purposes into charitable ones. A direction to provide a small sum of money to elementary school children on the last day of school is a benevolent purpose but not a charitable one. See Shenandoah Valley National Bank v. Taylor, 63 S.E. 2d 786 (Va. 1951).

2. Modification of Charitable Trusts

A charitable trust is not subject to the Rule Against Perpetuities and can last a long time. As the trust is administered, difficulties may develop due to restrictions imposed by the settlor when the trust was created. Sometimes problems develop in just a few years, and sometimes problems appear after decades of successful administration. The law developed two doctrines, *cy pres* and deviation, that permit a court to modify restrictions on the administration or purposes of a charitable trust. Each of these doctrines requires court approval. A trustee faced with a restriction that impairs the management of the trust can ask a court for a modification. The court will have to decide whether either of the doctrines permit a modification under the circumstances affecting the trust, and if the court modifies the restriction, the court will do so in keeping with the settlor's purposes for the trust.

Cy Pres

A settlor may create a charitable trust for a specific purpose and over time the purpose may become difficult to carry out. For example, a trust might provide for scholarships for mandolin students at a particular music school, and then years later the school might have no students interested in learning to play the mandolin or the school might close. If the terms of a trust do not provide for what should happen when changed circumstances affect a purpose restriction, *cy pres* permits a court to modify the restriction under certain circumstances. The term *cy pres* is short for the phrase *cy pres comme possible*, meaning "as near as possible." If the original purpose of a charitable trust may not be able to be accomplished according to its exact terms, a court may modify the restriction, but should do so in a way that is as close as possible to the settlor's original intent.

Historically, under the common law, a court had to find that a restriction had become illegal, impossible, or impracticable and that the settlor had a "general charitable intent" in order to apply *cy pres*. See Restatement (Second) of Trusts § 399 (1959). Courts applied *cy pres* strictly, interpreting "impracticable" to be nearly impossible. To make modification a little easier to obtain, UTC § 413 adds the term "wasteful." Courts' approval will still be necessary for a *cy pres* modification, and courts will have to interpret "wasteful," but the addition of the term may make modification more likely where a change would preserve assets for charitable purposes.

The requirement that a court find general charitable intent added time and expense to a *cy pres* proceeding. If a court did not find a general charitable intent, the property reverted to the settlor or the settlor's estate, so family members who might inherit had incentive to challenge an attempt to modify a charitable purpose. The doctrine assumed that if the settlor had general charitable intent, the settlor would want the restriction modified so that the trust could be used for another related charitable purpose. Because courts typically found general charitable intent, UTC § 413 removes the requirement of a finding of general charitable intent so that the issue does not need to be litigated.

Deviation

The doctrine of deviation is used to modify an administration restriction, in contrast with a purpose restriction, which would require *cy pres*. Deviation is sometimes referred to as "administrative deviation" or "equitable deviation." An administrative restriction relates to how the trust is managed or how the purpose is carried out. For example, a restriction on how property can be invested might be subject to modification through deviation. Deviation is said to further the settlor's intent, because a court uses the doctrine to modify a restriction that is impairing the accomplishment of the charitable purpose. Of course, sometimes the line between a purpose restriction and an administration restriction is fuzzy. In In re the Estate of Beryl Buck, No. 23259 (Cal. Super. Ct., Marin Cty., Aug. 15, 1986), a trust's geographical restriction on where distributions could be made was considered part of the purpose of the trust and could not be changed. In contrast, in In re Barnes Foundation, No. 58,788, 2004 Pa. Dist. & Cty. Dec. LEXIS 344, 2004 WL 2903655, a restriction that the art held in a charitable trust never leave the building constructed to house it was considered an administrative provision, subject to deviation.

The UTC provision on deviation, UTC § 412, applies to private trusts as well as to charitable trusts. Section 412 permits modification of both administrative and dispositive (purpose) terms, "if, because of circumstances not anticipated by the settlor, modification or termination will further the purposes of the trust." Chapter 11 discusses UTC § 412 in connection with private trusts.

3. Enforcement of Charitable Trusts

A private trust must have a beneficiary, because someone must be able to enforce the trust. If the trustee commits a breach of trust by engaging in self-dealing or violating the terms of the trust, the beneficiary has standing to bring a lawsuit against the trustee. A charitable trust has a charitable purpose but usually does not have an identifiable beneficiary. Who has standing to enforce the trust?

Attorney General

The state attorney general always has standing to take an action involving a charitable trust, but the attorney general may choose not to act, either because the attorney general determines that no action is warranted or because the office does not have sufficient resources to pursue the problem. Politics can play a role in these decisions. And note that while we describe the "attorney general" as having this power, the power could be held by another state regulator assigned to supervise charities.

Donor

In most situations only the attorney general has standing to enforce a charitable trust, but under some circumstances a donor—the settlor of a charitable trust—may be granted standing. When a donor makes a gift to a charity, the donor expects the charity to carry out the donor's intent with respect to the gift, based either on a specific restriction imposed by the donor or the assumption that the charity will continue the activities that caused the donor to contribute. If the charity uses the gift for some other purpose, the donor may be upset. Historically, the donor has not had standing to enforce the restriction and only the attorney general could do so. In most cases the answer is still that only the attorney general has standing. UTC § 405(c) now gives the settlor of a charitable trust standing to enforce the trust, but the UTC limits standing to a "settlor," so descendants would not have rights under this provision. This provision has not been extended to charities organized as nonprofit corporations. See Hardt v. Vitae Foundation, 302 S.W.3d 133 (Mo. App. 2009). A New York case, Smithers v. St. Luke's Roosevelt Hosp. Ctr., 723 N.Y.S.2d 426 (N.Y. App. Div. 2001), granted standing to the personal representative of a donor's estate, but that case has not been followed elsewhere. Some donors now include a standing provision in their gift agreements with charities, but the application of those provisions remains uncertain. A settlor may also have standing under the special interests doctrine, described next.

Special Interests Doctrine

Although beneficiaries of a charitable trust generally do not have standing as beneficiaries, courts have occasionally permitted identifiable beneficiaries to sue a charity by finding that the persons have a "special interest" in the charity. The plaintiffs must have a specific interest that will be directly affected by the charity's failure to carry out its purpose or by a breach of fiduciary duties. The persons with a special interest must be members of an identifiable class of beneficiaries of the charity and not merely members of the general public who are concerned that the charity be run properly. Courts have been willing to let such beneficiaries sue the charity to protect the "special interest" in a manner analogous to a suit by a beneficiary of a private trust, but the remedy sought must be a benefit to the charity itself and not money damages for the plaintiffs. See Restatement (Third) of Trusts § 94, cmt. g.

Chapter Summary

- A trust is a relationship created when a settlor assigns legal title in property to a trustee and beneficial title in that property to a beneficiary.
- A trust must have a valid purpose, one that is not illegal or against public policy.
- Any amount or type of property can be held in trust, but some amount of property is necessary to have a valid trust.

- A trustee has serious fiduciary duties, and the settlor should choose a trustee with care. Sometimes a family member is an appropriate trustee, and sometimes a corporate trustee will bring needed professional expertise.
- The settlor's intent to create a trust can be shown using any documents executed by the settlor as well as the circumstances surrounding the settlor and the property. Unlike a will, extrinsic evidence is permitted to understand the terms of the trust.
- Although a settlor can declare that the settlor holds property as trustee, a court will usually not save a gift that fails for lack of delivery by finding a trust. A promise to make a gift in the future or at death does not create a trust, and an outright transfer with precatory language concerning the use of the property does not create a trust.
- A trust must have an identifiable beneficiary unless it is a charitable trust, a trust for a purpose, or an animal trust. A court may recognize an honorary trust and permit the intended trustee to carry out the terms of a trust despite the lack of beneficiary.
- A trust for a pet will be enforceable by someone named in the trust instrument or by the court.
- No formalities of writing or execution apply to a trust, but an oral trust will be difficult to prove and cannot be used for real property.
- A revocable trust is used for incapacity planning as well as probate avoidance.
- A charitable trust must have a purpose that is charitable and not merely benevolent.
- A trustee can ask a court to use the doctrines of *cy pres* and deviation to modify a charitable trust.
- In most situations, only the Attorney General can enforce a charitable trust.

Applying the Concepts

1. William gives his sister, Elise, a check for $15,000 and asks her to keep the money for her daughter's college education. Elise puts the check in a separate bank account in her own name and leaves it there. After Elise's daughter graduates from college, the money (plus interest) is still in the bank. What should Elise do with the money?

2. Mustafa writes a letter to his cousin, Salome, that says, "I know you love the painting by our grandmother and I want you to have it after you finish school. I will keep it for you until then, but you should consider it yours." What is the effect of this letter?

3. Jackie's will contains the following provision: "I give all of my books to my neighbor, Garth, to distribute among my friends." Garth tells you that he and Jackie were in a book club with a group of ten people.

   a. Can Garth distribute the books among members of the book club?
   b. Can Garth keep all of the books himself?

4. Tiya owns a farm that has been in her family for three generations. Her daughter, Francine, has been farming the property with Tiya. Tiya's will says "I give the family farm to Francine because I know that she will keep it in the family." After Tiya dies, a real estate developer offers Francine a significant amount of money for the farm, which is just outside a rapidly growing city. Tiya wants to sell the farm, but her brother says she cannot. Can Tiya sell the farm?

5. Violet executes a revocable trust and a pour-over will that transfers all probate property into the revocable trust. Violet serves as trustee of the trust. The trust directs that on her death all her property should be distributed to her son, Darryl. She also has a daughter, Deanna, who receives nothing under the trust. When she dies, Darryl tells you that Schedule A, attached to the trust, lists "all my tangible personal property" and "my bank account at the Trustworthy Bank" as being in the trust. At her death, Violet has in her own name a house, a bank account at Trustworthy Bank, and an investment account with Vanguard.

   a. Must Darryl open a probate estate?
   b. As an intestate heir, can Deanna take a share of the property that was not transferred into the trust before Violet's death?
   c. Does the bank account go through probate?
   d. Can Darryl be the successor trustee of the trust if he is also the primary beneficiary after Violet's death? What if he is the sole beneficiary?

6. Wiley's will includes the following provision: "I give the sum of $10,000 to my friend, Donna, to hold for the benefit of my cat, Lucy. As long as Lucy lives, I direct Donna to provide Lucy with a safe place to live, plenty of food, and medical attention as needed. Donna may use the $10,000 for these purposes, in her sole discretion. When Lucy dies, Donna shall transfer any remaining money to the Humane Society."

   a. Does the gift to Donna create a trust? If not, what happens to the $10,000?
   b. What happens if Lucy lives with Donna but Donna does not take Lucy to the vet or provide basic medical attention for Lucy?
   c. What happens if Wiley's son learns that Donna plans to take Lucy to a shelter and pocket the $10,000?

7. Anthony creates a trust to protect polar bear habitat and names his friend Jill trustee.

   a. If Anthony discovers that Jill has been using some of the trust funds for llama habitat, what can he do?
   b. If Anthony dies and his son encourages Jill to use the trust funds for grizzly bear habitat, can she do so?
   c. If polar bears no longer live in the wild and live only in zoos, what should Jill do with the trust assets?

Trusts and Estates in Practice

1. Has the state in which you are going to law school adopted the UTC? If not, are there other statutory rules for trusts? What are they?

2. Do the statutes in the state in which you are going to law school provide for trusts for animals (which may be called pet trusts or animal trusts)?

3. A new client, Ruth, wants to create a trust to provide for her nieces and nephews. She needs advice on whom to designate as trustee. Ruth has two siblings, the parents of these nieces and nephews, and wonders whether she should appoint one of them as trustee or whether she should name a local bank as trustee. Ruth's sister, Bianca, is a full-time homemaker, caring for her spouse and three young children. Her spouse is an elementary school teacher. Ruth's brother, Mick, is an investment banker. Mick's spouse is a lawyer, and they have two young children. Advise Ruth. What are the advantages and disadvantages of naming Bianca, Mick, or the local bank as trustee?

4. Leonard has never accepted the fact that his child, Joel, is gay. His will includes a trust for Joel that directs the trustee to make distributions to Joel after Joel marries a woman. The trustee is directed to make a distribution to Joel each year he is married to a woman, and if any property remains in the trust at Joel's death to distribute the property to Leonard's college alma mater. After Leonard's death, his daughter, who was named as trustee of this trust, asks for your advice. Joel is married to a man and has no intention of marrying a woman. What should the trustee do with the property?

5. Draft a provision for inclusion in a will that would give the testator's tangible personal property to Arlo and Benita, with precatory language asking that they distribute the property among the testator's nieces and nephews.

6. Clive is 70 years old and is unmarried. Although Clive is in good health, he worries about the possibility of dementia, having seen his mother suffer for many years. Clive has two children. Mary lives nearby and helps Clive with chores around the house. Robert lives in another state, in a condo Clive owns. Clive worries about Robert because he has had problems with drug abuse in the past, although he is sober now. Clive has been able to keep Robert's problems private because Robert lives far away. Clive was a local television weather reporter until he retired, and he is a bit of a local celebrity. Clive has the following assets: the house Clive lives in, the condo Robert lives in, a bank account held in joint tenancy with Mary, and an investment account that names Mary and Robert as transfer-on-death beneficiaries.

    Explain to Clive whether you recommend a revocable trust or a will. Draft a letter to Clive (a lay person) explaining the advantages and disadvantages of using a revocable trust or a will in his situation.

7. Nate has three dogs, four cats, a turtle, and no spouse or children. He has plenty of money to provide for the animals after his death, but wonders about the best

way to do that. His best friend, Jamaal, loves animals and would provide a good home for the animals if asked. After providing for the animals and making a few gifts to friends, Nate will give the rest of his property to the University of Southern North Dakota at Hoople School of Law to fund a professorship in animal law. Advise Nate.

8. Adele would like to provide college scholarships to students attending the high school she attended. She wants to create her own trust to provide for the scholarships. How should you draft the trust? What additional information would you need from Adele?

9. Take a look at Exhibit 9.5, the Steven Hess Trust. Identify the elements of the trust: purpose, settlor, trustee, intent to create a trust, property, beneficiaries. What happens to the property while Steven Hess is alive? What happens if Steven develops dementia? What happens to the property when Steven dies?

EXHIBIT 9.5   **Revocable Trust**

Note: Do not use this document as a trust form. It was developed as a teaching tool, and some provisions normally included in a trust of this sort were deleted.

DECLARATION OF TRUST

I, Steven Hess, of Springfield, State of Bliss, as Settlor, declare myself Trustee of the property described in Schedule A attached hereto, and I hereby declare that I and my successors as Trustees shall hold and administer all such property and all other property at any time or times transferred (including any property transferred by reason of my death) to the Trustees, and the proceeds of all such property and all investments and reinvestments thereof (sometimes hereinafter called the "Trust Estate"), in trust, as follows:

ARTICLE I

NAME OF TRUST

This trust may be called the STEVEN HESS TRUST.

ARTICLE II

FAMILY

I am married to Julia Hess. We are the parents of Nina Hess, born January 2, 1978, and Ophelia Hess, born March 20, 1980. The provisions of this trust for the benefit of my children shall include those listed above, as well as any other child or children of mine born or adopted hereafter either before or after my death.

ARTICLE III

REVOCATION AND AMENDMENT

A. **Revocation/Withdrawals.** I reserve the right by written instrument signed by me as Trustor and filed with my Trustee to revoke this Declaration of Trust at any time or to withdraw from the trust estate, discharged of the trust, all or any part of the principal and accumulated income of the trust upon satisfying all sums due to my Trustee and indemnifying my Trustee to my Trustee's reasonable satisfaction against liabilities lawfully incurred in the administration of this trust.

B. **Amendment.** I reserve the right to alter or amend this Declaration of Trust at any time, by written instrument signed by me as Trustor and accepted by my Trustee.

C. **Rights Personal to Me.** The rights of revocation, withdrawal, alteration, and amendment reserved by me must be exercised by me personally and may not be exercised by any other person, including any agent, guardian, or conservator, or other person, except that amendment, withdrawal, or revocation may be authorized, after notice to the Trustee, by the court that appointed the conservator or by an agent acting under a durable power of attorney that specifically authorizes such action.

ARTICLE IV

DISPOSITION OF INCOME AND PRINCIPAL DURING MY LIFETIME

During my lifetime, the trust shall be administered and distributed as follows:

A. **Distributions.** My Trustee shall distribute to or for my benefit such portions of the income and principal of the trust as I may from time to time request in writing.

B. **Incapacity.** If I become incapacitated to the extent that I am unable to manage my business affairs, my Trustee shall distribute to or for my benefit income and principal in amounts determined by my Trustee to be necessary for my health (including but not limited to medical, dental, hospital, and nursing expenses), education, maintenance, or support to enable me to maintain the standard of living to which I am accustomed and in addition shall distribute to or for the benefit of my spouse such amounts of income and principal as my Trustee shall determine to be necessary for the health (including but not limited to medical, dental, hospital and nursing expenses), education, maintenance or support of my spouse to enable my spouse to maintain the standard of living to which my spouse is accustomed, and for the health, education, maintenance, or support of any my children who are under the age of majority.

ARTICLE V

SPECIFIC DISTRIBUTIONS FROM TRUST

A. **To Spouse, if Surviving.** After my death, if included as property of this trust, my Trustee shall distribute to my spouse, if my spouse survives me, all of my interest in all household furniture and furnishings, books, apparel, art objects, collections, jewelry and similar personal effects, sporting and recreational equipment; all other tangible property for personal use; all other like contents of my home and any vacation properties that I may own or reside in on the date of my death; animals; any motor vehicles that I may own on the date of my death; and any unexpired insurance on all such property.

B. **Otherwise, to Children.** If my spouse does not survive me, my Trustee shall distribute the property described above to my children who survive me, to be divided among themselves in such manner as they may determine and in as equal shares as may be practicable, taking into account my wishes as expressed to them during my lifetime or in any written memorandum that I may execute during my lifetime. Any such memorandum shall not create a trust or other obligation.

ARTICLE VI

DISTRIBUTION OF RESIDUE OF TRUST ESTATE

My Trustee shall distribute the residue of the trust estate to my spouse, if my spouse survives me, and if my spouse does not survive me, to my descendants who survive me, by right of representation.

ARTICLE VII

CONTINGENT BENEFICIARIES

If in any circumstances not provided for in this instrument there is any portion of the trust for which there is no named or described beneficiary, the portion shall be distributed to the Law Students Public Interest Fund of the State University Law School.

ARTICLE VIII

TRUSTEE PROVISIONS

A. **Successor Trustees.** In the event that I am unable or unwilling to continue to serve as Trustee for this trust or any trust created hereunder, my brother, Thomas Hess, shall serve as Trustee. If my brother is unable or unwilling to serve, or to continue to serve, Riverview Bank shall serve as Trustee.

B. **Resignation of Trustee.** A Trustee may resign at any time without court approval by giving written notice to the successor Trustee, or if there is no successor, to the beneficiaries, to their legal Guardians, or to the persons having the care or custody of minor beneficiaries.

C. **Removal of Settlor as Trustee.** Whenever Thomas Hess believes that I am incapable because of physical or mental disability, or for any other reason, of giving prompt and intelligent consideration to business matters, he shall have the right, by an instrument in writing, to remove me as Trustee.

D. **Responsibility of Successor.** A successor Trustee shall have the same rights, titles, powers, duties, discretions, and immunities and otherwise be in the same position as if the successor Trustee had been originally named as Trustee hereunder. No successor Trustee shall be personally liable for any act or failure to act of any predecessor Trustee or shall have any duty to examine the records of any predecessor Trustee. A successor Trustee may accept the account rendered and the property delivered to the successor Trustee by or on behalf of the predecessor Trustee as a full and complete discharge of the predecessor Trustee without incurring any liability or responsibility for so doing.

ARTICLE IX

MISCELLANEOUS PROVISIONS

A. **Distributions to Minors and Others.** If any beneficiary of the trust who is entitled to distributions of income or principal is incapacitated or under the age of majority, my Trustee may make distributions to which the beneficiary is entitled directly to the beneficiary, to a Guardian or Conservator of the beneficiary, to a Custodian for the benefit of a minor beneficiary, or to any person who or corporation that shall be furnishing health, education, maintenance, or support to the beneficiary. The receipt of any person to whom distributions are made as herein authorized shall be a sufficient voucher for the Trustee, and the recipient need not be required to account to my Trustee.

B. **Undistributed Income.** Unless otherwise provided in this will, income accrued, accumulated, or undistributed upon the termination of any interest under any trust shall pass to the beneficiary entitled to the next eventual interest. Any income that is not distributable shall be accumulated, added to, and thereafter administered as a part of the principal of the trust.

C. **Election to Defer Distribution.** A beneficiary may elect not to receive distribution of a share of a trust otherwise distributable to the beneficiary. In that event, my Trustee shall retain the distributable share in a separate trust. The separate trust shall be administered and distributed to or for the benefit of the beneficiary in accordance with the provisions of the trust established for that beneficiary, which by this reference are incorporated herein, and thereafter shall be subject to withdrawal by the beneficiary at any time.

D. **Spendthrift Protection.** No beneficiary shall have any power to sell, assign, transfer, encumber, or in any other manner anticipate or dispose of his or her interest in the trust or the income produced thereby prior to its actual distribution by my Trustee to said beneficiary or to another for the benefit of the beneficiary in the manner authorized by this Declaration of Trust. No beneficiary shall have any assignable interest in any trust created under this Agreement or in the income therefrom. Neither the principal nor the income shall be liable for the debts of any beneficiary. The limitations herein shall not restrict the exercise of any power of appointment or the right to disclaim.

E. **Rule Against Perpetuities.** Unless sooner terminated or vested in accordance with other provisions of this instrument, all interests not otherwise vested, including but not limited to all trusts and powers of appointment created hereunder, shall terminate twenty-one (21) years after the death of the last survivor of my spouse and my lineal descendants living on the date of my death, at the end of which time distribution of all principal and all accrued, accumulated, and undistributed income shall be made to the persons then entitled to distributions of income and in the manner and proportions herein stated (or, if not stated, equally), irrespective of their then-attained ages.

Executed this _____ day of _____, _____.

_____
Settlor/Trustee

Steven Hess Trust

SCHEDULE A

All of my tangible personal property
My bank account in the Worthy Bank, Springfield, State of Bliss
My investment account, #456890, at Oak Investment Company

10

Rights of Beneficiaries and Creditors in Trust Property

A trust beneficiary's rights depend on the terms of the trust. The terms of the trust delineate the beneficiary's rights to distributions of income and principal from the trust.

In making distributions of income or principal from a trust, the trustee is bound by the settlor's instructions and by a reasonableness or good-faith standard. A settlor can use different types of distribution provisions to guide the trustee, and legal rules help the trustee determine how to apply those distribution provisions and the scope of information to consider in making decisions to distribute income or principal.

Creditors may have claims to assets in a trust. Claims of a settlor's creditors depend on the circumstances of the trust's creation and the interests the settlor has retained in the trust. Claims of a beneficiary's creditors depend on the beneficiary's interests in the trust and on protections against creditors the settlor may have included in the trust instrument.

A challenge for the lawyer drafting the trust instrument is to provide enough direction so that the trustee knows what the settlor wants, yet give the trustee enough flexibility to make good judgments about when, to whom, and in what amounts to make distributions.

This chapter explains the different types of distribution provisions in trusts. These provisions provide guidance to trustees and delineate the rights of beneficiaries. We will examine how the trustees exercise the discretion

Key Concepts

- ■ The common standards of trust distribution and how courts interpret them
- ■ Duties of the trustee in making distributions from a trust
- ■ Ability of a beneficiary to challenge a trustee's decisions to make or not to make distributions
- ■ A trustee's underlying duty to act reasonably and in good faith
- ■ Obligations of a trustee in making distribution decisions
- ■ Rights of a settlor's creditors to property in a trust
- ■ Rights of a beneficiary's creditors to property in a trust
- ■ Planning to protect assets in a trust

325

over distributions, including the scope of the information they should consider. Because creditors of the settlor or of beneficiaries may be able to reach assets in or distributions from a trust, we look at the rights of creditors of the settlor and the beneficiaries. We also consider what settlors aided by estate-planning lawyers can do to limit the ability of creditors to get assets in a trust.

A. COMMON STANDARDS OF TRUST DISTRIBUTION

The beneficiaries' rights to distributions from a trust depend on the terms of the trust as set forth in the trust instrument, and the trustees' discretion follows from those provisions. The distribution provisions may be drafted in many different ways. The distribution provisions may be mandatory or discretionary. We will look at some of the standards commonly used in these distribution provisions and explore some difficulties that can arise in interpreting these standards.

1. Mandatory and Discretionary Distribution Provisions

Mandatory distribution provisions direct the trustee to pay *something* to a beneficiary. The trustee cannot exercise discretion as to the amount or the timing. For example:

> "I give these assets to Trevor, in trust, to pay the income to Samson for life annually and on Samson's death to pay the corpus to Delilah."

> Pursuant to this provision, Trevor must pay Samson all of the trust's income once per year (the trustee can decide on which date). When Samson dies, Trevor must transfer the remaining property to Delilah.

Note that a termination provision will usually be mandatory. That is, the terms of the trust will direct the trustee how to distribute the property when the trust terminates.

Discretionary provisions allow the trustee to exercise judgment in deciding what and how much to distribute, when to distribute, or to whom to distribute (or all of these). The trust instrument will usually provide guidance for the trustee. Discretionary standards can be narrow or broad, specific or general. A discretionary provision might provide:

> "I give these assets to Megan in trust, to distribute so much or all of the income and principal to one or more of my children as the trustee, in the trustee's discretion, determines is necessary for their health and education."

In this example, Megan must decide whether to distribute any principal to any of the children and, if so, to which children. The trustee must determine whether the children have health and education needs and, if they do, which expenses to pay. Megan's discretionary authority is not absolute and must meet the standard provided in the trust: distributions may be made only for the children's health and education and cannot be made for other reasons.

If the beneficiary thinks the trustee is not making distributions called for by the trust, the beneficiary can contact the trustee and urge the trustee to make the distributions the beneficiary thinks the beneficiary is entitled to receive. If the trustee refuses, the beneficiary can institute legal action to try to force a distribution.

Example of Trust with Both Mandatory and Discretionary Provisions

"I give these assets to Debra in trust, to pay all of the income at least quarterly to my children, in equal shares, and to distribute so much of the principal to one or more of my children as the trustee, in the trustee's discretion, determines is necessary for their health and education. When I have no living child under the age of 30 years, the trust shall terminate and the property be distributed to my descendants, per stirpes."

In this example, before the last child reaches age 30, the trustee must pay all the income to the children in equal shares (a mandatory provision) and must decide whether to distribute any principal to any of the children and, if so, to which children (discretionary). In order to exercise the discretion, the trustee must determine whether the children have health and education needs and, if they do, which expenses to pay; the discretion is limited to those purposes and not for other reasons. When the last child reaches age 30 (or dies), the trustee must distribute any remaining income and principal to the settlor's descendants, per stirpes (mandatory).

2. Support and Maintenance

If the distribution standard is limited to "support and maintenance," courts view this as an **ascertainable standard**. The court will start by looking at the beneficiary's basic needs, but "support and maintenance" goes beyond adequate food and housing. Courts typically look to the amount of property the settlor placed in the trust, the relationship between the settlor and the beneficiary, and the settlor's intent as expressed in the document. Unless there is a direction in the trust instrument that leads a court to find otherwise, the terms will usually be interpreted to imply the beneficiary's accustomed standard of living. *See* Restatement (Third) of Trusts § 50, cmt. (d)(3) (2003).

Ascertainable and Nonascertainable

Tax law uses these terms to identify when a trustee or a holder of a power of appointment (discussed in Chapter 12) who may distribute or appoint trust property to herself has a level of discretion so great that the apparent restriction in the standards is illusory.

An ascertainable standard, such as for health, education, maintenance, or support (HEMS), limits the trustee or powerholder's discretion. The standard is an objective one that a beneficiary can ask a court to enforce.

By contrast, a nonascertainable standard, like welfare and best interests, gives the trustee or powerholder nearly unlimited discretion. For that reason, tax law treats the trustee or powerholder of a nonascertainable standard exercisable for herself as being equivalent to the owner of the property.

Besides tax law, the significance of a standard being ascertainable or nonascertainable goes to the extent of the trustee's discretion and the degree to which a court will review the trustee's exercise of the discretion, as we discuss later.

Example of Trust with Distribution Standard for Support and Maintenance

"I give these assets to Edgar in trust, to distribute so much or all of the principal as the trustee shall determine to be necessary for the support and maintenance of my spouse."

In this example, the trustee must decide how much to distribute to the spouse from principal. The spouse may have a different view of amounts necessary for support than the trustee will have. Cases and the Restatement provide guidance on *how* the trustee should exercise this discretion.

The settlor could provide more guidance by saying, "I give these assets to Edgar in trust, to distribute so much or all of the principal as the trustee shall determine to be necessary for the support and maintenance of my spouse, to maintain my spouse in the standard of living we shared when I was alive."

3. Education

A standard that directs payments for education clearly covers college tuition. The term generally encompasses technical training as well as college or graduate education, depending on other evidence of the settlor's intent in the document. Ordinarily, it also includes room and board, books, fees, and other costs. See Restatement (Third) of Trusts § 50, cmt. (d)(3) (2003). Absent clear statements in the trust to the contrary, other costs for education, such as for private primary school, study abroad programs, and music lessons or sports instruction, are less likely to be viewed as within the term education.

If the settlor intends to limit or expand distributions for education in some way, that information can be stated in the trust instrument to avoid possible disagreements between the trustee and the beneficiary. However, the more specific the instructions to a trustee, the less flexibility the trustee will have. A direction to "pay the college tuition for each of my grandchildren" sounds clear, but what if the settlor has eight grandchildren and the first to attend college goes to a private school with high tuition? The trustee must consider the interests of all the beneficiaries (the duty of impartiality discussed in Chapter 11), but the grandchild heading off to college may expect the trustee to pay the entire tuition bill. The trustee's decision will be guided by additional factors, discussed in Section B.

4. Emergency

Emergency is considered a restrictive standard, one that is interpreted objectively to mean something most people would consider an emergency, rather than subjectively, or what the beneficiary might consider to be a personal emergency. The terms of the trust can, but normally do not, provide guidance as to the type of emergency covered, so the determination of what constitutes an emergency is usually left to the trustee's discretion, subject to court review.

As is generally true with respect to a trustee's exercise of discretionary powers (see discussion in Section B), courts tend to defer to the trustee's determination of whether an emergency has occurred and will define emergency narrowly when deciding whether the trustee acted unreasonably in not making a distribution.

Emergency—Trustee's Decision Not to Distribute Upheld

In In re Tone's Estates, 39 N.W.2d 401 (Iowa 1949), the beneficiary sought to force the trustee to make a distribution for legal expenses and attorney's fees incurred by the beneficiary and her husband to defend themselves against a civil assault claim, claiming this was an "unforeseen emergency."

The terms of the trust provided: "If at any time or times, on account of serious illness or other unforeseen emergency, any beneficiary [requires distribution of income of principal, the trustee is authorized to] expend for such purpose such an amount as in its discretion and judgment, it may think wise, prudent and necessary under the circumstances."

The court construed the provision in the trust, saying that an emergency is "a sudden or unexpected happening which calls for immediate action," and did not require the trustee to make the payment. The court did not think that "unforeseen" added anything.

Emergency—Trustee Should Distribute

In Shelley v. Shelley, 354 P.2d 282 (Or. 1960), a trust instrument directed the trustee "to make disbursements for the use and benefit of my son, Grant R. Shelley, or his children, in case of any emergency arising whereby unusual and extraordinary expenses are necessary for the proper support and care of my said son, or said children. . . ."

Grant had divorced twice and owed child support to children from both marriages when he disappeared. The children sought distributions from the trust.

The bank trustee argued that their request was for ordinary support and not for "unusual and extraordinary expenses."

The court construed the clause to include the circumstances faced by the children: being abandoned by their father and needing support. The court thought the settlor would have intended to cover this situation.

5. Welfare and Best Interests

Standards like "welfare," "best interests," "happiness," and "for any purpose" are considered nonascertainable for tax and state law purposes. Any of these standards give the trustee broad discretion. A trustee must act reasonably and in good faith, as explained in the next section, but the court gives the trustee significant latitude in the exercise of discretion. A trustee can choose to make or not make distributions for almost any purpose. Beneficiaries will find challenging a distribution under one of these standards difficult.

B. TRUSTEE'S EXERCISE OF DISCRETION

The more discretion the terms of the trust give the trustee, the less likely that the beneficiary will be successful in forcing the trustee, through a court proceeding, to make a particular distribution. Thus, if the standard for making distributions gives the trustee broad discretion (e.g., "the best interests of the beneficiary"), a court will rarely order a trustee to make any particular distribution. Instead, when reviewing a beneficiary's claims, a court will consider whether the trustee acted reasonably and in good faith in getting the information needed to exercise the discretion, considering the settlor's directions with respect to all beneficiaries, and applying the discretionary standard to the particular beneficiary's situation. When the trustee has acted reasonably and in good faith, the court will generally dismiss the claim. Even if the trustee has not done so, a court will generally just direct the trustee to exercise the discretion (gather information and apply the standard to the beneficiary), although the court may also make suggestions about the proper exercise of the discretion.

By contrast, the more precise the standard delineated in the trust, the greater the likelihood that the beneficiary can convince a court that the standard applies to her situation and is not being followed and that the court should require the trustee to make a distribution, even if the court will not dictate the amount of the distribution.

A trustee exercising discretion must keep in mind the fiduciary duties that apply to trustees. We examine these duties in Chapter 11. In general, a trustee must act with **prudence** and care. A trustee must act for the benefit of the beneficiaries and not for any self-interest of the trustee.

The trustee has a duty of impartiality and must treat the beneficiaries fairly and in accordance with the instructions given by the settlor. Thus, in making decisions about distributions, the trustee must consider the directions provided in the trust instrument and usually should get information about the beneficiaries' circumstances and needs. The fiduciary duties of trustees, including duties of **obedience**, **loyalty**, **impartiality**, and **care**, will affect decisions the trustees make about distributions.

A court will review a trustee's exercise of a standard of distribution to determine whether the trustee's exercise was consistent with the standard established by the settlor. Unfortunately, unless a provision is mandatory, predicting precisely how a court will interpret a provision is impossible. The best a lawyer advising a trustee about making distributions or advising beneficiaries about their rights can do is to understand the range of discretion encompassed by the words used in the document and the ways in which a court might intervene.

1. Reasonableness and Good Faith

If the trustee is given discretion in how and when to make distributions, the trustee must consider a variety of facts and circumstances before deciding whether to make a distribution. The trustee cannot simply do nothing. The trustee should act diligently in seeking information about the beneficiaries' needs and resources, unless the trust instrument relieves the trustee of that duty. After gathering the appropriate information, the trustee has the responsibility to determine how much to distribute, if anything, applying the standard of distribution based on the information gathered, the terms of the trust, and the trustee's own view of what the settlor would have wanted.

When a court reviews a trustee's decision to make a distribution or not make a distribution, the court will intervene only to prevent misinterpretation or abuse of the discretion. A court will not impose its own view of how a trustee should exercise discretion. The difficulty, as we will see, is that "abuse of discretion" tends to be one of those "I know it when I see it" concepts. It would be helpful, in advising trustees or beneficiaries, to be able to state what actions are within the trustee's scope of discretion and which are considered an abuse. Unfortunately, the best we can do is to consider examples of how courts have reviewed the exercise of discretion. The determination a court makes will be, necessarily, fact-specific.

In reviewing trustees' exercise of discretion, courts often use "reasonableness" as the standard, while the Uniform Trust Code (UTC) incorporates a "good-faith" standard. The standards are often interpreted to mean the same thing, but they could be applied differently. A court may apply either standard, or both, as it thinks best to protect the beneficiaries. If a trustee acts in bad faith, a court is likely to find a problem with the exercise of discretion, but even if the trustee acts in good faith, the court could find that the trustee did not exercise reasonable judgment.

Examples of Good Faith and Reasonableness

If a trustee has authority to distribute principal among the settlor's grandchildren for their "best interests," and some of the grandchildren are the trustee's children, a decision to distribute only to the trustee's own children may be in bad faith. If one of the trustee's children has serious medical problems, and the discretionary standard is to distribute for "any health emergency," a decision to distribute from the trust to the child with the medical problems could be in good faith.

If a trustee is directed to distribute trust property to the adult child of the settlor for the child's "best interests," the trustee could distribute the entire trust to the child. The trustee might decide to do so in good faith, thinking that the child could handle the money. However, if the child is only nineteen and still in college, a decision to transfer a significant amount of money to the child might not be reasonable.

EXHIBIT 10.1 **UTC § 814(a)**

Notwithstanding the breadth of discretion granted to a trustee in the terms of the trust, including the use of such terms as "absolute," "sole," or "uncontrolled," the trustee shall exercise a discretionary power in good faith and in accordance with the terms and purposes of the trust and the interests of the beneficiaries.

Comment to UTC § 814: Subsection (a) does not otherwise address the obligations of a trustee to make distributions, leaving that issue to the caselaw. . . . [W]hether the trustee has a duty in a given situation to make a distribution depends on the exact language used, whether the standard grants discretion and its breadth, whether this discretion is coupled with a standard, whether the beneficiary has other available resources, and, more broadly, the overriding purposes of the trust. . . .

The obligation of a trustee to act in good faith is a fundamental concept of fiduciary law. . . .

Consistent with this section, even when the settlor gives the trustee "absolute," "unlimited," or "sole and uncontrolled" discretion, a beneficiary can ask a court to review the exercise of discretion, and a court will require the trustee to act reasonably or in good faith.

---

2. Should the Trustee Consider a Beneficiary's Other Assets?

Absent specific direction in the trust, no specific legal rule determines whether a beneficiary's other assets should be a factor in the trustee's decision to make distributions. The Restatement (Third) of Trusts adopts as a default view that a trustee should consider other resources, but the Comment to the section indicates that no clear trend exists. Restatement (Third) of Trusts § 50, cmt. e (2003). Because no clear rule exists, in drafting a trust a lawyer will want to consider adding a direction to the trustee to make distributions either "without regard to any other income or assets of the beneficiary" or "after first taking into consideration any other income or assets of the beneficiary."

3. Duty to Inquire

Related to the question of whether and to what extent to consider the beneficiary's other resources in deciding whether to make distributions, another issue is the scope of the trustee's duty to inquire into the needs of the beneficiary rather than wait for the beneficiary to request distributions. As we see below in *Marsman*, the trustee has a duty to inquire, and the scope of the duty depends on the facts related to the trust. A trustee typically can rely on representations made by a beneficiary as to other available assets, but the trustee can also request the beneficiary to provide readily available information about other financial resources, especially if the trustee believes the beneficiary's representations are inaccurate.

Case Preview

Marsman

This case concerns whether a trustee charged by a trust instrument with making discretionary distributions to a beneficiary has a duty to inquire about the needs of the beneficiary before making decisions about distributions. Cappy was the beneficiary of a trust created for him by his wife, Sara. After Sara's death, Cappy needed money to be able to maintain even a reduced lifestyle, but the trustee discouraged him from requesting funds. Without adequate funds to pay expenses for his house, he transferred ownership of the house to Sara's daughter and the daughter's husband in exchange for their agreement to pay the expenses and let him live there. When Cappy died, his widow, Margaret, whom Cappy had married after Sara's death, argued that distributions from the trust would have enabled him to keep the house and give it to her on his death. The case examines the question of whether the trustee had a duty to inquire into Cappy's needs and raises a number of other issues. The trustee, James Farr, was also the lawyer who drafted the trust for Sara, and as a lawyer represented Sara, Cappy, Sara's daughter, Sally, and Sally's husband, Marlette. The interests of these clients conflicted, and yet the lawyer did not obtain conflict waivers from the clients. In addition, the trust contained an exculpatory clause relieving the trustee from liability for behavior that was not "willful negligence."

As you read the case, consider:

1. What was the standard of distribution? What do you think the settlor wanted the trustee to do?
2. Why do the interests of all of the parties involved raise questions about the trustee's ability to carry out the settlor's wishes?
3. Did the trustee act reasonably?
4. Why was the lawyer who drafted the trust acting as trustee?
5. What was the effect of the exculpatory clause?
6. What did Margaret receive? Why doesn't Sara get to keep the house?

Marsman v. Nasca
30 Mass. App. Ct. 789, 573 N.E.2d 1025 (1991)
rev. den., 411 Mass. 1102, 579 N.E.2d 1361

DEESON, J.

This appeal raises the following questions: Does a trustee, holding a discretionary power to pay principal for the "comfortable support and maintenance" of a beneficiary, have a duty to inquire into the financial resources of that beneficiary so as to recognize his needs? If so, what is the remedy for such failure? A Probate Court judge held that the will involved in this case imposed a duty of inquiry upon the trustee. We agree with this conclusion but disagree with the remedy imposed and accordingly vacate the judgment and remand for further proceedings.

1. FACTS. . . .

Sara Wirt Marsman died in September, 1971, survived by her second husband, T. Frederik Marsman (Cappy), and her daughter by her first marriage, Sally Marsman Marlette. Mr. James F. Farr, her lawyer for many years, drew her will and was the trustee thereunder.

Article IIA of Sara's will provided in relevant part:

> "It is my desire that my husband, T. Fred Marsman, be provided with *reasonable maintenance, comfort and support* after my death. Accordingly, if my said husband is living at the time of my death, I give to my trustees, who shall set the same aside as a separate trust fund, one-third (⅓) of the rest, residue and remainder of my estate ...; they shall pay the net income therefrom to my said husband at least quarterly during his life; and *after having considered the various available sources of support for him,* my trustees shall, if they deem it necessary or desirable from time to time, in their sole and uncontrolled discretion, pay over to him, or use, apply and/or expend for his direct or indirect benefit such amount or amounts of the principal thereof as they shall deem advisable for his *comfortable support and maintenance.*" (Emphasis supplied).

Article IIB provided: "Whatever remains of said separate trust fund, including any accumulated income thereon on the death of my husband, shall be added to the trust fund established under Article IIC. . . ." Article IIC established a trust for the benefit of Sally and her family. Sally was given the right to withdraw principal and, on her death, the trust was to continue for the benefit of her issue and surviving husband.

The will also contained the following exculpatory clause: "No trustee hereunder shall ever be liable except for his own willful neglect or default."

During their marriage, Sara and Cappy lived well and entertained frequently. Cappy's main interest in life centered around horses. An expert horseman, he was riding director and instructor at the Dana Hall School in Wellesley until he was retired due to age in 1972. Sally, who was also a skilled rider, viewed Cappy as her mentor, and each had great affection for the other. Sara, wealthy from her prior marriage, managed the couple's financial affairs. She treated Cappy as "Lord of the Manor" and gave him money for his personal expenses, including an extensive wardrobe from one of the finest men's stores in Wellesley.

In 1956, Sara and Cappy purchased, as tenants by the entirety, the property in Wellesley which is the subject of this litigation. Although title to the property passed to Cappy by operation of law on Sara's death, Sara's will also indicated an intent to convey her interest in the property to Cappy. In the will, Cappy was also given a life estate in the household furnishings with remainder to Sally.

After Sara's death in 1971, Farr met with Cappy and Sally and held what he termed his "usual family conference" going over the provisions of the will. At the time of Sara's death, the Wellesley property was appraised at $29,000, and the principal of Cappy's trust was about $65,600.

Cappy continued to live in the Wellesley house but was forced by Sara's death and his loss of employment in 1972 to reduce his standard of living substantially. He married Margaret in March, 1972, and, shortly before their marriage, asked her to read Sara's will, but they never discussed it. In 1972, Cappy took out a mortgage for $4,000, the proceeds of which were used to pay bills. Farr was aware of the transaction, as he replied to an inquiry of the mortgagee bank concerning the appraised value of the Wellesley property and the income Cappy expected to receive from Sara's trust.

In 1973, Cappy retained Farr in connection with a new will. The latter drew what he described as a simple will which left most of Cappy's property, including the house, to Margaret. The will was executed on November 7, 1973.

In February, 1974, Cappy informed the trustee that business was at a standstill and that he really needed some funds, if possible. Farr replied in a letter in which he set forth the relevant portion of the will and wrote that he thought the language was "broad enough to permit a distribution of principal." Farr enclosed a check of $300. He asked Cappy to explain in writing the need for some support and why the need had arisen. The judge found that Farr, by his actions, discouraged Cappy from making any requests for principal.

Indeed, Cappy did not reduce his request to writing and never again requested principal. Farr made no investigation whatsoever of Cappy's needs or his "available sources of support" from the date of Sara's death until Cappy's admission to a nursing home in 1983 and, other than the $300 payment, made no additional distributions of principal until Cappy entered the nursing home.

By the fall of 1974, Cappy's difficulty in meeting expenses intensified. Several of his checks were returned for insufficient funds, and in October, 1974, in order that he might remain in the house, Sally and he agreed that she would take over the mortgage payments, the real estate taxes, insurance, and major repairs. In return, she would get the house upon Cappy's death.

Cappy and Sally went to Farr to draw up a deed. Farr was the only lawyer involved, and he billed Sally for the work. He wrote to Sally, stating his understanding of the proposed transaction, and asking, among other things, whether Margaret would have a right to live in the house if Cappy should predecease her. The answer was no. No copy of the letter to Sally was sent to Cappy. A deed was executed by Cappy on November 7, 1974, transferring the property to Sally and her husband Richard T. Marlette (Marlette) as tenants by the entirety, reserving a life estate to Cappy. No writing set forth Sally's obligations to Cappy.

The judge found that there was no indication that Cappy did not understand the transaction, although, in response to a request for certain papers by Farr, Cappy sent a collection of irrelevant documents. The judge also found that Cappy clearly understood that he was preserving no rights for Margaret, and that neither Sally nor Richard nor Farr ever made any representation to Margaret that she would be able to stay in the house after Cappy's death.

Although Farr had read Sara's will to Cappy and had written to him that the will was "broad enough to permit a distribution of principal," the judge found that Farr failed to advise Cappy that the principal of his trust could be used for the expenses of the Wellesley home. The parsimonious distribution of $300 and Farr's knowledge that the purpose of the conveyance to Sally was to enable Cappy to remain in the house, provide support for this finding. After executing the deed, Cappy expressed to Farr that he was pleased and most appreciative. Margaret testified that Cappy thought Farr was "great" and that he considered him his lawyer.

Sally and Marlette complied with their obligations under the agreement. Sally died in 1983, and Marlette became the sole owner of the property subject to Cappy's life estate. Although Margaret knew before Cappy's death that she did not have any interest in the Wellesley property, she believed that Sally would have allowed her to live in the house because of their friendship. After Cappy's death in 1987, Marlette inquired as to Margaret's plans, and, subsequently, through Farr, sent Margaret a notice to vacate the premises. Margaret brought this action in the Probate Court.

After a two-day trial, the judge held that the trustee was in breach of his duty to Cappy when he neglected to inquire as to the latter's finances. She concluded that, had Farr fulfilled his fiduciary duties, Cappy would not have conveyed the residence owned by him to Sally and Marlette. The judge ordered Marlette to convey the house to Margaret and also ordered Farr to reimburse Marlette from the remaining portion of Cappy's trust for the expenses paid by him and Sally for the upkeep of the property. If Cappy's trust proved insufficient to make such payments, Farr was to be personally liable for such expenses. Both Farr and Marlette appealed from the judgment, from the denial of their motions to amend the findings, and from their motions for a new trial. Margaret appealed from the denial of her motion for attorney's fees. As indicated earlier, we agree with the judge that Sara's will imposed a duty of inquiry on the trustee, but we disagree with the remedy and, therefore, remand for further proceedings.

2. BREACH OF TRUST BY THE TRUSTEE

Contrary to Farr's contention that it was not incumbent upon him to become familiar with Cappy's finances, Article IIA of Sara's will clearly placed such a duty upon him. In his brief, Farr claims that the will gave Cappy the right to request principal "in extraordinary circumstances" and that the trustee, "was charged by Sara to be wary should Cappy request money beyond that which he quarterly received." Nothing in the will or the record supports this narrow construction. To the contrary, the direction to the trustees was to pay Cappy such amounts "as they shall deem advisable for his comfortable support and maintenance." This language has been interpreted to set an ascertainable standard, namely to maintain the life beneficiary "in accordance with the standard of living which was normal for him before he became a beneficiary of the trust."

Even where the only direction to the trustee is that he shall "in his discretion" pay such portion of the principal as he shall "deem advisable," the discretion is not absolute. "Prudence and reasonableness, not caprice or careless good nature, much less a desire on the part of the trustee to be relieved from trouble . . . furnish the standard of conduct."

That there is a duty of inquiry into the needs of the beneficiary follows from the requirement that the trustee's power "must be exercised with that soundness of judgment which follows from a due appreciation of trust responsibility." . . .

Farr, in our view, did not meet his responsibilities either of inquiry or of distribution under the trust. The conclusion of the trial judge that, had he exercised "sound judgment," he would have made such payments to Cappy "as to allow him to continue to live in the home he had occupied for many years with the settlor" was warranted.

4. REMAINDER OF CAPPY'S TRUST

. . . More than $80,000 remained in the trust for Cappy at the time of his death. As we have indicated, the trial judge properly concluded that payments of principal should have been made to Cappy from that fund in sufficient amount to enable him to keep the Wellesley property. There is no reason for the beneficiaries of the trust under Article IIC to obtain funds which they would not have received had Farr followed the testatrix's direction. The remedy in such circumstances is to impress a constructive trust on the amounts which should have been distributed to Cappy but were not because of the error of the trustee. Even in cases where beneficiaries have already been paid funds by mistake, the amounts may be collected from them unless the recipients were bona fide purchasers or unless they, without notice of the improper payments, had so changed their position that it would be inequitable to make them repay. Here, the remainder of Cappy's trust has not yet been distributed, and there is no reason to depart from the usual rule of impressing a constructive trust in favor of Cappy's estate on the amounts wrongfully withheld. . . .

5. PERSONAL LIABILITY OF THE TRUSTEE

Farr raises a number of defenses against the imposition of personal liability, including the statute of limitations, the exculpatory clause in the will, and the fact that Cappy assented to the accounts of the trustee. The judge found that Farr's breach of his fiduciary duty to inquire as to Cappy's needs and his other actions in response to Cappy's request for principal, including the involvement of Sally in distributions of principal despite Sara's provision that Cappy's trust be administered separately, led Cappy to be unaware of his right to receive principal for house expenses. The breach may also be viewed as a continuing one. In these circumstances we do not consider Cappy's assent. The judge also found that Margaret learned of Cappy's right to principal for house expenses only when she sought other counsel after his death.

The more difficult question is the effect of the exculpatory clause. . . . In view of the judge's finding that, but for the trustee's breach, Cappy would have retained ownership of the house, the liability of the trustee could be considerable.

Although exculpatory clauses are not looked upon with favor and are strictly construed, such "provisions inserted in the trust instrument without any overreaching or abuse by the trustee of any fiduciary or confidential relationship to the settlor are generally held effective except as to breaches of trust 'committed in bad faith or intentionally or with reckless indifference to the interest of the beneficiary.'" The actions of Farr were not of this ilk and also do not fall within the meaning of the term used in the will, "willful neglect or default."

Farr testified that he discussed the exculpatory clause with Sara and that she wanted it included. Nevertheless, the judge, without finding that there was an overreaching or abuse of Farr's fiduciary relation with Sara, held the clause ineffective. Relying on the fact that Farr was Sara's attorney, she stated: "One cannot know at this point in time whether or not Farr specifically called this provision to Sara's attention. Given the total failure of Farr to use his judgment as to [C]appy's needs, it would be unjust and unreasonable to hold him harmless by reason of the exculpatory provisions he himself drafted and inserted in this instrument."

Assuming that the judge disbelieved Farr's testimony that he and Sara discussed the clause, although such disbelief on her part is by no means clear, the conclusion that it "would be unjust and unreasonable to hold [Farr] harmless" is not sufficient to find the overreaching or abuse of a fiduciary relation which is required to hold the provision ineffective. We note that the judge found that Sara managed all the finances of the couple, and from all that appears, was competent in financial matters. . . . No claim was made that the clause was the result of an abuse of confidence.

The fact that the trustee drew the instrument and suggested the insertion of the exculpatory clause does not necessarily make the provision ineffective. No rule of law requires that an exculpatory clause drawn by a prospective trustee be held ineffective unless the client is advised independently.

The judge used an incorrect legal standard in invalidating the clause. While recognizing the sensitivity of such clauses, we hold that, since there was no evidence that the insertion of the clause was an abuse of Farr's fiduciary relationship with Sara at the time of the drawing of her will, the clause is effective.

. . .

The judgment is vacated, and the matter is remanded to the Probate Court for further proceedings to determine the amounts which, if paid, would have enabled Cappy to retain ownership of the residence. Such amounts shall be paid to Cappy's estate from the trust for his benefit prior to distributing the balance thereof to the trust under Article IIC of Sara's will.

So ordered.

Post-Case Follow-Up

The court found that the trustee, Farr, "did not meet his responsibilities either of inquiry or of distribution under the trust." The case was remanded to determine the amounts that Farr should have paid to Cappy. Those amounts would then be distributed to his estate, and ultimately benefit his widow, Margaret. Marlette kept the house, because he and Sally had fulfilled their obligations under the contract with Cappy.

Although the court found that Farr had breached his fiduciary duties, Farr paid no financial penalty for this failure. The trust contained an exculpatory clause providing that the trustee would be liable only for "willful negligence or default." Based in part on concerns about the outcome of this case, UTC § 1008 requires that if a trustee causes an exculpatory clause to be included in a trust instrument and later seeks to benefit from the clause, the trustee must prove that the settlor understood the clause and intended its use.

EXHIBIT 10.2 **UTC § 1008. Exculpation of Trustee**

(a) A term of a trust relieving a trustee of liability for breach is unenforceable to the extent that it:

(1) relieves the trustee of liability for breach of trust committed in bad faith or with reckless indifference to the purposes of the trust or the interests of the beneficiaries; or

(2) was inserted as the result of an abuse by the trustee of a fiduciary or confidential relationship to the settlor.

(b) An exculpatory term drafted or caused to be drafted by the trustee is invalid as an abuse of a fiduciary or confidential relationship unless the trustee proves that the exculpatory term is fair under the circumstances and that its existence and contents were adequately communicated to the settlor.

Marsman: Real Life Applications

1. If a trust provides for discretionary distributions to one or more of three adult children, what information should the trustee request before making a decision on distributions?

2. Based on *Marsman*, would you be willing to serve as trustee of a client's trust? If so, under what circumstances? If not, why not?

3. A trust provides for distributions from the principal for the "comfortable support" of several beneficiaries. The trustee sends a questionnaire each year to these beneficiaries, asking about their financial needs. Is sending the questionnaire and reviewing the responses enough to meet the trustee's duty of inquiry? What if a beneficiary fails to return the questionnaire, or returns it with only partial answers?

---

4. What if the Trustee Is a Beneficiary?

When the trustee is a beneficiary with interests different from those of other beneficiaries, difficulties can arise. The trustee must act in the interests of all the beneficiaries and must treat all beneficiaries equitably, but a trustee/beneficiary can take advantage of that position. In addition, other beneficiaries may assume the worst, even if the trustee/beneficiary is acting appropriately.

Example of a Trust for a Second Spouse

On his death, Daniel creates a trust for his second spouse, Wendy. The trust provides that the trustee should distribute all the income to Wendy and so much of the principal as the trustee determines to be in Wendy's best interests. On Wendy's death, the remaining property will be distributed to Daniel's children from his first marriage. If Wendy is the trustee, she will be managing the trust property for her own benefit. With broad discretion she can make distributions for herself for any purpose, but a court would likely require her to make distributions within the standard of living she had shared with Daniel.

If one of Daniel's children is the trustee, the child may be stingy with distributions from principal because anything left in the trust will eventually go to the three children. Wendy could try to get a court to require the trustee to make distributions, but with a broad standard of discretion, the court is unlikely to second-guess the trustee, unless Wendy can show that the trustee is acting unreasonably or in bad faith.

C. RIGHTS OF CREDITORS

When someone dies, the person may have property and also debts, including credit card debt, liens on property for past-due bills, and reimbursement owed the state government for expenditures made on behalf of the decedent, for example through Medicaid. Creditors typically have many sources from which to satisfy a claim, such as a debtor's checking accounts, wages, and stocks and securities. A trust in which a debtor has an interest as a settlor or beneficiary is certainly another potential source. Creditors frequently do not, however, attempt to attach an interest in a trust because the protections we are about to discuss make doing so difficult.

The effort to shelter assets, especially through the use of trusts, is referred to as **asset protection planning**. The most basic tool for asset protection, a **spendthrift clause**, prevents the beneficiary from selling or pledging any interest in a trust and prevents the beneficiary's creditors from getting access to the interest. Spendthrift clauses are included in almost all trusts created in the United States, at least all those drafted by lawyers.

A creditor has the same rights to property that a debtor has. If the debtor owns property in fee simple, a creditor can take possession of the property itself. Like the rights of beneficiaries, the rights of creditors vary, depending on whether a trust contains mandatory or discretionary distribution clauses. Regardless of the existence of a trust, however, creditors are free to pursue a beneficiary's other assets.

Law on Creditors Not Uniform

The UTC provisions on the rights of creditors, particularly § 504 (which provides that certain creditors may have access to property subject to a discretionary distribution standard), have not been adopted in all the states that have adopted the UTC. In addition, the common law on creditor rights has developed in different ways throughout the states. The result is that you will find significant variation in the rights of creditors to access trust property to satisfy their claims.

1. Creditors of a Beneficiary Who Is Not the Settlor

Mandatory Distributions

A trustee has no discretion over mandatory distributions, and a beneficiary entitled to mandatory distributions can force the trustee to make the distributions. For example, if the terms of the trust require the trustee to "pay income monthly to my spouse and, on her death, to pay the remaining principal to my son, Max," the distributions of income and principal are both mandatory. With respect to mandatory distributions, and absent a spendthrift clause covering such distributions, a creditor *can* get a court order attaching present or future mandatory distributions to or for the benefit of the beneficiary. UTC § 501. The trustee will then pay the creditor directly.

Discretionary Distributions

A creditor is unlikely to be able to reach a beneficiary's interest in distributions that are subject to the trustee's exercise of discretion. As we saw earlier in this chapter, a beneficiary has difficulty getting a court to intervene to force the trustee to make discretionary distributions. A creditor is in an even worse position, because a court will not force a trustee to make a discretionary payment to a creditor. UTC § 504(b) provides that even if the trustee abuses a standard of discretion, the ordinary creditor cannot compel a distribution. The creditor must wait, hope a distribution is made, and then go after the distribution in the hands of the beneficiary.

UTC § 504(c) creates an exception for certain preferred creditors: a child, spouse, or former spouse of the beneficiary with an order for support. If the trustee has not complied with a standard of distribution or has abused the standard, this statutory rule allows the court to direct the trustee to pay the amount that is "equitable under the circumstances." UTC § 504(c) changes the common law and is controversial. Some states that adopted the UTC did not enact § 504(c) or modified it. And many states have not adopted the UTC, so they will not have this provision.

How Does a Creditor Get Paid?

To attach property of an individual for repayment of a debt, the creditor needs first to obtain a judgment. With the judgment in hand, the creditor can have the sheriff place a levy on property owned by the debtor. With respect to trusts, the sheriff can seize whatever property has already been distributed. If the creditor wishes to garnish (seize) an interest of the settlor or a beneficiary that has not yet been distributed, the creditor might seek a court order requiring that money be paid directly to it, thus avoiding the time-consuming, costly, and often futile (if the money is already spent) procedure of garnishing the payments from the debtor after they have been distributed. The creditor is entitled to garnish only interests to which the debtor is entitled.

Existing Creditors of the Settlor

The Uniform Fraudulent Conveyance (or Transfer) Act, adopted in some form by every state, establishes that if someone who is already indebted transfers assets to another for less-than-adequate consideration, the transfer is generally considered in fraud of creditors, regardless of intent to defraud. Consequently, not only does the transferor-debtor remain liable to the creditors but so does the transferee, even if innocent. These rules apply to trusts, which means that a court can order the trustee to turn over the value of the transferred property to the extent of the debt incurred by the settlor. Fraudulent conveyance statutes apply whether or not the settlor is a beneficiary. Thus, property in a trust in which the settlor is not the beneficiary will still be subject to creditors of the settlor for debts incurred before the property was transferred into the trust.

Spendthrift Clauses

The basic rules—that a creditor can attach a mandatory distribution but not a discretionary distribution—apply only if the trust instrument does not include a spendthrift clause. Most trusts do include a spendthrift clause so an understanding of this tool is critical. A spendthrift clause prevents *both* voluntary and involuntary alienation of trust interests by the beneficiary. An effective spendthrift clause adopts a two-pronged approach: it precludes a beneficiary from assigning or selling any interest in a trust, and it prevents a creditor of the beneficiary from attaching the beneficiary's interest. The result is that the creditor must wait until after the payment is made and then attempt to collect from the beneficiary. The Comment to UTC § 506 adds: "The effect of a spendthrift provision is generally to insulate totally a beneficiary's interest until a distribution is made and received by the beneficiary."

EXHIBIT 10.3   **Sample Spendthrift Clause**

> No beneficiary shall have any right to anticipate, sell, assign, mortgage, pledge, or otherwise dispose of or encumber all or any part of any trust estate established for his or her benefit under this agreement. No part of such trust estate, including income, shall be liable for the debts or obligations of any beneficiary or be subject to attachment, garnishment, execution, creditor's bill, or other legal or equitable process.

To prevent a trustee and a beneficiary from collaborating to avoid a creditor by withholding a mandatory distribution of income or principal (including a distribution on termination of the trust to a remainder person), UTC § 506 allows a creditor to reach a mandatory distribution if it has not been made "within a reasonable time after the designated distribution date." In essence, at this point, "payments mandated by the express terms of the trust are in effect being held by the trustee as agent for the beneficiary and should be treated as part of the beneficiary's personal assets." UTC § 506, cmt.

Exceptions to Spendthrift Clauses

Most debtor-creditor relationships are created voluntarily after the creditor has had an opportunity to evaluate the risk of the debtor's nonpayment before extending credit. If these creditors rely on assets held for the debtor in trust, they are stuck with a spendthrift limitation.

However, some creditors' claims do not arise voluntarily and policy exceptions exist for certain family members owed support. A child trying to enforce a court order for child support makes a sympathetic plaintiff, as does a former spouse trying to enforce an order for alimony. The common law of numerous states has created exceptions to the spendthrift rule for these creditors, and now the UTC does as well.

Case Preview

Shelley v. Shelley

At the time of the *Shelley* case, creditors, including former spouses and children, typically could not reach assets held in trust for the debtor if the trust included a spendthrift clause. In *Shelley*, the beneficiary of a trust owed both spousal support and child support. The court was asked to decide whether assets in the trust could be distributed to the children and former spouses. The court had to consider whether a spendthrift clause precluded distributions to any creditor or whether an exception should be created for children and former spouses. The court also had to determine whether the children were entitled to discretionary distributions as beneficiaries of the trust.

As you read the case, consider:

1. Who are the beneficiaries of the trust?
2. What are the distribution standards in the trust?
3. What did the former spouses receive? Why?
4. What did the children receive? Why?
5. What distinctions does the court draw between income and principal of the trust?

Shelley v. Shelley
354 P.2d 282 (Or. 1960)

O'CONNELL, Justice.

. . . The trust involved in this suit was created by Hugh T. Shelley. The pertinent parts of the trust are as follows:

(4) . . . it is my desire, and I direct, that, the United States National Bank of Portland (Oregon), as trustee, shall continue this estate in trust and pay all income derived therefrom to my son, Grant R. Shelley, as long as he lives, said income to be paid to him at intervals not less than three (3) months apart; Provided, Further, That when my son, Grant R. Shelley, arrives at the age of thirty (30) years, my trustee may then, or at any time thereafter, and from time to time, distribute to said son absolutely and as his own all or any part of the principal of said trust fund that it may then or from time to time thereafter deem him capable of successfully investing without the restraints of this trust; Provided, However, That such disbursements of principal of said trust so made to my son after he attains the age of thirty (30) years shall be first approved in writing by either one of my brothers-in-law, that is: Dr. Frank L. Ralston, now of Walla Walla, Washington, or Russell C. Ralston, now of Palo Alto, California, if either of them is then living, but if neither of them is then living, then my trustee is authorized to make said disbursements of principal to my son in the exercise of its sole and absolute judgment and discretion; Provided, Further, That, said trust shall continue as to all or any part of the undistributed portion of the principal thereof to and until the death of my said son.

(5) I further direct and authorize my trustee, from time to time (but only upon the written approval of my said wife if she be then living, otherwise in the exercise of my trustee's sole discretion) to make disbursements for the use and benefit of my son, Grant R. Shelley, or his children, in case of any emergency arising whereby unusual and extraordinary expenses are necessary for the proper support and care of my said son, or said children. . . .

(8) Each beneficiary hereunder is hereby restrained from alienating, anticipating, encumbering, or in any manner assigning his or her interest or estate, either in principal or income, and is without power so to do, nor shall such interest or estate be subject to his or her liabilities or obligations nor to judgment or other legal process, bankruptcy proceedings or claims of creditors or others.

The principal question on appeal is whether the income and corpus of the Shelley trust can be reached by Grant Shelley's former wives and his children.

Grant Shelley was first married to [] Patricia C. Shelley. Two children were born of this marriage. Patricia divorced Grant in 1951. The decree required Grant to pay support money for the children; the decree did not call for the payment of alimony. Thereafter, Grant married the plaintiff, Betty Shelley. Two children were born of this marriage. The plaintiff obtained a divorce from Grant in August, 1958. The decree in this latter suit required the payment of both alimony and a designated monthly amount for the support of the children of that marriage.

Some time after his marriage to the plaintiff, Grant disappeared and his whereabouts was not known at the time of this suit. The defendant bank, as trustee, invested the trust assets in securities which are now held by it, together with undisbursed income from the trust estate. The plaintiff obtained an injunction restraining the defendant trustee from disbursing any of the trust assets. Patricia Shelley brought a garnishment proceeding against the trustee, by which she sought to subject the trust to the claim for support money provided for in the 1951 decree of divorce. . . .

The trial court entered a decree subjecting the accrued income of the trust to the existing claims of the plaintiff and Patricia Shelley; subjecting future income of the trust to the periodic obligations subsequently accruing by the terms of the decrees in the divorce proceedings brought by plaintiff and Patricia Shelley; and further providing that in the event that the trust income was insufficient to satisfy such claims, the corpus of the trust was subject to invasion.

We shall first consider that part of the decree which subjects the income of the trust to the claims of plaintiff and of,[]Patricia Shelley. The trust places no conditions upon the right of Grant Shelley to receive the trust income during his lifetime. Therefore, plaintiff and Patricia Shelley may reach such income unless the spendthrift provision of the trust precludes them from doing so.

The validity of spendthrift trusts has been established by our former cases. The question on this appeal is whether the spendthrift provision will be given effect to bar the claims of the beneficiary's children for support and the plaintiff's claim for alimony.

The question is whether a person should be entitled to enjoy the benefits of a trust and at the same time refuse to pay the obligations arising out of his marriage.

We have no hesitation in declaring that public policy requires that the interest of the beneficiary of a trust should be subject to the claims for support of his children. Certainly the defendant will accept the societal postulate that parents have the obligation to support their children. If we give effect to the spendthrift provision to bar the claims for support, we have the spectacle of a man enjoying the benefits of a trust immune from claims which are justly due, while the community pays for the support of his children. We do not believe that it is sound policy to use the welfare funds of this state in support of the beneficiary's children, while he stands behind the shield of immunity created by a spendthrift trust provision. To endorse such a policy and to permit the spectacle which we have described above would be to invite disrespect for the administration of justice. One who wishes to dispose of his property through the device of a trust must do so subject to these considerations of policy and he cannot force the courts to sanction his scheme of disposition if it is inimical to the interests of the state.

The justification for permitting a claim for alimony is, perhaps, not as clear. The adjustment of the economic interests of the parties to a divorce may depend upon a variety of factors, including the respective fault of the parties, the ability of the wife to support herself, the duration of the marriage, and other considerations. Whether alimony is to be granted and its amount are questions which are determined in light of these various interests. It is probably fair to say that the duties created by the marriage relation, at least as they are evaluated upon the termination of the marriage, are conceived of as more qualified than those arising out of the paternal relationship. On the theory that divorce terminates the husband's duty to support his former wife and that she stands in no better position than other creditors, some courts have held that the spendthrift provision insulates the beneficiary's interest in the trust from her claim. Recognizing the difference in marital and parental duties suggested above, it has been held that a spendthrift trust is subject to the claims for the support of children but free from the claims of the former wife. A majority of the cases, however, hold that a spendthrift provision will not bar a claim for alimony.

. . . The duty of the husband to support his former wife should override the restriction called for by the spendthrift provision. The same reason advanced above for requiring the support of the beneficiary's children will, in many cases, be applicable to the claim of a divorced wife; if the beneficiary's interest cannot be reached, the state may be called upon to support her. . . .

We hold that the beneficiary's interest in the income of the Shelley Trust is subject to the claims of the plaintiff for alimony and to the claims for the support of Grant Shelley's children as provided for under both decrees for divorce. These claims are not without limit. We adopt the view that such claimants may reach only that much of the income which the trial court deems reasonable under the circumstances, having in mind the respective needs of the husband and wife, the needs of the children, the amount of the trust income, the availability of the corpus for the various needs, and any other factors which are relevant in adjusting equitably the interests of the claimants and the beneficiary. . . .

The question of the claimants' rights to reach the corpus of the trust involves other consideration. For the reasons heretofore stated, the beneficiary's interest in the corpus is not made immune from these claims. But, by the terms of the trust, the disbursement of the corpus is within the discretion of the trustee (or, in some instances subject to the approval of others), and, therefore, Grant Shelley's right to receive any part of the corpus does not arise until the trustee has exercised his discretion and has decided to invade the corpus. Until that time, the plaintiff and Patricia Shelley cannot reach the corpus of the trust because the beneficiary has no realizable interest in it. It has been held that a discretionary trust for the "sole benefit" of the testator's son was enforceable by the son's destitute wife and children on the ground that the support of the son's family fell within the terms of the trust. But, assuming without deciding that such an interpretation is reasonable, it has not been extended to a case where there has been a divorce and the wife has ceased to be a member of the family and, therefore, has ceased to be a beneficiary of the trust. There is nothing in the trust before us which would indicate the testator's intent to make the plaintiff, either directly or indirectly, the beneficiary of the trust. Patricia Shelley could not be regarded as a beneficiary because the decree under which she claims called only for the payment of support money for the children and not alimony. . . . It follows that the decree of the lower court in making the corpus of the Shelley Trust subject to the plaintiff's claim for alimony was erroneous.

The claims for the support of Grant Shelley's children, provided for in the two divorce decrees, involve a different problem. The trust directed and authorized the trustee, in the exercise of its sole discretion upon the death of settlor's wife, to make disbursements for the use and benefit not only of Grant Shelley, but also for his children. The disbursements were to be made "in case of any emergency arising whereby unusual and extraordinary expenses are necessary for the proper support and care of my said son, or said children." Here the children are named as beneficiaries of the trust and need not claim derivatively through their father. However, they are entitled to a share of the corpus only if, in the trustee's discretion, it is determined that an emergency exists. The defendant bank contends that the expenses of supporting Grant Shelley's children claimed in this case were for the usual and ordinary costs of support and do not, therefore, constitute "unusual and extraordinary expenses" within the meaning of the trust provision. It is contended that there was no "emergency" calling for "unusual and extraordinary expenses" because there was no proof of an unexpected occurrence or of an unexpected situation requiring immediate action. We disagree with defendant's interpretation. We construe the clause to include the circumstances involved here, i.e., where the children are deserted by their father and are in need of support. We think that the testator intended to provide that in the event that the income from the trust was not sufficient to cover disbursements for the support and case of either the son or his children an "emergency" had arisen and the corpus could then be invaded. . . .

The decree of the lower court is affirmed and the cause remanded with directions to modify the decree in accordance with the views expressed in this opinion.

Post-Case Follow-Up

The court in *Shelley* created an exception to the rule that a spendthrift clause prevents a beneficiary's creditors from reaching assets in a trust held for the beneficiary. These exception creditors—former spouses and children—can still only reach distributions subject to a mandatory standard. They cannot reach assets held under a discretionary standard. The children in *Shelley* could get income as creditors, and they could also get distributions of principal as beneficiaries. The trust permitted distributions to the children in the event of an "emergency," and the court concluded that their need for support because they had been abandoned by their father constituted an emergency.

Shelley v. Shelley: Real Life Applications

1. Darrin is the beneficiary of a trust that directs the trustee to distribute so much or all of the trust's income and principal to Darrin for his maintenance and support. The trust includes a spendthrift clause. If Darrin owes child support and has no other assets, can his children obtain a distribution from any part of the trust?

2. When Emily and Forrest divorced, the court ordered Emily to pay spousal support to Forrest. After two years Emily stopped making the required payments. Forrest knows that Emily is a beneficiary of a trust created by her grandfather, and he wonders whether he can be paid from the trust. Write a letter to Forrest advising him as to his options.

A tort judgment creditor might seem like a sympathetic creditor, but the state legislatures have not looked upon tort creditors with the same favor as children and former spouses. Georgia and Louisiana currently provide exceptions from spendthrift protection for certain tort judgment creditors. Ga. Code Ann. § 53-12-80(d)(3); La. Rev. Stat. § 9:2005(3).

When a Mississippi court created an exception for a tort creditor, in Sligh v. First National Bank of Holmes County, 704 So. 2d 1020 (Miss. 1997), the Mississippi legislature quickly reversed this result. See Miss. Code Ann. § 91-9-503. In another case, Duvall v. McGee, 826 A.2d 416 (Md. 2003), the court refused to allow the tort creditor access to a trust held for the benefit of the tortfeasor. However, the dissent in Duvall v. McGee argued that public policy should require that a tortfeasor's mandatory interest in a trust be used to discharge his tort liability. The dissent noted that spendthrift trusts are considered valid because creditors have at least constructive notice that the beneficiary's interest in a trust is limited, but a tort victim is unable to protect herself in advance.

2. Creditors of a Beneficiary Who Is the Settlor

Revocable Trusts

With most revocable trusts, the settlor is also the trustee, the life income beneficiary, and the person with the power to invade principal without limitation. The settlor retains the power to amend or revoke the trust and thus controls the assets. In a practical sense, the settlor still has the equivalent of full ownership of the property in the trust. For that reason, whether there is a spendthrift provision or not, the assets of a revocable trust (and not merely the settlor's interests in the trust) remain reachable by the settlor's creditors, both during lifetime and at death. UTC § 505(a). If creditors could not reach assets in a revocable trust, these trusts would provide individuals withan easy creditor-avoidance tool.

Irrevocable Trusts

Under traditional trust law, there was little or no protection for a settlor who retained an interest in the trust. The basic rule, still in effect in a majority of states, is that whether or not a trust contains a spendthrift provision, a creditor of the settlor may reach the maximum amount that can be distributed to or for the settlor's benefit. UTC § 505(a)(2). For example, if Saraphina establishes a trust naming her friend, Theodore, as trustee, with the power to make distributions from income and principal to Saraphina for her welfare and best interests, her creditors can reach all of the property in the trust. This is true even though Saraphina cannot force the trustee to make a distribution to her.

A settlor seeking protection from creditors could transfer property to an irrevocable trust for someone else's benefit. A transfer to someone else, whether in trust or in fee simple, is an effective way for the settlor to avoid the claims of *future* creditors (although not present creditors). The obvious problem with this strategy is that the settlor loses the ability to enjoy the property.

Settlors and their advisors continue to search for ways to protect themselves from future creditors without giving up the use of their property. Asset protection trusts attempt to provide the settlor with continued access to the property and creditor protection.

Foreign and Domestic Asset Protection Trusts

In the 1980s, a number of "tax haven" countries created laws to encourage trust business by permitting nonresidents to establish irrevocable trusts that benefit the settlor while denying the settlor's creditors the right to reach the assets in those trusts. In the Cook Islands, the Cayman Islands, and various Caribbean and South Pacific islands, a settlor can establish a trust with a local trustee, knowing that the local courts will not enforce a judgment obtained elsewhere.

While the foreign courts will not require the assets to be used to pay the settlor's future debts, what remains uncertain is what U.S. courts will do when faced with a U.S. creditor, a U.S. settlor-beneficiary, and an offshore trust.

Lawyers using offshore asset protection trusts usually suggest that the settlor name someone other than the settlor as the trustee or trust protector. If the settlor is not the trustee, the settlor is yet another step removed from the assets. This structure helps mitigate the argument that the settlor has access to the trust assets. Offshore trusts continue to be used, but generally only for very wealthy clients, and, as the *Anderson* case shows, at some risk.

Domestic Asset Protection Trusts—Alaska's Statute

After watching trust business leave the United States, Jonathan Blattmachr, a New York estate-planning lawyer, and his brother, Douglas J. Blattmachr, who had trust and investment management experience, teamed up in 1997 to convince the Alaska legislature to amend state law to permit creditor protection for settlors in self-settled irrevocable spendthrift trusts if managed by an Alaskan trustee. The concept is this: permit a self-settled spendthrift trust to protect assets of the settlor-beneficiary from her creditors in the same way a spendthrift trust protects assets of a non-settlor-beneficiary.

Risks of Offshore Asset Protection Trusts

In 1995, Denyse and Michael Anderson set up an irrevocable trust in the Cook Islands. They served as co-trustees with a trust company licensed in the Cook Islands. After they illegally made over $6 million in a telemarketing Ponzi scheme, the Andersons deposited the money in the Cook Islands trust.

In 1998, the Federal Trade Commission charged them with violations of the Federal Trade Commission Act and the Telemarketing Sales Rule. The district court issued a temporary restraining order and an injunction, requiring the Andersons to repatriate any assets held for their benefit outside the United States. The Andersons sent a letter to the corporate trustee, asking the trustee to repatriate the assets, but the corporate trustee notified the Andersons that it would not do so.

Under a duress provision in the trust, the corporate trustee removed the Andersons as co-trustees. Nonetheless, the district court held the Andersons in contempt for refusing to repatriate the assets, and they served six months in jail before the court purged them of their contempt. Eventually, they settled with the FTC for $1.2 million, much less than the $20 million the FTC had sought. FTC v. Affordable Media, 179 F.3d 1228 (9th Cir. 1999).

Jonathan drafted the statute, and Douglas set up The Alaska Trust Company to serve as the Alaskan trustee. The Alaska statute provides that Alaska law will apply to assets held in an Alaskan trust by an Alaskan trustee; the settlor need not reside in Alaska. Alaska Stat. § 13.36.035.

After Alaska took the lead, Delaware quickly enacted similar legislation authorizing domestic asset protection trusts (DAPTs). Since then, numerous other states, including Delaware, Hawaii, Mississippi, Missouri, Nevada, New Hampshire, Ohio, Oklahoma, Rhode Island, South Dakota, Tennessee, Utah, Virginia, and Wyoming have enacted DAPT statutes. Each statute provides that a specified number of years after the creation of the trust, a spendthrift clause will be effective against creditors of the settlor whose claims did not exist at the time the settlor created the trust.

EXHIBIT 10.4   Common DAPT Requirements

- Shelter is not available for existing debts; only those liabilities that arise after the trust is established and funded are protected.
- The trust must be irrevocable.
- The settlor may not be a mandatory beneficiary, only a discretionary beneficiary.
- Some assets of the trust and a trustee must be located in the state where the trust is established and administered.

The application of conflict-of-laws rules with respect to asset protection trusts remains uncertain. Under general conflict-of-laws principles, a state need not apply law from another state if it violates the first state's public policy. For example, if a California resident sets up and transfers assets to an Alaskan trust, it is not clear whether California courts would agree to apply Alaska law if a California creditor sued the settlor in California. If the court considers transfers to a self-settled asset protection trust to be against the public policy of California, the court may permit a creditor of the settlor of the trust to obtain a judgment in California.

One case has considered the conflict-of-laws question in the context of federal law. In re Huber, 493 B.R. 798 (Bankr. W.D. Wash. 2013). Applying federal conflict-of-laws rules, a federal bankruptcy court looked to Restatement (Second) of Conflict of Laws § 270 (1971), which says that the laws of the state selected by the settlor will apply, so long as the application of that state's law "does not violate a strong public policy of the state with which, as to the matter at issue, the trust has its most significant relationship." In 2008, as the real estate market began to sink, a Washington man transferred his interests in numerous real estate companies as well as personal assets into an Alaska asset protection trust. The Alaska USA Trust Company and the settlor's son were the trustees. The settlor, his son, and all the beneficiaries lived in Washington, and all the assets other than a $10,000 certificate of deposit were in Washington. The court held that Washington law, and not Alaska law, applied. Under Washington law, the transfers were void against existing and future creditors, because Washington has a strong public policy against self-settled asset protection trusts. The case involved transfers made when the settlor already faced creditor problems and knew that more were coming, so the case may have involved fraudulent transfers, which are not protected by any of the asset protection statutes. Nonetheless, it provides the first examination of the conflict-of-laws issue.

Both the Restatement (Third) of Trusts § 58(2) (2003) and UTC § 505(a)(2) provide that a settlor's creditors can reach a self-settled spendthrift trust, explicitly rejecting the protections allegedly offered by an offshore or Alaska-style trust.

EXHIBIT 10.5   **Comment to UTC § 505(a)(2)**

Subsection (a)(2) . . . follows traditional doctrine in providing that a settlor who is also a beneficiary may not use the trust as a shield against the settlor's creditors. The drafters of the Uniform Trust Code concluded that traditional doctrine reflects sound policy. Consequently, the drafters rejected the approach taken in States like Alaska and Delaware, both of which allow a settlor to retain a beneficial interest immune from creditor claims. Under the Code, whether the trust contains a spendthrift provision or not, a creditor of the settlor may reach the maximum amount that the trustee could have paid to the settlor-beneficiary. If the trustee has discretion to distribute the entire income and principal to the settlor, the effect of this subsection is to place the settlor's creditors in the same position as if the trust had not been created.

Despite the rejection of DAPTs by the Restatement and the UTC and the continuing uncertainty over the conflict-of-laws question, interest in using these trusts continues to grow. Legislatures with an eye on attracting trust business continue to adopt statutes authorizing DAPTs, and at least some clients concerned about potential future lawsuits have decided they are worth the cost.

Chapter Summary

- Beneficiaries' rights in a trust depend on the terms of the trust expressed in the trust instrument.
- The rights of creditors of beneficiaries derive from the beneficiaries' rights.
- Distribution provisions can be mandatory or discretionary, and there are variations on how much discretion a trustee possesses—from absolute discretion to discretion based on an ascertainable standard.
- Even when a trust instrument gives a trustee "absolute discretion" in making decisions about distributions, the trustee must act reasonably and in good faith.
- Health, education, maintenance, support, and emergency are ascertainable standards; welfare, best interests, and happiness are nonascertainable standards.
- A trustee has a duty to inquire about the beneficiary's situation and needs in order to apply a standard of distribution appropriately.

■ For a beneficiary who is not the settlor, if a trust does not have a spendthrift clause, a creditor of the beneficiary can reach only those assets subject to a mandatory distribution standard.

■ For a beneficiary who is not the settlor, if a trust has a spendthrift clause, a creditor cannot reach assets in the trust, unless the creditor comes within an exception adopted by the state through case law or the UTC—a child or former spouse with a judgment. These exception creditors can reach mandatory payments under UTC § 503 and may be able to force discretionary distributions under UTC § 504. UTC § 504 has not been widely adopted.

■ A creditor of a settlor who is a beneficiary of a trust can reach all assets that may be distributed to the settlor, unless the trust meets the requirements of a Domestic Asset Protection Trust, permitted in a growing number of states.

Applying the Concepts

1. A trust directs the trustee to make distributions for the health, education, support, and maintenance of the settlor's five nieces and nephews. Answer the question twice, first assuming the trust holds $200,000 in assets and then assuming the trust holds $5 million in assets.

   a. Can the trustee make distributions to different nieces and nephews in response to requests for the following:
      i. Tuition to attend law school?
      ii. Expenses of a one-year trip around the world for a nephew who wants to educate himself through travel?
      iii. The down payment on a house?
      iv. Expenses of orthodontic treatment?
   b. For each of the requested distributions, what should the trustee do to establish reasonableness and good faith rather than an abuse of discretion for a decision to distribute or a decision not to distribute?

2. A trust provides: "The trustee shall distribute so much or all of the trust principal as is necessary for the health, education, maintenance, and support of my spouse. On my spouse's death, the trustee shall distribute the corpus of the trust to my descendants, by right of representation." For each request below, indicate whether the trustee can make the distribution. For each answer, discuss the analytical method the trustee should use to reach the appropriate conclusion. If the trustee makes the distribution, would you advise the other beneficiaries to sue and, if so, on what legal basis?

   a. A distribution to pay for elective cosmetic surgery.
   b. A distribution to pay expenses for the vacation house at the coast that the settlor and spouse had used together before the settlor's death.
   c. A distribution to pay for aerobics classes.
   d. A monthly stipend of $1,000 to help cover household expenses.

3. A trust provides: "The trustee shall distribute such amounts as the trustee determines, in the trustee's sole discretion, to be appropriate for Francine's happiness and welfare." Francine is a sister of the settlor. *Must* the trustee make distributions to cover the costs of a vacation for Francine? *Could* the trustee make a distribution for that purpose?

   a. What if the trust has a relatively small corpus?
   b. What if the trust has a substantial corpus?
   c. What additional information would you want?

4. Nicholas created an irrevocable, inter vivos trust for his nephew, Damien. The trust directs the trustee to distribute all the income to Damien, at least annually, and also directs the trustee to distribute the amounts the trustee determines to be necessary for Damien's health, education, maintenance, and support. Answer each of the following questions twice, first assuming that the trust agreement does not include a spendthrift clause and then assuming that the trust agreement includes a spendthrift clause.

   a. Damien has fallen behind on a bank loan he took out personally to help pay for law school. Can the bank look to the trust to satisfy Damien's outstanding debt and, if so, in what manner and to what extent?
   b. Damien used his credit card primarily to buy food, clothing, and other necessities. He also used it to travel to Hawaii for Christmas. He has fallen behind and cannot even make the monthly minimum payments. Can the bank look to the trust to satisfy Damien's outstanding debt and, if so, in what manner and to what extent?
   c. Damien was married and had a child. He dissolved the marriage three years ago and was ordered to pay child and spousal support. He has not paid either for two years. Can his child and former spouse look to the trust to satisfy Damien's outstanding debt and, if so, in what manner and to what extent?
   d. Damien asks the trustee to distribute some of the principal of the trust so that he can travel to his sister's wedding. Can the trustee do so? If the trustee makes a distribution, can the bank reach the money distributed?

5. Now assume that the trust in Problem 4 included the following provision: "My trustee may distribute to any child of Damien the amount the trustee determines to be necessary for the child's support in reasonable comfort." Does that provision change any of your answers?

Trusts and Estates in Practice

1. Does your state provide an exception from the spendthrift clause for former spouses or children with support orders? For anyone else?

2. What types of actions might cause a court to find a trustee to be acting in bad faith?

3. Indira wants to create a testamentary trust to provide for her spouse, Zane, for the rest of his life. At his death, she wants the assets remaining to go to her children from a prior marriage. All the children are adults. Indira has a substantial estate, but not a huge one. Zane has some income of his own but will need distributions from the trust to maintain his standard of living. Indira is concerned that income from her assets may not be enough to provide for Zane, and she is willing to allow for some distributions of principal to supplement his income. "But," she says to her lawyer, "it's important that something be left for my kids. I certainly wouldn't want Zane to spend all my money, and I especially don't want him using it to support a new wife and her family if he remarries!" Draft the terms of the trust that provide directions to the trustee for the distributions to Zane. You do not need to draft the provisions directing distribution on termination. You should draft only the provisions that tell the trustee when and what to distribute to Zane during his life. Indira's oldest child, Makayla, will be the trustee and Zane will not be the trustee.

4. Trent created a trust for his spouse, Noah. Noah is the trustee, and the trust provides, "the trustee shall, in the trustee's sole and absolute discretion, make such distributions as the trustee sees fit for my spouse's health, education, maintenance, or support. On the death of my spouse, the trustee shall distribute all remaining corpus to my niece, Johanna Marais." Noah made distributions for lengthy trips to exotic locations, a Maserati convertible, and lots of designer clothes. Johanna has come to you to ask whether she can curb his distributions. She asked Noah to distribute less, but he pointed out that he has broad discretion and can distribute whatever he thinks best. Advise Johanna.

5. If you had been the lawyer for Trent in Problem 4 what additional language might you have included in the trust? First assume that Trent wanted Noah to be able to distribute as much as he wanted without challenge by Johanna. Alternatively, assume that Trent did not want Noah to be able to distribute excessive amounts.

6. Alexander is concerned about his grandchild, James. James is 29, has graduated from college but has never held a full-time job, asks his parents for financial help from time to time, and has had a problem with substance abuse. Alexander wants to create a trust to provide a "safety net" for James, but he does not want James to be able to pressure the trustee to make distributions, and he does not want James's creditors to be able to reach the assets in the trust. How should the trust for James be structured? What sort of distribution standard would you recommend?

7. You are a state legislator. The legislature is considering a statute that would permit some or all of the following creditors to reach property held in trust despite a spendthrift clause. As a legislator, you are being asked to balance the rights of

creditors and trust beneficiaries. Which one or more of the following would you support? On what policy grounds?

- Under no circumstances can a creditor reach an interest of a beneficiary—no exceptions.
- A child support judgment creditor can reach an interest of a beneficiary.
- An ex-spouse enforcing an order for alimony can reach an interest of a beneficiary.
- A tort creditor can reach an interest of a beneficiary.
- The state government can reach an interest of a beneficiary to recover Medicaid payments.
- The federal government can reach an interest of a beneficiary to recover taxes due.
- Under all circumstances a creditor can reach an interest of a beneficiary. (In essence, this would abolish spendthrift clauses.)

Fiduciary Duties and Modification and Termination of Trusts

A trustee is responsible for managing trust property and for making distributions to beneficiaries. In the last chapter, we looked at the trustee's responsibilities relating to making discretionary decisions that affect beneficiaries, as directed by the terms of the trust. A trustee's responsibility to make distributions to beneficiaries is one part of the trustee's fiduciary duties. In this chapter, we examine the other fiduciary duties of a trustee. These fiduciary duties affect the way a trustee carries out the trustee's discretionary authority and govern the trustee's responsibilities in managing trust property. The duties include the duty of obedience, the duty of loyalty, the duty to inform and report, the duty of impartiality, the duty of care in managing trust property, and the duty to invest property as a prudent investor. The trustee must keep proper records of trust property, so we review the Uniform Principal and Income Act, which provides accounting rules for trustees.

After we explore the fiduciary duties that apply to trustees, we consider the remedies available to beneficiaries if a trustee breaches the fiduciary responsibilities in administering the trust. Finally, we consider the rules that allow a trust to be modified or terminated.

Key Concepts

- The duty of obedience to carry out the terms of the trust
- The duty of loyalty to act in the best interests of the beneficiaries
- The duty to provide information to beneficiaries
- The duty of impartiality to treat all beneficiaries fairly
- The duty of care to manage trust property for the beneficiaries
- The duty to invest property as a prudent investor would
- A court can authorize modification when some or all of the beneficiaries consent and when modification does not adversely affect a material purpose of the trust
- A trust typically terminates pursuant to its terms or when no assets remain

The modification or termination of a trust can affect various aspects of the trust's administration, including the timing of distributions and trustee powers and responsibilities.

A. FIDUCIARY DUTIES

Fiduciary duties developed in trust law to govern the behavior of the trustee. As we discussed in Chapter 9, the trustee holds legal title to the property and controls the property. Without strict duties allowing the beneficiary to seek court assistance if the trustee does not perform the fiduciary responsibilities appropriately, the trustee might be tempted to misbehave. The fiduciary duties seek to prevent a trustee from using trust property for the trustee's own benefit, or managing the property in a way that prefers the interests of one beneficiary over another, or harms the interests of all beneficiaries.

If the trustee acts in a way that breaches (violates) one of the above duties, the beneficiary can sue the trustee for **breach of trust**, and ask a court to enforce the trust and make sure the trust is carried out as the settlor intended. If the court finds that the trustee has violated any of the trustee's fiduciary duties, the court can direct the trustee to comply with the terms of the trust or provide information as requested by the beneficiary; the court can even replace the trustee with one that will do a better job.

History of Fiduciary Duties Involving Investments

Trust law and the law of fiduciary duties developed in England prior to the eighteenth century, at a time when trusts typically held land. Trustee powers were limited because the trustee's job was to manage the land, not to develop other investments. By the time trusts and trust law reached the United States, trusts frequently held assets other than land, but the fiduciary duties imposed on trustees in the eighteenth and nineteenth centuries continued to favor conservative investments.

In the United States, some states created statutory lists of approved investments for trusts, and investments in bonds were preferred over investments in stock. The goal was to preserve the value of the assets in the trust. Risk was low, but so was the return on investment, so trustees began to seek the ability to invest more in stocks and other riskier assets. During the twentieth century, trusts increasingly held complex investments, and trust law changed to accommodate the needs of trustees for greater management powers. The need for rapid changes in fiduciary duties resulted in new statutory law, because the incremental development of law through cases could not keep pace with the need for modification of the rules.

Some older trust documents still contain language that restricts trustee powers, particularly with respect to investment. Most modern documents, however, grant broad authority to trustees and rely on oversight by beneficiaries to protect the trust from trustee misbehavior.

Mandatory or Default Rules?

As discussed in Chapter 9, most rules in trust law are default rules. The settlor can decide which rules will govern the behavior of the trustee and can provide specific instructions about what the trustee can or should do. Even fiduciary duties can be altered by the settlor, and we will see examples of when a settlor might want the trustee to engage in behavior that would otherwise be a breach of a fiduciary duty. Although a settlor can limit or change individual duties, a settlor cannot abrogate all fiduciary duties. A trust must have some enforceable duties or no trust has been created. If the trustee has absolute control over trust property, without at least some restrictions imposed by fiduciary duties, the trustee is simply the owner of the property and not a trustee. See John H. Langbein, *Mandatory Rules in the Law of Trusts*, 98 Nw. U. L. Rev. 1105 (2004).

1. Duty of Obedience

A trustee must carry out the terms of the trust as the settlor directs in the trust instrument and based on the trustee's knowledge of the settlor's intent. The trustee must also comply with the law, for example by paying taxes and complying with any legal rules applicable to trust property. This **duty of obedience** underlies the other fiduciary duties.

A breach of the duty of obedience could occur if a trustee failed to make distributions required by the trust instrument or made distributions not permitted under the trust. For example, if a trust provided for the distribution of income to Andrea (a mandatory provision) and the distribution of principal to Betina for her health and support (a discretionary provision), the trustee could not refuse to distribute the trust income to Andrea. The trustee could not distribute trust principal to anyone other than Betina and could make distributions only for her health and support. A distribution of principal to Andrea's daughter for college tuition would be a breach of the trust.

2. Duty of Loyalty

In administering a trust, a trustee must always act "solely" in the interests of the beneficiaries. See Restatement (Third) of Trusts § 78 (2003). The **duty of loyalty** means that the trustee must not put the trustee's own interests (or the interests of others who are not beneficiaries) above those of the beneficiaries. The law of trusts developed strict rules governing transactions that violate the duty of loyalty because of the power and information imbalance between the trustee and the beneficiaries. The trustee has legal title to the property and control over management of the property, but beneficiaries might be unborn or incapacitated, or otherwise unable to monitor the trustees. Indeed, a settlor might have created a trust because the beneficiaries were not capable of protecting their own interests.

The duty of loyalty focuses on the existence of a conflict of interest, based on the assumption that beneficiaries cannot be expected to have the information or ability to review all transactions involving conflicts. The duty distinguishes between two types of conflicts, and we refer to one as self-dealing and one as conflict of interest.

A transaction between the trustee acting as trustee and the same person acting in an individual capacity is referred to as **self-dealing**. For example, if the trust holds a piece of land and the person acting as trustee buys the land from the trust, the person has engaged in self-dealing. A self-dealing transaction is voidable by the beneficiaries, even if the transaction was fair to the beneficiaries and the trust.

In contrast, when the trustee is influenced by the interests of someone close to the trustee, or the interests of a business with which the trustee is involved, we refer to that transaction as a **conflict of interest**. A conflict of interest transaction is presumptively voidable, but the trustee can overcome the presumption by establishing the fairness of the transaction.

EXHIBIT 11.1 **UTC § 802. Duty of Loyalty**

(a) A trustee shall administer the trust solely in the interests of the beneficiaries.

(b) . . . a sale, encumbrance, or other transaction involving the investment or management of trust property entered into by the trustee for the trustee's own personal account or which is otherwise affected by a conflict between the trustee's fiduciary and personal interests is voidable by a beneficiary affected by the transaction unless:

(1) the transaction was authorized by the terms of the trust;

(2) the transaction was approved by the court;

(3) the beneficiary did not commence a judicial proceeding within the [applicable] time;

(4) the beneficiary consented to the trustee's conduct, ratified the transaction, or released the trustee in compliance with [the UTC]; or

(5) the transaction involves a contract entered into or claim acquired by the trustee before the person became or contemplated becoming trustee.

(c) A sale, encumbrance, or other transaction involving the investment or management of trust property is presumed to be affected by a conflict between personal and fiduciary interests if it is entered into by the trustee with:

(1) the trustee's spouse;

(2) the trustee's descendants, siblings, parents, or their spouses;

(3) an agent or attorney of the trustee; or

(4) a corporation or other person or enterprise in which the trustee, or a person that owns a significant interest in the trustee, has an interest that might affect the trustee's best judgment.

Self-Dealing—Transactions for the Trustee's Personal Account

Subsection (a) of Uniform Trust Code (UTC) § 802 codifies the common law rule that a trustee must act "solely in the interests of the beneficiaries". Subsection (b) of UTC § 802 states that a transaction "affected by a conflict between the trustee's fiduciary and personal interests" is voidable, unless one of several exceptions listed in subsection (b) of UTC § 802 applies. Although the UTC does not use the term self-dealing, we will refer to this type of transaction as self-dealing. Such a transaction is *irrebuttably presumed* to be affected by a conflict and is therefore voidable even if the transaction is fair and reasonable to the beneficiaries.

The rule in subsection (b) of UTC § 802 is sometimes referred to as the **no further inquiry rule** because a beneficiary can void the transaction without proof of fraud on the part of the trustee or proof of harm to the trust. Even a transaction that benefits the trust and the beneficiaries remains voidable at the option of the beneficiaries under this rule. If no beneficiary voids the transaction, the transaction will stand.

Example: Self-Dealing

Conroy Lee is the settlor of the Lee Family Trust. The trust holds a variety of investment assets including undeveloped real property. Alan, a family friend of Conroy, serves as trustee of the trust. Alan would like to build a house for himself and thinks the property would be the perfect place. If Alan (acting for himself) buys the property from Alan (as trustee), the risk to the beneficiaries is that Alan may not pay a fair price for the property or may sell the property without accounting for the value of owning property versus another investment. If Alan does buy the property, then the beneficiaries could require Alan to undo the transaction, regardless of whether they determined that the transaction was unfair to them.

What if Alan gets three appraisals for the property and pays the trust the amount of the highest appraisal? Everyone agrees that the transaction is fair to the trust, and the beneficiaries are unlikely to seek to undo the sale. But then changes to neighboring property make the parcel that was sold much more valuable. Alan did not know that this would happen and this information did not figure into the appraisals. If the beneficiaries want to get the benefit of the increase in value, they can require Alan to undo the transaction. If instead the property drops in value, Alan cannot return the property to the trust. Only the beneficiaries have the power to void the transaction.

Conflicts of Interest—Transactions Involving Personal or Business Relationships

Subsection (c) of UTC § 802 provides the rule for a transaction that is not directly for the trustee's own individual benefit. If a trustee enters into a transaction with people or entities with whom the trustee has a family or business relationship, we refer to it as a conflict of interest. Under subsection (c), the transaction is rebuttably presumed to be affected with a conflict. In a conflict of interest situation, if the trustee can show that the transaction was fair to the trust and its beneficiaries, the transaction will not be voidable. See UTC § 802 cmt.

A conflict of interest transaction might involve a member of the trustee's family. For example, a trustee might want to hire a family member to perform services for the trust, to sell trust property to a family member, or to engage in a transaction with a business in which a family member holds a significant interest. The trustee's concern for the well-being of the family member could affect the trustee's ability to evaluate the transaction with only the interests of the trust beneficiaries in mind.

A conflict of interest transaction might involve a company with which the trustee has a business relationship. For example, if the trustee sits on the board of a company or holds a significant interest in the company, buying shares of that company as trustee or hiring that company to provide services to the trust would present conflicts of interest. If the company wanted to buy property owned by the trust, selling that property to the company would create a conflict for the trustee.

Because these indirect conflicts represent divided loyalty on the part of the trustee and may result in harm to the beneficiaries, UTC § 802(c) treats indirect conflicts as "presumed to be affected by a conflict between personal and fiduciary interests." Thus, indirect conflicts are presumptively voidable, not absolutely voidable (as a self-dealing transaction would be). If the trustee can show that the transaction was fair to the beneficiaries, the beneficiaries will not be able to void the transaction.

In states that have not adopted the UTC, a court may be willing to consider fairness to the beneficiaries in determining whether the transaction should stand. See, e.g., Culbertson v. McCann, 664 P.2d 388, 391 (Okla. 1983) (involving a sale to the fiduciary's sister).

Example: Conflict of Interest

Patricia is the trustee of a trust that holds several rental houses as assets. Patricia's son, Jordon, owns a company that manages apartment buildings and rental houses. Patricia needs someone to manage the rental houses owned by the trust, so she hires Jordon's company. Hiring a company owned by her son is a conflict of interest transaction, but if the terms of the contract are fair to the trust, the contract will not be voidable by the beneficiaries. UTC § 802(c) creates a presumption that the transaction was affected by the conflict, so Patricia will need evidence of fairness, such as bids from other potential property managers, to rebut the presumption if a beneficiary challenges her decision to hire Jordon's company.

Authorization of Self-Dealing and Conflicts of Interest

Trusts today hold many different types of property, and trustees may need to engage in transactions that benefit the trust but involve self-dealing or conflicts of interest. For this reason, the settlor, the beneficiaries, or a court may authorize these transactions. UTC § 802(b) codifies this rule. (See Exhibit 11.1 above.)

If, for example, a family business will be part of the property held in a trust and a family member active in the business will be trustee, the settlor may want to authorize the trustee to buy shares of stock from the trust, to vote shares in favor of the trustee or one of the trustee's immediate family members, and to engage in transactions between the trust and the family business. The settlor can authorize the trustee to engage in self-dealing or conflict of interest transactions with the trust. UTC § 802(b). For example, the trust instrument could permit the trustee to buy property from the trust or to borrow money from the trust.

A settlor who creates a trust that holds interests in a family business, and who also appoints a family member as trustee, might include a provision like the following:

> *Special Assets.* The Trustees of each trust created hereunder and the Personal Representatives of my estate are expressly authorized to continue to hold any stocks, bonds, or other securities issued by, or any other interests in [name of family business]. The Trustees and my Personal Representatives are also expressly authorized to make further investments therein from the trust estate of any trust or from my estate from time to time. These authorizations apply even though such stocks, bonds, securities or interests (hereinafter referred to as "special assets") may constitute all or substantially all of the trust estate of any trust created hereunder or my estate. The Trustees of each trust created hereunder and the Personal Representatives of my estate are further authorized, in addition to other powers herein granted to or conferred upon the Trustees and my Personal Representatives, to buy or sell any such special assets or any other assets. The Trustees and my Personal Representatives may make sales to and purchases from any one (1) or more of themselves, individually, or to or from any other person who is then acting as a Trustee of any other trust created hereunder or as a Personal Representative, or to or from any other person (including, without limitation, any individual, trust, estate, corporation, or partnership). Such sales or purchases may be at a price equal to the fair market value of such special assets or other assets at the time of such transaction, but in no event for less than adequate consideration in money or money's worth. No Trustee or Personal Representative shall be liable to any beneficiary hereunder or to any other person for any act or failure to act pursuant to this Article in the absence of the fiduciary's own bad faith.

UTC § 802(b)(2) permits a trustee to avoid liability for a breach of the duty of loyalty by seeking court approval before engaging in a transaction that would otherwise constitute a breach. Court approval protects the trustee from a later charge of fiduciary misconduct and also protects the beneficiaries, because a court will only authorize a transaction if it is fair and in the interests of the beneficiaries.

Under UTC § 802(b)(4), a trustee can also ask the beneficiaries to agree to a self-dealing or conflict of interest transaction. For the trustee to be protected, all beneficiaries of the trust must consent. If only some beneficiaries consent, then those beneficiaries cannot sue the trustee for breach of the duty of loyalty, but any beneficiaries who did not consent may still do so. If any beneficiaries are minor, or unborn children, or otherwise lack legal capacity, someone will have to represent the beneficiaries for purposes of consent. The common law has developed different types of representation rules, and the UTC has provisions on representation in UTC § 304. We discuss representation below in Section A.4 of this chapter.

Any payment of compensation to the trustee is self-dealing, because the person acting as trustee is receiving money from the trust. Although the trust instrument may prohibit trustee compensation, a trustee may be unwilling to provide services to the trust if the trustee cannot be paid. Trustee compensation is, therefore, routinely permitted, either by the terms of the trust or by statute. If compensation is permitted, the amount paid must be reasonable; excessive compensation will be considered a breach of the duty of loyalty.

Case Preview

Hosey v. Burgess

When Julian Watkins died, he left his farm in a trust that provided for his second wife, Florence Watkins, for her life and then directed the trustee to distribute the remainder to Leneva Hosey, his daughter from his first marriage. The case provides a good example of the complications that can develop when trustees are family members. In this case Leneva and her husband, N.R, are the trustees and make decisions that affect the income received by a trust beneficiary, while also providing a personal benefit to the trustees.

Leneva and N.R. had been farming Julian's property before his death. After Julian's death, N.R. stopped active farming, so Leneva and N.R. subleased the property to another farmer. Leneva and N.R. kept the income from the sublease, even though all income from the property in the trust should have gone to Florence, the income beneficiary of the trust. When Florence died, her daughter, Marysue Burgess, sued the trustees for breach of their fiduciary duties.

As you read the case, consider:

1. What harm did Florence suffer?
2. Leneva argues that the terms of the trust gave her permission to enter into transactions as trustee. What language does she point to?
3. Does Marysue have to show that Leneva acted intentionally to hurt Florence?

Hosey v. Burgess
890 S.W.2d 262 (Ark. 1995)

HOLT, Chief Justice.

This case involves an appeal from a decision by the Phillips County Chancery Court, finding that appellant Leneva Judy Hosey and her late husband, N.R. Hosey, as trustees for the late Florence R. Watkins (whose executrix was appellee Marysue Robinson Burgess), were guilty of self-dealing to the detriment of Mrs. Watkins by subleasing a farm and not giving Mrs. Watkins as the trust beneficiary the benefit of the enhanced rental. . . .

Julian J. Watkins, who owned a farm in Phillips County, Arkansas, married Florence Robinson on March 25, 1975, after the death of his first wife, Lonette Watkins. Several years later, he retired and, on April 10, 1980, entered into a twenty-five-year lease of his property with [] appellant Leneva Judy Hosey, and her husband N.R. Hosey, who owned a substantial farming operation. [] Mr. and Mrs. Hosey, as lessees, agreed to make annual payments of $35 per acre for the approximately 400 acres of cultivated land. Among the conditions set forth in the lease was a requirement that the lessees "not assign or sublet said premises, or any part thereof, without the consent, in writing, of Lessor first obtained. . . ."

On March 25, 1982, Julian Watkins executed his last will and testament and a codicil. In it, he named Mr. and Mrs. Hosey his co-executors. He also created a testamentary trust consisting of his land holdings, including the 400 leased acres, to be administered by Mr. and Mrs. Hosey, as trustees, on behalf of his wife:

> 5.1. If my spouse, Florence R. Watkins, survives me, I give, devise, and bequeath all the balance and residue of the real property of which I die seized and possessed to my trustees herein named, in trust, to hold, manage, and invest the same, to collect the income thereon, and to pay to, or apply for the benefit of, my spouse the net income thereof in quarterly or other convenient installments, but at least annually, for and during the term of my spouse's life.

> 5.2. Upon the death of my spouse, my trustees shall assign, transfer, and pay over the then principal of this trust to my then living issue, per stirpes. . . .

In 1989, Mr. Hosey, whose health was declining, ceased active farming. He and Mrs. Hosey, as lessors, entered into a lease with Dixie Hill Farms . . . . The lease, which embraced the farmlands owned by Mr. and Mrs. Hosey and involved a sublease of the 400 acres of Julian Watkins's farm, was to run for a three-year term from January 1, 1989, to December 31, 1991. The lease did not specify any rental on a per-acre basis for the two farms, which together contained approximately 1,316.5 acres; instead, the annual rental for all of the property was set at $88,000.

N.R. Hosey died on August 14, 1991, leaving his wife as the surviving trustee of the Watkins trust. In 1992, she entered into another three-year sublease of the trust land, extending through 1994, for the same rental amount.

On November 24, 1992, Mrs. Watkins died, leaving her daughter, appellee Marysue Robinson Burgess, as her sole beneficiary and executrix of her estate. Mrs. Burgess filed suit against Mrs. Hosey on March 5, 1993, seeking to recover the *pro rata* portion of the 1992 trust income and the difference between the rental under the twenty-five year lease and the amount received "at a rental greatly in excess of the rental paid to Florence R. Watkins" under the sublease for the years 1989, 1990, and 1991. . . .

Self-dealing by a trustee or any fiduciary is always suspect, and it is a universal rule of equity that a trustee shall not deal with trust property to his own advantage without the knowledge or consent of the *cestui que trust* [the beneficiary].

Mrs. Hosey cites the following exception to the general rule, stated in 76 Am. Jur. 2d Trusts §380 (1992), that a trustee, in administering a trust, is under the duty of acting exclusively and solely in the interest of the trust estate or the beneficiaries within the terms of the trust and is not to act in his or her own interest by taking part in any transaction concerning the trust where he or she has an interest adverse to that of the beneficiary:

> An exception exists to the well-recognized rule that a trustee may not place himself in a position where his interest may conflict with the interest of the trust property. When the conflict of interest is contemplated, created, and expressly sanctioned by the instrument, the conflict may be permitted. []

Id. See also Bogert, *The Law of Trusts and Trustees*, §543(U) (Repl. 1993): "In some cases where the settlor knew when his trust was drawn that the trustee whom he proposed to name was then in a position which, after acceptance of the trust, would expose him to a conflict between personal and representative interests, it has been held that there was an implied exemption from the duty of loyalty in so far as that transaction was concerned." . . .

Here, Mrs. Hosey was simultaneously trustee of the Watkins trust and remainder beneficiary under the testamentary trust established in the Watkins will. While the duality of identity is certainly not enough, in itself, to establish a violation of fiduciary duty, the circumstances of this case placed the trustee outside the bounds of fiduciary responsibility. The benefit to Mrs. Hosey was not merely coincidental but was, in fact, a breach of an explicitly defined duty to pay proceeds from the trust property to Mrs. Burgess.

Granted, the powers given Mrs. Hosey as trustee were exceedingly broad, as the sections quoted in the recitation of facts indicate. She was, for instance, empowered to "dispose of any . . . property, real or personal, . . . to any person . . . in such manner, and upon such terms and conditions as the executor or trustee shall deem advisable. . . ." Yet this general language was subject to the specific, overriding terms of §5.1 in Mr. Watkins's will, quoted earlier, in which the testator clearly set forth the extent of the duties of the trustees of the testamentary trust: "to hold, manage, and invest the same [real property], to collect the income thereon, and *to pay to, or apply for the benefit of, my spouse the net income thereof. . . .*" (Emphasis added.)

This court held, in *Hardy v. Hardy*, 263 S.W.2d 690, 694 ([Ark.] 1954), that:

> A trustee is at all times disabled from obtaining any personal benefit, advantage, gain, or profit out of his administration of the trust. . . . Any benefit or profit obtained by the trustee inures to the trust estate, even though no injury was intended and none was in fact done to the trust estate. . . .

In the present case, Mrs. Hosey and her late husband, however innocently, failed to adhere to the creating instrument's express directive that they apply the entire net income of the subject property to the benefit of Mrs. Watkins for her life. By the terms of the will, they were prohibited from deriving any personal monetary benefit from the 400 acres. . . .

We hold that the chancellor's findings that Mrs. Hosey and her husband engaged in self-dealing, albeit innocent and unintentional, were not clearly erroneous. . . .

Affirmed.

Post-Case Follow-Up

The court found that the trustees had breached their fiduciary duties, even though they did so unintentionally. In measuring damages, the court would probably have determined the value of the lease for the 400 trust acres, and then the Hoseys would have had to pay the trust the difference between the lease value and the amount the Hoseys had already paid to the trust on their lease. Because Leneva and N.R. acted innocently, the court would be unlikely to add a **surcharge**—a penalty for the breach.

Hosey v. Burgess: Real Life Applications

1. If a trust holds farm property and the best way to generate income for the trust is for the trustee to lease the property to the trustee, in the trustee's individual capacity, what steps should the trustee take to avoid a charge of self-dealing?

2. If Mr. Watkins had asked you to draft his trust, what issues would you have raised with him? Given what you know about his family, what suggestions for the trust would you have had?

Sole Interests or Best Interests?

The duty to act solely in the interests of the beneficiaries is not the same as the duty to act in the best interests of the beneficiaries. In an Illinois case, In re Will of Gleeson, 124 N.E.2d 624 (Ill. App. Ct. 1955), a trustee entered into a lease to prevent loss to the trust. Con Colbrook had leased farmland from Mary Gleeson before her death. When she died, she named Con as trustee of a trust holding her property, including the farm property, for her three children. Mary died 15 days before the start of planting season, so Con, as trustee, renewed the lease to himself. The trust suffered no loss and the court noted that the trustee had acted in good faith, but the court awarded the beneficiaries the profits the trustee earned in his individual capacity as a farmer leasing property from the trust. The trustee had acted in the best interests of the trust by making sure the land was farmed so the trust would receive income, but because the transaction involved a lease to himself, the trustee had not acted in the sole interests of the beneficiaries.

3. Duty to Inform and Report

Related to the duty of loyalty, the **duty to inform and report** requires the trustee to keep the beneficiaries informed about their interests and the administration of the trust. This duty helps the beneficiary enforce any interests in a trust; to do so, the beneficiary must have information about the trust, including its assets, transactions engaged in by the trustee, and income earned by the trust.

The common law requires the trustee to respond to requests for information from any beneficiary. The common law duty has been viewed as a reactive one—the beneficiary has to ask and has to know to ask.

Categories of Beneficiaries

The duties the trustee owes to beneficiaries depends on the category: permissible distributee, qualified beneficiary, or beneficiary. As discussed in Chapter 9, the more limited categories are subsets of the broader categories. All permissible distributees are qualified beneficiaries and beneficiaries. All qualified beneficiaries are beneficiaries. Recall that "qualified beneficiaries" means beneficiaries currently receiving or eligible to receive distributions ("permissible distributees"), beneficiaries who would step into that status if the interests of the permissible distributees ended, and beneficiaries who would be eligible to receive distributions if the trust terminated.

EXHIBIT 11.2   **UTC § 813. Duty to Inform and Report**

(a) A trustee shall keep the qualified beneficiaries of the trust reasonably informed about the administration of the trust and of the material facts necessary for them to protect their interests. Unless unreasonable under the circumstances, a trustee shall promptly respond to a beneficiary's request for information related to the administration of the trust.

(b) A trustee:

   (1) upon request of a beneficiary, shall promptly furnish to the beneficiary a copy of the trust instrument;

   (2) within 60 days after accepting a trusteeship, shall notify the qualified beneficiaries of the acceptance and of the trustee's name, address, and telephone number;

   (3) within 60 days after the date the trustee acquires knowledge of the creation of an irrevocable trust, or the date the trustee acquires knowledge that a formerly revocable trust has become irrevocable, whether by the death of the settlor or otherwise, shall notify the qualified beneficiaries of the trust's existence, of the identity of the settlor or settlors, of the right to request a copy of the trust instrument, and of the right to a trustee's report as provided in subsection (c); and

   (4) shall notify the qualified beneficiaries in advance of any change in the method or rate of the trustee's compensation.

(c) A trustee shall send to the distributees or permissible distributees of trust income or principal, and to other qualified or nonqualified beneficiaries who request it, at least annually and at the termination of the trust, a report of the trust property, liabilities, receipts, and disbursements, including the source and amount of the trustee's compensation, a listing of the trust assets and, if feasible, their respective market values. . . .

(d) A beneficiary may waive the right to a trustee's report or other information otherwise required to be furnished under this section. A beneficiary, with respect to future reports and other information, may withdraw a waiver previously given.

With changes in the types of assets held in trusts, and the increasingly complex duties of trustees, the UTC provides rules for better reporting by trustees. UTC § 813 incorporates the common law rule in paragraph (a) and then adds affirmative notification and reporting duties in (b) and (c). For states that have adopted UTC §§ 105(b)(8) and (9), certain of these duties are mandatory and cannot be removed by the settlor.

In some circumstances, a settlor may not want a beneficiary to know that the beneficiary has interests in a trust. A parent may be creating a trust for a child with a history of drug or alcohol abuse and may fear that the child will engage in undesirable behavior if the child knows that the trust is there as a safety net. Another parent may worry that if a child knows the extent of the assets held for the child's benefit, the child may lose the incentive to work hard and lead a productive life. A settlor may be concerned that a beneficiary will be reckless with the beneficiary's financial affairs knowing that a trustee will provide funds if needed.

For these and other reasons, a settlor may want to limit the duty to inform and report. However, the common law of trusts and the UTC provide that a settlor cannot keep a trust secret from a beneficiary, because the beneficiary needs information to be able to monitor the trustee and enforce the trust. To provide an option to keep a particular beneficiary from knowing about a trust, some jurisdictions have modified the UTC to allow the settlor to provide that notice can be given to another person instead of the beneficiary. See, e.g., D.C. Code § 19-1301.05(c); Or. Rev. Stat. § 130.020(3). The other person must be designated by the settlor and is charged with protecting the interests of the beneficiary. The settlor can provide that all information about the trust be sent to the designated person.

4. Representation

Beneficiaries who lack legal capacity or are not yet born need representation. The UTC permits representation by **fiduciaries**, which is consistent with law predating the UTC. In addition, the UTC provides for representation of minor and unborn children by a parent, or by a person who has an interest "substantially identical to" the interest of the person being represented.

 **EXHIBIT 11.3** **UTC § 303. Representation by Fiduciaries and Parents *and* UTC § 304. Representation by Person Having Substantially Identical Interest**

UTC § 303: To the extent there is no conflict of interest between the representative and the person represented or among those being represented with respect to a particular question or dispute:

(1) a [conservator] may represent and bind the estate that the [conservator] controls;
(2) a [guardian] may represent and bind the ward if a [conservator] of the ward's estate has not been appointed;
(3) an agent having authority to act with respect to the particular question or dispute may represent and bind the principal;
(4) a trustee may represent and bind the beneficiaries of the trust;
(5) a personal representative of a decedent's estate may represent and bind persons interested in the estate; and

(6) a parent may represent and bind the parent's minor or unborn child if a [conservator] or [guardian] for the child has not been appointed.

UTC § 304: Unless otherwise represented, a minor, incapacitated, or unborn individual, or a person whose identity or location is unknown and not reasonably ascertainable, may be represented by and bound by another having a substantially identical interest with respect to the particular question or dispute, but only to the extent there is no conflict of interest between the representative and the person represented.

The representation provisions under UTC § 303 apply only if the person representing another beneficiary does not have a conflict of interest. For example: a trust provides for income payments to Noah, for life, and on Noah's death, for distributions of the remaining principal to Noah's descendants. If representation is needed to approve a self-dealing sale of some property held in the trust to Trevor, the trustee, Noah can represent his descendants to approve the sale. Noah's interests are not in conflict with those of his descendants. If, however, representation is needed to terminate the trust early and distribute a portion of the property to Noah and a portion to his two children, Aaron and Ben, Noah cannot represent his descendants. His interest is in conflict with the interests of his children and other descendants. Aaron can represent Ben, because their interests are the same, but Aaron and Ben cannot represent their own children (Noah's grandchildren), because early termination would end the interests of Noah's descendants other than Aaron and Ben.

5. Duty of Impartiality

A trust typically provides for more than one beneficiary, and the beneficiaries' interests may occur at different times. For example, a trust might provide for income to a surviving spouse for life, with the remainder of the trust going to the settlor's children from a prior marriage. The **duty of impartiality** means that the trustee must manage the trust in a way that keeps the interests of all current beneficiaries and future beneficiaries in mind while making investment decisions or making distributions to any one beneficiary. The duty of impartiality is not, however, a duty to treat all beneficiaries in the same way. The trustee must consider the directions from the settlor to determine whether distributions should favor one beneficiary over another.

Example: Duty of Impartiality

Jayne creates a trust for her surviving spouse, Sheila, and provides that on Sheila's death, any property left in the trust should be distributed to Jayne's daughter from a prior relationship, Jamika. The trustee is directed to distribute all the income to Sheila, and to make distributions from principal to Sheila for her support and maintenance. Note that the type of investments will affect how much "income" is generated in the trust, and also that any distribution of principal to Sheila will affect the amount remaining in the trust for distribution to Jamika. The trustee must not only follow any relevant instructions within the trust's terms but also consider the interests of both Sheila and Jamika when exercising discretion as to how much principal to distribute and how to invest the trust assets.

6. Duty of Care

The **duty of care** is the duty to manage trust property and to administer the trust with "reasonable care, skill, and caution." See Restatement (Third) of Trusts § 77(2) (2003). This duty includes the duties to gather and protect the property, to keep proper records, to keep the property separate from the trustee's own property, and to invest prudently. The duty of care is now often referred to as the duty of prudence.

Protecting Trust Property

Before turning to a discussion of the trustee's duty to invest the trust property, we will review the basic rules for protecting the trust property. At the time the trust is created, the trustee must take control of all the assets in the trust and must take reasonable steps to protect the property. The trustee must take reasonable steps to collect assets that may be held by someone else, and should enforce claims of the trust if the trustee determines it will be cost effective to do so. The trustee need not enforce a claim, for example against a prior trustee, if the cost of doing so exceeds the benefit to the trust. The trustee should also defend the trust assets against claims if they arise, such as claims arising out of an accident that occurs on real estate held in the trust.

The trustee must keep all trust property separate from the trustee's own property (the **duty not to commingle**), and the title of the property should indicate that the trustee holds the property as trustee and not in the trustee's personal capacity (the **duty to earmark**). These duties are important to protect the property from any creditors of the trustee. The trustee must keep adequate records of the property and the administration of the trust.

Investing Trust Property—the Prudent Investor Rule

The legal understanding of what it means to invest prudently has evolved over the years. The duty has changed from strict rules with limited discretion for trustees, to the **prudent investor standard**, now codified in the **Uniform Prudent Investor Act (UPIA)**. The prudent investor standard applies throughout the United States, either through statutes or case law. UPIA has been widely adopted and is influential even where it has not been adopted, so we will use UPIA to understand the prudent investor standard.

UPIA directs a trustee to "invest and manage trust assets as a prudent investor would, by considering the purposes, terms, distribution requirements, and other circumstances of the trust." UPIA § 2(a).

A trustee must use "reasonable care, skill, and caution" in making investment decisions. Under this objective standard of prudence, a prudent trustee should make decisions that other similarly situated trustees would make. A prudent investor follows investment industry norms. The idea of what is prudent will continue to evolve.

A trustee must manage the trust's assets in a way that protects the value of the assets over time. For most trusts, the trustee will invest the assets with two goals:

1. to produce income for the income beneficiaries, and
2. to increase the value of the trust property for the remainder beneficiaries.

UPIA provides a list of factors to guide trustees, including factors related to the trust purposes and beneficiaries, as well as general economic factors. UPIA § 2. The trustee can, and should, make decisions with the entire portfolio in mind and should not make decisions on an asset-by-asset basis. That is, risk should be managed across the portfolio, and the trustee should be attentive to maintaining an appropriate balance of risk and reward.

In order to determine the appropriate level of risk, the trustee must consider the purposes and beneficiaries of the trust. A trust with limited assets and a beneficiary dependent on those assets for basic needs should be managed with a lower risk tolerance than a larger trust with a beneficiary who has other income and assets. UPIA emphasizes diversification of assets, because modern portfolio theory posits that diversification reduces risk in a portfolio.

In addition to changes relating to the standard for investment decision making, UPIA permits a trustee to delegate investment and management functions, as long as the trustee is careful in selecting and reviewing the investment advisor or other person. This represents a change from the common law rule, which limited the trustee's power to delegate.

Under the common law of trusts, a trustee can delegate **ministerial functions** (e.g., preparing tax returns) but not **discretionary functions** (e.g., decisions on distributions to beneficiaries). This nondelegation rule worked well historically, when trusts held only real property, but as the types of assets managed by trustees changed, the nondelegation rule presented significant problems for investment decision making. Investment decisions were not considered ministerial, so a delegation of decision making to investment advisors constituted a breach of the duty not to delegate. UPIA § 9 sets out the rules a trustee must follow when delegating authority to act.

Case Preview

In re Trust Created by Inman

The prudent investor standard encourages diversification, but sometimes the beneficiaries of a trust prefer to keep property with family significance in the trust. In the *Inman* case, the trustee sought court approval of a self-dealing transaction. The trustee wanted to buy property held in the trust for his individual purposes, and he argued that the court should authorize the sale because selling the property was necessary to comply with the duty to diversify under UPIA, which Nebraska had adopted. The trust held 189 acres of farmland, and the trustee wanted to sell 42 acres to himself and then invest that money in other investments. After the trial court refused to permit the sale because a number of beneficiaries, children and grandchildren of the settlor, objected, Brackett appealed. On appeal, he had an expert, Dr. David Volkman, testify about the prudent investor rule and whether the trust assets were invested prudently. This case provides a good discussion of the duty to diversify and the reasons nondiversification is sometimes preferred.

As you read the case, consider:

1. How does the trustee use the duty to diversify to argue that he should be allowed to buy land held in the trust?
2. How do other family members use UPIA's provision about nondiversification to support their argument that the property should stay in the trust?
3. What information does the court consider?
4. What does the court's opinion state about nondiversification?

In re Trust Created by Inman
693 N.W.2d 514 (Neb. 2005)

... Dr. David Volkman testified on behalf of Brackett [trustee of a revocable trust created by his grandfather, Harold Inman, now deceased] as an expert in economics and finance. Volkman reviewed the trust instrument, the assets held and income earned by the trust, the Nebraska Uniform Prudent Investor Act, information from the National Council of Real Estate Investment Fiduciaries, equity returns from a database, and the appraisals prepared by Wohlenhaus. Based upon this information, Volkman opined that because the assets of the trust were not diversified, the standards of the Nebraska Uniform Prudent Investor Act were not met. Volkman analyzed the diversification of the trust in relation to the return and risk of the investments and compared the rate of return on farmland as opposed to other types of investments. Asked to evaluate the risk associated with the trust assets as then held, Volkman stated:

> The greatest risk is that it's not diversified. It's invested all in one asset. And when you invest in one asset, you significantly increase the probability of not receiving the return that you would like to it. It would be similar if you went out and bought one stock and put all of your savings in one stock. There's a high probability you may not get the return that you want from that one stock.

Volkman further testified that farmland has a lower rate of return and higher risk for rate of return compared to the Dow Jones index, a higher rate of return and higher risk than treasury notes, and a significantly lower rate of return but also less risk than the NASDAQ Composite Index. He testified that the overall risk to the beneficiaries could be reduced by having a portion of the corpus invested in farmland and other portions in investments which would yield a higher rate of return.

Maryann Tremaine, [one of] Inman's [surviving children], testified as a spokesperson for the five beneficiaries who filed a written objection to the sale. She opposed the sale because of her belief that Inman intended the farmland to remain in trust for all of the beneficiaries and that it would increase in value over time. . . . Two beneficiaries who did not file written objections also testified in opposition to the sale. Peters opposed the sale because she believed the property should remain "in the family" and was satisfied with the current income. One of Inman's granddaughters who is a beneficiary of the trust testified that she opposed the sale because "I truly believe my grandfather left the property for everybody to enjoy. It has sentimental value to the whole family, not just one person." . . .

ASSIGNMENTS OF ERRORS

Brackett assigns, combined and restated, that by denying him authority to sell the trust property to himself, the probate court (1) failed to allow him to diversify the assets of the trust in compliance with the Nebraska Uniform Prudent Investor Act and (2) erroneously allowed principles against self-dealing to trump statutory law and trust provisions that authorized the requested sale. . . .

Resolution of the issue prescribed by this appeal requires an examination of the relationship between two separate legal duties owed by a trustee to the beneficiaries of the trust. . . . [We will discuss] the trustee's duties of loyalty and compliance with the prudent investor rule.

The record reflects that Brackett has purely personal reasons for seeking to acquire the 42-acre parcel from the trust. Brackett, who described himself as one who invests, remodels, and sells real estate, testified that he moved the farmhouse which he had purchased at auction to the trust property because he had "nowhere else to put it." He further acknowledged that he sought more land than was necessary for a home site because "I wanted my kids to have a good sized piece of land. I've always worked the land when I was a kid there and played up there. And it has some sentimental value, and I wanted more of a farmstead for my kids to grow up on." Brackett argues, however, that the county court should nevertheless have approved the sale because investment of the proceeds in something other than agricultural real estate would provide diversification of trust assets in a manner consistent with the prudent investor rule, thereby benefiting all the beneficiaries.

The prudent investor rule applicable to trustees is now codified at §§30-3883 to 30-3889. Included in that rule is the principle that a "trustee shall diversify the investments of the trust unless the trustee reasonably determines that, because of special circumstances, the purposes of the trust are better served without diversifying." §30-3885. On the record before us, we conclude that there was no absolute duty to diversify the trust assets which would compel court approval of the proposed sale. The prudent investor rule is a "default rule" which "may be expanded, restricted, eliminated, or otherwise altered by the provisions of a trust." §30-3883(b). It is true, as Brackett argues, that the trust instrument in this case gave the trustee broad powers in dealing with trust assets, including the power "[t]o receive, hold, manage and care for the property held in trust," and "[t]o sell publicly or privately for cash or on time, property, real or personal, held in trust. . . ." However, the trust instrument also conferred upon the trustee the power

> [t]o retain any property, whether consisting of stocks, bonds, other securities, participations in common trust funds, or of any other type of personal property or of real property, taken over by it as a portion of the trust, *without regard to the proportion such property or property of a similar character so held may bear to the entire amount of the trust,* whether or not such property is of the class in which trustees generally are authorized to invest by law or rule of court; *intending thereby to authorize the Trustee to act in such manner as will be for the best interest of the trust beneficiaries,* giving due consideration to the preservation of principal and the amount and regularity of the income to be derived therefrom.

(Emphasis supplied.) With respect to assets originally placed in trust, this provision modifies the general duty to diversify by authorizing the trustee to retain nondiversified assets if retention would be in the best interests of the beneficiaries.

Furthermore, the trustee's statutory duty to diversify trust assets is subject to the general "prudent investor" standard of care which requires a trustee to consider various circumstances relevant to the trust or its beneficiaries in investing and managing trust assets. §30-3884(c). These circumstances include "[a]n asset's special relationship or special value, if any, to the purposes of the trust or to one or more of the beneficiaries." §30-3884(c)(8). We agree with a commentator who has noted that a similar provision in the Nebraska Uniform Prudent Investor Act could be utilized as a basis for justifying "non-diversification" of a family farm or ranch held in trust in favor of retaining the asset "for future generations of the family." Ronald R. Volkmer, *The Latest Look in Nebraska Trust Law*, 31 Creighton L. Rev. 221, 246 (1997). Brackett's professed "sentimental" attachment to the farmland which has been in his family for many years is clearly shared by the other family members who are beneficiaries of the trust. Those who filed an objection or testified in opposition to the proposed sale expressed the view that excising a 42-acre parcel from the 189-acre farm would have a detrimental effect upon their special relationship with the asset without achieving any appreciable benefit. . . .

We conclude that the judgment of the county court conforms to the law, is supported by competent evidence, and is neither arbitrary, capricious, nor unreasonable. Finding no error appearing on the record, we affirm.

Post-Case Follow-Up

This case provides a good example of the balancing a trustee must do. UPIA requires a trustee to diversify investments—unless purposes of the trust are better served by not diversifying. UPIA also directs a trustee to consider an asset's special relationship to the purposes of the trust or the beneficiaries. Although beneficiaries may complain if a trustee sells an asset with special significance to the beneficiaries, they may also complain if the assets remain undiversified and the trust loses value. In In re J.P. Morgan Chase Bank, N.A., 41 Misc. 3d 1231(A) (2013) (unreported decision), the trustee held onto Kodak stock that constituted a significant part of the trust assets, probably due to the family's connections with the founding of the company. With the advent of digital photography, the stock lost value and the beneficiaries sued the trustee. The court ordered the trustee to pay more than $3 million in damages.

---

7. Investments, Trust Accounting, and the Duty of Impartiality

Income and Principal

Investments in a trust generate **revenue**, and special rules called **trust accounting rules**, codified in the **Uniform Principal and Income Act**, determine whether the revenue is treated as **income** or **principal**.

- If the revenue is considered income, then the *income beneficiary* gets a distribution.
- If the revenue is classified as principal, then the *remainder beneficiary* will get more when the trust terminates.
- If the trustee has discretion to distribute principal to one or more beneficiaries before the trust terminates, the extent of that discretionary authority will depend on how much principal is available.

So, what is considered income and what is considered principal for trust accounting? The trust accounting rules address many different types of investments, but we need only consider these rules in a general sense.

The assets transferred to the trustee by the settlor are *principal*. These assets are the initial property in the trust, and they, and any other assets contributed to the trust by the settlor, will remain principal.

Most receipts generated through investing the assets, less associated expenses including taxes, are considered *income* from a trust accounting perspective, with the big exception being **capital gains** (profit from sale of an asset). Thus, interest on bonds and on savings and checking accounts, dividends paid by corporations, the annual net profit of a business, and rents from real estate are all allocated to the *income account*.

However, any increase in the value of stocks, bonds, businesses, and real estate (appreciation in value) is allocated to principal. If a stock is sold, the shareholder will recognize "capital gain," the appreciation in the value of the stock from the time of purchase to the time of sale. Capital gains are income for income tax purposes, but will be allocated to the *principal account* for trust accounting purposes.

Note also that assets can decline in value, so the principal could shrink as the result of a capital loss.

Some Investments May Be More Likely to Generate Income or Principal

Some investments, such as bonds, generate returns in the form of interest (characterized as income) and do not appreciate or depreciate much. If the interest is paid to the income beneficiaries, they benefit, but when the remainder beneficiaries finally get the remainder, it may be worth an amount similar to its value when the investment was made. Given the risk of inflation, the remainder interest may have lost value over time.

Other investments may not generate income but may have a significant potential for appreciation in value. For example, a company may not pay dividends (characterized as income) because the company wants to invest all profits in the growth of the company. As the company grows, the stock price will increase in value (characterized as principal). This type of investment will benefit the remainder beneficiary, but the income beneficiary may receive little.

Duty of Impartiality Affects Investment Decisions

The duty of impartiality (discussed above) affects investment decisions, because the trustee must balance the need to generate income for the income beneficiaries with the need to preserve and increase the principal of the trust for the remainder beneficiaries. If a trustee chooses investments based on the likelihood that the investments will generate trust accounting income, in order to increase amounts going to the income beneficiary, the trustee may not be making decisions a prudent investor would make.

A prudent investor should invest in the way that will generate the greatest overall return within the risk tolerance of the portfolio. A prudent investor should not make investment decisions based on increasing returns for the income beneficiary or generating appreciation for the remainder beneficiary.

The Uniform Principal and Income Act

The Uniform Principal and Income Act starts with the traditional income and principal allocation rules described above. Then, if the basic allocation rules do not result in an appropriate division of income and principal, given the needs of the beneficiaries and the directions in the trust, the Uniform Principal and Income Act gives the trustee a **power to adjust**. The trustee can make adjustments in how receipts are allocated between the income and principal accounts. In deciding whether to make an adjustment, the trustee must consider all factors relevant to the purpose of the trust and the beneficiaries. The power to adjust is a significant change from prior statutes and allows the trustee to engage in prudent portfolio investing while maintaining fair allocations for both income and remainder beneficiaries.

In the statutes of some states, trustees can elect **unitrust treatment** as an alternative to continually making adjustments between the income and principal accounts. The Uniform Fiduciary Income and Principal Act, adopted by the Uniform Law Commission in 2018 and available for state adoption, also permits unitrust treatment. A unitrust pays the income beneficiary a fixed percentage of the value of the principal instead of trust accounting income. For example, the trustee of a trust governed by New York law may elect to pay 4 percent of the value of the trust, based on a three-year rolling average, as an alternative to paying trust accounting income or to exercising the power to adjust. N.Y. EPTL § 11-2.4. Like the power to adjust, a unitrust election aligns the investment incentives of income beneficiaries and remainder beneficiaries, and allows a trustee to invest for total return rather than to generate receipts that have a particular trust accounting identity as income or principal. A unitrust election may, therefore, help shield the trustee from liability stemming from a breach of fiduciary duty.

8. Remedies for Breach

The beneficiaries of a trust have standing to sue the trustee for a **breach of trust**—that is, a failure to comply with one or more fiduciary duties. Co-trustees, and, in the case of a charitable trust, the Attorney General, also have standing. If a trustee commits a breach of trust, the trustee will be personally liable to the beneficiaries for any loss to the value of trust assets caused by the breach and also for any profit the trustee obtained. UTC § 1002. Even if there has been no breach, the trustee will be liable for any profit made while administering the trust, other than reasonable compensation, but not for losses suffered by the trust. UTC § 1003.

The court has a variety of remedies available to address or prevent a breach:

- A court might enjoin the trustee from committing a breach of trust,
- compel the trustee to pay for a loss caused by a breach,
- require the trustee to restore property to the trust,
- order the trustee to account to the beneficiaries or the court,
- remove the trustee, or
- reduce or deny compensation owed to the trustee.

9. Removal of a Trustee

A court may remove a trustee for a variety of reasons. The most important basis for removal, both under the common law and the UTC, is a serious breach of trust. Failing to care for trust property, engaging in self-dealing with trust property, or refusing to provide information to beneficiaries despite repeated requests (over a period of time) can be grounds for removal. The more serious the breach, the more likely the court will be to remove the trustee.

A pattern of smaller breaches may also result in removal. A court may consider removing a trustee if co-trustees cannot or will not cooperate in managing the trust. For example, if a trust has two trustees (or any even number of trustees) and the two trustees cannot agree, no decisions can be made for the trust. The court may decide to remove one or both of the trustees. A pattern of being unable to make decisions for the trust would be considered a breach.

The UTC also makes removal possible in the event of substantially changed circumstances affecting the trust or the agreement of the beneficiaries that the trustee should be removed. The court must determine that removal is in the best interests of the beneficiaries and that removal is not inconsistent with a material purpose of the trust. If the settlor wanted a particular trustee to manage the trust, the settlor's choice of trustee might be considered a material purpose and make removal difficult. We look at the material purpose doctrine in connection with modification of trusts later in this chapter.

Trust documents themselves often grant to named individuals or beneficiaries the power to remove and replace trustees. In these cases, no court intervention or wrongdoing is necessary for a trustee to be removed.

EXHIBIT 11.4 **Sample Language to Remove and Replace a Corporate Trustee**

> Anything in this will to the contrary notwithstanding, a majority of the adult income beneficiaries of any trust hereunder shall have the right at any time and from time to time, by written instrument, to remove any corporate Trustee acting hereunder; provided, however, that they contemporaneously appoint a successor corporate Trustee.

---

10. Trust Director

A **trust director**, also called a **trust protector**, is someone named in a trust instrument with a specific power in connection with the trust. A settlor can give a trust director one or many powers, such as the power to remove the trustee and appoint a new trustee (other than the trust director); to make, direct, or veto investment decisions; to allocate sale proceeds between income and principal; to change the **situs** of the trust (the place the trust is administered); and to terminate the trust under specified conditions. A settlor might also give a trust director, rather than the trustee, the power to rearrange beneficial interests in keeping with the settlor's general intent.

The concept of trust director or trust protector has developed piecemeal, with confusion over the fiduciary status of trust directors and the trustees who are subject to direction. In 2017, the Uniform Law Commission completed the Uniform Directed Trust Act, which clarifies the fiduciary duties of both trust directors and **directed trustees**, who are trustees subject to direction from a trust director. Minimum fiduciary duties are mandatory for both, but the settlor can control the fiduciary requirements to a degree. The Uniform Directed Trust Act explains the powers and duties of a trust director and a directed trustee and provides rules for information sharing and monitoring among trust directors and trustees.

B. MODIFICATION AND TERMINATION

Over time, modification of the terms of the trust may become necessary to respond to changes in the beneficiaries' needs or circumstances, to address changes in the law, to obtain tax benefits, to fix mistakes in the original document, or for other purposes. A trust instrument can provide the circumstances under which a trust can be modified or terminated, but the trust document may not always do so. Early common law, with its emphasis on settlor intent, made modification at the request of beneficiaries difficult, but recent cases and the UTC increasingly provide beneficiaries greater opportunities for amendment or early termination of a trust.

In this section, we look first at revocable trusts; they permit modification by the settlor under a retained power to modify or revoke. We then examine the rules that apply to irrevocable trusts: first, when the settlor is alive; and second, after the settlor's death or when the settlor is otherwise unable to give consent to modification.

As you read the materials on modification, keep in mind that the rules on modification typically also apply to termination of a trust.

1. Revocable Trusts

UTC § 602 presumes a trust to be revocable unless the settlor states otherwise, and provides guidance on revocation if the trust instrument does not indicate what the settlor must do to revoke the trust. Because some states still apply the common law presumption that a trust is irrevocable unless the settlor retains the power to revoke or modify, a trust instrument should indicate whether the trust is revocable or irrevocable. A trust drafted by a lawyer normally will do so.

EXHIBIT 11.5   **UTC § 602. Revocation or Amendment of Revocable Trust**

(a) Unless the terms of a trust expressly provide that the trust is irrevocable, the settlor may revoke or amend the trust. This subsection does not apply to a trust created under an instrument executed before [the effective date of this [Code]]. . . .

(c) The settlor may revoke or amend a revocable trust:

   (1) by substantial compliance with a method provided in the terms of the trust; or

   (2) if the terms of the trust do not provide a method or the method provided in the terms is not expressly made exclusive, by:

      (A) a later will or codicil that expressly refers to the trust or specifically devises property that would otherwise have passed according to the terms of the trust; or

      (B) any other method manifesting clear and convincing evidence of the settlor's intent.

If a trust is **revocable**, the settlor can modify or revoke terms of the trust according to the means specified in the trust instrument. If the method set forth in the trust to amend or revoke is **exclusive**, the settlor must follow that method. But, if the method set forth in the trust to amend or revoke is **not exclusive**, other actions can suffice. For example, if the trust instrument requires that revocation be in writing, delivered to the successor trustee, and the settlor prepares a document revoking the trust and leaves it on a desk at home, where it is later found, the action on the part of the settlor is probably sufficient. Beneficiaries other than the settlor do not have a role in modification of a revocable trust, because the power to revoke gives the settlor complete control over modification and revocation.

EXHIBIT 11.6 **Sample Revocation Clause**

A. **Revocation and Amendment.** I reserve the right by written instrument signed by me as Settlor and delivered to my Trustee to revoke or amend this Trust Agreement at any time.
B. **Rights Personal to Me.** The rights of revocation and amendment reserved by me must be exercised by me personally and may not be exercised by any other person, including any agent, guardian or conservator, or other person, except that amendment or revocation may be authorized, after notice to the Trustee, by the court that appointed the conservator or by an agent acting under a durable power of attorney that specifically authorizes such action.

Can a Will Revoke a Trust?

The traditional rule is that a will cannot affect the disposition of a nonprobate asset. The UTC changes this rule for revocable trusts. UTC § 602(c)(2)(A) permits a will to alter provisions in a revocable trust if the will specifically refers to the trust or devises property that would have passed under the trust. Some states that have enacted the UTC take exception to UTC § 602(c)(2)(A), and they do not permit revocation by will.

  If the trust instrument provides that the settlor can revoke the trust by delivering a written revocation to the trustee, a will could constitute the required written revocation. For example, if Alexis is the settlor and trustee of a revocable trust that provides that it may be revoked by "delivery of a writing to the trustee," Alexis's will is a writing. If her will says "I revoke the Alexis Martinez Revocable Trust," when she executes the will, she has delivered a writing revoking the trust to herself. She possesses the document as testator, and she has received it as trustee. If Security Bank is acting as trustee of the Alexis Martinez Revocable Trust, then when Alexis executes her will, she does not revoke the trust unless she sends a copy of the will to Security Bank.

What if the Settlor Loses Capacity to Revoke?

A revocable trust does not necessarily become irrevocable if the settlor loses capacity. The settlor may regain capacity and be able to modify or revoke the trust, or a conservator or agent acting under a power of attorney may be able to modify or revoke the trust on the settlor's behalf.

Whether a conservator or agent can modify or revoke the trust raises difficult questions, however, because a settlor often creates a revocable trust to plan for the possibility of incapacity. UTC § 602 tries to limit disruption of the settlor's estate plan by providing safeguards for revocation or modification by others acting for an incapacitated settlor. These issues are addressed in Chapter 7.

2. Irrevocable Trusts

An irrevocable trust may be flexible enough that it will not need modification, and its terms will specify when it terminates. If, however, the trust is not sufficiently flexible and needs modification, then there are legal standards for modifying it. We look first at the rules for modification when the settlor is alive and then at the rules that apply when the settlor cannot consent to a modification, typically after the settlor's death. We consider modification to fix a mistake, modification for tax reasons, and termination when the value of property in the trust makes continued management uneconomic.

Building Flexibility into a Trust

Modification may be unnecessary if the trust has been created with enough flexibility to allow the trustee or beneficiaries to adapt to changes that occur over time. The following tools and strategies can add flexibility:

- Standards that give the trustee a broad range of discretion, such as absolute or unlimited discretion;
- A definition of spouse that would include only the person to whom the settlor or a beneficiary is currently married so that divorce will terminate any beneficial interest for the person;
- A provision giving the beneficiaries the power to replace the trustee with a different, independent trustee;
- A provision giving the trustee the power to make loans to beneficiaries;
- A provision giving the trustee the power to change nondispositive provisions of the trust;
- A provision giving a trust director (discussed earlier in this chapter) the power to change dispositive or nondispositive provisions; or
- A provision giving certain individuals a power of appointment (see Chapter 12).

Termination According to the Terms of a Trust

A trust will typically terminate according to the terms of the trust or because the trust has no more property. For example, a trust that directs the trustee to distribute income to Philip for life and on Philip's death to distribute the remaining principal to Philip's descendants, will terminate on Philip's death. If the trust includes the power to make distributions of principal to Philip for Philip's best interests, the trust could terminate earlier if the trustee made distributions of all the trust property.

Modification or Termination with the Settlor's Consent

The common law and the UTC provide that if the settlor and all the beneficiaries agree, they can modify (or terminate) an irrevocable trust without going to court to get approval. Because the settlor is included in the decision to modify, modification can occur even if the modifications are inconsistent with a material purpose of the trust. UTC § 411(a). (See discussion below on the material purpose doctrine.) Some lawyers worry that allowing a settlor to participate in a decision to terminate a trust will have adverse tax consequences, by causing the trust to be included in the settlor's estate for estate tax purposes because the settlor retained an interest in the trust. (The federal estate tax is discussed in Chapter 15.) For that reason, some trusts include a provision that prevents the settlor from modifying or terminating the trust or joining with others to do so.

Modification or Termination by Beneficiaries Without the Settlor's Consent

Often when a trust needs to be modified, the consent of the settlor is not available. The settlor may be dead or have lost capacity, or the terms of the trust may prevent the settlor from consenting to a modification. Without the settlor's consent, the beneficiaries will need to ask a court for approval to terminate the trust or modify its terms. The law makes modification after the settlor's death difficult, especially when the desired modification may conflict with a "material purpose" that the settlor had in establishing the trust. If the settlor is still alive and opposes a modification, modification will be even more difficult because the settlor can argue against it.

Material Purpose Doctrine

The common law doctrine is that modification by beneficiaries will be permitted only if the modification is not contrary to a "material purpose" of the settlor. This doctrine, established by Claflin v. Claflin, 20 N.E. 454 (Mass. 1899) and known as the *Claflin* doctrine or the material purpose doctrine, prevents modification of many common provisions in trusts. Anything the settlor considered an important reason for the trust may be considered material.

Claflin itself involved a provision that delayed termination of a trust until the beneficiary reached age 30. The beneficiary asked that the court terminate the trust when he reached age 21 and the court refused, noting that the settlor had the right to impose restrictions on property transferred in trust and to have those restrictions enforced.

Almost a hundred years later, in In re Estate of Brown, 528 A.2d 752 (Vt. 1987), the court denied modification citing the material purpose doctrine. In *Estate of Brown*, the beneficiaries wanted to terminate a trust and distribute the corpus to the lifetime beneficiaries who were the parents of the remainder beneficiaries. Even though the remainder beneficiaries consented to the request to terminate the trust, the court refused, finding that a material purpose of the settlor in setting up the trust was to have a professional manage the property for the lifetimes of the beneficiaries.

The management of trust assets for a beneficiary's lifetime or until a beneficiary attains a specified age is typically considered a material purpose. Another provision presumed to be a material purpose under the common law is a **spendthrift clause**. Lawyers routinely include a spendthrift clause in trusts they draft, thus precluding modification by beneficiaries. See Restatement (Second) of Trusts § 337 (1959). The UTC and Restatement (Third) of Trusts reverse the presumption, stating that the mere existence of a spendthrift clause does not mean it was intended as a material purpose. UTC § 411(c); Restatement (Third) of Trusts § 65, cmt. e (2003). Under UTC § 411(c), modification will be denied only if the court determines that the settlor intended that the spendthrift clause be considered a material purpose of the particular trust or that the modification would affect other material purposes of that trust.

Application of the material purpose doctrine always depends on the intent of the settlor when the trust was created. Delayed distribution of the principal or the inclusion of a spendthrift clause are often considered material purposes, but in some situations may not be material to a settlor. In any request for modification, the court will try to determine what mattered to the settlor. No bright-line rules exist for determining when a provision constitutes a material purpose.

If no material purpose of the trust would be frustrated by its termination or modification, the court will order modification if the beneficiaries agree to a

In re Trust Under Will of Flint

The absence of a trust director to advise the trustee was deemed a material purpose in In re Trust Under Will of Flint, 118 A.3d 182 (Del. Ch. 2015).

Wallace Flint, the brother of the founder of IBM, created a testamentary trust for his wife, and the trust continued after her death for their daughter, Katherine. At the time Katherine requested modification, she served as co-trustee with J.P. Morgan, and IBM stock constituted 81 percent of the value of the trust assets. The bank wanted to diversify, but the family (Katherine and her children) did not.

As a strategy to protect the bank, Katherine asked the court to modify the trust to create an Investment Advisor and then provide that the trustee would exercise its investment powers only as directed by the Investment Advisor. The court refused to authorize the modification, saying it violated a material purpose of the settlor, who "contemplated that the trustees would exercise judgment and discretion, not act as marionettes for the Investment Advisor."

modification and if *all* of the beneficiaries consent. UTC § 411(b). Even if all beneficiaries do not agree, a court may authorize modification or termination under certain conditions. UTC § 411(e).

EXHIBIT 11.7 | **UTC § 411. Modification or Termination of Noncharitable Irrevocable Trust by Consent**

(b) A noncharitable irrevocable trust may be *terminated* upon consent of all of the beneficiaries if the court concludes that continuance of the trust is not necessary to achieve any material purpose of the trust. A noncharitable irrevocable trust may be *modified* upon consent of all of the beneficiaries if the court concludes that modification is not inconsistent with a material purpose of the trust.

[(c)] A spendthrift provision in the terms of the trust is not presumed to constitute a material purpose of the trust.] . . .

(e) If not all of the beneficiaries consent to a proposed modification or termination of the trust under subsection (a) or (b), the modification or termination may be approved by the court if the court is satisfied that:

(1) if all of the beneficiaries had consented, the trust could have been modified or terminated under this section; and

(2) the interests of a beneficiary who does not consent will be adequately protected.

In order to obtain consent from all the beneficiaries, someone may need to represent minors, those not yet born, or beneficiaries under another legal disability. Common law trust doctrine provides some rules on representation for these beneficiaries, but the law in many states has not adequately addressed representation. As discussed earlier in this chapter, the UTC provides rules for several types of representation. In the absence of a conflict of interest, a parent can represent minor and unborn children, a conservator or guardian can represent the person he is appointed to protect, and a person with a "substantially identical interest" in the question or dispute can represent a beneficiary. These representation rules apply to modification and termination. If no other representation is possible, a court can appoint a representative. UTC § 305. A representative appointed by a court "may consider general benefit accruing to the living members of the individual's family" when making decisions. UTC § 305(c).

Modification or Termination Due to Changed Circumstances

The doctrine of **deviation**, also called **equitable deviation**, allows a court to modify a provision or terminate the trust to give effect to the primary intent the settlor had in creating the trust. The modification may change the settlor's directions to the trustee in some respect, but effectuate the settlor's overall intent with respect to the trust. Under this doctrine, a court can modify a provision not only due to changed circumstances, but also due to unanticipated circumstances—something the settlor did not know about when the settlor created the trust.

This approach applies to charitable trusts (discussed in Chapter 9) as well as to private trusts.

Courts have been more willing to use equitable deviation to modify administrative terms (those addressing operation of the trust) than dispositive terms (those addressing distributions). For example, in Donnelly v. National Bank of Washington, 179 P.2d 333 (Wash. 1947), the court allowed the modification of a termination provision imposed by the settlor. The settlor had directed that the trust created for his grandson's legal education be terminated when the grandchild reached a certain age. The grandson was drafted into the military and was unable to complete his legal education before the deadline. The court said that extending the trust furthered the settlor's intent to provide for the legal education of his grandson.

Historically, courts have been reluctant to authorize modification of dispositive provisions, but the Restatement (Third) of Trusts states that a modification that furthers the intent of the settlor should be permitted. Indeed, Restatement (Third) of Trusts § 66 (2003) now imposes a duty on the trustee to request modification of an administrative provision that might cause substantial harm to the trust.

Case Preview

In re Riddell

In this case the court relies on the Restatement (Third) to permit modification of a dispositive term in a trust. Ralph Riddell's parents had created trusts (consolidated into one trust by the time of the case) to provide for Ralph and his spouse for their lives and then to distribute the trust property to Ralph's children. The distributions to Ralph's children would be made only after the children attained age 35, and at the time of the case, both were older than 35. Ralph, as trustee, sought to modify the trust to provide that his daughter's share be distributed to a special needs trust for her benefit. A special needs trust is one that permits limited distributions to a beneficiary, for "special needs" and not for support; set up properly, a special needs trust can hold property for a beneficiary in a way that does not disqualify the beneficiary from government benefits for which the beneficiary has qualified. The change in *Riddell* involved a dispositive term, but the court concluded that permitting the change would further the settlor's intent.

As you read the case, consider:

1. What were the changed circumstances that led Ralph to seek the modification?
2. What would happen if the court did not permit the modification?
3. What did the trial court decide? Why?
4. Where did the appellate court find support for its view that modification would be consistent with the settlor's intent?

In re Riddell
157 P.3d 888 (Wash. Ct. App. 2007)

PENOYAR, J.

The Trustee of a consolidated trust, Ralph A. Riddell, appeals the trial court's denial of his motion to modify the trust and create a special needs trust on behalf of a trust beneficiary, his daughter, Nancy I. Dexter, who suffers from schizophrenia affective disorder and bipolar disorder. Ralph's deceased father and mother [established a trust]. Upon Ralph's death, the trust will terminate and Nancy will receive payment of her portion of the trust proceeds. . . . Ralph argues that the trial court has the power to modify the trust; that his daughter's disabilities are a changed and unanticipated condition; and that the purpose of the settlor will be preserved through the modification. We agree and remand to the trial court to reconsider an equitable deviation in light of changed circumstances and the settlors' intent that the beneficiaries receive both medical care and general support from the trust's funds.

FACTS

. . .

The Trustee . . . explained that, under the current trust, when her parents die, Nancy's portion of the principal will be distributed to her and the trust will terminate. He argued that a special needs trust is necessary because, upon distribution, Nancy's trust funds would either be seized by the State of Washington to pay her extraordinary medical bills or Nancy would manage the funds poorly due to her mental illness and lack of judgment. He argued that the modification would preserve and properly manage Nancy's funds for her benefit.

The trial court [] denied the motion to modify. It stated that it did not have the power to modify the trust unless unanticipated events existed that were unknown to the trust creator that would result in defeating the trust's purpose. The trial court found that the trust's purpose was "to provide for the education, support, maintenance, and medical care of the beneficiaries" and that a modification would only "permit[] the family to immunize itself financially from reimbursing the State for costs of [Nancy's medical] care." Relying on the Restatement (Second) of Trusts, it stated that it would not allow a modification "merely because a change would be more advantageous to the beneficiaries." Restatement (Third) of Trusts §66 cmt. b (2001). It did not issue factual findings or legal conclusions with its order but incorporated its reasoning from its oral ruling into the order.

Ralph moved for reconsideration, arguing that [Washington law] and the Restatement (Third) gave the trial court plenary power to handle all trusts and trust matters and the authority to modify the consolidated trust into a special needs trust. Ralph argued that, because the grandparents directed the trust proceeds to be distributed to their grandchildren when they reach the age of thirty-five, the settlors intended that their grandchildren attain a level of responsibility, stability, and maturity to handle the funds before receiving the distribution. He also argued that due to Nancy's mental illness, allowing a distribution to her would defeat the settlors' intent and the trust's purpose.

The trial court denied the motion for reconsideration. . . .

ANALYSIS

II. *Trust Modification*

Ralph asserts that the trial court had the authority to modify the trust under both the equitable deviation doctrine and under the plenary power granted by [state law, which] states that it is the Legislature's intent to give courts full and ample power to administer and settle all trust matters. . . . The trial court understood that it possessed the ability to modify the trust.

Next, Ralph contends that the trial court erred in declining to modify the trust. He explains that a modification would further the trust's purpose because, if George and Irene had anticipated that Nancy would suffer debilitating mental illness requiring extraordinary levels of medical costs and make her incapable of managing her money independently, they would not have structured the trust to leave a substantial outright distribution of the trust principal to her. He contends that the settlors instead would have established a special needs trust to protect the funds because Nancy's medical bills would be extraordinary and covered by state funding.

Ralph explains that the settlors conditioned the distribution of trust assets on her being at least thirty-five years old, indicating that they intended that their grandchildren have a level of maturity and stability before receiving the trust distribution. Ralph asserts that given Nancy's medical conditions and inability to handle her finances independently, she will never attain a level of maturity to handle the distribution of funds; therefore a special needs trust is appropriate.

Niemann [*v. Vaughn Cmty. Church*, 113 P.3d 463 (Wash. 2005)], is very instructive in this case. In *Niemann*, our Supreme Court held that trial courts may use "equitable deviation" to make changes in the manner in which a trust is carried out. The court outlined the two prong approach of "equitable deviation" used to determine if modification is appropriate. The court "may modify an administrative or distributive provision of a trust, or direct or permit the trustee to deviate from an administrative or distributive provision, if [(1)] because of circumstances not anticipated by the settlor [(2)] the modification or deviation will further the purposes of the trust." Restatement (Third) of Trusts §66(1) (2001). . . .

The first prong of the equitable deviation test is satisfied if circumstances have changed since the trust's creation or if the settlor was unaware of circumstances when the trust was established. Restatement (Third) of Trusts §66 cmt. a (2001). Upon a finding of unanticipated circumstances, the trial court must determine if a modification would tend to advance the trust purposes; this inquiry is likely to involve a subjective process of attempting to infer the relevant purpose of a trust from the general tenor of its provisions. Restatement (Third) of Trusts §66 cmt. b (2001).

The reason to modify is to give effect to the settlor's intent had the circumstances in question been anticipated. Restatement (Third) of Trusts §66 cmt. a (2001). Courts will not ordinarily deviate from the provisions outlined by the trust creator but they undoubtedly have the power to do so, if it is reasonably necessary to effectuate the trust's *primary* purpose. A trust settlor may possess a myriad of intentions in settling a trust, but the trial court must concern itself with their *primary* objective.

As stated above, we defer to the trial court's factual findings. In this case, the trial court did not issue formal factual findings, but it stated in the oral ruling that there was a showing of a changed circumstance in this case. This meets the first prong. The settlor's intent is also a factual question. The trial court found in its oral ruling that the "stated" purpose of the trust is to provide for the beneficiaries' education, support, maintenance, and medical care. Thus, it found that this trust's primary purpose was to provide for Nancy during her lifetime. Because the trust was to terminate at age thirty-five, it was also the settlors' intent that Nancy have the money to dispose of as she saw fit, which would include any estate planning that she might choose to do.

There is no question that changed circumstances have intervened to frustrate the settlors' intent. Nancy's grandparents intended that she have the funds to use as she saw fit. Not only is Nancy unable to manage the funds or to pass them to her son, but there is a great likelihood that the funds will be lost to the State for her medical care. It is clear that the settlors would have wanted a different result.

George and Irene both died without creating a special needs trust but did not know of Nancy's mental health issues or how they might best be addressed. They clearly intended to establish a trust to provide for their grandchildren's general support, not solely for extraordinary and unanticipated medical bills.

We remand to the trial court to reconsider this matter and to order such equitable deviation as is consistent with the settlors' intent in light of changed circumstances.

Post-Case Follow-Up

The court in *Riddell* permitted modification to further the settlors' purposes, based on changed circumstances relating to a beneficiary's need to qualify for government assistance for health care. In Oregon, the appellate court refused to permit modification in similar circumstances. In re Trust of Stuchell, 801 P.2d 852 (Or. Ct. App. 1990). Oregon estate planning lawyers responded by proposing legislation to permit a modification (or other non-judicial settlement agreement with respect to the trust) without court approval if the settlor (if living), the beneficiaries concerned with the subject of the agreement, and the trustee all consent. See Or. Rev. Stat. § 130.045.

In re Riddell: Real Life Applications

1. Which approach is more consistent with the settlor's intent: the Restatement (Second) position that is reluctant to change terms, or the Restatement (Third) approach that is more liberal? Which position would you advocate for your state to adopt as the default rule if you were working on a legislative committee?

2. If the settlors in *Riddell* had come to you for help in setting up the trust, what might you have suggested to build in flexibility? Nancy's disability appears to have arisen after their deaths, so assume that you, as their attorney, do not know that Nancy will need government benefits.

3. A client wants to create a trust for a child for life, with restrictive trust instructions on distributions and limited flexibility for the trustee. How would you counsel the client on the usefulness of flexibility? What examples might help a client understand the need for flexibility?

The UTC takes the same approach as that taken by the Restatement (Third) of Trusts. UTC § 412 provides that dispositive as well as administrative provisions may be modified due to changed circumstances. In fact, the UTC says that even termination of the trust is possible if doing so will further the purpose of the trust.

EXHIBIT 11.8 **UTC § 412. Modification or Termination Because of Unanticipated Circumstances or Inability to Administer Trust Effectively**

(a) The court may modify the administrative or dispositive terms of a trust or terminate the trust if, because of circumstances not anticipated by the settlor, modification or termination will further the purposes of the trust. To the extent practicable, the modification must be made in accordance with the settlor's probable intention.

(b) The court may modify the administrative terms of a trust if continuation of the trust on its existing terms would be impracticable or wasteful or impair the trust's administration.

(c) Upon termination of a trust under this section, the trustee shall distribute the trust property in a manner consistent with the purposes of the trust.

Modification to Fix a Mistake

The common law has always permitted reformation of inter vivos documents, including trusts, based on a mistake of fact or law. UTC § 415 extends this common law rule to testamentary trusts. If a trust provision resulted from a mistake, such as the wrong beneficiary or the wrong property description, then extrinsic evidence can be used to show the mistake. The statute requires clear and convincing evidence to establish that the mistake affected the settlor's intent and the terms of the trust. The mistake may be that the settlor was mistaken as to a fact or the law or the mistake may lie in the way the language in the document was drafted—the language may fail to carry out the settlor's intent.

Additional Modification Provisions in the UTC

Several UTC sections permit modification and termination based on best practices. These sections are modeled on provisions that have become common in well-drafted trusts, and provide the same benefits to trusts that lack these provisions. If the terms of a trust include authority for the trustee to modify or terminate the trust, these UTC provisions will be unnecessary.

Uneconomic trusts. UTC § 414(a) permits a trustee to terminate a trust when the value of the trust falls below $50,000, if the trustee determines that the value of the trust property is insufficient to justify the cost of administration. The trustee must first notify all qualified beneficiaries. The trustee may decide not to terminate a trust with property below the indicated value if the trust has an important purpose that makes continuation of the trust important, even if doing so is expensive relative to the value of the assets. If the value of the trust is greater than $50,000, UTC § 414(b) permits a court to modify or terminate a trust or change the trustee if the cost of administration is too great relative to the value of the trust.

Tax objectives. UTC § 416 permits a court to modify a trust to achieve the settlor's tax objectives, as long as the modification is not contrary to the donor's probable intent, particularly with respect to dispositive provisions.

Combining or dividing trusts. UTC § 417 makes combining or dividing trusts possible when the terms of the trust did not anticipate the need for doing so, if doing so would not adversely affect the purposes of the trust or any beneficiary. For example, a trustee might decide to combine two trusts to save administrative costs, or a trustee might want to divide a trust to keep the shares of beneficiaries separate for tax or management reasons.

3. Decanting

The term "**decanting**" is used for a process that involves pouring assets from one trust to another, removing unwanted provisions and adding more useful provisions. The philosophy behind decanting is that if the trustee has the power to distribute trust property to or for the benefit of one or more beneficiaries, the trustee can also exercise the power by distributing the property to a new trust. Decanting first surfaced in Florida when a court authorized the practice. Phipps v. Palm Beach Trust Co., 196 So. 299 (Fla. 1940).

A trust can provide the trustee with the authority to decant. If it does, the terms of the trust will outline the circumstances, procedures, and authority for decanting. If the trust does not address decanting directly, a decanting statute can provide the authority, and some states have already enacted decanting statutes. The Uniform Trust Decanting Act (UTDA), approved by the Uniform Law Commission in 2015, may spur more states to adopt decanting statutes, and may increase the uniformity of the statutes. As of early 2018 five states had adopted the Act, with three more introductions in the 2018 legislatures. The description of decanting that follows includes cites to UTDA, although most state decanting statutes were enacted before the uniform act was developed.

Any use of decanting must be consistent with the trustee's fiduciary duties. UTDA § 4. A trustee is exercising a discretionary power when decanting, and UTC § 814 (reprinted earlier) requires that the trustee exercise such power in "good faith." In addition, if the decanting adjusts beneficial interests, the trustee must consider the duty of impartiality, and if the trustee is a beneficiary of the trust, self-dealing may be an issue. Although any exercise of the decanting power must be consistent with fiduciary duties, UTDA makes clear that the existence of the power (under a statute) does not create a duty to consider decanting. UTDA § 4(b).

The basic concept of decanting is that if a trustee has discretionary power over distributions, the trustee can exercise that power to modify provisions in the trust, to the extent of the power the trustee has. If the discretion is limited, for example, the distributive power is subject to an ascertainable standard, most statutes limit changes to administrative ones. UTDA § 12. If the trustee has broad discretion, for example, a "best interests" or "welfare" standard, the new trust can have new dispositive provisions. UTDA § 11. Some states require the new trust to contain a distribution standard at least as restrictive as the one in the old trust, to protect the settlor's intent with respect to distributions. The decanting process can be used to remove beneficiaries but usually not to add new beneficiaries, and it cannot reduce or eliminate a vested interest. UTDA § 11(c). Some states prohibit acceleration of remainder interests, § 11(c), and generally the new trust cannot reduce a beneficiary's fixed income interest, except, in some states, in connection with the creation of a special needs trust. § 13. In general, the broader the trustee's authority is under the original trust, the more extensive the changes can be. UTDA restricts exercises of the decanting power that would be self-dealing by the trustee, including, for example, a modification to the compensation of the trustee or an increase in a limitation on the liability of the trustee. UTDA §§ 16, 17.

Because decanting developed based on the idea that the power was derivative of the trustee's power to make distributions, decanting involves distributing assets to a new trust. UTDA views decanting as a power to modify and thus permits a trustee to modify the existing trust, either by changing the terms of the existing trust or by distributing property to a second trust. A benefit of decanting, in contrast with modification under the UTC, is that decanting does not require court approval. Notice to qualified beneficiaries is required in most states, but consent of the beneficiaries is not required. UTDA § 7. In states that do not require notice to beneficiaries, elimination of interests can be controversial.

So when would decanting be useful? Decanting can address administration issues and might change the law governing the administration of the trust, add the ability to remove or appoint trustees without court approval, expand the power of the trustee to enter into more sophisticated investments, or permit the trustee not to diversify assets when the trust holds a family business. Changes to beneficial interests might restrict distributions to beneficiaries with substance abuse problems, remove a beneficiary, divide a trust for multiple beneficiaries into separate trusts for each branch of the family, or create a special needs trust for a beneficiary who requires government assistance. Decanting can also be used for tax-planning reasons, for example, to move a trust to a state with no income tax or facilitate tax planning for beneficiaries.

Chapter Summary

- A trustee must comply with strict fiduciary duties; failure to do so will result in a breach of trust.
- The fiduciary duties include the duty of obedience, the duty of loyalty, the duty to inform and report, the duty of impartiality, the duty of care in managing trust property, including the duty not to commingle and the duty to earmark, and the duty to invest property as a prudent investor.
- The duty of obedience is the duty to comply with the terms of the trust and applicable law.
- The duty of care requires a trustee to take control of trust property, segregate it from the trustee's own assets, and manage the property with "reasonable care, skill, and caution."
- A prudent investor considers the purposes of the trust, the needs of the beneficiaries, and economic conditions in making investment decisions.
- A prudent investor diversifies the trust holdings unless there are special circumstances that make nondiversification appropriate.
- A trustee must act impartially with respect to beneficiaries, treating all beneficiaries fairly, although not necessarily equally.
- When a trustee breaches a trust, a court can remove the trustee, require the trustee to prepare accountings for the beneficiaries, or impose a financial penalty on the trustee, among other remedies.
- A settlor can name a trust director to advise the trustee or make changes to the trust.
- If a settlor and all the beneficiaries agree, they can revoke or terminate an irrevocable trust; the settlor alone can revoke or terminate a revocable trust.
- Without the settlor's consent, a court can modify or terminate a trust if (1) all the beneficiaries agree (or beneficiaries who do not agree are adequately represented), and (2) the modification will not affect a material purpose. A court will determine whether a provision was a material purpose for the settlor in creating the trust.
- The common law doctrine of equitable deviation, also codified by the UTC, permits the modification of an administrative provision if the modification will further the settlor's intent.
- Depending on the authority provided in the trust instrument, a trustee may be able to use decanting to transfer a trust's assets to a new trust with modified terms.

Applying the Concepts

1. A trust's sole asset is an apartment building. The trustee collects rents and distributes them to the income beneficiaries, but the trustee does little to maintain the building, which is in declining structural condition. What should the remainder beneficiaries do?

2. A trust directs the trustee to pay the current beneficiary "all the income and as much of the principal as the trustee determines to be appropriate for the beneficiary's health, support, maintenance, and education." The trustee and current beneficiary is Sheila, the settlor's second spouse, and the remainder beneficiaries are children from a first marriage.

   a. If Sheila invests all the trust assets in corporate bonds that yield a good level of income but do not increase in value, has Sheila breached any of her fiduciary duties?

   b. The children have heard that Sheila has been taking expensive trips. They have asked her whether she is using trust funds for these trips, but she refuses to give them any information about the trust. What can the children do?

3. On his death, Ross leaves all the stock in the family business, which he built, in trust for his descendants. The terms of the trust direct the trustee to continue to hold the stock, even though the stock is the only asset in the trust. All the currently living beneficiaries want to authorize the trustee to sell the stock. What should they do?

4. Brian is the trustee of a trust created under the will of his wife, Mia. (Mia died two years ago.) Brian receives the income of the trust for his life, and on his death the remaining principal will be distributed to Mia's descendants. Mia had three children: Jesse (her son from a prior marriage) and two children with Brian.

   a. Brian invests the trust property in two rental houses. He does the work himself on the rentals and then distributes income based on the rents received, less the costs of maintaining the houses. He pays himself a fee for managing the houses but takes no fee as trustee.
      i. Is Brian acting as a prudent investor? (What additional information would you want to know?)
      ii. Is Brian complying with his duty of impartiality?
      iii. If Jesse requests a copy of the trust instrument, must Brian give him a copy?

   b. Assume that Brian resigns as trustee. Pursuant to the terms of the trust, a family friend, Lenora, becomes trustee. Lenora sells the houses and invests the proceeds in government bonds.
      i. How should the receipts from the house sales be reported for accounting purposes—as income or principal?
      ii. Is Lenora complying with the duty of impartiality?
      iii. To whom should Lenora send annual reports?
      iv. Can Lenora hire an investment advisor?

5. When Celestine died in an automobile crash, her will created a trust for her two children, who were eight and nine years old. The terms of the trust direct the trustee to use income and principal for the health, education, maintenance, and support of the two children. When neither child is under the age of 25, the

trust terminates and the trustee distributes the property to Celestine's then living descendants. Celestine's brother, Treyvon, is the trustee and is also the legal guardian for the children. With respect to each of the following additional facts, indicate whether Treyvon has breached any of his fiduciary duties, and, if so, which one(s). If you find a breach, what remedy might the court impose?

a. Treyvon has had good success with investments, so he puts the trust's money ($500,000) in his investment account. With the additional funds and economies of scale, the account makes an even better return that it had before.

b. Two years after the accident, Treyvon's broker tells him about a start-up company that is a "sure thing." Treyvon takes $100,000 of the trust's money and invests in the new company. Unfortunately, the company goes under and the investment is basically worthless.

c. When the younger child turns 25, Treyvon gives each child $25,000 and says that he has spent the rest of the trust money taking care of them. He notes that he gave them each $10,000 a year for college and that the rest of the money had been spent on housing, food, and clothing costs before they left for college.

6. Antonio created an irrevocable trust for his nephew, Nunzio. The trust provides for distributions for Nunzio's health, support, maintenance, and education until he turns 30, when the entire trust is distributed to him. If Nunzio dies before reaching age 30, the trust is distributed to his then living descendants, by representation, and if none, to Antonio's then living descendants, by representation. Natalie (Antonio's sister and Nunzio's mother) is trustee.

a. Nunzio is 26 and has finished college. The trust still has $60,000 in it. Antonio, Natalie, and Nunzio would all like to terminate the trust. How would you advise them to proceed? If Antonio is dead, how would you advise Natalie and Nunzio?

b. Assume the trust provides for distributions for Nunzio's health, support, maintenance, and education for his life. On Nunzio's death the remaining corpus will be distributed to his then living descendants, by representation. Antonio is no longer alive. The trust has $2 million in assets. How would you advise Nunzio, who is 45 and would like to terminate the trust? Does it matter whether Nunzio has children? How would you advise Natalie?

Trusts and Estates in Practice

1. When Jake dies, all of his farmland is distributed to his testamentary trust. Jake had leased the farmland to Evan for about ten years, ever since Jake could no longer handle the hard work of farming. Jake considered Evan the best person to continue to manage the farm, so he named Evan as the trustee. The trust will continue for ten years, and then when it terminates the assets will be distributed

to Jake's nieces and nephews. Jake wanted to keep the land in trust to give Evan an opportunity to save money and be able to buy the land.

    a. Jake dies in March, just two weeks before planting should begin and before Evan had entered into a lease for the season. Can Evan the farmer enter a lease with Evan the trustee? What should Evan do?

    b. Now assume that Jake comes to you to draft his will. What should you include about the farm when you draft the terms of the trust?

2. Serena established a trust under her will, making her son, Walker, the trustee. The trust directs the trustee to distribute income from the trust to Serena's second husband, Roger, for his life and then on Roger's death to distribute the remaining assets to Serena's descendants. Serena and her first husband had two children, Walker and William, and each of the sons has children. Roger has a daughter from his prior marriage. After Serena's death, Walker comes to you with the following questions:

    a. Walker would like to buy the family home from the trust. Roger has moved in with his daughter and is happy to have the house sold and the proceeds used for investments that will produce income. Can Walker buy the house? How should he proceed if William supports Walker's buying the house? What if William is opposed and wants to buy the house for himself?

    b. Serena and her first husband owned a natural foods store, which was incorporated. Walker has managed the store ever since his father's death; his brother is not involved in the business. After her first husband's death, Serena gave Walker and William each 20 percent of the voting stock, so at her death she gave her remaining 60 percent of the stock to the trust. Can Walker vote the shares held in the trust? Can Walker vote not to declare dividends (the business has paid dividends each year for the past eight years)? Can Walker buy stock from the trust?

    c. Can Walker pay himself a salary for serving as trustee? How would he decide how much to pay himself?

3. You represent Thomas, the trustee of the Cameron Owens Trust, which is now irrevocable because the settlor died. The trust provides that the trustee may distribute such parts or all of the income and principal for the health, education, maintenance, and support of the settlor's descendants while any child of the settlor is alive, and then must distribute any remaining principal to the surviving descendants. One grandchild of the settlor has developed a serious medical condition and the beneficiaries want to modify the trust to establish a special needs trust. Research the state law where your law school is located and determine whether there is a non-judicial method to modify the trust. If there is no non-judicial method, what should you advise the trustee to do? What is the likely outcome?

4. Monique creates a trust for her child, Heather. The trust provides income for Heather for life, with the remainder at her death to her then living descendants, by representation. Heather has two children, Isabelle and Jocelyn. Isabelle has two children, Keyshawn and Lana.

   a. Who is a qualified beneficiary?
   b. Who must receive an annual report?
   c. Who may request a copy of the trust document?
   d. If a trustee resigns and a successor becomes trustee, to whom must the new trustee give notice?
   e. If Heather becomes incapacitated, who can represent her to receive annual reports?
   f. If Lana is a minor, who can represent her to approve a self-dealing transaction if Isabelle is the trustee? If Heather's cousin is the trustee? Who can represent Lana in connection with a petition to modify the trust to permit different investments? To terminate the trust early?

12

Powers of Appointment

In this chapter, we explore a doctrine that is critical to estate planning: powers of appointment. A **power of appointment** allows the person who creates the power to give a third party the right to distribute property among a designated group of beneficiaries as circumstances and the text of the power dictate. It allows the person creating the power to build great flexibility into trusts and other asset dispositions.

Powers of appointment are common in estate planning because of their versatility. Consider that a trust may last for many years, and, rather than the settlor dictating specific terms that control the trust's operation and distributions, the settlor can delegate a power of appointment so that the powerholder can take into consideration changes in the family, the beneficiaries, or economic conditions.

Powers of appointment have their own terminology, so the chapter starts there, before examining how a power is created and how a power is exercised. Most of the legal disputes concerning powers of appointment relate to how they are exercised, so we consider a number of problems that can arise in connection with the exercise or nonexercise of a power of appointment. The chapter also includes a look at the rights of creditors in property subject to a power of appointment.

Key Concepts

- Creating a power of appointment
- Using a power of appointment in estate planning
- Effectively exercising a power of appointment
- Allowing a power of appointment to lapse and the consequences
- Understanding creditors' rights and tax implications of powers of appointment

A. WHAT IS A POWER OF APPOINTMENT?

Individuals can build flexibility into their estate planning in several ways. As discussed in Chapters 9 through 11, a settlor can use a trust that grants the trustee discretionary authority to make distributions to specified beneficiaries. The discretion can be substantial or limited. A power of appointment is another powerful tool that builds flexibility into estate planning by permitting the donor to delegate

Definition of Powers of Appointment

Historically, there has been little statutory law concerning powers of appointment. In 2013, the Uniform Law Commission approved the **Uniform Powers of Appointment Act** (UPAA). The Act is intended to provide consistency among states. Eight states have enacted the UPAA as of July 2018. The UPAA articulates a distinct terminology for powers of appointment doctrine, and in the interests of clarity and uniformity, we will use that terminology in this chapter. For example, while the holder of a power to appoint has traditionally been called the "donee" and the persons in whose favor a powerholder may exercise a power of appointment the "objects," the Act uses the terms "powerholder" and "permissible appointee." Many of the cases in the chapter use the older terms.

the authority to distribute property at some future time to a person who does not have fiduciary obligations.

1. General Terminology

Special language applies to powers of appointment. That terminology is useful in showing the creation of a power and the exercise or nonexercise of the power. While a power can be created without using these specialized words, this terminology helps make it clear when a power has been established and exercised.

- **Donor**: The person who creates a power of appointment.
- **Powerholder** (traditionally called the "donee of a power of appointment"): The person who is granted the power and makes decisions using the power. Unlike the trustee or the beneficiaries, the powerholder has neither legal ownership nor a beneficial interest in the property.
- **Appointive property**: The property subject to the power.
- **Permissible appointees** (or **objects of the power**): The persons/organizations in whose favor the power can be exercised.
- **Takers in default of appointment**: The persons or entities who will take the property if the powerholder fails to exercise the power before the powerholder's power terminates (often at death).

Testamentary Power of Appointment

A **testamentary power of appointment** can be exercised only by the will of the powerholder.

Presently Exercisable Power of Appointment

A **presently exercisable power of appointment** is a power that the powerholder can exercise during life, through an inter vivos instrument.

For example, Diego is the settlor of a trust. The Trust provides an income interest for Patrice, Diego's child, for life. The Trust also states: "Patrice has a power to appoint, by will, the property remaining in the Trust at Patrice's death to any descendant of Patrice. If Patrice does not exercise the power of appointment, then on Patrice's death, the property will be distributed to Patrice's descendants, by representation, or if no descendant is alive when Patrice dies, to the Municipal Food Bank."

In this example, Diego is the donor, Patrice is the powerholder or donee, the trust property is the appointive property, Patrice's descendants are permissible appointees, Patrice's descendants are also the takers in default, and the Municipal Food Bank is a contingent taker in default. The power is a testamentary power because Patrice can exercise the power only by will.

If Diego's trust had provided that Patrice could exercise the power at any time during her lifetime, in favor of any descendant of hers, by written instrument delivered to the trustee, then the power would be a presently exercisable power.

General Power of Appointment

A **general power of appointment** is the power to appoint in favor of the powerholder, the powerholder's estate, the powerholder's creditors, *or* the creditors of the powerholder's estate. A general power of appointment can be broad; it can allow the property to be given to anyone, or it can to be limited to allowing appointment only to one or more of the four categories listed—for example, to the powerholder.

Different tax and creditor consequences follow depending on whether a power is general or nongeneral. (See Section E below.)

In the example of Diego, if he granted to Patrice the power to appoint the property not just to her descendants but also "to her estate," this would be a general power of appointment. Even if Diego explicitly stated that Patrice could not appoint the property to creditors, this would still be a general power because Patrice holds the power to appoint to one of the four categories.

> ### Power to Descendants
>
> A trap for the unwary occurs when a donor gives one of his children the power to appoint among the donor's descendants, as compared to the powerholder's descendants. Since the powerholder is herself one of the donor's descendants, the donor may have unwittingly created in the powerholder a general power of appointment. Consider who is included in the powerholder's descendants!

Nongeneral Power of Appointment

A **nongeneral power of appointment** is a power that cannot be exercised in favor of the powerholder, the powerholder's estate, the powerholder's creditors, or creditors of the powerholder's estate. A nongeneral power can be broad—to anyone in the world other than those in the four categories—or it can be narrow, such as to the settlor's descendants or to a named person.

A nongeneral power is sometimes called a "special power" or a "limited power." In the original example, Diego granted Patrice a power to appoint, by will, the property remaining in the trust at Patrice's death to any descendant of Patrice. This is a testamentary nongeneral power because Patrice can appoint among any descendants, but the property cannot be appointed to Patrice, Patrice's creditors, Patrice's estate, or the creditors of the estate. The fact that one of Patrice's descendants could theoretically also be a creditor does not make this a general power.

Power of Withdrawal

The **power of withdrawal** gives the right to withdraw property, or a specified amount of property, from a trust. A power of withdrawal is a general power of appointment because the powerholder can withdraw property for her own benefit. See UPAA § 503. Diego could have provided Patrice with a power of withdrawal: "Patrice may withdraw from the Trust an amount not exceeding $5,000 each year. If Patrice does not exercise the power of withdrawal in any year, the power shall lapse." Patrice would have a general power of appointment to the extent of $5,000 per year (and, as discussed in Chapter 15, there are tax implications).

Exclusionary Power of Appointment

An **exclusionary power of appointment** is a nongeneral power of appointment that can be exercised in favor of one of a group of permissible appointees, to the exclusion of the other appointees.

Most powers are exclusionary powers. The default rule is that nongeneral powers are exclusionary. In the original example, Patrice has an exclusionary power of appointment because she can appoint the property "to any descendant." If she has two children and five grandchildren, she can appoint all of the property in the trust to one grandchild if she wants to do so. She does not need to appoint some amount to each child and each grandchild.

Nonexclusionary Power of Appointment

A **nonexclusionary power of appointment** is a power that must be exercised in favor of all permissible appointees, so that each member of the group receives something. There is no requirement of equal distribution, and the amount each appointee must receive can be the subject of controversy among the group of permissible appointees. Is $1 enough? Careful drafting should clarify the donor's intent as to how much must be distributed to each. Diego's trust could have provided: "to any descendant of Patrice, and when she exercises the power, she must appoint at least $1,000 to each of her living descendants."

Specific Reference

Specific reference is a requirement, often imposed by the donor in the granting instrument, that requires the powerholder to make specific reference to the instrument of power when the power is exercised. In our example, when establishing

Patrice's power, Diego could have provided: "In exercising this power, Patrice must make specific reference to Paragraph 3 of this Trust."

Specific reference is used to avoid inadvertent exercise of the power. Because powerholders often fail to follow the direction to make specific reference, this is a frequent source of litigation—as we will see in the next section.

Specific-Exercise Clause

A **specific-exercise clause** indicates the powerholder's intent to exercise the power, and explicitly refers to the particular power of appointment in question. For example, to comply with the specific reference requirement, Patrice's will might provide: "I exercise the power of appointment conferred upon me by Paragraph Three of Diego's Trust as follows: I appoint the property to my daughter, Amelia, or if she does not survive me, to my son, Juan."

Blanket Exercise Clause

A **blanket exercise clause** states that it exercises "any" power of appointment that the powerholder may have, and can be an effort to ensure that a powerholder does not inadvertently fail to exercise a power. For example, Patrice might provide: "I hereby exercise any power of appointment I may have as follows: I appoint the property to my descendants, per stirpes."

Blending Clause

A **blending clause** blends the appointive property and the powerholder's own property together in a common disposition. A blending clause may be in the form of a specific exercise, or, more commonly, a blanket exercise. It is often part of the residuary clause and it generally starts as follows: "All the residue of my estate, including property over which I have a power of appointment. . . ."

For example, Patrice might provide: "All the residue of my estate, including the property over which I have a power of appointment under Paragraph 3 of Diego's Trust, I devise to my daughter Amelia, or if she does not survive me, to my son Juan." That is an example of a blending clause with a specific exercise. By contrast, Patrice might provide: "All the residue of my estate, including any property over which I may have a power of appointment, I devise to my daughter Amelia, or if she does not survive me, to my son Juan." That is a blending clause with a blanket exercise.

2. Distinguishing Between a Power of Appointment and Fiduciary Power

A powerholder can choose to exercise the power or not; moreover, the powerholder can choose to exercise it in any matter, as long as the property subject to the power is given to a permissible appointee. By contrast, as discussed in

Chapter 11, the holder of a fiduciary power, such as a trustee, cannot act arbitrarily and is subject to specific fiduciary duties and responsibilities of loyalty, obedience, and prudence. Sometimes cases erroneously describe a trustee's discretionary power to distribute property as a power of appointment. However, the distinction between fiduciary distributive powers and nonfiduciary powers of appointment is well established. See Restatement (Third) of Trusts § 50, cmt. a (2003); Restatement (Third) of Property: Wills and Other Donative Transfers § 17.1, cmt. g (2011)

For example, Brady's mother transfers property to Mariko, as trustee. The trust instrument directs the trustee to distribute all income monthly to Brady and Brady's spouse, Didi, and so much of the principal as needed for Brady and Didi's support and maintenance to continue their accustomed standard of living. On Brady's death, the trust instrument directs the trustee to distribute the remaining principal to Brady's descendants. In addition, the trust instrument gives Didi the power to appoint so much or all of the trust property to anyone, during lifetime or at death.

Mariko, as the trustee, is a fiduciary. Mariko must distribute income monthly to Brady and Didi, and, upon Brady's death, Mariko must distribute the property in the trust to Brady's descendants. During the lifetime of Didi and Brady, Mariko can distribute trust principal only to them, and she must act in good faith to carry out Brady's intentions.

If Brady and Didi have been accustomed to a modest standard of living, Mariko should not make distributions to fund lavish expenses. Mariko has a fiduciary duty of impartiality, which means that she should treat the two current beneficiaries and the remainder beneficiaries fairly. She cannot decide to make distributions only to Didi because she likes Didi better. She may decide not to make distributions of principal, but that decision must be made after considering the circumstances of the beneficiaries, and the decision must be reasonable. See Chapter 11 for a discussion of the fiduciary duties.

Didi has a general power of appointment. Didi can appoint the trust property entirely to Brady, to herself, or to anyone Didi chooses. Didi can choose not to appoint the property and need not consider how the settlor would prefer that Didi use the power. The settlor has given Didi the power of appointment because the settlor expects Didi to exercise it appropriately, but Didi's decisions about the exercise are entirely up to Didi.

B. CREATING A POWER OF APPOINTMENT

As with the creation of a trust, the creation of a power of appointment requires that the donor of the power manifest the intention to create the power. See Restatement (Third) of Property: Wills and Other Donative Transfers § 18.1 (2011); UPAA § 201(a)(2). No special words are necessary, and the donor need not even use the words "power of appointment." As a result, sometimes disagreements arise about whether the donor intended to create a power of appointment or instead to give full ownership of property, combined with precatory language to use the property in a particular way. Much of what was discussed in Chapter 9 concerning intent to create a trust has equal relevance to intent to create a power of appointment.

For example, Edna's will provides: "I give my tangible property to Stephen, to divide among my children as Stephen thinks best." Is this an outright gift to Stephen, the creation of a power of appointment over the tangibles, or a trust with Stephen as the trustee? Consider what evidence would help you decide.

Donors have great flexibility when they create powers as to who holds the power, when and how it can be exercised, and in whose favor. One condition frequently imposed is that the powerholder make specific reference to the trust and to the power of appointment when exercising it (a "specific reference" clause discussed above).

C. EXERCISING A POWER OF APPOINTMENT

If a powerholder decides to exercise the power of appointment granted to her, she should be clear, in the language she uses, that she intends to exercise the power. In addition, the powerholder should follow any directions the donor specified, such as the requirement to make specific reference to the trust provision granting her the power or to exercise the power in a validly executed instrument. Depending on the particular requirement, courts may demand exact compliance or allow substantial compliance.

The UPAA codifies the rules for exercise of a power, as shown in Exhibit 12.1.

EXHIBIT 12.1   **UPAA § 301. Requisites for Exercise of Power of Appointment**

A power of appointment is exercised only:

(1) if the instrument exercising the power is valid under applicable law;
(2) if the terms of the instrument exercising the power:
    (A) manifest the powerholder's intent to exercise the power; and
    (B) subject to Section 304, satisfy the requirements of exercise, if any, imposed by the donor; and
(3) to the extent the appointment is a permissible exercise of the power.

The comments to § 301 of the UPAA recommend using a specific-exercise clause.

In addition to UPAA § 301, two other sections, shown in Exhibit 12.2, are important for the discussion that follows.

EXHIBIT 12.2 UPAA § 302. Intent to Exercise: Determining Intent from Residuary Clause & UPAA § 304. Substantial Compliance with Donor-Imposed Formal Requirement

UPAA § 302. INTENT TO EXERCISE: DETERMINING INTENT FROM RESIDUARY CLAUSE

(a) In this section:

    (1) "Residuary clause" does not include a residuary clause containing a blanket-exercise clause or a specific-exercise clause.

(b) A residuary clause in a powerholder's will, or a comparable clause in the powerholder's revocable trust, manifests the powerholder's intent to exercise a power of appointment only if:

    (1) the terms of the instrument containing the residuary clause do not manifest a contrary intent;

    (2) the power is a general power exercisable in favor of the powerholder's estate;

    (3) there is no gift-in-default clause or it is ineffective; and

    (4) the powerholder did not release the power.

UPAA § 304. SUBSTANTIAL COMPLIANCE WITH DONOR-IMPOSED FORMAL REQUIREMENT

A powerholder's substantial compliance with a formal requirement of an appointment imposed by the donor, including a requirement that the instrument exercising the power of appointment make reference or specific reference to the power, is sufficient if:

(1) the powerholder knows of and intends to exercise the power; and

(2) the powerholder's manner of attempted exercise of the power does not impair a material purpose of the donor in imposing the requirement.

All too frequently, powerholders (or, perhaps, the attorneys who are advising them) do not use a specific-exercise clause, do not follow the directions of the donor, or do not make clear their intent to exercise the power. The most common problems arise when the powerholder uses a residuary clause, because then it is not clear whether the powerholder intended to exercise the power or not. Some residuary clauses are blended with a blanket-exercise clause or a specific-exercise clause. Others are "pure" residuary clauses, with no mention of a power of appointment at all. The problem is determining whether there was an intent to exercise the power in the absence of any reference to it. Sometimes, the residuary clause of a will specifically excludes all property over which the testator held a power of appointment, and there the intent not to exercise is clear.

1. Parsing Powers of Appointment

Particularly because of the special terminology involved in powers of appointment, the material can be confusing. As you read the material and cases that follow, here are a few guiding questions.

1. Consider whether courts find the various types of exercise clauses to be adequate and why.
2. Examine both the document that creates the power and the document purporting to exercise the power. For example, does the grant require a specific reference? What is the manner in which the power is exercised?
3. Finally, ask what the estate planners should have done differently to be assured that what they intended to happen actually did happen and how doing so would have avoided unnecessary litigation.

2. Residuary Blending Clause with Blanket Exercise—Does It Satisfy a Specific Reference Requirement?

Case Preview

Motes/Henes Trust, Bank of Bentonville v. Motes

The next case considers what happens when the powerholder's will includes a blanket exercise clause but the drafting instrument requires a specific reference. Helen Henes drafted her will in 1979, including a clause that exercised any powers of appointment. Henes and her sister subsequently created a trust that created a power of appointment that required a specific reference in order for it to be effective.

As you read *Motes/Henes*, consider the following:

1. What language was used in the will concerning the power of appointment?
2. What are the two possible ways that the court identifies for construing the specific reference requirement?
3. What is the significance of the intent of the powerholder/testator?
4. Who made the decision that Ms. Henes did not need a new will after the trust was drafted? Why?

Motes/Henes Trust, Bank of Bentonville v. Motes
761 S.W.2d 938 (Ark. 1988)

HAYS, Justice.

The single issue presented by this appeal is whether a reference in the testator's will to a power of appointment was sufficient to exercise a power of appointment in a trust instrument.

Helen Fay Henes, deceased, executed a will in 1979 containing the following residuary clause:

> I give, devise and bequeath all of the remainder and residue of my estate together with property to which I may have a power of appointment at the time of my death, to the trustee hereinafter named, to be held in trust for the uses. . . .

In 1982, the Motes/Henes trust was established for Helen Fay Henes and her sister, Elizabeth Henes Motes, in which was placed approximately $6,000,000 from interests the sisters had redeemed from their ownership in certain businesses. The trust contained the following provision:

> This trust shall terminate with respect to the separate trust share of each grantor [the two sisters] upon the death of said grantor. Upon such termination, the remaining assets of said separate trust shall be paid to such person or persons or trusts as grantor may, by specific reference hereto, appoint in her Last Will and Testament. [Emphasis added.] Helen Fay Henes died in April 1983 . . .

The question is: When a power of appointment requires a specific reference to it, as does the trust in this case, will a general reference in the will be sufficient to exercise the power requiring specific reference?

The general rule is defined in Restatement (Second) of Property, Donative Transfers (1986):

§ 17.1 SIGNIFICANCE OF DONEE'S INTENT TO APPOINT

In order for a donee to exercise a power effectively it must be established—

(1) That the donee intended to exercise it; and
(2) That the expression of the intention complies with the requirements of exercise imposed by the donor and by rules of law.

The problem here concerns the second requirement and the question we must decide is whether Ms. Henes' will provision, making reference to "property to which I may have a power of appointment at the time of my death," is sufficient to exercise the power of appointment in the trust, or does the law require that she must have made reference to the trust instrument itself.

Finding no cases of our own on this topic, we have turned to other sources for guidance. The Reporter's Note to section 17.1 of the Restatement is primarily devoted to the problem in our case. While the Restatement discusses cases it classifies as "supporting" the rule and those "contrary" to the rule, a closer examination of those cases reveals that the division would be more aptly placed between those cases that construe the "specific reference" requirement literally, and those that favor a flexible interpretation, focusing more on the intent of the donee.

. . . We prefer the approach focusing on the intent of the donor, however, as we regard it as the better reasoned view. It is also in keeping with our general approach to the interpretation of wills, which has as its paramount principle that the intention of the testator will govern, as well as the rule that wills should be liberally construed. And in Moore v. Avery, 225 S.W. 599 (1920), in construing a will, we held that the phrase[] "all my property[]" was sufficient to refer to and exercise a power of appointment. While *Moore* does not involve a "specific reference" requirement, it nevertheless reflects the more liberal approach.

In Roberts v. Northern Tr. Co., 550 F. Supp. 729 (N.D. Ill. 1982), the court was faced with the same issue and reviewed Illinois law to determine the correct approach. The court found that in a significant power of appointment case, the Illinois court had drawn on three basic principles of will construction: 1) that the intent of the testator controls and courts should construe wills to give effect to that intention; 2) a devise or bequest should not be voided because of errors in describing the subject matter as long as enough remains to show the testator's intent; and 3) the court will use its equitable powers to correct technical defects in a will in order to effect the testator's intent. From those general rules the court fashioned the following test for the "specific reference" problem:

> Where the evidence of intent is powerful, the question of compliance should be examined in a light which favors fulfillment of both the donor's desire for assurance and the donee's intent. Where, however, evidence of the donee's intent is weak, a liberal construction of the condition of specific reference may well defeat the limitations of both donor and donee.

[W]e find the evidence of intent in this case is very strong and therefore have no problem with a more liberal construction of the "specific reference" requirement. The evidence of Fay Henes' [] intent came from the testimony of John L. Johnson, who was the attorney for both sisters. He had drafted the wills for both, and had also drafted the trust agreement. He testified that at the time of drafting the will he had discussed with Ms. Henes how she wanted to dispose of her property and she told him she wanted her sister to be benefitted and the property to go to her nieces and nephews, her sister's children. The will was drafted to effectuate that intent, giving her sister a life estate through the trust, for her enjoyment during her lifetime, with the property ultimately going to the nieces and nephews.

When Johnson drafted the trust agreement he reviewed Ms. Henes' will and decided there was no need to make any changes in it. He noted that the provision in the will on the power of appointment would operate to exercise all powers of appointment that Ms. Henes would have, to pass the property under a trust arrangement that was set up under her will. Johnson stated that this was absolutely consistent with his view and understanding of Ms. Henes' intent.

Johnson further commented that in drafting the trust, which was irrevocable, he wanted to avoid placing Ms. Henes in the position of being unable to change the beneficiaries of her estate by naming them in the trust instrument. By not putting final testamentary disposition provisions in the trust, it retained for Ms. Henes the ability at any point to change her mind as to the disposition of her estate.

The trial court noted that another significant factor was the problem of estate taxes. If the power was not exercised by the will, double taxation would result, and the trial judge observed that people do not intend tax consequences of that nature. We agree.

. . .

Affirmed.

Post-Case Follow-Up

Notwithstanding the requirement in the granting instrument for a specific reference, the court construed the powerholder's blanket exercise clause in her will to include exercise of a subsequently created power. The court focused on the issue of intent, one of the core issues throughout all of trust and estates law. Note that the donor and the powerholder were identical, so the intent was clear.

Motes/Henes Trust, Bank of Bentonville: Real Life Applications

1. Suppose Emma Henes had consulted you to set up the trust that granted her a power of appointment so that she could defer decision making on the ultimate taker of her property.

   a. She tells you that she does not want to change any other estate-planning documents, including her will, once you have drafted the trust. What advice do you give her about how to draft the trust?

   b. She is willing to make changes to other estate planning documents. What actions will you counsel her to take?

2. The *Motes/Henes* court could have chosen to require strict compliance with the specific reference clause. What impact would such a decision have had on the outcome?

3. Each of the following situations gives you an opportunity to work with the terminology involved in powers of appointment. For each problem, please identify: (i) the donor; (ii) the powerholder(s); (iii) the appointive property; (iv) the permissible appointees; (v) whether the power is general or nongeneral; (vi) whether the power is presently exercisable or testamentary; and (vii) whether the power includes a specific reference requirement. All of the examples are exclusive powers. Note that one instrument can create more than one power of appointment.

   a. Nancy's will creates a trust for her daughter, Angela, for life, and on Angela's death it continues for Angela's siblings. Nancy gives Angela the power to appoint the property in the trust to one or more of her siblings. The power is exercisable exclusively by will, and must state that Angela is appointing the property pursuant to the trust established by Nancy's will.

   b. Kieran's will establishes a trust naming his sister, Phoebe, as the trustee of a testamentary trust established under the will.
      i. The trust directs the trustee to pay income to Kieran's brother, Seamus.
      ii. Kieran's trust also provides that during Seamus's life, the trustee shall distribute up to $20,000 a year to any charity Seamus names in a writing that Seamus delivers to the trustee that refers to Kieran's trust.

    iii. On the death of Seamus, the trustee is directed to distribute all or some of the trust property to such person or persons as Seamus appoints by will. If Seamus fails to direct the distribution of all of the trust property, then the trustee is to distribute the property to Kieran's brother, Jervis, and if he is not then living, to Jervis's descendants.

4. Your client, Darrell, has asked you to represent him in claiming property that he believes has been appointed to him through a power of appointment. His father's will states, "All the residue of my estate, including any property over which I may have a power of appointment, I devise to Darrell." His father was the powerholder of a testamentary power pursuant to Darrell's mother's trust; the mother's trust created a nongeneral power of appointment that allowed appointment to her descendants but that also required a specific reference to the mother's trust. Darrell has asked you to assess his likely success in claiming the appointive property.

5. Your client, Darrell, has learned that his father was also the powerholder of a power created by his second wife (Darrell's stepmother); the stepmother's trust created a nongeneral power of appointment that allowed appointment to her family members but that also required a specific reference to the stepmother's trust. Darrell has asked for your assessment of his likely success in claiming the appointive property.

---

3. Can a Powerholder Exercise the Power by a "Pure" Residuary Clause?

In *Motes/Henes*, Helen Fay Henes exercised her power of appointment in a residuary clause blended with a blanket exercise that included "any power of appointment." Consider the following clause in a powerholder's will:

> I give the residue of my estate to my descendants, by representation.

Does this clause, which does not contain a blanket-exercise clause or in fact any reference to a power, indicate the testator's intent to exercise the power? The majority of states follow the rule that a general or "pure" residuary clause like the one in the example does not exercise a power of appointment held by the testator, regardless of whether the donor required a specific reference. If the general residuary clause is not treated as a valid exercise, the takers in default receive the property that was subject to the power.

    UPAA § 302 and Restatement (Third) of Property: Wills and Other Donative Transfers § 19.4 (2011) both note that a pure residuary clause, without more, will not exercise a power. They provide exceptions if (i) the power is a general power, and (ii) the donor did not provide for takers in default. Why? The policy behind these provisions is to limit exercise to situations in which permitting the residuary clause to exercise the power is likely to accord with the donor's intent.

A minority of jurisdictions, however, take an even more expansive approach when there is no specific reference requirement, finding additional circumstances in which a pure residuary clause is deemed to exercise a power of appointment. The next case follows the majority approach.

Case Preview

Cessac v. Stevens

In Cessac v. Stevens, the court considered whether the decedent's attempt to devise the appointive property was effective. Ms. Christiansen was the beneficiary of three trusts created by her father. The terms of the power allowed her to appoint the trusts' assets through her will, but those terms required a specific reference to the trust. Ms. Christiansen's will included a residuary clause that bequeathed the remainder of her property to Joanne Cessac. In another provision in the will, Ms. Christiansen referred to her father's trusts as part of her probate assets, but she did not refer to the power of appointment created by those trusts.

As you read Cessac v. Stevens, consider:

1. What is the role of Ms. Christiansen's intent? Of her father's intent?
2. The will referred to the trusts that created the powers of appointment; why was that reference insufficient?
3. Who benefits from the failure of the exercise?

Cessac v. Stevens
127 So. 3d 675 (D. Ct. App. Fl. 2013)

Wetherell, J.

. . .

The decedent died in January 2011. Her will devised $5,000 to Appellee Sharon Peeples and devised "the rest and remainder of [her] estate, both personal and real property" to Appellant Joanne Cessac. The will also included a provision stating:

> Included in my estate assets are the STANTON P. KETTLER TRUST, FBO, SALLY CHRISTIANSEN, under will dated July 30, 1970, currently held at the Morgan Stanley Trust offices in Scottsdale, Arizona, and two (2) currently being held at Northern Trust of Florida in Miami, Florida.

The will did not contain any other references to the trusts, nor did it mention any powers of appointment held by the decedent.

The trust referred to by name in the will included a provision authorizing the decedent to direct who would receive the assets in the trust upon her death. This power of appointment provided:

> Upon the death of my daughter, SALLY, the Trustees shall transfer and deliver the remaining principal of this share of the trust, together with any accumulated or undistributed income thereon to or for the benefit of such one or more persons, corporations or other organizations, in such amounts and subject to such trusts, terms and conditions as my daughter may, by her will, appoint, making specific reference to the power herein granted. . . .
>
> If my daughter, SALLY, predeceases me, or having survived, dies without exercising the power of appointment granted herein, SALLY's share of this trust shall be divided into equal shares so that there shall be one share for each child of my daughter who is then living and one share for each child of my daughter who has predeceased her but is represented by issue. . . .

Nearly identical language was included in the two other trusts of which the decedent was a beneficiary. . . .

The decedent's will was admitted to probate. Appellee Marcia Stevens, the decedent's daughter, filed a petition in the probate case for declaratory judgment, construction of the will, and other relief. The petition sought a declaration that the assets in the trusts are not the property of the estate because the decedent's will did not properly exercise the powers of appointment granted by the trusts. The effect of such a declaration would be that the assets in the trusts would be distributed to Ms. Stevens and the decedent's son, Appellee Christopher Evans, in accordance with the terms of the trusts, rather than to Ms. Cessac.

. . .

We begin our analysis with Talcott v. Talcott, 423 So. 2d 951 (Fla. D. Ct. App. 1983), which appears to be the only Florida decision involving a power of appointment similar to those granted by the trusts in this case. There, a widow and personal representative of the estate of her deceased husband sought a declaration of her rights under a trust agreement executed by her father-in-law. *Talcott*, 423 So.2d at 952. . . . The trust agreement required that the husband exercise the power of appointment by making a specific reference to the power in his will. Id. The husband died testate and in his will devised all of his estate to his wife without specific reference to the trust or the power of appointment given therein. Id.

The [court] held that evidence of the husband's intent to exercise the power of appointment was immaterial in light of his failure to comply with the specific reference requirement of the trust.

The circumstances of this case differ from those in *Talcott*. There, the will not only failed to make specific reference to the power of appointment granted by the trust, but it failed to mention the trust at all. Here, the decedent's will included a reference to one of the trusts by name and identified the other two trusts by reference to a location where the assets were held.

Although we agree with Appellants that *Talcott* is distinguishable, we find the analysis in the opinion persuasive and agree with its holding that whether a donee has validly exercised a power of appointment depends not on the intent of the donee, but on whether the power was exercised in the manner prescribed by the donor. . . .

Thus, the donee's failure to abide by the donor's requirements invalidates an exercise of a power of appointment.

Appellants urge this Court to adopt an equitable construction standard and construe the "specific reference" requirements in the trusts to demand only a reasonable substantive compliance. Under this theory, Appellants argue we should hold that the language in the decedent's will substantively complied with the requirements in the trusts and, thus, the trusts' assets became part of the decedent's estate, passing to Ms. Cessac. In support of this argument, Appellants cite out-of-state cases that are factually distinguishable because the wills in each of those cases made at least a general reference to powers of appointment held by the donees.

. . .

[I]n In re Strobel, 717 P.2d 892, 893-94 (Az. 1986), Mr. Strobel created two trusts, each of which gave Mrs. Strobel a power of appointment which required specific reference in her will. Mrs. Strobel's will stated that she had been given a power of appointment in Mr. Strobel's will rather than the trust documents and that, pursuant to such power, she appointed all of the trust assets to her estate. Id.

The *Strobel* court noted that the general rule is that an exercise of a power of appointment must comply with the specific requirements imposed by the donor. Id. at 896-97. However, the court adopted the view of the Restatement of Property § 346 (1940) that "equity will 'aid the defective execution of a power'" if the defect was due to mistake, the appointment approximately met the requirements of the manner of exercise, and the appointee was a natural object of affection. Id. The court concluded that the evidence showed that Mrs. Strobel clearly intended to exercise the power of appointment and that the invalidity of her exercise of the power was due to mistake. Id. at 897. The court then, after concluding that granting equitable relief would not defeat Mr. Strobel's purpose in imposing the requirements on exercising the power of appointment, gave effect to the defective exercise of appointment in light of Mrs. Strobel's approximate compliance with the requirements. Id. at 899.

Here, unlike the aforementioned cases (and the other authorities cited by Appellants), the decedent's will did not include even a general reference to the powers of appointment held by the decedent. Without such, the decedent's will failed to even substantially comply with the "specific reference" requirements of the trusts.

. . .

In sum, we conclude that to properly exercise a power of appointment such as the powers provided for in the trusts at issue in this case, the decedent must at least make reference in his or her will to the powers of appointment held by the decedent. Here, the mere reference to one of the trusts and to the location of the property of the other two trusts was not sufficient to even substantially comply with the "specific reference" requirements in the trusts. Accordingly, because the decedent failed to comply with the requirements of the trusts when attempting to execute her powers of appointment, the assets in the trusts did not become part of her estate and must pass to the decedent's children, as directed in the original trusts, rather than to Ms. Cessac as provided in the decedent's will.

We recognize the seemingly harsh result of our conclusion that Ms. Cessac will not receive the assets the decedent apparently intended for her to receive. However, this result is a function of the intent of the original donor, who had the right to place whatever restrictions he desired on the disposition of his property. The decedent was obligated to comply with these restrictions, and compliance would not have been difficult here, as all that was necessary was some reference to powers of appointment in the decedent's will.

For the reasons stated above, the trial court correctly determined that the trusts' assets are not the property of the decedent's estate. Accordingly, the order on appeal is AFFIRMED.

Post-Case Follow-Up

This case summarizes the majority approach that, where a specific reference is required, a general residuary clause in a will, or a will making general disposition of all the testator's property, does not exercise a power of appointment. To exercise the power, the testator must make specific reference to the power or there must be some other indication of intent to include the property subject to the power. While the need for specific reference may seem formalistic, it protects against unintended consequences and respects the intent of the donor.

Cessac v. Stevens: Real Life Applications

1. Suppose that Ms. Christiansen consults you about writing her will to appoint the property in the trusts to Ms. Cessac. What language will you draft to include in the will? Why do you select this language?

2. What if Ms. Christiansen's will had included a blending clause, similar to the one you read in *Motes/Henes*?

3. Changing the facts of the case, suppose that the trusts did not require a specific reference in order for the powers to be exercised. Based on the language in Ms. Christiansen's will, what arguments would you make on behalf of Ms. Cessac that the will serves as an effective exercise?

4. What Is Required for Substantial Compliance?

As mentioned earlier, some states will recognize a power as being exercised even when there has not been strict compliance with the requirements in the instrument granting the power of appointment. In these states, "substantial" compliance is sufficient. What crosses the threshold of substantiality, however, is debatable. Courts must often engage in a facts-and-circumstances analysis to determine whether what the powerholder did was sufficient. Courts focus on whether there is evidence that the powerholder intended to exercise the power, and seek to ensure that the exercise is consistent with the donor's goals. Thus, a requirement of an inter vivos exercise may be satisfied through a will. Restatement (Third) of Property: Wills and Other Donative Transfers § 19.10, illus. 4 (2011)

From a counseling perspective, a lawyer ought to instruct strict compliance with any requirements in the granting document to avoid controversy and minimize the risk of litigation. Yet that's not necessarily what happens.

Case Preview

In re Estate of Carter

In *Cessac*, the powerholder referred to her father's trusts that had created the power. In the next case, however, the testator, Lucile Clark, neither referenced the power nor her husband's will that granted the power and required a specific reference. She did not use any of the words typically employed by powerholders, like "power" or "appoint." The court was asked to determine whether the exercise was effective.

As you read *Carter*, consider:

1. What is the role of intent?
2. Who are the permissible appointees? What is the relationship between the powerholder and the persons to whom she hopes to give the property? Does the powerholder want to give all of the property subject to the power to those appointees?
3. What does the applicable statute provide with respect to exercising a power? Did Ms. Carter comply with that statute?
4. Why does the court believe Ms. Carter exercised the power?

In re Estate of Carter
760 N.E.2d 1171 (Ind. Ct. App. 2002)

GARRARD, Senior Judge.

This appeal is from a determination by the Clinton Circuit Court that in her last will and testament Lucile Rogers Clark validly exercised a power of appointment given to her under the will of her deceased husband, James Cedric Carter. It is contended that . . . the will of Lucile failed to exercise the power.

James Cedric Carter died testate in 1981. James' will established a testamentary trust to provide for his wife, Lucile, during her lifetime and which contained the following provision:

4. Upon the death of my wife after my death, the trustee shall distribute the trust property, as then constituted, to or in trust among the class of persons consisting of Robert R. Carter, Anne Fenton Carter, Junior Brownfield, Virgie Brownfield, and the then living descendants of any of such persons, upon such conditions and estates, with such powers, in such manner, and at such times as my wife appoints and directs by will specifically referring to and exercising this limited power of appointment. Nothing in this provision shall be construed as empowering my wife to appoint any of the trust property to herself, her estate, her creditors, or the creditors of her estate.

The trust then provided for a disposition of the trust property upon the death of James' wife "to the extent that she does not effectively exercise the foregoing limited power of appointment" (or upon James' death if his wife did not survive him).

Lucile died on August 9, 2000 [and her will was admitted to probate]. Item III of her will leaves 16.19 acres of real estate, which is specifically described by metes and bounds, to Junior Brownfield and Virgie Brownfield, husband and wife. It is undisputed that the 16.9 acres is a portion of 80 acres left by James in trust and over which Lucile had a limited power of appointment, and it is undisputed that Junior Brownfield and Virgie Brownfield belong to the class of persons to whom Lucile could appoint by her will. It was also shown that on the same date Lucile executed her will, she executed a warranty deed in which she purported to convey the same 16.9 acres to Junior Brownfield and Virgie Brownfield, husband and wife. This deed was recorded in Tippecanoe County where the real estate was located.

Since Item III of Lucile's will did not expressly state that she was thereby intending to exercise the power of appointment granted her under James' will, the personal representative of her estate petitioned the court to construe her will and instruct it on how to proceed.

After a hearing the court found that Junior Brownfield and Virgie Brownfield were husband and wife. Within days of executing her will Lucile had adopted them as adults. They had lived on the 16.19 acres for more than thirty years, most of the time without direct payment of rent which was pursuant to the wishes of the Carters, and over the years they had made several improvements to the realty[,] some of which they furnished and some of which the Carters furnished. The court then determined that in spite of Lucile's failure to specifically characterize the devise to the Brownfields as an "exercise of her limited power of appointment" her intention to do exactly that was clear and should be given effect. It then ordered the described tract conveyed to the Brownfields by Bank One Trust Company, N.A., the personal representative of Lucile's estate and the testamentary trustee of James' testamentary trust.

The appellant, Roger Carter, (hereinafter "Roger") [challenges the outcome].

C. EXERCISING A POWER OF APPOINTMENT

In probate law it is axiomatic that the primary rule of construction is that the intention of the testator should govern (providing this can be done without contravening public policy or some inflexible rule of law.)

In the present case it is clear that James intended that Lucile have a limited power of appointment to dispose of certain assets by her will. The question thus arises as to whether she exercised that power.

I.C. § 29-1-6-1(f) directs that a will will not operate as exercising a power of appointment "unless by its terms the will specifically indicates that the testator intended to exercise the power." . . .

Roger contends that in order to have exercised the power Lucile's will must have explicitly stated that it was her intent to do so. He relies heavily upon the comment of the Probate Study Commission which stated,

> This subsection provides that the mere making of a will devising property over which the testator has a power of appointment will not constitute an exercise of such power of appointment unless the testator specifically indicates by the use of appropriate words his intention to exercise such power. It is believed that this rule of construction will avoid litigation.
>
> . . .

There can be little doubt that the general purpose of the statute is to resolve questions concerning the possible unintentional or accidental exercise of powers of appointment. The prime example is, no doubt, a general bequest of "all the rest, residue and remainder of my estate. . . ." Yet Indiana legal history has long displayed an aversion to any notion that some shibboleth should be required for the exercise of powers of appointment. Thus, our supreme court in the early case of Bullerdick v. Wright, 47 N.E. 931, 932-22 (1897)[,] . . . concluded, "The authorities uniformly affirm the doctrine that it is not essential to refer in express terms to the power, if an intention to execute it otherwise plainly appears; and any words or expressions indicating an intention to exercise the power will operate to that effect."

. . .

As already set forth, the court found that because Lucile's will specifically described property that was subject to the power and gave it to beneficiaries within the class permitted by the power and because of the other facts and circumstances surrounding her execution of the will it was clearly her intent to exercise her power of appointment. Roger's argument in opposition simply contends that in order to exercise the power, Lucile's will had to expressly state that she was thereby exercising her limited power of appointment. Since we have already held herein that express reference to the power is not the only manner of indicating that a testator intended to exercise it, this argument must fail. Moreover, we determine that the court's findings are sufficient to sustain its conclusion that the will did exercise the power of appointment granted under James' will.

Affirmed.

Post-Case Follow-Up

There is no question of Lucile's intent, even though she did not comply with the formal requirements established by the instrument that created the power. The result in this case is supported by the Restatement, which provides that an attempted exercise should be effective if evidence shows that: (i) the powerholder intended to exercise the power; and (ii) the way in which the powerholder exercised the power did not impair the donor's reason for imposing a requirement on the manner of exercise. Restatement (Third) of Property: Wills and Donative Transfers § 19.10 (2011). If the reason for the requirement is to avoid inadvertent exercise, then substantial compliance should be sufficient.

In re Estate of Carter: Real Life Applications

1. Assume that you had been the lawyer advising Lucile and drafting her will. Draft a will provision exercising her power that gives the property to the Brownfields in a manner that leaves no room for a challenge to the exercise.

2. Dara has one child, Shirley. Dara's will creates a trust that distributes all trust income to Shirley for life, with remainder as Shirley may appoint by an inter vivos instrument. Shirley's will exercises the power in favor of "my spouse, Jordan." Jordan would like to know whether the appointment is valid. In Indiana, how do you think a court would rule?

3. Evelyn had one child, Lin. Evelyn's will devised property to the Evelyn Trust, which granted Lin a testamentary general power of appointment. Upon Lin's death, Lin's family finds a memorandum that states: "I know this is not a legal document, but I hope that my issue will give half of the property from Evelyn's trust to my spouse." Lin's issue have asked for your advice on what to do with the property they have received from Evelyn's trust.

---

5. Exercise in Further Trust

A general power of appointment may be exercised to appoint the property in fee simple as well as subject to further trust or to a new power of appointment. Since the powerholder of a general power could appoint to herself and then use the property to establish a trust or give the property to a permissible appointee subject to a further power, the law permits the powerholder of a general power of appointment to accomplish this result directly without the intermediate step of appointing the property to herself.

If the power is a nongeneral power, however, the powerholder may be able to appoint in further trust only if the grant of the power so provides, depending on case law in the state. Some courts have held that the powerholder of a nongeneral power can appoint in trust so long as the trust is one for the benefit of the permissible appointees. See Loring v. Karri-Davies, 357 N.E.2d 11 (Mass. 1976).

Good drafting associated with the granting of the power should specify whether the powerholder has the authority to appoint in further trust. Here is an example of a power of appointment that includes the power to appoint in further trust, followed by an example of an exercise of the power in further trust:

EXAMPLE: I, Joan Flynn, grant to my husband, Edward Flynn, the power to cause all or any part of the Trust to be paid to such one or more of our joint descendants, at such times, in such proportions and in such manner, in valid trust or otherwise, and with such powers of appointment, general or special, as he may appoint by his will, executed after my death, specifically referring to this power of appointment, and valid wherever probated.

EXAMPLE: I, Edward Flynn, hereby exercise the power of appointment granted me under the will of Joan Flynn and direct that all the property subject to that power be distributed to my friend, Eugene Tanaka ("trustee"), to be held by him as trustee for the benefit of Ruben Saldana, the grandson of Joan and Edward Flynn. The trustee shall distribute to Ruben so much or all of the income and principal of the trust as the trustee determines to be in Ruben's best interests. On Ruben's death, the trustee shall distribute any remaining assets to the descendants of Joan and Edward Flynn, by representation.

6. Rule Against Perpetuities and Powers

In states that still follow the Rule Against Perpetuities, which establishes limitations on the duration of property interests, the Rule applies to an exercise of a power of appointment. The date of the gift of the power is the starting date for the Rule, and a gift in further trust may violate the Rule if the trust extends too far in the future. If the power is a general power, then the powerholder is treated as the owner and the Rule begins to run from the time of exercise rather than the time of creation, extending the period. In the example above, the gift is a general power, so the Rule starts to run when Edward dies and appoints the property.

If the power is a nongeneral power, then the power runs from the date of creation of the power, but facts at the date of the exercise control. Assume that in her will, Joan gave Edward the power to appoint the trust property to his descendants. The date of her death is the controlling date for purposes of the Rule. If Ruben is born before Joan dies, the trust for Ruben will not violate the Rule even though the power is a nongeneral power. If Ruben is born after Joan dies, however, he will not be a life in being for purposes of the trust, and exercising the power in further trust for Ruben's life would violate the Rule.

Problems with Appointees

The powerholder may not appoint the property to permissible appointees, or the appointees may have died. Both of those circumstances are discussed below.

Exercise in Favor of Impermissible Appointees

A power of appointment can be exercised only in favor of the permissible appointees. If a powerholder attempts to exercise the power in favor of someone who is not a permissible appointee, the attempted exercise is invalid. The property will go to the takers in default.

For example, Valerie holds a power to appoint among the descendants of her father, the donor of the power. Valerie's will exercises the power, appointing the trust property subject to the power to "my children, Jacob, Noah, Caleb, and Liam." Noah, Caleb, and Liam are all descendants under the state definition of descendants, but Jacob is the child of Valerie's spouse, and Valerie has not adopted him. Although Valerie thinks of him as one of her children, he is not a permissible appointee (unless the document creating the power of appointment modified the state's definition of descendant). The attempted exercise in favor of Jacob is invalid. His one-fourth share will go to the takers in default.

Case Preview

BMO Harris Bank N.A. v. Towers

BMO Harris Bank addresses the consequences of appointing to an impermissible appointee. Martin Jr. was the power-holder of two different powers of appointment from his parents. There is no issue with respect to the form in which he exercised the powers.

As you read the case, consider the following questions:

1. To whom—or what—did Martin Jr. exercise the power? Why was that appointment impermissible?
2. Who is responsible for Martin Jr.'s impermissible exercise?
3. Why doesn't it matter that no property subject to the power was ever actually distributed to an impermissible appointee?

BMO Harris Bank N.A. v. Towers
43 N.E.3d 1131 (Ill. App. Ct. 2015)

JUSTICE LAMPKIN delivered the judgment of the court, with opinion.

. . .

We hold that: As the trust donee, Martin Jr.'s exercise of his limited testamentary powers of appointment in favor of himself was ineffective and therefore void because he was not a permissible appointee. . . .

Mary and Martin Cornelius, Sr., created two trusts with the Bank as trustee that were to be administered for the benefit of their son, Martin Jr., during his lifetime. Each trust granted Martin Jr. a limited testamentary power of appointment. Under the terms of the Mary trust, Martin Jr. could appoint assets to or in further trust for his spouse, Mary's descendants other than Martin Jr., or the spouses of such descendants. Under the terms of the Martin Sr. trust, Martin Jr. could appoint assets to or in further trust for his spouse, his lineal descendants and their spouses, Martin Sr.'s other lineal descendants and their spouses, or any charitable organization. [I]f the powers of appointment were not effectively exercised, then distributions would be made to the descendants of Martin Jr. living at the time of his death.

During his lifetime, Martin Jr. created a revocable living trust (the Martin Jr. trust). Martin Jr. [] was survived by his spouse and four children, Harry, Martin III, Camilla, and Dagmar. Martin Jr.'s last will and testament, dated 1991, was admitted to probate. . . . In sections 2.2 and 2.3 of his will, Martin Jr. exercised his limited powers of appointment under the Mary and Martin Sr. trusts by appointing all the property to the trustee of the Martin Jr. trust.

. . .

Section 5.3 of the [Martin Jr.] trust agreement directed the trustee, upon Martin Jr.'s death, to pay from the "original trust . . . all debts, expenses of administration, and death taxes (estate, inheritance, and like taxes, including interest and penalties but not including any generation-skipping transfer taxes) that are payable as a result of [Martin Jr.'s] death." Section 5.5 of the trust agreement provided that "[a]t any time during the continuance of the original Trust after [Martin Jr.'s] death, the trustee may distribute to [Martin Jr.'s] probate estate, as a beneficiary of the Trust, cash or other property out of any assets then held by the Trust." [Upon termination,] the remaining assets of the trust would be paid in equal shares to Martin Jr.'s son Harry and three of Martin Jr.'s grandchildren. Martin Jr. explicitly stated that his children Dagmar and Martin III were omitted as residuary beneficiaries.

. . .

The [defendants, consisting of the trustee of Martin Jr.'s revocable trust and three of Martin Jr.'s four living children] assert that Martin Jr. properly segregated the assets from his parents' trusts because after Martin Jr.'s death no assets were ever withdrawn from the [parents'] trusts, used for any improper purpose, or distributed to any improper beneficiary. The Towers defendants acknowledge that Martin Jr., as the donee of his parents' powers appointment, could not make the property subject to that power part of his estate for all purposes, and argue that the terms of Martin Jr.'s will and trust and extrinsic evidence establish that he intended to fulfill his parents' wishes without making the assets of their trusts part of his estate for all purposes.

. . .

. . . . The same rules that pertain to the construction of a will also pertain to the construction of a trust, with the intention of the testator being of supreme importance. "A power of appointment is not an absolute right of property, nor is it an estate, for it has none of the elements of an estate." People v. Kaiser, 137 N.E. 826 (1922). . . . A special power of appointment is only valid if it was exercised in compliance with any conditions established by the donor. . . . [T]he plain language controlling the powers of appointment for both the [parents'] trusts establishes that Martin Jr. could not exercise the powers of appointment in favor of himself because he was not within the class of permissible beneficiaries designated by his parents. [T]he plain terms of Martin Jr.'s will and trust agreement provided that the assets from his parents' trusts would be commingled with the assets of his original trust and then his trustee would pay "all debts" that were payable as a result of Martin Jr.'s death from the original trust. No language in the Martin Jr. trust agreement segregated the assets from his parents' trusts from the assets of Martin Jr.'s original trust, and Martin Jr.'s creditors could have used the commingled assets to satisfy Martin Jr.'s debts.

. . . We conclude that Martin Jr. blended his own property with the appointed property for all purposes. Contrary to the [] defendants' argument on appeal, the plain language of section 5.3 of Martin Jr.'s trust agreement establishes that it was Martin Jr.'s intent to pay all his debts from his original trust, which included the assets appointed from the [parents'] trusts. Because Martin Jr. exercised his powers of appointment in favor of himself and he was not within the class of permissible beneficiaries under the limited powers of appointment designated by his parents, his impermissible exercise of his powers of appointment rendered the act of conveyance void. Accordingly, the trial court correctly instructed the Bank to distribute the appointed property per stirpes to Martin Jr.'s four children who were living at the time of his death, in compliance with the terms of the Mary and Martin Sr. trusts in the event the powers of appointment were not effectively exercised.

The [] defendants also argue extrinsic evidence establishes that no debts of Martin Jr.'s estate were ever paid from the assets of his parents' two trusts, and Martin Jr.'s spouse paid all the debts, expenses and taxes directly from Martin Jr.'s estate without taking any money from the parents' two trusts held by the Bank. This happenstance, however, is not controlling in the determination of whether Martin Jr. improperly exercised the powers of appointment. [] Regardless of how the trustee actually performed his duties, the intent and validity of a will is determined at the time of death, and the will and trust agreement here dictated that Martin Jr.'s debts would be paid from the original trust, which contained the commingled assets of both Martin Jr.'s estate property and the assets from his parents' trusts. This was the intent of Martin Jr., and the fact that Martin Jr.'s creditors never actually accessed the assets of his parents' trusts does not remedy the invalid conveyance.

Affirmed.

Post-Case Follow-Up

When the donor creates the power, the donor will also define the group of permissible appointees. If the donee attempts to appoint to anyone other than a permissible appointee, as Martin Jr. did here, then that exercise is ineffective. Because Martin Jr. attempted to appoint all of the property to the trust, the entire exercise was invalid. In most states, if Martin Jr. had appointed some of the property to permissible and some to impermissible appointees, only the attempted appointments to the impermissible appointees would be invalid; the appointment to permissible beneficiaries would be effective, and the property appointed to the impermissible appointees would go to the takers in default. See Restatement (Third) of Property: Wills and Other Donative Transfers § 19.15 (2011). The property that has not been appointed to permissible appointees goes to the taker-in-default.

BMO Harris Bank N.A. v. Towers: Real Life Applications

1. Identify what terms in the trust created the problems discussed in *BMO Harris Bank*. If Martin Jr. had wanted to exercise the power in favor of his trust, what steps might he have taken?

2. If Martin Jr. had wanted to exercise the power of appointment in favor of his trust beneficiaries, without changing his trust, how might he have done so?

3. Imagine that Martin Jr. consults you and wants to know if the powers of appointment can be exercised in further trust. What advice do you give him?

4. The Bank, as the trustee of the parents' trust, has asked you for advice on what to do with the property remaining in the trusts. What is your advice?

7. Predeceased Appointees

What happens if an appointee is alive when the powerholder executes a valid will exercising a power of appointment in favor of the appointee but the appointee then dies before the powerholder? Just as a beneficiary of a will must survive the testator to take under a will, an appointee must survive the powerholder in order to take appointed property.

Uniform Probate Code (UPC) § 2-603(b)(5) applies the anti-lapse rule to powers of appointment, and a number of states have adopted similar statutes. The Restatement (Third) of Property: Wills and Other Donative Transfers § 19.12 (2011) urges courts to apply a general anti-lapse statute to powers of appointment even if the state statute does not explicitly apply to powers. The UPAA concurs. See UPAA § 306, cmt. Under an anti-lapse statute, if the appointee is related to the donor or the powerholder as prescribed by the statute and the appointee predeceases the powerholder, the property will go to the appointee's descendants. The question of applying anti-lapse statutes to powers of appointment is tricky because doing so may mean that the property will be distributed to persons who were not named by the donor as permissible appointees. For example, if the power is exercisable in favor of the powerholder's siblings and an appointee sibling predeceases the powerholder, an anti-lapse statute would give the property to the deceased sibling's descendants. A donor can provide that the anti-lapse statute will not apply, but should do so specifically. The comment to UPAA § 306 takes the view that naming takers in default should not be construed to mean that the donor did not want the anti-lapse statute to apply.

A different problem arises when the powerholder attempts to appoint directly to an impermissible appointee because the permissible appointee is deceased at the time the powerholder makes the appointment. For example, if a testamentary power is exercisable in favor of the powerholder's brother and the brother is deceased when the powerholder executes his will, can the powerholder exercise the power in favor of anyone else?

UPAA § 306 extends the anti-lapse rule so that a powerholder can appoint property to the descendants of any deceased permissible appointee. In contrast with the anti-lapse provision, the UPAA does not limit this alternative exercise provision to appointees related to the donor or the powerholder. Consequently, application of § 306 could add permissible appointees not identified by the donor. To avoid application of the rule, the donor would have to state specifically that she did not want this rule to apply. See also Restatement (Third) of Property: Wills and Other Donative Transfers § 19.12, cmt. f (2011).

For example, Robin gave Jamie a testamentary power to appoint trust property to Robin's friend, Alix, and to Robin's child, Sasha. In default, the property subject to the power goes to Robin's other child, Dora. Jamie executes a will appointing one-half of the property to each of Alix and Sasha. After Jamie executes the will, but before Jamie dies, Alix and Sasha die. Under the rule in many states, the attempted exercise for each of them is ineffective, and Dora will take the property. Under UPAA § 306(a), assuming the state has also adopted UPC § 2-603(b)(5), Sasha's descendants will take Sasha's share, but Alix's descendants will not (Alix is a friend, and is not related to Jamie as required by the anti-lapse statute).

If Alix and Sasha are already deceased when Jamie executes the will, their descendants are permissible appointees under UPAA § 306(b). Jamie could appoint the property subject to the power to any one or more of Alix's children (even though Alix is not related to Jamie) and Sasha's children (or further descendants).

8. Selective Allocation

The doctrine of selective allocation may fix, at least partially, a problem created by an ineffective exercise of a power. A powerholder's residuary clause may combine property subject to a power and the powerholder's own property. If the powerholder's beneficiaries are not all permissible appointees, the doctrine of selective allocation will distribute the property in the way that best carries out the powerholder's intent. See Restatement (Third) of Property: Wills and Other Donative Transfers § 19.19 (2011); UPAA § 308.

For example, in his will, Luis grants Rafael a testamentary power to appoint among Rafael's "descendants." Rafael's will includes the following residuary clause: "I give all of the property I own at my death together with all property subject to a power of appointment I hold under the will of Luis Rodriguez, to my three children, Alma, Bruno, and Camilla." Alma and Bruno are Rafael's genetic children, and Camilla is Rafael's unadopted stepchild. Camilla does not qualify as a descendant because Camilla and Rafael do not have a legalized parent-child relationship. The powerholder's intent to benefit Alma, Bruno, and Camilla seems clear on the face of the will. The doctrine of allocation would allocate Rafael's own assets (up to one-third of the total) to Camilla and the appointed assets to Alma and Bruno. If the appointive property was $220,000 and Rafael's own property was $80,000, Camilla would receive $80,000 and Alma and Bruno would each receive $110,000. If the appointive property was $80,000 and Rafael's property was $220,000, each child would receive $100,000 (Camilla would receive $100,000 of Rafael's property, and Alma and Bruno would divide the remaining $120,000 of Rafael's property and each receive half of the appointive property).

D. RELEASE, FAILURE TO EXERCISE, AND AN EXPRESS STATEMENT OF NONEXERCISE

A holder of a power of appointment often chooses to exercise it consistently with the terms of the grant, as discussed above. But a powerholder is not, however, required to exercise the power. Instead, she can (1) release it, (2) not exercise it, or (3) expressly indicate her decision not to exercise it (each of these is defined below). The Restatement of Property refers to all of these situations as a lapse of the power; in other words, the powerholder did not exercise the power, so the power lapsed. See Restatement (Third) of Property: Wills and Other Donative Transfers § 19.22 (2011). A power of appointment can only be exercised by the named powerholder. If the powerholder dies without exercising the power, then the power does not pass to the powerholder's heir or devisees.

Just as it is important for the powerholder to be clear about the intent to exercise a power of appointment by using a specific-exercise clause, it is important to be clear about one's intention not to exercise a power. The law has developed rules that apply to all three forms of lapse in the same way. The text sets out definitions of the three types of lapse and then considers what happens to the property when the power lapses. The consequences of lapse vary, depending on the terms of the grant of the power.

- **Release**: If the holder of a power of appointment releases it by giving notice to the trustee, then the powerholder no longer has the power to decide who will take it. A powerholder may decide to release a power in order to prevent creditors from reaching the appointive property, or there may be tax benefits for doing so. After the release, the takers in default, if there are any, whose interests were contingent now have vested remainder interests.

  For example, Jamie has a life income interest in a trust, with a testamentary power of appointment to distribute the trust property among Jamie's siblings and their descendants. The trust provides that if Jamie fails to exercise the power, the property will go to Jamie's first cousin, Nicky. If Jamie notifies the trustee in writing that she releases the power, Jamie will have no further rights with respect to the power, and Nicky will have a vested remainder in the property. Nicky will still wait until Jamie's death to have possession of the trust property.

- **Nonexercise**: For a variety of reasons, the powerholder may not exercise the power. The powerholder may think the takers in default should take the property, may forget to exercise the power, or may not know about the power. If the powerholder does not expressly release the power and does nothing that could constitute an exercise of the power, then the powerholder has failed to exercise the power.

- **Expressly refraining from exercise**: Because a residuary clause may sometimes be considered to exercise a power of appointment, even without a specific reference to the power, the holder of a power may want to clarify in her will that she does not intend to exercise the power. The will might say, "I expressly do not exercise the power of appointment I have under the will of Hayden Richardson."

1. Who Gets the Property?

Takers in Default Stated

If the original grant of a power provides for takers in default, the takers in default will receive the property if the power lapses for one reason or another. See UPAA § 310(1) (general power); § 311(1) (nongeneral power). The takers in default are determined at the time set for distribution, so if the takers are a class (children or descendants), the determination of membership in the class will be made at the time of distribution. Here are two examples.

For example, Jacob created a testamentary trust for his child, Izzy, with distributions during Izzy's life. The trust provides that on Izzy's death, the property will be distributed to such one or more charities as Izzy appoints, or, if Izzy does not exercise her power of appointment, to Izzy's two siblings equally. If Izzy does not exercise her power of appointment, the two siblings will receive the property when Izzy dies.

As another example, Rajan and Deepal were married. During the marriage, Rajan created an irrevocable trust that granted Deepal an income interest in the trust property for life along with a power to appoint the principal remaining at her death to anyone other than Deepal, Deepal's creditors, Deepal's estate, or the creditors of Deepal's estate (a broad, nongeneral power). The trust provides that the takers in default are Rajan's descendants. When Rajan and Deepal divorce, Deepal agrees to release the power. When Deepal releases the power, Rajan's living descendants take a vested interest in the property, although which descendants will take depends on who is alive at Deepal's death. Deepal will no longer be able to appoint the property.

No Takers in Default Stated

If the donor did not provide for takers in default, then who will take the property if the power lapses depends on whether the power was general or nongeneral.

If the power is nongeneral, the property will be distributed to the permissible appointees, if those permissible appointees are a defined and limited class. If the class is so broad that specific members cannot be determined, then the property will be distributed to the donor's estate as a reversionary interest. See UPAA §§ 310(2), 311(2).

For example, Daniel creates a trust for his daughter, Jeanne, with distributions during her life. The trust provides that on Jeanne's death, the property will be distributed to such one or more charities as Jeanne appoints. The trust does not provide who will take the property if Jeanne does not exercise the power. Although this is a nongeneral power, the class of permissible appointees includes any charity, and it is not sufficiently specific for a gift to those appointees. If the power lapses, the property will revert to Daniel or to Daniel's estate.

As another example, Daniel creates a different trust for Jeanne. This trust provides that on Jeanne's death the property will be distributed to such one or more of Jeanne's descendants as Jeanne appoints. This is a nongeneral power with a defined class. When Jeanne died, she had two living children and two grandchildren who are the children of one of her deceased children. If the power lapses, on Jeanne's death the trust property will be distributed as it would be distributed to Jeanne's descendants under the state's intestacy statute, unless the document defines descendants in some other way. Thus, the trustee will distribute the property in three shares, one to each living child and one divided equally between the two grandchildren.

If the power is general and the powerholder fails to exercise it, the property will be distributed to the powerholder's estate, unless the terms of the grant of the power provide otherwise. The idea behind this rule is that because the powerholder could control the power, the default rule should be to distribute it through the powerholder's estate.

If the powerholder releases the power, however, or expressly states that he does not exercise it, that affirmative action by the powerholder indicates his desire not to control the disposition of the property. In that situation the property is distributed to the donor or the donor's estate, as a reversionary interest. See Restatement (Third) of Property: Wills and Other Donative Transfers § 19.22 (2011); UPAA § 310.

For example, Daniel creates yet another trust for Jeanne and gives her a general power of appointment, to appoint to anyone including herself. The trust does not provide for takers in default. If Jeanne releases the power, the trust property will be distributed to Daniel's estate. If Jeanne takes no action with respect to the power (i.e., does not exercise the power), the trust property will be distributed to Jeanne's estate.

Capture

If a general power is ineffectively exercised, the doctrine of capture causes the property subject to the power to be distributed through the powerholder's estate. See Restatement (Third) of Property: Wills and Other Donative Transfers § 19.21 (2011); UPAA § 309. This might happen if the powerholder exercises the power in favor of a permissible appointee who has died without leaving any descendants.

2. Contract to Exercise a Power

The holder of a power of appointment that can be exercised currently can enter into a contract to exercise the power on behalf of a permissible appointee. The contract is valid so long as it "does not confer a benefit on an impermissible appointee." UPAA § 405.

For example, Morgan is given a power to appoint among the settlor's children, during lifetime or at death. One of the children, Danielle, would like to buy a house, and she would like Morgan to agree to appoint some of the trust property to her if she becomes unable to pay the mortgage. If Morgan agrees, his promise will be an enforceable contract, because he could currently appoint property to her as a permissible appointee. Now assume that Morgan promises the bank that if Danielle defaults on her mortgage payments, Morgan will pay the bank directly from the trust.

Although the guarantee benefits the bank, an impermissible appointee, Danielle is the actual beneficiary, and the benefit is incidental to the bank's business of providing loans, so the contract is enforceable. See Restatement (Third) of Property: Wills and Other Donative Transfers § 21.1, cmt. a (2011).

The holder of a testamentary power cannot enter into a contract to exercise the power in the future. If a donor creates a testamentary power of appointment, the donor intends the powerholder to be able to continue considering the best way to exercise the power until the donor dies. A contractual agreement to exercise it in a particular way operates like a current exercise because the powerholder cannot change her mind later. Consequently, a court will not enforce an agreement requiring that the power be exercised in a certain way.

The traditional rule is that even if a permissible appointee enters into a contract with the powerholder to exercise a testamentary power on behalf of the person, and the powerholder fails to exercise the power as required by the contract, the contract will not be enforced against the property. Instead, the person contracting will have a claim of restitution based on the unjust enrichment of the powerholder. If the powerholder has no assets, then the person contracting is out of luck.

This lack of enforceability was the situation in Seidel v. Werner, 364 N.Y.S.2d 963, *aff'd on opinion below*, 376 N.Y.S.2d 139 (1975). Steven Werner held a testamentary general power of appointment over property in a trust created by his father. His four children, from two marriages, were the takers in default. Werner agreed, as part of a divorce settlement, to exercise the power of appointment in favor of the two children of the marriage being dissolved. He died with a will that exercised his power in favor of his next wife (she was wife number three). The court refused to uphold the contract to appoint against the property of the trust and said that the children's only remedy was a claim for restitution against Werner's estate. The trust property could not be used to satisfy that claim because the trust property did not belong to Werner, who had only held a power of appointment over the property.

If the person hoping to get the property subject to a testamentary power is named as a taker in default, then having the powerholder release the power may be better than entering into a contract to exercise the power. In *Seidel*, a release would have meant that Werner's four children (the takers in default) would have received the property.

The Restatement and the UPAA treat a contract to exercise a testamentary power in favor of permissible appointees as a release to the extent necessary to carry out the contract. See UPAA § 403, cmt.; Restatement (Third) of Property: Wills and Other Donative Transfers § 20.3, cmt. d (2011). In *Seidel*, the result under the Restatement or the UPAA would have been to treat the power as released with respect to half the property, because the two children would have taken half the trust property as takers in default. The safer strategy for the lawyer representing the divorcing spouse would have been to insist on a release.

E. RIGHTS OF CREDITORS

The holder of a general power of appointment may appoint some or all of the property to himself to the extent consistent with the grant. This may be viewed as the functional equivalent of ownership. Since the powerholder can make the trust property his own, one question that arises is whether his creditors can look to the trust as a source to collect debts.

Under the common law, the holder of a general power of appointment has traditionally been treated as not owning the property until he exercises the power. See Restatement (Second) of Property: Donative Transfers § 13.2 (1986). Under this rule, the powerholder's creditors cannot reach the appointive property before he appoints it to himself. The court in *Seidel v. Werner, supra*, followed this traditional rule in holding that the trust property could not be used to satisfy the children's claim.

The Uniform Trust Code (UTC) and trust statutes in several states have changed this rule. UTC § 505(b) and UPAA § 501 provide that creditors of the holder of a general power of appointment can reach property subject to the power in much the same manner as they could have proceeded against the settlor of a revocable trust. The comments to UTC § 505 state:

> If the power is unlimited, the property subject to the power will be fully subject to the claims of the powerholder's creditors, the same as the powerholder's other assets. If the powerholder retains the power until death, the property subject to the power may be liable for claims and statutory allowances to the extent the powerholder's probate estate is insufficient to satisfy those claims and allowances. For powers limited either in time or amount, such as a right to withdraw a $10,000 annual exclusion contribution within 30 days, this subsection would limit the creditor to the $10,000 contribution and require the creditor to take action prior to the expiration of the 30-day period.

Importantly, with respect to the claims of creditors, UPAA § 502(b) treats what might otherwise qualify as a general power of appointment as a nongeneral power of appointment—and thus not subject to the claims of creditors—if the power to appoint to oneself was "created by a person other than the powerholder [and] is subject to an ascertainable standard relating to an individual's health, education, support, or maintenance. . . ."

A split exists between the uniform laws and the Restatement regarding whether transferees of nonprobate assets are liable for the claims of creditors of the decedent if the probate property is insufficient to satisfy those claims. The comments to UPC § 6-102 state that the definition of "nonprobate transfer . . . does not include a transfer at death incident to a decedent's exercise or nonexercise of a presently exercisable general power of appointment created by another person." By contrast, the above-referenced Restatement says, "property subject to a general power of appointment that was exercisable by the donee's will is subject to creditors' claims to the extent that the donee's estate is insufficient to satisfy the claims of creditors of the estate and the expenses of administration of the estate."

One thing the uniform laws and the Restatement agree on is that the creditors of a holder of a nongeneral power of appointment have no rights against the property subject to the power. The law basically views the powerholder as no more than an agent of the donor and a conduit through whom the property passes to a select group of appointees. The powerholder has no rights in or quasi-ownership of the property that a creditor can attach.

1. Be Careful About Tax Consequences!

Federal estate and gift tax law, discussed in Chapter 15, has a distinct way of treating powers of appointment. General powers of appointment can affect income taxation of trusts as well. While tax issues are not discussed in depth in this chapter, it is important to understand that there are tax consequences for powers of appointment. Indeed, in some circumstances, a trustee's fiduciary powers may be taxed as a power of appointment.

For example, regardless of whether the power to distribute is held in a fiduciary capacity by a trustee, or is held as a powerholder, a distribution to a person other than the person with the right to make the distribution is treated as a transfer subject to gift or estate tax—but only if distributed by a person who possesses a general power of appointment or a comparable fiduciary power. Internal Revenue Code §§ 2514 and 2041. Further, if the person holding the power can distribute property to herself, even in a fiduciary capacity and even if the power is not exercised, the property may be included in her estate for estate tax purposes. In contrast, no estate or gift tax consequences follow from the exercise or nonexercise of a nongeneral power of appointment.

Chapter Summary

- A power of appointment allows the owner of property to give someone else (the powerholder) the authority to designate a new owner of the property. The powerholder does not hold title to the property and has no fiduciary obligations. A power of appointment can be created in a trust, a will, or in another document.
- A "general" power of appointment can be exercised in favor of any one or more of the following: the powerholder, the powerholder's estate, a creditor of the powerholder, or a creditor of the powerholder's estate.
- A nongeneral power of appointment cannot be exercised to appoint the property to the powerholder, the powerholder's estate, a creditor of the powerholder, or a

creditor of the powerholder's estate, but the powerholder may have the authority to exercise the power in favor of anyone else.

- The donor may require that the powerholder exercise the power in a certain way, such as inter vivos or by will, and may require a specific reference to the power. The document in which the power is exercised must itself be valid, must indicate the powerholder's intent to exercise the power, and must be in favor of a permissible appointee. Typically, a powerholder must substantially comply with the formal requirements for exercise.

- Regardless of whether specific reference is required, the clearest way to exercise a power of appointment is through a specific exercise clause that specifically refers to the power and the document that created it. For example, "I exercise the power of appointment conferred upon me by [my father's will] as follows: I appoint [fill in details of appointment]."

- A blending clause purports to blend the appointive property with the powerholder's own property in a common disposition. The exercise portion of a blending clause can take the form of a specific exercise or, more commonly, a blanket exercise, such as "any property over which I may have a power."

- In most circumstances a residuary clause that does not refer to a power in any way does not manifest an intent to exercise a power of appointment.

- If a powerholder does not want to exercise a power, she is not required to do so. She can, but is not required to, explicitly release the power. If the power lapses, then the takers in default (if any) receive the property.

- Creditors cannot reach property subject to a nongeneral power of appointment. Although the traditional rule is that creditors cannot reach property subject to a general power of appointment, the modern trend is to allow more rights to creditors in such property.

Applying the Concepts

1. Amir's will created a trust with the following provision:

> The trustee shall distribute all the income to Jasmine, at least monthly. The trustee shall also distribute so much or all of the principal of the trust to Jasmine, as the trustee determines necessary for her health, maintenance, and support. On Jasmine's death, the trustee shall distribute the remaining trust corpus to such one or more of my descendants, in trust or otherwise, as Jasmine appoints by will, and if Jasmine fails to exercise this power of appointment, to my then living descendants, by representation.

When Amir died, he was married to Jasmine. They had two children, Damien and Fatima. After Amir died, Jasmine married Ibrahim. They had a child, Nadia. To whom should the trustee distribute the trust property if, when Jasmine died, her probated will contained the following provision:

a. "I appoint all property in the trust created under Article Five of my deceased husband's will and over which I hold a power of appointment to my husband, Ibrahim."

b. "I appoint all property in the trust created under Article Five of my deceased husband's will and over which I hold a power of appointment in equal shares to my three children."

c. "I give the residue of my estate to my descendants, by representation."

d. "I give the residue of my estate, including any property subject to a power of appointment, to my daughter, Fatima."

2. The facts are the same as in Problem 1, except assume that Jasmine died intestate. Five years before she died, Jasmine signed a document that said, "I hereby release the power of appointment I hold under the will of my former husband, Amir." To whom should the trust property be given?

3. Elvira created a trust for her daughter, Aubrey. The trust instrument directs the trustee to distribute the property to Aubrey, for her welfare and best interests. The trust instrument also directs the trustee to distribute property as Aubrey appoints either by an instrument executed during her lifetime or by will. If Aubrey fails to exercise the power of appointment, the trustee is to distribute the property to the nonprofit organization Doctors Without Borders.

   Aubrey enters into a contract with George, in connection with their divorce, in which she agrees to exercise her power of appointment in favor of their child, Bruno. When Aubrey dies, her will contains the following provision: "I hereby exercise the power of appointment I was given under the will of my mother, Elvira, and appoint all remaining trust property to my partner-in-life, Hannah." To whom should the trustee distribute the property?

4. Dori transfers property to Theo in trust, directing Theo to pay the income to Shannon (Dori's child) for life, with a general testamentary power in Shannon to appoint the principal of the trust, and in default of appointment the principal is to be distributed "to Shannon's descendants who survive Shannon, by representation, and if none, to State University." Shannon dies, leaving a will that does not exercise the power, but she does have descendants who survive her. What happens to the principal?

5. Celeste and Marina executed a joint revocable trust, providing that on the death of the first spouse, the trust would become irrevocable. The survivor had the power to appoint so much or all of the trust assets as the survivor "shall appoint and direct by specific reference to this power of appointment in her last Will admitted to probate by a court of competent jurisdiction. If the power is not exercised, then the property shall be given to our children." The trust included the family home and various bank accounts.

   Two years after Celeste's death, Marina executed a document that purported to be an amendment to the trust. The document provided that on Marina's death, the family home would go to a friend, Tomas, who had taken care of Marina. Marina signed the document, and her lawyer notarized it.

a. Has Marina exercised the power of appointment?

b. What arguments can Tomas make that he should receive the family home?

Trusts and Estates in Practice

1. Has your state enacted the Uniform Powers of Appointment Act? If not, what laws control the creation and exercise of powers of appointment?

2. Pursuant to your state's laws, under what circumstances will a residuary clause exercise a power of appointment?

3. Under your state's laws, can creditors ever reach a power of appointment? Under what circumstances?

4. Develop a brief description, suitable for a client, that defines a power of appointment and explains when and why it might be useful.

5. Your client wants to release her power of appointment. How can she do so?

6. Warren's trust contained the following provision: "My daughter, Violet, shall have the power during her lifetime or at death to appoint the trust property to any one or more of her descendants." Violet has three children: Axel, Morgan, and Claude. Axel has a child, Magda, and Morgan has a stepchild, Norine. Draft the following:

   a. A current exercise of the power giving the trust corpus to Magda and Norine.

   b. A testamentary exercise of the power giving the trust corpus to Axel, Morgan, and Claude.

7. Your client, Jane, has been given the following power by the Barry Kane Trust dated May 2, 2018. Section 4.1 of the Trust states: "My daughter, Jane, has the right to distribute the trust property to, or direct that it be held for the benefit of, any person or persons, in such amounts as Jane shall appoint by deed or by will, and such deed or will shall refer specifically to the power given Jane by this Trust. If Jane does not appoint the trust property by deed or by will, the trust property shall be distributed to my descendants, per stirpes." Jane would like to exercise the power in favor of her children.

   a. What are her options for doing so?

   b. Advise her on what issues, beyond the legal implications, she might want to consider as she decides what to do with the appointive property.

   c. Draft a specific-exercise clause that appoints the property to her living children in equal shares.

13

Professional Ethics in Trusts and Estates

Throughout the textbook, you have seen lawyers in a variety of roles, acting both competently and incompetently. This chapter explores lawyers' obligations to act ethically and appropriately. Rather than reviewing all of the professional responsibility rules applicable to lawyers, this chapter focuses on the rules of conduct of particular importance to the trusts and estates practitioner due to the frequency with which they are encountered. These rules include those relating to competence, diligence, client communications, reasonable attorneys' fees, confidentiality, conflicts of interest between current and former clients, client capacity, and multi-jurisdictional practice and the unauthorized practice of law.

The rules in nearly all states are based at least in significant part upon the Model Rules of Professional Conduct (Model Rules of Prof'l Conduct (2013) (MRPC)) as adopted by the American Bar Association, although local variations are common. Trusts and estates lawyers often find the Commentaries to the Model Rules developed by The American College of Trust and Estate Counsel (ACTEC) to be particularly helpful because they provide additional guidance on how to apply the MRPC in the estate planning and administration context. See Am. Coll. of Trust & Estate Counsel, ACTEC Commentaries on the Model Rules of Professional Conduct (5th ed. 2016) (hereinafter ACTEC Commentaries). The ACTEC Commentaries are cited frequently in this chapter.[1]

Key Concepts

- Attorneys' duties to clients and non-clients
- How to reduce malpractice exposure
- Upholding the standards of competence and diligence
- Maintaining proper communication with a client
- Reasonable attorney fees
- Managing confidentiality
- Conflicts of interest
- Client capacity levels

---

[1]References in this chapter to rules of professional conduct are citations to the Delaware Lawyers' Rules of Professional Conduct, which closely track the language of the Model Rules of Professional Conduct and can be found at http://courts.delaware.gov using the Rules link. Excerpts from rules are often edited and do not include the entire rule.

A. THE IDENTITY OF THE CLIENT, MALPRACTICE LITIGATION, AND LIABILITY TO NON-CLIENTS

Most of the standards of professional ethics discussed in this chapter address the duties an attorney owes to a client. But the initial question is: Who is the client? This is a matter that may be more complicated in the practice area of trusts and estates, where individuals are playing fiduciary roles and the person who is the obvious "client" cannot survive to oversee the proper administration of the estate. The following section discusses the identification of the client in trusts and estates practice and the additional individuals or entities to whom the lawyer may owe professional obligations.

1. Who Is the Client in Estate Planning and Estate Administration?

The primary client in estate planning is the testator or donor. When representing multiple clients, such as spouses or multiple members of the same family, a lawyer must pay close attention to conflicts of interest and matters of confidentiality in these joint representations. Although the testator or donor is the client of the lawyer, parties other than the client may have the right to bring malpractice claims, a point discussed in more detail in Section A.3.

The identity of the client in estate administration is somewhat more difficult. The client can no longer be the testator or donor, who is now deceased. So who does the attorney represent? The estate itself? The personal representative (in an individual capacity, a fiduciary one, or both)? The heirs or beneficiaries? Does estate administration even require an attorney? States vary as to the answers to all of these questions, although the most common rule is that the attorney represents the personal representative, rather than the beneficiary or the estate. For more information, see Michael Hatfield, *Pro Se Executors—Unauthorized Practice of Law, or Not?*, 59 Baylor L. Rev. 329, 347-48 (2007). Even in states that suggest that the estate itself is the client, duties are generally owed to the personal representative, beneficiaries, and creditors. Recall that the personal representative also owes obligations to the creditors and beneficiaries or heirs to administer the estate prudently, so a lawyer overseeing the administration of the estate must remain aware of the needs of a variety of stakeholders.

2. Common Grounds for Malpractice

The savvy and conscientious lawyer naturally wants to avoid professional negligence that could trigger malpractice litigation. To what, then, must the attorney pay particular attention? Professor Gerry Beyer collects a list of common causes of action for estate planning litigation in his article, *Avoid Being a Defendant: Estate Planning Malpractice and Ethical Concerns*, 5 St. Mary's J. Legal Mal. & Ethics 224

(2015). The most common claims are broken down into five main categories by Professor Beyer: (1) poor client interactions, (2) will drafting errors, (3) improper will execution, (4) trust drafting errors, and (5) other "troublesome mistakes." The discussion below draws on Professor Beyer's framework and article.

With respect to poor client interactions, these claims include matters such as failing to gather information fully and completely. It also includes poor client communication and lack of timeliness. Believing the client without supporting outside evidence can also be risky, as can failing to document strange requests and failing to notice situations that ultimately trigger will contests.

Will drafting errors are also a common malpractice trap. Best practice is always to proofread documents carefully, as proofreading mistakes can lead to litigation. Failure to include important provisions in the will, such as those addressing pretermitted, adopted, and nonmarital children; exoneration; abatement; ademption; and lapse also lead to malpractice claims. Other common failures relate to the survival period, tax apportionment, tax planning, integration, and incorporation by reference. Lawyers also face liability for ambiguous language choice, insufficient provisions for the personal representative, and everyone's favorite: the Rule Against Perpetuities.

Improper will execution is another common cause for malpractice claims. Flaws in execution include having a procedure for the execution ceremony that does not comply with state law, not having the testator sign properly, and failure to make sure sufficient witnesses sign. Completing the self-proving affidavit improperly can lead to claims, as can directing the testator to execute duplicate original wills.

Errors in trust drafting are as risky as errors in will drafting. Many of the same issues with respect to will drafting may arise, but additional traps include failure to include principal and income provisions, leaving out the spendthrift provision, and improperly stating the power to revoke. Finally, lawyers may encounter "other troublesome mistakes" that lead to litigation based on violation of their responsibilities as an estate planner. These include failure to plan for disability, failure to use appropriate disclaimers, and not providing the client with sufficient instructions following delivery of the estate plan. Improper preservation of documents rounds out the list.

Certainly, there are many pitfalls for trusts and estates attorneys and many opportunities for mistakes to arise. But the client is dead, so there's no one left to sue, right? Not so fast. Read on.

The Fall of Privity and the Rise of Malpractice Claims

Professor Martin Begleiter explains in *First Let's Sue All the Lawyers—What Will We Get: Damages for Estate Planning Malpractice*, 51 Hastings L.J. 325, 326-27 (2000) (footnotes omitted):

Until 1960, rarely was an attorney subject to liability to disappointed beneficiaries in a will case, regardless of the error made by the attorney. The reason was that only those in privity with the drafter of the will had standing to sue the drafter for malpractice. The beneficiaries under a defectively executed will or the intended beneficiaries under a deficiently drafted will had no contractual relationship with the drafting attorney and therefore could not bring an action against the attorney. In 1961, the famous California case of Lucas v. Hamm changed that rule by making the question of whether the beneficiaries could sue the attorney a question of public policy. . . . As of 1999, only six states retained a rule of absolute privity prohibiting beneficiaries under a will or trust from bringing a malpractice action against the drafting attorney. . . .

3. Duties to Non-Clients and the Privity Defense

Lawyers across practice areas are liable for negligence in their failure to represent clients competently. Estate planning presents a unique dynamic, however, because it is generally not the client who learns of a lawyer's malpractice, but someone who expected to benefit from the estate. The matter is complicated further by the fact that the estate itself may suffer no damages by the lawyer's malpractice; the value of the estate is the same, it just gets divided among different beneficiaries than the client intended. A drafting error that leads to avoidable taxation harms the estate, but a drafting error that names the wrong sibling merely shifts who receives the property, not its value. If there is no loss to the estate itself, and no living client to complain, how can a drafting attorney be held accountable?

For quite a while, the effective answer was that lawyers were not held accountable for estate planning malpractice because no one had standing to sue. The majority rule is now that a lawyer is liable not only to the client, but to intended third-party beneficiaries, both for damages to the estate as a whole as well as losses caused to individual beneficiaries by the lawyer's negligence. In a few states, questions still remain about whether a lawyer's duty extends to intended beneficiaries or only to the client who was in privity with the lawyer.

Case Preview

O'Bryan v. Cave: Appellate Brief

Consider the following excerpt from an appellate brief. The brief pertains to a case where a nephew alleged that a lawyer was negligent in preparing a deed and will for his client, the nephew's uncle. The appellate court found that the lawyer did indeed breach a duty to the non-client family member, but the Kentucky Supreme Court reversed, finding that summary judgment was appropriate because no evidence was produced that the lawyer committed any negligent act, regardless of whether the client or the nephew had standing to bring the claim. Cave v. O'Bryan, 2004 WL 869364 (Ky. App. 2004), reversed by O'Bryan v. Cave, 202 S.W.3d 585 (2006). In the midst of this controversy, counsel for the lawyer filed the appellate brief below, arguing (among other matters) that there are three approaches to the privity defense and that strict privity is the preferable rule.

As you read the brief, consider:

1. What are the primary approaches states take to extending duties to intended beneficiaries of an estate plan?
2. Which approach is most efficient in minimizing lawyer malpractice?
3. How does protecting the beneficiaries' rights function as a proxy for protecting the client's rights?

O'Bryan v. Cave: Appellate Brief
2005 WL 5406327 (Ky.) (Appellate Brief)

Supreme Court of Kentucky.
George R. O'Bryan, Appellant/Cross-Appellee,
v.
Dwight V. Cave, Appellee/Cross-Appellant.

No. 2004-SC-0407-DG.
June 14, 2005.
Brief for the Appellant/Cross-Appellee, George R. O'Bryan
Eugene L. Mosley, M. Thomas Underwood, Mosley, Sauer & Townes, PLLC, One Riverfront Plaza, 401 W Main Street, Suite 1900, Louisville, Kentucky 40202, (502) 589-4404 (Tel.), (502) 589-4405 (Fax).

I. INTRODUCTION

This case involves a claim of legal malpractice brought by a beneficiary under a will against the attorney who drafted the will for the testator. The attorney appeals the decision of the Court of Appeals, which held that an attorney who drafts a will owes a duty to certain beneficiaries of that will. . . .

IV. STATEMENT OF THE CASE

This case involves a claim of legal malpractice brought by a beneficiary under a will against the attorney who drafted the will for the testator. In July, 1997, Claude Cave ("Claude") and his wife, Doris Cave ("Doris"), met with the Appellant, George O'Bryan, an attorney ("O'Bryan"), in regard to drafting a Deed and a Will. (TR 95.) This July meeting was the first of only two meetings between O'Bryan and Claude. (TR 96.) During the course of the meeting, Claude informed O'Bryan that he "wanted to draw a will and a deed." (TR 97.) O'Bryan talked to Claude "at some length about Doris' right to renounce the Will," advising Claude that Doris would certainly have the right to renounce her interest in the Will under Kentucky law. (TR 100.)

At this July meeting, Claude requested O'Bryan to prepare a Deed that gave Doris joint interest, with the right of survivorship, in Claude's home at 5002 Invicta Drive, Louisville, Kentucky. O'Bryan advised Claude that execution of the Deed with the right of survivorship would cause the property to pass to Doris without having to go through probate. (TR 99.) O'Bryan also advised Claude that Doris could later renounce the Will. (O'Bryan Depo., p. 8.) Nevertheless, Claude indicated that he was fine with that and still wanted to draw up both the Deed and the Will because he wanted there to be "no problems or hassles" [with Doris receiving the real estate] when Claude died. (TR 97.)

On August 12, 1997, Claude returned to O'Bryan's office to execute the Deed and Will that O'Bryan had prepared pursuant to Claude's request. (TR 96.) The Deed transferred ownership of the house at 5002 Invicta Drive to both Claude and Doris as joint owners with the right of survivorship. (TR 88-90.) The Deed, on its face, sets forth Claude's intent that for "love and affection" he wished his wife to have a survivorship interest in his Invicta Drive home. Claude also executed a Last Will and Testament prepared by O'Bryan pursuant to Claude's instructions. (TR 86-87.) Under the Will, Claude devised and bequeathed all of his real estate to Doris. (Item 2 of Will.) The Will devised and bequeathed the residuary of his estate to Claude's sisters, Dorothy Ming, Della Burress and Dora Landrum, and to his nephews, Leroy Kilby and the Appellee, Dwight Cave ("Cave"), to share and share alike. (Item 3 of Will.)

On August 2, 1999, Claude died. (TR 66.) On August 30, 1999, the Will was submitted to probate. (TR 66.) On January 28, 2000, Doris executed and recorded a release under KRS 392.080 renouncing her interest in Claude's Will. (TR 66.) O'Bryan never advised Doris of her renunciation right, nor has he ever represented Doris, but he did prepare the renunciation in his capacity as the attorney for the Estate of Claude Cave. (O'Bryan Depo., pp. 16-18.)

On October 10, 2002, Cave filed suit against O'Bryan, alleging that O'Bryan was negligent in drafting the Will and Deed. . . On October 29, 2002, the trial court entered an order granting Summary Judgment in favor of O'Bryan, finding (1) that Cave had presented no evidence to refute O'Bryan's assertion that he abided by his duty, and (2) that Cave lacked standing to bring the malpractice action. . . Cave subsequently appealed to the Court of Appeals.

On April 23, 2004, the Court of Appeals rendered its Opinion, reversing the Jefferson Circuit Court's Summary Judgment and remanding the matter to the trial court, on the grounds that an attorney who drafts a will owes a duty to certain beneficiaries of that will, and that genuine issues of material fact existed. On February 9, 2005, this Court granted O'Bryan's Motion for Discretionary Review on the issues of whether: (1) an attorney who drafts a will for his client owes a duty of care to beneficiaries of the will; (2) a plaintiff's inability to produce evidence to support his claim(s) will justify the granting of a defendant's summary judgment; and, (3) the Court of Appeals can reverse a summary judgment on the basis of matters not raised by the parties in their pleadings. On April 13, 2005, this Court granted Cave's Motion for Discretionary Review on the issue of whether O'Bryan should have been required to admit the standard of care.

V. ARGUMENT

A. In Kentucky, an attorney who drafts a will for his client owes a duty of care to the client, but not to the beneficiaries of the will

The Court of Appeals held that "an attorney owes a duty of care to the direct, intended, and specifically identifiable beneficiaries of the estate planning client, notwithstanding a lack of privity." (Opinion, p. 8.) In doing so, the Court of Appeals adopted what is known as the "third party beneficiary rule", a standard previously unheard of in Kentucky.

1. Three approaches to determining an attorney's liability to non-clients

The question of whether an estate planning attorney may be sued by beneficiaries of the will after the testator's death appears to be one of first impression in Kentucky. In other jurisdictions where the issue of an attorney's liability to non-clients has been addressed, three approaches have developed: (1) the third party beneficiary rule; (2) the balancing of factors theory; and, (3) the strict privity rule.

Third party beneficiary rule. Under the third party beneficiary rule, adopted by the Court of Appeals in this case, in order for an attorney to owe a duty to a non-client, the non-client must show that the intent of the actual client to benefit the non-client was a direct purpose of the transaction or relationship. Noble v. Bruce, 709 A.2d 1264, 1273 (Md. 1998).

Balancing of factors approach. The "balancing of factors" approach was announced by the California Supreme Court in Biakanja v. Irving, 49 Cal. 2d 647, 320 P.2d 16, 19 (1958), and was later modified in Lucas v. Hamm, 56 Cal. 2d 583, 364 P.2d 685, 15 Cal. Rptr. 821 (1961), cert. denied, 368 U.S. 987, 82 S. Ct. 603, 7 L. Ed. 2d 525 (1962). In determining whether the beneficiaries of a will have a cause of action against the attorney who drafted the will, this approach considers the following factors: (1) the extent to which the transaction was intended to affect the plaintiff, (2) the forseeability of harm to the plaintiff; (3) the degree of certainty that the plaintiff suffered injury; (4) the closeness of the connection between the defendant's conduct and the injury; (5) the policy of preventing future harm; and, (6) whether imposing liability imposes an undue burden on the legal community. 364 P.2d at 687-688.

The balancing of factors approach has been criticized by some courts as being too broad, see, e.g., Pelham v. Griesheimer, 92 Ill. 2d 13, 440 N.E.2d 96, 100, 64 Ill. Dec. 544 (1982), and by others as "so unworkable that it has led to 'ad hoc determinations and inconsistent results.'" Noble at 1271, citing Guy v. Liederbach, 501 Pa. 47, 459 A.2d 744, 749 (1983).

Strict privity rule. This traditional rule generally holds that a third party not in privity with an attorney has no cause of action against the attorney for negligence in the absence of fraud or collusion. National Savings Bank v. Ward, 100 U.S. 195, 205-206, 25 L. Ed. 2d 621, 625 (1879). As the Court of Appeals pointed out, Kentucky slightly modified this rule in Rose v. Davis, 288 Ky. 674, 157 S.W.2d 284, 284-285 (1941), to reflect that an attorney is not ordinarily liable to a third party for acts committed in the representation of a client unless those acts are fraudulent or tortious and result in injury to the third party.

. . .

There are many compelling justifications for selecting the strict privity rule in estate planning situations. . . .

Post-Case Follow-Up

Note that the case was resolved on grounds related to lack of evidence of negligence and not privity. The brief discusses the approaches to privity states can take and argues for the continuation of a strict privity rule, but that fortress is crumbling. The substantial majority of states do not require privity between a lawyer and a client for the lawyer to be held liable for damages to an intended third-party beneficiary.

O'Bryan v. Cave: Appellate Brief: Real Life Applications

1. You work for a state legislator who is deciding to vote on a statute establishing one of the three approaches listed above as the state's rule for when non-clients may sue estate planning lawyers. Pick an approach and defend it.

2. You are a new associate in a firm that represents Rox Tarr, a famous musician. In reviewing Rox's will, you realize that a senior partner failed to oversee the execution ceremony properly and there is only one witness. Rox leaves his entire estate to the Rock and Roll Hall of Fame, cutting out his children who would take by intestacy. Respectfully advise the senior partner why there may be cause for concern if the firm does not confess the mistake and have Rox return to execute the will properly.

It remains the status of the law in most states that a trusts and estates attorney is subject to malpractice claims brought by intended beneficiaries and not just the individual (deceased) estate planning client. Malpractice insurance is a reality of a modern lawyer's practice, and exercising care and diligence is not just a matter of comporting with professional ethics—it's a matter of avoiding lawsuits for negligence.

B. COMPETENCE AND DILIGENCE

Lawyers who draft estate planning documents need to be aware of rules of professional conduct. Those who violate standards of professional conduct may find themselves as litigants in cases with plaintiffs seeking damages against the attorney in contract or in negligence tort claims. They may settle such claims out of court, with the help of their unhappy (and increasingly expensive) malpractice insurance carriers—or they may not. In addition to the risk of being sued for malpractice, attorneys who violate ethical standards may face disciplinary proceedings of the state bars of which they are members. Pursuant to these proceedings, lawyers can suffer various penalties including loss of the hard-earned license to practice law.

Claims against the lawyer can arise in several contexts and we will discuss the variety of duties a trusts and estate lawyer has. We will begin with a common one: competent and diligent representation. An attorney who accepts the representation of a client in estate planning, estate administration, or any fiduciary matter must comply with professional conduct standards relating to competent representation and diligence in performance of legal services. Although the standards of competence and diligence exist throughout the range of practice areas in which a lawyer may operate, there are special concerns for the trusts and estates practitioner.

The Rules of Professional Conduct require both competence and diligence in the representation of a client. Competence includes the "legal knowledge, skill, thoroughness and preparation" needed to represent a client. The standard of diligence includes both diligence itself and timeliness. See Exhibit 13.1.

A lawyer must maintain ethical standards of both competence and diligence with respect to a client. Diligence and promptness are particularly critical when a client wants to execute or change estate planning documents when death may be imminent, which is not uncommon. In terms of malpractice liability to intended third parties, however, courts often distinguish between finished but flawed representation (malfeasance, tied to competence) and failing to complete the representation in time (nonfeasance, tied to diligence). A client is entitled to take the estate planning process at a pace appropriate for the client, without being rushed by concerns of potential beneficiaries, and may change the plan at any time before execution. It is therefore less appropriate for beneficiaries of a draft document to sue the lawyer for malpractice when a client does not execute a document because it is incomplete at the client's death than it would be for beneficiaries of an executed document to sue the lawyer for a complete but badly drafted document. See *Hall v. Kalfayan*, 190 Cal. App. 4th 927 (Ct. App. 2010).

Public Reprimands

Violations of professional conduct standards can result in a variety of consequences, including public reprimand. In Warren Cty. Bar Assn. v. Clifton, Slip Opinion No. 2016-Ohio-5587, the disciplinary committee found that an estate planning lawyer had added the name of the decedent's daughter to a will after it was signed to avoid embarrassment for mistakenly omitting the name. The addition did not change the way in which the estate was distributed. Public reprimand was published as below:

The Supreme Court of Ohio

CASE ANNOUNCEMENTS

September 1, 2016

[Cite as *09/01/2016 Case Announcements*, 2016-Ohio-5604.]

MERIT DECISIONS WITH OPINIONS

2015-2001. Cincinnati Bar Assn. v. Fernandez, Slip Opinion No. 2016-Ohio-5586.
On Certified Report by the Board of Professional Conduct, No. 2015-039. Justin Enrique Fernandez, Attorney Registration No. 0062974, is hereby publicly reprimanded.
　　O'Connor, C.J., and Pfeifer, O'Donnell, Lanzinger, Kennedy, French, and O'Neill, JJ., concur.

2016-0250. Disciplinary Counsel v. Kendrick, Slip Opinion No. 2016-Ohio-5600.
On Certified Report by the Board of Professional Conduct, No. 2015-038. Linda Louise Kendrick, Attorney Registration No. 0078797, is hereby suspended from the practice of law for one year, fully stayed on conditions.
　　O'Connor, C.J., and Pfeifer, O'Donnell, Lanzinger, Kennedy, French, and O'Neill, JJ., concur.

2016-0258. Warren Cty. Bar Assn. v. Clifton, Slip Opinion No. 2016-Ohio-5587.
On Certified Report by the Board of Professional Conduct, No. 2015-040. Parker Lee Clifton, Attorney Registration No. 0081815, is hereby publicly reprimanded.
　　O'Connor, C.J., and Pfeifer, O'Donnell, Lanzinger, Kennedy, French, and O'Neill, JJ., concur.

2016-0259. Disciplinary Counsel v. Simmonds, Slip Opinion No. 2016-Ohio-5599.

EXHIBIT 13.1 **Competence and Diligence Rules**

Rule 1.1: COMPETENCE

A lawyer shall provide competent representation to a client. Competent representation requires the legal knowledge, skill, thoroughness and preparation reasonably necessary for the representation.

Rule 1.3: DILIGENCE

A lawyer shall act with reasonable diligence and promptness in representing a client.

Competence and diligence are required of all attorneys. Although certainly general practitioners may draft estate planning documents (trusts and estates practice is not limited to specialists), lawyers must invest the necessary skill, thoroughness, and preparation that estate planning requires. In order to meet the needs of a client, lawyers without significant expertise in trusts and estates may need to invest more time in research or learning before undertaking the representation. Relying on other professionals for guidance can also help a lawyer attain the level of skill necessary for competent representation.

One important step in diligent and competent representation is to review previously executed estate planning documents of the client, as well as other documents that could be relevant (such as divorce settlements or marital agreements). Sometimes the estate planning lawyer may need to get consent from the client to obtain documents from a prior lawyer if the client does not have them. If the client needs advice with respect to certain documents, it is particularly important to have full facts and information to provide sufficient advice.

Competent representation for an estate planning attorney may require overseeing the execution of estate planning documents. As we saw in Chapter 3, it is easy for clients (or careless or inexperienced practitioners) to fail to comply with statutory formalities that are less than intuitive, and a document may be denied probate based on failure to execute it properly. Following a consistent procedure when overseeing document execution can protect against making mistakes. Lawyers and firms often develop something along the lines of a script—a series of steps lawyers consistently repeat to ensure compliance with laws regulating execution of estate-planning documents.

The standard of competence requires not only good faith, but also the exercise of sufficient skill in the drafting and execution of estate planning documents. This requires attentiveness to language choice in the document as well as knowledge of state-specific procedures for document execution. Lawyers who lack such skill and draft insufficient documents may find themselves subject to professional discipline.

Case Preview

In re J. Sinclair Long

In the case of *In re J. Sinclair Long*, a lawyer who drafted a will was brought before the D.C. bar for disciplinary proceedings. The lawyer did not possess the necessary competence to draft the will, as it was outside of his primary area of practice, and he did not seek help from attorneys experienced in trusts and estates.

As you read the case, consider:

1. What actions did the lawyer take (or fail to take) that demonstrated lack of competency?
2. The lawyer charged his client only a nominal fee. Did that save him from professional discipline?
3. The lawyer's primary motive in drafting the will was to help a friend, rather than financial gain. Is it still an ethical violation if one's motives are noble?

In re J. Sinclair Long
902 A.2d. 1168 (D.C. 2006)

The Board on Professional Responsibility has recommended that J. Sinclair Long, a member of the Bar of this court since 1992, be suspended from the practice of law for thirty days. Although Long's professional legal career was in government service and criminal law, he personally became involved with legal affairs of an aged family friend, Mrs. Lessie T. Lowery, and her relative and caretaker, Mr. Wilbert Harris. In doing so, he had no self-serving intent; his actions reflected his desire to be helpful. The only money Long ever received from either of them was the $75 that Mrs. Lowery paid him to prepare her will.

The Board ruled, and Long concedes, that when he drafted the will for Mrs. Lowery, he incompetently represented her interests. . . . On appeal, Long excepts only to the Board's recommended sanction. He contends that the Board misconstrued *In re Boykins*, 748 A.2d 413 (D.C. 2000), a case involving similar charges, when it refused to stay the thirty-day suspension in favor of probation, as was done in *Boykins*. We agree with Long that *Boykins* is controlling. Before entering into a discussion of *Boykins*, we set forth, in an abbreviated fashion, the facts of this case.

I.

Long was admitted to the District of Columbia bar on June 1, 1992. He is also a member of the Bar of the State of Pennsylvania, having been admitted on May 12, 1978. At the time of the hearing, Long was an assistant general counsel at the District of Columbia Department of Consumer and Regulatory Affairs. In the past, he served as counsel for the Fraternal Order of Police, and maintained a criminal law practice. He has no history of disciplinary violations.

At the time of the events at issue, Long had been friends with Wilbert Harris for approximately 25 years. Through Harris, Long became friends with the elderly Mrs. Lowery and her husband. After the passing of Mrs. Lowery's husband, Harris moved into her home and assumed the responsibility of her care. Long had occasion to socialize with Mrs. Lowery when he visited Harris at her home. To Long, it appeared that Harris took appropriate care of Mrs. Lowery and that the two had a good relationship. Long believed that Harris was Mrs. Lowery's sole living relative.

At some point in the spring or summer of 1996, Harris approached Long with a form book in hand, and requested that Long draft a will in which Mrs. Lowery would leave all her assets to Harris. Long agreed to draft the will, despite his having no experience in estate planning. Long edited the form will in an attempt to comply with the requirements of District of Columbia law. He did not seek the advice of other attorneys more experienced with estate planning nor did he perform any legal research on the subject. Long prepared two drafts of the will, the second of which he submitted to Harris for his approval. After correcting a few errors, Long gave the final draft to Harris, instructing him to have Mrs. Lowery sign the will in front of two witnesses.

Sometime before Long produced the final draft of the will, he spoke with Mrs. Lowery at her home. Long remarked that he understood that she intended to "turn[] over the farm to Mr. Harris." Mrs. Lowery responded, "yes, [h]e's been taking care of me." Long did not become knowledgeable about the existence or identity of Mrs. Lowery's other relatives, he had no specific knowledge of her finances, and he did not discuss her intentions in anything more than this perfunctory manner. He took no special precautions in light of Mrs. Lowery's advanced age and medical condition in anticipation of a challenge to the will. Long charged Mrs. Lowery $75 for preparing her will, which she paid for by a check dated August 15, 1996. Ten days later, Mrs. Lowery signed the will in the presence of two witnesses.

On December 27, 1997, Mrs. Lowery died. Several nieces and nephews contested the will that Long had drafted. The contest ended in a settlement in which Harris received 40% of the estate and Mrs. Lowery's other heirs received 60% of the estate . . .

II.

The Hearing Committee recommended that Long be informally admonished for his misconduct. In support of this recommendation, the Hearing Committee noted that the underlying incident represented Long's first ethical violations, there were no aggravating factors, and Long cooperated with Bar Counsel's investigation and acknowledged his misdeeds. The Hearing Committee further noted that Long's misconduct arose from his desire to assist close friends.

The Board, however, rejected the recommended sanction, pointing out that Long had committed multiple violations. Instead, the Board emphasized that "suspensions of varied lengths have been imposed when conflicts of interest are combined with more serious violations, such as dishonesty." The Board . . . declined to stay Long's suspension.

III.

This court typically adopts the "recommended disposition of the Board unless to do so would foster a tendency toward inconsistent dispositions for comparable conduct or would otherwise be unwarranted." *In re Delate,* 579 A.2d 1177, 1179 (D.C. 1990); *see also* D.C. Bar R. XI, § 9(g). Our concern here is that, in our judgment, the Board was mistaken in its analysis of the factors it relied on to differentiate Long's case from *Boykins.*

The Board reasoned that Boykins had deserved leniency because he had been a member of the Bar for only two years prior to the disciplinary proceedings. To us, this factor cuts both ways: while Long certainly cannot claim the status of a newcomer, his record as an attorney remained unblemished for more than twenty years. We have held repeatedly that an attorney's record, or more accurately a lack thereof, may be considered a mitigating factor when fashioning an appropriate sanction. *See, e.g., In re Shay, 756 A.2d 465, 484, 486 (D.C. 2000).*

Second, the Board believed that the stress of managing a private practice mitigated Boykin's misconduct, and by implication, considered that because Long failed to demonstrate that his misdeeds resulted from similar pressure, he was undeserving of leniency. We interpret the occurrence of Long's violations in a personal context outside his usual practice—assistant general counsel at the Department of Consumer and Regulatory Affairs—to be a mitigating rather than an aggravating factor in the *Boykins* analysis. Unlike Boykins, Long did not hold himself out on a regular professional basis with the requisite expertise over an extended period of time. Long's foray into estate planning represented a one-shot event of a personal nature. Conversely, Boykin's misconduct extended over several months in his regular professional legal practice open to the public and included several separate transactions. On numerous occasions, we have noted that an isolated violation of the Rules may be considered a mitigating factor. *See, e.g., In re Miller, 553 A.2d 201, 205-06 (D.C. 1989); In re Harrison,* 511 A.2d 16, 19 (D.C. 1986). Remembering a primary purpose for the Rules and their enforcement—protecting the public—and given Long's cooperation with Bar Counsel in this disciplinary proceeding and acknowledgment of his transgressions, we think that the chances for recurrence are minimal.

We agree with the Board, however, in rejecting the proposed sanction of an informal admonition. An attorney who undertakes to act in a legal capacity, albeit on a personal basis and even if entirely gratis, is not exempt from the ethical rules governing the legal profession. Moreover, incompetent representation [is a] significant breach. . . .

Accordingly, J. Sinclair Long is hereby suspended from the practice of law for thirty days, stayed in favor of probation. . .

So ordered.

Post-Case Follow-Up

Suspension from the practice of law, even if the penalty is stayed in favor of probation, is discipline for misconduct that is noted on an attorney's record. The effect of a negative disciplinary record can be significant loss of business for an attorney in private practice, and a negative impact on the ability of a lawyer to find work in the business and government sectors as well. The discipline imposed by the bar is not the only penalty—it is the implications of having the penalty imposed that create the most damage for the lawyer failing to exercise the proper standard of competence. In most if not all jurisdictions, disciplinary records for lawyers are searchable online, and most clients will want a lawyer with a clean record.

In re J. Sinclair Long: Real Life Applications

1. You have just learned that you passed the bar exam and will start your job in a small family law private practice next month. Your roommate asks you to draft her estate plan. Can you provide competent representation? What factors affect whether this is the case? What steps can you take to ensure competent representation if you are not confident in your abilities?

2. It is 20 years in the future and your Wills class is just a fond memory, as you have found your calling as in-house corporate counsel to a company that manufactures flying cars. Your aunt's friend asks you to draft her will. What should you do? Does it matter whether or how much you charge her for your services?

Diligence is rationally related to the standard of competence, because competent representation is necessarily timely. The task of estate planning may be particularly time-sensitive when a client is ill or aged. The lawyer should avoid unreasonable delay and complete the representation promptly—or it may not be possible to complete at all. The ACTEC Commentaries highlight some of the ways in which the duty of diligence is encountered in the context of estate planning or administration.

> *Timetable.* [I]t is usually desirable, early in the representation, for the lawyer and client to establish a timetable for completion of various tasks. . . Many clients engaged in estate planning are elderly or are facing medical emergencies. There is thus an enhanced risk that the client might die or otherwise become incapable of completing an estate plan if the estate planner takes more time than is reasonable under the circumstances to do the work requested. In such cases the client may be harmed, and intended beneficiaries may not receive the benefits the client intended them to have.
>
> *Planning the Administration of a Fiduciary Estate.* Lawyers retained to assist in the administration of an estate too frequently succumb to the temptation to delay this kind of work, where rigid court deadlines may not be imposed, in favor of what they

consider more pressing matters. The lawyer and the fiduciary should plan the administration of an estate or trust in light of the fiduciary's obligations to the courts, tax authorities, creditors and beneficiaries. . . .

C. ATTORNEY-CLIENT COMMUNICATIONS

Effective communication between a lawyer and client is essential for effective representation. This is true in the case of a representation of a testator or donor in the estate planning context as well as the fiduciary throughout the process of estate administration.

The Rules of Professional Conduct provide guidance as to the standards of communication between a lawyer and a client. Exhibit 13.2 includes the relevant rule.

EXHIBIT 13.2   **Rule 1.4: Communication**

(a) A lawyer shall:
  (1) promptly inform the client of any decision or circumstance with respect to which the client's informed consent, as defined in Rule 1.0(e), is required by these Rules;
  (2) reasonably consult with the client about the means by which the client's objectives are to be accomplished;
  (3) keep the client reasonably informed about the status of the matter;
  (4) promptly comply with reasonable requests for information; and
  (5) consult with the client about any relevant limitation on the lawyer's conduct when the lawyer knows that the client expects assistance not permitted by the Rules of Professional Conduct or other law.
(b) A lawyer shall explain a matter to the extent reasonably necessary to permit the client to make informed decisions regarding the representation.

Maintaining high standards for client communication is of utmost importance in the very personal practice of estate planning. In order to provide sound counseling and advice to the client, a lawyer must encourage open communication between the client and lawyer. The client should understand how the standard of confidentiality (discussed later) protects their discussions, and that understanding may encourage more open and honest discussion.

The ACTEC Commentaries advise that a lawyer meet personally with a client at the beginning of a representation, and not merely with a third party claiming to represent the client's interests. This initial meeting is important for gathering information from the client and providing guidance to the client to support informed decisions. Clients should not be simply provided with model forms, but should be guided through a discussion of the overall plan, with the lawyer committing the plan to paper. The lawyer is more than a mere scrivener and should serve as a counselor and advisor to the client.

Some estate planning documents, particularly those that include tax planning, may be difficult for a client to understand independently. Therefore, the drafting attorney should explain in plain terms, ideally both orally and in writing, what the documents do. The lawyer should also be sure to communicate to the client what steps the client needs to take to implement the plan, such as changing beneficiaries of nonprobate transfers as appropriate or executing documents to convey property to a trustee. Communication is normally most active during the initial drafting phases of the engagement, and the ACTEC Commentaries provide useful guidance on how to manage the representation during that phase:

> *Communications During Active Phase of Representation.* . . . . The lawyer's duty to communicate with a client during the active period of the representation includes the duty to inform the client reasonably regarding the law, developments that affect the client, any changes in the basis or rate of the lawyer's compensation. . . and the progress of the representation. The lawyer for an estate planning client should attempt to inform the client to the extent reasonably necessary to enable the client to make informed judgments regarding major issues involved in the representation. . . . If the lawyer determines that the client has some degree of diminished capacity, the lawyer should proceed carefully to assess the ability of the client to communicate his or her intentions and to understand the advice being given and the documents being drafted by the lawyer. The lawyer should also be alert to the possibility that after the commencement of a representation, the client might lose sufficient capacity for the lawyer to continue.

D. FEES

Certainly, most lawyers want and expect to be compensated for the legal services they provide within the practice of trusts and estates law. Compensation is appropriate so long as it is reasonable and properly structured within the boundaries of professional ethics standards. The Rules of Professional Conduct provide guidance as to appropriate methods of developing fees for legal services and limitations on the ways fees should be structured. The relevant rule is shown in Exhibit 13.3.

EXHIBIT 13.3   **Rule 1.5: Fees**

(a) A lawyer shall not make an agreement for, charge, or collect an unreasonable fee or an unreasonable amount for expenses. The factors to be considered in determining the reasonableness of a fee include the following:

(1) the time and labor required, the novelty and difficulty of the questions involved, and the skill requisite to perform the legal service properly;

(2) the likelihood, if apparent to the client, that the acceptance of the particular employment will preclude other employment by the lawyer;

(3) the fee customarily charged in the locality for similar legal services;

(4) the amount involved and the results obtained;

(5) the time limitations imposed by the client or by the circumstances;

(6) the nature and length of the professional relationship with the client;

> **(7)** the experience, reputation, and ability of the lawyer or lawyers performing the services; and
> **(8)** whether the fee is fixed or contingent.
> **(b)** The scope of the representation and the basis or rate of the fee and expenses for which the client will be responsible shall be communicated to the client, preferably in writing, before or within a reasonable time after commencing the representation, except when the lawyer will charge a regularly represented client on the same basis or rate. Any changes in the basis or rate of the fee or expenses shall also be communicated to the client. . .

Whether a trusts and estates lawyer bills by the hour or charges a flat fee for certain services, the overall amount must comply with state laws for reasonableness as well as ethical standards for fee structures. Contingency fees have no meaningful place in trusts and estates work, so the primary concerns become whether the fee is reasonable given the factors in state statutes or ethics codes. Keep in mind that the trusts and estates lawyer may be earning fees in a variety of contexts, including drafting documents and representing or even serving as fiduciary of a trust or an estate. If a lawyer is serving in both a legal and a fiduciary role, she should not double-charge for her time. (Note also that an attorney nominating himself or herself as fiduciary in a document that attorney drafted raises ethical issues of its own, which are discussed in the section on conflicts of interest.)

When charging a client for services, the lawyer must advise the client as to the basis of the reasonable fee (whether flat-rate or hourly) and get the client's agreement to the fee arrangement. The fee structure is often provided as part of the engagement letter when the representation begins. The client must also be informed of additional expenses beyond the attorney fee, such as charges for paralegal or secretarial work, duplication or postal costs, court filing fees, and other expected costs that may arise during the representation.

One area of ethics where the estate planning attorney must take special care is with respect to payment of fees by third parties. Although it is ethical for the lawyer's bill to be paid by a person or entity other than the client, the lawyer's focus must be on the client alone. The client must have the exclusive right to direct the lawyer in providing appropriate services and the lawyer must keep the confidences of the client as agreed, even if that means withholding information from the person who is paying the bill. The engagement letter provides an opportunity for the lawyer to explain these matters to the client.

E. CONFIDENTIALITY

Maintaining confidential information obtained from a client is important in all areas of practice, but perhaps particularly challenging in trusts and estates matters where a lawyer accepts joint representation of spouses or other related parties. The rules on conflicts of interest are also triggered by such joint representations, but we will first consider the rules relating to confidentiality and the conditions under which it can be waived.

The Rules of Professional Conduct explain the lawyer's duty of confidentiality with respect to client information, which can become more complicated in the matter of joint representation of multiple clients. Joint representation of multiple clients is a common practice in estate planning due to the cost savings for the clients (it takes less than double the time to create documents for a couple than in would to create documents for two separate clients). That said, joint representation raises thorny ethical issues and some lawyers believe the safest course of action is to avoid it. The relevant rule is shown in Exhibit 13.4.

EXHIBIT 13.4 **Rule 1.6: Confidentiality of Information**

(a) A lawyer shall not reveal information relating to representation of a client unless the client gives informed consent, the disclosure is impliedly authorized in order to carry out the representation or the disclosure is permitted by paragraph (b).

(b) A lawyer may reveal information relating to the representation of a client to the extent the lawyer reasonably believes necessary:

(1) to prevent reasonably certain death or substantial bodily harm;

(2) to prevent the client from committing a crime or fraud that is reasonably certain to result in substantial injury to the financial interests or property of another and in furtherance of which the client has used or is using the lawyer's services.

(3) to prevent, mitigate or rectify substantial injury to the financial interests or property of another that is reasonably certain to result or has resulted from the client's commission of a crime or fraud in furtherance of which the client has used the lawyer's services.

(4) to secure legal advice about the lawyer's compliance with these Rules;

(5) to establish a claim or defense on behalf of the lawyer in a controversy between the lawyer and the client, to establish a defense to a criminal charge or civil claim against the lawyer based upon conduct in which the client was involved, or to respond to allegations in any proceeding concerning the lawyer's representation of the client; or

(6) to comply with other law or a court order.

(7) to detect and resolve conflicts of interest arising from the lawyer's change of employment or from changes in the composition or ownership of a firm, but only if the revealed information would not compromise the attorney-client privilege or otherwise prejudice the client.

(c) A lawyer shall make reasonable efforts to prevent the inadvertent or unauthorized disclosure of, or unauthorized access to, information relating to the representation of a client.

Confidentiality is perhaps the most difficult standard to uphold given the frequency with which trusts and estates lawyers represent members of the same family, such as married couples, who may have different expectations as to how information will be shared among the parties. These issues are most commonly moderated by using an engagement letter at the beginning of the client relationship, giving the parties a choice as to whether confidences acquired in the course of the representation are to be shared with the other family members. Clients most commonly choose joint representation in which all confidences are shared among the parties, but they may instead choose separate representation, where information is not shared with other clients (including between spouses). Where the rules have not been agreed upon ahead of time, resolving a conflict is often more difficult than preventing one, and withdrawal from representation is sometimes necessary.

As an initial matter, the lawyer has the responsibility to preserve confidences of the client and must make reasonable efforts toward that end. This includes proper supervision of outsourced work as well as security of electronic storage or message transmission. Remember that the client may be sharing very sensitive information with the lawyer, including information about finances, family members, Social Security numbers, and tax forms. The lawyer does have the implied right to disclose information to courts, administrative agencies (including the IRS), and others with whom the lawyer needs to share information in order to represent the client effectively. As in other areas of representation, a lawyer may also share confidential information if necessary to prevent death or severe harm.

One area of confidentiality that is particularly difficult to navigate occurs in the common situation where a lawyer represents both spouses or other members of the same family. Here, the clients must decide to what extent the lawyer will keep confidential information shared by each client from the other client. The ACTEC Commentaries provide the following advice:

> *Joint and Separate Clients.* [A] lawyer may represent more than one client with related, but not necessarily identical, interests (e.g., several members of the same family, more than one investor in a business enterprise). The fact that the goals of the clients are not entirely consistent does not necessarily constitute a conflict of interest that precludes the same lawyer from representing them. . . . Thus, the same lawyer may represent a husband and wife, or parent and child, whose dispositive plans are not entirely the same. When the lawyer is first consulted by the multiple potential clients, the lawyer should review with them the terms upon which the lawyer will undertake the representation, including the extent to which information will be shared among them. . . . In the absence of any agreement to the contrary (usually in writing), a lawyer is presumed to represent multiple clients with regard to related legal matters jointly, but the law is unclear as to whether all information must be shared between them. As a result, an irreconcilable conflict may arise if one co-client shares information that he or she does not want shared with the other. Absent special circumstances, the co-clients should be asked at the outset of the representation to agree that all information can be shared. The better practice is to memorialize the clients' agreement and instructions in writing, and give a copy of the writing to the client. . .

> *Confidences Imparted by One Joint Client.* As noted earlier, except in special circumstances, joint clients should be advised at the outset of the representation that information from either client may be required to be shared with the other if the lawyer considers such sharing of information necessary or beneficial to the representation. . . Absent an advance agreement that adequately addresses the handling

of confidential information shared by only one joint client, a lawyer who receives information from one joint client (the "communicating client") that the client does not wish to be shared with the other joint client (the "other client") is confronted with a situation that may threaten the lawyer's ability to continue to represent one or both of the clients. As soon as practicable after such a communication, the lawyer should consider the relevance and significance of the information and decide upon the appropriate manner in which to proceed. The potential courses of action include, *inter alia*, (1) taking no action with respect to communications regarding irrelevant (or trivial) matters; (2) encouraging the communicating client to provide the information to the other client or to allow the lawyer to do so; and, (3) withdrawing from the representation if the communication reflects serious adversity between the parties. . . .

Opinion Preview

Professional Ethics Opinion of the Florida Bar Opinion 95-4

In the ethics opinion that follows, the Florida Bar offers advice to attorneys in joint representation agreements when one spouse reveals information that he wants kept secret from the other spouse. It is a delicate situation that arises more often than one might hope. The opinion discusses hypothetical and common scenarios and explains how an attorney should ethically respond.

As you read the opinion, consider:

1. What must a lawyer do if he represents both spouses and one spouse reveals information that she wants the lawyer to hold confidentially and not share with the other spouse?
2. May a lawyer reveal confidential information received from one spouse to the other spouse?
3. Must a lawyer provide procedures for the sharing (or not sharing) of confidential information or conflicts of interest before such a situation arises? If not, is it a good idea to do so anyway?

Professional Ethics Opinion of the Florida Bar Opinion 95-4
(May 30, 1997)

The Estate Planning, Probate, and Trust Law Professionalism Committee (the "RPPTL Professionalism Committee") of the Florida Bar's Real Property, Probate, and Trust Law Section has requested a formal advisory opinion regarding some ethical issues that trusts and estates practitioners face in day-to-day practice. The RPPTL Professionalism Committee has presented the following generalized situation, reflecting a common type of estate planning representation. . . .

SITUATION PRESENTED

Lawyer has represented Husband and Wife for many years in a range of personal matters, including estate planning. Husband and Wife have substantial individual assets, and they also own substantial jointly-held property. Recently, Lawyer prepared new updated wills that Husband and Wife signed. Like their previous wills, the new wills primarily benefit the survivor of them for his or her life, with beneficial disposition at the death of the survivor being made equally to their children (none of whom were born by prior marriage).

Husband, Wife, and Lawyer have always shared all relevant asset and financial information. Consistent with previous practice, Lawyer met with Husband and Wife together to confer regarding the changes to be made in updating their wills. At no point since Lawyer first started to represent them did either Husband or Wife ever ask Lawyer to keep any information secret from the other, and there was never any discussion about what Lawyer might do if either of them were to ask Lawyer to maintain such a separate confidence.

Several months after the execution of the new wills, Husband confers separately with Lawyer. Husband reveals to Lawyer that he has just executed a codicil (prepared by another law firm) that makes substantial beneficial disposition to a woman with whom Husband has been having an extra-marital relationship. Husband tells Lawyer that Wife knows about neither the relationship nor the new codicil, as to which Husband asks Lawyer to advise him regarding Wife's rights of election in the event she were to survive Husband. Lawyer tells Husband that Lawyer cannot under the circumstances advise him regarding same. Lawyer tells Husband that Lawyer will have to consider Lawyer's ethical duties under the circumstances. Lawyer tells Husband that, after consideration, Lawyer may determine to withdraw from representing Husband and Wife. Lawyer further tells Husband that, after consideration, Lawyer may determine to disclose to Wife the substance of Husband's revelation if Husband does not do so himself.

ISSUES PRESENTED

The following ethical questions have been asked by the RPPTL Professionalism Committee:

1. Prior to Husband's recent disclosure, did Lawyer owe any ethical duty to counsel Husband and Wife concerning any separate confidence which either Husband or Wife might wish for Lawyer to withhold from the other?
2. Assuming that Husband does not make disclosure of the information [referred to in Issue 1] to Wife:

   a) Is Lawyer required to reveal voluntarily the information to Wife?
   b) May Lawyer in Lawyer's discretion determine whether or not to reveal the information to the Wife? If so, what are the relevant factors which Lawyer may or should consider?
   c) If Lawyer does not reveal the information to Wife, is Lawyer required to withdraw from the representation? If so, what explanation, if any, should Lawyer give to Wife?

3. May Lawyer continue to represent Husband alone if Lawyer notifies Wife that Lawyer is withdrawing from the joint representation and will no longer represent Wife? If so, is disclosure to Wife necessary in order to obtain her informed consent to Lawyer's continued representation of Husband?
4. Assuming that adequate disclosure is made to Wife, may Lawyer continue to represent both Husband and Wife if they both wish for Lawyer to do so?

The RPPTL Professionalism Committee views Lawyer's representation of Husband and Wife as a "joint representation." The committee concurs in this view in reaching the opinion expressed below.

DISCUSSION

From the inception of the representation until Husband's communication to Lawyer of the information concerning the codicil and the extra-marital relationship (hereinafter the "separate confidence"), there was no objective indication that the interests of Husband and Wife diverged, nor did it objectively appear to Lawyer that any such divergence of interests was reasonably likely to arise. Such situations involving joint representation of Husband and Wife do not present a conflict of interests and, therefore, do not trigger the conflict of interest disclosure-and-consent requirements of Rules 4-1.7(a) and 4-1.7(b), Rules Regulating The Florida Bar. It is important to recognize, however, that some spouses do not share identical goals in common matters, including estate planning. For example, one spouse may wish to make a Will providing substantial beneficial disposition for charity but the other spouse does not. Or, either or both of them may have children by a prior marriage for whom they may wish to make different beneficial provisions. Given the conflict of interest typically inherent in those types of situations, in such situations the attorney should review with the married couple the relevant conflict of interest considerations and obtain the spouses informed consent to the joint representation.

In view of the conclusions reached in the remainder of this opinion, we conclude that, under the facts presented, Lawyer was not ethically obligated to discuss with Husband and Wife Lawyer's obligations with regard to separate confidences. While such a discussion is not ethically required, in some situations it may help prevent the type of occurrence that is the subject of this opinion.

We now turn to the central issue presented, which is the application of the confidentiality rule in a situation where confidentiality was not discussed at the outset of the joint representation. A lawyer is ethically obligated to maintain in confidence all information relating to the representation of a client. Rule 4-1.6. A lawyer, however, also has a duty to communicate to a client information that is relevant to the representation. Rule 4-1.4. These duties of communication and confidentiality harmoniously coexist in most situations. In the situation presented, however, Lawyer's duty of communication to Wife appears to conflict with Lawyer's duty of confidentiality to Husband. Thus, the key question for our decision is: Which duty must give way? We conclude that, under the facts presented,

Lawyer's duty of confidentiality must take precedence. Consequently, if Husband fails to disclose (or give Lawyer permission to disclose) the subject information to Wife, Lawyer is not ethically required to disclose the information to Wife and does not have discretion to reveal the information. To the contrary, Lawyer's ethical obligation of confidentiality to Husband *prohibits* Lawyer from disclosing the information to Wife.

The lawyer-client relationship is one of trust and confidence. *Gerlach v. Donnelly*, 98 So.2d 493 (Fla. 1957). Rule 4-1.6 recognizes a very broad duty of confidentiality on the part of a lawyer. Save for a few narrow exceptions set forth in the rule, a lawyer is prohibited from voluntarily revealing any "information relating to the representation" of a client without the client's consent. Rule 4-1.6. The duty of confidentiality "applies not merely to matters communicated in confidence by the client but also to all information relating to the representation, whatever its source" and "continues after the client-lawyer relationship has terminated." Comment, Rule 4-1.6.

It has been suggested that, in a joint representation, a lawyer who receives information from the "communicating client" that is relevant to the interests of the non-communicating client may disclose the information to the latter, even over the communicating client's objections and even where disclosure would be damaging to the communicating client. The committee is of the opinion that disclosure is not permissible and therefore rejects this "no-confidentiality" position. The argument for a "no-confidentiality" approach—which is a departure from the usual rule of lawyer-client confidentiality—is premised on two bases: (1) that joint clients have an expectation that everything relating to the joint representation that is communicated by one client to the joint lawyer will be shared by the lawyer with the other client (i.e., that joint clients have no expectation of confidentiality within the joint representation); and (2) that the law governing the evidentiary attorney-client privilege sets (or should set) the standard for the lawyer's ethical duties in the joint representation setting. Both of these foundations, in the committee's opinion, are flawed. . . .

The ethical duty of confidentiality assures a client that, throughout the course of the representation and beyond, the lawyer ordinarily may not voluntarily reveal information relating to the representation to anyone else without the client's consent. In contrast, the evidentiary privilege becomes relevant only after legal proceedings have begun. The privilege is a limited exception to the general principle that, in formal legal proceedings, the legal system and society should have all relevant information available as part of the search for truth. . . . The committee is of the opinion that the law of privilege does not, and should not, set the ethical standard of lawyer-client confidentiality.

It has been argued in some commentaries that the usual rule of lawyer-client confidentiality does not apply in a joint representation and that the lawyer should have the *discretion* to determine whether the lawyer should disclose the separate confidence to the non-communicating client. This discretionary approach is advanced in the *Restatement*, sec. 112, comment *l*. This result is also favored by the American College of Trusts and Estates in its *Commentaries on the Model Rules of Professional Conduct* (2d ed. 1995) (hereinafter the "ACTEC Commentaries"). The *Restatement* itself acknowledges that no case law supports the discretionary approach. Nor do the *ACTEC Commentaries* cite any supporting authority for this proposition.

The committee rejects the concept of discretion in this important area. Florida lawyers must have an unambiguous rule governing their conduct in situations of this nature. We conclude that Lawyer owes duties of confidentiality to both Husband and Wife, regardless of whether they are being represented jointly. Accordingly, under the facts presented Lawyer is ethically precluded from disclosing the separate confidence to Wife without Husband's consent.

The conclusion we reach is consistent with the Rules of Professional Conduct and with prior committee decisions. For example . . . in Opinion 92-5 we concluded that a lawyer who was faced with a federal law purporting to require the lawyer to disclose client information that was confidential under Rule 4-1.6, but not protected by the attorney-client privilege, could not disclose the information without client consent until compelled to do so by legal process.

Our conclusion is also supported by out-of-state authorities. Facing an issue quite similar to that presented by the instant inquiry, the Committee on Professional Ethics of the New York State Bar Association in its Opinion 555 concluded that the lawyer's duty of confidentiality to the communicating joint client (a partner in a two-partner partnership) must take precedence over the lawyer's duty to provide relevant information to the non-communicating joint client (the other partner). That committee reasoned that the mere joint employment of a lawyer does not imply consent on the part of the joint clients to reveal a communication to the non-communicating joint client where disclosure would be adverse to the communicating client. See American Bar Association Formal Opinion 91-361; New York State Bar Association Opinion 674; Monroe County (N.Y.) Bar Association Opinion 87-2. See also *Study Committee Report*, at 788.

The committee further concludes that Lawyer must withdraw from the joint representation under the facts presented. An adversity of interests concerning the joint representation has arisen. This creates a conflict of interest. Many conflicts can be cured by obtaining the fully informed consent of the affected clients. Rule 4-1.7. Some conflicts, however, are of such a nature that it is not reasonable for a lawyer to request consent to continue the representation. . . .

In the situation presented, the conflict that has arisen is of a personal and, quite likely, emotionally-charged nature. Lawyer's continued representation of both Husband and Wife in estate planning matters presumably would no longer be tenable. Rule 4-1.16 thus requires Lawyer's withdrawal from representation of both Husband and Wife in this matter.

In withdrawing from the representation, Lawyer should inform Wife and Husband that a conflict of interest has arisen that precludes Lawyer's continued representation of Wife and Husband in these matters. Lawyer may also advise both Wife and Husband that each should retain separate counsel. As discussed above, however, Lawyer may not disclose the separate confidence to Wife. The committee recognizes that a sudden withdrawal by Lawyer almost certainly will raise suspicions on the part of Wife. This may even alert Wife to the substance of the separate confidence.

Regardless of whether such surmising by Wife occurs when Lawyer gives notice of withdrawal, Lawyer nevertheless has complied with the Rules of Professional Conduct and has not violated Lawyer's duties to Husband. . .

Post-Case Follow-Up

Note that the outcome of the situation where one spouse discloses confidential information intended to be secret from the other is an unhappy one for all parties involved—withdrawal from both representations. The lawyer can be paid for work already completed, but if the clients are not leaving with documents in hand, they are unlikely to be satisfied. Note also that the withdrawal itself raises suspicions in the spouse not responsible for it—or should, anyway. Still, the predominant modern rule is to recommend withdrawal. See, e.g., A. v. B. v. Hill Wallack N.J. (1999).

Professional Ethics Opinion of the Florida Bar Opinion 95-4: Real Life Applications

1. You are just beginning to represent a married couple, Jan and Robin, in estate planning. What steps do you take?

2. You have been representing a married couple in multiple matters, including joint management of a real estate venture and their estate planning. One spouse indicates an interest in talking to you separately about the estate planning. Should you try to stop the conversation from happening? What if you warn her about confidentiality rules and withdrawal procedures at this point, after she has asked to speak with you privately but before any secrets have been revealed? Is this zealous representation of either of your clients?

F. CONFLICTS OF INTEREST

As mentioned in the prior section, lawyers in the estate planning practice may often represent spouses or multiple members of a family. The goals of multiple family members will sometimes conflict with each other. In other cases, the incentives of the lawyer may be at odds with those of the client. The professional ethics standards provide guidance as to how to navigate these conflicts.

The Rules of Professional Conduct articulate standards for managing conflicts of interest, including details on conflicts between current clients as well as specific guidance where a conflict may exist between the client's interest and those of the lawyer. The relevant rule is shown in Exhibit 13.5:

EXHIBIT 13.5 **Conflict of Interest Rules**

Rule 1.7: CONFLICT OF INTEREST: CURRENT CLIENTS

(a) Except as provided in paragraph (b), a lawyer shall not represent a client if the representation involves a concurrent conflict of interest. A concurrent conflict of interest exists if:

   (1) the representation of one client will be directly adverse to another client; or

   (2) there is a significant risk that the representation of one or more clients will be materially limited by the lawyer's responsibilities to another client, a former client or a third person or by a personal interest of the lawyer.

(b) Notwithstanding the existence of a concurrent conflict of interest under paragraph (a), a lawyer may represent a client if:

   (1) the lawyer reasonably believes that the lawyer will be able to provide competent and diligent representation to each affected client;

   (2) the representation is not prohibited by law;

   (3) the representation does not involve the assertion of a claim by one client against another client represented by the lawyer in the same litigation or other proceeding before a tribunal; and

   (4) each affected client gives informed consent, confirmed in writing.

Rule 1.8: CONFLICT OF INTEREST: CURRENT CLIENTS: SPECIFIC RULES

(a) A lawyer shall not enter into a business transaction with a client or knowingly acquire an ownership, possessory, security or other pecuniary interest adverse to a client unless: (1) the transaction and terms on which the lawyer acquires the interest are fair and reasonable to the client and are fully disclosed and transmitted in writing to the client in a manner that can be reasonably understood by the client; (2) the client is advised in writing of the desirability of seeking and is given a reasonable opportunity to seek the advice of independent legal counsel on the transaction; and (3) the client gives informed consent, in a writing signed by the client, to the essential terms of the transaction and the lawyer's role in the transaction, including whether the lawyer is representing the client in the transaction. . . .

(c) A lawyer shall not solicit any substantial gift from a client, including a testamentary gift, or prepare on behalf of a client an instrument giving the lawyer or a person related to the lawyer any substantial gift, unless the lawyer or other recipient of the gift is related to the client. For purposes of this paragraph, related persons include a spouse, child, grandchild, parent, grandparent or other relative or individual with whom the lawyer or the client maintains a close, familial relationship.

Potential conflicts between clients must be navigated with care. As mentioned in Part D of this chapter discussing the ethics of fees, lawyers must be particularly careful if one client attempts to engage the lawyer to draft documents for a different client, especially if the estate plan of the new client will benefit the existing client. Third-party payment of fees can be appropriate. In such cases, the lawyer must be sure the representation is attuned to the needs of the client for whom the documents are drafted, and not for the benefit of an existing client, no matter who pays the bill. For example, a parent may pay for estate planning services for an adult child, but the lawyer must be sure the documents reflect the wishes of the child as the client.

Normally, representation in estate planning matters is not adversarial. It is therefore often ethical to represent multiple clients, such as drafting estate plans for spouses or multiple members of a family, representing co-trustees, or advising multiple trust beneficiaries. If a lawyer does represent multiple parties with related interests, she should discuss whether representation ought to be joint or separate. In joint representation, all information is shared among all parties and individual clients do not keep confidences from each other. In separate representation, client confidences will be concealed from other clients.

The second category of conflicts is when the lawyer's personal interests are at stake. One area where conflicts arise between the interest of the client and the interest of the lawyer is with respect to exculpatory clauses, discussed in more detail in Chapter 10. Exculpatory clauses limit the liability of a fiduciary to beneficiaries. If the lawyer is the fiduciary, the exculpatory clause benefits the lawyer. A lawyer should only include an exculpatory clause if it is the choice of the client to do so, and must obtain informed consent of the client for its inclusion.

One particularly delicate matter of conflict is when a client desires to make a gift to a lawyer in an estate planning document. A lawyer must not ask for gratuitous transfers from a client or prepare documents that implement gratuitous transfers to the lawyer. However, a lawyer may prepare documents that give the lawyer a substantial benefit if the lawyer has a close familial relationship with the client. Even in cases of close relationship, the lawyer should be careful (and consider referring the client to independent counsel) if the gift is disproportionately large compared to others who are related to the client in the same way. For example, once you pass the bar, it is not an ethical violation to draft wills for your parents—but don't create a document that leaves 90 percent of the estate to you and divides the remainder among your three siblings. Normally, documents that give a lawyer no more than the share the lawyer would have received under intestacy are considered to comply with ethical standards. Counseling your family members may raise emotional or personal issues, however, and often having an objective outside attorney draft the documents is worth the cost.

Case Preview

Cooner v. Alabama State Bar

In the case that follows, an attorney drafts a trust in which he names himself as a beneficiary. Although the lawyer was related to the client through marriage, the lawyer's wife had died, so there was no longer any official familial relationship. The Alabama state bar disciplinary board ordered the lawyer to be disbarred for drafting the document creating the transfer for his own benefit, and the lawyer brought an appeal before the Alabama Supreme Court.

As you read the opinion, consider:

1. Under what circumstances is it a violation of professional ethics for a lawyer to prepare a document that makes a gratuitous transfer to himself?
2. Under what circumstances, if any, is it appropriate for a lawyer to draft a document making a beneficial transfer to himself?

Cooner v. Alabama State Bar
59 So. 3d 29 (Ala. 2010)

STUART, Justice.

On February 17, 2010, the Disciplinary Board of the Alabama State Bar, Panel III ("the Board"), ordered that Douglas H. Cooner be disbarred from the practice of law in the State of Alabama. . .

. . .

Cooner contends that the Board erred in concluding that in preparing a trust instrument for his uncle, William B. Riley, he violated Rule 1.8(c), Ala. R. Prof. Cond. It is undisputed that Cooner was related to Riley by marriage, not by blood [and that Cooner's wife is dead, thereby dissolving the familial tie]; that Cooner drafted an irrevocable trust for Riley; and that Cooner was named as one of the 13 beneficiaries of Riley's residual estate in the trust instrument. Cooner maintains that the preparation of this trust by which he would or could receive a gift at Riley's death does not violate Rule 1.8(c), Ala. R. Prof. Cond., because, he says, he was related to Riley. Cooner states that he presents a question of law this Court has not previously addressed: whether an uncle-nephew relationship established by marriage is encompassed within the term "related" as that term is used in Rule 1.8(c), Ala. R. Prof. Cond.

The State Bar maintains that the Board did not err in finding Cooner guilty of violating Rule 1.8(c), Ala. R. Prof. Cond., because, it says, Cooner is not "related" to Riley. The State Bar argues that the terms "relative" or "related" as used in Rule 1.8(c), Ala. R. Prof. Cond., "refer to those only who are connected by blood." Consequently, the State Bar reasons, because Cooner was related to Riley only by marriage, Cooner's preparation of the trust instrument for Riley, which provided that Cooner, at a minimum, would receive a l/13th share of the residuary of Riley's estate, violated Rule 1.8(c), Ala. R. Prof. Cond.

Cooner and the State Bar agree that because this issue does not involve a question of fact, but instead a question of law, this Court's review is de novo.

A "relative" is "[a] person connected with another by blood or affinity; a person who is kin with another." *Black's Law Dictionary* 1315 (8th ed.2004). Thus, a person is "related" to another person, when the person is connected with another person by blood or affinity. In *Kirby v. State,* 89 Ala. 63, 69, 8 So. 110, 111 (1889), this Court defined "affinity" as "the tie which arises from marriage betwixt the husband and blood relatives of the wife, and between the wife and the blood relatives of the husband." Therefore, we conclude that "related" as that term is used in Rule 1.8(c), Ala. R. Prof. Cond., includes relationships by blood and by marriage and that an affinity relationship between an uncle and his nephew is within the meaning of the term "related."

Moreover, we decline to hold, as the State Bar urges us to do, that, for purposes of Rule 1.8(c), Ala. R. Prof. Cond., an affinity relationship arising from the marriage between a husband and blood relatives of the wife terminates with the death of the wife...

The undisputed evidence indicates that Cooner was related to Riley by marriage; therefore, Cooner's preparation of the trust instrument did not violate Rule 1.8(c), Ala. R. Prof. Cond. The Board's decision that Cooner violated Rule 1.8(c), Ala. R. Prof. Cond., is reversed. . .

CONCLUSION

Based on the foregoing, the judgment of the Board is reversed, and this cause is remanded for proceedings consistent with this opinion.

REVERSED AND REMANDED WITH DIRECTIONS. . .

Post-Case Follow-Up

Note that the Board originally voted to disbar the attorney for his actions in drafting the estate planning documents that benefitted him. The Court overrides the decision only because of the family relationship. Notice also that even though there is a family relationship present, the other relatives are quite rankled by the generous transfer to the nephew. Even though the lawyer escaped bar discipline in this instance, it is possible that grounds may exist for allegations of undue influence.

As the Opinion points out, the Restatement and ACTEC Commentaries would permit the lawyer to disclose the confidence in this situation. A lawyer who encounters this conflict should look to state ethics rules, and many bar associations offer ethics hotlines or other helpful resources.

Cooner v. Alabama State Bar: Real Life Applications

1. You have graduated from law school and have passed the bar exam in your state. At a dinner celebrating your admission to the bar, your parents strongly hint that because they helped support you through law school, you ought to draft their estate planning documents for them free of charge. Assuming you have the competence to create a plan sufficient to address their financial situation, should you draft the documents? Does it matter whether your parents want to treat all of their children equally in terms of gratuitous bequests, or if they genuinely want to give you a larger share than your siblings because of special circumstances?

2. You have been practicing in an estate planning boutique for five years after law school graduation and have been engaged to a dentist named Parker, whom you plan to marry in six months. Is it a violation of professional ethics to create estate planning documents for Parker that benefit you before the two of you are married?

G. CLIENT CAPACITY

Although clients require a threshold level of capacity to enter into a contract with a lawyer to provide trust and estate services, clients with diminished capacity remain entitled to vigorous representation and continued respect for their autonomous choices. The rules provide guidance on special issues that may arise when a client has limited or diminished capacity. This may be common in estate planning clients who seek to execute a will later in life, where Alzheimer's disease or other mental challenges associated with aging may have developed.

The Rules of Professional Conduct explain the heightened standards of care a lawyer has when dealing with a client who may have diminished capacity, which is not an uncommon occurrence in the estate planning practice. Exhibit 13.6 shows the relevant rule.

EXHIBIT 13.6 **Diminished Capacity Rule**

Rule 1.14: CLIENT WITH DIMINISHED CAPACITY

(a) When a client's capacity to make adequately considered decisions in connection with a representation is diminished, whether because of minority, mental disability or for some other reason, the lawyer shall, as far as reasonably possible, maintain a normal client-lawyer relationship with the client.

(b) When the lawyer reasonably believes that the client has diminished capacity, is at risk of substantial physical, financial or other harm unless action is taken and cannot adequately act in the client's own interest, the lawyer may take reasonably necessary protective action, including consulting with individuals or entities that have the ability to take action to protect the client and, in appropriate cases, seeking the appointment of a guardian ad litem, conservator or guardian.

(c) Information relating to the representation of a client with diminished capacity is protected by Rule 1.6. When taking protective action pursuant to paragraph (b), the lawyer is impliedly authorized under Rule 1.6(a) to reveal information about the client, but only to the extent reasonably necessary to protect the client's interests.

Navigating the standard of client capacity requires a delicate balance between ensuring the autonomy of a client who wishes to implement a plan and protecting clients lacking capacity from implementing a plan that does not truly reflect their preferences. While a client has full capacity, the lawyer can take measures to plan for management of assets or personal care during incapacity, such as through durable powers of attorney, revocable trusts, health care proxies, and advanced directives. After a client's capacity declines, however, representation becomes trickier.

As discussed in Chapter 6, a client must have mental capacity in order to execute estate planning documents. A lawyer should not draft documents for a client who clearly does not meet the test for capacity. If the client's capacity is borderline, representation remains ethical. In determining whether the client has sufficient capacity to execute documents, the lawyer may consult with the client's family members or others as needed. The ACTEC commentaries suggest that in assessing a client's level of capacity, a lawyer "may consider the client's overall circumstances and abilities, including the client's ability to express the reasons leading to a decision, the ability to understand the consequences of a decision, the substantive appropriateness of a decision, and the extent to which a decision is consistent with the client's values, long term goals and commitments. In appropriate circumstances, the lawyer may seek the assistance of a qualified professional."

Chapter Summary

- In most states, a lawyer remains potentially liable to third-party beneficiaries for negligence under a malpractice claim.
- A trusts and estates lawyer must uphold the standards of professional ethics of the states in which the lawyer is admitted to the bar. Most states base their standards on the Model Rules of Professional Conduct, but often with variations, so practitioners should be alert to local modifications of the rules.
- A lawyer must provide competent representation to clients. This requires "the legal knowledge, skill, thoroughness and preparation reasonably necessary for the representation."
- A lawyer must provide diligent representation to clients, which includes responsiveness within a reasonable time frame.
- A lawyer must maintain appropriate communications with clients. This includes obtaining informed consent from clients, consulting with the client about the means used to accomplish the client's goals, keeping the client reasonably informed about the status of the representation, complying promptly with requests for information, and informing clients of the limits of the representation.
- A lawyer may charge only reasonable fees for services and expenses and should explain to the client how fees and costs are calculated.
- With limited exceptions, a lawyer must maintain the confidentiality of client communications and not disclose client information without informed consent.
- A lawyer must manage conflicts of interest between the client and prior or current clients, which is particularly tricky where a lawyer represents spouses or multiple members of the same family. A lawyer must also manage conflicts of

interest between the client and the lawyer, and generally should avoid gratuitous transfers from clients who are not also close family members.

■ A lawyer should remain mindful of the potentially diminished capacity of clients, particularly those who are elderly or disabled, while recognizing the autonomy of individuals who do possess baseline levels of capacity.

Applying the Concepts

Note: The material in this chapter, dealing with professional ethics, is critical to the practice of law. It is also material tested on the Multistate Professional Responsibility Exam (MPRE). Therefore, the Applying the Concepts questions are posed in the multiple-choice MPRE style, whereas the In Practice section follows our traditional problem-based format. For discussion purposes, however, be prepared to defend your answer even though it is presented in multiple-choice format.

1. Charles, Shaundra, and Kim are partners in a multi-discipline practice. The bulk of Shaundra's practice consists primarily of drafting wills and administering estate matters for clients. For the upcoming partnership's fiscal year, trips to continuing legal education (CLE) conferences will no longer be expensed by the firm. Instead, each partner will be financially responsible for attending the conferences, should they choose to do so. Shaundra decides that to save money, she will not attend any conferences for the year, but will instead keep abreast of changes in the law through searching the Internet.
   Which answer is most correct?

   a. Per MRPC 1.3, Shaundra will be deemed to satisfy her professional responsibility to keep abreast with new developments in the law.
   b. Shaundra must make a good-faith effort to attend as many CLE conferences as possible.
   c. As long as Shaundra makes a concerted effort to remain informed of new developments in the law, sole use of online means should satisfy Rule 1.1.
   d. Shaundra may use the internet to keep informed of new developments in the law. However, she should also check with her state licensing bar to inquire as to any mandatory attendance requirements for CLE programs.

2. Michael, a practicing attorney, receives a visit from his distant nephew, Jorge. Jorge is now married with a newborn and asks if Michael would draft a will for him. As a courtesy, Jorge says that he wants to leave Michael a piece of land that he inherited from his mother, Michael's sister. What should Michael do in preparing the will?

   a. Insert the bequest into the will and thank the nephew for his generosity.
   b. Make certain that his nephew is fully informed of his decision to pass the property to Michael by providing full written disclosure, which Jorge should sign.

c. Decline the bequest, instead suggesting to his nephew to leave him any cash proceeds from the sale of the land, as the Model Rules of Professional Conduct treat cash and land differently.

d. Decline the bequest or the representation. Jorge may choose to engage a different attorney, but if Michael drafts the document, he should not include the bequest to himself. *family excep. does not apply. [closer relatives only]*

3. Shaun and Dedra have come to Roberta McKinney, Esq., to revise their estate plans. Roberta has agreed to represent both jointly in the matter, but did not establish any disclosure agreement beforehand. Dedra, having inherited a substantial amount of money from her parents, wishes to leave it all to Shaun. Under her existing estate plan, Dedra maintained an insurance policy with a significant death benefit, which named Shaun as the sole beneficiary. After the initial client meeting, Dedra calls Roberta confessing that she has allowed the life insurance to lapse, and that Shaun will not receive any proceeds from it upon her death. Dedra directs Roberta not to tell this to Shaun.

   What is the most appropriate course of action for Roberta to take in this scenario? *conflict w/ disclosure v. confidence → withdraw*

   a. Explain to Dedra that it is in her best interest to disclose the news to Shaun, but that as her attorney, she will respect her decision.

   b. Urge Dedra to disclose the news to Shaun, while maintaining that if she does not, she will withdraw from joint representation altogether.

   c. Explain to Dedra that the offsetting inheritance she will leave to Shaun in the will should mitigate any issues that might later arise due to not informing Shaun of the matter.

   d. Suggest to Dedra that she revise the terms of the will to leave more assets to Shaun so as to ameliorate any resentment Shaun may have toward her if and when he discovers that the policy has lapsed. Otherwise, no immediate action need be taken.

4. Gerald is an older gentleman who has sought out James, an attorney who specializes in practicing elder law. During the client meeting, Gerald supplies James with the needed information for him to accurately prepare a new will. A week later during their follow-up meeting, Gerald informs James that he wishes to change the named beneficiary of a large amount of his estate. Instead of leaving a majority of his assets to his children, James now wants to leave them all to his favorite charity, State University. What, if any, steps should James take under MRPC Rule 1.14?

   a. Notify authorities that James suspects State University to be unlawfully exploiting Gerald.

   b. Seek out Gerald's children who are mentioned in his will and inform them of Gerald's change of heart.

   c. Consult with Gerald to confirm his intentions and inform him of the corresponding consequences.

   d. Terminate the representation of Gerald.

5. Aware that his mother is elderly and has never taken any form of estate planning measures, Travis consults with Sheila, an attorney, about setting up basic estate devices for his mother. Travis asks about Sheila's fee, stating that he intends to pay for all expenses incurred on behalf of his mother. All he asks in return is that Sheila keep him informed of the progress. At this point, what course of action is appropriate for Sheila to take?

   a. Agree to keep Travis informed of her progress and discussions with his mother.

   b. Explain that normally Sheila is not allowed to disclose clients' matters to third parties. However, because he is related and paying the legal costs of the work to be performed, an exception is allowed.

   c. Agree to take the case, upon receipt of consent from Travis's mother regarding the payment arrangement, subject to Travis understanding that she will not be allowed to disclose to him any matters discussed with his mother.

   d. Decline representation, as she can prospectively determine that the representation will be more trouble than it is worth.

Trusts and Estates in Practice

1. A new client has come to your office to discuss engaging you to draft a will and trust. Taking into account Model Rule of Professional Conduct 1.5, what matters regarding your fee should you discuss? On a related note, what are some things you could look to in setting your fee? (Rule 1.5(a)(1)-(8).)

2. Research the Rules of Professional Conduct set forth by the licensing bar of the state in which you intend in practice law. Does your state follow the MRPC? In particular, research any rule addressing the receipt of gifts from clients by bequest. Do any exceptions exist that might allow an attorney to prepare a will and still receive a testamentary gift? (Rule 1.8 (c).)

3. You have an estate planning practice that generally focuses on clients of moderate wealth. Your friend from college, Quinn, has become a highly-compensated professional athlete who wants to hire you for estate planning, but Quinn will require tax planning to make a transfer to a non-citizen spouse. You have a good form book and feel you could select an appropriate form to accomplish Quinn's goals, but don't understand the underlying tax law enough to explain it well. Assuming that you can establish that you have the requisite level of competence, are there any other professional ethics limitations on your ability to represent Quinn? Draft a short paragraph explaining what ethical limits there are on your representation. (Rule 1.4.)

4. Read MRPC Rule 1.14 and the accompanying comments. Assume you are assisting a client with planning her estate, including drafting a will. Although she

is able to speak somewhat coherently, she seems uncertain about her answers to your questions, causing you to repeat each question multiple times. Make a list of certain topics you may want to be on the lookout for in determining whether your client is indecisive or has a genuine cognitive impairment. (Rule 1.14, cmt. 6.)

5. You are serving as the fiduciary to an estate. Within the estate there is property that you are interested in purchasing. What mandatory steps, if any, must you take in attempting to purchase the property? Do you believe such requirements are sufficient to mitigate any conflicts of interest that may arise? (Rule 1.8(a).)

14

Estate Administration and the Probate Process

At a person's death, the estate plan "matures" into an administration and the process of probating the estate can begin. The overall process of administering a decedent's estate is fairly similar whether there is a valid will or distribution based on intestacy statutes, although this chapter will flag the important differences that do exist. The administration process generally involves appointing a personal representative, probating and proving the will if there is one, managing the assets and inventory, dealing with creditors, and distributing property to the entitled heirs or beneficiaries. Many years or decades often pass between the date a will is executed and the testator's date of death. This means it is often not the same attorney who drafted the estate plan that sees the estate through probate. The probate process lasts at least six months, due to the need to notify and pay creditors, and often takes a year or two to complete. Probate proceeds through several distinct phases and culminates with the termination of the estate through the distribution of property in the estate and the release of the personal representative.

KEY CONCEPTS

- Court appointment of a personal representative and grant of authority to act
- Probating and proving a will (if there is one)
- Management of assets and inventory throughout administration
- Creditor rights and claims
- Nonprobate and tax matters
- Estate termination and concluding administration

A. ACTIONS BEFORE COMMENCING ADMINISTRATION

When a person dies, many tasks must be completed before the estate is distributed to the heirs or beneficiaries. The **probate process**—the steps required to administer an estate—is a series of actions designed to protect the rights of heirs or beneficiaries (and creditors of the estate) while the personal

What Court Is Appropriate for Probate?

As noted above, most administrations will take place at the probate court in the county where the decedent was domiciled when she died. Not all states, however, refer to this court as the "Probate Court." It is not unusual, for example, to call it a "Surrogate's Court" or "Orphan's Court," and in some jurisdictions a chancery court or other court of equity will handle probate matters. Many courts that oversee administration of estates have jurisdiction over other matters as well, such as adoptions, guardianships, involuntary commitments, and sometimes even elections or other matters not directly related to probate law.

representative manages and distributes the assets of the estate. Before the official process of probating an estate can begin, the attorney must identify key players and determine the initial track of the probate process. In some jurisdictions, estate administration may proceed without an attorney, particularly for estates of limited size. Administrations that do involve a lawyer are of primary interest to the practicing attorney, so the discussion here will focus primarily on those scenarios. The probate of an estate generally takes place in the county probate court in which the decedent was domiciled; however, an additional probate proceeding (called **ancillary probate**) may also be necessary if the decedent owned probate real property in another state. The administration process is form-intensive; forms used will also vary by jurisdiction, and some of them may be found online.

1. Determine the Personal Representative

The first step in the probate process is to determine which individual or entity will manage (or "represent") the **estate**. To assume legal responsibility over the estate, that person will typically need legal confirmation, either by a court or a clerk's office. Terminology varies by state, but the representative of an intestate estate is usually called an **administrator**, whereas a testate estate's representative is called an **executor**. The term **personal representative** applies broadly to both types of estates. The Uniform Probate Code (UPC) and some states use the term personal representative rather than the more specific terms. In a testate estate, a will most commonly nominates an individual (or entity, like a bank) to serve as executor, and a court will generally give that nominee priority to serve. See UPC § 3-203. Sometimes a will does not nominate an executor or the nominated executor does not serve; in such a case, the probate court appoints a personal representative to fill the vacancy. For an intestate estate, the court will appoint an administrator. In making its decision, the court looks to the requisite state statute that designates the hierarchy of individuals who should be considered, typically giving precedence to close family members. For example, section 3-203 of the Uniform Probate Code gives the spouse first priority to administer an intestate estate, followed by other heirs and finally creditors. Appointed personal representatives must meet certain minimum qualifications, which generally relate to age, capacity, eligibility for bond (insurance), and the confirmation that fiduciary authority will not be abused.

2. Establish the Client Relationship

The personal representative may select an attorney to represent him throughout the process of administering the estate. As in any attorney-client relationship, when a lawyer accepts new business, she should discuss the scope of the representation with the client and record the agreement in an engagement letter. The engagement letter will establish fees, whether flat rate or hourly, as well as define any actions the attorney may take in the probate administration. Often the attorney retained by the personal representative will provide services beyond mere probate, such as those relating to nonprobate matters or tax. Matters such as these should be covered in the letter to avoid future misunderstandings. Drafting the documents of the decedent does not automatically entitle the attorney to serve as lawyer to the estate, and retaining original copies of estate planning documents should not, as a matter of professional ethics, be used to persuade clients to use the firm for estate administration services. The attorney-client relationship for the estate administration is a new one and not a continuation of the representation of the decedent in estate planning, and it is within the rights of the personal representative to select his own legal counsel. The commentaries published by the American College of Trust and Estate Counsel (ACTEC) provide very useful guidance on ethical considerations in representation throughout the probate process, and the ACTEC website also includes model engagement letters for such representation. The ACTEC commentaries on the Model Rules of Professional Responsibility are discussed in more detail in Chapter 13, and you can see the variety of model engagement letters available to trusts and estates practitioners at www.actec.org.

3. Weigh Costs and Benefits to Determine Whether Probate Is Necessary

Probate is not always necessary, and sometimes skipping the probate process may be the better choice for a client. The primary benefits of the probate process are threefold. First, the process generates evidence regarding the transfer of title for certain assets. This can be important when retitling real estate or other property and may be of substantial value to the new owners. Second, probate provides a window of time during which creditors of the estate must speak or forever hold their peace. This set period of time protects creditor rights as well as affords assurance to the surviving heirs or beneficiaries that there will be no claims against the estate after the assets have been distributed. Third, by nature, probate provides a court-supervised process, which better ensures the honest and efficient collection of estate assets and proper distribution of those assets. In many circumstances, the process of probate does offer significant benefits to estates. See David Horton, *In Partial Defense of Probate: Evidence from Alameda County, California*, 103 Geo. L.J. 605 (2015).

There is no requirement that an estate be probated. In certain estates, the benefits of probate fail to outweigh the costs. Costs include court document filing fees, payment for services of the attorney and personal representative, and other costs associated with administration, like mailing, copying, and phone calls. In very small estates, the entirety of the estate's assets could be depleted through attorney fees and court costs, with nothing left to distribute to the heirs or beneficiaries. Estates without substantial creditor interaction or property needing clear title may not gain much benefit from the process. In some estates, nearly all of the value passes through nonprobate transfers, so there is little probate property to manage. If no interested parties advocate for estate administration there is no need, which is why many estates are not probated. However, states commonly have a statute requiring individuals in possession of a decedent's will to deliver it to the appropriate probate court whereupon any interested party may initiate probate. That said, if there is no expressly shown interest in probating an estate, there is no necessity for it to begin. An alternative to probate is an informal family settlement, which under proper circumstances can be effective in getting the property where it belongs at a reduced cost as compared to formal legal proceedings. Upon encountering small estates, attorneys should counsel the personal representative on the benefits of probate against the costs in particular cases.

4. Small Estate Administration or Informal Probate

For smaller estates, many states offer alternatives to formal estate administration. These alternative procedures generally require less paperwork and may be completed at a lower cost than formal probate. These processes are best suited to estates with no existing or expected substantial conflict among the beneficiaries or heirs. The beginning of an estate's administration can start on the informal track (sometimes called "in common form") and later switch to the formal track (sometimes called "in solemn form") should conflict arise or upon request of the personal representative, heirs, or beneficiaries.

One variety of informal probate is a small estate administration procedure, which is available to estates below a certain value (and sometimes only those that exclude real estate). Small estate procedures have minimal filing costs, less court oversight, and can often be accomplished without the involvement of an attorney. For example, Tennessee offers a Small Estates Act procedure for estates under $50,000. See Tenn. Code Ann. § 30-4-102. These small estates in Tennessee, whether there is a will or not, may be administered by survivors filing a simple affidavit (and perhaps a few other forms) with the probate court setting forth the relevant facts of the estate. Tenn. Code Ann. § 30-4-103. Small estate administration may be a viable alternative for a family who is considering avoiding probate altogether due to cost constraints.

The Uniform Probate Code makes a clear distinction between "Informal Probate and Appointment Proceedings; Succession without Administration" (covered in

UPC sections 3-301 to 3-322) and "Formal Testacy and Appointment Proceedings" (covered in UPC sections 3-401 to 3-414) paired with "Supervised Administration" (covered in UPC 3-501 to 3-505). This format of parallel tracks to administer an estate allows clients flexibility in choosing whether they need the informal path for a simpler estate or the formal one for estates involving controversy or otherwise requiring substantial court oversight. States vary as to the extent to which informal administration is permitted, but all states have a formal administration procedure.

5. Determine Whether Estate Is Testate or Intestate

The attorney must also make another initial assessment, which is to determine whether the decedent died **testate** (with a valid will) or **intestate** (with no valid will). The status of the estate as testate or intestate will influence certain steps in the probate process, such as the forms to file to appoint the personal representative, the parties entitled to notice, and how the property should be distributed. An estate initially believed to be testate may become intestate following a successful will contest. In that case, amended forms must be submitted to the probate court demonstrating the new character of the estate and the appointment of a new personal representative, if the administrator is different than the original executor.

6. Cremation or Burial of Decedent and Planning for Surviving Minors

One of the earliest actions to be taken upon the death of a person is determining the proper treatment of remains. Some individuals leave instructions relating to burial, cremation, donation of organs, funeral instructions, and other matters. See Karen J. Sneddon, *Memento Mori: Death and Wills*, 14 Wyo. L. Rev. 211, 238-48 (2014). Sometimes a person will engage in "pre-need" funeral planning and pay costs of burial or other services in advance, as well as make plans relating to how the funeral should proceed. In the event the decedent left no directions, state law normally leaves such decisions to the surviving spouse, or to the adult children, or to other next of kin. See, e.g., Al. Code 34-13-11 (2013). If the body of the decedent cannot be found, there are state procedures to declare a missing individual as deceased, and probate proceedings may then be commenced, although with additional complications. See Bradley Richardson, *Presumed Dead: Laying to Rest the Whereabouts Unknown*, 58 S.D. L. Rev. 375 (2013).

If the decedent died leaving behind minor children, the surviving parent assumes sole legal guardianship, and no additional action is required to maintain that role. However, if there is no surviving parent, the court must appoint a guardian for the minor children. State statutes provide courts with criteria to guide the selection, generally favoring those adults with a close familial relationship to the child, but often allowing the court substantial discretion in determining which guardian is in the best interests of the child. See Alyssa A. DiRusso & S. Kristen Peters, *Parental Testamentary Appointments of Guardians for Children,* 25 Quinnipiac Prob. L.J. 369 (2012). Where the last-to-die parent has included nominations of a guardian in his will, those nominations are often, but not always, respected. For more information on handling matters involving minors at the death of a parent, see Naomi Cahn & Alyssa A. DiRusso, *Planning for the Daily Care of a Minor in the Event of an Adult's Incapacity or Death, in* Tax, Estate, and Lifetime Planning for Minors (ed. Carmina Y. D'Aversa, 2019).

B. AUTHORIZING THE PERSONAL REPRESENTATIVE

Once the client relationship is established and the style of probate determined, the personal representative must be granted the formal authority to act by the probate court. The document conveying authority to the personal representative to act is generally called *Letters*—**Letters Testamentary** in the case of a will and **Letters of Administration** in an intestate estate, although terminology may vary by state. In most states, temporary Letters may be granted if time is of the essence.

1. Petition for Letters and Grant of Letters

In order to receive Letters Testamentary or Letters of Administration, the personal representative must file a form with the probate court requesting that Letters be granted. The form is usually titled the Petition for Letters (Testamentary/of Administration). The form will require details needed to determine whether the personal representative is eligible to serve, including age, capacity, and certain other personal information. The form will also include a list of heirs (and beneficiaries, if any), entitled to receive notice of the personal representative's appointment. An official copy of the decedent's death certificate is generally filed along with the Petition for Letters, although sometimes it is instead filed with the Petition to Probate the Will. For a sample death certificate, see Exhibit 14.1. The personal representative generally needs several original copies of the death certificate to use in connection with probate filings and gathering of nonprobate assets.

EXHIBIT 14.1   Sample Death Certificate

STATE OF NEW JERSEY

B0008910356

NEW JERSEY DEPARTMENT OF HEALTH
CERTIFICATE OF DEATH

STATE FILE NUMBER
20170020016

1a. Legal Name of Decedent (First, Middle, Last, Suffix)
Doris Virginia McCunney

LIMB ONLY ☐

1b. Also Known As (AKA), If Any (First, Middle, Last, Suffix)

2. Sex	3. Social Security Number	4a. Age	5. Date of Birth (Mo/Day/Yr)
Female	189-16-3473	93 Years	03/23/1924

6. Birthplace (City & State/Foreign Country)
Philadelphia, Pennsylvania

7a. Residence-State	7b. County		7c. Municipality/City	
New Jersey	Atlantic		Linwood City	

7d. Street and Number	7e. Apt No.	7f. Zip Code	7g. Inside City Limits?
432 Central Ave		08221	Yes

8a. Ever in US Armed Forces?	8b. If Yes, Name of War:	8c. War Service Dates (From/To):
No		

9. Domestic Status at Time of Death	10. Name of Surviving Spouse/Partner (Name given at birth or on birth certificate)
Divorced	

11. Father's Name (First, Middle, Last)
Johann Haas

12. Mother's Name Prior to First Marriage (First, Middle, Last)
Adolfine Smykal

13a. Name of Informant	13b. Relationship to Decedent
Richard McCunney	Son

13c. Mailing Address (Street and Number, City, State, Zip Code)
6304 Cormorant Court, Bradenton, FL 34203

14. Method of Disposition	15. Place of Disposition (name of cemetery, crematory, other)	16. Location- City & State/Foreign Country
Cremation	Seaside Crematory	Upper Township, New Jersey

17. Name and Complete Address of Funeral Facility
Adams-Perfect Funeral Home Inc, 1650 New Road, Northfield, NJ 08225-1108

18. Electronic Signature of Funeral Director	19. NJ License Number
Jared Andrew Kirschenbaum	23JP00471600

20. Decedent Education	21. Decedent of Hispanic Origin?	22. Decedent Race
High school graduate or GED completed	Not Spanish / Hispanic / Latino	White

23. Occupation of Decedent (Type of work done most of life, even if retired)	24. Kind of Business/Industry
Bank Manager	Banking

25. Name and Address of Last Employer
First Pennsylvania Bank, Philadelphia, NJ

26. Date Pronounced Dead (Mo/Day/Yr)	28. Name of Person Pronouncing Death
04/03/2017	*Joe Maalouf*

27. Time Pronounced Dead (24-hr)	29. License Number	30. Date Signed (Mo/Day/Yr)
1631	Medical Resident	04/03/2017

31. Date of Death (Mo/Day/Yr)	32. Time of Death (24-hr)	33. Was Medical Examiner Contacted?	34. Place of Death
04/03/2017	1631	No	Hospital: Inpatient

35a. Facility Name (if not institution, give street and number)
Mainland Division-AtlantiCare Regional Medical Center

35b. Municipality	35c. County
Galloway Township	Atlantic

CAUSE OF DEATH: **36a. PART I -** IMMEDIATE CAUSE - final disease or condition resulting in death. Subsequently list conditions, if any, leading to the cause listed on Line a. Enter the UNDERLYING CAUSE (disease or injury that initiated the events resulting in death) LAST.

	Interval Between Onset and Death
Immediate Cause a. **respiratory arrest**	15 minutes
Due to (or as a consequence of): b. **Bradycardia**	15 minutes
Due to (or as a consequence of): c. **Ventricular tachycardia**	15 minutes
Due to (or as a consequence of): d. **Chronic systolic and diastolic heart failure**	15 minutes

36b. PART II - Enter other significant conditions contributing to death but not resulting in underlying cause given in PART I.	37. Was an Autopsy Performed? No
	38. Were Autopsy Findings Available to Complete Cause of Death? Not Applicable

39. Date of Injury (Mo/Day/Yr)	40. Time of Injury (24-hr)	41. Place of Injury (e.g. home, construction site, restaurant)	42. Injury at work?

43a. Location of Injury (Number and Street, Zip Code)	43b. Municipality	43c. County	43d. State

44. Describe How Injury Occurred	45. If Transportation Injury:

Record Contains Amendment ☐

46. Manner of Death	47. Did Decedent Have Diabetes?	48. Did Tobacco Use Contribute to Death?	49. If Female, Pregnancy State
Natural	No	Unknown	Not applicable

50. Certifier Type	51. Name, Address, and Zip Code of Certifier
Certifying Physician or APN	Sanjay Shetty 2 St Meena Avenue, Manahawkin, NJ 08050

52. Electronic Signature of Certifier	53. License Number	54. Date Certified (Mo/Day/Yr)
Sanjay Shetty	25MA08391200	04/03/2017

55. Electronic Signature of Local Registrar	56. District No.	57. Date Received	Case ID Number
Robin Atlas	V0168	04/05/2017	1908811

DATE ISSUED: *April 05, 2017*

ISSUED BY:
Northfield City

Robin Atlas, Local Registrar

This is to certify that the above is correctly copied from a record on file in my office.
Certified copy not valid unless the raised Great Seal of the State of New Jersey or the seal of the issuing municipality or county, is affixed hereon.

Vincent T. Arrisi
Vincent T. Arrisi
State Registrar
Office of Vital Statistics and Registry

REG-42B
JUN 14

THIS DOCUMENT HAS MULTIPLE SECURITY FEATURES TO DETER FRAUD; VOID IF ALTERED

If the personal representative meets all the requirements, the probate judge who received the Petition for Letters will grant Letters (Testamentary/of Administration) to the personal representative. The Letters consist of a simple form that gives the personal representative authority to act. Often third parties interacting with the estate, such as banks and creditors, will require the presentation of the Letters. Letters remain in force until they are revoked or until the personal representative no longer serves the estate. For a sample grant of Letters Testamentary, see Exhibit 14.2.

EXHIBIT 14.2   **Sample Grant of Letters Testamentary (Washington)**

SUPERIOR COURT OF WASHINGTON
FOR _____ COUNTY

Estate of	
_____,	**NO. _____**
	LETTERS TESTAMENTARY
	(RCW 11.28.090)
_____ **Deceased.**	

On _____, the last *Will* of the above named Decedent was duly exhibited, proven, and filed in the foregoing Superior Court.

In the *Will*, Decedent named *(name:)*_____ to act as its Executor, who, by Order of this Court, is authorized to execute the *Will* according to law.

Witness my hand and the seal of this Court on

_____
Clerk of the Superior Court

By: _____
Deputy Clerk

Letters Testamentary   Name:
RCW 11.28.090   Address:
Page 1 of 1   Phone:

2. Bond (Surety) for Personal Representative

In some circumstances, a personal representative is required to obtain a bond (also called a surety) as a condition to the granting of Letters by the probate court. The bond acts as insurance that provides benefits to the estate in the event the personal representative conducts an improper administration of the estate causing loss. A will can waive the requirement that a personal representative purchase a bond, but intestate estates and testate estates with no express waiver generally do require insurance. The cost of the bond is borne by the estate. The personal representative enters into a contract for insurance with the bonding company before filing for Letters and often provides proof of the bond as part of that filing.

3. Notice

An important part of the probate process is making certain that the **interested persons**—those who have or may have a financial stake in the outcome of the administration—are kept informed of the important parts of the process. The interested persons generally include "heirs, devisees, children, spouses, creditors, beneficiaries, and any others having a property right in or claim against a trust estate or the estate of a decedent, ward, or protected person." See UPC § 1-201(23). The personal representative should provide **notice** of potential appointment to the interested persons, particularly beneficiaries specified in the will (if any) and to the heirs who would take the property in an intestate estate. This information allows the heirs or beneficiaries to protect their interests by knowing who to contact with respect to estate matters, as well as to object to the appointment upon legitimate grounds. For a sample notice of appointment of a personal representative, see Exhibit 14.3.

EXHIBIT 14.3   **Sample Notice to Interested Parties of Appointment of Personal Representative (Ohio)**

LEGAL NOTICE
IN RE: ESTATE OF
JEANNE C. TULL
LORAIN COUNTY
PROBATE COURT
CASE NO. 2016 ES 00842

To all persons interested in the Estate of Jeanne C. Tull, Deceased, Lorain County Probate Court,

Case No. 2016 ES 00842:

This notice is given to all unknown heirs and/or next of kin of the decedent who have not already received notice and who would be entitled to inherit from the decedent, if the decedent had died intestate.

You are hereby notified that Jeanne C. Tull died on November 3, 2015. An Application for Authority to Administer Estate was filed with the Lorain County Probate Court on August 24, 2016. The Probate Court has scheduled the Application for hearing before Judge James T. Walther for October 13, 2016 at 1:30 p.m. The hearing will be held at the Lorain County Common Pleas Court, Probate Court Division, 225 Court Street, 6th Floor, Elyria, Ohio 44035.

Timothy N. Toma is applying to be appointed Administrator of the Estate.

The attorney for the Estate is Katherine B. McCoy(#0093714), Toma & Associates,

L.P.A., Inc.,33977 Chardon Road #100, Willoughby Hills, Ohio 44094, (440) 516-0200 x 206.

C.T. 9/8-15-22/16
20561458

4. Removal, Replacement, or Succession of Personal Representatives

As discussed in a previous section, a state's statute normally determines which family member will be appointed as administrator, and a will generally designates who should serve as executor. Wills often also include successor executors if the original selection is or becomes unable or unwilling to serve. Once the procedure for nominations in the will has been exhausted, a probate court will resort to procedures for appointing administrators to find a replacement personal representative.

There may also be a provision in the will that allows certain individuals the right to remove and replace the executor. If these provisions are included, those with the right to remove and replace may use it as freely as the provision allows. In the absence of such a provision, the probate court will determine whether the behavior of a personal representative merits removal. Probate courts give substantial deference to the selection of fiduciary made by the decedent and traditionally have allowed removal of the personal representative only for evident cause. However, there has been a trend in favor of allowing removal of the personal representative when it is in the "best interests" of the beneficiary. This trend brings wills law in conformity with trust law under the Uniform Trust Code.

Case Preview

In re Estate of Mason D. Robb

In this case, a son of the decedent was appointed as executor of his father's estate and trustee of associated trusts. After the son accepted a $50,000 death-bed transfer and did not include it in the account of estate assets, comingled estate assets with his own, and failed to prepare proper accountings, the other beneficiaries of the estate had him removed. The son appealed his removal from his fiduciary roles and argued that removal was improper.

As you read the case, consider:

1. What was the standard used by the court to determine whether the personal representative should be removed?
2. To what extent was the standard for removal in this case any different for the personal representative of an estate than it would be for the trustee of an irrevocable trust?
3. Why do you think the personal representative was selected by the decedent to serve? How do you think a testator typically decides who should serve as executor?

In re Estate of Mason D. Robb
21 Neb. App. 429 (2013)

RIEDMANN, Judge.

Theodore J. Robb appeals the order of the county court for Hall County removing him as the personal representative of his deceased father's estate and as the trustee of his father's inter vivos trust. The issue raised is whether the trial court erred in determining that it was in the best interests of the estate and the trust to remove Theodore from his fiduciary positions. Because Theodore's individual interests conflicted with the interests of the estate and the trust, we affirm the trial court's decision to remove him from his fiduciary positions.

Mason D. Robb passed away in March 2010. Pursuant to his last will and testament and his trust documents, his son, Theodore, became the personal representative of his estate and the trustee to the inter vivos Mason D. Robb Revocable Living Trust (the Trust). The Trust included three pieces of real estate: the Tri Street house, the Hall County farm, and the Sherman County pastures.

The Trust declared that the trustee should hold and use the Trust property for two purposes: to pay administrative costs and the settlor's debts and for the benefit of the Mason D. Robb [] Family Trust (the Family Trust). The Trust directed the trustee to separate the funds in the Family Trust into two equal shares: one for the benefit of Theodore and one for the benefit of Theodore's sister, Linda Hahn (Linda). The share created for Theodore was to be delivered to him outright, and the share created for Linda was to be held in trust for Linda's benefit. The Family Trust stated that Linda should receive income from her share of the Family Trust periodically throughout her lifetime.

In September 2011, Linda and her son, Shawn Eichman (Shawn), filed a motion to remove Theodore as the personal representative. In December, Linda and Shawn filed an additional motion to remove Theodore as the trustee.

The evidence presented at trial indicates that Theodore received a $50,000 "death-bed transfer" from his father. Theodore admitted receipt of the payment and agreed that the payment should be treated as an estate asset, but he stated that he had not deposited it in the estate account at the time of trial. Theodore also failed to include it in either the inventory or the amended inventory filed with the court.

The evidence also reveals that Theodore sold several items of personal property belonging to his father, in the amount of approximately $900, but that he had not included that amount in any accounting filed with the court as of the date of the hearing. Theodore had, however, deposited the funds into the estate account.

Theodore was also untimely in his filing of his original inventory and accounting. Despite a court order, Theodore failed to file an amended inventory or an accounting that included funds and assets through June 15, 2012; rather, his amended filings were current through only 2011.

The court found that Theodore should be removed from his positions as the personal representative and as the trustee, because his actions in commingling his individual funds with the funds and assets of the estate and the Trust caused irreconcilable conflict and could continue to do so. Accordingly, the trial court determined that removing Theodore from his positions as the personal representative and as the trustee was in the best interests of the estate and the Trust.

This timely appeal followed.

On appeal, Theodore argues that the county court erred in removing him from his role as the personal representative and as the trustee, because removal was not in the best interests of the estate and the Trust. We disagree.

Neb. Rev. Stat. § 30-2454(a) (Reissue 2008) states that a court may remove a personal representative from an estate if "removal would be in the best interests of the estate, or if it is shown that a personal representative . . . has mismanaged the estate or failed to perform any duty pertaining to the office." When an executor has a personal interest in the administration of an estate and in the disposition of the estate property, and when the circumstances disclose that those interests prevent him from performing his duties in an impartial manner, he should be removed.

In this case, Theodore failed to impartially perform his duties as the personal representative. In particular, as the personal representative, Theodore was entrusted with the duty to manage and properly account for the property that was part of the estate. The record reveals that Theodore has failed to properly account for estate assets, particularly the $50,000 "deathbed transfer." While Theodore acknowledged that this money should be considered property of the estate, he had not deposited it into the estate's account during the 2½ years between his father's death and the hearing. In addition, Theodore sold items of personal property belonging to his father without notification to the remaining heirs and had not accounted for the income. Furthermore, Theodore did not timely file his original inventory and accounting, nor was it complete. These actions disclose that Theodore's personal interest in the estate prevented him from impartially performing his duties as the personal representative. We agree with the trial court that allowing Theodore to continue as the personal representative was not in the best interests of the estate and that his removal was proper.

The trial court did not err in removing Theodore from his positions as the personal representative and as the trustee, because his actions reveal that his interests irreconcilably conflicted with the interests of the estate and the Trust. Accordingly, the decision of the trial court is affirmed.

AFFIRMED.

Post-Case Follow-Up

Note that although the court applies the more modern "best interest" standard for removal, Theodore's actions justify removal under the traditional "for cause" standard as well. His failures as personal representative include misappropriation of assets for his own benefit as well as missed filing deadlines. Although it would normally be in the "best interest" of the beneficiaries to remove a fiduciary who abuses the role, the standard is broad enough to allow removal of the personal representative who has done no wrong. A "best interest" standard could be used to remove a personal representative where the estate has an opportunity for minimizing fiduciary fees (such as when a bank's fee schedule is not competitive), whereas a "for cause" standard could not. State laws vary, with the "for cause" standard still in place in many states and the "best interest" standard a modern trend.

In re Estate of Mason D. Robb: Real Life Applications

1. You represent an estate planning client who has named his spouse to serve as executor and has named no alternates. What do you counsel him on the importance of naming alternate or successor executors and the circumstances that could result in one being needed?

2. You are a member of your firm's model document revision task force. Should your firm's model will include a provision allowing for removal and replacement by certain individuals in their own discretion, or should the matter of removal be left to the court? Why?

3. You represent a bank that serves as executor of many estates and trustee of a variety of trusts. If the bank performs its duties in good faith, under what circumstances can it still be removed? What standards for removal are likely to apply?

C. PROBATE THE WILL (TESTATE ADMINISTRATIONS ONLY)

Some parts of the probate process are unique to testate administrations. Obviously, for intestate estates, there is no will to probate and subsequently no need to probate it. Where a will is present, the personal representative must complete certain steps in order to admit the will to probate, begin proving proper execution of the will, and provide adequate notice to all interested parties.

1. Petition to Probate the Will

To begin the probate of a will, a personal representative completes a form often called a **Petition to Probate the Will**. The form includes information about the decedent, the personal representative, and the designated beneficiaries. The personal representative files the Petition, along with the original will and all codicils to it, in the county probate court where the decedent was domiciled. In some states, the personal representative may alternatively file the will in a county where the decedent died, lived, or held property. The Petition to Probate the Will is usually filed at roughly the same time as the Petition for Letters Testamentary, because the will is needed to identify the executor.

2. Notice Requirements

As discussed above, beneficiaries and heirs are entitled to notice at certain points throughout the probate process. When the Petition to Probate the Will is filed, the beneficiaries and heirs are entitled to notice. This allows the heirs or beneficiaries an opportunity to contest the will before admission to probate is final.

3. Proving the Will (and Self-Proved Wills)

Part of admitting the will to probate involves the executor proving that the will was executed in compliance with statutory formalities, whether it is an attested will or a holographic will. Professionally drafted wills often include a **self-proving affidavit** and therefore qualify as **self-proved wills** (as discussed in Chapter 3). The self-proving affidavit is a statement signed by the testator and witnesses in front of a notary public, which recites that the will was executed in compliance with statutory formalities. A self-proving affidavit normally acts as conclusive evidence of due execution. An interested party may provide evidence to contradict the terms of the affidavit with respect to capacity or lack of testamentary intent, however, so the self-providing affidavit is not a guarantee against all will contests.

If the will has an attestation clause reciting the facts surrounding the signature of the will by the testator and witnesses, but does not have a self-proving affidavit, this provides prima facie evidence of due execution. If no one objects, the court may accept the finding of due execution. If a party alleges that the execution was improper, the process for admitting the will to probate follows the path of wills lacking an attestation clause described in the next paragraph.

If the will is merely signed by the witnesses without any recitation of the facts surrounding the execution, the executor (with the help of an attorney) is expected to gather evidence regarding facts surrounding the execution of the will from all surviving witnesses in order to determine whether it was executed appropriately. Often, such evidence is gathered outside of court, and witnesses will be asked to sign an affidavit to be entered into evidence that recites the conditions of the will execution. Sometimes lawyers use interrogatories to provide evidence surrounding the facts of execution. Occasionally, predominately during a will contest, witnesses to the execution of the will may be called to testify. Sometimes, no witnesses survive the testator and there is no evidence of due execution, so the will is denied probate.

4. Order Admitting Will to Probate

The probate judge will enter an order admitting the will to probate upon a successful Petition to Probate the Will. An interested party may contest the will at any time before the will is officially admitted. If a will contest occurs, a party often has the option to remove the matter from probate court to circuit court. A circuit court will generally permit a jury trial, whereas in probate court, a judge generally decides the case. Also, not all probate judges are lawyers, whereas circuit court judges almost uniformly have been admitted to practice law.

D. MANAGING THE ASSETS AND INVENTORY

Once administration of the estate has begun and the personal representative has gained authority to act, the first responsibility is to manage the assets of the estate. As discussed earlier in the chapter on fiduciary duties, a trustee's responsibilities include collecting and protecting assets, maintaining proper accounts, and prudently investing funds under the control of the fiduciary. These obligations apply to a personal representative as well. In addition to upholding the fiduciary duties they share with trustees, executors and administrators must complete paperwork and filings that are unique to the probate process, such as filing an inventory, appraisal, and perhaps additional accountings.

1. Possession and Control of Assets

Shortly following the death of the decedent, the personal representative should take steps to secure the probate property of the estate. Remember that probate administration applies only to *probate* assets—nonprobate assets, such as life insurance, financial accounts with pay-on-death or transfer-on-death designations, retirement plan benefits, and other nonprobate assets are not subject to administration by the personal representative nor appropriately possessed by him in his fiduciary capacity. The personal representative must take possession of the probate property and prevent any misappropriation that may occur from other individuals (most commonly family members who believe they are entitled to current possession of the property). Title to most probate assets will vest in the personal representative until the probate process determines whether the heirs or beneficiaries—or creditors—are entitled to final ownership.

EXHIBIT 14.4   **What Gives the Personal Representative Authority to Take Possession of Estate Assets?**

UPC SECTION 3-709. DUTY OF PERSONAL REPRESENTATIVE; POSSESSION OF ESTATE

Except as otherwise provided by a decedent's will, every personal representative has a right to, and shall take possession or control of the decedent's property, except that any real property or tangible personal property may be left with or surrendered to the person presumptively entitled thereto unless or until, in the judgment of the personal representative, possession of the property by him will be necessary for purposes of administration. The request by a personal representative for delivery of any property possessed by an heir or devisee is conclusive evidence, in any action against the heir or devisee for possession thereof, that the possession of the property by the personal representative is necessary for purposes of administration. The personal representative shall pay taxes on, and take all steps reasonably necessary for the management, protection and preservation of, the estate in his possession. He may maintain an action to recover possession of property or to determine the title thereto.

In addition to taking physical possession of the assets of the probate estate, the personal representative should take prompt action to secure their continued safety. This may include maintaining adequate insurance as well as implementing appropriate security measures such as locks.

2. Opening Estate Accounts

Upon gaining possession of the estate's financial assets, the personal representative is expected to open fiduciary accounts. The accounts should be earmarked as estate funds and not titled solely in the name of the personal representative. For example, the executor should open an account titled "Estate of Doris Haas" with himself as executor on the signature card. Aside from a reasonable amount maintained in cash reserves for ongoing expenses, the funds in the account should be invested to produce income throughout the administration process, and the personal representative must monitor the ongoing welfare of the accounts.

3. Filing Inventory and Appraisal

Shortly after taking possession of the assets of the estate, the personal representative should prepare an **inventory** of the items in the probate estate. The inventory must include a description of all listed assets as well as their fair market value. Assets of substantial value, such as real property, often require a professional **appraisal** in which an expert prepares a report estimating the asset's fair market value. States vary as to when an inventory of the estate should be filed with the probate court, but the usual time falls several months after the personal representative receives Letters. The valuation of assets for probate purposes is generally consistent with valuation of assets for tax purposes. The comparative valuations make the Internal Revenue Code and Regulations (and sources discussing them) useful as to guidance for how to value specific types of assets, including most common financial holdings.

4. Liquidation and Investment of Assets

A personal representative's authority to manage estate assets without court approval varies depending on state law and on whether there is a will that specifically authorizes independent action. The UPC grants a personal representative fairly broad powers of administration, but not all states are as generous. For intestate estates, particularly during formal administration, a personal representative will sometimes need to obtain court approval to sell or buy substantial assets such as real estate, and occasionally less valuable assets as well. Wills often provide a personal representative with more authority, but the default rule of court approval applies to testate estates where a will has not authorized an action and the statute governing executor powers does not authorize the action in question. The personal representative must therefore determine the scope of her authority, under either the will or state law, to buy and sell assets within the estate and seek approval from the probate court for actions exceeding the scope of that authority. Even if the personal representative believes an action is within the scope of authority, it may still be best practice to get court approval if an action is contentious. Liquidation of assets may become necessary to pay creditors or costs of administration, but often assets are retained for the course of the administration, and the personal representative can later distribute those assets in kind to the heirs or beneficiaries.

As mentioned above, the powers and rights of a personal representative will vary significantly by state. That is one reason why, in drafting, it is often best practice to include very broad powers for the executor within the will itself. Compare the broad rights of a personal representative to sell property under the UPC with the restrictions under the Alabama Code:

EXHIBIT 14.5 **Comparing Statutory Powers of a Personal Representative**

UPC SECTION 3-704. PERSONAL REPRESENTATIVE TO PROCEED WITHOUT COURT ORDER; EXCEPTION

A personal representative shall proceed expeditiously with the settlement and distribution of a decedent's estate and, except as otherwise specified or ordered in regard to a supervised personal representative, do so without adjudication, order, or direction of the court, but he may invoke the jurisdiction of the court, in proceedings authorized by this [code], to resolve questions concerning the estate or its administration.

ALA. CODE SECTION 43-2-410—POWER OF SALE CONFERRED

Any part of the personal property of a decedent, including land warrants and choses in action, may be sold only by order of the court, on the written application of the executor or administrator, verified by affidavit, in the following cases, unless, in such cases, power to sell is conferred by the will:

(1) For the payment of debts.
(2) To make distribution among the distributees or legatees.
(3) To prevent the waste or destruction of property liable to waste, or of a perishable nature, if it is proved that the sale would be beneficial to the estate.

5. Periodic Accountings and Partial Settlements

Throughout the administration of the estate, the personal representative should make periodic accountings (at least annually) to the beneficiaries or heirs. Some estate administrations may be concluded within six months to a year, in which case the annual accounting and the final accounting would be the same document, but many estate administrations take one to two years and some take even longer. All accountings are filed with the probate court. The accountings depict which assets have come into the estate, which assets have left the estate (what bills were paid, creditors satisfied, or beneficial distributions made), and the remaining balance. When an estate is clearly solvent, there is the option for **partial settlements**, which means that certain assets may be distributed to the heirs or beneficiaries before the completion of administration. A personal representative should not make a partial settlement until the expiration of the creditors' claim period and only based on a determination that the estate is clearly solvent. A settlement should also not be made that exceeds the balance remaining for beneficial claims after debts (including taxes) are paid. The personal representative needs to retain enough assets in the estate for the final settlement, in which attorneys' fees and personal representative costs are approved; the personal representative can make final distributions to heirs and beneficiaries at that point.

E. MANAGING CREDITORS' CLAIMS AND TAXES

A decedent's beneficiaries and heirs are not the only parties who have a stake in where the money goes—the creditors of the decedent do too. Keep in mind that one of probate's purposes is to vet the claims of creditors and ensure that the decedent's valid debts are paid in the appropriate order of priority. State statutes generally require that creditors bring claims within a specific time frame, usually beginning to run upon death or notice of death and lasting sometimes as little as four to six months. Triggering this short statute of claims generally requires both providing **actual notice**, where the personal representative personally notifies any known creditors in writing of their opportunity to bring a claim against the estate, and **publication notice**, where the personal representative prints notice of the death in a local newspaper to attempt to reach unknown creditors.

1. Publication of Notice to Creditors

A decedent may have creditors of which the personal representative has no knowledge (and could not become aware with reasonable effort). The personal representative must attempt to notify these unknown creditors by publishing notice of the decedent's death, appointment of the personal representative, and the limited nature of the time period in which claims may be presented. Notice should be published in a newspaper in general circulation where the decedent lived, often over the period of several weeks. Some states require newspapers to upload their legal notices to the internet. See, e.g., Ohio Rev. Code 7.10-7.12. Another requirement that some states enforce is the posting of a physical copy at the courthouse. Some probate courts will arrange for publication, and in others, the responsibility falls to the personal representative or her attorney. It is entirely possible these methods will not be effective in reaching many estate creditors. Regardless, it remains a part of the process and may potentially prevent unknown creditors from raising late claims as long as the personal representative complies with the requirements for publication notice under the applicable state statute. For sample notice to creditors forms, see Exhibit 14.6.

EXHIBIT 14.6   **Sample Publication Notices to Unknown Estate Creditors (Ohio/Texas)**

NOTICE OF APPOINTMENT OF FIDUCIARY

On 08/31/2016, in the PROBATE COURT OF NOBLE COUNTY Case No. 20161055, Ruth Annette Reed, 17045 Black Stocking Rd., Caldwell, OH 43724, was appointed as Executor of the estate of Dana H. Reed, deceased, late of 17045 Black Stocking Rd., Caldwell, OH 43724. Creditors are required to file their claims with said fiduciary within 6 months from date of death.

Judge John W. Nau
Attorney William C. Hayes

NOTICE TO CREDITORS
Notice is hereby given that original Letters Testamentary for the Estate of Judith Swayze, Deceased, were issued on August 22, 2018 in Docket No. 18-0724-CP4, pending in the County Court at Law Number Four of Williamson County, Texas, to:
Patrick Dell Swayze
The residence of the Independent Executor is in Leander, Williamson County, Texas, but the post office address for notice is as follows:
c/o AKINS, NOWLIN & PREWITT, L.L.P. 306 N.
Lampasas Street
P. O. Box 249
Round Rock, Texas
78680-0249
All persons having claims against the Estate which is currently being administered are required to present them within the time and in the manner prescribed by law.
DATED the 23 day of August, 2018.
AKINS, NOWLIN & PREWITT, L.L.P.
306 N. Lampasas Street
P. O. Box 249
Round Rock, Texas 78680
(512) 244-0001
FAX: (512) 244-9733
By:/S/ Wesley Prewitt
Wesley Prewitt
State Bar No. 24007872
ATTORNEYS FOR ESTATE

2. Personal Notice to Creditors

While notice by publication will suffice for creditors that are unknown, creditors that the personal representative knows or could reasonably know are entitled to actual notice of the death of the decedent, appointment of personal representative, and limit on time to bring a claim. Known creditors not provided with actual notice may bring a claim even after the statute of limitations has run. See Jones v. Golden, 176 So. 3d 242 (Fla. 2015) (stating that actual notice must be given to known creditor; known creditor not barred without such notice). The personal representative therefore must remain conscientious in discerning the creditors of the estate and providing them actual written notice. Although the time frame during which creditors must respond after receiving notice varies by state, the fact that known creditors are to receive actual notice does not.

Case Preview

Tulsa Professional Collection Services v. Pope

In this case, the United States Supreme Court weighs in on the issue of whether it violates the due process rights of a creditor when a state statute requires only publication notice to creditors and a short statute of limitations in which to make to make a claim against the estate. *Pope* has been extremely influential in shaping the statutes requiring notice to creditors that you see in probate codes today.

As you read the case, consider:

1. What notice is a known creditor of an estate entitled to receive?
2. Why is a known creditor entitled to notice?
3. What are the constitutional restrictions on a state passing a law that limits a creditor's receiving notice of the death of a debtor?

Tulsa Professional Collection Services v. Pope
485 U.S. 478 (1988)

Justice O'CONNOR delivered the opinion of the Court.

This case involves a provision of Oklahoma's probate laws requiring claims "arising upon a contract" generally to be presented to the executor or executrix of the estate within two months of the publication of a notice advising creditors of the commencement of probate proceedings. The question presented is whether this provision of notice solely by publication satisfies the Due Process Clause.

I

Oklahoma's Probate Code requires creditors to file claims against an estate within a specified time period, and generally bars untimely claims. . . . Such "non-claim statutes" are almost universally included in state probate codes. See Uniform Probate Code § 3-801, 8 U.L.A. 351 (1983). Giving creditors a limited time in which to file claims against the estate serves the State's interest in facilitating the administration and expeditious closing of estates. Nonclaim statutes come in two basic forms. Some provide a relatively short time period, generally two to six months, that begins to run after the commencement of probate proceedings. Others call for a longer period, generally one to five years that runs from the decedent's death. Most States include both types of nonclaim statutes in their probate codes, typically providing that if probate proceedings are not commenced and the shorter period therefore never is triggered, then claims nonetheless may be barred by the longer period.

The specific nonclaim statute at issue in this case, Okla. Stat., Tit. 58, § 333 (1981), provides for only a short time period and is best considered in the context of Oklahoma probate proceedings as a whole. . . .

[T]he executor or executrix is required to "give notice to the creditors of the deceased." § 331. Proof of compliance with this requirement must be filed with the court. § 332. This notice is to advise creditors that they must present their claims to the executor or executrix within two months of the date of the first publication. As for the method of notice, the statute requires only publication: "[S]uch notice must be published in some newspaper in [the] county once each week for two (2) consecutive weeks." § 331. A creditor's failure to file a claim within the 2-month period generally bars it forever. § 333. The nonclaim statute does provide certain exceptions, however. If the creditor is out of State, then a claim "may be presented at any time before a decree of distribution is entered." § 333. Mortgages and debts not yet due are also excepted from the 2-month time limit. . . .

II

H. Everett Pope, Jr., was admitted to St. John Medical Center, a hospital in Tulsa, Oklahoma, in November 1978. On April 2, 1979, while still at the hospital, he died testate. His wife, appellee JoAnne Pope, initiated probate proceedings in the District Court of Tulsa County in accordance with the statutory scheme outlined above. The court entered an order setting a hearing. After the hearing the court entered an order admitting the will to probate and, following the designation in the will, named appellee as the executrix of the estate. Letters testamentary were issued, and the court ordered appellee to fulfill her statutory obligation by directing that she "immediately give notice to creditors." Appellee published notice in the Tulsa Daily Legal News for two consecutive weeks beginning July 17, 1979. The notice advised creditors that they must file any claim they had against the estate within two months of the first publication of the notice.

Appellant Tulsa Professional Collection Services, Inc., is a subsidiary of St. John Medical Center and the assignee of a claim for expenses connected with the decedent's long stay at that hospital. Neither appellant, nor its parent company, filed a claim with appellee within the 2-month time period following publication of notice. In October 1983, however, appellant filed an Application for Order Compelling Payment of Expenses of Last Illness. *Id.*, at 28. In making this application, appellant relied on Okla. Stat., Tit. 58, § 594 (1981), which indicates that an executrix "must pay . . . the expenses of the last sickness." Appellant argued that this specific statutory command made compliance with the 2-month deadline for filing claims unnecessary. The District Court of Tulsa County rejected this contention, ruling that even claims pursuant to § 594 fell within the general requirements of the nonclaim statute. Accordingly, the court denied appellant's application.

The District Court's reading of § 594's relationship to the nonclaim statute was affirmed by the Oklahoma Court of Appeals. Appellant then sought rehearing, arguing for the first time that the nonclaim statute's notice provisions violated due process. In a supplemental opinion on rehearing the Court of Appeals rejected the due process claim on the merits.

Appellant next sought review in the Supreme Court of Oklahoma. That court granted certiorari and, after review of both the § 594 and due process issues, affirmed the Court of Appeals' judgment. . . We noted probable jurisdiction, and now reverse and remand.

III

[S]tate action affecting property must generally be accompanied by notification of that action: "An elementary and fundamental requirement of due process in any proceeding which is to be accorded finality is notice reasonably calculated, under all the circumstances, to apprise interested parties of the pendency of the action and afford them an opportunity to present their objections." In the years since *Mullane* the Court has adhered to these principles, balancing the "interest of the State" and "the individual interest sought to be protected by the Fourteenth Amendment." The focus is on the reasonableness of the balance, and, as *Mullane* itself made clear, whether a particular method of notice is reasonable depends on the particular circumstances. . . .

Appellant's interest is an unsecured claim, a cause of action against the estate for an unpaid bill. Little doubt remains that such an intangible interest is property protected by the Fourteenth Amendment. . . . Appellant's claim, therefore, is properly considered a protected property interest.

The Fourteenth Amendment protects this interest, however, only from a deprivation by state action. Private use of state-sanctioned private remedies or procedures does not rise to the level of state action. Nor is the State's involvement in the mere running of a general statute of limitations generally sufficient to implicate due process. But when private parties make use of state procedures with the overt, significant assistance of state officials, state action may be found. The question here is whether the State's involvement with the nonclaim statute is substantial enough to implicate the Due Process Clause.

It is true that nonclaim statutes generally possess some attributes of statutes of limitations. They provide a specific time period within which particular types of claims must be filed and they bar claims presented after expiration of that deadline. Many of the state court decisions upholding nonclaim statutes against due process challenges have relied upon these features and concluded that they are properly viewed as statutes of limitations.

The State's interest in a self-executing statute of limitations is in providing repose for potential defendants and in avoiding stale claims. The State has no role to play beyond enactment of the limitations period. While this enactment obviously is state action, the State's limited involvement in the running of the time period generally falls short of constituting the type of state action required to implicate the protections of the Due Process Clause.

Here, in contrast, there is significant state action. The probate court is intimately involved throughout, and without that involvement the time bar is never activated. The nonclaim statute becomes operative only after probate proceedings have been commenced in state court. The court must appoint the executor or executrix before notice, which triggers the time bar, can be given. Only after this court appointment is made does the statute provide for any notice; § 331 directs the executor or executrix to publish notice "immediately" after appointment. Indeed, in this case, the District Court reinforced the statutory command with an order expressly requiring appellee to "immediately give notice to creditors." The form of the order indicates that such orders are routine. Finally, copies of the notice and an affidavit of publication must be filed with the court. It is only after all of these actions take place that the time period begins to run, and in every one of these actions, the court is intimately involved. This involvement is so pervasive and substantial that it must be considered state action subject to the restrictions of the Fourteenth Amendment.

Where the legal proceedings themselves trigger the time bar, even if those proceedings do not necessarily resolve the claim on its merits, the time bar lacks the self-executing feature that *Short* indicated was necessary to remove any due process problem. Rather, in such circumstances, due process is directly implicated and actual notice generally is required. . . . In sum, the substantial involvement of the probate court throughout the process leaves little doubt that the running of Oklahoma's nonclaim statute is accompanied by sufficient government action to implicate the Due Process Clause.

Nor can there be any doubt that the nonclaim statute may "adversely affect" a protected property interest. In appellant's case, such an adverse effect is all too clear. The entire purpose and effect of the nonclaim statute is to regulate the timeliness of such claims and to forever bar untimely claims, and by virtue of the statute, the probate proceedings themselves have completely extinguished appellant's claim. Thus, it is irrelevant that the notice seeks only to advise creditors that they may become parties rather than that they are parties, for if they do not participate in the probate proceedings, the nonclaim statute terminates their property interests. It is not necessary for a proceeding to directly adjudicate the merits of a claim in order to "adversely affect" that interest. . .

In assessing the propriety of actual notice in this context consideration should be given to the practicalities of the situation and the effect that requiring actual notice may have on important state interests. As the Court noted in *Mullane,* "[c]hance alone brings to the attention of even a local resident an advertisement in small type inserted in the back pages of a newspaper." Creditors, who have a strong interest in maintaining the integrity of their relationship with their debtors, are particularly unlikely to benefit from publication notice. As a class, creditors may not be aware of a debtor's death or of the institution of probate proceedings. Moreover, the executor or executrix will often be, as is the case here, a party with a beneficial interest in the estate. This could diminish an executor's or executrix's inclination to call attention to the potential expiration of a creditor's claim. There is thus a substantial practical need for actual notice in this setting.

At the same time, the State undeniably has a legitimate interest in the expeditious resolution of probate proceedings. Death transforms the decedent's legal relationships and a State could reasonably conclude that swift settlement of estates is so important that it calls for very short time deadlines for filing claims. As noted, the almost uniform practice is to establish such short deadlines, and to provide only publication notice. Providing actual notice to known or reasonably ascertainable creditors, however, is not inconsistent with the goals reflected in nonclaim statutes. Actual notice need not be inefficient or burdensome. We have repeatedly recognized that mail service is an inexpensive and efficient mechanism that is reasonably calculated to provide actual notice. As the Court indicated in *Mennonite,* all that the executor or executrix need do is make "reasonably diligent efforts," to uncover the identities of creditors. For creditors who are not "reasonably ascertainable," publication notice can suffice. Nor is everyone who may conceivably have a claim properly considered a creditor entitled to actual notice. . . .

On balance then, a requirement of actual notice to known or reasonably ascertainable creditors is not so cumbersome as to unduly hinder the dispatch with which probate proceedings are conducted. Notice by mail is already routinely provided at several points in the probate process. . . . Indeed, a few States already provide for actual notice in connection with short nonclaim statutes. We do not believe that requiring adherence to such a standard will be so burdensome or impracticable as to warrant reliance on publication notice alone. . . .

Whether appellant's identity as a creditor was known or reasonably ascertainable by appellee cannot be answered on this record. Neither the Oklahoma Supreme Court nor the Court of Appeals nor the District Court considered the question. Appellee of course was aware that her husband endured a long stay at St. John Medical Center, but it is not clear that this awareness translates into a knowledge of appellant's claim. We therefore must remand the case for further proceedings to determine whether "reasonably diligent efforts," would have identified appellant and uncovered its claim. If appellant's identity was known or "reasonably ascertainable," then termination of appellant's claim without actual notice violated due process.

IV

We hold that Oklahoma's nonclaim statute is not a self-executing statute of limitations. Rather, the statute operates in connection with Oklahoma's probate proceedings to "adversely affect" appellant's property interest. Thus, if appellant's identity as a creditor was known or "reasonably ascertainable," then the Due Process Clause requires that appellant be given "[n]otice by mail or other means as certain to ensure actual notice." *Mennonite, supra,* at 800, 103 S. Ct., at 2712. Accordingly, the judgment of the Oklahoma Supreme Court is reversed and the case is remanded for further proceedings not inconsistent with this opinion.

It is so ordered.

Post-Case Follow-Up

The U.S. Supreme Court's decision in Tulsa Professional Collection Services v. Pope had a predictably powerful impact on probate codes across the country. All states now require actual notice to be served upon known or reasonably ascertainable creditors in order to trigger the short statute of limitations for creditors' claims. Notice is generally given by first-class mail, with return receipt requested to ensure delivery has been made. States also require publication notice, often in a newspaper in circulation in the decedent's domicile, to attempt to notify unknown creditors.

Tulsa Professional Collection Services: Real Life Applications

1. Since reasonably ascertainable creditors are entitled to actual notice before the statute of limitations begins to run against a claim, how does this affect the timeline for when a personal representative should begin to distribute assets to heirs or beneficiaries?

2. From the perspective of businesses who are frequent providers of services on credit to the elderly or ill, how does the law on estate creditor claims affect the way in which a business should keep tabs on customers?

---

3. Responding to and Disputing Claims

Most claims made by creditors against the estate are valid and should be paid by the personal representative promptly upon proper evidence of the debt, provided that the estate is solvent and will have sufficient funds to pay all valid debts. Some claims are unclear or unenforceable. When the personal representative is not confident a creditor's claim should be paid, the personal representative may dispute the claim, and the probate court will determine whether the debt is enforceable or not.

4. The Insolvent Estate

If an estate lacks sufficient funds to pay all valid and enforceable debts against it, the estate is **insolvent**. An insolvent estate operates rather like a bankruptcy, where claims are paid in order of priority and some claims may be paid partially or not at all. States have statutes dictating the pecking order of claims against an insolvent estate which do prioritize funds for legal representation over most other claims. When an estate is insolvent, the beneficiaries or heirs do not receive any beneficial distributions, except to the extent a surviving spouse or dependent children can exercise preferential rights as described in the next section.

F. FAMILY PROTECTION AND POSTMORTEM PLANNING

The topics of family protection and postmortem planning are considered more in depth in Chapter 8, but a brief reminder of the key issues and the role they play in probate administration is flagged in this section.

1. Elective Share

Recall that even if a spouse is deliberately omitted from a will, separate property states almost unanimously provide the surviving spouse with a right to a share in the decedent's estate. A surviving spouse can exercise this right by filing a Petition for an Elective Share (or similar document) with the probate court after the Petition to Probate the Will has been filed. There may be a hearing on the petition if there is controversy as to whether the spouse is entitled to the elective share (if, for example, the right was allegedly waived). The personal representative is responsible for allocating assets to the surviving spouse to fund the elective share. The distribution of the elective share maintains a priority status over other beneficial distributions, but not over creditor claims against the estate.

2. Omitted Spouse and Children

Spouses married after the execution of either party's respective will and children (and sometimes other descendants) omitted from a will may be entitled to a share of the decedent's estate. Before an estate's assets are distributed according to the terms of a will, the personal representative should determine whether the rights of an omitted spouse or child override the distribution pattern set forth in the will.

3. Homestead, Personal Property Set-Aside, and Family Allowance

During probate administration, a surviving spouse may also exercise the protective rights granted by statute to widows or widowers (or often to dependent children of the decedent, if there is no surviving spouse). The homestead allowance varies significantly by state and can protect as much as an unlimited value of a home to a small cash allowance in lieu of a distribution of real property. Likewise, the value of the Personal Property Set-Aside differs among states, but generally allows a set budget to the surviving spouse with regards to certain personal effects of the decedent. The family allowance is often subject to judicial discretion as to value, but it is routinely awarded so that the family may continue paying ongoing expenses while the property is held up in probate administration. The surviving spouse may exercise all three of these rights by filing the relevant forms with the probate court overseeing the estate's administration. All three of these rights maintain priority over the claims of creditors.

Consider the examples of statutory authority for homestead, exempt property, and a family allowance under the UPC (Exhibit 14.7):

EXHIBIT 14.7   **Examples of Statutory Authority for Surviving Family Benefits**

UPC SECTION 2-402. HOMESTEAD ALLOWANCE

A decedent's surviving spouse is entitled to a homestead allowance of [$22,500]. If there is no surviving spouse, each minor child and each dependent child of the decedent is entitled to a homestead allowance amounting to [$22,500] divided by the number of minor and dependent children of the decedent. The homestead allowance is exempt from and has priority over all claims against the estate. Homestead allowance is in addition to any share passing to the surviving spouse or minor or dependent child by the will of the decedent, unless otherwise provided, by intestate succession, or by way of elective share.

UPC SECTION 2-403. EXEMPT PROPERTY

In addition to the homestead allowance, the decedent's surviving spouse is entitled from the estate to a value, not exceeding $15,000 in excess of any security interests therein, in household furniture, automobiles, furnishings, appliances, and personal effects. If there is no surviving spouse, the decedent's children are entitled jointly to the same value. If encumbered chattels are selected and the value in excess of security interests, plus that of other exempt property, is less than $15,000, or if there is not $15,000 worth of exempt property in the estate, the spouse or children are entitled to other assets of the estate, if any, to the extent necessary to make up the $15,000 value. Rights to exempt property and assets needed to make up a deficiency of exempt property have priority over all claims against the estate, but the right to any assets to make up a deficiency of exempt property abates as necessary to permit earlier payment of homestead allowance and family allowance. These rights are in addition to any benefit or share passing to the surviving spouse or children by the decedent's will, unless otherwise provided, by intestate succession, or by way of elective share.

UPC SECTION 2-404. FAMILY ALLOWANCE

(a) In addition to the right to homestead allowance and exempt property, the decedent's surviving spouse and minor children whom the decedent was obligated to support and children who were in fact being supported by the decedent are entitled to a reasonable allowance in money out of the estate for their maintenance during the period of administration, which allowance may not continue for longer than one year if the estate is inadequate to discharge allowed claims. The allowance may be paid as a lump sum or in periodic installments. It is payable to the surviving spouse, if living, for the use of the surviving spouse and minor and dependent children; otherwise to the children, or persons having their care and custody. If a minor child or dependent child is not living with the surviving spouse, the allowance may be made partially to the child or his [or her] guardian or other person having the child's care and custody, and partially to the spouse, as their needs may appear. The family allowance is exempt from and has priority over all claims except the homestead allowance.

(b) The family allowance is not chargeable against any benefit or share passing to the surviving spouse or children by the will of the decedent, unless otherwise provided, by intestate succession, or by way of elective share. The death of any person entitled to family allowance terminates the right to allowances not yet paid.

4. Disclaimer

Before an heir or beneficiary accepts the estate's property, the person should consider whether disclaiming the property would create any personal, tax, or creditor benefits. An heir or beneficiary can disclaim probate property by delivering a simple written document to the personal representative. This must be completed during the time allowed by state statute, which usually ranges between six to twelve months from the date the decedent died. Disclaimer rules vary by state, but several have adopted the Uniform Disclaimer of Property Interests Act. See Glenn M. Karisch, Thomas M. Featherston, Jr. & Julia E. Jonas, *Disclaimers Under the New Texas Uniform Disclaimer of Property Interests Act*, 8 Est. Plan. & Community Property L.J. 179 (2015). For federal tax purposes, disclaimers must be final within nine months of the decedent's death, even if state law permits a longer period. The person disclaiming property cannot accept any benefits from the property before disclaiming. Once the heir or beneficiary takes a benefit, for example cashes the check for a rent payment on a rental property, the gift cannot be disclaimed. The personal representative needs to be attentive to disclaimers as they can change who is entitled to distributions from the estate.

G. NONPROBATE AND TAX MATTERS

The attorney assisting the personal representative in the administration of the estate is often called upon to provide services beyond probate administration. For example, the attorney may deal with a variety of nonprobate assets, such as life insurance, retirement plan benefits, joint tenancy property, financial assets held as transfer-on-death or payable-on-death, and contractual matters. A lawyer may also assist with small business succession issues. Tax matters are usually either handled by the attorney or an outside accountant, depending on the circumstances. All estates are required to file the decedent's final income tax return, nearly all estates will need an estate income tax return, and some estates will also need to file an estate tax return (and perhaps additional transfer tax returns, such as the portability election). For more information on taxes, see Chapter 15.

H. FEES FOR THE ATTORNEY AND PERSONAL REPRESENTATIVE

Both the personal representative (whether executor or administrator) and the attorney are entitled to be compensated for their contributions to the estate administration process. The attorney fees are generally governed by a standard of reasonableness in most states and should be covered in the engagement letter when an attorney agrees to assist in the administration of an estate. State-specific rules may apply, and the standards for collection depend on the attorney's role in the process (for example, a routine estate administration as opposed to probate litigation). See Robert J. Augsburger, *Getting Paid in Probate Court*, 44 St. Mary's L.J. 425 (2013). The fees for personal representatives also differ among states, but commonly are either tied to reasonableness or a percentage of the value of the estate assets, sometimes with a cap. For example, in Florida, a personal representative is entitled to a reasonable fee, and the fee is presumed to be reasonable if it is no more than 3 percent of the first $1 million, 2.5 percent for the amount between $1 million and $5 million, 2 percent for the amount between $5 million and $10 million, and 1.5 percent for any amount over $10 million. See Florida Code 733.612. The personal representative may also receive additional compensation for extraordinary services, such as maintaining an ongoing business or engaging in estate litigation. Id. The norm is for the estate to pay attorney fees periodically throughout the administration process (unless agreed otherwise), while personal representative fees usually await the conclusion of the administration and approval of the fees by the probate court.

Case Preview

Andrews v. Gorby

In the case that follows, an attorney drafted a will for an elderly neighbor that appointed the attorney as executor of the estate. The will included a clause that the executor would be paid according to a bank's standard fee schedule, which resulted in a generous bill for the lawyer's services. The lower court awarded the attorney about a third of the fees he sought for his services as lawyer and executor, and he appealed, seeking payment according to the provisions of the will.

As you read the case, consider:

1. Does it matter that the executor drafted the will? Might the outcome have been different if a lawyer at another firm drafted the document?
2. What is the standard for compensation of a personal representative?
3. What is the standard for compensation of an attorney in an estate administration case?
4. Is it troublesome that the plaintiff is seeking to be compensated as both personal representative and attorney? If one is attempting such dual compensation, what record-keeping practices should be maintained? How is the line drawn between actions an individual is taking as the personal representative and ones she is taking as attorney?

Andrews v. Gorby
237 Conn. 12 (1996)

The following [] issues are raised in this appeal: whether the Probate Court and the Superior Court on appeal therefrom are bound by a testator's direction in his will that the executor of his estate, who drafted the will, be compensated in accordance with a specified fee schedule; and [] whether the attorney for the decedent's estate is required to maintain time records in order to receive compensation for legal services performed for the estate.

The plaintiff, Gordon C. Andrews, is the executor of the estate of the decedent and testator, John Stark Gorby (testator). The plaintiff also acted as the attorney for the estate. The named defendant, John T. Gorby, is the son of the testator and a beneficiary of his estate. In the final account of the estate, the plaintiff sought credit and an allowance in the amount of $45,898.31 as an executor's fee and $28,064 as an attorney's fee. [The lower courts] allowed the plaintiff an executor's fee in the amount of $28,000 and disallowed his request for an attorney's fee.

We reverse [] and order a new trial.

. . .

Although the Superior Court heard evidence for two days and filed a lengthy memorandum of decision, its factual findings were limited to the conclusion that "the requested executor fees of $45,898.31 in the present case *would not be just and reasonable.*" (Emphasis added.) We look to the transcript in order to put these issues within a factual context.

The plaintiff is an attorney admitted to practice in Connecticut. During the period for which he sought compensation, he was employed full-time as general counsel for a corporation in Woodbridge, New Jersey. He also engaged in private practice, providing legal services for friends and neighbors for a fee.

The plaintiff was the testator's neighbor for fourteen years, during which time they formed, according to the plaintiff, a "very close" relationship. The plaintiff first provided legal services to the testator when he probated the estate of the testator's wife when she died in 1986, at which time he also assisted the testator with his duties as executor. The plaintiff charged the testator $1000 for these services. At that time, the testator was eighty years old and had a will in which the plaintiff was not named as either trustee or executor. The plaintiff subsequently prepared a new will and two codicils for the testator. The new will, executed in February, 1987, named the defendant as executor and appointed Union Trust Company as trustee and successor executor. The only direction regarding compensation was that the trustee "shall be entitled to the compensation to which testamentary trustees shall be from time to time entitled under the laws of the State of Connecticut."

The first codicil, executed in October, 1987, named "my good and loyal neighbor," the plaintiff, as both executor and trustee. The defendant was named as successor executor, and the Union Trust Company as successor trustee. It also contained a provision that provided that the "[e]xecutor . . . shall be entitled to compensation in accordance with fees then payable for Estate Settlement services as published by said UNION TRUST COMPANY in its then effective Personal Trust Fee Schedule. . . ." (fee schedule). Under the fee schedule, the executor's fee was to be calculated as a percentage of the estate's valuation for federal estate tax purposes. The second codicil, executed in October, 1988, also named "my good and loyal neighbor," the plaintiff, as both executor and trustee, and further gave the plaintiff the power of appointment to name a successor executor and trustee.

The testator died in March of 1989. His estate was admitted to probate on April 6, 1989, with the plaintiff acting as executor. The estate consisted of a gross estate valued at $748,656 and assets reported for tax purposes of $614,621. At the close of the probate proceedings, the plaintiff submitted an accounting to the Probate Court seeking approval of executor's and attorney's fees, each for approximately $28,000. The defendant objected to the requested fees. In response, the plaintiff raised his fee request for executor fees to the full amount provided for in the fee schedule, or $45,898.31. The Probate Court approved an executor's fee of $28,000, but did not award any attorney's fees. The plaintiff appealed from that decision to the Superior Court.

The plaintiff testified before the Superior Court that he did not believe that he had ever discussed with the testator the magnitude of the executor's fee under the fee schedule or how attorney's fees associated with the probate of the testator's will would be calculated. The plaintiff did not present evidence such as time records or documents showing the nature or extent of his services either as executor or attorney. With respect to his executor's fee claim, the plaintiff testified that he "claimed the full executor's fee pursuant to the Union Trust schedule." He also testified as to the nature and extent of his duties both as executor and as attorney.

A

With respect to the testamentary direction on fiduciary fees, we address the narrow question of whether the Probate Court and the Superior Court on appeal are bound by the direction of the testator in a will prepared by the named executor.

We begin our analysis with the fiduciary relationship between the lawyer who drafts the will and the testator. This relationship falls within the attorney-client sphere, and thus raises the concerns typically found in that area. "The judicial system has a significant interest in regulating attorneys and the attorney-client relationship. . . . In so doing, courts have been mindful that the relationship between an attorney and client must involve personal integrity and responsibility on the part of the lawyer and an equal confidence and trust on the part of the client. . . . The relationship between an attorney and his client is highly fiduciary in its nature and of a very delicate, exacting, and confidential character, requiring a high degree of fidelity and good faith." (Citations omitted; internal quotation marks omitted.)

This fiduciary relationship has always demanded a high degree of scrutiny. For example, we have held with respect to the attorney-client relationship in general that "[p]roof of a fiduciary relationship therefore imposes a twofold burden upon the fiduciary. Once a [fiduciary] relationship is found to exist, the burden of proving fair dealing properly shifts to the fiduciary. . . . Furthermore, the standard of proof for establishing fair dealing is not the ordinary standard of fair preponderance of the evidence, but requires proof . . . by clear and convincing evidence. . . ." (Citations omitted; internal quotation marks omitted.)

The necessity for heightened scrutiny is highlighted by the facts of this case. The eighty-year-old testator and the plaintiff were good friends. The testator and his wife had been married for sixty years and, as the plaintiff testified, the testator "was a very dedicated husband." The defendant characterized the testator as "kind of adrift" after his wife's death. The plaintiff had acted as the attorney for the estate of the testator's wife, and had assisted the testator with his duties as executor, for which services the plaintiff charged $1000. The will and the two codicils, which directed that the plaintiff be named executor and granted him the power of appointment for successor executors and trustees, were drafted by the plaintiff and executed by the testator during the period following his wife's death. While these events may reflect a well placed trust, and even though in this case the plaintiff assumed these fiduciary duties against his wishes at the testator's insistence, the fiduciary relationship is the overriding consideration.

Further, although ostensibly the plaintiff was not a beneficiary under the will, compensation in excess of that which is reasonable is, in the words of the

Superior Court, "the functional equivalent of a bequest to the plaintiff." If the testator had wanted to make such a bequest to his attorney who drafted the will, he would have so provided in the will. Therefore, we conclude that the testator intended to provide a measure of reasonable compensation for the executor, and not a bequest.

We conclude that, as a matter of public policy, an attorney who drafts a will that names the attorney as executor and contains a fee schedule for his compensation as executor is limited to reasonable compensation, irrespective of the schedule. . . . Further, the burden rests on the attorney to prove the reasonableness of the compensation requested by a preponderance of the evidence.

B

The Superior Court made no award of attorney's fees, finding that the Probate Court did not abuse its discretion when it denied attorney's fees because the plaintiff had failed to maintain time records for services provided as an attorney. . . .

Time spent is but one factor in determining the reasonableness of an attorney's fee. Although the better practice is for an attorney for the estate to maintain time records, the failure to do so does not preclude the court from determining and awarding an attorney's fee. . . . The Superior Court should, therefore, have considered whether an attorney's fee should have been awarded and, if so, the reasonable amount of that fee.

III

We conclude in summary: . . . that the Probate Court and the Superior Court on appeal are not bound by the testator's direction in his will that the executor, who drafted the will, be compensated in accordance with a specified schedule but, rather, must order reasonable compensation not to exceed that provided for in the schedule; and. . .that an executor who also acts as the attorney for the estate is not precluded from reasonable attorney's fees solely because he failed to keep time records for his services.

The judgment is reversed and the case is remanded to the Superior Court for a new trial.

Post-Case Follow-Up

Notice that the attorney is entitled to compensation both for his role as executor and for his attorney fees, but that both of these charges must be "reasonable" even if the document is more generous. Keep in mind that although the outcome for the executor-attorney here was (relatively) favorable, there were potential professional responsibility breaches on these facts, and the attorney could be subject to sanctions for drafting a will that provided such a generous fee schedule.

Andrews v. Gorby: Real Life Applications

1. Note the provision in the will that fees will be paid according to a published fee schedule of a financial institution. If you are drafting a document that names the financial institution as fiduciary, should you include such a provision in the will? What if the financial institution the client wants will decline the business if the provision is not included? Do you need to specify that the fee schedule applies only to the bank or its successors, or should it apply to any fiduciary who serves?

2. Gordon Andrews drafted the will that named himself executor of the estate. Consider the excerpt below from the comments following MRPC 1.7 on Conflicts of Interest in the ACTEC Commentaries and draft a policy for your firm concerning when, if ever, attorneys should be named as executors or trustees in estate-planning documents prepared at the firm.

> *Selection of Fiduciaries.* The lawyer advising a client regarding the selection and appointment of a fiduciary should make full disclosure to the client of any benefits that the lawyer may receive as a result of the appointment. In particular, the lawyer should inform the client of any policies or practices known to the lawyer that the fiduciaries under consideration may follow with respect to the employment of the scrivener of an estate planning document as counsel for the fiduciary. The lawyer may also point out that a fiduciary has the right to choose any counsel it wishes. If there is a significant risk that the lawyer's independent professional judgment in the selection of a fiduciary would be materially limited by the lawyer's self interest or any other factor, the lawyer must obtain the client's informed consent, confirmed in writing. If the client is selecting a fiduciary that is affiliated with the lawyer, such as a trust company owned by the lawyer's firm, the lawyer must obtain the client's informed consent, confirmed in writing.

Am. Coll. of Tr. & Est. Couns., ACTEC Commentaries on the Model Rules of Prof'l Conduct (5th ed. 2016).

I. CLOSING THE ESTATE: DISTRIBUTION, FINAL SETTLEMENT, AND DISCHARGE OF THE PERSONAL REPRESENTATIVE

Once the personal representative has paid all the estate's debts as well as set aside sufficient funds for remaining fees, the beneficiaries or heirs receive their assets from the estate. In connection with these terminating distributions, the personal representative will file for final settlement or similar acknowledgement of the full and proper distribution of assets. Upon the court's approval of the final settlement, the personal representative will be discharged from her duties. The final distribution of all assets and release of the personal representative signifies the termination of the estate and the end of the probate process.

1. Distribution

As discussed earlier, the personal representative pays valid debts of solvent estates throughout the administration process and may make partial distributions to heirs or beneficiaries once the creditor claim period has closed and the estate is clearly sufficient to cover expenses. The personal representative may also make distributions throughout the course of administration to satisfy the homestead allowance, exempt property set-aside, or family allowance. At the culmination of the estate administration process, the personal representative distributes all remaining assets in the estate to those entitled to receive them.

If the estate is intestate, the personal representative will distribute the assets among the heirs according to the intestacy statutes in the state in which the decedent was domiciled. If the estate is testate, he will make distributions according to the terms of the will. Recall that rules of abatement, discussed in Chapter 5, determine the priority for distributions to beneficiaries if some assets were liquidated to satisfy debts. Because the personal representative may be personally liable—or may have to make a claim on her bond—if she distributes property to beneficiaries or creditors in the wrong priority, a personal representative should never make distributions until entitlements are clear.

2. Final Settlement

In connection with the final distribution of assets in the estate to heirs or beneficiaries, the personal representative will also complete a final accounting of all actions as fiduciary. This is generally referred to as a final settlement. This filing is similar to a periodic accounting, showing the assets received by the personal representative and paid out to creditors, heirs, or beneficiaries. There may be a court hearing on the final settlement, which gives the interested parties an opportunity to approve or disapprove of the actions the personal representative took during the course of administration. A hearing may, in fact, not be necessary if heirs or beneficiaries consent to the settlement in writing and waive their right to a hearing. If the interested persons do not approve of the personal representative's actions, they could bring a lawsuit based on any uncovered breaches of fiduciary duty, discussed in more detail in Chapter 11. In most cases, the interested parties approve the settlement, pending the court's approval. Upon the court's approval of the final settlement, the personal representative is released from liability for actions appropriately disclosed in the paperwork and approved by the heirs or beneficiaries.

3. Discharge of the Personal Representative

Along with the final settlement paperwork, the personal representative will submit a filing to the probate court to formally terminate his role as personal representative. Once the assets in the estate are distributed, the personal representative has no property to manage, so the role is complete. The discharge of the personal representative represents the formal end of her fiduciary role and is generally accompanied by the court-approved payment of fees for administering the estate. The personal representative does not have authority to act on behalf of the estate once the personal representative has been discharged, so a **special administrator** would need to be appointed by the court later if a reason to reopen the estate arises.

4. The Termination of the Estate

When the assets of the estate have been fully distributed to creditors and heirs or beneficiaries and the personal representative has been discharged from her post by the probate court, the estate terminates. From start to finish, the administration of an estate normally takes at least six months, due to the creditor claim period, but often may take several years, particularly if there is a will contest or complicated tax matters. This chapter, remember, focuses on state probate law concerns, so lawyers handling tax matters for an estate will be completing additional tasks throughout the administration process relating to both state and federal tax filings for the estate or decedent.

The termination of the estate is also often the termination of the attorney-client relationship between the lawyer and the personal representative. The lawyer should complete a closing letter for the client clarifying that representation has ended and a new engagement will be required for legal assistance in other matters.

Chapter Summary

- Probate administration is an extended process that proceeds through specific phases to ensure that all parties benefiting from the estate, from creditors to heirs or beneficiaries, have their interests adequately protected.
- Initial considerations before beginning probate include determining whether there is a valid will (and therefore a testate rather than intestate administration procedure) and assessing whether alternatives to formal probate are appropriate.
- The probate process begins with the appointment of a personal representative, who is the fiduciary of the estate. A will normally nominates an executor, but the administrator of an intestate estate is normally decided by statute and based on family relationship to the decedent. The personal representative files for and is granted Letters Testamentary or Letters of Administration to authenticate the position of authority for the estate.

■ In a testate estate, the personal representative must offer the will for probate by filing a Petition to Probate the Will. The will must be "proved" by showing proper execution of the document or an appropriate self-proving affidavit. The personal representative gives notice to interested parties of the Petition to Probate the Will, which allows plaintiffs to bring a will contest at this point in the process.

■ Throughout the administration of the estate, the personal representative is responsible for managing the assets of the estate. This includes prudent management of estate assets as well as providing an initial inventory of the estate and periodic accountings or partial settlements.

■ The personal representative must manage the obligations of the estate to the creditors of the decedent through providing actual notice to reasonably ascertainable creditors and publishing notice to unknown creditors. Providing notice starts the claims period during which creditors must assert their debt against the estate or be barred from collecting payment. Creditors should be paid only when the claims period has ended, so a personal representative can ensure that the estate is solvent and able to pay all creditors in full.

■ The estate administration process is the time during which the family protection rights discussed earlier in this book come to fruition. Matters such as the elective share, personal property set-aside, homestead exemption, family allowance, and omitted spouses or descendants may affect who receives distributions from the estate.

■ Most attorneys also handle an assortment of nonprobate matters on behalf of their client during the probate process. This may include tasks such as collecting life insurance proceeds, updating deeds held in joint tenancy with right of survivorship, and managing employee benefits. Some attorneys will also handle tax matters for the estate, including the final income tax return of the decedent, annual income tax returns for the estate, and the estate tax return. In other estates, an accountant handles tax matters.

■ Both the personal representative and the attorney are generally entitled to a fee for the services provided during the course of the estate administration. Personal representative fees are sometimes statutory and based on a percentage of the estate. Attorneys' fees are often governed by a "reasonableness" standard. Some states require court approval of attorneys' and/or personal representatives' fees before they can be paid.

■ When it is time to close the estate, the personal representative distributes the property remaining in the estate after creditors are paid to the heirs or beneficiaries. Closing the estate requires the filing of final settlement paperwork that provides an accounting to all interested parties of what assets came into the care of the personal representative and to whom the assets have been distributed. After the interested parties are given the opportunity to review the final settlement, the court officially discharges the personal representative from her duties. The estate administration is complete.

Applying the Concepts

1. Carlotta has died, survived by her husband and two young children. The family would like to avoid probate if possible.

    a. Why might it be beneficial to the family to avoid probate? Why might it be beneficial to pursue probate?

    b. How might the family avoid formal probate if Carlotta has left no real property and her entire probate estate totals $15,000?

    c. Assume instead that Carlotta has died with an estate of significant size. Must all of her assets pass through probate? List typical assets that are considered to be nonprobate assets and explain how they will be distributed outside of the probate process.

2. Haiyan died last month leaving a decades-old will in which she nominated her daughter Ming as personal representative. Ming is overwhelmed and has decided she does not want to act as personal representative of her mother's estate. She requests that Bob, Haiyan's surviving spouse, take over the role as representative, but he declines. She then asks Tamara, her sister. Tamara agrees to replace Ming as personal representative. Can Tamara administer the estate in place of Ming or Bob? What needs to be done in order to change the personal representative of Haiyan's estate?

3. Jeff has brought a claim as a creditor against the estate of Susie. Before Susie's death, she borrowed $100,000 from Jeff so she could buy a nice Jet Ski for her new lake house. Susie died in a Jet Ski accident last summer and her son Liam, whom she had named personal representative, promptly petitioned to probate the will and was appointed as executor. Liam administered Susie's estate and distributed it within six months. Two months after the estate closed, Jeff tries to contact Susie to request overdue payment on the debt and learns of Susie's death. Consider the following:

    a. Jeff produces a promissory note that was signed by both parties and he claims Susie also had a copy. What kind of notice was Jeff entitled to receive from Liam and when?

    b. Due to the lack of notification, Jeff has brought his claim a week after the claims period expired. Can he still assert a claim as a creditor?

    c. Assume that Jeff is still able to assert his claim. Liam is having trouble locating the promissory note that Jeff asserts Susie signed. Despite his constant complaints about lack of payment, Jeff dodges any questions about the note's whereabouts when Liam asks to see his copy of it. Liam is not sure there even is a promissory note. How would you advise Liam about what actions to take with respect to Jeff's claim?

4. Assume you are a probate judge. Maria has been nominated as the executor under a will that has been amended by two codicils. She files with the court her

Petition for Letters Testamentary along with the Petition to Probate the Will, the decedent's death certificate, and the will and both codicils. The will and first codicil have self-proving affidavits, but the second codicil does not have one. What documents should you admit to probate? Should you grant Maria Letters Testamentary?

5. Consider the following scenarios regarding a personal representative's managing of Nia's estate assets and inventory. Evaluate whether the personal representative, Nia's sister Imani, has been properly fulfilling her duty to the estate and whether any of the actions taken raise any potential legal issues.

   a. Imani knows she must first gather all the decedent's assets. She is aware that the house is empty and located in a transitional neighborhood. She receives a call from Nia's neighbor, Alli. Alli offers to live in the house and look after Alli's real and personal property until the estate is closed. Imani agrees.

   b. Imani hears about an investment opportunity from her accountant boyfriend. Apparently, it's a little risky, but she is almost certain that it is a good investment. She has access to the estate's accounts and decides that she will invest the funds.

   c. The estate administration is approaching conclusion and it is time for Imani to submit her accounting records to the court as personal representative. She realizes she has completely forgotten to record anything. Imani quickly types up a timeline of transactions and files it with the court.

   d. Would your consideration of the executor's behavior change if the executor were Great Big National Bank as opposed to a family member? What if Imani were an attorney?

Trusts and Estates in Practice

1. You are an associate at a law firm. You will be handling the estate administration of the recently deceased Yogi. Yogi has left behind his wife Millie and their two young children. Draft a client letter to Millie, who will serve as personal representative of the estate, establishing representation. Remember to address the following points: (i) duties to be performed by counsel; (ii) terms of payment; (iii) consent; and (iv) a list of documents that you will need to administer the estate. Also consider what actions you should take with regard to any non-clients who are also heirs or devisees of Yogi's estate.

2. Refer back to Problem 1. Assume you have been retained as counsel throughout the entirety of the estate's administration and it is now time to close the estate. Compose a closing letter terminating representation. Consider the extent to which a closing letter completing the engagement should refer back to the engagement letter establishing it.

3. Kamiah's wife has recently died and her valid will nominated her sister, Nanea as personal representative; the local probate court granted Letters to Nanea. Kamiah comes to you because he is very concerned about Nanea's competence serving as executor. He is also aware of several creditors that have been waiting to receive payment for weeks now. The estate may not have adequate monetary assets to pay the creditors. He would like to know whether he could have Nanea removed as personal representative because of Nanea's behavior. Assuming the estate is currently unable to pay off its creditors, what options are left? Write a letter to Kamiah answering these questions and give your opinion on what he should do.

4. Léonie has taken some of her mother's jewelry while her estate is still under administration. Because Léonie is the beneficiary entitled to receive the jewelry under the will, she does not understand why she needs to wait to take possession of it. You represent the executor of the estate, who has asked that you write an email message to Léonie explaining the timing of distribution of assets from the estate. Write the message.

5. You are a lawyer representing Nye Doore, personal representative of the estate of his brother, Jason. Judge Rand McNally of the Jefferson County Probate Court of your state has grated Letters Testamentary to Nye on January 4 of this year. Using one of the sample Notice to Creditors forms in Exhibit 14.6, draft a document that Nye can use to publish notice to creditors of the estate.

15

Introduction to Federal Estate and Gift Taxes

The federal estate tax and the federal gift tax are each assessed upon gratuitous transfers of property. These two transfer taxes are "unified" in that they work in connection with each other to ensure that gifts made during life and those made at death share the same rate table and combined amount that can pass free of tax. Additional wealth is freed from tax through the use of deductions and exclusions, including the gift tax annual exclusion, the unlimited marital deduction, and the unlimited charitable deduction. Any gratuitous transfers made during life or at death are potentially subject to tax, but very few taxpayers actually must pay the tax because of the scope of deductions and exclusions.

Although the transfer taxes affect very few people, for individuals or couples with net worth in the eight figures, lawyers need to structure estate plans strategically in order to minimize the application of a tax of 40 percent of the amount not sheltered by deductions or exclusions. Increasingly, estate planning for high-net-worth families includes income tax planning as well as strategies to minimize transfer taxes. These rules come from the Internal Revenue Code (IRC or Code), and all quotes of statutes in this chapter are from the Code unless otherwise noted. Although under current law only the wealthiest taxpayers are affected, historically the amount that could pass tax-free has been much lower. For that reason, the

Key Concepts

- Which transfers and interests in property are subject to the estate and gift tax
- The meaning of a gift for gift tax purposes
- How to shelter transfers from tax through the unified transfer tax credit
- Which lifetime gifts are free from tax due to the annual exclusion
- Which transfers during life or at death are free from tax under the marital deduction or charitable deduction
- How estate-planning techniques can minimize taxes

existence of the federal estate tax over the past century has left a footprint on estate-planning documents already executed that you may come across as you begin your career. A good number of states also have estate or inheritance taxes that use rules that are similar to the federal estate tax, although often with lower exemption amounts. This discussion will lead you through the basics of federal transfer taxation, from gift tax to estate tax, with a brief introduction of the generation-skipping transfer tax, and some basics for planning to minimize tax.

A. THE FEDERAL GIFT TAX

The federal gift tax is a **transfer tax**—an assessment made against the gratuitous transfer of property from one person to another. It is a tax on the transaction, like a sales tax, as opposed to a tax on the property itself. Various exclusions, deductions, and credits make many gifts trigger no tax obligation. As of 2019, the tax rate applied to taxable gifts is 40 percent. In this section, we will discuss what counts as a taxable gift, the annual exclusion from gift tax, and other exclusions and deductions that reduce the tax liability of most people to nothing.

1. Taxable Gifts

The Internal Revenue Code and Regulations set out the definitions of what constitutes a **taxable gift**: a taxable gift is any transfer of property for less than full and adequate consideration. The focus is the gap in value between what the donor parted with and what the donor received in exchange, if anything. Whether the donor intends that the transfer be a gift is entirely irrelevant. Section 2012(b) of the IRC describes a gift as follows:

> (b) Where property is transferred for less than an adequate and full consideration in money or money's worth, then the amount by which the value of the property exceeded the value of the consideration shall be deemed a gift, and shall be included in computing the amount of gifts made during the calendar year. . . .

The definition makes sense when you realize that the gift tax is designed to work together with the estate tax, so the definition of a gift is tied to the amount by which the transfer would lower the value of the estate later subject to tax. Without the gift tax, a person could avoid the estate tax with lifetime gifts, so the estate tax would be unable to generate revenue for the government. While any transfer for which the donor does not receive sufficient consideration is potentially subject to the gift tax, the Code provides many exclusions and exemptions. We set out the most important ones, including the annual exclusion and the unlimited marital and charitable deductions, below.

2. The Annual Exclusion from Gift Tax

Perhaps the most important exclusion from the gift tax is the **annual exclusion** (the amount each taxpayer can give away tax-free each year). IRC § 2503(b) provides that:

> [i]n the case of gifts (other than gifts of future interests in property) made to any person by the donor during the calendar year, the first $10,000 of such gifts to such person shall not, for purposes of subsection (a), be included in the total amount of gifts made during such year.

There is a lot of detail in this compact language. First, note that the annual exclusion is *per year*—every January 1 the taxpayer is alive, the annual exclusion regenerates and the taxpayer starts with the full amount for the year. The annual exclusion is use it or lose it, and amounts from prior years cannot be carried over.

Second, note that the annual exclusion is allowed *per donor*. Each individual is allowed his or her own annual exclusion. A married couple is not treated as one taxpayer, even if they are treated as one taxpayer for federal income tax purposes. (In fact, taxpayers who are married even enjoy an advantage over single taxpayers in that they can split gift tax liability between each other. See IRC § 2513.)

Third, note that the exclusion is allowed *per donee*. Every donor may give the annual exclusion amount to an unlimited number of beneficiaries. There is no cumulative or overall cap. Your client has ten children and thirty grandchildren? Swell—she can give the annual exclusion amount to each of them, each year.

Fourth, note that the excluded gift must be of a *present interest*—in the language of the statute, gifts of "future interests in property" do not qualify. This means your client must structure the gift in a way in which the beneficiary has the immediate right to use and possess the property. The present interest requirement eliminates the ability of most gifts in trust to qualify. Some gifts in trust, however, can qualify for the present interest exclusion if the trust is structured in ways explicitly authorized by the Code or includes certain withdrawal rights for beneficiaries.

Finally, note that the amount excluded each year—$10,000, but indexed for inflation; $15,000 as of 2019—is designed to eliminate the tax on small transfers—but, if used strategically, can eliminate tax on large transfers. Consider how effective the gift tax annual exclusion is in eliminating tax liability in the following case.

 Case Preview

Estate of Maria Cristofani, Deceased, Frank Cristofani, Executor v. Commissioner of Internal Revenue

In the case that follows, Maria Cristofani makes a gift to a trust benefiting her two children and five grandchildren. The children and grandchildren have only a very limited amount of time to withdraw the contribution she has made to the trust, and some of the grandchildren are too young to act without a representative being appointed for them. The court has to address whether this limited right to withdraw the property is enough to create a present interest in property so as to qualify the transfer for the annual exclusion from gift tax. The *Cristofani* case relies on an earlier case, *Crummey v. Commissioner*, which held that a right to withdraw property from a trust was a present interest in property.

As you read the case, consider:

1. What rights to property, specifically, triggered the treatment of the transfers as being covered by the present interest annual exclusion?
2. Must it be realistic that a beneficiary will exercise rights to possess property?
3. What is the cumulative impact on the size of an estate if gifts to multiple beneficiaries can pass gift-tax-free each year?
4. Does the present interest annual exclusion only function to eliminate small-scale transfers and only those where the donor cannot postpone a beneficiary's possession or enjoyment of the property?

Estate of Maria Cristofani, Deceased, Frank Cristofani, Executor v. Commissioner of Internal Revenue
97 T.C. 74 (1991)

RUWE, JUDGE:

Respondent determined a deficiency in petitioner's Federal estate tax in the amount of $49,486. The sole issue for decision is whether transfers of property to a trust, where the beneficiaries possessed the right to withdraw an amount not in excess of the section 2503(b) exclusion within 15 days of such transfers, constitute gifts of a present interest in property within the meaning of section 2503(b).

FINDINGS OF FACT

[The court explains that Maria Cristofani established an irrevocable trust for the benefit of her children (Frank and Lillian) and her five grandchildren. Frank and Lillian each had the right, for the fifteen days following any contribution to the trust, to withdraw an amount equal to the section 2503(b) annual exclusion. Maria's five grandchildren each had the same withdrawal rights. Frank and Lillian were also entitled to mandatory net income and discretionary distributions of principal from the trust during Maria's life.

At Maria's death, the trust was to be divided into shares for each child who survived her by 120 days or died leaving issue who survived her by 120 days. The shares were to be distributed to the surviving children or grandchildren.

Maria conveyed a one-third interest in certain property, valued at $70,000, to the trust in 1984, and another one-third interest in the same property, also valued at $70,000, in 1985. She planned to convey the last third of the property in 1986, but died in December of 1985, so it remained in her estate.

No child or grandchild ever exercised a withdrawal right from the trust, although there was no express agreement that they would not. The IRS permitted the annual exclusion for the two children, but argued it should not be allowed for the five grandchildren, who held only the withdrawal right and a contingent remainder interest (the grandchildren would receive property only if their parent predeceased Maria).]

OPINION

Section 2001(a) imposes a tax on the transfer of the taxable estate of every decedent who is a citizen or resident of the United States. . . . Section 2503(b) provides that the first $10,000 of gifts to any person during a calendar year shall not be included in the total amount of gifts made during such year. A trust beneficiary is considered the donee of a gift in trust for purposes of the annual exclusion under section 2503(b). The section 2503(b) exclusion applies to gifts of present interests in property and does not apply to gifts of future interests in property. The regulations define a future interest to include "reversions, remainders, and other interests or estates, whether vested or contingent, and whether or not supported by a particular interest or estate, which are limited to commence in use, possession or enjoyment at some future date or time." The regulations further provide that "An unrestricted right to the immediate use, possession, or enjoyment of property or the income from property (such as a life estate or term certain) is a present interest in property. An exclusion is allowable with respect to a gift of such an interest (but not in excess of the value of the interest)." Sec. 25.2503-3(b), Gift Tax Regs.

In the instant case, petitioner argues that the right of decedent's grandchildren to withdraw an amount equal to the annual exclusion within 15 days after decedent's contribution of property to the Children's Trust constitutes a gift of a present interest in property, thus qualifying for a $10,000 annual exclusion for each grandchild for the years 1984 and 1985. Petitioner relies upon Crummey v. Commissioner, 397 F.2d 82 (9th Cir. 1968), revg. on this issue T.C. Memo. 1966-144. [The IRS argues that the gift is of a future interest.]

Relying on these powers [to withdraw the contributions], the settlors claimed the section 2503(b) exclusion on transfers of property to the trust for each trust beneficiary. Respondent permitted the settlors to claim the exclusions with respect to the gifts in trust to the beneficiaries who were adults during the years of the additions. However, respondent disallowed exclusions with respect to the gifts in trust to the beneficiaries who were minors during such years. Respondent disallowed the exclusions for the minor beneficiaries on the ground that the minors' powers were not gifts of present interests in property. . . .

In the instant case, respondent has not argued that decedent's grandchildren did not possess a legal right to withdraw corpus from the Children's Trust within 15 days following any contribution, or that such demand could have been legally resisted by the trustees. In fact, the parties have stipulated that "following a contribution to the Children's Trust, each of the grandchildren possessed the SAME RIGHT OF WITHDRAWAL as . . . the withdrawal rights of Frank Cristofani and Lillian Dawson." (Emphasis added.) The legal right of decedent's grandchildren to withdraw specified amounts from the trust corpus within 15 days following any contribution of property constitutes a gift of a present interest. Crummey v. Commissioner, supra.

On brief, respondent attempts to distinguish *Crummey* from the instant case. Respondent argues that in *Crummey* the trust beneficiaries not only possessed an immediate right of withdrawal, but also possessed "substantial, future economic benefits" in the trust corpus and income. Respondent emphasizes that the Children's Trust identified decedent's children as "primary beneficiaries," and that decedent's grandchildren were to be considered as "beneficiaries of secondary importance.". . .

In the instant case, the primary beneficiaries of the Children's Trust were decedent's children. Decedent's grandchildren held contingent remainder interests in the Children's Trust. Decedent's grandchildren's interests vested only in the event that their respective parent (decedent's child) predeceased decedent or failed to survive decedent by more than 120 days. We do not believe, however, that *Crummey* requires that the beneficiaries of a trust must have a vested present interest or vested remainder interest in the trust corpus or income, in order to qualify for the section 2503(b) exclusion.

As discussed in *Crummey*, the likelihood that the beneficiary will actually receive present enjoyment of the property is not the test for determining whether a present interest was received. Rather, we must examine the ability of the beneficiaries, in a legal sense, to exercise their right to withdraw trust corpus, and the trustee's right to legally resist a beneficiary's demand for payment. Crummey v. Commissioner, 397 F.2d at 88. Based upon the language of the trust instrument and stipulations of the parties, we believe that each grandchild possessed the legal right to withdraw trust corpus and that the trustees would be unable to legally resist a grandchild's withdrawal demand. We note that there was no agreement or understanding between decedent, the trustees, and the beneficiaries that the grandchildren would not exercise their withdrawal rights following a contribution to the Children's Trust.

Respondent also argues that since the grandchildren possessed only a contingent remainder interest in the Children's Trust, decedent never intended to benefit her grandchildren. Respondent contends that the only reason decedent gave her grandchildren the right to withdraw trust corpus was to obtain the benefit of the annual exclusion.

We disagree. Based upon the provisions of the Children's Trust, we believe that decedent intended to benefit her grandchildren. Their benefits, as remaindermen, were contingent upon a child of decedent's dying before decedent or failing to survive decedent by more than 120 days. We recognize that at the time decedent executed the Children's Trust, decedent's children were in good health, but this does not remove the possibility that decedent's children could have predeceased decedent.

In addition, decedent's grandchildren possessed the power to withdraw up to an amount equal to the amount allowable for the 2503(b) exclusion. Although decedent's grandchildren never exercised their respective withdrawal rights, this does not vitiate the fact that they had the legal right to do so, within 15 days following a contribution to the Children's Trust. Events might have occurred to prompt decedent's children and grandchildren (through their guardians) to exercise their withdrawal rights. For example, either or both of decedent's children and their respective families might have suddenly and unexpectedly been faced with economic hardship; or, in the event of the insolvency of one of decedent's children, the rights of the grand-children might have been exercised to safeguard their interest in the trust assets from their parents' creditors. In light of the provisions in decedent's trust, we fail to see how respondent can argue that decedent did not intend to benefit her grandchildren.

Finally, the fact that the trust provisions were intended to obtain the benefit of the annual gift tax exclusion does not change the result. . . .

Based upon the foregoing, we find that the grandchildren's right to withdraw an amount not to exceed the section 2503(b) exclusion, represents a present interest for purposes of section 2503(b). Accordingly, petitioner is entitled to claim annual exclusions with respect to decedent's grandchildren as a result of decedent's transfers of property to the Children's Trust in 1984 and 1985.

Decision will be entered for the petitioner.

Post-Case Follow-Up

The IRS has acquiesced in result only with this case, which means that the Service may continue to challenge trusts where a beneficiary has only a withdrawal right and no other substantial interest in the trust. More conservative draft-ing attorneys will ensure that beneficiaries have additional rights, such as discretionary distributions from income or principal, paired with the withdrawal right, and will also give a longer and more realistic window for beneficiaries to make the withdrawal. Still, it is the *right* to immediate possession and enjoyment of the property, and not the possession itself, that characterizes this transfer in trust as a present interest.

Estate of Cristofani: Real Life Applications

1. You represent an unmarried grandfather with an estate worth $17,000,000. He wants to benefit his three children and seven grandchildren. Assuming that the annual gift tax exclusion is $15,000, how could you design a transfer in trust that would remove $1,500,000 from his estate over the course of ten years? Does a $15,000 annual exclusion still seem small when creating estate plans for million-aires?

2. Continuing your representation of the grandfather in the problem above, assume that the grandfather favored certain children and grandchildren over others during his lifetime, and wants one child and three grandchildren to be the primary beneficiaries of his estate. Can you structure a plan to meet the grandfather's personal goals as well as attain tax savings? How do you weigh the relative importance of tax savings with respect to accomplishing overall cli-ent goals?

3. Additional Exclusions and Deductions from Gift Tax

In addition to the annual present interest exclusion, several other exclusions and deductions virtually assure that the vast majority of American taxpayers never encounter the gift tax. To understand how these exclusions and deductions work, let's look at the transfer tax system as a whole first. It is initially important to understand that the estate tax and the gift tax are a **unified transfer tax system**, meaning that they share a rate table and a credit to be used against the payment of taxes on gift and/or estate taxes (the **unified transfer tax credit**). The unified transfer tax credit provides a large enough exclusion that most people never have to pay estate or gift tax.

Under the unified transfer tax system, gifts that would be subject to gift tax or transfers at death that would be subject to estate tax are sheltered by the unified transfer tax credit. IRC § 2010. The unified transfer tax credit is the amount it would take to pay taxes on $11,000,000 (indexed for inflation; $11,400,000 as of 2019). The transfer taxes have a progressive rate structure, meaning that lower values of transfers are subject to lower-percentage-rate taxes (beginning at 18 percent) and higher values of transfers are subject to higher-percentage-rate taxes (topping out at 40 percent). Using the rate tables to calculate the credit, it is $345,800 (which represents the tax on the first $1,000,000 using the progressive rates) plus 40 percent of the amount over $1,000,000. See IRC § 2001 for the rate tables.

In addition to the unified transfer tax credit, there are certain types of transfers that don't count as gifts under the Internal Revenue Code. A parent paying a minor child's support expenses is not a gift, because it is a legal obligation of the parent. A legitimate business transaction, even if there is a disparity between the amount paid and the amount received, is not subject to gift tax—so a good deal on electronics on Black Friday is not a gift from the store to the consumer. Treas. Reg. § 25.2512-8. Gifts paid on behalf of any individual, of any amount, that are medical expenses (paid directly to the provider) or tuition (paid directly to the educational institution), are free from gift tax. IRC § 2503(e). A few other exclusions are also available, so this description serves only as an introduction.

On top of the unified transfer tax credit and various transfers that are free from gift tax, several key deductions can reduce gift tax liability, often to nothing. A **deduction** is an amount the taxpayer may subtract from the **tax base** (the amount that would be subject to tax) before calculating the amount owed. Among the most common deductions is the **marital deduction**—a properly structured transfer to a U.S. citizen spouse is eligible for a deduction unlimited in amount. IRC § 2056. Likewise, under the **charitable deduction**, a properly structured transfer to a qualifying charitable organization is eligible for a deduction unlimited in amount. IRC § 2055. Both the marital deduction and the charitable deduction are discussed later, in connection with the estate tax.

4. Calculating Gift Taxes

Estimating how much gift tax a client will pay is pretty simple: if the exclusion amount is still available to shelter the gift, no tax is owed, and if the exclusion amount (and other deductions and exclusions) are exhausted, the effective tax will be 40 percent of the fair market value of the gift. It is only after the credit amount is exceeded (and other offsetting credits and deductions have run dry) that any gift tax is actually assessed and paid to the IRS. To the extent a taxpayer does not entirely deplete the exclusion amount during life (very common), the balance is available to offset any tax liability under the estate tax.

Calculating exact gift taxes for purposes of the gift tax return can be rather complex, because the cumulative impact of several years of past gifts must be considered and progressive rates, rather than a flat rate, determine what the tentative tax liability would be. First the taxpayer should combine the current year's taxable gifts with all prior years' taxable gifts. Then, the taxpayer assesses the tax on cumulative gifts (using the rate table in Section 2001) and subtracts any gift tax paid on prior gifts, which results in a tentative gift tax owed. Finally, the taxpayer applies the unified transfer tax credit remaining, and any balance due is the tax owed.

When a person makes a taxable gift during life, it triggers the need to file a gift tax return—Form 709—but only rarely results in the actual payment of tax, because the gifts are often sheltered by the credit amount or other exclusions or deductions. Form 709 documents the amount of the gift and any tax owed. See Exhibit 15.1 for the first page of a sample Form 709.

> ### Who Pays the Gift Tax?
>
> Because the gift tax is a transfer tax and it is the donor who initiates the transfer, the donor has primary liability to pay the tax. The tax is not on the receipt of property, but on the transaction of giving it away. This means that the donor, who has just parted with property, may have an additional cost to bear. The recipient is secondarily liable for the tax debt if the donor fails to pay.

EXHIBIT 15.1 Federal Gift Tax Return: Form 709 (First Page)

Form **709**	**United States Gift (and Generation-Skipping Transfer) Tax Return**	OMB No. 1545-0020
Department of the Treasury Internal Revenue Service	► Go to *www.irs.gov/Form709* for instructions and the latest information. (For gifts made during calendar year 2017) ► See instructions.	2017

Part 1—General Information

1	Donor's first name and middle initial	2 Donor's last name	3 Donor's social security number
4	Address (number, street, and apartment number)		5 Legal residence (domicile)
6	City or town, state or province, country, and ZIP or foreign postal code		7 Citizenship (see instructions)

		Yes	No
8	If the donor died during the year, check here ► ☐ and enter date of death _____ , _____		
9	If you extended the time to file this Form 709, check here ► ☐		
10	Enter the total number of donees listed on Schedule A. Count each person only once ►		
11a	Have you (the donor) previously filed a Form 709 (or 709-A) for any other year? If "No," skip line 11b		
b	Has your address changed since you last filed Form 709 (or 709-A)?		
12	**Gifts by husband or wife to third parties.** Do you consent to have the gifts (including generation-skipping transfers) made by you and by your spouse to third parties during the calendar year considered as made one-half by each of you? (see instructions.) (If the answer is "Yes," the following information must be furnished and your spouse must sign the consent shown below. **If the answer is "No," skip lines 13–18.**)		
13	Name of consenting spouse	14 SSN	
15	Were you married to one another during the entire calendar year? (see instructions)		
16	If 15 is "No," check whether ☐ married ☐ divorced or ☐ widowed/deceased, and give date (see instructions) ►		
17	Will a gift tax return for this year be filed by your spouse? (If "Yes," mail both returns in the same envelope.)		
18	**Consent of Spouse.** I consent to have the gifts (and generation-skipping transfers) made by me and by my spouse to third parties during the calendar year considered as made one-half by each of us. We are both aware of the joint and several liability for tax created by the execution of this consent.		

Consenting spouse's signature ►   Date ►

Part 2—Tax Computation

19	Have you applied a DSUE amount received from a predeceased spouse to a gift or gifts reported on this or a previous Form 709? If "Yes," complete Schedule C		
1	Enter the amount from Schedule A, Part 4, line 11	1	
2	Enter the amount from Schedule B, line 3	2	
3	Total taxable gifts. Add lines 1 and 2	3	
4	Tax computed on amount on line 3 (see *Table for Computing Gift Tax* in instructions)	4	
5	Tax computed on amount on line 2 (see *Table for Computing Gift Tax* in instructions)	5	
6	Balance. Subtract line 5 from line 4	6	
7	Applicable credit amount. If donor has DSUE amount from predeceased spouse(s) or Restored Exclusion Amount, enter amount from Schedule C, line 5; otherwise, see instructions	7	
8	Enter the applicable credit against tax allowable for all prior periods (from Sch. B, line 1, col. C)	8	
9	Balance. Subtract line 8 from line 7. Do not enter less than zero	9	
10	Enter 20% (.20) of the amount allowed as a specific exemption for gifts made after September 8, 1976, and before January 1, 1977 (see instructions)	10	
11	Balance. Subtract line 10 from line 9. Do not enter less than zero	11	
12	Applicable credit. Enter the smaller of line 6 or line 11	12	
13	Credit for foreign gift taxes (see instructions)	13	
14	Total credits. Add lines 12 and 13	14	
15	Balance. Subtract line 14 from line 6. Do not enter less than zero	15	
16	Generation-skipping transfer taxes (from Schedule D, Part 3, col. H, Total)	16	
17	Total tax. Add lines 15 and 16	17	
18	Gift and generation-skipping transfer taxes prepaid with extension of time to file	18	
19	If line 18 is less than line 17, enter **balance due** (see instructions)	19	
20	If line 18 is greater than line 17, enter **amount to be refunded**	20	

Attach check or money order here.

Sign Here	Under penalties of perjury, I declare that I have examined this return, including any accompanying schedules and statements, and to the best of my knowledge and belief, it is true, correct, and complete. Declaration of preparer (other than donor) is based on all information of which preparer has any knowledge.	May the IRS discuss this return with the preparer shown below (see instructions)? ☐ Yes ☐ No
	► Signature of donor Date	

Paid Preparer Use Only	Print/Type preparer's name	Preparer's signature	Date	Check ☐ if self-employed	PTIN
	Firm's name ►			Firm's EIN ►	
	Firm's address ►			Phone no.	

For Disclosure, Privacy Act, and Paperwork Reduction Act Notice, see the instructions for this form.   Cat. No. 16783M   Form **709** (2017)

B. THE FEDERAL ESTATE TAX

The federal estate tax works in connection with the gift tax to cover gratuitous transfers effective upon death. The reach of the estate tax is quite broad, including not only probate transfers but a wide variety of other interests in property as well. Like the gift tax, the taxpayer's ultimate liability is significantly reduced by the use of deductions and credits. The estate tax owed is reported on Form 706, due nine months after death, although a filing extension for six months is routinely granted. See Exhibit 15.2 for a sample of the first page of Form 706.

EXHIBIT 15.2 Federal Estate Tax Return: Form 706 (First Page)

Form **706**
(Rev. August 2017)
Department of the Treasury
Internal Revenue Service

United States Estate (and Generation-Skipping Transfer) Tax Return

▶ Estate of a citizen or resident of the United States (see instructions). To be filed for decedents dying after December 31, 2016.
▶ Go to *www.irs.gov/Form706* for instructions and the latest information.

OMB No. 1545-0015

Part 1—Decedent and Executor

1a Decedent's first name and middle initial (and maiden name, if any)	**1b** Decedent's last name
	2 Decedent's social security no.
3a City, town, or post office; county; state or province; country; and ZIP or foreign postal code.	**3b** Year domicile established **4** Date of birth **5** Date of death
	6b Executor's address (number and street including apartment or suite no.; city, town, or post office; state or province; country; and ZIP or foreign postal code) and phone no.
6a Name of executor (see instructions)	
6c Executor's social security number (see instructions)	
	Phone no.

6d If there are multiple executors, check here ☐ and attach a list showing the names, addresses, telephone numbers, and SSNs of the additional executors.

7a Name and location of court where will was probated or estate administered   **7b** Case number

8 If decedent died testate, check here ▶ ☐ and attach a certified copy of the will.   **9** If you extended the time to file this Form 706, check here ▶ ☐

10 If Schedule R-1 is attached, check here ▶ ☐   **11** If you are estimating the value of assets included in the gross estate on line 1 pursuant to the special rule of Reg. section 20.2010-2(a)(7)(ii), check here ▶ ☐

Part 2—Tax Computation

1	Total gross estate less exclusion (from Part 5—Recapitulation, item 13)	**1**	
2	Tentative total allowable deductions (from Part 5—Recapitulation, item 24)	**2**	
3a	Tentative taxable estate (subtract line 2 from line 1)	**3a**	
b	State death tax deduction	**3b**	
c	Taxable estate (subtract line 3b from line 3a)	**3c**	
4	Adjusted taxable gifts (see instructions)	**4**	
5	Add lines 3c and 4	**5**	
6	Tentative tax on the amount on line 5 from Table A in the instructions	**6**	
7	Total gift tax paid or payable (see instructions)	**7**	
8	Gross estate tax (subtract line 7 from line 6)	**8**	
9a	Basic exclusion amount **9a**		
b	Deceased spousal unused exclusion (DSUE) amount from predeceased spouse(s), if any (from Section D, Part 6—Portability of Deceased Spousal Unused Exclusion). **9b**		
c	Restored exclusion amount (see instructions) **9c**		
d	Applicable exclusion amount (add lines 9a, 9b, and 9c) **9d**		
e	Applicable credit amount (tentative tax on the amount in 9d from table A in the instructions) **9e**		
10	Adjustment to applicable credit amount (May not exceed $6,000. See instructions.) **10**		
11	Allowable applicable credit amount (subtract line 10 from line 9e)	**11**	
12	Subtract line 11 from line 8 (but do not enter less than zero)	**12**	
13	Credit for foreign death taxes (from Schedule P). (Attach Form(s) 706-CE.) **13**		
14	Credit for tax on prior transfers (from Schedule Q) **14**		
15	Total credits (add lines 13 and 14)	**15**	
16	Net estate tax (subtract line 15 from line 12)	**16**	
17	Generation-skipping transfer (GST) taxes payable (from Schedule R, Part 2, line 10)	**17**	
18	Total transfer taxes (add lines 16 and 17)	**18**	
19	Prior payments (explain in an attached statement)	**19**	
20	Balance due (or overpayment) (subtract line 19 from line 18)	**20**	

Under penalties of perjury, I declare that I have examined this return, including accompanying schedules and statements, and to the best of my knowledge and belief, it is true, correct, and complete. Declaration of preparer other than the executor is based on all information of which preparer has any knowledge.

Sign Here	▶ Signature of executor	Date
	▶ Signature of executor	Date

Paid Preparer Use Only	Print/Type preparer's name	Preparer's signature	Date	Check ☐ if self-employed	PTIN
	Firm's name ▶			Firm's EIN ▶	
	Firm's address ▶			Phone no.	

For Privacy Act and Paperwork Reduction Act Notice, see instructions.   Cat. No. 20548R   Form **706** (Rev. 8-2017)

In this section, we will first introduce the wide variety of gratuitous transfers included in the base subject to estate tax. We will then discuss the unified transfer tax credit that shelters a generous budget of transfers, meaning that only multimillionaires ultimately wind up paying estate tax. We discuss the marital deduction and portability, which generally result in tax being owed, if ever, only upon the death of the surviving spouse of a marriage. We will mention the charitable deduction and a handful of other deductions that can further reduce estate tax liability. Finally, we will explain the basic mechanics of calculating the estate tax a client may owe.

1. Transfers Included in the Estate Tax Base

The first step in determining a decedent's estate tax liability is to determine what assets make up the gross estate—the initial base against which the tax will be assessed (later suitable deductions will be allowed). A wide range of interests in property held by the decedent make up the gross estate. Although there are exceptions, as a general rule, if the decedent had a hand in or a hand on—if the decedent benefited from the property roughly until death or controlled the right to determine who would get that property—one of the tax code provisions will reach the property.

A substantial variety of interests in property will be subject to inclusion in the gross estate. Of course, part of the fun of estate planning is finding the exceptions. For now, let's start with what is included:

- § 2033 Property owned at death
- § 2034 Dower or curtesy
- § 2035 Certain transfers within 3 years of death
- § 2036 Transfers with retained life estate or retained controls
- § 2037 Transfers taking effect at death (reversions)
- § 2038 Revocable transfers
- § 2039 Annuities and death benefits
- § 2040 Property passing by right of survivorship
- § 2041 Property over which decedent had a general power of appointment
- § 2042 Life insurance
- § 2043 Transfers for a partial consideration
- § 2044 Transfers for which a QTIP was previously allowed

The first and most obvious type of property that is subject to inclusion in the gross estate is probate property. Any property the decedent could control the conveyance of by will or that would pass by intestacy is included in the gross estate under Section 2033. Note that this is the first of eleven code sections on inclusion, which tells you that many nonprobate transfers are subject to the estate tax base as well.

Section 2034 refers in its title to dower and curtesy, but what this code section does is include in the gross estate property that is passing to the surviving spouse through means of an elective share statute or similar right. This inclusion will have an offsetting marital deduction, so won't result in any tax liability.

Section 2035 brings in certain gratuitous transfers made within three years of death. This limits the ability of a client to purge assets from the estate shortly before death and avoid estate tax on them. The same code section brings in gift tax paid within three years of death, to avoid the technique of making death-bed transfers to lower the value subject to estate tax.

Section 2036 brings in property where the decedent made a transfer during life, but retained the right to use and enjoy the property herself—or to pick who does—until death (or for a period tied to death). For example, if O from your first-year property class conveyed Blackacre to O for life and then to A, poor O is subject to estate tax on the entire value of Blackacre. Likewise, if O put Blackacre in trust and retained the right to determine whether A or B would receive it at his death, the property is included. Limiting rights and discretions may grant decedents reprieve from this rule.

Section 2037 brings back into the gross estate certain reversionary interests in property. Suppose a transfer is structured so that: (1) the transferor gives an interest in property to a transferee, who can only receive that property by surviving a third party; (2) if the transferee does not survive that third party, then the donor gets it back; and (3) the probability of that happening is 5 percent or greater. If so, then the property interest remains in the gross estate. Right, it doesn't happen all that often.

Section 2038 brings in all revocable transfers. This includes all revocable trusts. Revocable trusts have many roles in estate planning, but avoidance of estate tax is not one of them. The estate tax reaches a transfer the decedent makes where she retains the right to alter, amend, revoke, or terminate that interest. Again, some exceptions apply.

Section 2039 brings in certain annuities and death benefits. The most common type of asset reached here is retirement plan benefits. Because defined contribution retirement plans generally make payments to the employee throughout retirement and, upon the employee's death, distribute the balance to a beneficiary the employee selected, these assets are subject to the estate tax.

Section 2040 includes in the gross estate joint tenancies. This section includes joint tenancies in real estate as well as other assets, such as bank accounts. Where the joint tenancy is between spouses, such as in a tenancy by the entirety, half of the property is included in the gross estate. Where the joint tenancy is between individuals other than spouses, the proportion of the asset that does not represent the survivor's contribution is included.

Section 2041 brings in property over which the decedent held (or in some cases exercised or released) a general power of appointment. A power of appointment is the right to determine who receives property that is not one's own. A power of appointment is general if that right can be exercised in favor of one's self, one's creditors, one's estate, or a creditor of one's estate.

Section 2042 brings into the gross estate life insurance—under certain circumstances. Life insurance proceeds are includable in the gross estate if they are payable to the estate or if the decedent retained "incidents of ownership" over the policy—things like the right to benefit economically from the policy, the right to change the beneficiary designation, and other powers. If the estate is not the beneficiary and the decedent retained no problematic rights, the insurance proceeds are not included.

Section 2043 applies to part-bequests, part-sales. Not surprisingly, the portion of the transfer that is gratuitous is subject to tax, and the part that represents a sale for fair market value is not (but remember that those proceeds will be included as an asset of the gross estate).

Section 2044 brings into the gross estate property for which a qualified terminable interest property (QTIP) election has been made. This means that the property was transferred in a manner designed to qualify for the marital deduction at the death of the first spouse to die, and the remaining balance will be included at the death of the surviving spouse. The QTIP election is explored in more detail in the *Clancy* case later in this chapter.

As the discussion above shows, many interests in property are subject to estate tax. Even interests in property that are not currently in the decedent's possession at death may be subject to tax. Consider how broad the reach of the gross estate is in the following case.

Case Preview	***Estate of Russell Badgett, Jr., Deceased, Bentley Badgett, Jr., Executor v. Commissioner of Internal Revenue***

In the case that follows, a taxpayer was owed an income tax refund but had not received it as of the time of his death. The question arose as to whether the expected refund ought to be subject to estate tax, given that the taxpayer did not possess it at death.

As you read the case, consider:

1. What is the basis for including the income tax refund owed to the decedent in the gross estate?
2. Did the decedent have any use or enjoyment of the refund proceeds during life?
3. Did the decedent have the ability to transfer the refund proceeds once he (or his estate) did receive them?

Estate of Russell Badgett, Jr., Deceased, Bentley Badgett, Jr., Executor v. Commissioner of Internal Revenue
T.C. Memo. 2015-226

JACOBS, Judge:

The issue for decision is whether Federal income tax refunds for 2011 and 2012 due Russell Badgett, Jr. (decedent), at the time of his death are includible in the value of his gross estate. Respondent (Internal Revenue Service or IRS) claims they are and thus determined an estate tax deficiency of $146,454; decedent's estate (estate) claims they are not.

BACKGROUND

The stipulation of facts and the exhibits attached thereto are incorporated herein by this reference.

Decedent died on March 8, 2012.... On May 1, 2012, a Form 1040, U.S. Individual Income Tax Return, for 2011 was filed for decedent reflecting . . . an overpayment of $429,315. . . . The IRS applied the $25,000 estimated tax payment to decedent's 2012 Federal income tax on April 15, 2012, and refunded $404,315 to the estate on May 28, 2012.

On December 13, 2012, the estate filed a Form 706, United States Estate (and Generation Skipping Transfer) Tax Return. The 2011 Federal income tax refund due decedent was not included in the value of the gross estate.

On April 15, 2013, a Form 1040 for 2012 was filed for decedent reflecting total tax of $10,874, total payments of $25,000, and an overpayment of $14,126. On May 13, 2013, the IRS issued a refund of $14,126 to the estate. The $14,126 refund for 2012 was not included in the value of decedent's gross estate as reflected on the Form 706.

On January 6, 2015, the IRS mailed a notice of deficiency to the executor of the estate determining a deficiency in estate tax; the entire amount of the deficiency is the result of the estate's not including the amounts of the 2011 and 2012 Federal income tax refunds in the value of decedent's gross estate.

DISCUSSION

Section 2031(a) provides that "[t]he value of the gross estate of the decedent shall be determined by including to the extent provided for in this part, the value at the time of his death of all property, real or personal, tangible or intangible, wherever situated." Section 2033 provides that "[t]he value of the gross estate shall include the value of all property to the extent of the interest therein of the decedent at the time of his death."

To determine a decedent's interest in property, we first look to State law:

State law creates legal interests and rights. The federal revenue acts designate what interests or rights, so created, shall be taxed. Our duty is to ascertain the meaning of the words used to specify the thing taxed. If it is found in a given case that an interest or right created by local law was the object intended to be taxed, the federal law must prevail no matter what name is given to the interest or right by state law. . . .

The estate asserts that under Kentucky law, property must be in existence on the tax assessment date to be subject to tax and cannot be a mere possibility or expectancy.

The estate acknowledges that decedent overpaid his 2011 and 2012 income tax but posits that an "overpayment" does not create a right to an income tax refund. The estate argues that there is no property interest until the refund has been declared by the Government. Continuing, the estate postulates that even if decedent had an expectancy to receive the income tax refunds, "under Kentucky state law, a mere expectancy is not the same as an interest in property." The estate cites a number of cases to support its position, but these cases are distinguishable from the case before us. . . .

[T]he IRS has discretion in determining whether overpayments should be refunded to the taxpayer or applied to outstanding tax (or other) liabilities of the taxpayer. Because there was no guarantee that the IRS would refund the full amounts of the overpayments to the taxpayers, we, in *Estate of Bender,* and the bankruptcy court, in *In re Pigott,* concluded that the overpayments could not be treated as taxpayer property.

However, we reached a different conclusion in another case where a deceased taxpayer had no tax liabilities to which a tax overpayment could be offset. In *Estate of Chisolm v. Commissioner,* 26 T.C. 253 (1956), the taxpayer died before his Federal income tax return was filed. We determined therein that the full value of the deceased taxpayer's viable but unasserted income tax refund claim was an asset of the estate, stating:

The entire taxes on the income of Harvey [the deceased taxpayer] and his wife for 1950, as disclosed on the return filed for that year, were paid by Harvey. He was dead at the time the return was filed and of course did not join in filing it. However, the type of return that was filed for that period is immaterial as is the crediting of the overpayment as requested on that return. The fact is that Harvey had overpaid not only his own taxes but those of himself and his wife. The resulting overpayment was really his. It was valuable property and a part of his estate at the time he died. It was includible in his estate under section 811(a) [a precursor to the current section 2033], and incidently would have been includible in his estate even if it represented jointly held property since he had supplied the entire consideration therefor. . . .

Id. at 257; *see Estate of Swezey v. Commissioner,* T.C. Memo. 1976-361 (Federal and State tax refunds for year of decedent's death were includible in value of decedent's gross estate); *Estate of Law v. Commissioner,* T.C. Memo. 1964-257 (Federal tax refund received by decedent's widow was includible in value of decedent's gross estate even though decedent died before tax return was filed).

We believe it proper to herein follow the holdings in these cases. Simply stated, if no offsetting liability exists, section 6402(a) is clear: The statute mandates that the IRS "shall" refund any balance to the taxpayer. In the matter herein, there is no indication that decedent was subject to any liability or obligation against which the IRS could offset his overpayments. The status of the tax refund is more than a mere expectancy; the estate has the right to compel the IRS to issue a refund for the years for which decedent overpaid his tax. Thus, we hold that the overpayments in question attained the status of independent assets for estate tax purposes; they constitute decedent's property for estate tax purposes.

The estate maintains that *Estate of Chisolm* and its progeny are not herein applicable because the "[d]ecedent [in *Chisolm*] knew before he died he was entitled to an income tax refund". But the facts in *Estate of Chisolm* do not support that conclusion. The facts in *Estate of Chisolm* merely state that the decedent overpaid his tax, and the Court concluded that the overpayment constituted valuable property that was includible in the value of the decedent's gross estate.

The estate also argues that "a taxpayer has 'no legal right' to a tax refund unless and until the taxpayer files a successful suit within the permitted statutory periods against the IRS for that tax refund after meeting all conditions precedent." *See, e.g., Commissioner v. Lundy,* 516 U.S. 235, 237 (1996) (Tax Court lacks jurisdiction to award refund of tax paid more than two years prior to date on which Commissioner mailed taxpayer notice of deficiency in a case where taxpayer failed to file return); *Hampton v. United States,* 513 F.2d 1234, 1243 (Ct. Cl.1975) (filing claim for refund is condition precedent to maintenance of any suit for recovery of wrongfully assessed tax); *Bank of Cal., Nat'l Ass'n v. Commissioner,* 133 F.2d 428 (9th Cir. 1943) (decedent's claim for refund was property and includible in the value of her gross estate). *Ebert v. United States,* 66 Fed. Cl. 287, 290 (2005) (taxpayer bears burden of establishing she is entitled to refund and exact amount thereof). These cases do not support the estate's contention. Rather, they merely discuss the requirements imposed on a taxpayer of prosecuting a tax refund action.

We therefore hold that decedent had property interests in the values of his 2011 and 2012 Federal income tax refunds and consequently the refunds are included in the value of decedent's gross estate for Federal estate tax purposes. . . .

Decision will be entered for respondent.

Post-Case Follow-Up	Note that the fact that the taxpayer never had possession or enjoyment of the amount he was owed by the IRS was no bar to including it in his gross estate. The fact that he had the right to receive it was enough. The question of to what extent contingent rights to receive property should be included in a gross estates raises a valuation issue that is better left to more advanced classes.

Estate of Russell Badgett, Jr.: Real Life Applications

1. You represent a sole proprietor business owner who often sells on credit. Are the amounts receivable included in the gross estate? Could you argue that their fair market value ought to be less than face value due to possibility of nonpayment? Is a business debt different from a tax refund in the likelihood the payor will default?

2. Under *Badgett,* the income tax refund is clearly includable in the gross estate. Does this mean it is an asset that Badgett could convey through his will or otherwise through his estate plan? How can a client convey an asset at death that he does not yet have?

As the discussion above details, the estate tax casts a wide net in defining assets that are includable in the gross estate and potentially subject to tax. Fortunately for the taxpayer, there are a variety of deductions and exemptions that are taken into account before calculating actual estate tax liability.

2. The Unified Transfer Tax Credit and the $11 Million Exemption

As discussed in the section on gift taxes, under the unified transfer tax system, gifts that would be subject to gift tax or transfers at death that would be subject to estate tax are sheltered by the unified transfer tax credit. IRC § 2010. The unified transfer tax credit is the amount it would take to pay taxes on roughly $11,000,000 worth of transfers, indexed for inflation. The full amount of the credit will be available at death if all gifts were covered by other exclusions or deductions, but if the decedent generated taxable gifts during life, those gifts will eat into the exemption amount.

The transfer tax credit is taken into account at the end of the estate tax calculation. It is large enough to wipe out any tax liability for the vast majority of estates. Larger estates are better served by combining the power of the unified transfer tax credit with various other deductions designed to delay or eliminate tax liability.

3. The Marital Deduction and Portability

One of the most important and commonly used deductions is the marital deduction of Section 2056. Under this section, a properly designed transfer to a surviving spouse is free from tax at the death of the first spouse to die. The property is included in the gross estate, but then subtracted from the tax base because of the marital deduction.

A variety of transfers qualify for the marital deduction, but they must be carefully structured to comply with the requirements of tax law. Outright transfers to a U.S. citizen spouse always qualify, but only certain transfers in trust or partial interest transfers qualify. Generally, if the transfer is a "terminable interest," creating a risk that the spouse will not receive the property, the deduction is not permitted. However, interests in trust that are structured as "qualified terminable interest property" (or "QTIP") do qualify, because the balance of the property remaining in the trust will be subject to tax at the death of the second spouse to die. Certain other structures of marital trusts will qualify for the deduction as well. Special rules apply for the marital deduction when a spouse is not a United States citizen.

Because the marital deduction is unlimited in amount, it is possible to reduce the estate tax to zero at the death of the first spouse by sheltering part of the estate with the unified transfer tax credit and the balance with the marital deduction (and other deductions). More on this technique is covered in the estate-planning techniques section near the end of this chapter.

Another benefit that spouses have under the estate tax is portability. Portability is the right of a surviving spouse to elect to make use of a decedent spouse's unused exclusion amount (called the DSUE—deceased spouse's unused exclusion). Unfortunately, this right applies only to an individual's most recently deceased spouse, so later marriages can foil the use of a spouse's exclusion amount. For example, if Sven survives his wife Daisy, then finds love again and marries Parker, Sven can use Daisy's exclusion amount only if he dies before Parker (if Sven survives Parker, Parker becomes Sven's most recently deceased spouse). Still, portability takes some pressure off the use-it-or-lose-it nature of the unified transfer tax credit. Only a surviving spouse can benefit from portability—no other family members have this entitlement.

4. The Charitable Deduction and Other Deductions

In addition to the unlimited marital deduction, the estate tax system also offers various other important deductions. A taxpayer receives an unlimited charitable deduction under § 2055. While the deduction is unlimited in amount, there are restrictions in the way it must be structured. First, the transfer must be to a qualified organization, such as a tax-exempt charity. Second, it also must be structured in a "qualified" manner. Outright bequests qualify, but there are limitations as to when partial interests or interests in trust qualify. Certain other transfers qualify under this code section too. More on this topic is discussed in connection with estate-planning techniques at the end of the chapter.

Aside from the marital and charitable deductions, the most critical deduction is the Section 2053 deduction for debts and expenses. This deduction ensures that property that passes to pay bills, such as debts of the estate and costs of administration, is not taxed as if it were a gratuitous transfer. Attorney fees are included in this deduction as well. A handful of other deductions, which arise less frequently, may also reduce overall tax liability.

5. Calculating Estate Taxes

To calculate the taxes owed on an estate, a lawyer must take into account both gift taxes and estate taxes, because it is a unified system. The first step of the process is to determine which assets constitute the gross estate. As discussed earlier, this includes a wide range of interests in property where the decedent either used or enjoyed the property or had the ability to control ownership of it.

After the lawyer has determined which assets are included in the gross estate and at what value, the next step is subtracting any allowable deductions. A married decedent often makes transfers to the spouse that qualify for the marital deduction. Transfers to charities can qualify for the charitable deduction. Debts of the estate and costs of administration may be subtracted here as well. The lawyer should also determine whether any other deductions may apply and subtract them. Subtracting the allowable deductions from the gross estate leaves the balance as the taxable estate.

To the taxable estate, the lawyer must add in adjusted taxable gifts made during the taxpayer's lifetime. Gifts are taken into account, even if tax has already been paid on them, to unify the system and ensure a full run-up of the progressive rate structure. The sum of the taxable estate and the adjusted taxable gifts is the estate tax base.

Once the lawyer has calculated the estate tax base, the next step is applying the rate tables in Section 2001 to calculate the tentative tax owed. The rate table is progressive, meaning that lower amounts are taxed at lower rates. Fortunately, the table includes the effect of the progressive rates, so calculating the actual amount becomes a matter of adding a set dollar amount to a percentage of the amount the balance exceeds the rate threshold. Under 2019 law, that means adding $345,800 to 40 percent of the amount the estate exceeds $1,000,000.

After calculating the tentative tax, the lawyer applies any credits for which the estate qualifies. The most common and valuable is the unified transfer tax credit. For most estates, this will reduce the tax owed to nothing. The balance remaining after subtracting the credits is the amount owed.

C. THE GENERATION-SKIPPING TRANSFER TAX

In addition to the federal estate and gift tax, a third type of tax, called the **generation-skipping transfer tax** or GST tax, applies to a gratuitous transfer that skips over a generation (such as from grandparent to grandchild). A **generation-skipping transfer**, in simple terms, is one that is made from an individual in an older generation to one who is at least two generations younger. In more technical terms, it is a transfer to a **skip person**, which means someone who bears a certain familial relationship to the donor (grandchild, grand-niece, etc.) or who is unrelated and more than 37.5 years younger than the donor.

The GST tax was designed to ensure that very wealthy families could not avoid the reach of the estate tax at the death of each generation merely by transferring wealth to much younger generations. For example, if Daddy Bigbucks transfers his estate to Annie, and she transfers her estate to her children, the estate is taxed twice—once at Daddy's death and once at Annie's. If instead Daddy passes the entire estate to Annie's daughter (let's say she is named Sandy), no tax is imposed at Annie's death. The GST tax is designed to thwart this planning technique.

1. Forms of Generation-Skipping Transfers

Generation-skipping transfers can come in one of three forms: a **direct skip**, a **taxable distribution**, or a **taxable termination**. IRC § 2612. A direct skip is a transfer that is subject to the gift tax or estate tax and that is made to a skip person. Certain transfers in trust may also count as gifts to a skip person and therefore be treated as a direct skip. A taxable termination occurs at the end of an interest in property held in trust if after the termination only skip persons have interests in the trust. A taxable distribution is a distribution from a trust to a skip person, if the transfer is not otherwise a direct skip or taxable termination. All three types of generation-skipping transfers can subject the donor to GST tax.

2. Exemptions, Deductions, and Exclusions from the GST Tax

Fortunately, as is the case for the gift and estate tax, there are multiple exemptions, deductions, and exclusions that mean that very few people ever pay the GST tax. First, there is the lifetime credit, which is the same amount as the unified transfer tax credit for estate and gift tax. The GST tax credit functions a little differently than the unified transfer tax credit, though, because donors may choose when to use their GST tax credit rather than chipping away at their budget automatically. The exemptions discussed earlier for gift and estate tax—like the annual exclusion and the exclusion for directly paid tuition and medical expenses—also apply to generation-skipping transfers.

3. Calculating the GST Tax

The generation-skipping transfer tax applies at the highest estate and gift tax rate in effect at the time of the transfer (currently 40 percent). IRC § 2641. Calculating the GST tax is a little different, however, because a donor may choose to save all or part of his exclusion from GST tax. Therefore, it is possible to have a transfer that is partially excluded from GST tax and partially taxable. To calculate the tax on these hybrid transfers, one must use the inclusion ratio, which is the proportion of the transfer that is taxable (calculated by using the value of the transfer as the denominator and the amount of GST tax exemption allocated to the transfer as the numerator). For example, if Grandma made a transfer of $2,000,000 to D'Shawn and allocated $1,000,000 of her exemption to the transfer, the inclusion ratio would be one-half, making the effective tax rate half of 40 percent or 20 percent (to be applied to the $2,000,000 transfer). In the gift and estate tax, the exemption is automatically allocated as soon as a taxpayer makes a gratuitous transfer, but in the GST tax, a client can choose when to use it and when to save it.

D. ESTATE PLANNING TECHNIQUES

One of the primary goals of estate planning is to minimize or eliminate taxes while furthering the gratuitous transfer goals of the client. The term **estate planning** involves counseling clients on wealth management, including tax-efficient transfers both during life and upon death. What techniques will work best depend on the wealth of the client and the client's risk tolerance, family structure, and intended beneficiaries. Some strategies are available only to married clients and some will be relevant only for those with philanthropic goals. Others are available to a broader base and can be widely used. Increasingly, estate planning also emphasizes minimizing income tax consequences to the donor, the donor's estate, or the donor's beneficiaries. A class in Estate Planning, often taken after a course in Estate and

Gift Tax, will provide a much broader grounding in these strategies than this chapter provides. The following discussion will provide a basic introduction.

1. Efficient Use of Lifetime Gifts

As discussed earlier, the annual exclusion from gift tax for lifetime gifts can be a powerful tool to reduce the value of an estate that is subject to tax. Whether made outright or through a trust where beneficiaries hold withdrawal rights (often referred to as a *Crummey* Trust and described in the *Cristofani* case discussed earlier in this chapter), a systematic program of making annual gifts to a large group of beneficiaries can reduce the size of the estate subject to tax without any gift tax cost to the donor.

Other lifetime gifts can be structured to offer another potential advantage over holding onto property until death when it is subject to estate tax. The tax assessed against gratuitous transfers is based on the fair market value of the property. Therefore, property that is prone to appreciate in value, such as real estate or some closely held business interests, may benefit from the "freeze" that applies when the value is assessed at the time of the gift (and not years later at the time of the donor's death, when the value is predicted to be higher). The price of this strategy, however, is that property that stays in the donor's estate benefits from an adjustment to date-of-death basis under Section 1015 of the Internal Revenue Code. Because the basis is the amount against which the beneficiary's gain or loss will be measured for income tax purposes, the cost of lowering the estate tax for the donor may be to increase the income tax liability for the beneficiary. Because the income tax rates on capital gains tends to be lower than the estate and gift tax rate, sometimes the trade-off is worth making.

For example, say Orville is a very wealthy individual who will be subject to the estate tax (assume he has otherwise used the annual exclusion and unified credit so they do not affect these transactions). Orville owns Pop's Popcorn stock that he bought for $900,000, which is currently worth $1,000,000 but is projected to grow in value to $2,000,000 in five years. If Orville makes a gift of the stock to his movie star friend Penelope, and Penelope immediately sells the stock for $1,000,000, she will owe a 20 percent capital gains tax of $20,000. Orville will have generated gift tax on a $1,000,000 transfer and owe taxes of 40 percent on that, or $400,000. If Orville instead leaves Penelope the stock in his will, then when he dies five years later and the stock is worth twice as much, the stock will be included in his estate at a $2,000,000 value and will generate $800,000 of tax. If Penelope then sold the stock for its $2,000,000 value, she will pay no income tax because the stock got a new basis on Orville's death. In a case like this, saddling Penelope with a $20,000 income tax liability was a good deal, in that it eliminated $400,000 of estate tax liability.

With fewer estates subject to the estate tax at all, planning to move assets out of the estate has become less critical. Under the current estate tax structure, the benefits of carryover basis are available to all taxpayers, while the estate tax will apply to very few. Imagine now that Orville's estate, in the example above, consists of the Pop's Popcorn stock and $8,000,000 in other assets. If he keeps the stock until he dies, the estate is worth $10,000,000. That's a lot of money, but no estate tax will be imposed on the estate. When he gives the stock to Penelope under his will, Penelope will take the stock with a basis of $2,000,000. If Penelope sells the stock before it increases in value, she will owe no capital gains tax.

Gifts that actually trigger the payment of gift tax—meaning those that have exceeded the amount sheltered by the unified credit and all other available deductions and exclusions—can result in additional estate tax savings if the gift is final more than three years before death. See IRC § 2035. This is because the amount that goes to pay the gift tax is not included in the estate tax base and itself subject to tax.

For example, if Patrice has a taxable estate of $21,400,000, and makes a lifetime gift of $1,000,000 to her niece, Patrice will pay gift tax of $400,000 when the transfer is final (assuming Patrice has already exceeded the transfer tax credit amount). At her death, say, five years later, Patrice will have only $20,000,000 against which to assess the estate tax. If Patrice instead waited until death to make the $1,000,000 transfer, the $400,000 that would have gone to pay gift tax is itself subject to 40 percent estate tax, resulting in an additional $160,000 liability that could have been avoided.

Problems with this technique include not knowing if the client will survive the three-year term (the gift tax is brought back into the estate if not) and continued hope that the estate tax may be repealed or made more generous. With that in mind, estate planners often are reluctant to advise paying tax now because the tax may be avoided altogether if the property owner waits.

2. Efficient Use of the Marital Deduction and Unified Credit

As described above, the primary goal of estate tax planning is to shelter transfers with deductions and exclusions to generate as little tax as possible. Perhaps the most common way to accomplish this goal is through strategic application of the combination of the unified credit and the marital deduction. By using both the unified credit and marital deduction, an estate planner can ensure that no estate tax is paid on the death of the first spouse. Under this plan, the minimum amount necessary to reduce the estate tax liability to zero passes to the surviving spouse, and the balance of the estate (generally whatever portion of the unified transfer tax credit budget remains) passes to others or to a trust that is structured in a way to avoid inclusion in the estate of the second spouse to die, such as in a trust that includes no powers or rights for the surviving spouse that would trigger the inclusion of the assets. With portability now available, the amount sheltered by the decedent's unified credit could go directly to the surviving spouse, along with an election to transfer the DSUE to the surviving spouse. In some estates giving the surviving spouse control of all the assets makes sense, but in other estates, especially those involving a spouse who is not the parent of the decedent's children, creating a trust will still be appropriate.

Qualifying for the marital deduction is not completely straightforward, however. If there are problematic limitations on the spouse's right to the property, or allocation of debts to be paid from the surviving spouse's share, all or part of the property intended to qualify for the marital deduction may instead be subject to tax. To minimize that risk, careful drafting is essential. Sometimes lawyers include a savings clause in the trust document, to ensure that any ambiguous language cannot be interpreted in a way that would squander qualification for the marital deduction.

Case Preview

Michelle Bandy et al. v. Alexandra Clancy

In the case that follows, the famous author Thomas Clancy left an estate plan that included significant tax planning. The widow and the children argued as to whether the language included in the document was sufficient to eliminate all liability for transfer taxes from the share passing to the surviving spouse.

As you read the case, consider:

1. How was formula language used to make efficient use of both the marital deduction and the unified transfer tax credit amount?
2. How was the trust drafted to ensure that the transfer to the surviving spouse would qualify for the marital deduction?

Michelle Bandy et al. v. Alexandra Clancy
449 Md. 577 (Ct. App. 2016)

BATTAGLIA, J.

"The avoidance of taxes is the only intellectual pursuit that still carries any reward."—John Maynard Keynes

"The legal right of a taxpayer to decrease the amount of what otherwise would be his taxes, or altogether avoid them, by means which the law permits, cannot be doubted."—Justice George Sutherland

Acclaimed author Thomas L. Clancy, Jr., ("Decedent" and "Testator") died in October of 2013, survived by his second wife, Alexandra M. Clancy ("Mrs. Clancy") and a minor child by that marriage, as well as four adult children ("The Older Children") from Mr. Clancy's first marriage. Mr. Clancy died, leaving a will, as well as various amendments; the issue before us involves the interpretation of Mr. Clancy's Will, as amended by a Second Codicil, with respect to not only the payment of federal estate taxes, but also to the question of upon which beneficiaries the burden of such taxes should be placed at the time of Mr. Clancy's death.

Federal estate taxes may be imposed on a decedent's real and personal property and any property interests in excess of five million dollars, an amount adjusted annually since 2011 for the "cost of living", 26 U.S.C. § 2010(c)(3); the threshold for the imposition of Federal estate taxes in 2015 was $5,430,000. Federal estate tax is calculated on a graduated basis, on the value of the estate above the threshold, starting at 18% for the first ten thousand dollars. Which beneficiaries, if any, are obligated to pay a portion or all of the federal estate taxes is a matter of State law, and, in Maryland, may be provided for under the Will. . . .

Essentially, then, an estate can avoid adverse tax consequences upon the death of the testator through the use of the marital deduction, because the marital deduction "reflects a strongly held policy that it is inappropriate to assess transfer taxes on transfers of property between spouses." Federal estate taxes may be reduced when property is transferred to the surviving spouse upon the death of the decedent, but the value of the property conveyed that remains at the time of the death of the surviving spouse is subject to federal estate tax.

To qualify for the marital deduction, the property must be that which would have been includable in the gross estate of the decedent and which passes, or has passed, to the surviving spouse by operation of law or otherwise.15 26 U.S.C. § 2056(a). "Terminable" property interests, interests given to a surviving spouse for a limited time, however, do not qualify for the marital deduction, unless the interest qualifies as one of the exceptions provided in Section 2056 of the Internal Revenue Code, including the Qualified Terminable Interest Property (QTIP), 26 U.S.C. § 2056(b)(7). . . .

Any property used to pay federal estate taxes, however, will not qualify for the marital deduction. 26 U.S.C. § 2056(b)(4)(A). If property allocated to the marital deduction is used to pay federal estate tax, the marital deduction is reduced by the amount of the payment made, thereby increasing the federal estate tax imposed on the estate. Id.

One way to protect the marital deduction from adverse tax consequences and receive the full federal estate tax benefit for property transferred to the surviving spouse is to use a "savings clause" in the will. That type of savings clause, often referred to as an "interpretive aide savings clause", restricts actions taken by the personal representative that could reduce the tax benefit of the marital deduction and assists with the interpretation and explanation of the testator's intent with respect to preventing adverse tax consequences. . . . The interpretive aide savings clause, therefore, can express the testator's intent that any authority granted to the personal representative is void should it reduce the efficacy of the marital deduction. . . .

Mr. Clancy's Will, executed June 11, 2007, contained fourteen items that named his personal representative, instructed with respect to the payment of estate taxes, left Mr. Clancy's personal and real property to Mrs. Clancy and, with respect to the remainder of his estate, created three residuary trusts: a Marital Trust for the benefit of Mrs. Clancy representing one-third of the residuary; a Family Trust for the benefit of Mrs. Clancy and their minor child equal to one-half of the residue that remained after the creation of the Marital Trust; and the final, two Older Children's Trusts into which the remaining one-half of the residue after the creation of the Marital Trust was to be deposited.

[The court proceeded to discuss the conflict that arose between Item Third in the Will, which provided that:

"All estate, inheritance, legacy, succession and transfer taxes (including any interest and any penalties thereon) lawfully payable with respect to all property includible in my gross estate or taxable in consequence of my death . . . shall be paid by my Personal Representative out of my residuary estate, subject, however, to the provisions hereinafter contained in Item SIXTH hereof with respect to the Marital Share therein created . . . ."

and Item Twelfth D, as amended, which provided:

"No asset or proceeds of any assets shall be included in the Marital Share or the Non-Exempt Family Residuary Trust as to which a marital deduction would not be allowed if included. Anything in this Will to the contrary notwithstanding, and whether or not any reference is made in any other provision of this Will to the limitations imposed by this Paragraph D, neither my personal representative nor my trustee shall have or exercise any authority, power or discretion over the Marital Share or the Non-Exempt Family Residuary Trust or the income thereof, or the property constituting the Marital Share or the Non-Exempt Family Residuary Trust, nor shall any payment or distribution by my personal representative or my trustee be limited or restricted by any provision of this Will, such that, in any such event, my estate would be prevented from receiving the benefit of the marital deduction as hereinbefore set forth. My Wife shall have the power at any time by written direction to compel my trustee to convert unproductive property held in the Marital Trust into income producing property. Likewise, my Wife shall have the power at any time by written direction to compel my trustee to convert unproductive property held in the Non-Exempt Family Residuary Trust into income producing property."

The issue, then, was whether the "savings clause" in the second provision listed above would override the direction in the will to pay taxes out of the residue, such that the full value of the marital deduction would be preserved.]

Mr. Clancy's Older Children assert that their father intended that federal estate taxes should be paid out of the residuary estate, including that which was allocated to the Family Trust, when he executed his Will, because ITEM THIRD of the Will directed that, "All estate, inheritance, legacy, succession and transfer taxes . . . shall be paid by my personal representative out of my residuary estate[.]" They argue that federal estate taxes can be paid out of the Family Trust and still preserve the property allocated to that trust for the marital deduction.

Mrs. Clancy does not dispute that ITEM THIRD of the Will says what it says, but asserts that the Savings Clause expressly excepts any property from the residuary estate allocated to the marital deduction from having to bear the burden of estate taxes.

The parties' disagreement, then, centers on the impact of the Second Codicil's qualification of the Family Trust for the marital deduction and, moreover, the interpretation of the restrictions in the Savings Clause as amended by the Second Codicil, juxtaposed against ITEM THIRD of the Will, which indicated that federal estate taxes are to be paid from the residuary estate.

When construing a will and any codicils, "[t]he will and codicils must be construed as one instrument, and effect must, if possible, be given to every part of them." Lederer v. Safe Deposit & Trust Co. of Baltimore, 182 Md. 422, 428, 35 A.2d 166, 169 (1943); Hutton v. Safe Deposit & Trust Co. of Baltimore, 150 Md. 539, 551, 133

A. 308, 312 (1926) ("The general rule of construction requires us to give a meaning and purpose to every part of the will and codicil."). "It is a settled rule of construction that a will and its codicils must be interpreted as one instrument, and the provisions of the will are to be given effect except to the extent only to which they are revoked by the codicils, either in terms or by clear inconsistency between the earlier and later expressions of the testator's intention." Associated Professors of Loyola College of City of Baltimore v. Dugan, 137 Md. 545, 552, 113 A. 81, 84 (1921).

The Older Children and Mrs. Clancy, as well as the personal representative, all agree that the Second Codicil qualified the Family Trust for the QTIP election, because Mrs. Clancy became the income beneficiary of the Family Trust for life; she could not transfer her income nor was she given a limited power of appointment, but she could request that the trustee invade the corpus of the trust for her needs, which would reduce the value of the Family Trust passing upon her death. All the parties also agree that the Second Codicil contained a Savings Clause that amended the Savings Clause in the Will to restrict the actions of the personal representative and trustee to qualify the portion of the residuary trust allocated to the Family Trust for the marital deduction.

The Second Codicil did not, however, specifically address, in any way, the Will provision that instructed that taxes were to be paid out of the residuary estate of which the Family Trust was a part.

To resolve the ambiguity and apparent conflict, we rely on the interpretive aide of the Savings Clause to elucidate Mr. Clancy's intent. In so doing, we determine, as did the Orphans' Court, that the Savings Clause contained in the Second Codicil which prevented the personal representative from exercising any "authority, power, or discretion" to disqualify any portion of the Family Trust from the marital deduction, such as the payment of federal estate taxes, "trumps" ITEM THIRD of the Will relating to payment of taxes from the residuary estate. We reach this conclusion for a number of reasons, the first of which is because of the decisions in similar circumstances by other courts, as well as the Internal Revenue Service's decision in Revenue Ruling 75-440. . . .

Our determination that the Savings Clause in the Second Codicil clarifies Mr. Clancy's intention that the Family Trust not be charged with any federal estate taxes also is supported by Revenue Ruling 75-440, supra. In that case, the Service concluded that its savings clause that provided that, "Notwithstanding anything herein contained to the contrary, any power, duty, or discretionary authority granted to my Fiduciary hereunder shall be absolutely void to the extent that either the right to exercise or the exercise thereof, shall in any way affect, jeopardize or cause my estate to lose all or any part of the tax benefit afforded my estate by the Marital Deduction under either Federal or State Laws.", Rev. Rul. 75-440 at 2, operated to void any power given to the trustees that would disqualify the marital deduction. Id. at 3. The savings clause, as interpreted by the Service, permitted it to displace the provision of the will that had directed estate taxes to be paid from the residuary estate of which the marital property qualifying for the deduction was a part.

Were the Family Trust in the instant case to bear the burden of any portion of the payment of the federal estate tax, that payment would reduce the marital deduction as noted in the tax regulation. . .

The Savings Clause in the Second Codicil, nevertheless, explicitly directs that the personal representative not act to adversely impact the benefit of the marital deduction of the Marital Trust and the Family Trust. To burden the Family Trust with payment of federal estate taxes at the time of Mr. Clancy's death when the property is conveyed in trust for the benefit of Mrs. Clancy would be in direct derogation of Mr. Clancy's intent manifested in the Savings Clause....

We agree with the Older Children that it is clear that a testator could direct that the burden of inheritance taxes could be placed on legatees who otherwise would not have to pay such taxes, as well as payment of estate taxes on the marital share, as the Older Children have asserted. Mr. Clancy, however, in his estate documents did not burden the marital share with payment of federal estate taxes.

Moreover, were the Family Trust to bear the burden of federal estate taxes, at the time of Mr. Clancy's death, the corpus of that trust would be subject to imposition of federal estate taxes twice, at the time of Mr. Clancy's death as well as when Mrs. Clancy died. The establishment of the QTIP Trust in Mr. Clancy's Will insures that the Younger Child will have to pay estate taxes when Mrs. Clancy dies. 26 U.S.C. § 2044. Certainly, as each party agrees, Mr. Clancy intended to minimize the impact of federal estate taxes in the entirety of his Will, an intent that would be eviscerated by double taxation.

Finally, the Older Children question having the burden of federal estate taxation being placed on them, to the benefit of Mrs. Clancy. Mr. Clancy, however, clearly intended, by the establishment of the QTIP Trust, to benefit Mrs. Clancy to the detriment of the Younger Child, whose remainder could be diminished by Mrs. Clancy's invasion of corpus for need. As a result, all of Mr. Clancy's children are burdened for the benefit of Mrs. Clancy and to avoid federal estate tax.

In conclusion, we hold that the property conveyed in the Family Trust as identified in Mr. Clancy's Will and Second Codicil cannot be burdened by the payment of federal estate taxes.

JUDGMENT OF THE ORPHANS' COURT AFFIRMED; COSTS IN THIS COURT TO BE PAID BY APPELLANTS.

[Dissent ommitted.]

Post-Case Follow-Up

Note the conflict of financial interest between the older children and the surviving spouse: the children want the less tax-efficient result, because it means the spouse and not the older children would bear the cost of the tax and the older children would receive more money. Don't assume that all beneficiaries share the goal of tax minimization for the estate. Particularly in cases of multiple marriages or blended families, individual financial well-being may motivate beneficiaries to bring litigation intended to foil a tax-efficient plan.

Clancy: Real Life Applications

1. You represent the adult Clancy children. Assume there is no savings clause in the trust but that the overall structure of the estate as described in the case remains the same. Make the argument that the taxes should be paid from the Family Trust even though it reduces the marital deduction and increases the tax liability of the estate.

2. Instead, represent Mrs. Clancy, but also assume no savings clause. Can you still argue that the trust should be construed for tax-optimal results?

3. You are a member of your firm's form drafting committee. Should you routinely include a savings clause in trusts that are drafted to qualify for the marital deduction? What questions might you want to raise with clients when you include such clauses?

3. Valuation Planning

The amount subject to estate or gift tax is the fair market value of the property transferred. Fair market value, for tax purposes, is the amount at which property would change hands between a willing buyer and a willing seller, neither being under any compulsion to buy or sell and both having full knowledge of relevant facts. This objective test of a hypothetical transaction can lead to many formulations as to what the actual value of an item might be. Experts often disagree on value. There are steps clients can take that depress value, such as adding restrictions or affecting the marketability of an asset. For purposes of this introductory chapter, we introduce the topic of valuation, but leave the details for more advanced study.

4. Charitable Giving Techniques

Qualifying transfers to appropriate charitable organizations can trigger a deduction from estate tax (and gift tax). Outright transfers to charity always qualify, and it is therefore possible to structure a gift to a charitable organization to zero-out the estate tax of a philanthropically minded client, much like the technique one uses for marital deduction planning. It is never necessary for a client to pay federal estate tax; he or she may always make a qualified charitable contribution instead, while also passing the amount sheltered by the unified transfer tax credit to family members or other loved ones.

In addition to outright bequests, clients can also consider more sophisticated charitable giving options that may generate additional tax benefits. These strategies generally involve split-interest trusts, in which a qualifying charity is the beneficiary of one part of the gift and an individual is the beneficiary of another part (or the donor retains a part). Split-interest trusts must be structured very specifically in order to qualify, and the following discussion will give a brief introduction without including every qualification that would be needed for the technique to pass tax muster.

The first type of charitable transfer that a client could consider is a charitable remainder trust. Under a charitable remainder trust, a non-charity (most commonly an individual beneficiary) receives the lead interest in a trust for either life (or lives) or a term of up to 20 years, and the charity receives the remainder at the end of the term. The lead interest must be either an annuity interest, meaning a fixed percentage of the initial value of the trust, or a unitrust interest, meaning a fixed percentage of the value of the trust, revalued from year to year. A trust with an annuity interest is called a charitable remainder annuity trust or CRAT, and a trust with a unitrust interest is called a charitable remainder unitrust or CRUT.

The second type of charitable transfer that a client could consider is a charitable lead trust. This technique is just an inversion of the CRAT and CRUT discussed above. Under a charitable lead trust, the charity receives the lead unitrust or annuity interest for a term of up to 20 years, and an individual beneficiary receives the remainder at the end of the term of the CLAT or CLUT. Like the CRAT or CRUT, some of the tax benefit comes from the fact that actuarial tables are used to calculate the value of the charitable benefit and the individual gift, and that may underestimate the value of the gift and overstate the value of the charitable deduction, depending on the property with which the trust is funded and how well it performs.

There are additional charitable giving techniques that estate planners may consider that can have estate tax benefits as well as the potential for income tax savings. Strategies may include charitable gift annuities, pooled income funds, conveyances of conservation easements, and more advanced strategies covered in an upper-level Estate Planning course.

5. Other Wealth Management Planning Strategies

Increasingly, wealth management is not solely about minimizing estate taxes. Instead, the focus has expanded to awareness of income tax costs—for both the client and beneficiaries. Income taxes apply not only at the federal level, but often at the state and local levels as well. Choice-of-law matters have come center stage as advisors seek attractive jurisdictions for trusts. Because some states are more aggressive at taxing trusts or their beneficiaries than others, trustees may change the situs of the trust or **decant** the trust (pour its contents into a new one with more favorable terms, if permitted by the instrument) to chase attractive tax jurisdictions.

In addition to the growing emphasis on income tax planning, trusts and estates lawyers may also be involved with counseling regarding wealth management. Beyond urging compliance with long-standing rules relating to prudent investment and diversification, lawyers may help clients connect with alternative investment opportunities, including through offshore trusts. The modern goal in wealth management is not just to minimize estate taxes, but to minimize other taxes as well while seeking investment options that grow the overall value of the estate.

Chapter Summary

- The gift tax is assessed upon any transfer for less than adequate consideration. The subjective intent of the donor is irrelevant; it is the gap in value that matters.

- The annual exclusion from gift tax exempts gifts of up to $10,000 (indexed for inflation; $15,000 in 2019). The exclusion applies for each donor, for each recipient, for each tax year during life. Only gifts of a present interest in property qualify.

- The gift tax and the estate tax share the same tax rate table. The table appears to be progressive graduated rates, but only the highest rate of 40 percent is ever effective because of the unified transfer tax credit.

- The unified transfer tax credit shelters gift and estate tax transfers so that the first $11 million (indexed for inflation) for each taxpayer is free from tax.

- The estate tax base includes not only assets held by the decedent at death and transferred through the probate estate, but a wide collection of transfers or interests in property where the decedent had rights to enjoy the property or control the ultimate owner of it.

- The unlimited marital deduction means that properly structured transfers to a spouse who is a U.S. citizen will not be subject to transfer taxes, whether during life or at death. Efficient use of the marital deduction ensures that no taxes will be owed for a married couple until the death of the second spouse. Portability of the exclusion amount between spouses also minimizes the likelihood that any tax will be owed on the death of the first spouse.

- The unlimited charitable deduction means that properly structured transfers to a charity will not be subject to gift or estate taxes. Charitable transfers often convey income tax benefits as well.

- Additional deductions or exclusions, such as amounts paid to settle enforceable debts, further reduce the amount of an estate subject to taxes.

- The generation-skipping transfer tax is an additional level of tax that applies when a transfer that is taxable under the estate or gift tax is made to a person two or more generations younger than the donor. The tax is applied at the highest estate and gift tax rate. Every individual has an exclusion of $11 million from GST tax transfers that can shelter a combination of lifetime and estate transfers. Additional deductions and exemptions may lower the GST tax further.

- Sophisticated estate-planning techniques, often involving the use of trusts, can lower the value of property subject to transfer taxes or lower the overall estate tax owed. Wealth management strategies consider a broad range of techniques that can sustain wealth throughout generations, coordinating transfer tax, income tax, and investment matters.

Applying the Concepts

1. You have a new client and need to explain the basics of the amount an individual can pass without triggering transfer taxes. Explain the following concepts:

   a. What is the current dollar amount of the unified transfer tax credit?
   b. What does the excludable dollar amount represent?
   c. Is this a static amount, or is it subject to change?

2. Jamele agrees to deed title to her house to her son, Charles. The property is currently valued at $130,000. Both agree that in return for Jamele deeding the property, Charles will pay $100,000 to his mother. Will Jamele owe any gift tax for this transaction?

3. Harmony is the recipient of a life estate interest in the income produced by assets within an irrevocable trust established by her grandmother. Upon Harmony's death, the remainder passes to Harmony's brother. Will either the value of the trust's assets or the value of the income stream be includable in her gross estate for tax purposes?

4. Ava Grace's mother established a trust in which Ava Grace has received a life estate. Under the trust agreement, Ava Grace is permitted to choose which of her three children receive the assets of the trust at her death. Knowing that Ava Grace is a small business entrepreneur, Ava Grace's mother also inserted a clause within the agreement allowing Ava Grace to withdraw specified amounts of trust assets to fund her ventures. At Ava Grace's death, will any amount of the assets remaining in the trust be included within Ava Grace's estate?

5. For the current year, Peyton, age 40, will make a gift of $25,000 to a trust established for the benefit of her best friend's newborn son. Assume Peyton has not made any prior gifts to the newborn for this year, but has no remaining amount of the unified transfer credit. Will any gift tax be owed on the gift? Is gift tax the *only* tax Peyton might owe? Why?

Trusts and Estates in Practice

1. You have determined that for estate planning purposes, use of a trust will be beneficial to your client, Emma Kate, who has two minor children. Assume you are drafting a trust instrument to comply with all legal requirements so that Emma Kate may benefit from the annual gift tax exclusion amount for transfers made to the trust for the benefit of her two children. Draft a provision setting forth what rights, if any, *must* be afforded to the beneficiaries of the trust in the instrument.

2. After many years of investing, Blake has amassed a sizeable fortune. Although he is relatively young, he has asked you to develop a plan as to how he may begin decreasing his estate through coordinated gifting without using any of his unified transfer exclusion amount. Blake is not married and has one child (for whom he currently pays $1,200 per month child support), two siblings, and four nieces and nephews. In addition, he has many friends he would like to help. In one paragraph, explain to Blake the possibilities of how he may give money. Be certain to include not only to whom he may give money, but also the amounts that he may give. Try also to address any other aspects of Blake's situation that may reduce his assets without using any of his unified exclusion amount.

3. Suppose two grandparents, Mark and Kim, consult you about monetary gifts they each wish to make to their two grandchildren. Each grandchild will be attending college within the next calendar year. Being mindful of the generation-skipping transfer tax, draft a short statement to Mark and Kim suggesting any means by which they may give money without incurring tax.

4. You are assisting your client, Jalen, with coordinating a strategy to minimize estate tax liability. Jalen's main question pertains to whether he should wait until death for assets to pass to his specified beneficiaries, or proceed with making gifts right away. How do you respond? Are there any benefits or drawbacks to gifting property during life as opposed to waiting until death?

5. You are a new associate at a law firm that maintains a sizeable trusts and estates practice. Your supervising partner has asked you to write a short client letter to Ashley and Jordan Perrie, who wish to establish a trust to accomplish their dual goals of affording the surviving spouse with a steady stream of income for life while also donating assets to Teenage Dramatists, Inc., their preferred charity. The letter is not to exceed two paragraphs in length and should focus solely advising the clients as to how a charitable remainder trust or a charitable lead trust could meet their estate planning goals.

GLOSSARY

120-Hour rule   A survival rule imposed by statute

Abatement   A doctrine that determines to what extent devises under a will are reduced if the estate is without sufficient assets to make all distributions provided for in the will

Accessions   A doctrine that traces changes in shares of stock owned by the testator at death and provides rules to determine how many shares the devisee of the stock will receive

Acts [or events] of independent significance   Any fact, act, or event existing or occurring outside the four corners of the will so long as it is an otherwise objective event that occurs without regard to the testator's plan of disposition

Actual notice   Personalized written notice delivered to the receiver; occurs when a personal representative notifies any known creditor in writing of their opportunity to bring a claim against the estate

Adeemed   The term used to describe what happens to property that was specifically devised under a will but was not in the decedent's possession at death

Ademption   The doctrine that says what happens if an asset that was specifically devised under a will is not in the decedent's possession at death

Ademption by extinction   Ademption that happens when at death the testator does not own an item of property specifically devised under the will; also called ademption

Ademption by satisfaction   Ademption that happens when at death the testator does not own an item of property specifically devised under the will because the testator gave the property to the devisee named to take the property; also called satisfaction

Administrator (or Administratrix)   The personal representative of an intestate estate

Advance medical directive   Sets out an individual's medical wishes in the case of incapacity

Advancement   A pre-payment that diminishes the child's inheritance

Agent   Person acting on behalf of another person

Ambiguous   Susceptible to multiple reasonable meanings

Amended   Altered

Ancillary probate   An additional probate proceeding required if the decedent owned probate real property in a state other than the decedent's domicile

Annual exclusion   The amount each individual can give to an unlimited number of recipients every year without incurring gift tax

Annuity   An insurance product that an individual purchases in order to receive fixed amounts at a later date

Antilapse   A rule of construction, which dictates that property goes to a devisee's descendants if the devisee is related to the donor or the powerholder as prescribed by the statute

Appointive property   The property subject to the power of appointment

Apportionment   A determination of whether taxes are paid by the residue of the estate or are shared by (apportioned among) all bequests in the will or by all nonprobate transfers

Appraisal   The process in which an expert prepares a report estimating an asset's fair market value

Ascertainable standard   A distribution standard that can be enforced by a court under state law; under tax law, health, education, support and maintenance

Asset protection planning   The effort to shelter assets from creditors

Attest   To authenticate a testator's execution or documentation of a will

Attestation   To sign as a witness to authenticate the action

Attorney-in-fact   Term for person appointed to act as an agent pursuant to a power of attorney

Augmented estate   Under the UPC, the combined value of both spouses' assets for purposes of the elective share

Beneficiary   The person who holds equitable or beneficial interests in property held in trust

Blanket exercise clause   A clause that states that it exercises "any" power of appointment that the powerholder may have

Blending clause   A clause that blends the appointive property and the powerholder's own property together in a common disposition

Breach   A violation by a trustee of a fiduciary duty

Breach of trust   A violation by a trustee of a fiduciary duty

Capacity   The ability to govern one's self and own affairs; *see* mental capacity and legal capacity

Capture   When a general power is ineffectively exercised, the property subject to the power is distributed through the powerholder's estate

Charitable deduction   A properly structured transfer to a qualifying charitable organization that may be subtracted from the tax base, reducing the amount subject to tax

Charitable trust   A trust created for a charitable purpose

Codicil   A document that amends or supplements a prior will

Collateral heirs/relatives   Family members of a decedent who are not descendants or ancestors

Common law system   Treats the title to property as determinative of the power to dispose of that property

Community property system   Provides built-in protections for the surviving spouse (and others classified as a spouse pursuant to state law) by assuming that earnings acquired during marriage are joint

Conflict of interest   When the trustee enters into a transaction involving trust property with a family member or a business associate

Conscious-presence   When a will can be validated if witnesses are within the range of any of the testator's senses

Conservator   A fiduciary appointed by the court to make financial decisions for an incapacitated person

Constructive trust   An equitable remedy that a court can use to transfer title as required by law to the legal owner but direct that the legal owner holds the property subject to a constructive trust, with the duty to transfer the property to the rightful owner; typically used to prevent unjust enrichment

Construe   Interpret language in a document

Contesting the will   Bringing litigation to show that a will is not entitled to probate

Contingent beneficiary   Beneficiary who is eligible to take a distribution only if the first-named beneficiaries have predeceased

Convenience account   An account that provides lifetime rights for the party added to the account but does not provide after-death rights

Counterpart or duplicate   One of two corresponding copies of a legal instrument

Curtesy   A protection for surviving husbands, through which they received a life estate in all of their deceased wife's property if one child had been born during the marriage

Cy pres   A doctrine in which a condition of a transfer made to a charity is modified because the condition has become impossible, illegal, impracticable, or wasteful

Dead hand control   The disposition established by a will

Decanting   When used with a trust, a process that involves pouring assets from one trust into another, removing unwanted provisions and adding more useful provisions

Decedent   The person who has died

Declaration of trust   A trust document in which the settlor will serve as the initial trustee

Deduction   An amount the taxpayer may subtract from the tax base before calculating the amount owed

Defined benefit plan [pension]   A retirement plan in which employees receive a guaranteed level of fixed monthly payments based on a formula that considers several factors, such as length of employment and salary

Defined contribution plan   A retirement plan that provides payments based on the amount of money contributed and the rate of return on the money invested

Demonstrative devise   A gift from a specific source

Dependent relative revocation   A doctrine that applies when revocation was conditional upon a mistaken understanding of the testator and has the effect of reversing the revocation of a will

Descendants   A multiple-generation class, beginning with children and also including all subsequent generations down the decedent's descending line; synonymous with issue

Deviation   Also called equitable deviation, a doctrine that allows a court to modify a provision or terminate the trust to give effect to the settlor's primary intent in creating the trust

Devise   To make a gift at death of property in whatever proportions the testator wants and to whomever the testator wishes

Digital assets   Electronic property like computer files, web domains, digital communications, and virtual currency

Direct skip   A transfer that is subject to the gift tax or estate tax and that is made to a skip person

Directed trustees   Trustees subject to the authority of a trust director

Disclaim   The refusal to accept a gift

Disclaimant   A person who disclaims a gift

Discretionary   Instructions that may be followed; action is within the discretion of the person receiving the instructions

Discretionary functions   A trustee's functions that involve decision making

Discretionary provision   A provision in a trust that gives the trustee discretion over distributions

Distributees or permissible distributees   Beneficiaries to whom the trustee may or must make distributions

Donee   With respect to a power of appointment, the holder of a power to appoint

Donor   With respect to a power of appointment, the person who creates a power of appointment

Dower   A life-estate in one-third of a woman's husband's real property

Durable power of attorney   Power of attorney that is effective immediately and lasts throughout the principal's incapacity

Duress   A wrongdoer performs or threatens to perform a wrongful act that coerces the transferor to make a transfer that the transferor would not otherwise have made

Duty not to commingle   Fiduciary duty to keep the trustee's individual property separate from trust property

Duty of care   The fiduciary duty to manage and administer a trust with reasonable care, skill and caution

Duty of impartiality   The fiduciary duty to treat all beneficiaries fairly

Duty of loyalty   The fiduciary duty to act in the sole interests of the beneficiaries

Duty of obedience   The fiduciary duty to carry out the terms of the trust

Duty of prudence   The fiduciary duty to manage and administer a trust with reasonable care, skill, and caution

Duty to earmark   Fiduciary duty to indicate that trust property is held by the trustee in the trustee's fiduciary capacity

Duty to inform and report   The fiduciary duty to provide information to beneficiaries

Elective share   A minimum amount to which the surviving spouse may be entitled

Elements of a trust   The requirements for a valid trust

Emancipated minors   Minors that have been legally released from parental control

Emancipation   Being granted adult status as a minor

Equitable adoption (or adoption by estoppel or de facto adoption)   A process that allows a child to inherit even without having been formally adopted

Equitable deviation   A doctrine that allows a court to modify a provision or terminate the trust to give effect to the primary intent the settlor had in creating the trust; also called deviation

Escheat   The decedent's property is transferred to the state because no heir can be found

Estate   The assets owned by the decedent

Estate plan   Involves documentation of the tasks that manage and dispose of an individual's assets in the event of their incapacitation or death

Estate planning   Counseling clients on wealth management as well as planning for death or incapacity

Exclusionary power of appointment   A nongeneral power of appointment that can be exercised in favor of one of a group of permissible appointees to the exclusion of the other appointees

Exclusive   When used to refer to a power to revoke a trust, this means the settlor must follow the procedure provided in the terms of the trust

Executor   The individual appointed by the court to collect, manage, and distribute the property of the decedent; the UPC refers to this individual as the "personal representative"

Exoneration   A doctrine that determines whether a devise of property will pass subject to a debt attached to the property

Exordium   The first clauses in the will

Express revocation   Revoking a will by using a writing specifically stating a will is revoked

Expressly refraining from exercise   When the holder of a power clarifies expressly in her will that she does not intend to exercise the power

Extrinsic evidence   Evidence beyond the document itself

Fiduciary   Someone who represents the interests of someone else

Fiduciary duties   The duties the law imposes on a trustee and on any fiduciary who manages property for another

First-generation statutes   Statutes governing holographic wills that require that the testator write the entire will

Fraud   When a person deliberately misleads the testator as to the nature or contents of the will or relevant external facts; *see* fraud in the execution and fraud in the inducement

Fraud in the execution   A misrepresentation about the nature or contents of the document the testator is signing

Fraud in the inducement   A misrepresentation about an external fact relevant to the pattern of distribution among beneficiaries

Freedom of donative intent   Allows property owners to do what they want with their property during life and at death

Freedom of testation   Allows property owners to do what they want with their property during life and at death

General devise   A gift of property payable from any asset in the testator's estate

General power of appointment   A power to appoint in favor of the powerholder, the powerholder's estate, the powerholder's creditors, or the creditors of the powerholder's estate

Generation-skipping transfer   A transfer that is made from an individual in an older generation to someone who is at least two generations younger

Generation-skipping transfer tax (GST tax)   A type of tax that applies to a gratuitous transfer that skips over a generation

Guardian   A fiduciary who is legally responsible for the person and property of a minor or an incapacitated adult

Half-blood relationship   A relationship between individuals who share one, but not both, parents

Harmless error   This doctrine excuses compliance with the formalities if the testator's intent is clear

Healthcare power of attorney   Document that identifies an agent to serve as a healthcare decision maker for the principal

Holographic will   A will that is in the testator's writing

Hotchpot   A method to calculate whether the heir who received an advance has already received the amount to which she is entitled, or whether she is entitled to more

Identity theory   If the will makes a gift of specific property and the testator does not own the property at death, the gift is adeemed and the beneficiary receives nothing

Illusory transfer   Fraud on the widow's share to apply the elective share to property held in revocable trusts

Incapacity   The inability to manage one's own property and business affairs

Income   In a trust, the amount distributed to a beneficiary who receives "all the income"; income under UPIA includes interest, dividends, rents, and short-term capital gains among other revenue, but a trustee can make adjustments between the income and principal accounts

Individual retirement account (IRA)   Retirement savings accounts that can offer various tax breaks

Incorporation by reference   Permits a will to include a separate writing that has not been executed with the testamentary formalities

Inherit through   When an individual does not inherit directly from a certain relative but needs to establish a connection with that relative in order to inherit from someone else

Insane delusion   A false belief that the testator is fixated upon even in the face of overwhelming contrary evidence and that affects the testator's will

Insolvent   When an estate lacks sufficient funds to pay all valid and enforceable debts against it

Integration   The process of establishing the testator's will by piecing together all of the testator's wills, codicils, and other testamentary instruments

Inter vivos trust   A trust created by a settlor during life

Interested witness   A beneficiary of the will who authenticates the testator's execution or documentation of a will

Interested persons   Persons who have or may have a financial stake in the outcome of the administration of the will

Intestacy   When an individual dies without a will

Intestate   The status of being without a will

Inventory   A description of all listed assets in the probate estate and their fair market value

Irrevocable trust   A trust the settlor cannot change

Issue   Descendent

Joint will   One document executed by both spouses that governs the disposition of assets of the couple

Joint tenancy   Shared ownership of an account or property by two or more parties

Joint tenancy with right of survivorship   A means for co-ownership of property that entitles a surviving co-owner to the share of a deceased co-owner

Legal capacity   Having attained a certain age or substitute for maturity under the state statute

Lapse   The doctrine that provides for what happens to a gift to a donee who does not survive under the terms of the document

Lapse of power   When the powerholder did not exercise the power, either through releasing it, not exercising it, or expressly indicating the decision not to exercise it

Latent ambiguity   Extrinsic evidence is needed to expose a latent ambiguity

Letters of administration   A document conveying authority to the personal representative to act in an intestate estate

Letters testamentary   A document conveying authority to the personal representative to act in the case of a will

Life insurance   Insurance on the life of a person that typically takes the form of a contract that guarantees payment if the insured person dies

Living will   Document in which an individual specifies preferences regarding life-sustaining medical care in case of incapacity that is limited to end-of-life decision making

Lucid interval   A time at which the tests for capacity are met even if only for a short while

Mandatory   Instructions that must be followed

Mandatory distribution provision   A provision in a trust that directs the trustee to distribution something without discretion

Marital deduction   A properly structured transfer to a spouse that results in that amount being subtracted from the tax base of the transferring spouse

Marital presumption   Offspring of a married couple (regardless of the sex of the spouses) are presumed to be the children of their parents

Married Women's Property Act   Provided married women with property rights

Material provisions   Dispositive provisions

Medicaid   Jointly-funded federal-state program that provides health coverage for people with low incomes and few resources

Medicare   The federal health care insurance program that provides coverage for people 65 and older and for people under age 65 with selected ailments

Mental capacity   When the testator understands the consequence of the will she is executing, the natural objects of her bounty, what property she has to convey, and how those three elements relate to each other

Merger   A doctrine that causes the interests of the trustee and the beneficiary to merge and the trust to cease to exist if the trustee and the trust's only beneficiary are the same person

Ministerial functions   A trustee's functions that do not involve discretion

Mistake   A word that does not reflect the testator's true intent

No-contest clause   A provision in a will that states that any beneficiary who brings a will contest or similar challenge will forfeit any bequest in his favor under the will; also called an *in terrorem* clause or a *forfeiture* clause

No further inquiry rule If a trustee engages in a self-dealing transaction, the beneficiary can void the transaction without evidence of fraud on the part of the trustee or loss to the trust

Non-ademption statutes Statutes that create a substitute gift for a beneficiary in some circumstances when a gift is adeemed

Non-exclusive When used to refer to a power to revoke a trust; means the settlor may use methods to revoke the trust beyond the procedure provided in the terms of the trust

Nonexclusionary power of appointment A power that must be exercised in favor of all permissible appointees so that each member of the group receives something

Nonexercise When the holder of a power does nothing that could constitute an exercise of power

Nongeneral power of appointment A power that cannot be exercised in favor of the powerholder, the powerholder's estate, the powerholder's creditors, or creditors of the powerholder's estate

Nonprobate transfers or will substitutes Gratuitous grants of property that are made without a will

Notice Affords interested parties an opportunity to contest the will or otherwise intervene in the administration of an estate; *see* actual notice and publication notice

Nuncupative will Oral will

Objects of the power The persons/organizations in whose favor a power of appointment can be exercised

Parentala Consists of the line of blood relatives, including the ancestor and that ancestor's surviving descendants

Partial settlements The process in which certain assets are distributed to the heirs to beneficiaries before estate administration is complete

Patent ambiguity The ambiguity appears on the face of the document

Pension Retirement plan in which a specific amount is paid every month to a retiree

Per capita Per head or per person; statutes use this term to distinguish ways of inheriting through an ancestor

Per stirpes Per bloodlines or per roots or stocks; statutes use this term to distinguish ways of inheriting through an ancestor

Permissible appointees The persons/organizations in whose favor the power can be exercised

Personal representative The representative of an estate

Personalty All property that is not real property, money, or investments

Petition to probate the will A form completed by a personal representative to begin the probate of a will

Power of appointment   Allows the person who creates the power to give a third party the right to distribute property among a designated group of beneficiaries as the third party determines

Power of attorney   Delegates financial decision making to another entity

Power of withdrawal   The right to withdraw property, or a specified amount of property, from a trust

Power to adjust   A power under UPIA for the trustee to move amounts between the income and principal accounts, considering the needs of the beneficiaries, the purposes of the trust, and the sources of revenue

Powerholder   The person who is granted a power of appointment and makes decisions using the power; unlike the trustee or the beneficiaries, the powerholder has neither legal ownership nor a beneficial interest in the property

Premium   The amount of money paid to obtain an insurance policy

Prenuptial agreement   Contract entered into before marriage; also called a premarital agreement

Presence   Being in the line of sight of the testator when signing; can also include when the testator did not see the witness, but the testator could have done so without changing her position

Presently exercisable power of appointment   A power the powerholder can exercise during life, through an inter vivos instrument

Pretermitted   Unintentionally omitted members of a will

Principal   Person who signs the power of attorney and authorizes another person (the agent) to act on the principal's behalf

Principal   In a trust, the amount distributed to a remainder beneficiary and the amount subject to discretionary distributions of principal; under UPIA, principal includes amounts contributed to the trust and long-term capital gains, but a trustee can make adjustments between the income and principal accounts

Private express trust   A trust created intentionally by the owner of property for private beneficiaries and not for a charitable purpose

Probate process   The steps required to administer an estate

Prudent investor standard   Duty to manage and invest trust funds as a prudent investor would

Publication   The testator must declare to the witnesses that "this is my will"

Publication notice   When the personal representative prints notice of the death in a local newspaper to attempt to reach unknown creditors

Putative spouse   A person who cohabited with the decedent in the good-faith but mistaken belief that he or she was married to the decedent

Qualified beneficiaries   Beneficiaries who, on the date the determination of who the beneficiaries are is made, are beneficiaries to whom the trustee may or must make distributions (distributees or permissible distributees), would be distributees or permissible distributees if the interests of the first group ended, or would be distributees or permissible distributees if the trust terminated

Quasi-community property   Property that was acquired in common law state that would have been community property

Reforming a will   Using extrinsic evidence to fix a mistake in a will

Release   When the holder of a power of appointment loses the power by giving notice to the trustee that she is releasing the power

Representation   A system by which lower-generation descendants take shares of the estate when the descendant is not living at the time of the decedent's death

Republication   The process of treating the earlier will as though it had been executed as of the date of the codicil

Requirement of survival   A beneficiary under a will and an heir under intestacy must survive to take a share of a decedent's estate

Residuary beneficiary   The recipient of any money and assets remaining in the estate once estate expenses, taxes, and all other bequests have been satisfied

Residuary devises   A bequest where all assets remaining after the other devises and estates debts have been satisfied are distributed

Resulting trust   When a trust fails to make a complete disposition of property or can no longer be administered because it lacks a valid purpose, the trust property returns to the settlor

Revenue   In a trust, receipts from investments

Revive   To re-execute a will

Revival   Provides that a will that has previously been revoked is reinstated to legal enforceability

Revocable   When used in connection with a trust, the settlor can modify or revoke a trust

Revocable trust   A trust the settlor can modify or revoke

Revocation by inconsistency   Revoking a will with a later document containing terms that override an earlier document

Revoked   Voluntarily retracted by the testator

Rule against perpetuities   Establishes limitation on the duration of property interests

Rule of construction   Typically either a judicial doctrine or statute that can help a court give meaning when the intent is unclear

Second-generation statutes   Statutes that require that the signature and the material provisions be in the handwriting of the testator

Selective allocation   A doctrine that distributes property in the way that best carries out the powerholder's intent, when the powerholder's beneficiaries are not all permissible appointees

Self-dealing   When the trustee enters into a transaction as a fiduciary and in the trustee's individual capacity

Self-proved will   A will containing a self-proving affidavit

Self-proving affidavit   A statement signed by the testator and witnesses in front of a notary public, which recites that the will was executed in compliance with statutory formalities

Settlor   Person who creates a trust

Situs   The place a trust is administered

Skip person   A person who is at least two generations younger or who is unrelated and more than 37.5 years younger than the transferor, for purposes of the generation-skipping transfer tax

Slayer statutes   Statutes that prevent a beneficiary or heir who killed the decedent feloniously and with intent from taking property as the result of the decedent's death

Special administrator   An administrator that is appointed by the court if the court reopens the estate once the personal representative has been discharged

Specific devise   Refers to a particular item given under a will

Specific reference   When the powerholder makes specific reference to the trust and to the power of appointment when exercising it

Specific-exercise clause   A specific exercise clause indicates the powerholder's intent to exercise the power, and explicitly refers to the particular power of appointment in question

Spendthrift clause   A provision in a trust that prevents a beneficiary from selling or pledging trust property and prevents a beneficiary's creditors from getting trust assets

Springing power of attorney   A power of attorney that only becomes effective upon the principal's incapacity

Substantial compliance   This doctrine asks whether a will has substantially complied with the formalities

Supplemental amount   A minimum amount for the surviving spouse

Survive   Live beyond a specified date

Takers in default of appointment   The persons or entities who will take the property if the powerholder fails to exercise the power before the powerholder's power terminates (often at death)

Tax base   The amount that would be subject to tax before deductions

Taxable distribution   Distribution from a trust to a skip person, if the transfer is not otherwise a direct skip or taxable termination

Taxable gift   A transfer of property for less than full and adequate consideration

Taxable termination   The triggering of generation-skipping transfer tax at the end of an interest in property held in trust if after the termination only skip persons have interests in the trust

Tenancy by the entirety   A special form of joint tenancy with right of survivorship available only for married couples

Testacy   The rules that govern one's ability to direct the allocation of property at death by drafting a will

Testamentary capacity   Individuals "of sound mind"

Testamentary intent   When the decedent intended the document to be a will and to become operative on her death

Testamentary power of appointment   A power that can be exercised only by the will of the powerholder

Testamentary trust   A trust created under a will

Testate   When the decedent dies with a valid will

Testator   Person who makes the will

Tortious interference with an expectancy   A tort claim in which the plaintiff must prove the existence of an expectancy; intentional interference with the expectancy through tortious conduct, causation, damages; and that the probate remedies were exhausted through no fault of the wronged party

Totten trust   An account created when the transferor puts money into a bank account and designates that, at the transferor's death, the account passes to a named third party

Transfer tax   An assessment made against the gratuitous transfer of property from one person to another; the transfer taxes include the gift tax, the estate tax, and the generation-skipping transfer tax

Transferor's intent   Intent of the individual who is disposing of the property

Trust   A legal relationship whereby property is held by one party for the benefit of another

Trust accounting rules   Rules that tell a trustee whether receipts should be classified as income or principal

Trust agreement   A trust document in which the settlor will not serve as the sole initial trustee precatory; language that suggests a wish or desire; not mandatory

Trust director   Someone named in a trust instrument with a specific power in connection with the trust

Trust protector   Someone named in a trust instrument with a specific power in connection with the trust

Trustee   The person who has legal title to property held in trust and manages the property for the benefit of the beneficiary

Undue influence   The plan of the decedent is overcome by substantial and forceful outside influence

Unified transfer tax credit   A tax credit that shelters gifts and transfers that would be subject to tax

Unified transfer tax system   A tax system in which taxes share a rate table and a credit to be used against the payment of other taxes

Uniform Determination of Death Act   A uniform act that provides rules for determining when and whether death has occurred

Uniform Premarital Agreement Act   Validates the parties' choices concerning the financial term of their marriage

Uniform Principal and Income Act (UPIA)   Codification of the trust accounting rules

Uniform Probate Code   A model act that sets out a state's approach to handling an individual's property at death

Uniform Trust Code   A model law that provides statutory rules for trusts

Unintentional disinheritance   Being prevented from inheriting

Unitrust   A trust that distributes a fixed percentage of the value of the trust, recomputed annually, to the unitrust beneficiary

Ward   Person for whom a conservator or guardian is appointed

Will   A legal document that expresses an individual's wishes concerning property distribution at death

Will substitute   A legal means to pass property at death other than through a will

Table of Cases

Index